Site	URL
U.S. Census Bureau Tiger Map Service	http://tiger.census.gov
Dun & Bradstreet	http://www.dbisna.com
Vietnam Online	http://www.govietnam.com
LANIC (Latin America)	http://lanic.utexas.edu
China	http://www.yahoo.com/regional/countries/china/business
Europa (European Union)	http://www.cec.lu/welcome.html
REESWeb (Russia/Eastern Europe)	http://www.pitt.edu/~cjp/rees.html
MSU Weather Map	http://wxweb.msu.edu/weather
Dilbert	http://www.unitedmedia.com/comics/dilbert/
Levi Strauss	http://www.levi.com
JobTrak	http://www.jobtrak.com
Online Career Center	http://www.occ.com
E-Span's Interactive Employment Network	http://www.espan.com
Canada/British Columbia Business Service Centre	http://www.sb.gov.bc.ca/smallbus/sbhome.html
CorpFiNet	http://www.corpfinet.com
AccountingNet	http://www.accountingnet.com
Venture Information Network for Entrepreneurs	http://www.thevine.com
FinanceHub	http://www.financehub.com
Small Business Resource Center	http://www.webcom.com/seaquest/sbrc/reports.html
U.S. Business Advisor	http://www.business.gov
OSHA	http://www.osha.gov
FedWorld	http://www.fedworld.gov

Hatten's SMALL BUSINESS Homepage

Be sure to check out this textbook's home page at:

http://www.prenhall.com/~hattensb

*Please note that URLs (Website addresses) can change often. If you find that one of the above URLs doesn't work, try finding the site through Yahoo, Lycos, Webcrawler, or one of the other search engines.

D1384636

Small Business: Entrepreneurship and Beyond

Timothy S. Hatten

with the assistance of
Mary Coulter

Prentice Hall, Upper Saddle River, N.J. 07458

Acquisitions Editor: Natalie Anderson
Development Editor: Carol Wood
Associate Editor: Lisamarie Brassini
Editorial Assistant: Crissy Statuto
Editor-in-Chief: James Boyd
Director of Development: Steve Deitmer
Marketing Manager: Sandra Steiner
Production Editor: Louise Rothman
Production Coordinator: David Cotugno
Managing Editor: Carol Burgett
Manufacturing Supervisor: Arnold Vila
Manufacturing Manager: Vincent Scelta
Senior Designer: Ann France
Design Director: Patricia Wosczyk
Interior Design: Lisa Jones
Cover Design: Donna Wickes
Illustrator (Interior): ElectraGraphics, Inc.
Composition: Progressive Information Technologies
Cover Illustration: Robert Neffson/"Waverly"/1990, 40″ × 44″, oil on canvas

Photo Credits xx Mauch Portrait Studio/Timothy S. Hatten; **2** Boston Beer Company; **28** James Schnepf Photography, Inc.; **62** Scott Goldsmith Photography; **92** Robert Holmgren; **122** Auntie Anne's, Inc.; **150** Allan Penn; **176** Andy Freeberg Photography; **200** Tim Wright/Gamma-Liaison, Inc.; **230** T. Michael Keza/Nation's Business Magazine; **254** Tom Stillo; **286** David Butow/SABA Press Photos, Inc.; **310** Ken Touchton; **340** Roger Mastroianni; **368** Allan Penn; **400** Bayside Precision Gearheads; **422** John Dowling; **444** Chris Stewart; **474** Eric Millette; **500** Tom Salyer

Copyright © 1997 by Prentice-Hall, Inc.
A Simon & Schuster Company
Upper Saddle River, New Jersey 07458

All rights reserved. No part of this book may be reproduced, in any form or by any means, without written permission from the Publisher.

Library of Congress Cataloging-in-Publication Data
Hatten, Timothy S.
   Small business : entrepreneurship and beyond/Timothy S. Hatten.
     p. cm.
   Includes index.
   ISBN 0-13-180340-9 (hardcover)
   1. Small business—Management—Handbooks, manuals, etc.
 I. Title.
 HD62.7.H38 1997
 658.02′2—dc20   96-13018
                                              CIP

Prentice-Hall International (UK) Limited, London
Prentice-Hall of Australia Pty. Limited, Sydney
Prentice-Hall Canada, Inc., Toronto
Prentice-Hall Hispanoamericana, S.A., Mexico
Prentice-Hall of India Private Limited, New Delhi
Prentice-Hall of Japan, Inc., Tokyo
Simon & Schuster Asia Pte. Ltd., Singapore
Editora Prentice-Hall do Brasil, Ltda., Rio de Janeiro

Printed in the United States of America

10 9 8 7 6 5 4 3 2

To Jill, Paige, Brittany, and Taylor

Brief Contents

Contents

Part IV: Marketing the Product or Service 229

Chapter 9: Competitive Advantage and Marketing Research 231

Chapter 10: Marketing for Small Business 255

Chapter 11: Pricing and Credit Policies   287

Chapter 12: Global Small Business   311

Chapter 19: The Legal Environment 501

Preface

Small Business: Entrepreneurship and Beyond is organized into six parts. **Part One—The Challenge** sets the stage. **Part Two—Planning in Small Business** explains the importance and practice of looking ahead. **Part Three—Early Decisions** discusses topics that arise before you open the doors of your business. **Part Four—Marketing the Product or Service** walks you through the process of finding out what your customers want and determining how you can reach them. **Part Five—Managing Small Business** helps you put yourself at the helm of your dream . . . a business of your own. **Part Six—Financial and Legal Management** provides you with useful information on technical aspects of running your business.

The Theme of This Book

The theme of this book revolves around creating and maintaining a *sustainable competitive advantage* when you are running your small business. Of course, the process of starting a business is covered, but the emphasis of the book is on the on-going process of managing a small business. Running a small business is difficult in today's rapidly evolving environment and at no other time has the importance of holding a competitive advantage been greater. Every chapter in this book can be used to create yours whether your location, your marketing, your production, or any other facet is the key to your business.

Running a small business is like being in a race with no finish line. You must strive for continual improvement to satisfy the changing wants and needs of your customers. This book can help you run your best race.

Integrated throughout this book you will find the importance of **global opportunities, workforce diversity, service, quality,** and **technology** to small businesses.

Several unique approaches were taken in writing this book. For example, the topics of social responsibility, ethics, and strategic planning may seem to be an unusual combination, but are included in the same chapter because they work together to form the core essence of what your business stands for and where it is going.

The writing style is personal and conversational. I have tried to avoid the excessive use of jargon by explaining topics in simple, understandable language. The book is written in first person, present tense because I, the author, am speaking directly to you, the student.

I believe that a good example can help make the most complex concept more understandable and interesting to read. Examples were carefully selected from the business press and from small business owners I have known to strengthen the flow of the material and to reinforce important points.

Features

The pedagogical features of this book are designed to complement, supplement, and reinforce material from the body of the text. In order to enhance critical thinking and show practical applications of running a small business you will find:

- ✔ Two complete **business plans** written by undergraduate business students—one for a service business, one for a retail establishment.
- ✔ Small business-related information is popping up all over cyberspace—tap into it with **Entering the Internet** feature boxes.
- ✔ Highlight boxes featuring **Global Small Businesses** are included in each chapter.
- ✔ Small business is not an abstract, theoretical subject so the **Chapter Opening Vignettes, Reality Checks,** and extensive use of examples throughout the book show you what *real* small businesses are doing.
- ✔ The importance of technology to small businesses is shown in each chapter in **Computer Applications** highlight boxes.
- ✔ Service related businesses have a major impact on our economy and small businesses are well represented as shown in **Small Business in the Service Industry** highlight boxes.
- ✔ **Manager's Notebooks** provide business-tested, nuts and bolts tips for running your small business.
- ✔ Each chapter begins with a **Chapter Focus** which provides objectives for students to concentrate upon while reading the chapters. These same objectives are then revisited and identified in the chapter summaries.
- ✔ A **Running Glossary** in the margins to bring attention to important terms as they appear in the text.

✔ **Critical Incidents** at the end of each chapter are included to stimulate classroom discussion.

✔ **Take It to the Net** exercises at the end of each chapter direct students to a case (as up-to-date as today's newspaper!) with Web-related exercises. See our home page at: **http://www.prenhall.com/~hattensb**

Acknowledgments

I would like to sincerely thank the people who made this book possible and those who made it better. Projects of this magnitude do not happen in a vacuum and even though my name is on the cover, a lot of talented people have contributed their skills. The list begins with Lynn Guza, the wonderful PH book rep who started this whole thing. All the Prentice Hall sales force have a major impact on the success of this book and I appreciate them.

Natalie Anderson is the Acquisitions Editor who has believed in me and my book from the beginning. She has never failed to be encouraging, supportive, creative, and excited. I am lucky to have found an excellent editor who has become a good friend.

Every person on the team of professionals I work with from Prentice Hall has used their special skills to make this book better than it would have been without them. Carol Wood, my Developmental Editor, pored over every word, bringing organization and a different point of view to this project. Steve Deitmer coordinated the developmental process. Lisamarie Brassini coordinated the supplements. Louise Rothman supervised production. Donna Mulder copyedited the manuscript.

Thanks to Mary Coulter for her outstanding ability to find just the right person or company to highlight in the boxed features and end-of-chapter cases. Tom Lietz, Fred Hiedrich, and Morgan Bridge made tremendous contributions, each in his or her area of specialty. Becky Finch helped put on the finishing touches. My colleagues at Mesa State College provided a sounding board for much of my thinking. Mark Springsteel, Karl Hall, Mike Hyatt, and Shawn Serviss are students who did a great job writing the business plans included in the appendix.

I would like to thank my colleagues who reviewed this manuscript and provided feedback concerning their and their students' needs.

Michael Cicero, Highline Community College, Des Moines, WA

Richard Cuba, University of Baltimore, Baltimore, MD

William Soukoup, University of San Diego, San Diego, CA

Marty St. John, Westmoreland County College, Youngwood, PA

Milton Miller, Carteret Community College, Morehead City, NC

Rudy Butler, Trenton State College, Trenton, NJ

Warren Weber, California Polytechnical, Pomona, CA

Paul Lamberson, University of Southern Mississippi, Hattiesburg, MS

Bill Motz, Lansing Community College, Lansing, MI

Alan Zieber, Portland State University, Portland, OR

Arlen Gastinau, Valencia Community College West, Orlando, FL

Joe Salamone, SUNY Buffalo, Buffalo, NY

Nancy Payne, College of Dupage, Glen Ellyn, IL
Doug Hamilton, Berkeley College of Business, White Plains, NY
MaryLou Lockerby, College of Dupage, Glen Ellyn, IL
Charles Tofloy, George Washington University, Washington, DC

Finally, to my family. . . . Saying thanks and giving acknowledgment is not enough for the patience, sacrifice, and inspiration you have provided. My wife, Jill, daughters Paige and Brittany, and son Taylor—you are the best. The perseverance and work ethic needed for a job of this magnitude were instilled in me by my father, Drexel, and mother, Marjorie—I don't know how you did it, but I appreciate it. Thank you, Jesus.

About the Author

Timothy S. Hatten is Assistant Professor and Chair of Business Administration at Mesa State College in Grand Junction, CO. He received his Ph.D. from the University of Missouri—Columbia. He earned his M.A. at Central Missouri State University and his B.A. from Western State College in Gunnison, CO.

Dr. Hatten has been passionate about small and family businesses his whole life. He grew up with the family-owned International Harvester farm equipment dealership in Bethany, MO, which his father started. Later, he owned and managed a Chevrolet, Buick, and Cadillac dealership with his father, Drexel, and brother, Gary.

Since entering academia, he has been active bringing students and small businesses together through the SBA's Small Business Institute program. He counsels and leads small business seminars through the Western Colorado Business Development Corporation. Dr. Hatten approached writing this textbook as if it were a small business. His intent was to produce a product (in this case, a book) which would benefit his customers (students and faculty).

Dr. Hatten's adopted home on the western slope of Colorado has provided him the opportunity to share his love of the mountains with his children. Between teaching, writing, and consulting he tries to maintain balance in his life by camping, fishing, and hunting with his wife Jill, daughters Paige and Brittany, and son Taylor.

Please send questions, comments, or suggestions to: **thatten@mesa5.mesa. colorado.edu**

VIDEO CASE
The Steel Comeback

THE AMERICAN STEEL INDUSTRY has historically been dominated by massive companies such as U.S. Steel, Inland, Bethlehem Steel, and LTV. However, expensive labor, outdated plants, and low quality led these familiar names to some of the largest losses of money in corporate America. For example, U.S. Steel was losing $100 million a month in the mid-1980s. A decade later, the steel industry has turned its inferior products and staggering losses into world-class steel and profit. Who has led this turnaround? Small, agile mini-mills have.

Mini-mills, such as those operated by Nucor, perform standard steel milling functions but on a much smaller scale than do traditional mills. In the relatively short time they have existed, mini-mills have taken over one third of the market—and more are on the way. These corporate Davids are winning against well-established Goliaths by streamlining operations, introducing state-of-the-art technology, and providing powerful incentives to workers rather than divisive union rules. Because mini-mills operate more efficiently, they are able to hold their costs down and price their steel considerably lower than can large steel producers or foreign exporters. *Source: Adapted from* The Wall Street Journal Report, *Show #682, Oct. 21, 1995.*

Discussion Questions

- What similarities do you see between the mini-mills in this video and the micro-breweries like Boston Beer Company discussed in Chapter 1? What differences between the two industries do you see for the future?
- How do small businesses compete with large competitors? Could you expect results in other industries similar to those in the steel industry?

Chapter Focus

After reading this chapter, you should be able to:

- Describe the characteristics of small business.
- Recognize the role of small business in the U.S. and global economies.
- Understand the importance of diversity in the marketplace and the workplace.
- Illustrate the causes of small business failure.
- Suggest ways to court success in a small business venture.

1 Small Business: An Overview

O N PATRIOT'S DAY 1985, Jim Koch (pronounced cook) started Boston Beer Company. Koch brewed his beer, Samuel Adams, according to a family recipe from the 1870s. Although he had never been in the beer business before, he became at age 37 a sixth-generation brewer. Intending to compete directly with the best imports, Koch advertised beer with patriotic slogans like "Declare your independence from foreign beer." The namesake of the beer was a revolutionary war hero who helped organize the Boston Tea Party.

Like many entrepreneurs, Koch started his business on a shoe-string: $100,000 from personal savings and $250,000 borrowed from family and friends—a small amount for a brewery. To reduce over-head expenses, he arranged to use the excess capacity of a brewery in Pittsburgh. For the first several years, Koch was the company's only salesperson traveling from bar to bar enticing bartenders to taste samples of Samuel Adams that he carried in his briefcase. Sometimes up to 15 calls were needed before getting the sale. Even after the company had grown to revenues of $7 million with 28 employees, Koch still spent two-thirds of his time making sales.

Samuel Adams was not made for the mass market. At first it was brewed in batches of only 6,500 cases each. Koch marketed the beer to people tired of drinking "ordinary" beer and willing to pay for premium quality. Koch enjoyed saying that major breweries spill more beer in a minute than he made in a year. Quality was his focus, not quantity.

Samuel Adams has been voted Best Beer in America at the Great American Beer Festival four times in its ten-year existence. It was the first American beer in the twentieth century to satisfy the stringent German purity laws enabling it to be sold in the German market. Premium ingredients costing up to ten times more than those used by competitors are needed to maintain this level of quality. Appropriately, Boston Beer Company ads stress product and process—not image—by not featuring muscle-bound men or bikini-clad women. Because Samuel Adams was the first beer to have a freshness date stamped on its label, Koch wrote a radio ad touting that "Maybe other beer commercials want you to think that if you drink their beer, you'll get lucky. But I can guarantee with Samuel Adams, you'll always get a date."

In a short time, from austere beginnings, Boston Beer Company has become a $50 million business. Samuel Adams is no longer brewed in small batches, but the quality remains high. The company is the first to enter the chasm between *micro*brewery and *major* brewery. Its incredible growth and success have come from its fanatical attention to quality, its use of marketing tools that no other microbrewery had used—advertising, merchandising, and hard selling—and the perseverance of its founder, Jim Koch, an entrepreneur with a vision. *Source: Adapted from Jennry McCune, "Brewing Up Profits," Management Review (April 1994), pp. 16–20. James Koch, "Portrait of the CEO as Salesman," Inc. (March 1988), pp. 44–46. Gerry Khermouch, "Marketers of the Year—Jim Koch," Brandweek, November 8, 1993, p. 42. Stanley Angrist, "Brewing America," Forbes, April 6, 1987, p. 172. John Persinos, "Heady Brews: Amber Waves of Grain," Venture (January 1988), pp. 58–61. Laura Loro, "The Marketing 100—Jim Koch," Advertising Age, July 5, 1993, p. s-22.*

What Is Small Business?

As the driver of the free enterprise system, small business generates a great deal of energy, innovation, and profit for millions of Americans. According to the Internal Revenue Service, more than 21 million tax returns were filed in 1992 that included income from a small business.[1] As of 1991, over 98 percent of all businesses have a payroll of fewer than 500 people.[2] These figures exclude farmers,

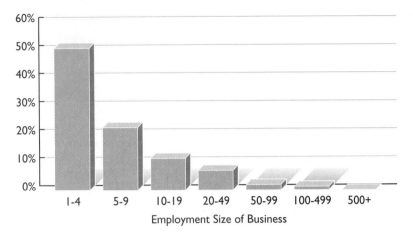

FIGURE 1-1
Almost All Businesses Are Small Businesses
Percent of Enterprises by Employment Size
U.S. Small Business Administration, 1991, NFIB Foundation/VISA Business Card, as shown in William J. Dennis, Jr., A Small Business Primer, *1993, National Federation of Independent Business, p. 11.*

who constitute another 2 million people whose primary occupation is operating a small business. (See Figure 1-1.)

Small businesses include everything from the stay-at-home parent who provides day care for other children to the factory worker who makes after-hours deliveries, to the owner of a chain of fast-food restaurants. Over 9 million Americans operate "sideline" businesses, part-time enterprises that supplement the owner's income. Another 12 million people make owning and operating a small business their primary occupation. Seven million of these employ only themselves—as carpenters, independent sales representatives, freelance writers, or other type of single-person businesses. Nearly 5 million businesses have fewer than 100 employees. About 80,000 businesses have 100 employees or more, while only 15,000 businesses have 500 or more workers on their payroll.

Size Definitions

The definition of **small business** depends on the criteria for determining what is "small" and what qualifies as a "business." The most common criterion used to distinguish between large and small businesses is the number of employees. Other criteria include sales revenue, the total value of assets, and the value of owners' equity. The Small Business Administration (SBA), a federally funded agency that provides loans and assistance to small businesses, has established definitions of business size that vary by industry. (See Table 1-1.) These definitions are based on annual sales revenues or number of employees and are assigned by Standardized Industrial Code (SIC) to each of seven main industries: construction, manufacturing, mining, transportation, wholesale trade, retail trade, and service.[3] In general, manufacturers with fewer than 500 employees are classified as small, as are wholesalers with fewer than 100 employees, and retailers or services with less than $3.5M annual revenue.

Why is it important to classify businesses as big or small? Aside from academic discussion of the contributions of each, these classifications are important in that they determine whether a business may qualify for SBA assistance and for government set-aside programs, which require a percentage of each government agency's purchases to be made from small businesses.

small business A business is generally considered small if it is independently owned, operated, and financed, has fewer than 100 employees, and has relatively little impact on its industry.

TABLE 1 ▪ 1   How Big Can a Small Business Be?

SIC CODE	DESCRIPTION BY INDUSTRY	ANNUAL SALES OR NUMBER OF EMPLOYEES
1521	General building contractor	$17M
2311	Fabric apparel manufacturer	500 employees
2511	Wood furniture manufacturer	500
3411	Metal can fabrication	1,000
3571	Electronic computer manufacturer	1,000
4724	Travel agency	$ 0.5M
4212	Local trucking without storage	$12.5M
5072	Hardware (wholesale)	100 employees
5311	Department store	$13.5M
5511	Motor vehicle dealer (new and used)	$17M
5641	Children's and Infants' clothing store	$ 3.5M
5944	Jewelry store	$ 3.5M
7011	Hotel and motel	$ 3.5M
7311	Advertising agency	$ 3.5M
7841	Videotape rental	$ 3.5M

Source: Code of Federal Regulations 13:121 *(Washington, DC: U.S. Government Printing Office, January 1, 1994), pp. 354–367.*

Types of Industries

Some industries lend themselves to small business operation more than others do. In construction, for instance, 86.8 percent of companies in the industry are classified as small by the SBA. Manufacturing industries have long been associated with mass employment, as well as mass production, yet SBA data show that 28.9 percent of manufacturers are classified as small.

Over 60 percent of all retail businesses are small, employing a total of 10.6 million people in selling goods to ultimate consumers. More than three out of every four wholesale businesses are small, as 4.5 million people are employed by these intermediaries.

The industry that employs the greatest number of people in small business, however, is services. Over 13 million people (51.5 percent of the total) are employed by small businesses that provide a broad range of services from restaurants to lawn care to telecommunications.

As indicated by industry percentages and by sheer numbers of employees, small businesses are important to every industry sector. (See Figure 1-2.)

For purposes of discussion in this book, we will consider a business to be small if it:

- **is independently owned, operated, and financed.** One or very few people run the business.
- **has less than 100 employees.** While SBA standards allow up to 500 or more for some types of businesses, the most common limit is 100.
- **has relatively little impact on its industry.** Boston Beer Company described in the chapter opener has sales of $50 million. While this is an impressive figure, it is still classified as a small business because it has little influence on Anheuser-Busch or Miller breweries with 1994 sales of $11.5 billion and $2.92 billion, respectively.[4]

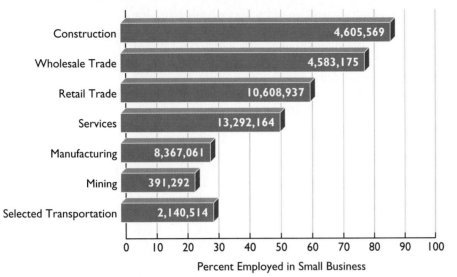

FIGURE 1-2
Small Business Employment Statistics, 1992
Percentage of work force, and total number of workers, employed in small business.
Source: The State of Small Business: A Report of the President Transmitted to the Congress *(Washington: U.S. Government Printing Office, 1992), p. 224.*

Small Business in the American Economy

Until the early 1800s, all businesses were small in the way just described. Most goods were produced one at a time by workers in their cottages or in small artisanal studios. Much of the U.S. economy was based on agriculture. But with the Industrial Revolution mass production became possible. Machinery like Samuel Slater's textile machinery, Eli Whitney's cotton gin, and techniques like Samuel Colt's use of interchangeable parts in producing firearms, changed the way business was conducted. Factories brought people, raw material, and machinery together to produce large quantities of goods.

Though early manufacturers were small, by the late 1800s businesses grew rapidly in industries which relied on economies of scale for their profitability. *Economy of scale* is the lowering of costs through production of larger quantities: The more units you make, the less each costs. For example, Andrew Carnegie founded U.S. Steel, Henry Ford introduced the assembly line for manufacturing automobiles, and Cornelius Vanderbilt speculated in steamships and railroads. Although the individuals had begun as entrepreneurs, their companies eventually came to dominate their industry. The costs of competing with them became prohibitively high as the masses of capital they had accumulated formed a barrier to entry for newcomers to the industry. The subsequent industrialization of America decreased the impact of new entrepreneurs over the first half of the twentieth century.[5] Small businesses still existed during this period, of course, but the economic momentum that large businesses gathered kept small businesses in minor roles.

The decades following World War II also favored big business over small business. Industrial giants like General Motors and IBM and retailers like Sears flourished during this period by tapping into the expanding consumer economy.

In the late 1950s and early 1960s another economic change began. Businesses began paying more attention to consumer wants and needs, rather than a sole focus on production. This paradigm shift was called the **marketing concept;** finding out what people want and then producing that good or service, rather than making products and then trying to convince people to buy them. With this shift came an increased importance of the service economy. The increased em-

marketing concept The business philosophy of discovering what consumers want and then providing the good or service that will satisfy their needs.

service sector Businesses that provide services, rather than tangible goods.

phasis on customer service of businesses adopting the marketing concept started to provide more opportunities for small business. The **service sector** of our economy is made up of jobs that produce services for customers rather than tangible products. The growth of this sector is important to small businesses because they can compete well in it.

In 1960, just over half of our nation's jobs were in the service sector, and by 1995, that figure had grown to 80 percent.

Small Business IN THE Service Industry

The service industry is growing by leaps and bounds. As we approach the twenty-first century, service businesses dominate the economies of the United States, Canada, Australia, and Western Europe. What factors have led to this phenomenal growth? Part of the growth in services can be traced to the fact that the post-World War II economic boom years provided consumers with more money but less time to perform many of the services that they had previously performed for themselves. They had money to pay to have these services done for them. In addition, consumers' increased income meant they could acquire more possessions, which led to increased demands for maintaining and preserving those possessions. Finally, rapid advances in telecommunications and computer technology have inaugurated entire new industries devoted to organizing, storing, and transmitting information for both personal and commercial uses. Because service organizations comprise such a large proportion of U.S. economic activity, in each chapter of the book we'll look at specific ways in which small businesses are innovating and prospering in this field.

The importance of service businesses is illustrated by changes in traditional measuring tools. The prestigious Fortune 500 list of the largest businesses in the United States radically changed by including service businesses for the first time in 1995.[6]

Recent Growth Trends. By the early 1970s, corporate profits had begun to decline while costs increased. Entrepreneurs like Steve Jobs of Apple Computer and Bill Gates of Microsoft started small businesses and created entirely new industries that had never before existed. Managers began realizing that bigger is not necessarily better; that economy of scale does not guarantee lower costs. Other start-ups like Wal-Mart and The Limited dealt serious blows to retail giants like Sears because their organizational structures were flatter, they were faster in responding to customers' changing desires, and they were more flexible in changing their products and services.

In the 1980s U.S. business saw a period of "merger mania," when businesses acquired other businesses purely for the sake of growth, not because a natural fit would be created. This period was short-lived because most of the mergers and acquisitions were financed heavily, often with *junk bonds*—funds borrowed at very high interest rates. This debt left the newly expanded businesses at a disadvantage and was often followed by a string of bankruptcies and

R eality Check

Maximum Efficiency

What's your image of the U.S. steel industry? If you think of cavernous buildings, housing giant blast furnaces capable of transforming iron ore, coal, and limestone into millions of tons of molten metal every single year, you're seeing only part of the picture. During the early 1980s, the major U.S. steel producers were battered by foreign competitors who capitalized on their weaknesses: oversized, outdated production facilities, high costs, and inflexible and overly bureaucratic management structures. However, in the last decade, the steel industry has been magically transformed by an aggressive group of small firms, called *minimills*, that produce between 200,000 and 1 million tons of steel per year.

A minimill is a relatively small, electric-powered steel mill that melts down scrap steel to manufacture various steel products. This radically different production process saves money on costly labor, raw materials, and the expensive machinery needed to produce steel from iron ore. (However, a major concern of minimill manufacturers is maintaining product quality, since their raw materials consist of scrap steel containing a variety of impurities and alloys.) These small firms concentrate on producing only a few products and are usually much more efficient than most of their larger rivals. Because of their efficiency, they have been growing and adding capacity while larger U.S. steel companies have been restructuring, downsizing, and otherwise struggling to survive in a changed global environment.

What's the story behind the success of these steel minimills? To better understand the role of these small businesses in the turnaround of the steel industry, let's take a closer look at one—Nucor Corporation of North Carolina. Nucor operates several minimills that produce basic steel products such as joists, decking, and steel bars. Nucor is extremely efficient at making steel—its sales revenues have grown at an annual compounded rate of more than 20 percent during the last decade. The company began with the reorganization of a nearly bankrupt company called Nuclear Corporation of America. To help control both quality and costs, Ken Iverson, who was chosen as the company's chief executive officer (CEO), designed a decentralized company structure with only four management levels. At the top level is Iverson and the company's president. The second level includes vice presidents, each of whom serves as a general manager of one of the company's minimills, joist plants, or other divisions. At the third level are the department heads—sales managers, division controllers, or managers of melting or casting. And the fourth level includes the first-line supervisors.

Iverson delegated all decisions dealing with manufacturing operations to the individual plants. He believed that managers closest to the action had the knowledge to best deal with changes and to take appropriate steps. Iverson also tied worker compensation directly to production, awarding bonuses for each extra ton of production. These bonuses can sometimes almost double a production worker's paycheck. Managers' financial rewards are similarly dependent on continued productivity. Finally, Nucor's workers have excelled in suggesting innovative ideas for improving productivity and quality. So, although Nucor has reached over $2 billion in annual sales, it continues to prosper by "acting small."

Sources: Donald F. Barnett and Robert W. Crandall, Up From the Ashes: The Rise of the Steel Minimill in the United States *(Washington, DC: The Brookings Institution, 1986); John Ortman, "Nucor's Ken Iverson on Productivity and Pay,"* Personnel Administrator *(October 1986), pp 46–108;* The Wall Street Journal, *May 10, 1991, pp. A1 and A4; F. C. Barnes, "A Nucor Commitment," in James M. Higgins and Julian W. Vincze,* Strategic Management: Text and Cases, *5th ed. (Ft. Worth, TX: Dryden Press, 1993); and John A. Byrne, "How Entrepreneurs Are Reshaping the Economy—And What Big Companies Can Learn,"* Business Week, Enterprise Edition *(October 1993), pp. 12–18.*

downsizing The practice of reducing the size of a business. Downsizing impacts small businesses in two ways—people who have lost their jobs often start their own businesses and small businesses often provide services that downsized businesses no longer perform themselves.

layoffs and a relatively new term entered the business vocabulary—**downsizing.** Downsizing involves the reduction of a business's work force in order to shore up dwindling profits. Between 1987 and 1993, more than 6 million permanent jobs were eliminated, and the trend appears to be continuing.[7] Any segment of a business in which its owner does not have special skills is put up for sale, eliminated, or given to someone else to do (known as *outsourcing*). The impact of downsizing on small business is twofold. Many people who have lost their jobs with large businesses have started small businesses of their own. These new businesses often do the work that large businesses no longer perform themselves—temporary employment, cleaning services, and independent contracting, for example.

The trend of people working in their homes either via telecommuting or as the owner of their own home-based business may put the study of the history of business into perspective. Have we now come full circle to where we were in the early 1800s with all business conducted in private cottages? We probably will not continue that far, but the question does illustrate the importance of studying history—it can repeat itself.

Large businesses will always be needed, but in an environment in which competition, technology, and desires of the marketplace change quickly, as it does in the economy of the 1990s, entry barriers fall. Small businesses are better able to take advantage of changing conditions. As Ted Stolberg, a venture capitalist who invests in small businesses, says, "The capital advantage big businesses sometimes have is being eliminated. The technology is helping smaller companies beat up the big guys."[8]

Increased Business Startups.   Indeed, the rate of small business growth has more than doubled in the last 25 years. In 1970, 264,000 new businesses were started.[9] In 1980, that figure had grown to 532,000, reaching 647,000 by 1990! While a lot of attention tends to be paid to the failure rate of small businesses, many more people are going into business for themselves. Nine new businesses are formed for every one that fails.[10]

FIGURE 1-3
Small Businesses Create the Most Net New Jobs
Employment share and average net new employment share by employee size of business, 1977 to 1990
U.S. Small Business Administration, 1992, NFIB Foundation/VISA Business Card Primer, as shown in William J. Dennis, Jr., A Small Business Primer, 1993, National Federation of Independent Business, p. 17.

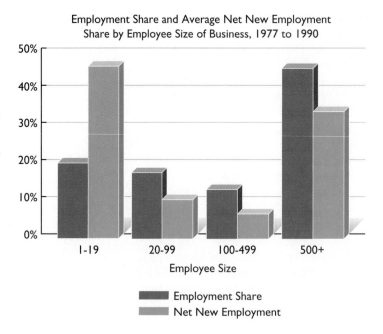

Small Business as Employer.   Small businesses generate employment when they are started and when they expand. Figure 1-3 shows that the smallest businesses (1–19 employees) produced an increasingly large proportion of new jobs from 1977 to 1990, while that produced by all other sizes of businesses fell. Of the net new jobs (jobs created minus jobs lost) generated from 1970 to 1990, small businesses created two-thirds of them.[11] This contribution is even more impressive when you consider that the total number of U.S. jobs increased by 50 percent during this period. According to research conducted by Cognetics Inc. of Cambridge, MA, firms with up to 500 employees created all 5.8 million new jobs from 1987 to 1992. During the same five-year period, firms with 500 or more employees had a net loss of 2.3 million jobs.[12]

SBA data show that the trend continued in 1993. Small businesses created 1.3 million new jobs (71 percent of total), while large businesses generated 0.6 million new jobs (29 percent).[13] So while large businesses have begun growing again, small businesses are growing even faster. Among small businesses, the most jobs created in 1993 were in the following industries.

Personnel supply services—(such as temporary employment agencies)	296,100 jobs
Eating and drinking places	281,400
Special trade contractors—(electricians, plumbers, and so on)	156,400
Wholesale trade—durable goods	65,900
Employment agencies	61,300
Medical offices and clinics	56,100
Miscellaneous retail stores	40,300
Agriculture services	39,800

Increasing Interest at Colleges and Universities.   The growing economic importance of small business has not escaped college and university campuses. In 1971, only 16 schools in the United States offered courses in entrepreneurship. By 1993, that number had grown to 370.[14]

What can explain this phenomenal growth of interest in small business? For one thing, it parallels the explosion in small business formation. For another, mistakes made in running a small business are expensive in terms of both time and money. More students today are present or prospective business owners who want to make as many of those mistakes as possible on paper and not in reality.

Work Force Diversity

The U.S. work force is becoming more diverse. The perceived homogeneity of the business world, as depicted in television shows of the 1950s, will be sharply contrasted by the reality of the 1990s. (See Table 1-2.) The U.S. Labor Department report, *Workforce 2000*, predicted that of the 25 million people entering the work force by the year 2000, 85 percent would be women, minorities, and immi-

TABLE 1 ▪ 2   The U.S. Work Force Is Changing

	1965	1980	1990
Women	35.0%	42.0%	45.0%
Blacks	6.5	9.4	10.1
Hispanics	N/A	5.6	7.5
Asians	N/A	1.0	2.6

Source: U.S. Department of Labor, Bureau of Labor Statistics, 1991.

grants.[15] Trends like an aging population, increasing birthrate of minority groups, more attention to the needs and abilities of people with handicaps, and more women entering the work force are changing the way our nation and our businesses operate. The intent of most civil rights laws (covered in Chapter 14) is to ensure that all groups are represented and that discrimination is not to be tolerated. Wheels of change tend to move slowly and inequities exist for all groups of people, but progress is being made. (See Table 1-3.)

Business Responds to Diversity. The response by businesses to the diversification of the work force has been mixed. Research has shown that many companies are aware of and concerned about the effects of demographic shifts on their work force and markets. Yet their response so far has concentrated more on the recruitment of minorities than on initiatives to improve their long-term retention, such as training, education, and support.[16] A 1992 study of 1,400 companies by the Hay Group reported that nearly two-thirds responded that adapting to work force diversity over the next two years was either "important but not a priority" or "not very important."[17] Still, some businesses have proven how variety in the work force can pay off.

Certain large companies like Levi Strauss and Hoechst Celanese have turned diversity to their own advantage. Levi's has established a strict set of corporate goals, or "aspirations," for its work environment. Levi's states that it will "value a diverse work force (age, sex, ethnic group, and so on) at all levels of the organization. . . . Differing points of view will be sought; diversity will be valued and honestly rewarded, not suppressed."[18] Levi's believes that a varied work force will lead to unique and creative perspectives among its workers. Levi's chairman and CEO, Robert Haas, great-great-grandnephew of the company's founder Levi Strauss, believes in multiformity not because it is "politically correct," but because of the interconnection between the personal success of the people involved and the success of the company.[19] So far, the connection between diversity and profit has not been proven, but Levi's adheres to its vision.

Ernest Drew, CEO of chemical producer Hoechst Celanese, learned the value of diversity during a company conference. A group of 125 top company officials, primarily white men, were separated into groups with 50 women and minority employees. Some of the groups comprised a variety of races and gender; some were composed of white men only. The groups were asked to solve a prob-

TABLE 1 ▪ 3   Percent of Population by Cultural Group and Age

AGE	WHITE	BLACK	HISPANIC	ASIAN/ PACIFIC ISLANDER	NATIVE AMERICAN	OTHER RACES
0–9	74.8	15.0	12.6	3.3	1.1	5.9
10–19	75.1	15.1	11.6	3.3	1.1	5.4
20–29	77.3	13.1	11.5	3.3	0.8	5.5
30–39	79.9	12.0	8.9	3.3	0.8	4.0
40–49	82.9	10.4	7.1	3.1	0.7	2.9
50–59	84.4	10.1	6.4	2.6	0.6	2.3
60–69	87.4	8.8	4.8	1.9	0.5	1.5
70–79	89.3	7.9	3.5	1.4	0.4	0.9
80+	90.4	7.5	3.2	1.0	0.3	0.8
All Ages	80.3	12.1	9.0	2.9	0.8	3.9

Source: U.S. Bureau of Census, 1990.

Note: Because Hispanic may include different races, percentages may not equal 100 percent.

lem concerning corporate culture and how to change it. According to Drew, the multiformed teams produced the broadest solutions. "They had ideas I hadn't even thought of," he recalled. "For the first time, we realized that diversity is a strength as it relates to problem solving."[20] Drew now believes that a varied work force is needed at every level of an organization. Drew's realization, of course, applies to businesses of any size. Talent and teamwork are among the most valued qualities to look for in an employee.

Small Business's Opportunity for All.   How does diversity affect small business ownership? Businesses owned by women and minorities are growing at a faster rate than all businesses combined. According to the Small Business Administration, women own and operate one-third (over 5.5 million) of all proprietorships in the United States.[21] From 1982 to 1987, the rate of women entering business increased 82 percent; black-owned businesses grew by 37.6 percent; Hispanic-owned businesses grew by 80.5 percent; and Asian-owned companies rose 89.3 percent.[22] The growth rate for all firms during the period was 14.2 percent. These data show that when faced with the choice of working for someone else or working for themselves, people from widely varied backgrounds are finding opportunities in small businesses.

Considering the number of problems that most small business owners face, perhaps more small business owners will find the same answer that Ernest Drew found—that diversity in the workplace can provide creative problem-solving ideas.

The Expanding Marketplace

It may come as a surprise, but big businesses need small businesses. Actually, a symbiotic relationship exists between large and small businesses. For instance, John Deere Company relies upon hundreds of vendors, many of which are small, to produce component parts for its farm equipment. Deere's extensive network of 3,400 independent dealers comprising small businesses provides sales and service for its equipment. These relationships enable Deere, the world's largest manufacturer of farm equipment, to focus on what it does best, while at the same time creating economic opportunity for hundreds of individual entrepreneurs.

Small businesses perform more efficiently than larger ones in several areas. For example, while large manufacturers tend to enjoy a higher profit margin due to their economies of scale, small businesses are often better at distribution. Most wholesale and retail businesses are small to link more efficiently large manufacturers with the millions of consumers spread all over the world.

Downsizing, Outsourcing, and Strategic Alliances.   As large businesses continue to trim the size of their organizations, many turn to outsourcing as a way to do more with fewer employees. **Outsourcing** means that a company hires another, usually smaller, business to produce components and perform needed activities. None of the major U.S. automobile manufacturers make more than half of the parts used to build their cars and trucks. Chrysler outsources two-thirds of its components.[23] Nike makes none of its own shoes.[24] If you choose the right outsourcer, the people in your business are free to concentrate on what they know best. Through outsourcing, small and large businesses form what is called a *strategic alliance*—a contract or commitment to work together to produce goods and services.

Honda Motor Corporation provides a clear illustration of how outsourcing and strategic alliances can lead to more efficient modes of production. Honda

outsourcing Occurs when a company hires another business to provide goods or services rather than producing them itself.

Flying Solo

Jody Severson got tired of managing employees, shuffling paperwork, and "sweating payroll every Sunday night." Bill Collier lost his job of 33 years at IBM. Ellen Leanse could not imagine raising her children while working 80-hour weeks as an executive at Apple Computer. Paul Farrow found himself at a crossroads the day that his job as vice president of finance and manufacturing for an environmental service company no longer existed. What do these four people have in common? More than you might think. They are all new business soloists.

Severson, Collier, Leanse, and Farrow each started a business that allowed them to do what they do very well. They work for themselves—by themselves. Severson became a political consultant in South Dakota thriving on the independence and advantages a solo business provides: low overhead, no worries about anyone else's salary, and picking the work he wants to do. Severson, like many soloists, depends on technology to communicate with customers and distribute his service. His laptop computer, fax machine, and cordless phone counter any geographical disadvantage he might face from being located in South Dakota.

Collier provides an example of the situation that 600,000 salaried personnel or managers faced in 1993. Forced from his previous position due to corporate downsizing, he turned to self-employment for survival. Collier formed Multiprocessor Diagnostics, where he produces and markets software that test-programs computer multiprocessors.

Leanse has maintained many of her business contacts from Apple, which have developed into an ever-increasing web of referrals and new business. She now provides marketing consultation to high-tech companies.

While Farrow was on a family vacation in Maine, he chanced upon the opportunity for a new career and a new identity for himself. He wanted more than to own his own company. He wanted to be the company, all by himself. So Farrow created a *virtual corporation* making kayaks for the masses.

Farrow used his knowledge of manufacturing, his passion for the environment, and his observation of a large unsatisfied market to produce an inexpensive kayak made of recycled plastic for people who had never considered kayaking. Virtual corporations like Farrow's Walden Paddlers require many strategic partnerships by using the skills of many other people and organizations to complement the skills of the entrepreneur. This allows one person, like Paul Farrow, to design, produce, and market a technically sophisticated kayak by himself.

Soloists are a new hybrid of business owner and their numbers are growing. It is estimated that 20 million Americans' primary occupation is now owner of a solo business. Soloists are not empire builders. They are not getting rich, but by offering specialized professional services they are changing the way business is done. And they are inventing new varieties of self-employment.

Source: Adapted from Anne Murphy, "Do-It-Yourself Job Creation," Inc. (January 1994), pp. 36–48; and Edward O. Wells, "Virtual Realities," Inc. (August 1993), pp. 50–58.

chose Donnelly Corporation of Holland, Michigan to produce external mirrors for its U.S.-made cars. Although Donnelly did not make external mirrors at the time (only internal ones), Honda liked how Donnelly treated its workers—encouraging them to make use of their intelligence and imagination, as well as their manual labor skills. This type of working philosophy, Honda's managers believed, amounts to a partnership with suppliers as opposed to an adversarial relationship. The payoff to Donnelly was big—$5 million in sales the first year to an expected $60 million by 1997.[25]

If the trend toward outsourcing continues, today's large corporations may be transformed into companies with a relatively small core of permanent employees. The rest of a company's work force may become temporary employees hired to complete specific jobs of limited duration plus a network of vendors (small businesses).[26]

Just as many small businesses today perform specific tasks for large businesses, small business owners are increasingly turning to other companies for needed goods and services. A survey of 400 CEOs of fast-growing businesses showed that 68 percent outsourced their payroll responsibilities, 48 percent hired another business to handle their tax compliance, and 46 percent farmed out their employee benefits and claims administration.[27]

The chairman of General Electric, John G. Welch, Jr., has said that "Size is no longer the trump card it once was in today's brutally competitive world—a marketplace that is unimpressed with logos and sales numbers but demands, instead, value and performance."[28] Since they are flexible and efficient, today's small businesses can provide the "value and performance" that the market demands.

Computer Applications

Technology is rapidly changing the way we work and play. In fact, it's changing the way we live our lives, from daybreak to day's end. Because computers and technology are transforming society, we want to show you how you can benefit from technology. In this feature, throughout the book, we'll be "capturing" the importance of technology to small business by describing many useful computer tools—primarily software programs and CD-ROMs—that you can use to be more effective and efficient. Let's look at this chapter's example.

Gaining a competitive advantage can be made easier with the use of a multimedia CD-ROM called CRUSH from Hands-On Technology of Burlingame, California. This CD-ROM helps you analyze your competition and the market-

place and then organizes the information into a meaningful format. With this information, a small business owner can identify areas of competitive advantage and specify ways to build on company strengths, address company weaknesses, and "CRUSH" the competition. Keep in mind, however, that running CD-ROMs such as CRUSH typically requires a computer system that has adequate memory, dual-speed (or faster) CD-ROM drive, an adequate monitor with graphics capability, and a compatible sound system, such as SoundBlaster. But if you have the required computer hardware and software capability, CD-ROMs such as CRUSH can be a powerful tool for small business owners and managers.

Source: Dennis James, "Shortcut to Success," Success *(November 1995), pp. 67–70.*

Niche Marketing. The flexibility of small businesses to respond to the needs of their customers, whether they be large businesses, consumers, or located in another country, is their ability to market to niches. **Niche marketing** is defined as serving a small segment or group of customers. Small businesses enjoy the advantage of being able to profitably serve smaller niches than their larger counterparts. For example, Olmec Corporation, maker of ethnic toys, has chosen a niche in the gigantic toy market. Olmec was one of the first to produce ethnic toys and still has the niche largely to itself. Currently, the large toy manufacturers are not making toys for this market because they believe there is not enough demand to justify large production runs or national marketing campaigns. Therefore, Olmec could put itself in danger if it succeeds in creating a much larger market for minority-oriented toys because larger competitors might be attracted to enter the field.

niche marketing Identifying and serving small groups, or segments, of a market.

Small Business in a Global Marketplace. The same competitive advantages (unique skills, talents, and products) that have made your business successful in local markets may also create advantage in foreign markets. Since small businesses are especially suited to satisfying niche markets quickly, they are and will continue to be important players in international trade. As the world becomes more of a global marketplace, many opportunities are emerging for small businesses, especially those that can take advantage of technological advances.

 Global Small Business

Consider the example set by Edward Kaplan and Gary Cless, two electromechanical engineers. Working at Teletype, a subsidiary of AT&T's Western Electric, the two men were designing teleprinters, a precursor to fax machines. Because they didn't like working for a large corporation, they decided to go into business together. One of their products was a paper-tape punch machine that punched out designs to program machine tools, and by 1982, they were the market leaders in that industry. But Kaplan and Cless were closely monitoring how computers and technology were changing the way businesses worked. They believed that the newly emerging business of bar coding was what they should focus on in the future.

Kaplan and Cless started their next company, Zebra Technologies, in 1982, to make industrial bar code label printers. And the demand for their products positively exploded! Today bar codes produced by Zebra software and printed on Zebra printers can be found everywhere, from hospitals to zoos to steel plants. And inevitably, the company attracted global competitors because of its success. However, Zebra continues to prosper by selling high-end printers while their competitors sell mostly cheaper models.

Kaplan and Cless nonetheless recognize that they must cultivate more mid-size companies to broaden their customer base. To this end, they've introduced a more moderately priced line of bar code printers that smaller companies can afford. Obviously, the two founders of Zebra Technologies are people who know how to "change their stripes"— that is, how to survive in a rapidly evolving marketplace. *Source: Toddi Gutner Block, "Riding the Waves," Forbes, September 11, 1995, pp. 182–183.*

Of the 105,000 manufacturers involved exporting products in 1993, about 96 percent had fewer than 100 employees; 63 percent had fewer than 20 employees.[29] (In terms of quantities of goods exported, however, large companies still predominate.) In 1994, the top 100 exporters accounted for over half of the goods sent abroad.[30] But manufacturing isn't the only area in which small businesses are advancing globally. In Chapter 12, we will discuss how small businesses are involved in exporting, international licensing, international joint ventures, establishing operations in other countries, and importing.

Secrets of Small Business Success

When large and small businesses compete directly against each other, it may seem that large businesses have a better chance of winning. However, small businesses have certain inherent factors that work in their favor. You will improve your chances of success in running a small business if you identify your competitive advantage, remain flexible and innovative, cultivate a close relationship with your customers, and strive for quality.

Competitive Advantage

To be successful in business, you have to offer your customers more value than your competitors do. That value gives the business its **competitive advantage.** For example, say that you are a printer whose competitors offer only black-and-white printing. An investment in color printing equipment would give your business a competitive advantage, at least until your competitors purchased similar equipment. The stronger and more sustainable your competitive advantage, the better your chances of winning and keeping customers. You must have a product or service that your business provides better than the competition, or the pressures of the marketplace may make your business obsolete. (See Chapter 9.)

competitive advantage The facet of a business that is done better than everyone else. A competitive advantage can be built from many different factors.

Flexibility. In order to take advantage of economies of scale, large businesses are usually concerned with devoting resources to produce large quantities of products over long periods of time. This commitment of resources limits their ability to react to new and quickly changing markets as small businesses do. Imagine the difference between making a sharp turn in a loaded 18-wheel tractor trailer and a small pickup. Now apply the analogy to large and small businesses turning in new directions. The big truck has a lot more capacity, but the pickup has more maneuverability in reaching customers.

Innovation. Real innovation has come most often from independent inventors and small businesses. The reason? The research and development departments of most large businesses tend to concentrate on the improvement of the products the company already makes. This practice makes sense for companies trying to profit from their large investments in plants and equipment. At the same time, it tends to discourage the development of totally new ideas and products. For example, telecommunications giant AT&T has an incentive to improve its existing line of telephones and services to better serve its customers. But the idea of inventing a product that would make telephones obsolete would threaten its investment.

By striving for flexibility, creativity, and closeness to the customer, small businesses deliver satisfaction along with quality products and services.

Small businesses have contributed many inventions that we use daily. The long list would include zippers, air conditioners, helicopters, computers, instant cameras, and automobiles, most of which were later produced by large manufacturers. In fact, many say that the greatest value of entrepreneurial companies is the way they force larger competitors to respond to innovation. Small businesses innovate new technology, markets, products and ideas.

creative destruction The replacement of existing products, processes, ideas, and businesses with new and better ones.

Economist Joseph Schumpeter called the replacement of existing products, processes, ideas, and businesses with new and better ones **creative destruction.** It is not an easy process. Though change can be threatening, it is vitally necessary in a capitalist system.[31] Small businesses are the driving force of change in the development of new technology.

Recently the SBA researched types of innovation and the role played by small businesses. The four types of innovation are:

- *Product innovation:* Developing a new or improved product.
- *Service innovation:* Offering a new or altered service for sale.
- *Process innovation:* Inventing a new way to organize physical inputs to produce a product or service.
- *Management innovation:* Creating a new way to organize business's resources.

The most common types of innovation relate to service and product. Thirty-eight percent of all innovations are service related, and 32 percent are product related. Interestingly, the majority of innovations were found to have originated from the smallest businesses, those with 1 to 19 employees. Over three-fourths of service innovations are generated by very small businesses, which also generate 65 percent of both product and process innovations.[32]

The process of creative destruction is not limited to high technology or to the largest companies. A small business owner who does not keep up with the market risks being left behind. Creative destruction occurs in mundane as well as exotic industries, such as chains of beauty salons replacing barber shops.[33] Knowledge is the key to innovation and advancement. For this reason, it is important for you to keep current with business literature by reading periodicals such as *Inc., Success,* or *Fortune,* that cover small business topics and any specialized trade journals that exist for your type of business. Many business schools also have executive education programs, which range from two days to a year or longer, specifically designed for small business owners.[34]

Close Relationship to Customers. Small business owners get to know their customers and neighborhood on a personal level. This closeness allows small businesses to provide individualized service and gives them firsthand knowledge of customer wants and needs. By contrast, large businesses only get to "know" their customers through limited samples of marketing research (which may be misleading). Knowing customers personally can allow small businesses to build a competitive advantage based on specialty products, personalized service, and quality, which enable the small business to compete with the bigger business's lower price gained through mass production. For this reason, you should always remember that the rapport you build with your customers is what makes them come back again and again.

Product Quality. One of the management buzzwords of the 1980s was *total quality management* (TQM). Companies have adopted TQM principles as a way to demonstrate their commitment to quality on every level of the business. The philosophy of total quality management is based on the work of W. Edwards Deming, who developed a list of 14 points for managers to follow in achieving world-class quality (described in Chapter 13). Basically, **quality** refers to all the features and characteristics of a product or service that affect its ability to satisfy a customer's wants and needs.

quality The features and characteristics of a product that allow it to exceed customer expectations.

Val Verutti is quality support manager for Granite Rock Company, a construction materials manufacturer. For Verutti, the key to producing quality is being able to measure the results. "If you set goals and lofty ideals, without means of measuring," he states, "you're just kidding yourself."[35] Verutti should know something about quality—Granite Rock won the 1992 Malcolm Baldrige National Quality Award for the small business category.

Some companies subscribing to the TQM philosophy have found that it can be expensive, time-consuming, and complex. It can result in more attention being paid to administering the TQM program than to customers or to products. Many managers, especially small business owners who are strapped for resources, now look for **return on quality** (ROQ), which means paying the closest attention to parts of your product or business that are most important to your customers and your bottom line. Quality for its own sake, in areas that don't matter to customers or which don't produce a payoff in improved sales, profits, or increased market share, waste the company's effort and resources.[36] (See Chapter 13.)

return on quality The act of concentrating attention to produce quality in areas most important to customers.

Getting Started

Before starting your business, you will want to make sure you have the tools to succeed. Look for a market large enough to generate a profit, sufficient capital, skilled employees, and accurate information.

Market Size and Definition.   Who will be buying your product or service? Marketing techniques help you find out what consumers want and in what quantity. With this information, you can make an informed decision about the profitability of offering a particular good or service. Once you conclude that a market is large enough to support your business, you will want to learn what your customers have in common and about their likes and dislikes in order to serve them better and remain competitive.

Gathering Sufficient Capital.   Too often, entrepreneurs try to start a business without sufficient startup capital. The lifeblood of any young business is cash; starting on a financial shoestring hurts your chances of success. Profit is the ultimate goal, but inadequate cash flow cuts off the blood supply. (See Chapter 17.)

You may need to be creative in finding startup capital. A second mortgage, loans from friends or relatives, a line of credit from a bank or credit union, or a combination of sources may be sufficient. Thorough planning will give you the best estimate of how much money you will need. Once you have made your best estimate, double it—or at least get access to more capital. You'll probably need it.

Finding and Keeping Effective Employees.   Maintaining a capable work force is a never-ending task for small businesses. Frequently, small business owners get caught up in urgency to "fill positions with warm bodies" before spending enough time on the selection process. You should hire, train, and motivate your employees before opening for business. (See Chapter 14.)

Once established, you must understand that your most valuable assets walk out the door at closing time. Your employees are valuable assets because it is their skill, knowledge, and information that make your business successful. These intangible assets are called **intellectual capital.**

intellectual capital The valuable skills and knowledge that employees of a business possess.

Getting Accurate Information.   Managers at any organization will tell you how difficult it is to make a decision before acquiring all the relevant information. This difficulty is compounded for the aspiring small business owner, who does not yet possess the expertise or experience needed to oversee every functional area of the business, from accounting to sales. Consult a variety of sources of information, from self-help books in your local library to experts in your nearest Small Business Development Center. A more accurate picture can be drawn if you consider several vantage points.

Entering the Internet

You can't read a magazine or watch a news program these days without seeing or hearing references to it. What is *it?* "It" is the Internet and, of course, its more popular cousin—the World Wide Web. In this feature, throughout the textbook, we'll show you useful and interesting sites on the Internet (and particularly, on the Web) that can help you plug into a vast array of electronic resources. But first, we need some basics. Just what are the Internet and the World Wide Web?

Put simply, the Internet is a vast network of computers located at universities and government agencies around the world (estimated at more than 50,000 computers in 90 countries in 1995). Connections between them are made across phone lines to which computers are attached by a modem. Computers on the network share a common language format for routing data from one computer to another. Home computers aren't typically part of the Internet, although home users can dial into it by subscribing to any of the national commercial services such as America Online, Prodigy, CompuServe, GEnie, or Delphi.

Most Internet users are interested in one of the Internet's most popular components, the World Wide Web (known as the Web or WWW). The Web has opened up the vast array of available information and product resources to a more general audience. Before the Web was created, users needed sophisticated computer skills and knowledge of arcane computer language to search and retrieve information on the Internet. Now, with a computer, modem, and Web browser software such as Netscape or Mosaic (easy-to-use computer programs that help you navigate the Web), even novices can avail themselves of the thousands of information sources on the Web. Information on the Web is found on a "Web page"— a publicly available computer file, stored on a computer attached to the Internet. Web pages can consist of text, sound, or graphics, even video! They usually contain hypertext—highlighted words or graphics in the Web site that link to other information stored on the Web.

All in all, a small business owner can use the Net and the Web to market products, to find important information, to talk to other small business people, or just to check the weather! We know you'll enjoy learning about the Internet and the World Wide Web. Have fun "surfing the Web"! *Sources: John W. Verity and Robert D. Hof, "The Internet: How It Will Change the Way You Do Business,"* Business Week, *November 14, 1994, pp. 80–88; Vince Gelormine, "Selling in Cyberspace,"* Success *(May 1995), pp. 61–68; Stephen H. Wildstrom, "Feeling Your Way Around the Web,"* Business Week, *September 11, 1995, p. 22; "Good Question,"* Inc. *(October 1995), p. 16; and Philip E. Ross and Nikhil Hutheesing, "Along Came the Spiders,"* Forbes, *October 23, 1995, pp. 210–216.*

Note: Throughout the book we provide the names and addresses of sites on the Internet and the World Wide Web that we think you'll find useful. We have made every effort to assure their accuracy. However, because these computer networks are constantly evolving, some of the addresses may have changed by the time you pick up this book. If you find an incorrect address, you can find the correct one by going to one of the Web search tools, such as Yahoo or Lycos, and keying in the name of the site that you're trying to reach.

Understanding the Risks of Small Business Ownership

The decision to start your own business should be made with a full understanding of the risks involved. If you go in with both eyes open, you will be able to anticipate problems, reduce the possibility of loss, and increase your chances of success. The prospect of failure should serve as a warning to you. Many new businesses do not get past their second or third years. Running a small business involves much more than simply getting an idea, hanging out a sign, and opening for business the next day. You need a vision, resources, and a plan in order to take advantage of the opportunity that exists.

What Is Business Failure?

Even though business owners start their ventures with the best of intentions and work long, hard hours, some businesses do fail. Dun & Bradstreet, a financial research firm, defines a *business failure* as a business that closes:

- due to actions such as bankruptcy, foreclosure, or voluntary withdrawal from the business *with a financial loss to a creditor,* or
- any business involved in court action like receivership (taken over involuntarily) or reorganization (receiving protection from creditors).

According to this definition, 107 out of 10,000 businesses failed in 1991.[37] More detailed information on failure rate by industry for 1991 is shown in Figure 1-4. You can see that businesses within the agriculture, forestry, and fishing industries enjoy the lowest industry failure rate, while businesses within the transportation industry suffer the highest rate. Still, a considerable variance of failure

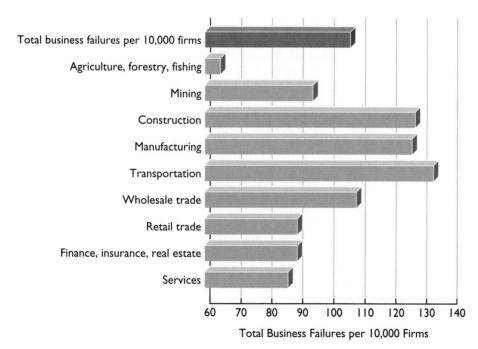

FIGURE 1-4
Business Failure Rate per 10,000 Firms, 1991
Source: Statistical Abstract of the United States, *1993, p. 540.*

M anager's Notebook

Risky Business

Riskiest Types of Business	Business Failure Rate per 10,000 (1990)	Safest Types of Business	Business Failure Rate per 10,000 (1990)
Amusement and recreation services	578	Personal services	39
Oil and gas extraction	166	Insurance agents and brokers	28
Lumber and wood manufacturing	106	Legal services	25
General building contractors	101	Health services	21
Furniture and home furnishing stores	99	Private educational services	13

Source: Bruce Phillips, Small Business Administration Office of Economic Research, cited in Inc. State of Small Business, *May 16 1995, p. 20.*

rates exists within industries. The table in the Manager's Notebook box illustrates the five riskiest and the five safest businesses in 1990. If you are considering starting an amusement or recreation service business, the failure rate of 578 businesses per 10,000 carries much more meaning to you on the risk you face than the figure of 75 per 10,000 for all businesses.

Causes of Business Failure

The rates of business failure vary greatly by industry and are affected by factors such as type of ownership, size of the business, and expertise of the owner. The most common causes of business failure, however, are inadequate management and financing. (See Figure 1-5.)

While financial problems are listed as the most common cause of business failure, consider management's role in controlling them. Could business failure due to industry weakness be linked to poor management? Yes, if the owner tried to enter an industry or market with no room for another competitor or was slow to respond to industry changes. High operating expenses and an insufficient profit margin also reflect ineffective management. Finally, business failure due to insufficient capital also suggests inexperienced management.

Inadequate Management. Business management is the efficient and effective use of resources. For small business owners, management skills are especially desirable—and often especially difficult to obtain. Lack of experience is one of their most pressing problems. Small business owners must be generalists; they do not have the luxury of specialized management. On the one hand, they may not be able to afford to hire the full-time experts who could help avert costly mistakes. On the other hand, their limited resources will not permit them to make many

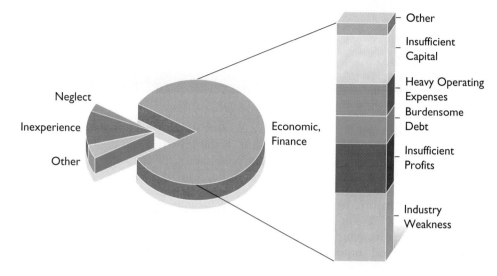

FIGURE 1-5
The Causes of Business Failures Are Many and Complex
Causes of business failure, 1990.
Business Failure Record, *The Dun & Bradstreet Corporation, NFIB Foundation/VISA Business Card Primer, as shown in William J. Dennis, Jr.,* A Small Business Primer, *1993, National Foundation of Independent Business, p. 23.*

mistakes and stay in business. As a small business manager, you will probably have to make decisions in areas in which you have little expertise.

The manager of a small business must be a leader, a planner, and a worker. You may be a "top gun" in sales, but that skill could work against you. You might be tempted to concentrate on sales while ignoring other equally important areas of the business such as recordkeeping, inventory, or customer service.

Inadequate Financing. Business failure due to inadequate financing can be caused by improper managerial control as well as shortage of capital. On the one hand, if you don't have adequate funds to begin with, you will not be able to afford the facilities or personnel you need to start up the business correctly. On the other hand, if you do possess adequate capital but do not manage your resources wisely, you may be unable to maintain adequate inventory or keep the balance needed to run the business.

There are a lot of ways to fail in business. You can extend too much credit. You can fail to plan for the future or not have strategic direction. You can overinvest in fixed assets or hire the wrong people. Identifying mistakes that can be made is only part of the problem. Figuring out how to avoid them is the hard part.[38]

Business Termination

There is a difference between a **business termination** and a **business failure.** A *termination* occurs when a business no longer exists for any reason. There are many reasons for a business to be terminated. The owner may have an opportunity to sell his or her business to someone else for a healthy profit. The owner may be ready to move on to a new business or to retire, or may have simply lost interest in the business. The market for the business's product may have changed or become saturated. Perhaps the owner decided it was more attractive to work for someone else. In other cases, businesses may change form. A partnership may be restructured as a corporation, or a business may simply move to a new location. Businesses that undergo such changes are considered terminated even though they continue in another form.

business termination When a business ceases operation for any reason.

business failure When a business closes with a financial loss to a creditor.

Manager's Notebook

Entrepreneurial Mistakes

No one likes to think about failing. Yet many small business owners invite failure by ignoring basic rules for success. One of the most common mistakes is failing to look toward the future, in the belief that planning is too hard or time-consuming. Planning what you want to do with your business, where you want it to go, and how you're going to get it there are prerequisites for a sound business. But that doesn't mean you can't change your plans as circumstances dictate. Rather, your plan should provide a roadmap for your business, showing you both the express-ways, the scenic route—and, of course, the detours.

Another common mistake is failing to understand the commitment and hard work that are required for making a business a success. Having to work long hours and do things you do not enjoy because there's no one else to do them are part and parcel of owning a small business. But often, when you have the freedom of being your own boss, the hard work and long hours don't seem so demanding!

Another mistake that small business owners make, particularly in rapidly growing businesses, is not hiring additional employees soon enough or not using existing employees effectively. There comes a point in the growth of a business when it's no longer possible for the manager to do it all, and it's often difficult for the manager to give up control. Yet it's important to recognize that delegating tasks to others isn't giving up control—it's giving up the execution of details.

The last type of mistake that we want to look at involves the financials. Inaccurate estimates of cash flow and capital requirements can swamp a business quickly. Figuring the correct amount of money needed for starting a business is a tough balancing act. Asking for too little may hinder growth and may actually jeopardize survival. But asking for too much might cause lenders or investors to hesitate. An important rule to remember in terms of arranging financing or calculating cash flow projections is to figure the unexpected into your financial plans. In this way, you can have more of a cushion to fall back on when things don't go exactly according to plan. After all, without the right amount of capital, it's impossible to succeed.

Sources: Udayan Gupta, "How Much?" The Wall Street Journal, May 22, 1995, p. R7; and Stephanie N. Mehta, "Small Talk: An Interview with Wendell E. Dunn," The Wall Street Journal, May 22, 1995, p. R16+.

Failure-Rate Controversy

Most everyone has heard the story about the supposedly high rate of failure for small businesses. "Did you know that 90 percent of all new businesses fail within one year?" the story usually begins, as if to confirm one's worst fears about business ownership. For educators and businesspeople, this piece of modern folklore is known as the "myth that would not die." Actually, only about 18 percent of all new businesses are forced to close their doors with a loss to creditors.[39] The rest either closed voluntarily or are still in business.

Sometimes researchers include business terminations in their failure-rate calculations, resulting in an artificially high number of failures. Economic consultant David Birch describes the misinterpretation of economic data as "like being at the end of a whisper chain. It's a myth everyone agrees to."[40] Fortunately for small business owners, the myth is not a fact.

Starting a business does involve risk, but the assumption of risk is part of life. The divorce rate in 1992 was 48 per 10,000.[41] Of every 10,000 students who start college, how many fail to graduate? Would you decide not to get married because the divorce rate is too high? Were you afraid to go to college because of the drop-out rate? The point to remember is that if you have a clear vision, know your product and your market, and devote the time and effort needed, small businesses can and do succeed.

Over the last ten years, the number of new businesses that have opened has exceeded the number that have closed. Table 1-4 shows a net business formation for a recent 20-year period. Data from the SBA show that the average new firm formation rate averaged 13 percent for the years 1982–1993.[42] More recently, Dun & Bradstreet reported that the number of business failures peaked in 1992 at 97,069 and fell to 85,982 in 1993.[43]

TABLE 1 ▪ 4   U.S. Startups versus Failures

	NUMBER OF NEW INCORPORATIONS	NUMBER OF FAILURES
1970	264,000	10,748
1975	326,000	11,432
1980	532,000	11,742
1985	663,000	57,078
1990	647,000	60,747

Source: Statistical Abstract of the United States, 1993, p. 539.

What's Ahead?

Because small businesses vary so greatly, it is difficult to generalize about them. Examples and illustrations used to describe how to operate a small business may be appropriate for most but still not fit the exact business you have in mind. The following chapters will attempt to lead you through the process of starting and operating your own successful small business.

Summary

■ The characteristics of small business.

Small businesses include a wide variety of business types which are independently owned, operated and financed. While specific size definitions exist for each type of business, manufacturers with fewer than 500 employees, wholesalers with fewer than 100 employees and retailers or services with annual revenue of under $3.5M are considered small. By itself, each individual small business has relatively little impact in its industry.

■ The role of small business in the U.S. and global economies.

Small businesses provided the economic foundation on which the U.S. economy was built. Small businesses are creating new jobs while large businesses are eliminating jobs. Small businesses are more flexible in the products and services they offer. Most real product innovations come from small businesses. Small businesses are rapidly becoming important players in international trade.

■ The importance of diversity in the marketplace and workplace.

Small businesses are responding as the population becomes more diverse. Businesses owned by women and minorities are growing at a faster rate than the overall rate of business growth.

■ The causes of business failure.

Ineffective and inefficient management, which shows up in many ways, is the number one cause of business failure. Inadequate financing, industry weakness, inexperience, and neglect are other major causes.

■ Ways to court success in a small business venture.

To prevent your small business from becoming another casualty in business failure statistics, you must begin with a clearly defined competitive advantage. You must offer a product or service that people want and are willing to buy. You must do *something* substantially better than your competition. You must remain flexible and innovative, stay close to your customers, and strive for quality.

Questions for Review and Discussion

1. How would you define *small business?*
2. Name a company that seems large but might be classified as small because it has relatively little impact on its industry.
3. Large businesses depend on small businesses. Why?
4. Define *outsourcing,* and describe its impact on small business.
5. Why are small businesses more likely than large businesses to be innovative?
6. Explain the term *creative destruction.*
7. How can being close to your customers give you a competitive advantage?
8. How would you show that small business is becoming a more important part of the economy?
9. The text compares the failure rate of small business with the divorce rate in marriage and student failure rate in college. Are these fair comparisons?
10. Describe four causes of small business failure. How does the quality of management relate to each of these causes?
11. Describe the techniques that a business you are familiar with has used to prevent business failure.
12. How would the computer industry be different today if there were no businesses under 500 employees? Would personal computers exist?
13. Predict the future of small business. What industries will it be involved in? What trends do you foresee? Will the failure rate go up or down? Will importance of small business increase or decrease by the year 2010?

Critical Incident

Clark Childers is all of 17 years old and already he's president of his own successful small business, QuikSkins Boat Covers of Corpus Christi, Texas. Even at such a young age, Childers pulled together several key ingredients to launch his business: a comprehensive business plan, product prototypes, available funding, and an untapped market.

Childers loves to sail. But one thing he hates about the hobby is taking his small Sunfish sailboat apart after sailing and packing up all the boat's parts. This chore could easily consume 15 to 20 minutes each time. Then Childers realized that he could make his pasttime much more enjoyable if he found a way to cover his Sunfish in just a few minutes. So he designed a fabric cover to fit around the mast, cover the boat, and protect the boat's removable parts (rudder, centerboard, and tiller). The cover even included a pocket for the sail.

Childers's first product prototype worked well, but his initial attempts at mail order and marketing to local boat shops weren't as successful. Demand was so small that only a family friend was needed to hand-sew the boat covers as they were ordered. However, Childers knew he had a good product that other Sunfish enthusiasts would be excited about. So he wrote to the president of the boat's manufacturer, Sunfish/Laser Inc., describing his product. And his strategy paid off with an order for 300 boat covers!

To begin production, Childers first had to find financing. He obtained a bank loan, cosigned by his mother. Then he had to find an affordable production facility which could turn out the product quickly and reliably. Childers wanted to ensure that paying production expenses didn't eat up all his profits. And he had only six weeks from the time he signed the contract with Sunfish/Laser to deliver the 300 covers. He considered manufacturers in Corpus Christi, which he realized would allow him only to break even on his expenses. After someone suggested that he look to Mexico for a possible partner, he found a firm in Piedras Negras called Tight Stitches, which not only met the production deadline, but charged $30 less per cover than the lowest bid he had received in Corpus Christi. That 300-cover order propelled QuikSkins Boat Covers to 1994 sales of $45,000, with profits topping $20,000.

What advice does Clark Childers have for other small business owners? He says the main lesson he learned was to be open to nontraditional ways of operating. Childers continued working with Tight Stitches, but also partnered with a Corpus Christi workshop for people with disabilities to manufacture some of his other products. Using a foreign factory or a manufacturing shop made up of workers with disabilities may *sound* risky to some small business owners, but for Childers, it has proven profitable. *Source: Clark Childers and Susan Biddle Jaffe, "Setting Sail on a New Venture,"* Nation's Business *(October 1995), p. 6.*

Questions

1. Pretend that you're Clark Childers and your business is facing shutdown if you don't get some customers for your product. Write a letter to the president of Sunfish/Laser Inc. that would persuade the president to place an order.

2. Break into teams and discuss what Childers did correctly in getting his business started. What problems could he possibly run into and how could he address them?

Take it to the Net

We invite you to visit the Hatten page on the Prentice Hall Web site at: http://www.prenhall.com/~hattensb for this chapter's World Wide Web exercise.

Chapter Focus

After reading this chapter, you should be able to:

- Articulate the differences between the small business manager and the entrepreneur.
- Explain how entrepreneurial skills benefit the small business owner.
- Enumerate the advantages and disadvantages of self-employment.
- Characterize the three main forms of ownership, sole proprietorship, partnership, or corporation and their unique features.
- Discuss the steps in preparing for small business ownership.

2 Small Business Management, Entrepreneurship, and Ownership

S A COLLEGE PROFESSOR, Robert Nourse never dreamed that he would one day own one of the hottest retail businesses in North America. But today Nourse is president and CEO of the Bombay Company, which sells replicas of eighteenth- and nineteenth-century English furniture. In 1993 he was named Entrepreneur of the Year by *Inc.* magazine.

Nourse had managed several businesses but felt he was ready to run one of his own, and he was looking for just the right opportunity. Nourse first heard of the Bombay Company from a friend who had invested in the small mail-order company and who encouraged Nourse to take a look. Bombay sold attractive reproductions of eighteenth- and nineteenth-century English furniture at reasonable prices. A unique advantage of the furniture was that it was unassembled and packed in flat boxes (called "knock-down" in the furniture business) that reduced shipping and storage costs. Nourse met with Brad Harper, the company's founder, to investigate. Since Bombay had not entered the Canadian market, Nourse bought the Canadian rights to

Bombay for $1 plus 4 percent royalties. The two men penned the deal with entrepreneurial flair on the back of a napkin.

In running the business in Canada, Nourse made his first strategic change by eliminating the mail-order distribution and opening stores in shopping malls. In this way, customers could take the furniture right to their cars after purchasing it, rather than having to wait 6 to 12 weeks for delivery. Nourse risked his entire life savings of $125,000 and another $125,000 in bank loans to open the first location in Toronto's Eaton Centre. Sales were impressive, but 1980 interest rates of 20 percent prevented expansion to other locations.

Meanwhile, Harper sold U.S. operations to a holding company called Tandy Brands, which was interested in the Canadian operations. Unable to afford the cost of expanding, Nourse sold his distribution rights to Tandy Brands. However, the terms of the buyout allowed Nourse to manage the Canadian operations and to use Tandy's financing to allow him to build 13 stores by 1983. While Nourse's stores were profitable, Tandy's stores were not. Carson Thompson, Tandy CEO, merged U.S. and Canadian units and promoted Nourse to president. The combined companies, with Nourse as president, went from a $3 million loss in 1984 to a $500,000 profit in 1985, then a $2 million profit the next year. By 1994, sales from 383 Bombay Company stores reached $232 million. Bombay ranked sixteenth largest out of approximately 50,000 North American home furnishing retailers. Nourse says, "Our original ambition was to have 400 to 500 stores. Now that we are almost there, we never dreamed that we'd just be scratching the surface of a whole new generation of growth."

Robert Nourse believes that "a business, and certainly a retail business that changes so quickly, has to keep reinventing itself or it will wither and die." He is living proof of that belief. Instead of relaxing and enjoying his overwhelming success, he is rolling out a whole new retailing concept called Alex & Ivy, which features French and American country furniture and accessories.

Nourse has a rare combination of skills. He is both a successful entrepreneur and a skillful long-term business manager. As we will see in this chapter, the talent to be a successful entrepreneur does not automatically mean a person will be as successful as a long-term business manager. *Source: Jay Finegan, "Survival of the Smartest," pp. 78–88. Adapted with permission, INC. magazine, December 1993. Copyright 1993 by Goldhirsh Group, Inc., 38 Commercial Wharf, Boston, MA 02110.*

The Entrepreneur/Manager Relationship

What is the difference between a small business manager and entrepreneur? Aren't all small business owners also entrepreneurs? Don't all entrepreneurs start as small business owners? The terms are often used interchangeably, and while there is overlap between them, there are enough differences to be studied separately. Entrepreneurship and small business management are both *processes,* not isolated incidents.

Entrepreneurship is the process of identifying opportunities for which marketable needs exist and assuming the risk of creating an organization to satisfy them. An entrepreneur needs the vision to spot opportunities and the ability to capitalize on them. Small business management, by contrast, is the ongoing process of owning and operating an established business. A small business manager must be able to deal with all the challenges of moving the business forward—hiring and retaining good employees, reacting to changing customer wants and needs, making sales and keeping cash flow positive, for example.

The processes of entrepreneurship and small business management each present challenges and rewards as the business progresses through different stages.

What Is an Entrepreneur?

An entrepreneur is a person who sees an opportunity and assumes the risk of starting a business to take advantage of the opportunity or idea. The risks that go with creating an organization can be financial, material, and psychological. The term *entrepreneur,* a French word that dates from the seventeenth century, translates literally to "between-taker" or "go-between."[1] It originally referred to men who organized and managed exploration expeditions and military maneuvers. The term has evolved over the years into a multitude of definitions but most include the following behaviors:

- *Creation:* A new business is started.
- *Innovation:* The business involves a new product, process, market, material, or organization.
- *Risk assumption:* The owner of the business bears the risk of potential loss or failure of the business.
- *General management:* The owner of the business guides the business and allocates the business's resources.
- *Performance intention:* High levels of growth and/or profit are expected.[2]

All new businesses require a certain amount of entrepreneurial skill. The degree of entrepreneurship involved depends on the amount of each of these behaviors that is needed.

An entrepreneur is a person who takes advantage of a business opportunity by assuming the financial, material, and psychological risks of starting or running a company.

Entrepreneurship and the Small Business Manager

Entrepreneurship involves the startup process. Small business management focuses on running a business over a long period of time. While you cannot study one without the other, they are different. In managing a small business, most of the "entrepreneuring" was done a long time ago. Of course, a good manager is always looking for new ways to please customers, but the original innovation and the triggering event that launched the business make way for more stability in the maturity stage of the business.

The manager of a small business needs perseverance, patience, and critical thinking skills to deal with the day-to-day challenges that arise in running a business over a long period of time.

Manager's Notebook

Staying Fresh

What happens to that opportunity-seeking, entrepreneurial spirit as a small business grows? Does achieving stability mean the end of entrepreneurship? What can you, as a small business manager, do to maintain the creative, daring, innovative approaches that made your business successful in the first place while building a "business that lasts"?

Often, as a small business achieves marketplace and financial successes and grows in size, it loses those bold, ingenious risk-seeking attitudes, actions, and approaches that helped make it successful. For instance, employees may, for whatever reasons, become resistant to taking risks and making changes. But it doesn't have to be that way! A successful and growing small business can be well structured, organized, under control, and yet still maintain an organizational environment where entrepreneurial attitudes can flourish. How? Let's look at some suggestions that can help small businesses preserve that spirit of entrepreneurship.

Develop an Appropriate Control System. It's important to get feedback about decisions that have been made by employees. Yet your control system should imply trust, so that employees can make decisions without feeling like someone's always looking over their shoulders.

At Indus Group, a management software developer in San Francisco, founder Bob Felton wanted employees to use their judgment, not bureaucratic rules, to guide their actions. He uses electronic mail to keep up with them. Every Friday, all employees type up a one-page summary of what they worked on that week, what their plans are for the coming week, and what obstacles they'd run into.

Emphasize Responsibility, Not Just Authority. In a young firm, employees tend to feel personally responsible for what happens to the company. In older firms, where authority is centralized in levels of management, people often feel less inclined to pursue opportunities and change on their own initiative. How can you instill a sense of employee commitment in your established firm?

At BAI International, a Tarrytown, New York–based market research firm, employees are encouraged to "make things work" by improving both the work environment and the work product. President and owner Kathy Knight asks employees to get involved by speaking up about work-related decisions. Because they are involved in these decisions, employees feel a sense of responsibility to the company.

Determine the Kinds of Failure your Company Can Tolerate. Failure and mistakes are an inevitable part of business life. One of the hallmarks of an entrepreneurial company is that failures are seen as valuable learning experiences. Of course, lapses in ethical decision making can have serious consequences and should not be tolerated. Yet when individuals fail because they lack the skills, or application of effort needed, or because of uncontrollable external influences, managers should look for ways to address the causes and remedies of those mistakes so they can be avoided in the future.

Create and Nurture Teams and Teamwork. A growing company inevitably becomes more complex. The number of its products and the size of its markets have probably increased, and it may pursue new technologies or aggressive growth strategies. Organizing employee teams offers a way to empower employees to stay on top of all the changes for you. Teams facilitate empowerment in varying ways, some by cross-training employees to increase the general skill level, others by asking employees to specialize in a certain area. However they are structured, teams assist problem solving by giving employees a sense of direction.

At Published Image, a small Boston firm that publishes documents for shareholders of 11 mutual fund companies, president and founder Eric Gershman reorganized employees into four self-managed teams. Gershman says that creating the teams helped to halt chronically high employee turnover and to keep customers coming back while increasing profits. Gershman feels that it was the teams' close focus on clients' needs that helped his company manage its rapid growth.

Encourage Functional Excellence in All Positions. While every manager wants quality people in all functional areas, hiring specialists is typically cost prohibitive for the small business. So you may have to try other options. At Playground Environments Inc., a small maker of playground equipment in Speonk, New York, all core employees are trained to do several jobs. From product innovation to developing marketing plans to taking turns cooking lunch for everyone in the office, employees are expected to contribute in different functions as needed. By working in these different jobs, the company's employees get to see how all

the pieces fit together and why it is important for each job to be done in an excellent manner.

Promote Continuous Adaptive Organizational Change. To build a company atmosphere that supports opportunity-seeking behavior and change, the small business manager should reward individuals who come up with bold, innovative ideas. Nothing can kill the risk-taking spirit faster than criticizing employees who want to try something new. Restless invention, not staid complacency, should be the credo of a growing business that wants to maintain that entrepreneurial spirit.

Sources: Howard Stevenson and José Carlos Jarrillo-Mossi, "Preserving Entrepreneurship as Companies Grow," The Journal of Business Strategy (Summer 1986), pp. 10–23. Leslie Brokaw, "Thinking Flat," Inc. (October 1993), p. 88. Roberta Maynard, "Are Your Employees Helping Your Company Grow?" Nation's Business (April 1994), p. 10. Michael Selz, "Testing Self-Managed Teams, Entrepreneur Hopes to Lose Job," The Wall Street Journal, January 11, 1994, p. B1+. Gail Buchalter, "Making a Difference," Forbes, May 9, 1994, pp. 164–165.

A Model of the Startup Process

The processes of entrepreneurship and small business management can be thought of as a spectrum with six distinct stages that can be identified for each. (See Figure 2-1.)[3] The stages of the entrepreneurship process are innovation, a triggering event, and implementation. The stages of the small business management process are growth, maturity, and harvest.

The **entrepreneurial process** begins with an *innovative* idea for a new product, process, or service, which is refined as you think it through. You may tell your idea to family members or close friends to get their feedback as you develop and cultivate it. You may visit a consultant at a local Small Business Develop-

entrepreneurial process The stage of a business's life which involves innovation, a triggering event, and implementation of the business.

FIGURE 2-1
The Startup Process
The stages of entrepreneurship and small business management.
Source: Based on, with additions to, Carol Moore, "Understanding Entrepreneurial Behavior: A Definition and Model," in J. A. Pearce, II and R. B. Robinson, Jr. (eds.), Academy of Management Best Paper Proceedings. *Forty-sixth Annual Meeting of the Academy of Management, Chicago, pp. 66–70. Also see William Bygrave, "The Entrepreneurial Paradigm (I): A Philosophical Look at Its Research Methodologies,"* Entrepreneurship: Theory and Practice *(Fall 1989), pp. 7–25.*

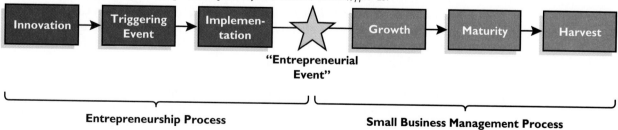

ment Center for more outside suggestions for your innovative business idea. Perhaps you even wake up late at night thinking of a new facet to your idea. That is your brain working through the creative process subconsciously. The time span for the innovation stage may be months or even years before the potential entrepreneur moves on to the next stage. Usually a specific event or occurrence sparks the entrepreneur to proceed from thinking to doing—a triggering event.

When a **triggering event** occurs in the entrepreneur's life, he or she begins bringing the organization to life. This event could be the loss of a job, the successful gathering of resources to support the organization, or some other factor that sets the wheels in motion.

Implementation is the part of the entrepreneurial process when the organization is formed. This can also be called the "entrepreneurial event."[4] Risk increases at this stage of the entrepreneurial process because a business is now formed. The innovation goes from being an idea in your head to committing resources to bring it to a reality. The commitment needed to bring an idea to life is a key element in entrepreneurial behavior. Implementation involves one of the following: (1) introducing new products; (2) introducing new methods of production; (3) opening new markets; (4) opening new supply sources; or (5) industrial reorganization.[5]

Entrepreneurship is the creation of new organizations.[6] By defining entrepreneurship in terms of the organization rather than the person involved, entrepreneurship ends when the creation stage of the organization ends. This is the point where **small business management** begins. The rest of this text will concentrate on the process of managing a small business from growth through harvest.

small business management process The stage of a business's life which involves growth, maturity, and harvest.

The small business manager guides and nurtures the business through the desired level of **growth.** The growth stage does not mean that every small business manager is attempting to get his or her business to *Fortune* 500 size. A common goal for growth of small businesses is to reach a critical mass, a point at which an adequate living is provided for the owner and family with enough growth remaining to keep the business going.

The **maturity** stage of the organization is reached when the business is considered to be well established. The survival of the business seems fairly sure, although the small business manager will still face many other problems and challenges. Many pure entrepreneurs do not stay with the business until this stage. They have usually gone on to other new opportunities before this point. Small business managers are more committed to the long haul. This stage could be as short as a few months (in the case of a fad product) or as long as decades. Maturity in organizations can be similar to maturity in people and in nature. It is characterized by more stability when compared to the growth and implementation stages. Of course, organizations should not become too complacent or stop looking for new ways to evolve and grow, just as people should continue learning and growing throughout their lives.

In the **harvest** stage, the owner removes himself or herself from the business. Harvesting a business can be thought of as picking the fruit of years of labor. In his book *The Seven Habits of Highly Effective People,* Steven Covey says that one of the keys of being effective in life is "beginning with the end in mind."[7] This advice applies to effectively harvesting a business also. Therefore, it is a time that should be planned for carefully.

Harvest can take one of many forms. The business can be sold to another individual who will step into the position of manager. Ownership of the business could be transferred to its employees via an **employee stock ownership plan (ESOP).** It can be sold to the public via an **initial public offering (IPO).** The business could merge with another existing business to form an entirely new business. Finally, the harvest could be due to failure, in which case the doors are closed, the creditors paid, and the assets liquidated. Although made in a different context, George Bernard Shaw's statement "Any darned fool can start a love affair, but it takes a real genius to end one successfully" can also apply to harvesting a business.

Not every business reaches all stages. Maturity cannot occur unless the idea is implemented. A business cannot be harvested unless it has grown.

Figure 2-2 adds **environmental factors** to our model to show what is going on outside the business at each stage of development. Management guru Peter Drucker points out that innovation occurs as a response to opportunities within several environments.[8] For example, other entrepreneurs serve as role models when we are in the innovation and triggering event stages. Businesses in the implementation and growth stages must respond to competitive forces, consumer desires, capabilities of suppliers, legal regulations, and other forces. The environmental factors a business must operate within change from one stage to the next.

The **personal characteristics** of the entrepreneur or the small business manager that are most significant in running a business will vary from one stage to the next. As you will see in the following section, personal characteristics or traits are not useful in predicting who will be a successful entrepreneur or small business manager, but they do affect our motivations, actions, and effectiveness in running a small business. (See Figure 2-3.) For example, in the innovation and triggering event stages, a high tolerance for ambiguity, a strong need to achieve, and a willingness to accept risk are important for entrepreneurs. In the growth and maturity stages, the personal characteristics needed to

environmental factors Forces that occur outside the business which have an impact upon the business and its owner.

personal characteristics The traits of a business owner which affect the development of the business.

FIGURE 2-2
Environmental Factors Affecting the Startup Process
At each stage in the startup process, the small business person must confront a new set of concerns. Here the arrows show what those concerns are and how they overlap.
Source: Based on, with additions to, Carol Moore, "Understanding Entrepreneurial Behavior: A Definition and Model," in J. A. Pearce, II and R. B. Robinson, Jr. (eds.), Academy of Management Best Paper Proceedings. *Forty-sixth Annual Meeting of the Academy of Management, Chicago, pp. 66–70. Also see William Bygrave, "The Entrepreneurial Paradigm (I): A Philosophical Look at Its Research Methodologies,"* Entrepreneurship: Theory and Practice *(Fall 1989), pp. 7–25.*

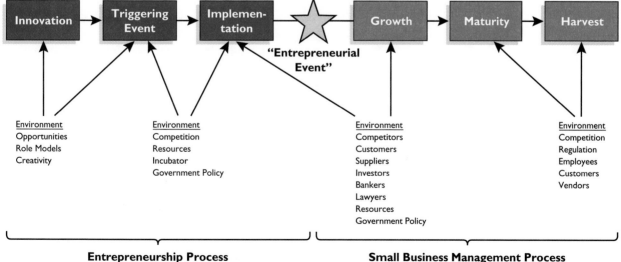

be a successful small business manager are different than those needed to be a successful entrepreneur. For example, the small business manager needs to be persevering, committed to the long run of the business, a motivator of others, and a leader.

The business changes as it matures also. In the growth stage, attention is placed on team building, setting strategies, and creating the structure and culture of the business. In the maturity stage, more attention can be directed to specific functions of the business. The people within the business gravitate toward, specialize in, and concentrate on what they do best, be it marketing, finance, or managing human resources.

FIGURE 2-3

A Model of the Entrepreneurship/Small Business Management Process
In each stage of the startup process, different personal characteristics will be more important to the owner, as the business takes on new attributes. This model shows how entrepreneurial skills are required early in the process, giving way to management skills once the business is established.
Source: Based on, with additions to, Carol Moore, "Understanding Entrepreneurial Behavior: A Definition and Model," in J. A. Pearce, II and R. B. Robinson, Jr. (eds.), Academy of Management Best Paper Proceedings. Forty-sixth Annual Meeting of the Academy of Management, Chicago, pp. 66–70. Also see William Bygrave, "The Entrepreneurial Paradigm (I): A Philosophical Look at Its Research Methodologies," Entrepreneurship: Theory and Practice *(Fall 1989), pp. 7–25.*

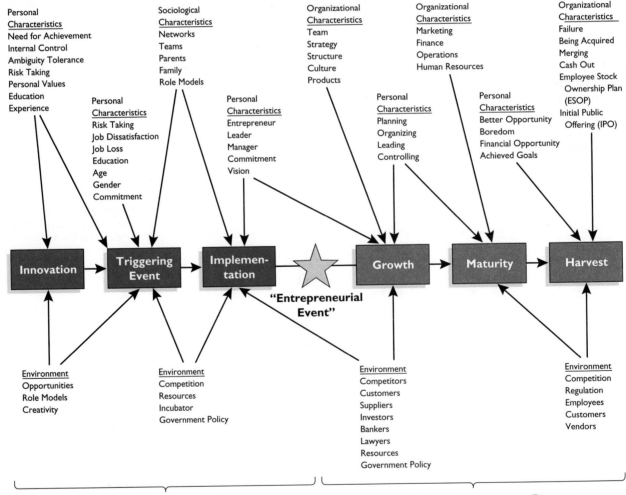

The purpose of the entrepreneurship and small business management model is to illustrate the stages of both processes and factors that are significant in each. The subtitle of this book is *Entrepreneurship and Beyond* because its purpose is to assist you as you proceed from the innovation stage through the management of your successful business to a satisfying harvest.

Your Decision for Self-Employment

Because you have chosen to study small business management, you may be considering the prospect of starting your own business now or at some time in the future. What are some of the positive and negative aspects of self-employment? Why have other people chosen this career path? What do they have in common? What resources did they have available? How can you prepare yourself for owning a small business? The answers to these questions may help you decide if owning a small business is right for you.

Pros and Cons of Self-Employment

Owning your own business can be an excellent way to satisfy personal as well as professional objectives. Before starting your own business, you should be aware of the payoffs and drawbacks involved.

Most people starting their own businesses seek the opportunities of independence, an outlet for their creativity, a chance to build something important, and rewards of money and recognition. (See Figure 2-4.)

Opportunity for Independence. To many people, starting their own businesses means having control over their own lives. That is why owning their own businesses is attractive to so many people. They don't feel working for someone else will enable them to reach their full potential. They feel restrained by the organi-

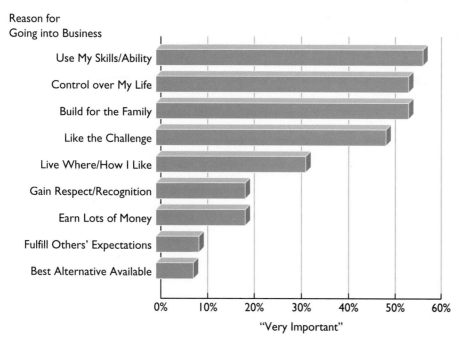

Reason for
Going into Business

| Use My Skills/Ability |
| Control over My Life |
| Build for the Family |
| Like the Challenge |
| Live Where/How I Like |
| Gain Respect/Recognition |
| Earn Lots of Money |
| Fulfill Others' Expectations |
| Best Alternative Available |

0% 10% 20% 30% 40% 50% 60%
"Very Important"

FIGURE 2-4
Independence Is the Primary Reason Most People Go Into Business for Themselves
Reasons for going into business by relative importance.
Source: Arnold C. Cooper, et al., New Business in America, *1990, NFIB Foundation/VISA Business* Card *Primer as shown in William J. Dennis, Jr., A Small Business* Primer, *1993, National Federation of Independent Business, p. 31.*

independence The feeling of control a person has over his or her own destiny.

zation or by their bosses. For such people, business ownership can offer a way to realize their talents, ambitions, or vision. The search for **independence** has led many people to leave jobs with large corporations to strike out on their own.

Small Business IN THE Service Industry

Take, for instance, Seija Goldstein of New York City. At one time she was the director of acquisitions for CBS's magazine division. She had also served a stint as chief financial officer for a small publisher. Now Goldstein utilizes her financial knowledge and skills as a self-employed financial consultant. She loves the freedom and independence that come from running her own business.

Source: Brian O'Reilly, "The New Face of Small Business," Fortune, May 2, 1994, p. 84.

Opportunity for a Better Lifestyle. The desire to use one's own skills fully is the most common motivation for self-employment. It may enable you to provide a good or service that other people need while enjoying what you do. The lifestyle provided by owning your own business can make going to work fun. Starting a business could be a creative outlet that would give you the opportunity to use a combination of your previously untapped talents.

Global Small Business

Paul Hsu initially came to the United States from Taiwan in 1969 to pursue a career in social work. Five years later, Hsu decided to put his knowledge of Asian culture and traditions to work by starting his own business, Hsu's Ginseng Enterprises. He began exporting North American ginseng to Asia, where the plant is used as a treatment for a variety of ailments. Within a year, Hsu's small part-time business had become a full-time job. The company has since expanded into farming its own ginseng, even opening a division in Malaysia. By starting this business, Hsu found a way to profit from his skills and knowledge *and* to do something he enjoyed! *Source: Paul Hsu, "Profiting from a Global Mindset," Nation's Business (June 1994), p. 6.*

The challenge presented by running a business is attractive to most entrepreneurs who may be bored working for someone else. The only limitations you face arise from a challenge to your own perseverance and creativity, not from barriers placed before you by other people or the constraints of an organization.

About half of small business owners are motivated by familial concerns. (See Figure 2-4.) They may feel that self-employment is the best way to provide for their children, or they may wish to have a legacy to pass on. Children, in turn, may enter the family business out of self-interest or to help ease their parents' burden.

Opportunity for Profit. Less than 20 percent of business owners expressed a desire to earn lots of money. Most people do not start businesses to get rich, but to earn an honest living. Nonetheless, the direct correlation between effort and compensation is a powerful motivation to work hard. The fact that you can keep all the money you earn is a powerful motivator for many entrepreneurs.

R eality Check

From Accidental Startup to Sure Thing

Small business owners go into business for incredibly varied reasons and means. Here are two examples to illustrate how differently two businesses can start up; one by design and planning, one by chance and luck.

Dan Hoard and Tom Bunnell were on a quest for fun and adventure while backpacking in Australia. The sun was hot so Hoard did what any self-respecting, uninhibited free spirit would do (or anyone that thought of it)—he cut off his pant leg and stuck in on his head. He was just having fun; he didn't intend to create a $3 million clothing business. "We would sit in front of the mirror and cry laughing," remembers Bunnell.

Thus was born the Mambosok ("it sounded festive," Hoard explains). Research and development consisted of driving around the Pacific Northwest in a beat-up van. Their business plan didn't exist. They were flying by the seat, er—leg of their pants.

Bunnell was a bartender and expected to sell a few of their first 1,000 Mambosoks to his bar patrons. They were gone in two weeks! This success led Bunnell to formulate two hypotheses:

1 The market for this product does exist.
2 Drinking impairs your judgment. (Could be a combination.)

Hoard and Bunnell sold $200,000 worth in six months. They sold $1 million worth in the second year and $3 million in 1993. They even picked up some business savvy along the way. Hoard and Bunnell realized that the product life cycle for Mambosoks would probably be rather short and competition would certainly enter with knock-off products. This led the Seattle funsters to extend their product line to more than 60 items of Mambosok wear. Amazing what doing something fun and funky can turn into! Perhaps you have the next big, fun, accidental business just waiting to happen to you.

By sharp contrast, if any startup company ever looked like a "sure thing" it would be Cardinal Technologies. Harold Krall, now CEO of Cardinal, and six other managers from RCA left the company together to form their new business to manufacture computer-related equipment like modems, monitors, and desktop systems. Without even realizing it at the time, they followed a path that is prototypical of how the most successful U.S. companies begin.

First, they knew their industry inside and out and they knew how to run a business. They started with a full slate of management—a CEO and specialists in marketing, finance, manufacturing, engineering, sales, and systems. Most had grown up in family businesses before taking management positions with RCA. Second, they had contacts within the industry: suppliers, marketing allies, and contacts who would become customers. They began the business as a team and have forged even stronger bonds.

Third, even though they were beginning a capital-intensive business, they had a healthy financial start. The seven partners and the 13 other former RCA employees pooled $800,000 of their own money to get things rolling. They were also wise enough to trade away some equity for cash. A healthy respect for debt has kept the company virtually debt free.

A real key to Cardinal's success is that they didn't ever look like a startup. The experience of the team kept them from ever being mistaken for novices. Even though the business was new, the players were not. While the founders surely went through most of the same traumas that any founders experience, the outside world didn't see them.

Sources: Adapted from Anne Murphy, "Founded on Frolic" in "Where Great Ideas for New Businesses Come From," Inc. (September 1993), pp. 54–57; and Leslie Brokaw, "Guaranteed Success," Inc. (March 1993), pp. 66–68.

Risks of Self-Employment. Small business ownership offers ample opportunities to satisfy your material and psychological needs, yet it also poses certain risks of which you should be aware. Personal liability, uncertain income, long working hours, and frequently limited compensation while the business grows are some of the disadvantages of self-employment. Not having anyone looking over your shoulder may leave you with fewer places to turn for advice when the going gets tough. And even though you are your own boss, you still are answerable to many masters. You must still respond to customer demands and complaints, keep your employees happy, obey government regulations, and grapple with competitive pressures.

The uncertainty of your income is one of the most challenging aspects of starting a business. There is no guaranteed paycheck at the end of the pay period as exists when you are working for someone else. Your young business will require you to pump any revenue generated back into it. As the owner, you will be the last person to be paid, and you will probably have to live on your savings for a while. Going through the first year of business without collecting a salary is common for entrepreneurs.[9]

The reliable, if dull, 9-to-5 work schedule is another luxury small business owners must do without. To get your business off the ground during the critical startup phase, you may find yourself being the company president during the day and its janitor at night. Owning and running a business require a tremendous commitment of time and effort. You must be willing to make sure that everything that must be done gets done.

When you own a business, it becomes an extension of your personality. Unfortunately, it can also take over your life, especially at the beginning. Families, friends, and other commitments must sometimes take a back seat to the business. This problem is complicated by the fact that people often start businesses in their child-rearing years. Married couples going into business together face a volatile mix of business and marital pressures that do not always lead to happy endings.

Traits of Successful Entrepreneurs

Since the early 1960s researchers have tried to identify the personal characteristics that will predict those people who will be successful entrepreneurs. The conclusions of 30 years of research indicate that there are no personality characteristics that predict who will be a successful entrepreneur before entering business. Successful small business owners and entrepreneurs come in every shape, size, color, and from all backgrounds. Still, in this section we will briefly examine some characteristics seen among individuals who tend to rise to the top of any profession. The point to remember when you are considering owning a business is that no combination of characteristics guarantees success. People possessing all these traits have experienced business failure.

What are some prerequisites for becoming a successful entrepreneur? You need a **passion** toward what you are doing. Caring very deeply about what you are trying to accomplish through your business is imperative. If you go into business with a take-it-or-leave-it, it-will-go-or-it-won't attitude, you are probably wasting your time and money. **Determination** is also critical. You must realize that you have choices and are not a victim of fate. You need to believe that you can succeed if you work long enough and hard enough. Finally, you need a deep **knowledge** of the area in which you are working. Your customers see you as a re-

R eality Check

Not All Happy Endings

Mary and Phil Baechler started their company, Racing Strollers, in 1984 with a rented garage and a phone listing in *Runner's World* magazine. A devoted runner, Phil had designed a stroller, the Baby Jogger, with three bicycle wheels that enabled him to take their six-month-old child with him when he went running. The product was very successful and the business grew quickly. Within ten years, Racing Strollers had become a $5 million company. Unfortunately, the Baechlers differed in their levels of interest in the business. This compounded the strain of living and working together. Mary became hooked on the challenges of running a growing business, while Phil wanted to cultivate a life away from work. Phil couldn't understand why Mary always chose work over family. Mary couldn't understand why Phil would not always put in the extra effort for the business. Can two people with different obsessions live in peace?

Mary thinks the secret might be in accepting the other person the way he or she is, but they couldn't do that for each other. Mary wanted to change Phil into a manager, embroiled in every detail of the business. Phil longed for the sweet girl he had met 15 years earlier. At some point, Mary chose the business over her marriage. The pressure she felt to build the business is common to entrepreneurs. She used typical rationalizations like "as soon as this current problem is over, I'll spend more time with the family" and "I just gotta get through this month" to justify her actions to herself.

Small problems in the marriage accumulated, building a wall one brick at a time—critical comments made in passing, patterns of neglect here and there. Soon the success of the business brought in offers from prospective buyers and very different reactions from the Baechlers. Phil saw the business as a winning lottery ticket to be cashed in. Mary couldn't let go of it.

The Baechlers' marriage ended because they had different answers to the fundamental question "Why are we here?" Phil is an artist and designer who wanted financial security from the business that would allow him to play golf and paint in Hawaii. Mary loved being needed by the business. She needed the thrills and magic that problems and victories of running a business provided. They still loved each other, but they couldn't love each other *and* run a business together.

Can you separate family and business? How can you maintain a balance between them? When is enough sacrifice enough?

Source: Mary Baechler, "Death of a Marriage," Inc. *(April 1994), pp. 74–78.*

liable source in solving their wants and needs. These are three characteristics that virtually every successful entrepreneur possesses.[10] Having perseverance, the technical skills to run a business, and belief in yourself are more important than a specific psychological trait you could exhibit.

A pioneer in entrepreneurial research, David McClelland identified entrepreneurs as people with a higher **need to achieve** than nonentrepreneurs.[11] People with high need to achieve are attracted to jobs that challenge their skills and their problem-solving abilities. They avoid goals that they think would be almost impossible to achieve or ones that would guarantee success. They prefer tasks in which the outcome depends upon their individual efforts.

need to achieve The personal quality linked to entrepreneurship in which people are motivated to excel and choose situations in which success is likely.

Reality Check

Expanding Horizons for Small Business Owners

The number of women and minorities in small business has grown exponentially since 1960 (see Chapter 1, p. 11). The appeal of small business—independence, challenge, personal freedom—is the same for women and minorities as for anyone else. Yet these qualities are especially desirable for individuals who have been faced with discrimination in the workplace, whether it was deliberate or unintentional.

Women sometimes leave large corporations because they feel they have hit a glass ceiling, an invisible, unspoken barrier that prevents women from rising above a certain level in the organization.

The glass ceiling is also familiar to many minority members. According to Joshua Smith, chairman of the U.S. Commission on Minority Business Development, African-Americans are often motivated to start their own businesses because of lack of alternatives when employers are reluctant to hire, promote, or reward them on the basis of their skills.

Some of the hottest businesses of the 1990s have been started by women. For example, in 1981 when Judy Figge bought In Home Health, a provider of at-home nursing care, annual revenues ran about $300,000. Several lending institutions were skeptical about lending money to a registered nurse, but Figge was determined to start her own business and persevered until she found financing. By 1993 In Home Health was providing nursing care and pharmaceutical sales in 19 markets with annual revenues of $104 million.

Judie Eakins founded and is president of Omega Studios Inc. Southwest of Irving, Texas. Since 1987, she has run the design and photography business after her previous position as head of a similar Dallas subsidiary was eliminated. Within the first two years, annual revenue was up to $4 million and she had 67 employees, but those are not her measures for success. Her goal in starting her business was never to make a lot of money. She is more interested in self-satisfaction and enjoyment of what she is doing. "If you're having fun," she says, "the people working for you are having fun and you're satisfying your customer base, that spells success for me."

Eakins's need for self-fulfillment appears to be a common motivation for female entrepreneurs, according to the Avon Report, which surveys women in business across the country every year. Of the 319 women surveyed, only 12 identified profits as their leading measure of the success of their businesses. Self-fulfillment was the most common answer with 106 (33 percent), followed closely by achievement with 96 (30 percent), and helping others with 64 (20 percent).

William Thompson is now an inspiring entrepreneur with four successful businesses, and it took only a single magazine article to start him in that direction. Thompson was a pilot in the Air Force in 1976. He was walking across the tarmac when he spotted the magazine that would change his life laying on the ground. He picked it up and saw an article on executive compensation. The lowest-paid executive in the article made $169,000. The young African-American captain earning $20,000 had had no idea that businesspeople made that much money, but he instantly knew he wanted in on his share.

Thompson's first business was the result of another article he read in a magazine about a man in Canada who made $100,000 selling roses. At a local outdoor bazaar, Thompson paid five female friends commission to sell flowers for $1 each. After paying $100 for a business license, he took home 40 cents per rose sold. This totaled only a couple of hundred dollars per week, but he was on his way.

Thompson sold the flower business when he decided to go to law school in Boston. While studying tax law, he worked as a commercial pilot for Delta Airlines. After graduating in 1992, he kept flying for Delta, but he also started a tax and financial planning company with two partners. The business prospered and he eventually gained sole ownership by buying out his two partners. A group of businesspeople sought Thompson's tax advice on a shopping center they were planning to build. Thompson ended up joining this group to form a development company that peaked with 450 residential and commercial properties worth $36 million.

With the healthy financial base established from selling his real estate holdings, Thompson and a partner formed Summit Programming. They designed computer software and provided programmers for corporations and government agencies, eventually landing contracts with McDonnell Douglas, the city of Boston, and others. Much of their work involved government contracts, which require a percentage of contractors and subcontractors to be minority-owned businesses. This requirement spelled opportunity for Summit.

With experience in writing government contracts under his belt, Thompson saw more opportunity coming up in the area of hazardous waste cleanup. That led him to form Summit Drilling, which provides soil samples to companies bidding for hazardous waste cleanup projects.

Thompson recently moved in yet another direction by opening the first black-owned Subway Sandwich and Salad franchise in Massachusetts in 1991. He has plans for many more.

What do a financial planning business, a computer programming business, a soil sample business, and a sandwich shop all have in common? Not much beyond the fact that they are owned by the same man. What they show us is the ability that William Thompson possesses to recognize and take advantage of opportunity. That is the hallmark of an entrepreneur. These four businesses generate about $3 million in annual sales for the man who founded them. People who create businesses not only provide income for themselves; they power our nation's economy, create jobs, and serve as role models for others to follow.

Source: Terri Scandura, "Women Can Shatter Job Barriers," USA Today (May 1994), p. 68; Andrew Serwer, "Lessons from America's Fastest-Growing Companies," Fortune, August 8, 1994, pp. 42–60; Dorothy Gaiter, "Short-term Despair, Long-term Promise," The Wall Street Journal—Black Entrepreneurship Special Report, April 3, 1992, p. R1; and Lisa Fried, "A New Breed of Entrepreneur—Women," Management Review (December 1989), pp. 18–25.

Locus of control is a term used to explain how people view their ability to determine their own fate. Entrepreneurs tend to have a stronger **internal locus of control** than people in the general population.[12] People with high internal locus of control believe that the outcome of an event is determined by their own actions. Luck, chance, fate, or the control of other people (external factors) are less important than one's own efforts.[13] When faced with a problem or a difficult situation, internals look within themselves for solutions. Internal locus of control is the force that compels many people to start their own businesses to gain independence, autonomy, and freedom.

locus of control A person's belief concerning the degree to which internal or external forces control his or her future.

Successful entrepreneurs and small business owners are innovative and creative. **Innovation** results from the ability to see, conceive, and create new and unique products, processes, or services. Entrepreneurs see opportunities in the marketplace and visualize creative new ways to take advantage of them.

How do entrepreneurs tend to view **risk taking?** A myth about entrepreneurs is that they are wild-eyed, risk-seeking, financial daredevils. While acceptance of financial risk is necessary to start a business, the prototypical entrepreneur tends to accept moderate risk only after careful examination of what he or she is about to get into.

A small business manager needs perseverance, patience, and intelligence to meet the ongoing challenges of keeping a company vibrant.

Scott Schmidt does not see himself as reckless. Schmidt is the entrepreneurial athlete who started what has become known as "extreme skiing." Basically, he jumps from 60-foot cliffs on skis for a living. He is sponsored by ski-equipment companies for endorsements and video production. If you saw him from the ski lift, you would say "that guy is a maniac for taking that risk." The same is often said of other entrepreneurs by people looking in from outside the situation. Actually, Schmidt very carefully charts his takeoff and landing points. An analogy can be drawn between Schmidt's adventurous style of skiing and the risks of starting a new business.

Entrepreneurs carefully plan their next moves in their business plans. Once they are in the air, entrepreneurs must trust their remarkable talent to help them react to what comes their way as they fall. Entrepreneurs don't risk life and limb because they look for ways to minimize their risks by careful observation and planning, just as Schmidt precisely plans his moves. They commonly do not see unknown situations as risky because they know their strengths and talents, are confident of success, and know the playing field. In similar fashion, Scott Schmidt doesn't consider himself to be reckless. He considers himself very good at what he does.[14] That is a typical entrepreneurial attitude.

Other traits that are useful in owning your own business are: **high level of energy, confidence, orientation toward the future, optimism, desire for feedback, high tolerance for ambiguity, flexibility/adaptability, and commitment.**

Jon Goodman is director of the Entrepreneur Program at the University of Southern California. When asked to describe the characteristics of the entrepreneurial personality, she responded, "Just one: *incredible tenacity*."[15]

Preparing Yourself for Business Ownership

How do you prepare for an undertaking like owning your own business? Do you need experience? Do you need education? The answer to both questions is always "yes." What kind and how much? These are tougher to answer because it depends on the type of business you plan to enter. The experience you would need to open a franchised bookstore would be different than that needed for an upscale restaurant.

Entrepreneurs and small business owners have higher education levels than the general public. About 60 percent of new business owners have had at least some college.[16] (See Figure 2-5.) Exceptions exist—people have dropped out of

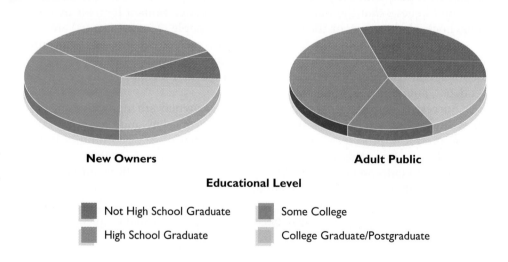

FIGURE 2-5
Education Level of New Business Owners
Although individual exceptions exist, as a group, small business owners have more formal education than the general population.
Source: The NFIB Foundation and Statistical Abstract of the United States, *1986, as shown in* Small Business Primer, *National Federation of Small Business, p. 15.*

New Owners   **Adult Public**

Educational Level

■ Not High School Graduate   ■ Some College

■ High School Graduate   ■ College Graduate/Postgraduate school and have gone on to start successful businesses, so it is difficult to generalize. But in a majority of cases, we can conclude that more education increases the chances of success.

Entrepreneurship and small business management are the fastest-growing subjects in business schools across the country.[17] In 1971, Karl Vesper of the University of Washington found that 16 U.S. schools offered a course in entrepreneurship. In his 1993 update, that number had grown to 370.[18] Some of the nation's top business schools like Babson College, The Wharton School of the University of Pennsylvania, Harvard Business School, University of Southern California, University of California at Los Angeles, many other four-year colleges, and community colleges are offering degrees in entrepreneurship and small business management.[19] Up until very recently, leaders of most business schools argued that entrepreneurship could not be taught. However, the increased academic attention is constructing a body of knowledge on the processes of starting and running small businesses, which proves that entrepreneurial processes can and are being learned.[20]

SBA and other nonacademic agencies offer start-your-own-business seminars to prospective entrepreneurs. Executive education programs offered through college extension departments are providing curricula specifically designed for entrepreneurs and small business owners.[21] These one-day to one-year programs provide valuable skills without a degree.

Obtaining practical experience in your type of business is an important part of your education. You can learn valuable skills from all types of jobs that will prepare you for owning your own business. For example, working in a restaurant, in retail sales, or in a customer service department can hone your customer relations skills, which are crucial in running your own business but difficult to learn in a classroom.

The analytical and relational skills that you learn in formal education settings are important, but remember that your future development depends on lifelong learning. (Commencement, after all, means "beginning"—the beginning of your business career!) Finally, don't overlook hobbies and other interests in preparing for self-employment. Participating in team sports and student organizations, for instance, can cultivate your team spirit and facility in working with others. Your marketing skills can be improved through a knowledge of languages or fine art. Sometimes an avocation can turn into a vocation. For example, more than one weekend gardener has become a successful greenhouse owner. Many small business owners get their ideas for what types of businesses they want to run from their favorite pastimes.

No amount of experience or education can completely prepare you for owning your own business. Because every person, situation, and business are different, you are certainly going to encounter situations for which you could not have prepared. Get as much experience and education as you can, but at some point you must "take off and hang on." You have to find a way to make your business go.

Forms of Business Organization

One of the first decisions you will need to make in starting a business is choosing a form of ownership. This section will lead you through your options and will present the advantages and disadvantages of each.

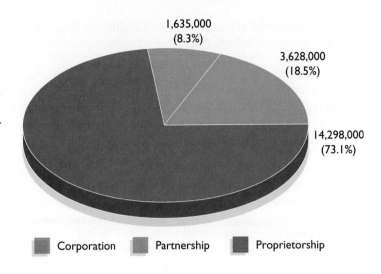

FIGURE 2-6
Ownership Forms of U.S. Businesses

While the sole proprietorship is the most common business form in the United States, corporations produce the majority of revenue and net income.

Source: Statistical Abstract of the United States, *1993, p. 531.*

1,635,000
(8.3%)

3,628,000
(18.5%)

14,298,000
(73.1%)

■ Corporation   ■ Partnership   ■ Proprietorship

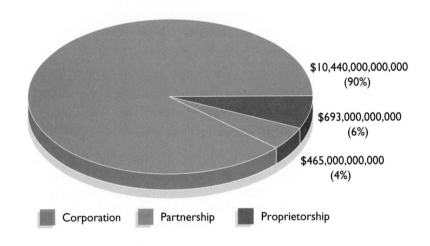

FIGURE 2-7
Sales Revenue by Ownership Type

Source: Statistical Abstract of the United States, *1993, p. 531.*

$10,440,000,000,000
(90%)

$693,000,000,000
(6%)

$465,000,000,000
(4%)

■ Corporation   ■ Partnership   ■ Proprietorship

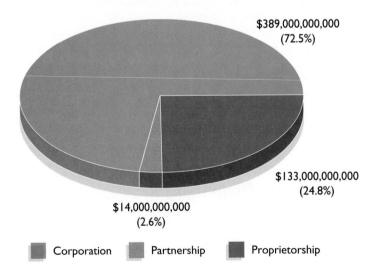

FIGURE 2-8
Net Income by Ownership Type

Source: Statistical Abstract of the United States, *1993, p. 531.*

$389,000,000,000
(72.5%)

$133,000,000,000
(24.8%)

$14,000,000,000
(2.6%)

■ Corporation   ■ Partnership   ■ Proprietorship

Several issues should be considered when making this decision. To what extent do you want to be personally liable for financial and legal risk? Who will have controlling interest of the business? How will the business be financed? The three basic legal structures you can choose for your firm are sole proprietorship, partnership, or corporation, with specialized options of partnerships and corporations available.

About 73 percent of all businesses that exist in the United States are sole proprietorships, making them the most common form of ownership. (See Figures 2-6, 2-7, and 2-8.) Although a majority of businesses are proprietorships, they account for only about 6 percent of the total revenue generated and about 25 percent of the net profits earned. Corporations bring in 90 percent of business-generated revenue and 72.5 percent of the net income earned, although they make up only about 18 percent of the total. Partnerships are a minority with 8 percent of the total number, 4 percent of the revenue, and less than 3 percent of the net income earned.

Figure 2-9 shows that proprietorships increased in number and as a percentage of the total of the 21 million small businesses that existed in the United States from 1980 to 1992. This illustrates the rise of very small businesses. The number of corporations grew gradually, while the number of partnerships remained relatively constant. Changes in tax laws have an effect on the number of businesses of each type that are formed.

There is no single best form of organization. The choice depends on your short- and long-term needs, your tax situation, and your personal preferences, abilities, and resources. Don't confuse legal form of ownership with the size of the business. When you walk into a small neighborhood business, can you assume that it is a sole proprietorship? Not necessarily. A one-person flower shop may be a corporation or a multimillion-dollar factory could be a sole proprietorship.

The Sole Proprietorship

A **sole proprietorship** is a business that is owned and operated by one person. There are no legal requirements to establish a sole proprietorship. In most states, if you are operating under a name other than your full first and last legal names,

sole proprietorship A business owned and operated by one person.

FIGURE 2-9
Growth in the Business Population
Business tax returns filed by form of business and year.
Source: Internal Revenue Service, NFIB Foundation/VISA Business Card Primer, as shown in William J. Dennis, Jr., A Small Business Primer, 1993, National Federation of Independent Business, p. 7.

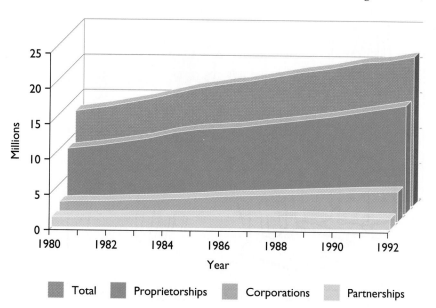

Total   Proprietorships   Corporations   Partnerships

you must register the business as a trade name with the state Department of Revenue. (See Table 2-1.)

Advantages.   As the owner of a sole proprietorship, you have complete control of the business. The sole proprietorship is well suited to the aspiring entrepreneur's desire for independence. You don't have to consult with any partners, stockholders, or boards of directors. As a result of this independence, you are free to respond quickly to new market needs. Since you make all the decisions and bear all the responsibility, you do not have to share profits with anyone. You may have a smaller pie, but it's all *your* pie. As Mel Brooks in the movie *History of the World, Part 1* said, "It's good to be the king." No one else in the business tells you what to do, criticizes your mistakes, or second guesses your decisions.

A sole proprietorship is easy to set up. There are fewer legal requirements and restrictions than with a partnership or a corporation. Legal and license costs are at a minimum. An inexpensive business license from the city or county clerk is all that is usually required, unless your type of business requires special permits. For example, businesses selling food must be inspected by health departments. Otherwise, you need only hang your sign on the door and let the world know you are in business. The fast, simple way in which a proprietorship can be formed reduces startup costs and stress.

The Internal Revenue Service (IRS) regards business and owner in a sole proprietorship as a single entity. If your business shows a loss the first year or two (which is common), those losses can be deducted from any other income for the year. This tax advantage is short-lived, however. The tax code states that your business must make money three out of five years. According to the IRS, only money-making ventures are considered businesses. Anything else is a hobby. Still, this deduction can give you a boost if you are starting your business on a part-time basis and have other income.

Just as proprietorships are easy to open, they are easy to close. If you choose, you can liquidate your assets, pay your bills, turn off the lights, and take

Source: The Wall Street Journal, *February 25, 1994, p. A14.* Permission, Cartoon Features Syndicate.

"You can't call in sick, Harold, you're self-employed"

TABLE 2 ▪ 1 Balancing the Advantages and Disadvantages of Sole Proprietorships

ADVANTAGES	DISADVANTAGES
Independence	Unlimited liability
Easy to set up	Limited resources
Easy to close	Limited skills
Tax benefits	Lack of continuity

your sign off the door, and you are out of business. This is not the case with partnerships and corporations.

Disadvantages.   The biggest disadvantage of sole proprietorships is **unlimited liability.** This means that as a sole proprietor, you are personally liable for all debts incurred by the business. If the business should fail, you could lose more than you invested in it. Personal assets, such as your home and car, might have to be liquidated to cover the business debt. Thus, while there are few caps on the potential for return with a sole proprietorship, there are similarly few caps on the amount you could lose.

unlimited liability The potential to lose more than an owner has invested in a business.

The sole proprietorship is the most difficult form of business for which to raise capital from outside sources. As one individual, you have access to fewer financial resources than a group of people could gather. Lenders believe that their chances of seeing a return on their investment are reduced in a sole proprietorship and, therefore, they are not as likely to loan money.

The total responsibility of running a sole proprietorship may mean independence, but it can also be a disadvantage. As you are limited to the amount of capital you can raise, you are also limited to and by your own skills and capabilities. You may be an expert in some areas of running a business but be deficient in others.

Total responsibility can also mean a lack of continuity in the business. If you should become unable to work through illness, disability, or death, the business will cease to exist. Long vacations can become virtually impossible to take.

Entering the Internet

The U.S. government's Small Business Administration makes a wide variety of information available on the Internet. The SBA Online offers guidelines, advice, statistics, bibliographies, and listings of local offices and other resources for people who run small businesses and those who are thinking of doing so. You can access the SBA Online through its home page (a computer screen image that functions as a starting point) on the World Wide Web. At this site, you will find information that could be useful for those individuals who want to go into business for themselves or for individuals who need help or advice in managing an existing small business. For instance, topics included in the General Information and Publications section range from advertising your business to pricing your products to using the metric system in your business. This information is free, although you must have access to the Internet and World Wide Web to obtain it.

SBA Online: http://www.sbaonline.sba.gov

The Partnership

If two or more people are going into business together, they have two choices: form a partnership or a corporation. A partnership is defined as an association of two or more persons to carry on as co-owners of a business for profit. Legally you can have a partnership without a written agreement (although it is not recommended) so the paperwork requirements for starting a partnership are about the same as a proprietorship.

When you form a partnership with friends, family, or associates, you may not think it is necessary to have a written agreement because you are so familiar with each other. You do. Problems are inevitable for every partnership. An agreement that is well thought out when the partnership is formed can save the business—and a friendship—later. Without a written agreement, a partnership operates according to the rules of the state under the Uniform Partnership Act (UPA). The intent of the UPA is to settle problems between partners. For example, without a written agreement that states otherwise, each partner shares equally in the profit and management of the business.

Partners should bring complementary skills and resources to the alliance to give it a better chance of success. For instance, if one partner has creative abilities, the other partner should have a good business sense. Partners may also complement one another by providing different business contacts or amounts of capital. Think of the relationship this way: If both partners possess the same qualities, one of them probably isn't needed.

general partnership A business structure in which the business owners share the management and risk of the business.

There are two types of partnerships: general and limited. Most of this discussion will focus on the **general partnership,** which is more common. In a general partnership, each partner faces the same personal liability as a sole proprietor. In a limited partnership, at least one of the partners has limited liability. This section will concentrate on general partnerships, with limited partnerships discussed at the end of the section.

Advantages.   The biggest advantage of partnerships should be the pooling of managerial talent and capital to create a product or service that is better than any of the partners could have created individually. (See Table 2-2.)

Access to additional capital is an advantage of partnerships. Partners can pool their money, and credit is easier to obtain than for a proprietor. The reason for this is that the creditor can collect the debt from any one or all of the partners. Partnerships can benefit from more management expertise in decision making.

The tax advantages of a partnership, like a proprietorship, are usually advantageous since partners pay taxes as individuals. The partnership must file an informational return that reports how much money the partnership earned or lost during the tax year and what share of the income or loss belongs to each partner. Therefore, profits are taxed only once on each partner's share of the income.

TABLE 2 ▪ 2   **Balancing the Advantages and Disadvantages of Partnerships**

ADVANTAGES	DISADVANTAGES
Pooled talent	Unlimited liability
Pooled resources	Potential for management conflict
Easy to form	Less independence than proprietorships
Tax benefits	Continuity or transfer of ownership

Partnerships are easy to create. Like a proprietorship, all you need are the appropriate business licenses, a tax number, and you are in business—for better or for worse.

Disadvantages.   As with sole proprietorships, a disadvantage of partnerships is that the general partners carry the burden of unlimited liability. Each general partner's liability is not limited to the amount of his or her investment but extends to his or her personal property as well. Even if the partnership agreement specifies a defined split in profits, each partner is 100 percent responsible for all liabilities.

In a partnership, you may be held liable for the negligence of your partners. A lot of trust, a comprehensive agreement, and a good lawyer are needed. Similarly, each partner may act as an agent of the partnership. This means that any partner can enter into a contract for the partnership incurring debt or other responsibilities, or selling assets, unless limited by the articles of partnership. The choice of a business partner is much like choosing a partner for marriage. You need to know and be able to live with the other person's character, work habits, and values to make sure you are compatible.

The potential for managerial conflict within the partnership is one of the most serious problems that can threaten its viability. If partners disagree on matters that involve core issues, such as future direction of the business, the partnership could literally split at the seams.

The four Sasson brothers were looking ahead when they started Scopus Technology, a high-tech firm, in 1991. Recognizing that each had a strong ego, they minimized managerial overlap by each taking on a different function of the business—one in marketing, one in operations, another in technology, and the fourth controlled the financial management of the business. After three years, Scopus Technology had 70 employees and annual revenue of $8 million. They consider the secret of their success to be the fact that they had so clearly divided responsibilities among themselves, and had hired a salaried president to act as referee.[22]

If a common reason to go into small business is independence, going into a partnership limits that independence. For example, what happens if you want to reinvest profits in the business, but your partner wants to start having your business meetings in Hawaii and have the company buy each of you new cars? Some resolution must be found or the entire business could be in jeopardy. Being a partner requires compromise and cooperation.

While the ability to raise capital is higher with a partnership than with a proprietorship, a partnership still cannot usually gather as many resources as a corporation.

Another financial problem could occur when the partnership decides to retain some of its income and reinvest it in the business. All partners must still pay income tax on their share of the partnership's income, even if they do not receive those funds. This could be financially difficult for some partners.

Continuity can be a problem for partnerships. Difficulties arise if a partner wants to withdraw from the partnership, dies, or becomes unable to continue in the business. Even if the partnership agreement identifies the value of each owner's share, the remaining partners may not have the financial resources to buy out the one who wants to leave. If a partner leaves, the partnership is dissolved. The remaining partners must either find a new partner to bring in, contribute additional capital themselves, or terminate the business. This problem can be aided in advance with a buy-sell agreement in the articles of partnership. This agreement spells out what will happen if one of the partners wants to leave voluntarily, becomes disabled, or dies. A sensible solution is a "right of first refusal" clause, which requires the selling partner to give the remaining partners first chance at buying the share. This proactive solution is highly recommended for all partnerships and corporations.

The Limited Partnership. The **limited partnership** was created to avoid some of the problems of a general partnership while retaining its basic benefits. A limited partnership must have at least one general partner who retains unlimited liability and all other responsibilities discussed in the general partnership section. Any number of limited partners with limited liability are allowed. Limited partners are usually passive investors. All they can lose is the amount they invest in the business. With very few exceptions, limited partners cannot participate in management of the business without losing their protection. Limited partnerships are a good way for the general partner(s) to acquire capital—from the limited partners—without giving up control, taking on debt, or going through the process of forming a corporation.

The cost and complication of organizing a limited partnership can be as high as forming a corporation. A document called a limited partnership agreement is required in most states. This agreement identifies each partner's potential liability and the amount of capital each partner supplies. Most limited partnerships are formed for real estate investment because of the tax advantages to the limited partners, who can write off depreciation and other deductions from their personal taxes.[23]

The Uniform Partnership Act (UPA). Signed in 1914, the UPA covers most legal issues concerning partnerships and has been adopted by every state in the union except Louisiana. The intent of the UPA is to settle problems that arise between partners. The best way for partners to protect their individual interests and the interests of the business is to draft their own articles of partnership. But since partnerships can be formed by two people verbally agreeing to hang up a sign and start a business, not all of them write such articles. Even if the partners do not draw up a written agreement, the UPA provides an amount of protection and regulation for them including:

- All partners must agree to any assignment of partnership property.
- Each partner has one vote, no matter what percentage of the partnership he or she owns unless a written agreement states otherwise.
- Accurate bookkeeping records are required and all partners have the right to examine them.
- Each partner owes loyalty to the partnership by not doing anything that would intentionally harm the partnership or the other partners.
- Partners may draw on their share of the profits. This provides partners access to their own capital.
- Salaries must be part of a written agreement. If a loss is incurred, partners must pay their share.[24]

Articles of Partnership. The formal contract between the principals, or people forming a partnership, is called the **articles of partnership.** The purpose of the contract is to outline partners' obligations and responsibilities. As a legal document, it helps to prevent problems from arising between partners and to provide

limited partnership A business structure in which one or more of the owners may be granted limited liability as long as one partner is designated as a general partner with unlimited liability.

articles of partnership The contract between partners of a business which defines obligations and responsibilities of the business owners.

a mechanism for solving problems that do arise. A partnership agreement can save your business and your friendship. Articles of partnership usually specify:

- The name, location, and purpose of the partnership.
- The contribution of each partner in cash, services, or property.
- The authority of each partner and the need for consensual decision making. For example, large purchases (over $5,000) or contracts could require the approval of a majority of the partners.
- The management responsibilities of each partner. For example, all partners shall be actively involved and participate equally in the management of the operation of the business.
- The duration of the partnership. Many partnerships are created to last indefinitely. Partnerships that exist for a specific period of time or for a specific project, such as building a new shopping center, are called **joint ventures.**
- The division of profits/losses. Distribution of profits or losses does not have to be exactly equal. Distribution could be allocated according to the same percentages that the partners contributed to the partnership. If not exactly equal, division must be clearly stated.
- The salaries/draws of partners. How will partners be compensated? After the decision is made on how to divide profits/losses at the end of the accounting period, you need to specify how each will be paid. A draw is the removal of expected profits by a partner.
- The procedure for dispute settlement/arbitration. Even with a partnership agreement, disputes can still arise. Providing an agreement for mediation or arbitration to solve serious disagreements can save a costly trip to court.
- The procedure for sale of partnership interest. This section should provide veto power to partners should a partner try to sell his or her interest in the business.
- The procedure for addition of a new partner. You should specify whether the vote for adding a new partner will have to be a simple majority or unanimous.
- The procedure for absence or disability of a partner. No one likes to consider an accident, illness, or death of a partner, but provisions should be defined.
- The procedure and conditions for dissolving the partnership.

joint venture A partnership that is created to complete a specified purpose and is limited in duration.

The Corporation

The **corporation** is the most complicated business structure to form. In the eyes of the law, a corporation is an autonomous entity, which has the legal rights of a person, including the ability to sue and be sued, to own property, and to engage in business transactions. A corporation must act in accordance with its charter and the laws of the state in which it exists. These laws vary by state.

This section is concerned with the type of corporation most common among small businesses—a **closely held corporation.** This means that relatively few people (usually fewer than ten) own stock. Most owners participate in management and those that don't are usually family or friends. By contrast, corporations that sell shares of stock to the public and are listed on a stock exchange are called

corporation A business structure which creates an entity that is separate from its owners and managers.

closely held corporation A corporation which is owned by a limited group of people. Stock is not traded publicly.

public corporations. Public corporations must comply with more detailed and rigorous federal, state, and Securities Exchange Commission regulations, such as disclosing financial information in the company's annual report. These are different animals than the closely held corporations of small businesses.

This discussion will begin with the regular or C corporation. Later we will look at variations called the S corporation and the limited liability company.

C Corporation. The C corporation is a separate legal entity which reports its income and expenses on a corporate income tax return and is taxed on its profits at corporate income tax rates.

Advantages. By far the biggest advantage of forming a corporation is the limited liability it offers its owners. In a corporation, the most you stand to lose is the amount you have invested in it. If the business fails or if it is sued, your personal property is protected from creditors. (See Table 2-3.)

An example of how limited liability can be an advantage to a small business can be shown in the case of Kathy, owner of a local brew pub. Kathy is worried that one of her employees might inadvertently or intentionally serve alcohol to a minor or to an intoxicated person. If the intoxicated person were to get into an automobile accident, Kathy could be sued. In addition to buying liability insurance, Kathy has also incorporated her business so her personal assets will be protected in the event of a lawsuit.

Corporations generally have easier access to financing because bankers, venture capitalists, and other lending institutions tend to regard them as being more stable than proprietorships or partnerships. Corporations have proved to be the best way to accumulate large pools of capital.

Corporations can take advantage of the skills of several people and draw on their increased human and managerial resources. Boards of directors can bring valuable expertise and advice to small corporations.

Finally, since a corporation has a "life" of its own, it continues to operate even if its stockholders change. Transfer of ownership can be completed through the sale of the stock.

Disadvantages. Complying with requirements of the state corporate code poses disadvantages not faced by proprietorships or partnerships. Even the smallest corporation must file articles of incorporation with the secretary of state, adopt bylaws, and keep records from annual stockholder and director meetings. Directors must meet to show that they are setting policy and are actively involved in running the corporation. All these requirements are needed to prevent the IRS, creditors, or lawsuits from removing the limited liability protection. If a corporation does not operate as a corporation, the limited liability protection of the directors and stockholders could be denied, holding them personally responsible for corporate liabilities. This process is referred to as "piercing the corporate veil."[25]

TABLE 2 ▪ 3   **Balancing the Advantages and Disadvantages of Corporations**

ADVANTAGES	DISADVANTAGES
Limited liability	Expensive to start
Increased access to resources	Complex to maintain
Transfer of ownership	Double taxation

The legal and administrative costs incurred in starting a corporation can be a sizable disadvantage. Self-incorporation kits exist, but be careful about going through the incorporation process without the aid of an attorney. The cost of incorporating can easily reach $1,000 before the business is even open.

Corporate profits face double taxation in that the profits are taxed at the corporate level first and can be taxed again once the profits are distributed to stockholders. If a stockholder also works in the corporation, he or she is considered to be an employee and must be paid a "reasonable wage," which is subject to state and federal payroll taxes.

Even the limited liability a corporation affords does not completely protect your personal property. If you use debt financing or borrow money, lenders will probably expect you to secure the loan with your personal property. Therefore, if the business must be liquidated, your personal property can be attached.

If you sell stock in your corporation, you are giving up some control of your business. The more capital you need to raise, the more control you must relinquish. If large blocks of stock are sold, you may end up as a minority stockholder of what used to be your own business. Raising capital in this way may be necessary for growth, but you will have to relinquish some control.

Forming a Corporation. The process for incorporating your business includes the following steps. You must prepare **articles of incorporation** and file them with the secretary of state in the state in which you are incorporating. You must choose a board of directors, adopt bylaws, elect officers, and issue stock. At the time you incorporate, you must also decide whether to form a C corporation, an S corporation, or a limited liability company.

articles of incorporation A document to describe the business which is filed with the state in which a business is formed.

You are not required to use an attorney to file articles of incorporation, but attempting the process and making a mistake could end up costing you more than an attorney would have charged for the job. Although states vary in their requirements, articles of incorporation usually include:

- *The name of your company.* The name you choose must be registered with the state in which it will operate. This registration prevents companies from operating under the same name, which could create confusion for the consumer. Your corporation's name may not be deceptive about its type of business.

- *The purpose of your corporation.* You must state the intended nature of your business. Being specific about your purpose will give financial institutions a better idea of what you do. Incorporating in a state that permits very general information in this section allows you to change the nature of your business without reincorporating.

- *The names and addresses of the incorporators.* Some states require at least one incorporator to reside in that state.

- *The names and addresses of the corporation's initial officers and directors.*

- *The address of the corporation's home office.* You must establish headquarters in the state from which you receive your charter or register as an out-of-state corporation in your own state.

- *The amount of capital required at time of incorporation.* You may need to deposit a specified percentage of the par value (the value that you place on your stock) of the capital stock in a bank before incorporation.

- *Capital stock to be authorized.* In this section, you specify the types of stock and the number of shares that the corporation will issue.

- *Bylaws of the corporation.* A corporation's bylaws are the rules and regulations by which it agrees to operate. Bylaws must stipulate the rights and powers of shareholders, directors, and officers; the time and place for the annual shareholder meeting, and the number needed for a quorum (the number needed to transact business); how the board of directors is to be elected and compensated; the dates of the corporation's fiscal year; and who within the corporation is authorized to sign contracts.
- *Length of time the corporation will operate.* Most corporations are established with the intention that they will operate in perpetuity. However, you may specify a duration for the corporation's existence.

Specialized Forms of Corporations

You have two other options to consider in addition to the C corporation. S corporations and limited liability companies are corporations that are granted special tax status by the Internal Revenue Service. A competent tax advisor can assist you to determine whether one of these options could provide a tax advantage for your business.

S corporation A special type of corporation in which the owners are taxed as partners.

S Corporation. An S corporation provides you with the limited liability protection of a corporation while enjoying the tax advantages of a partnership. Forming an S corporation will allow you to avoid the double-taxation disadvantage of regular corporations, and to offset losses of the business against your personal income tax. The S corporation files an informational tax return to report its income and expenses, but it is not taxed separately. Income and expenses of the S corporation "flow through" to the shareholders in proportion to the number of shares they own. Profits are taxed to shareholders at their individual income tax rate. To qualify as an S corporation you must meet the following requirements:

Computer Applications

Some small business owners minimize the legal costs of forming a corporation by doing much of the background work themselves. Software companies have jumped on this do-it-yourself bandwagon. For instance, the *PC Law Library*, published by Cosmi Corporation of Rancho Dominguez, California, contains over 200 legal documents for both business and personal situations. Nolo Press of Berkeley, California, a publisher of legal reference books, has developed Nolo's Partnership Maker®. This software provides 84 standard and alternative clauses that can be included in a partnership agreement. It also provides step-by-step help for understanding each clause in a partnership agreement.

If you decide to go this route, it is highly advisable to have an attorney familiar with your state's incorporation or partnership laws review your papers just to make sure that all the required information has been covered.

- Shareholders must be individuals, estates, or trusts—no other corporations.
- Nonresident aliens may not be shareholders.
- Only one class of outstanding common stock can be issued.
- All shareholders must consent to the election of the S corporation.
- State regulations specify the portion of revenue that must be derived from business activity, not from passive investments.
- There may not be more than 35 shareholders.[26]

Limited Liability Company (LLC). A relatively new form of ownership is the **limited liability company.** Recognized by the IRS in 1988. LLCs offer the protection of a corporation and the tax advantages of a partnership without the restrictions of an S corporation. It is now authorized in 47 states and the District of Columbia, although there are significant differences from state to state. (Currently Hawaii, Massachusetts, and Vermont have not enacted statutes allowing LLCs.) The owners of an LLC are called members. Unlike C and S corporations, the ownership by the members is not represented by shares of stock. Rather the rights and responsibilities of members are specified by the operating agreement of the LLC, which is like a combination of bylaws and a shareholder agreement in other corporations.

> **limited liability company (LLC)** A relatively new type of corporation which taxes the owners as partners yet provides a more flexible structure than an S corporation.

LLCs offer small business owners greater flexibility than either C or S corporations. This flexibility is provided to the members of the LLC by their writing of the operating agreement. The operating agreement can contain any provision for the LLC's internal structure and operations. LLCs are not constrained by regulations imposed on C and S corporations, such as who can and cannot participate, what the LLC can or cannot own, or how profits and losses are allocated to members. For example, the owners of an LLC can allocate 50 percent of the profit to a person who owns 30 percent of the business.[27] This is not allowable in C or S corporations.

LLCs should be considered seriously if you need flexibility in the legal structure of your business, desire limited liability, and prefer to be taxed as a partnership rather than a corporation.

The Nonprofit Corporation. The **nonprofit corporation** is a tax-exempt organization formed for religious, charitable, literary, artistic, scientific, or educational purposes. Nonprofit corporations depend largely on grants from private foundations and public donations to meet their expenses. People or organizations that contribute to a nonprofit can deduct that contribution from their own taxes. Assets dedicated to nonprofit purposes cannot be reclassified. If its directors decide to terminate the corporation, its assets must go to another nonprofit organization.[28] The details of forming and running a nonprofit corporation are beyond the interest of most readers of this book. To learn more about this business form, consult the sources listed in the endnotes.

> **nonprofit corporation** A tax-exempt corporation which exists for a purpose other than making a profit.

Summary

■ The differences between the small business manager and the entrepreneur.

An entrepreneur is a person who recognizes an opportunity and assumes the risk involved in creating a business for the purpose of making a profit. A small business manager is involved in the day-to-day operation of an established business. Each faces significant challenges, but they are at different stages of development in the entrepreneurship/small business management model.

■ The stages of entrepreneurship and of small business management.

The entrepreneurship process involves an *innovative* idea for a new product, process, or service. A *triggering event* is something that happens to the entrepreneur that causes him or her to begin bringing the idea to reality. *Implementation* is the stage in which the entrepreneur forms a business based on the idea. The first stage of the small business management process is *growth*, which usually means the business is becoming large enough to generate enough profit to support itself and its owner. The *maturity* stage is reached when the business is stable and well established. The *harvest* stage is when the small business manager leaves the business either through its sale, merger, or failure.

■ The advantages and disadvantages of self-employment.

The advantages of self-employment include the opportunity for independence, the chance for a better lifestyle, and the potential for significant profit. The disadvantages include the personal liability you face should the business fail, the uncertainty of an income, and the long working hours.

■ The characteristics of the forms of small business ownership.

There are several choices for the form of ownership of your small business. The most common is the sole proprietorship. If you choose a partnership, you could form a general partnership, in which all partners are fully liable for the business, or a limited partnership, in which at least one partner retains unlimited liability. A corporation offers its owners limited liability. In forming a corporation, you are creating a legal entity that has the same rights as a person. Variations of corporations include S corporations and limited liability companies.

Questions for Review and Discussion

1. What do entrepreneurs do that distinguishes them from any other person involved in business?
2. How could a person be both a small business manager and an entrepreneur?
3. Why may personality characteristics be good predictors of who may be a successful entrepreneur?
4. If a friend told you that entrepreneurs are high risk takers, how would you set the story straight?
5. Describe the significance of triggering events in entrepreneurship. Give examples.
6. How is small business management different from entrepreneurship?
7. Why would an entrepreneur be concerned about harvesting a business that has not been started yet?
8. Explain why people who own a small business may not enjoy pure independence.
9. In light of your answer to question 8, why is the desire for independence such a strong motivator for people to become self-employed?
10. If personal characteristics or personality traits do not predict who will be a successful entrepreneur, why are they significant to the study of entrepre-

neurship or small business management? Which characteristics do you think are most important? *studies indic - determ; knowledge, innov .*

11. Is a college degree in entrepreneurship an oxymoron?

12. Sole proprietorships make up 76 percent of all U.S. businesses and generate 6 percent of all business revenue. Only 18 percent of all sole proprietorships are incorporated, but they generate 90 percent of all revenue. What do these statistics tell you about the two forms of ownership?

13. Under what conditions would you consider joining a partnership? Why would you avoid becoming a partner? *1 gen. part. - others LTD. (passive invest. v/ LTD. liab.)*

14. What is the difference between limited and general partners?

15. When would forming a limited liability company be more advantageous than a C corporation or a partnership? *Ltd. liab. taxed like partnership (part. rate)*

Critical Incident

"Gardeners love this crap." That's the slogan for Pierce Ledbetter's Memphis, Tennessee–based company, Zoo Doo. In 1990, while still a student at Cornell University, Ledbetter returned home to Memphis and talked the managers at the local zoo into selling him composted animal manure from the enormous amounts produced by the zoo's animals daily. Why would any sane individual want animal manure? Well, it's extremely rich in soil nutrients. Wanting to cash in on the gardening craze just beginning to sweep across the United States, Ledbetter saw a marketing opportunity. He began selling his "Zoo Doo" in attractively designed pails. He even had the unique idea of having the manure compressed into various animal-shaped sculptures that gardeners could place in their gardens to decompose naturally and organically. His designs caught the eye of garden centers and mass merchandisers across the United States. Ledbetter's Zoo Doo now claims sales of about $1.5 million.

But having a great product and a great slogan isn't enough to make any small business a success. It's important to choose a form of business ownership that best meets your individual needs, goals, and constraints. Factors such as availability of adequate funding, amount of management expertise, product liability possibilities, and willingness to share decision making can influence which form of ownership is most appropriate. *Source: Thomas Jaffe and Damon Darlin, "Ah, The Sweet Smell of Manure!" Forbes, May 22, 1995, p. 92.*

Questions

Collaborative Learning

1. Put yourself in Pierce Ledbetter's shoes (and watch where you step)! Discuss the advantages and disadvantages of organizing Zoo Doo as a sole proprietorship, a partnership, or as a corporation. Think of all the possible factors that might influence your choice.

2. Now that you've looked at the various ways to organize Zoo Doo, it's time to convince your management professor at Cornell University of your decision. Write a letter describing the approach you've decided to take in organizing your Zoo Doo business and why.

Take it to the Net

We invite you to visit the Hatten page on the Prentice Hall Web site at: http://www.prenhall.com/~hattensb for this chapter's World Wide Web exercise.

VIDEO CASE
Au Revoir Les Bistros?

BISTROS—THE SMALL NEIGHBORHOOD restaurants that are as important as symbols of France as is the Eiffel Tower—are in trouble. Approximately 4000 of them fail per year due to steadily declining sales. Bistro owner Jean-Pierre Cachau says that all a good bistro used to need was a good, strong coffee, a good draft beer, and a good wine. But now French people are no longer awakening over a bistro's strong coffee or lingering through a long, leisurely lunch of stew and a bottle of wine.

The French economy is evolving from being farm-based to service-based, and as a result the pace of life has quickened. More people in France are living in urban areas and are opting to eat at foreign fast-food restaurants rather than at bistros. Although their customers have changed, French bistros continue to operate as they have for centuries. *Source: Adapted from* The Wall Street Journal Report, *Show #656, April 22, 1995.*

Discussion Questions

- How can business planning help save France's bistros?
- Jean-Pierre Cachau said that he has raised prices in his bistro by three or four percent. Do you see this as the answer for the problems facing bistro owners? What do you think they need to do?

Chapter Focus

After reading this chapter, you should be able to:

- Recognize the relationship between social responsibility, ethics, and strategic planning.
- Identify the levels of social responsibility.
- Discuss how to establish codes of ethics for your business.
- Suggest ways of influencing the organizational culture of your new business.
- Recognize the differences between strategic planning and business planning.
- List the steps in the strategic planning process.

3 Social Responsibilities, Ethics, and Strategic Planning

STEVE MARIOTTI IS NOT LIKE entrepreneurs who start enterprises to satisfy desires to make money. Mariotti's entrepreneurial fires were kindled in 1981 after he was brutally mugged. The former Ford executive who then ran an import-export business wanted to teach teens, like the two who beat him up, a real lesson—how to run a business.

Mariotti's theory was that the troubled inner-city youths who attack people are potential entrepreneurs. They just need help identifying different opportunities and the tools to help them rechannel their energies to more legitimate pursuits. He wanted to provide those tools. First, he quit his job in the import-export business so he could become a teacher. In ghetto classrooms, he saw firsthand the need for a curriculum that focused on practical applications of business topics. That need led him to develop a comprehensive course in the free enterprise system that got kids involved in business. He says he wanted to show them "there is more markup in lingerie than in drugs," so students wrote business plans for buying and selling neckties at a profit.

In 1987 Mariotti sought backing to form a nonprofit business to market his course to other schools. His students helped write the prospectus for the National Foundation for Teaching Entrepreneurship (NFTE). A $60,000 donation from a New Jersey philanthropist got him going.

In 1994 the business generated $4.5 million with 2,650 students enrolled in ten cities. Some success stories of the 7,000 graduates to date include a founder of a prosperous inner-city sports store and the president of a new rap music company. The NFTE has expanded offerings to include a "mini-MBA" course, which provides startup capital, entrepreneur profiles, and a briefcase to potential entrepreneurs. Many of the 2,600 low-income participants are on welfare and 10 percent have been convicted of crimes. Fourteen percent of the businesses that graduates have started survive, but that figure is hardly the only way to measure success. Many more participants have changed the direction in which their lives were heading. Mariotti does not make as much money as he did with his previous jobs, but he states "to me, each child is worth a billion dollars. So I consider myself very wealthy."

Mariotti has a strategic plan and a social conscience that show that an entrepreneur can make a living and a difference at the same time. *Source: Adapted from Mary Lord, "Making a Difference and Money, Too," U.S. News and World Report, October 31, 1994, pp. 103–105.*

Social Responsibilities of Small Business

What do concepts like social responsibility and ethics have to do with strategic planning in business? They are rarely covered together in textbooks, but they do have a connection. Strategic planning is the guiding process used to identify the mission, goals, and objectives for your business. It provides the manager with strengths and weaknesses of her business while identifying opportunities and threats that exist in the operating environments. Strategic planning spells out a long-term game plan for operating your business.

social responsibility The obligations of a business to have a positive impact on society on four levels—economic, legal, ethical, and philanthropic.

Corporate **social responsibility** (CSR) means different things to different people. In this chapter we will define it as the managerial obligation to take action to protect and improve society as a whole while achieving the goals of the business.[1] The manager of a CSR business should attempt to make a profit, obey the law, act ethically, and be a good corporate citizen.

Your level of commitment to these responsibilities and the strategic planning process you conduct form the heart of your business, the foundation and philosophy the business rests upon. Knowing what is important to yourself, your business, and everyone affected by its actions (social responsibility), is significant in deciding where you want to go and how to get there (strategic planning). The business you start or operate takes on a culture or a set of shared beliefs of its own. When you create a business, *your* values have a strong influence on the culture of the business you create. The values and culture of your business are demonstrated by your socially responsible (or irresponsible) actions.

Social responsibilities are the obligations of a business to maximize the pos-

FIGURE 3-1
The Pyramid of Social Responsibility
The four interconnected areas in which businesses are expected to act in a responsible manner.
Source: Archie Carroll, "The Pyramid of Corporate Social Responsibility," reprinted from Business Horizons *(July/August 1991), pp. 39–48.* © 1991, Foundation for the School of Business at Indiana University. Used with permission.

itive impact it has on society and minimize the negative impact. There are four levels of social responsibility: economic, legal, ethical, and philanthropic. (See Figure 3-1.)[2] While the primary responsibility of a business is economic, our legal system also enforces what we, as a collective group or society, consider proper behavior. Each firm and person decide what is ethical, or what is right beyond legal requirements. Finally, a business can be expected to act like a good citizen and help improve the quality of life for everyone. While all four of these obligations have always existed, ethical and philanthropic issues have received considerable attention recently.

Economic Responsibility

economic responsibility
The view that a business must make a profit in order to survive and make any other contributions.

As a businessperson in a free enterprise system, you have not only the fundamental right but the responsibility to make a profit. You are in business because you are providing a good or a service that is needed. If you do not make a profit, how can you stay in business? If you don't stay in business, how can you provide that good or service to people who need it?

Historically, the primary role for business has been economic. Entrepreneurs assume the risk of getting into business because profit is their incentive. If you don't attend to the economics of your business, you can't take care of anything else. Therefore, the economic responsibilities of your business would include a commitment to being as profitable as possible; to making sure employees, creditors, and suppliers are paid; to maintaining a strong competitive position; and to maintaining efficient operation of your business.

Economist Milton Friedman emphasizes the economic side of social responsibility. Friedman contends that business owners should not be expected to know what social problems should receive priority or how many resources should be dedicated to solving them. He states, "There is one and only one social responsibility of business: to use its resources and energy in activities designed to increase its profits so long as it stays within the rules of the game . . . [and] engages in open and free competition, without deception and fraud."[3] His point of view is that business revenues that are diverted to outside causes raise prices to consumers, decrease employee pay, and may support issues with which some of the business's stakeholders do not agree. Basically, Friedman's argument is that businesses should produce goods and services and let concerned individuals and government agencies solve social problems.

Legal Obligations

legal obligation The level of responsibility to obey the law.

Above making a profit, we are each expected to comply with the federal, state, and local laws that lay the ground rules in which we must operate. Laws can be seen as society's codes of right and wrong which exist to ensure that individuals and businesses do what is considered right. These codes change all the time as laws are added, repealed, or amended in an attempt to match public sentiment. Regulation of business activity generally falls into four groups of laws that protect: (1) consumers, (2) competition, (3) the environment, and (4) equality and safety.

The category of **consumer protection** became popular when Ralph Nader started the consumer movement in the early 1960s. Beginning with his safety campaign in the automotive industry, Nader and the consumer activist group he formed, Nader's Raiders, have fought to protect the safety and rights of consumers. Consumer activism has taken the form of letter-writing campaigns, lobbying of government agencies, or boycotting companies that are perceived to be irresponsible. Laws protecting consumers from unsafe business practices go back to 1906 when the Pure Food and Drug Act was passed. Today government agencies such as the Consumer Product Safety Commission and the Food and Drug Administration (FDA) set safety standards and regulations for consumer products, food, and drugs.

Laws that protect **competition** go back to the Sherman Antitrust Act of 1890, which prohibits monopolies. These laws see competition and unrestrained trade as checks and balances in businesses providing quality products and services at reasonable prices. The Federal Trade Commission (FTC) enforces many of these laws.

Laws protecting the **environment** were passed beginning in the 1960s also to set minimum standards for business practices concerning air, water, and noise. The Environmental Protection Agency (EPA) was created to enforce many of these laws.

The 1960s saw the passage of legislation regarding **equality** in the workplace. The Civil Rights Act of 1964 prohibits discrimination in employment on the basis of race, color, sex, religion, or national origin. The Equal Employment Opportunity Commission (EEOC) enforces these laws. While the Americans with Disabilities Act of 1990, equal employment opportunity (EEO), and affirmative action regulate diversity in the workplace (see Chapter 14 for more details on these issues), a small business owner must keep the big picture in mind. The key to managing diversity is to see people as individuals with strengths and weaknesses and to create a climate where everyone can contribute to the best of their ability.[4]

Sexual harassment is a problem in small businesses, although it generally doesn't receive as much public attention as multimillion-dollar corporate settlements. Sexual harassment can damage a person's dignity, productivity, and eagerness to come to work, which is costly to that person and to the business.[5] EEOC guidelines define sexual harassment as unwelcome sexual advances, requests for sexual favors, and other verbal or physical conduct of a sexual nature when: (1) sexual activity is required to get or keep a job, or (2) a hostile environment is created where work is unreasonably difficult.[6] The legal costs associated with a sexual harassment lawsuit average $200,000 per complaint for those investigated and found to be valid before it ever gets to court. Sexual harassment is expected to cost U.S. businesses over $1 billion in legal fees and actual damages from 1994 to 1999.[7] To help keep your small business free of harassment, the American Management Association recommends that you:

- Have a clear written policy prohibiting sexual harassment.
- Hold mandatory supervisory training programs on policies and prevention of harassment.
- Ensure that the workplace is free of offensive materials.
- Implement a program for steps to take when a complaint of harassment is received.
- Keep informed of all complaints and steps taken.
- Make sure the commitment against harassment exists at every level.[8]

Ethical Responsibility

While economic and legal responsibilities are shown in Figure 3-1 as separate levels of obligation, they actually coexist because they represent the minimum threshold of socially expected business behavior. Ethics are the rules of moral values that guide decision making by groups and individuals. They are a person's fundamental orientation toward life—what she sees as right and wrong. Ethical responsibilities of a business are how its decisions and actions show concern for what its stakeholders (employees, customers, stockholders, and the community) consider fair and just.

ethical responsibility
The obligation of individuals and businesses to do what is right.

Changes in ethical standards and values usually precede changes in laws. As shown in the previous section on legal obligations, society's expectations changed dramatically (civil rights, consumer, and environmental movements) in the 1960s, which led to new laws. Changing values cause constant interaction between the legal and ethical levels of social responsibility.

Even businesses that set high ethical standards and try to operate well above legal standards have difficulty keeping up with expectations that perpetually rise.

As a case in point, late in 1994 The Body Shop encountered direct and specific criticism of some of its business practices. Critics began to question whether or not The Body Shop was being honest in its advertising and its public image. One of the most vocal critics was journalist Jon Entine. A year-long investigation by Entine led him to make certain allegations against The Body Shop in the September–October 1994 issue of *Business Ethics*. Selected allegations follow:

- Despite its reputation as an innovative natural cosmetics company, cosmetics experts say the company uses many outdated, off-the-shelf product formulations filled with nonrenewable petrochemicals.
- The company has a documented history of quality control problems, including selling "contaminated" products and products that contain

formaldehyde. These assertions were made by former Body Shop quality control managers and one of its own consulting scientists.

- The Body Shop's charitable contributions and its progressive environmental standards don't match up to what the company claims it does.

About three weeks after the publication of these allegations, T. Gordon Roddick (founder Anita Roddick's husband and chairman of The Body Shop) responded with a letter to subscribers of *Business Ethics* disputing the information in the article. He stated that, "Of the 22 sources named in the article, 10 were disgruntled former employees or franchisees, current competitors, or disappointed bidders for our business, all of whom obviously have personal reasons for wanting to make The Body Shop look bad."

But, that wasn't the end of this intriguing story. In the middle of November 1994, subscribers to *Business Ethics* received a letter from the publisher stating that The Body Shop had obtained the mailing list of the magazine through deceptive means, used it without permission to send Roddick's letter to subscribers, and that Entine and the publisher stood by the facts stated in the article.

It's hard to know whether or not the criticisms against The Body Shop were fully justified or whether it's a situation where a company that's loudly and visibly pronounced itself as socially responsible and ethical was just an easy target for critics. But the fact remains that a business that makes such claims about itself had better be able to stand up to scrutiny. It's a lesson that The Body Shop learned the hard way.[9]

In addition to Roddick, other owners and their businesses that began small and have led the way in social responsibility include Paul Hawkin of Smith & Hawkin, Ben Cohen and Jerry Greenfield of Ben and Jerry's Ice Cream, and Yvon Chouinard of Patagonia.[10]

Ethics and Business Strategy. Business ethics mean more than simply passing moral judgment about what should and should not be done in a particular situation. It is part of the conscious decisions you make about the directions you want your business to take. It is a link between morality, responsibility, and decision making within the organization.[11]

The American public has serious concerns about the ethical standards of people they deal with and the decisions they make. Figure 3-2 shows the perception of the American public that the ethical standards of small business owners

FIGURE 3-2
Groups Perceived to Have Unethical Standards
Source: Harris Poll of 1,256 adults, data printed in "USA Snapshots," USA Today, September 3, 1992, p. 1A. © 1994, USA TODAY. Reprinted with permission.

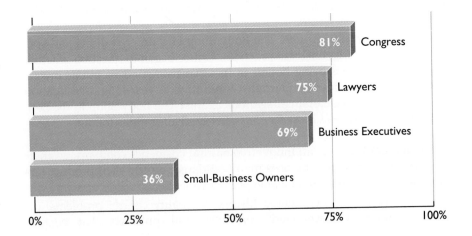

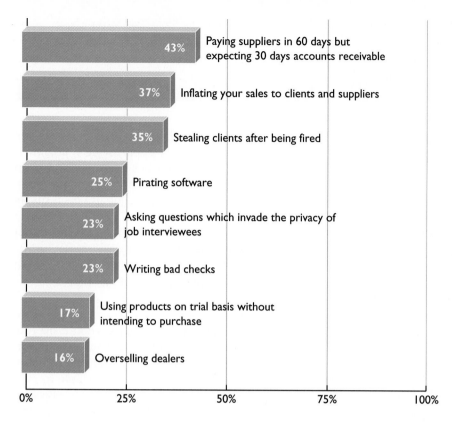

FIGURE 3-3
What Is Acceptable Conduct?
Percentage of businesspeople who regard questionable practices as acceptable.
Source: Adapted with permission, INC. *Magazine, December 1992, p.16. Copyright 1994 by Goldhirsh Group, Inc., 38 Commercial Wharf, Boston, MA 02110.*

are considerably higher than members of Congress, lawyers, and large business executives.

A poll by *Inc.* magazine asked people who run small businesses whether they found certain business practices to be acceptable or unacceptable. Compare their responses to your own. Inflating your sales to clients and suppliers means telling people you sell more than you really do. Overselling dealers means requiring the dealers who are under contract for your goods to purchase more than they would voluntarily choose to. This practice inflates your sales at the expense of increasing your dealers' inventory levels. (See Figure 3-3.)

Codes of ethics. A code of ethics is a formal statement of what your business expects in the way of ethical behavior. It can serve as a guide for employee conduct to help employees determine what behaviors are acceptable. Since the purpose of a code of ethics is to let everyone know what is expected and what is considered right, it should be included in an employee handbook (see Manager's Notebook).

Your **code of ethics** should contain a reflection of *your* ethical ideals, be concise in order to be remembered, be written clearly, and apply equally to all employees regardless of level of authority.[12] Your expectations and the consequences of breaking the code should be communicated to all employees.

An explicit code of ethics and the expectation that employees must adhere to it can reap many benefits for your small business including:

1. Obtaining high standards of performance at all levels of your work force.
2. Reducing anxiety and confusion over what is acceptable employee conduct.

code of ethics The tool with which the owner of a business communicates ethical expectations to everyone associated with the business.

Employee Handbooks

How do you communicate your mission statement, your code of ethics, and your policies on topics such as discrimination and sexual harassment to your employees? Many small businesses are writing employee handbooks that explain company policies and help to orient employees while covering legal notification requirements to prevent lawsuits.

Wendy Rhodes, a partner with Hewitt Associates, a benefits and compensation consulting firm, suggests including the following sections in your employee handbook:

- *Employment Policies.* Describe work hours, regular and overtime pay, performance reviews, vacations and holidays, equal employment opportunities, and other items that affect employment.
- *Benefits.* Relate insurance plans, disability plans, workers' compensation, retirement programs, and tuition reimbursement.
- *Employee Conduct.* Explain your expectations on everything you classify as important from personal hygiene to dress codes to employee development.
- *Glossary.* Every company has its own terms and jargon. Explain terminology important to your business. For example, Ashton Photo distinguishes between *late* ("not completed on time in a given department"), *delayed* ("production of a job has been suspended, awaiting information from the customer"), and *on hold* ("production of a job has been suspended for accounting reasons").
- *Organization Chart.* Include charts and job descriptions to give employees a sense of their place in the organization and how all the parts of the business fit together.

In your employee handbook, don't try to spell out specifics on what people should do in every possible situation. You just want to communicate your broader principles of what the company believes in and how you expect people to perform.

You do not want to give the impression that providing an employee a handbook guarantees lifetime employment, so lawyer Robert Nobile recommends including a disclaimer to the effect of: "This handbook is not a contract, express or implied, guaranteeing employment for any specific duration. Although we hope that your employment relationship with us will be long term, either you or the company may terminate this relationship at any time, for any reason, with or without cause or notice."

Source: Adapted from Tom Ehrenfeld, "The (Handbook) Handbook," Inc. (November 1993), pp. 57–64

3. Allowing employees to operate as freely as possible within a defined range of behavior.
4. Avoiding double standards that undermine employee morale and productivity.
5. Developing a public presence and image that are consistent with your organization's ideals.[13]

If you want to maintain and encourage ethical behavior in your business, it must be part of your company's goals. By establishing ethical policies, rules, and standards in your code of ethics, you can treat them like any other company goal, such as increasing profit or market share. Establishing ethical goals allows you to take corrective action by punishing employees who do not comply with company standards and rewarding those who do. If your code of ethics is supported and strictly enforced by you and your management team, it will become part of your company's culture and will improve ethical behavior. If your managers and employees see your code of ethics as a window-dressing façade, it will accomplish nothing.

Ethics Under Pressure. Businesses face ethical dilemmas every day. How can they maintain high ethical standards when the effects will hit their bottom line?

> You run a construction company and receive a bid from a subcontractor. You know a mistake was made and the bid is accidently 20 percent too low. If you accept the bid, it could put the subcontractor out of business. But accepting it will improve your chance of winning the contract for a big housing project. *What do you do?*[14]

Robert George, CEO of Medallion Construction Company of Merrimack, New Hampshire, was the manager who faced this dilemma. Medallion was bidding to become the general contractor of a $2.5 million public housing contract. An electrical contractor from the area submitted a bid that was $30,000 or 20 percent, lower than the quotes from four other subcontractors. Subcontractor bids come in only a few hours before the general contractors must deliver their bids so that subcontractors can't be played against each other. Robert George was tempted to take the bid he knew was a mistake because it would have almost guaranteed that Medallion would win the contract. Then he reconsidered for several reasons. Accepting the bid could have caused problems if the subcontractor went belly-up once the project was underway. Then he would have to find a replacement, which would cause time delays and cost overruns.

Aside from pragmatic problems, George was troubled by the ethical ramifications. He asked himself, "Is it fair to allow someone to screw up when they don't know it and you do?" He decided that the money was not worth the damage to his reputation or putting a fellow small business person under. George called the subcontractor and said, "Look, I'm not going to tell you what your competitors bid, but your number is very low—in my opinion, too low." The subcontractor withdrew his bid. Medallion still won the contract.

A year later the same subcontractor submitted another low bid on a different project. This time the low bid was intentional. The subcontractor offered a 2 percent discount because he remembered how honestly George had treated him earlier. Sometimes high ethics can have material rewards. Having a reputation for high ethical standards can give you an "ethical edge," a competitive advantage for your business. Being known for doing what is right can help you attract talented people, win loyal customers, forge relationships with suppliers, and earn the public's trust.

> You spend months trying to negotiate a deal to sell your equipment in Japan. You deliver your product, as agreed, but the Japanese distributor tells you it is not what the customer expected. The distributor wants you to re-engineer the equipment even though it clearly meets the written specifications. *What do you do?*[15]

David Lincoln is president of Lincoln Laser Company, a manufacturer located in Phoenix. Lincoln thought he had a done-deal with a distributor from Japan who had spent months scrutinizing Lincoln's $300,000 machine that scans

Ethical dilemmas can be magnified by differences in language, culture, and business practices.

Reality Check

Can You Serve Two Bottom Lines?

When Tom and Gun Denhart moved from Connecticut to Portland, Oregon to start their own business, they had modest goals. Tom wanted to get out of the high-pressure rat race of advertising he faced with Ogilvy & Mather in New York. Tom and Gun wanted to make a living selling high-quality Swedish products for children. They created what quickly became the ideal workplace. Unfortunately, they found that putting the needs of their employees, the community, and society first can be hazardous to the health of a business.

The business they created is called Hanna Andersson (named after Gun's grandmother). They sold upscale children's clothing made from Swedish cotton via mail order. Tom used his advertising skills to create award-winning, understated masterpieces of direct mail. The market of successful baby boomers was ripe in the early 1980s. They were ready to spend money on their young children. Competition didn't exist, so Hanna Anderson flourished. Their startup could have come from a storybook. Operating out of their garage and a spare room until their second year, Hanna soon reached $40 million annual sales while retaining the atmosphere of a family-run shop. Sales and number of employees doubled annually for the first five years. They were not only creating a company, they were creating their own counterculture. From the start the company was not about baby clothes or money, it was about serious social responsibility, creating opportunities for people to be fulfilled at work and "doing the right thing."

By conscious design, the workplace created was one of perks, benefits, and contributions. Local charities received 5 percent of pretax profits. When profits were in the millions, this yielded six-figure gifts. Their crown jewel initiative was the Hannadown program. Customers would receive 20 percent discount on their next purchase for returning used Hanna clothing. The returned goods were distributed to needy children across the country. Employee benefits were incredible. Half of all child care costs were paid by the company. Part-time and seasonal employees working 30 hours per week received full benefits. They had flextime, family-leave time, sick time, and even lunchtime was subsidized with a light gourmet employee cafeteria. They were paid cash bonuses, had profit-sharing and tuition reimbursement programs, and deep product discounts. Employee parking cost the company $80,000 per year.

Success was calculated by what the Denharts and other socially responsible entrepreneurs called the "double bottom line": one for profit; one for good works. Profits, revenue, and good works flowed freely and Gun thought that the money would always flow to them as long as they did the right thing—but it didn't. The tide started to turn, not because of a single problem, rather a combination of problems. Two years of recession made customers less willing to shell out $38 for overalls for a two-year-old. There had been management mistakes in trying to fix things that weren't broken, like radical changes to a great catalog. When the company started in 1984, they were alone in the market. By 1991, they realized that worthy competitors like Lands' End, L.L. Bean, Oshkosh, Gymboree, and Gap Kids were out there. Most companies could have made adjustments to compensate for the competition, but most companies were not saddled with cost structures that paid for sky-high benefits and contributions. Mary Roberts, now company president, said, "We thought we were immune to worldly cares. Suddenly, we had to face the fact that we were part of the real world."

Costs had to be reduced and inefficiencies had to be improved. Benefit cuts and even some layoffs sent tremendous shock waves through the culture used to protection and pampering. Gail

Johnson, vice president of operations, stated that "Topping the to-do list was reeducating employees and weaning them of the sense of entitlement that years of prosperity had bred." The many cost-cutting adjustments are helping the company get back on its feet. Sales are climbing slowly and attention is being paid to the bottom line. Values are not being abandoned, just modified. Gun realizes that having high values is easy; maintaining them is difficult when the going gets tough. Doing the right thing by employees is not the same as doing the smart thing for the business.

What do you do when the current well-being of employees clashes with the future well-being of the company? How do you tell what the "right" thing to do is at any given time? Would a strategic plan have helped management to be socially responsible and to monitor changing competitive and customer environments so adaptations could have been made *before* serious problems existed?

Source: Anne Murphy, "Too Good to Be True?" Adapted with permission, Inc. magazine, July 1994, pp. 34–43. © 1994, Goldhirsh Group, Inc., 38 Commercial Wharf, Boston, MA 02110.

printed circuit board wiring for very small cracks or breaks. The distributor finally ordered eight machines. Unfortunately, the Japanese client was not happy after delivery. Lincoln said, "They thought it should inspect *every type* of printed circuit board, even though we explained repeatedly that it was suitable only for a certain class of boards." To change the machine so it could inspect every type of

Reality Check

Catering to the Community

Why do restaurants and hotels routinely throw away leftover food when there are people in their communities going hungry? The problem has always been the administrative costs of getting the food delivered to the people who need it. Enter Bruce Feldman, president of Economy Linen and Towel Service, who came up with an idea that won him the 1993 *Inc.* Socially Responsible Entrepreneur of the Year award.

In applying his business skills to help solve a social problem, Feldman arranged for restaurants and hotels to donate their surplus food. When Economy Linen drivers were making linen and towel deliveries to these businesses, they would place the donated food into insulated food carriers that had been installed in the linen trucks. The food was then deposited in a freezer at Economy Linen's warehouse. From there the Emergency Food Bank, a nonprofit agency working in tandem with Feldman, directed the food to community kitchens, homes for runaway children, and shelters for battered women.

Bruce Feldman identified a goal and strategically worked through problems in setting up the process to achieve that goal: to get once wasted food to people who need it. He says modestly of the idea that "it seemed to be a way for private industry to harness the assets we have in place already in the community." Bruce Feldman used strategic management in an ethical way to demonstrate his social responsibility.

Source: Adapted from Leslie Brokaw, "Moving Force," Inc. (December 1993), pp. 119–120.

Manager's Notebook

Green Marketing

Efforts of businesses to act in a socially responsible manner toward the environment are usually called *green marketing*. Small businesses can show concern for the environment (and cut costs at the same time) by recycling paper products and office supplies, by using environmentally benign products, and by using environmentally safe product packaging. Each business must decide how it can have the greatest positive environmental impact. Not every business can affect the air pollution from vehicles or ozone depletion, but every business must recognize the power of the green movement and the rise in environmental consciousness. Incorporating a green marketing program can be aided by the following guidelines:

- Environmentalism is not a passing fad. It is strongly supported.
- The number of people concerned about environmental issues is growing. They buy environmentally friendly products.
- Green marketing can be a sustainable competitive advantage leading to long-term profit.
- A successful green marketing strategy depends on effective communication and continuous monitoring.
- Green marketing needs to be integrated into the strategic planning process.

Source: Ted Rakstis, "Business Rethinks, Refines, Recycles, and Recoups," Kiwanis Magazine (August 1993), pp. 43–49, and Stephen McDaniel and David Rylander, "Strategic Green Marketing," Journal of Consumer Marketing, Vol. 10, no. 3 (1993), pp. 4–10.

circuit would require Lincoln to have the software rewritten, to pull engineers from another project, and to borrow funds to pay for the additional work.

Lincoln's first instinct was to say, "This is what you agreed to, we supplied what we said we would. You bought it, pay up." He could have said "no" and been acting ethically according to common business practices in the United States, but he decided to go beyond his basic obligation and do what he felt was the right thing. Lincoln reflected upon the differences between American and Japanese customers. Lincoln had expected Japanese customers to act like American clients without realizing the differences in adaptation levels between the two groups. The company hadn't taken time to become sensitive to cultural differences. Fortunately, Lincoln was able to secure financing to accommodate its customers—keeping its ethical principles, its credibility, and the Japanese market intact.

Philanthropic Goodwill

philanthropic goodwill
The level of social responsibility in which a business does good without the expectation of anything in return.

Philanthropy is the highest level illustrated on the social responsibility pyramid of Figure 3-1. This includes businesses participating in programs that improve the quality of life, raise the standard of living, and promote goodwill. The difference between ethical responsibility and philanthropy is that the latter is seen not so much as obligations but as contributions to society to make it a better place. Businesses that do not participate in these activities are not seen as unethical, but those that do tend to be seen in a more positive light.

Philanthropic activity is not limited to the wealthy or to large corporations writing seven-digit donation checks. Average citizens and small businesses can be and are philanthropic. A small business can sponsor a local Special Olympics meet, contribute to a Habitat for Humanity project, lead a community United Way campaign, or sponsor a Little League baseball team.

Fernando Mateo, owner of a small New York City carpet business, Carpet Fashions, had an idea that has made the streets of his city a little safer to walk. Mateo and his 14-year-old son were watching a television program about the increase in violence in the United States. The son said he would give up his Christmas presents if it would stop violence. That sparked an idea in Mateo's mind—why not trade guns for toys? He bought $5,000 worth of gift certificates from Toys "R" Us and began advertising his offer to exchange a $100 gift certificate for every gun turned in—no questions asked—in the high-crime section of Manhattan called Washington Heights.

The $5,000 went to 500 takers quickly, but the positive publicity led Toys "R" Us, Foot Locker, Dial-A-Mattress, and other companies to add $160,000 to the program. In ten days 1,502 weapons were turned in to police precincts. While

Reality Check

Making Good

Do you have to be the owner of a big corporation, flush with cash, to be able to make a contribution to your city or neighborhood? Not necessarily. Small businesses all over the country are recruiting their modest resources—including their products, skills, customers, and suppliers—to help make their communities better places. Not every small business can mount a national campaign against social problems as Ben & Jerry's or The Body Shop have done. But your commitment and creativity can make a contribution to your community more important than money.

Giving your product away may be a starting point. Laury Hammel is general manager and principal owner of Longfellow Clubs, a health and recreation company in Wayland, MA. Hammel has founded five nonprofit foundations, is involved in ten such organizations, and participates in many local charities and community events. But his favorite charitable act is donating the use of Longfellow Club facilities to kids with special needs. In his Handi-Racket Tennis Program, handicapped kids learn to play tennis. Hammel has similar programs for swimming and basketball. The three programs bring in about 50 disabled children from the Wayland area each week. Although Hammel estimates that he gives up about $3,000 per year in court and club fees, he says his program takes more initiative than money. Hammel is committed to working with these children, even if the programs sometimes get in the way of club members' desires.

No matter how large or small, a social purpose injects humanity into your business. The perception of business as being soulless has existed for so long that many owners love a chance to show an amount of social concern through their company.

Source: Adapted from Ellyn Spragins, "Making Good," Inc. *(May 1993), pp. 114–122.*

the program may only affect a small percentage of the total number of handguns on the street, it has had a positive impact. Michael Goldstein, CEO of Toys "R" Us, said, "We thought that Fernando's program of toys for guns was a wonderful attempt by a well-meaning individual to try to do something to curb violence in the Bronx, and since he used our gift certificates, we agreed to assist him."[16] One small business owner can make a difference!

Strategic Planning

strategic plan A long-term planning tool used for viewing a business and the environments in which it operates in broadest terms.

Recall from Chapter 1 that poor management is the major cause of business failure. The first function of good management, therefore, is good planning. Strategic planning is a long-range management tool that helps small businesses be proactive in the way they respond to environmental changes. The process of strategic planning provides an overview of your business and all the factors that may affect it in the next three to five years. This will help you formulate goals for your business to take advantage of opportunities and avoid threats. From your goals you can determine the most appropriate steps you need to take to accomplish them—an action plan.

At the beginning of this chapter, the question was posed about the connection between social responsibility, ethics, and strategic planning. If the intent of the strategic planning process is to produce a working document for your business to follow, the relationship can be seen in the following way. When you assess your company's external environment for opportunities and threats, you identify what you *might do*. When you look at the internal strengths and weaknesses, you see what you *can do* and *cannot do*. Your personal values are ingrained into the business; these are what you *want to do*. Your ethical standards will determine what is *right for you to do*. Finally, in responding to everyone that could be affected by your business, social responsibility guides what you *should do*.[17] When viewed in this manner, not only are social responsibility, ethics, and strategic planning connected, it is not possible to separate them.

The Strategic Planning Process

Writing a strategic plan generally involves a six-step sequential process. Figure 3-4 shows that the strategic planning process begins with (1) formulating your mission statement, (2) completing an environmental analysis, (3) perform-

FIGURE 3-4
The Strategic Planning Process
The six sequential steps to drafting a strategic plan.

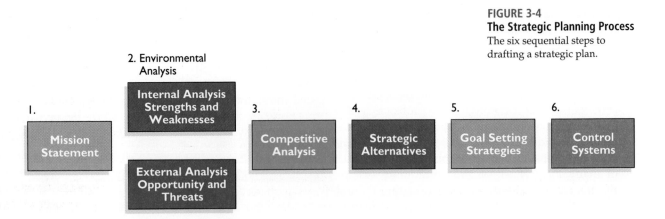

2. Environmental Analysis

Internal Analysis Strengths and Weaknesses

External Analysis Opportunity and Threats

1. Mission Statement

3. Competitive Analysis

4. Strategic Alternatives

5. Goal Setting Strategies

6. Control Systems

Computer Applications

Computer software products that are on the market today can help the small business manager or owner cope more easily with the demands of strategic planning. For instance, Inspiration by Inspiration Software (503-245-9011) is a visually based planning tool that is ideal for the novice planner. The Business Insight Software available from Business Resource Software (800-423-1228) can guide you through uncovering the potential problem areas in your business, which is part of the environmental analysis step in strategic planning. However, at a suggested retail price of $495, it might be cost prohibitive to many small businesses. Another useful program (but even more expensive at $995) is the Business Planning Advisor by Enterprise Support Systems (770-441-

3190). Even though this software is called "business" planning, it functions as a strategic planning tool by providing a step-by-step process for strategic planning and business development. One person who's had a positive experience with Business Planning Advisor is John V. Giordano, the vice president and general manager of DRS Military Systems of Oakland, New Jersey. The program helped him implement a more structured approach to planning, narrow the company's strategic focus, and get more people involved in planning.

Sources: Ripley Hatch and Jon Pepper, "They Could Just As Well Be Giants," Nation's Business *(July 1995), pp. 50–51; Dennis James, "Shortcut to Success,"* Success *(November 1995), pp. 67–70; and Arden Hoffman, "Perfect Picks,"* Working Woman *(November 1995), pp. 63–68.*

ing a competitive analysis, (4) analyzing your strategic alternatives, (5) setting your goals and strategies, and (6) setting up a control system.

Mission Statement. A **mission statement** provides direction for the company by answering the question, "What business are we really in?" The mission statement should be specific enough to tell the reader something about the business and how it operates. It should *not* be a long, elaborate document that details all of your business philosophies. By carefully identifying the purpose, scope, and direction of your business, the mission statement communicates what you want your business to do and to be. It is the foundation upon which all other goals and strategies are based.

mission statement
The reason an organization exists.

Another value of a mission statement is the commitment you make by printing and publicizing your strategy and philosophy. You have more incentive to stick to your ideas and expect others to follow them if they are written and shared than if you keep them to yourself.

Management consultant and author Tom Peters writes that a company's mission statement should be 25 words or less in length.[18] This brevity will allow everyone in the organization to understand and articulate it.

The mission statement of Starbucks Coffee Co., a Seattle company, reads:

Our mission is . . .
    To establish Starbucks as the premier purveyor of the finest coffee in the world while maintaining our uncompromising principles as we grow.

This mission statement then explains the principles it wishes to maintain:

The following five principles will help us measure the appropriateness of our decisions:
—Provide a great work environment and treat each other with respect and dignity.
—Apply the highest standards of excellence to the purchasing, roasting, and fresh delivery of our coffee.
—Develop enthusiastically satisfied customers all of the time.
—Contribute positively to our communities and our environment.
—Recognize that profitability is essential to our future success.[19]

Good mission statements, such as Starbucks', maintain a balance between ideas and reality. From Starbucks' statement, you can tell what it wants to achieve and how. It says what the business is and is not. Does Starbucks intend to diversify into flavored teas and soft drinks to become a major force in the beverage industry? No, the company intends to focus on making and selling the best coffee possible.

Since the mission statement is the heart of the strategic planning process, you can see in Starbucks' statement and principles the connection between strategic planning and social responsibility. You can even see evidence of the pyramid of social responsibility in its stated principles. The importance of making a profit identifies economic responsibility. The principle of treating each other with respect and dignity incorporates ethics into its strategic plan. The company's prin-

Manager's Notebook

Strategic Cabinetry

The importance of having a strategic plan cannot be overemphasized. Even very small businesses can benefit from developing one. One company that recognized the importance of strategic planning early is Woodpro Cabinetry, Inc. of Cabool, Missouri, a small bathroom cabinet manufacturer located in the rolling hills of the Missouri Ozarks. Owner and president LeRoy Walls knew that competition was heating up and that the marketplace was changing. He realized that to help ensure future prosperity his company needed a document to guide its decisions. So in the early 1990s, LeRoy and several Woodpro employees began developing in earnest a strategic plan for the company. The results of their hard work can be found

in a document of 200+ pages entitled "Woodpro Strategic Plan." The document, contained in a three-ring binder, covers a wide variety of important information, such as:

- *The Mission Statement.* One of the first elements that you see in Woodpro's strategic plan is its mission statement, which establishes that Woodpro seeks to be the **best** on-time producer and distributor of affordable quality bath cabinetry. But, having a Mission Statement is just the first step in a strategic plan.
- *The Environmental and Competitive Analysis.* Formulating appropriate strategies also requires an environmental and competitive

analysis. Woodpro's strategic plan describes what the company's managers see as its strengths (positive internal characteristics and resources) and weaknesses (negative internal characteristics and lack of resources); opportunities (positive external environmental trends), and threats (negative external environmental trends). Woodpro's strategic plan, internal strengths and weaknesses and external opportunities and threats are analyzed for each of the company's functional areas (marketing, manufacturing, human resources, and communication). For instance, its Marketing Threats section warns that "Competitors are broadening their product offerings" and that "More manufacturers are targeting home center stores." The company's 15 top competitors are then analyzed by products, services, customers, and operations with the information presented in eight separate tables. The Operations Weaknesses section notes that the company's "raw material usage volumes are too low to capture industry competitor cost advantages" and that a "preventive maintenance program is not yet in place." Woodpro's managers can use this vital information to strengthen the company's productivity and assure the stability and growth of its market share. Woodpro's managers admit that gathering competitor data hasn't been a high priority of theirs for very long, but they recognize the importance of knowing what the competition is doing. The competitor analysis in the strategic plan provides a good start to knowing the competition.

- *Strategic Alternatives, Goals, and Chosen Strategies.* Each of the functional sections in Woodpro's strategic plan ends with a description of specific strategies and desired outcomes. Thus, the goal stated under the topic of Marketing Promotion, in the Marketing Section is: "To increase awareness of Woodpro's attributes, philosophies, product offerings, and how we help sell our cabinetry, we will establish better communication and rapport with customers, potential customers, and neighbors." To accomplish this goal, the plan states that its strategy is to become better known in the American Midwest through advertising

and trade shows, and to use public relations tactics to gain recognition among cabinet retailers and cabinet manufacturers. In the Human Resource section, one stated goal is: "To provide a computerized system for entry and reporting of innovations, personal reminders, things to do, and strategies and plans." The strategies for achieving this goal are to improve reporting and control of project teams and process teams. Another strategy is to turn the strategic planning group into a team with ongoing responsibilities.

- *Putting Strategies into Action.* A written plan by itself isn't enough to ensure success. It needs to be put into action. Woodpro's strategic plan describes specific details for implementing each strategy. For instance, the Marketing Section asserts that to become better known in mid-America through advertising and trade shows, managers must develop direct-mail advertising programs, attend national trade shows, and use national magazine advertising.

- *Setting Up Controls.* This is one area where Woodpro's strategic plan isn't as thorough as it could be. Although the plan does identify specific actions that will be monitored, specific control techniques aren't described. In the case of the Marketing Section, Woodpro is to monitor the accomplishment of its strategies by determining if a direct-mail advertising program was developed, if national trade shows were attended, and if national magazine advertising was used. However, the means for evaluating the degree of success are not stated.

Once Woodpro's strategic plan was completed, it wasn't thrown on a shelf to gather dust. Instead, it was openly shared with all company employees, directors, and financial partners. It is constantly used. Whenever decisions need to be made or problems crop up, the strategic plan reminds employees and managers alike what Woodpro is striving to achieve.

Source: Woodpro Business Plan, Woodpro Cabinetry, Inc., Cabool, Missouri, 1993–1996.

ciple to contribute positively to the community and the environment shows ethics and philanthropy.

Environmental Analysis. Large and small businesses must operate in constantly changing environments. The ability to adapt to change is a major determinant of success or failure for any business in a free enterprise system. Essentially, environmental analysis is the process in which a manager examines what is going on within any sector that could affect the business, either within the business or outside of it.

Environmental analysis is also called **SWOT analysis** because you examine **S**trengths, **W**eaknesses, **O**pportunities, and **T**hreats. An analysis of the *internal* environment identifies strengths and weaknesses that exist within your own business. An analysis of the *external* environment identifies opportunities and threats—factors outside your control—that may affect your business.

Because of their speed, flexibility, and sensitivity to customer preferences, small businesses are in a position to take advantage of changes in the environment rapidly. Environmental analysis is important to small businesses because they have fewer resources to risk. No business can afford many mistakes, but the larger the operation, the more breadth it generally has to absorb the cost of errors. A small business may be significantly affected by environmental changes that a larger business could more easily weather.

External Analysis. Opportunities are positive alternatives that you may choose to help attain your company's mission. While you should always be scanning for opportunities, you cannot pursue every one. Your strategic plan will help you identify those that are right for your business.

Threats are obstacles to achieving your mission or goals. They are generally events or factors over which you have no personal control. A change in interest rates, new government regulation, or a competitor's new product might threaten your business. You may not be able to control these threats, but you can prepare for them or take positive action to cope with them. Threats and opportunities can be found by scanning developments in the following environments:

- *Economic.* A lot of economic data readily available on the international and national levels are very valuable to small businesses operating in smaller, more isolated markets. As a small business owner, you need to be aware of economic conditions that affect your target markets, such as unemployment rates, interest rates, total sales, and tax rates within your community.
- *Legal/regulatory.* Some factors can affect small businesses in more than one environment. For example, the passage of the North American Free Trade Agreement (NAFTA) changes regulations and the competitive environment. With regulations altered to encourage trade between the United States, Canada, and Mexico, many small businesses find a wealth of new opportunity in new markets. Other businesses see the changes as a threat with new competition. The voice of small business was also heard in Washington, as delegations of small business representatives from all 50 states brought nearly 300 policy recommendations when they met for the White House Conference on Small Business in the summer of 1995.
- *Sociocultural.* What members of society value and desire as they pass from one life stage to another has an effect on what they purchase. For example, an increased popularity of tatoos for teens and twenty-somethings, means

SWOT analysis The step of strategic planning in which the managers identify the internal strengths and weaknesses of a business and the opportunities and threats that exist outside the business.

Entering the Internet

Looking for the information you need on the Web can be both exciting and nerve-wracking. But you can make the search less frustrating by familiarizing yourself with the more effective Web search tools. These Web navigators (as they're called) can be particularly useful for doing an environmental analysis in your strategic planning. By plugging in specific keywords or topics from your environmental analysis—for example, tax law, venture capital, or country-western music—you can locate sites on the Web related to those areas. Once you've found a site or document that includes material you can use, you can usually find related material by clicking on the highlighted material (that's the miracle of hypertext!). What are the most popular Web search tools? Yahoo is a search tool that's set up as a directory—meaning that it lists Web sites by topic in a menulike format. (The Web addresses for Yahoo and all of the other search tools follow.) Other search tools are set up to let you find specific documents through keyword searches. One of the most useful of these is Lycos, which claims to have "indexed" 90 percent of Web sites. Another search tool is WebCrawler, America Online's proprietary search tool. WebCrawler provides a listing of Web sites, which may be accessed for free by anyone on the Net. (American Online subscribers may use the tool to access more detailed and descriptive listings of Web sites.) There are other search tools available, but these three tend to be the most popular. Happy hunting!

Yahoo	http://www.yahoo.com
Lycos	http://www.lycos.com
WebCrawler	http://www.webcrawler.com

Sources: Stephen H. Wildstrom, "Feeling Your Way Around the Web," Business Week, September 11, 1995, p. 22; and Philip E. Ross and Nikhil Hutheesing, "Along Came the Spiders," Forbes, October 23, 1995, pp. 210–216.

opportunity for skin artists who are able to provide this service in a small business.

- *Technological.* Technology is the application of scientific knowledge for practical purposes. Few environmental forces have caused as much excitement in the business community as the creation of the "information superhighway." Entrepreneurs are scrambling to find ways to take advantage of the perceived opportunities in linking computers all over the globe.

- *Competitive.* Actions of your competitors are considered forces within your competitive environment. You face a difficult task in not only tracking what your competitors are currently doing, but also in predicting their reactions to your moves. If you drop the price of your product to gain more market share, will competing business managers react by holding their prices constant or by cutting their prices below yours? This could escalate into an expensive price war.

Are opportunities and threats easy to identify? No, and they never have been. Writer Mark Twain once said, "I was seldom able to see an opportunity until it had ceased to be one."

Internal Analysis. An internal analysis assesses the strengths and weaknesses of your company. It identifies what it is that your company does well and what it could do better. Internal analysis is important for two reasons. First, your personal opinion of your own business will be biased, at best, and could provide an unrealistic view of the capacity and potential of your business. We tend to look at ourselves through proverbial rose-colored glasses.

Second, internal analysis is important in matching the strengths of your business with opportunities that exist. The idea is to put together a realistic profile of your business to determine if you are able to take advantage of opportunities and react to the threats identified in the environmental analysis. This is not as easy as it sounds because you have to view your environments not as if they are snapshots, but as several videos playing at once. The key is to match opportunities that are still unfolding with resources that are still being acquired.[20]

While most of us have no problem identifying our strengths, some of us may need help realizing our weaknesses. The following diagnostic tests can help you evaluate your business realistically:

- Visit your newest, lowest-level employee. Can he or she tell you why the business exists? Name major competitors? Say what you do well? List major customers? If not, your vision isn't coming across.
- Can that same employee describe what he or she is doing to contribute to your competitive advantage?
- Ask a long-term employee how things went yesterday. If you get answers like "OK," or "Fine . . . just fine," you may have a potential problem. If you hear specifics, consider it a good sign.
- Observe what the business looks like after hours. Are things neat and orderly, or does it look like a tornado struck? While neatness doesn't guarantee success, you should be able to find the checkbook, phonebook, and most of the furniture.
- Observe your business during work hours. Invent a reason to be where you can watch and hear what goes on. What impression do you get of the business?
- Select a few customers at random to call or visit. Ask them how they were *honestly* treated the last time they were in your business.
- Call your business during the busiest part of the day. How quickly is the phone answered? Is the response efficient, friendly, surly, or overly chatty?
- Ask a friend to visit your business as a mystery shopper. Would he or she come back again?[21]

Competitive Analysis/Competitive Advantage. Without analysis, competition can also be viewed with bias. Competitors are rarely as slow, backward, and inferior in all areas as we would like to believe they are. Competition should be viewed as formidable and serious. In the competitive analysis, you are trying to identify *competitive weaknesses*. In what areas is the competition truly weak and therefore vulnerable? Some bias may be removed if you are as specific as possible in writing your competitive analysis. For example, instead of saying your competitors offer poor service, qualify your remarks with references to return policies, delivery, schedules, or fees.

The heart of your company's strategy and reason for being in business is your *competitive advantage*. You must do *something* better than everyone else, oth-

Competitive Analysis: How to Beat the Competition

Rank your business and the four competitors you have identified for each of the following areas. Rank the businesses from "1" to "5", with "5" being the lowest and "1" the highest. Assign only one "1" per area, one "2", and so on through "5." No ties are allowed so you end up with a ranked list of the five companies. This exercise can help you improve your competitive position.

Areas of Comparison

1. *Image.* How do consumers perceive the reputation and the physical appearance of the business?

2. *Location.* Is the business convenient to customers for distance, parking, traffic, and visibility?

3. *Layout.* Are customers well served with the physical layout of the business?

4. *Atmosphere.* When customers enter the business, do they get a feeling that is appropriate for your type of business?

5. *Products.* Can customers find the products they expect for your type of business?

6. *Services.* Do customers receive the quantity and quality of services they expect?

7. *Pricing.* Do customers perceive the prices charged to be appropriate for the quality of the products sold? Do they receive the value they expect?

8. *Advertising.* Does the advertising of the business reach its target market?

9. *Sales methods.* Are customers comfortable with the methods the business uses to sell products?

AREAS OF COMPARISON	YOUR BUSINESS	COMPETITOR A	B	C	D
1. Image					
2. Location					
3. Layout					
4. Atmosphere					
5. Products					
6. Services					
7. Pricing					
8. Advertising					
9. Sales methods					
TOTALS					

erwise your business is not needed. (See Chapter 9.) Your competitive advantage must be sustainable over time to remain a benefit to you. If it can be easily copied by competitors, you have to find a new way to stay ahead.

Sometimes people mistake a gimmick for competitive advantage. For example, suppose a microbrewery accidently adds blue food coloring to a vat of beer, which becomes a surprise hit with its regular customers. Could this brewery sustain this advantage? No, it's really a gimmick because competitors could just as easily add blue food coloring to their beer with little lapse of time, negating the microbrewery's advantage. By contrast, the microbrewery might find greater competitive advantage by using unique combinations of ingredients when brewing its beer or refining its process of production to be truly distinctive.

Competitive advantage can be enhanced through *positioning*. Positioning is creating an image for your business or its products and is achieved by differentiating your good or service from your competition's offering. Positioning and images are created in people's minds through comparing your products or services with those of competing companies. The more unique people view your product to be when compared with others, the stronger your position will be in the market. You accomplish positioning through your marketing efforts. (See Chapter 10.)

How can you analyze the competition? The process of gathering competitive intelligence does not have to be prohibitively expensive. A little effort and creativity combined with keeping your eyes open can yield a lot of information. Here are common ways that can help small business owners gather information for compiling their competitive analyses:

- Read articles in trade publications. A proliferation of specialized publications in every industry makes your gathering easier. For example, *Progressive Grocer* if you are selling food products or *Lodging Hospitality* if you are interested in travel accommodations.

- Listen to what your customers and salespeople say about competitors. These groups make the most frequent comparisons of you and the competition.

- Keep a file on key competitors. Information is useless unless you can access it easily. Include published information, notes of conversations, or competitors' sales, product, or service brochures. These readily available sources of information can help you determine how competitors position themselves.

- Establish a regular time, perhaps a monthly meeting, to meet with key employees to evaluate the information in these competitive information files.

- Attend industry trade shows, exhibits, and conferences. A lot can be learned from competitors' booths and through the networking (or socializing) that goes on at such events.

- Buy competitors' products and take them apart to determine their quality and other advantages. Consider incorporating the best elements of competing products into your products. This process is called *reverse engineering* and is part of a process of establishing comparison standards called *benchmarking*.

- Consult published credit reports on your competitors. Companies like Dun & Bradstreet (D & B) make standard credit reports available. See what D & B says about the competition.[22]

Global Small Business

Everyone agrees that the Asian market is positively teeming with business opportunities. One person who jumped in early was Michael Dunne. He started his company Automotive Resources Asia Ltd. (ARA) in Bangkok, Thailand in the summer of 1990. Today his company is absolutely thriving! Dunne had the foresight and admittedly good luck to start his business when Detroit's car companies were just starting to look seriously at the potential of the Asian market. What does ARA do? It provides strategic research for other automotive and automotive-related companies wanting to do business in Asia. And obviously, these companies have been willing to pay for the strategic knowledge and experience that Dunne's ARA has gained. Not only did Michael Dunne recognize and jump on the opportunities available in this global market, but he's also helping others do the same while making his business a big success! *Source: Edith Hill, "He Came, He Saw, He's Conquering," Business Week/Enterprise, November 20, 1995, pp. ENT 20–ENT 22.*

Strategic Alternatives.   The process of defining strategic alternatives begins by identifying problems based on information gained in earlier steps. The process continues with drafting a list of alternatives; thus, it is a two-step process—identify what is wrong and what can you do about it.

Problem identification is the most difficult part of strategic planning. It takes thorough SWOT and competitive analyses and a lot of analytical thinking to pinpoint problems like a current strategy that no longer suits your environment or a mismatch between your strengths and an opportunity that you have identified. Bracing one of your weaknesses and preparing for an upcoming threat are problems that demand your attention. If completion of your SWOT and competitive analyses identifies no major problems or new strategies needed, don't fix anything. Always look to be proactive, but don't ignore the status quo either.

Few problems can be solved with a single solution or the first one that comes to mind. Therefore, after you have identified a problem, your next step is to generate a list of alternative solutions. Try to come up with as many alternatives as possible. Once you've exhausted the possibilities, evaluate whether they would solve your particular problem or work in your company. However, don't evaluate possibilities as you generate ideas, as this stifles creativity. Once your list of alternative strategies is compiled, you need to anticipate the result of each and consider the impact on your company's resources, environment, and people.

While there is a strong temptation to list alternatives and strategies informally in one's mind, research has shown that getting ideas down on paper creates a wider range of strategies and alternatives.[23] Most strategic theorists stress that creativity and insightful thinking are the bases for strategic change.[24]

Goal Setting and Strategies.   Your mission statement sets the broadest direction for your business. SWOT and competitive analyses help you refine and/or change direction. The goals that you set must stem from your mission statement. Goals are needed before you can build a set of strategies. As the cliché goes, "If you don't put up a target, you won't hit anything." Goals need to be:

- *Written in terms of outcomes rather than actions.* A good goal states where you want to be, not how you want to get there. For example, a goal should focus on increasing sales rather than your intention to send one of your brochures to every address in town.
- *Measurable.* You must be able to tell if you accomplish a goal or not. To do this, you must be able to measure the outcome you want to accomplish.
- *Challenging yet attainable.* Goals that are too easy to accomplish are not motivating. Goals that are not likely to be accomplished are self-defeating and also decrease motivation.
- *Communicated to everyone in the company.* You will find a team effort is difficult to produce if some of your players don't know the goals.
- *Written with a time frame for achievement.* Performance and motivation increase when people have goals with a time frame as compared with open-ended goals.

Writing usable goals is not easy at first. If you state that your goal is to be successful, is that a good goal? It sounds positive, it sounds nice. But is it measurable? No. How can you tell whether or not you achieve your goal? You can't because there is no defined outcome. There is also no time frame. Do you intend to be successful this year? By the time you are 90? Goals need the characteristics listed previously to be useful.

Although you will have only one mission statement, you will have several business-level goals that apply to your entire organization. Each functional area of your business (for example, marketing, human resources, production, and finance) will have its own set of specific goals that will relate directly to achieving your business-level goals. (See Figure 3-5.) Even if you are the only person performing marketing, human resource management, production, and finance duties, these areas of your small business must still be addressed individually.

- Your *mission statement* describes who you are, what your business is, and why it exists.
- A *business-level goal* describes what you want your overall business to accomplish in order to achieve your company mission.
- A *function-level goal* describes the performance desired of specific departments (or functional areas, such as marketing, production, and so on) in order to achieve your business-level goals.
- A *strategy* is a plan of action that details how you will attain your function-level goals.

In the final stage of goal setting, specific strategies are developed to accomplish your goals. For example, a marketing *strategy* would be to hire Jerry Seinfeld to be spokesperson for your new stand-up comedy computer program. This strategy should help you attain your *function-level marketing goal* of capturing 20 percent market share of the total comedy software market. Your marketing goal should help you attain your *business-level goal* of increasing third-quarter profits

FIGURE 3-5
3-D-5 Levels of Goals
The goals you set for each functional area of your small business should help you achieve the overall goals of your business, which, in turn, focus on your mission statement.

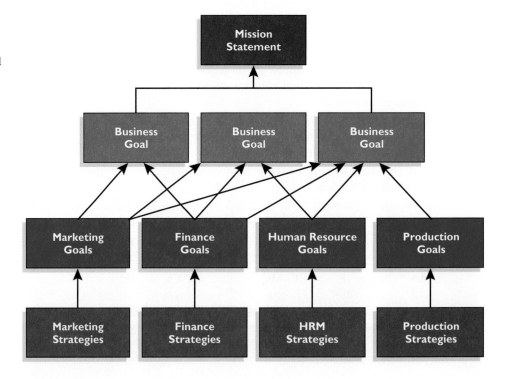

by 8 percent, which in turn ensures that you accomplish your company *mission* of satisfying the entertainment needs of lonely computer operators, and thereby earning a profit.

Function-level goals and strategies must coordinate with one another and with business-level goals for the business to run smoothly. For example, the marketing department may develop a strategy of advertising on the Internet that will bring in orders from all over the globe. This is great as long as the production department can increase capacity, the human resource department can hire and train enough new employees, and all other areas of the business are prepared. Each functional area must see itself as an integral part of the entire business and act accordingly.

Control Systems.   Planning for the future is an inexact science. Very rarely do the actual outcomes of your plans match exactly what you anticipated. When things don't turn out as you planned, you must ask "Why was there a deviation?" Having a control process built into the planning process will help answer this question.

Your strategic plan, including all of its separate parts, sets a standard of comparison for your business's actual performance. The purpose of control systems is to provide you with information to start the planning process all over again. After checking your controls, you either readjust the standards of your plan or create new goals for your plan, and off you go for another planning period. This is why goals must be: written in terms of outcomes rather than actions; measurable, challenging, yet attainable; communicated; and written with a time frame for achievement. You need to collect accurate data about what you have done so you can compare this information with your planned standards. Control systems do not need to be expensive and elaborate. They should be simple enough to become a natural part of your management process.

Strategic Planning in Action

Strategic plans are different than business plans. (See Chapter 4.) Business plans and strategic plans support each other and overlap to a degree but seek to accomplish different purposes. Business plans are written primarily to test the feasibility of a business idea, acquire financing, and coordinate the startup phase. Strategic plans are needed both before the business is started and continuously while it is in operation to match the direction of the business with changes that occur within its environments.

Strategic planning addresses strategic growth—where you are going. Business planning addresses operational growth—how you will get there. Strategic planning looks outward from the business at the long-term prospects for your products, your markets, your competition, and so on. Business planning or organizational growth focuses on the internal concerns of your business such as capital, personnel, and marketing. Eventually, the two plans converge as your long-term strategic goals will be strongly influenced by operational decisions made when the business was started.[25] Strategic planning requires you to broaden your thinking and forces you to look at general issues over the next three to five years—countering the realities of the competitive world with concrete plans instead of wishful thinking. Most sections will not be extremely detailed but will provide outlines for direction. Business planning, on the other hand, needs to be as detailed as possible.

Strategic planning requires you to broaden your thinking and forces you to look at the general issues over the next 3 to 5 years—countering the realities of the competitive world with concrete plans instead of wishful thinking.

Planning is difficult and many small business owners would like to ignore it. The reason the planning process is difficult is because it forces you to identify realities that exist in a competitive world rather than rely on emotions, guesses, and assumptions.

What is the best kind of strategic or business plan to write? The ones that you will *use!* A balance must be struck between floundering with no direction and drowning in a detached, strangling planning process based on hard data that really are not hard. You need to remember that the *planning process* is actually more important and valuable than the plan that is created because of the *strategic thinking* required to write it.

When you begin writing the first draft of your plan, don't worry about the fine points of its structure—simply get your ideas on paper. Once written, you should revise your plan to reorder your ideas into a logical and clear format. An informal plan written in a format that you are comfortable with and will use is 100 percent better than a formal plan that fits someone else's definition of "correct" form but sits on a shelf.

Get advice and suggestions from as many sources as practical when you are formulating your plans. Talk to colleagues, bankers, accountants, other executives, and lawyers for their input. If your business is already in operation, including employees in decisions is a great way to show them their opinions count. They can all provide valuable insight to your plans.

Establishing a Business Culture

Organizational culture can be defined as a set of values, beliefs, goals, norms, and rituals that members of the organization share. You can say that culture is "the way we do things around here." Culture is created by a manager's belief about how to manage himself or herself, the employees, and how to conduct business.[26]

Small Business IN THE Service Industry

She was named the 1994 Small Business Person of the Year by the U.S. Small Business Administration after winning the state award for Utah. Lorraine Miller owns and operates a plant store in Salt Lake City called Cactus and Tropicals. Her company sells unusual and unique plants, both at the wholesale and retail levels. In addition, some of her 35 employees tend about 2 million plants under commercial maintenance contracts. Not wanting to rest on her laurels, so to speak, Miller devised a goal to reenergize herself and her company. She decided that she wanted Cactus and Tropicals to go from $1 million in sales per year to $5 million. And she also wanted to create a business culture in which employees would continue to be motivated and committed to the customer. To accomplish these goals, Miller started off by drafting a six-point mission statement that reflected ambitions for the company *and* for her employees. Miller says, "I wanted to create a space where my employees can grow, too. . . ." So, even small business owners who have received visible and very public tributes to their success must still deal with putting their plans into action. *Source: Michael Barrier, "Profits in Bloom,"* Nation's Business *(October 1995), p. 14.*

If you expect ethical behavior, you must act ethically yourself and reward ethical behavior. If you do not express and model desired behavior and goals, a culture will evolve on its own. If ethical behaviors are not valued by your business, you may be rewarding unethical behavior.

Gaps between your ethical beliefs and those of your employees can develop. For example, you may believe that the culture of your business encourages respect for each other, but your reward system may communicate to your employees that you want them to compete against one another. Because of this belief, they may intentionally or unintentionally sabotage each others' work to win the reward.[27] Rewards and punishments need to be consistent with your business's true culture. A basic premise of management is "the things that get rewarded are the things that get done."

Summary

◼ Recognize the relationship between social responsibility, ethics, and strategic planning.

The social responsibility and ethics of your business are the commitments you make to doing what is right. Strategic planning is the process of deciding where you want your business to go and how it will get there. All three concepts work together to form the foundation upon which your entire business rests.

◼ Identify the levels of social responsibility.

You have an economic responsibility to make your business profitable. Without profit, your business could not contribute anything else. Your legal obligation to obey the law shows the minimum behavior expected to be part of society. Your ethical responsibility covers your obligation to do what is right, without intentionally harming others. Philanthropic goodwill is contributing to others without expecting anything in return.

◼ Discuss how to establish a code of ethics for your business and the reasons for such a code.

A code of ethics is a way for you to communicate your ethical expectations to everyone involved in your business. The code should represent your ethical ideals, be concise enough to be remembered, be written clearly, and apply to everyone in the organization.

◼ Recognize the differences between strategic planning and business planning.

Strategic planning concentrates more on internal and external factors which concern your business and where the business is going. Strategic plans view long-term issues that will affect your business for the next three to five years. Business plans address the operations of your business—how your business will accomplish its strategies. Business plans are generally written to test the feasibility of a business idea, to acquire financing, and to get the business organized.

◼ List the steps in the strategic planning process.

The strategic planning process includes defining your mission statement, conducting an environmental analysis (internal and external, or SWOT analysis), analyzing the competition, identifying strategic alternatives, setting goals, and establishing systems to measure effectiveness.

Questions for Review and Discussion

1. Write a brief summary of the connection between strategic planning, ethics and corporate responsibility in a small business setting.

2. Discuss the four groups of laws which generally regulate business activity in this country and give some historical background on the major laws that affect all entrepreneurs today.

3. Define the purpose of a code of ethics and write a brief code that would be suitable for a small business.

4. Although a certain practice may be widely accepted in the business community and be perfectly legal, does that necessarily mean it is *always* moral? Qualify your answer with examples.

5. Write a mission statement for a small business which not only functions as a strategic planning guide, but also incorporates the company's philosophy of social responsibility and ethical standards.

6. Explain how cultural differences between countries can have either a positive or negative effect on an entrepreneur who is pursuing a contract either outside the United States or with persons of different ethnic backgrounds in the United States.

7. Why is environmental analysis more crucial to the small business owner than to larger corporations?

8. You are an entrepreneur and wish to perform a "self-evaluation" of your business environment. How would you go about this task? Be specific about what you hope to discover through the evaluation of your employees, product, management, and so on.

9. What is the value of competitive analysis to the small business owner? What sorts of things should you know about your competition and what analytical methods can you use to find out this information?

10. What does strategic planning mean to the small business owner? How does the size of the organization affect the strategic planning process and how much input should be sought from outside sources while outlining the strategic plan?

11. Goal-setting is a major part of the entrepreneur's business plan. Outline specific methods for setting goals that are both realistic, fit into the overall mission of the company, and can be related to the strategic planning process that is in place at the organization.

12. Discuss the concept of organizational culture as it relates to the small business environment. What is the role of the manager/owner in the organizational culture?

Critical Incident

Some small businesses, by the very nature of what they produce or market, find it difficult to clarify how they're going to fulfill the four levels of social responsibility (economic, legal, ethical, and philanthropic). However, by using strategic planning, even companies in somewhat controversial and questionable industries can define how they're going to be socially responsible. Take, for instance, Grand Casinos of Minneapolis. As more and more states have legalized gambling in selected locations, Lyle Berman, CEO of Grand Casinos, has been there to develop and manage the casinos. His company has been so successful that it ranked first on *Fortune's* list of America's 100 fastest-growing companies. Yet Grand Casino's business—gambling—still tends to arouse definite controversy. Obviously, Berman could use strategic planning to help identify areas in which his company could fulfill its social responsibilities.

Let's take a look at another small business that's in an industry that often is publicly criticized for its products. Boisset USA is a producer and marketer of high-quality, affordable wines. Yet Jean Charles Boisset, president of Boisset USA, has committed his company to supporting charitable causes—one in particular the company supports is Oklahoma-based Feed the Children. Since September 1994, 10 percent of gross profit on every bottle of two of the company's products, Christophe Vineyards and the French-imported J.C. Boisset, goes to Feed the Children. By September 1995, that amounted to funding for 3 million meals for needy children. Their goal is to fund 5 million meals by the end of 1998, and the company appears to be on track to meet that particular goal.

Here we have two companies, both in industries that often arouse public criticism and controversy. How can they connect social responsibility, ethics, and strategic planning? *Sources: Richard S. Teitelbaum, "America's 100 Fastest-Growing Companies," Fortune, April 17, 1995, pp. 75–84; and Lynn Keillor, "Fighting Hunger with Wine," Business Ethics (July/August 1995), p. 25.*

Questions

1. You're in charge of strategic planning for Grand Casinos. The company has plans to open and manage a casino in rural Iowa. You and your strategic planning team have been asked by community residents to attend a town meeting to discuss the casino. You'll need to prepare a description of how your company is fulfilling its social responsibility. (Use Figure 3-1 as a guide.) Other members of the class will act as community residents. Prepare your questions and concerns for confronting the Grand Casinos team.

2. You've been hired by Boisset USA to prepare a strategic plan. Draft an outline of a strategic plan for the company that takes into consideration all the components of strategic plans, including the social responsibility and ethics aspects.

Take it to the Net

We invite you to visit the Hatten page on the Prentice Hall Web site at: http://www.prenhall.com/~hattensb for this chapter's World Wide Web exercise.

Chapter Focus

After reading this chapter, you should be able to:

- Explain the importance of the business plan.
- Describe the components of a business plan.
- Identify what *not* to do when writing a business plan.
- Recognize where to get help in writing a business plan.

4 The Business Plan

IT'S GOT TO BE A DREAM OF business students everywhere—to write a business plan for a class project assignment that not only nabs an A but will one day give rise to a business bringing fame and fortune. Ken Hawk, a 1993 graduate of Stanford Business School, realized that dream by starting a successful business that earned him an article in *Inc.* magazine. After receiving an A+ on his business plan as a class project, Hawk later used the plan to get partial financial backing from an investor in helping him get his company, Power Express, off the ground. By 1995, just two years after starting up, Power Express hit revenues of $2.1 million, and sales revenues for 1997 are projected at $7.5 million. What did Hawk's business plan for Power Express look like and what role did it play in the company's successful start?

First, Hawk's plan very clearly and specifically described his concept of what Power Express was to become: the top retail source of replacement rechargeable batteries for users of notebook computers, cellular phones, and video cameras. Marketing and distribution were to be an important differentiating factor for the company, the plan stated. Power Express would make it easy for customers to shop by using a mail-order catalog, online services, the Internet, and a 24-hour service hotline. Of course, Hawk's business plan included the requisite financial projections and marketing research. But, in addition, Hawk did an extremely thorough study of the rechargeable battery industry and potential competition to see how these factors might impact his company.

By using his business plan to clarify how Power Express would diverge from the traditional distribution channels of getting batteries from manufacturers to the end users, Hawk was able to identify Power Express's competitive advantage—a database that allows the company to quickly locate any hard to find batteries most replacement battery shoppers needed. Also, since Power Express would be the direct link between the battery manufacturers and the customer, it would enjoy lower costs by eliminating warehousing and inventory expenses. But the plan also pinpointed two of Power Express's early hurdles—finding customers willing to use the 800 line and good telephone sales representatives to service it. As Hawk states, "Helping callers figure out which battery they need, out of thousands available, is a tough job."

In this chapter, we'll be looking at why it's so important to have a business plan and the specifics of developing an effective business plan. We hope you'll be motivated to follow in Ken Hawk's footsteps and develop your own winning business plan! *Source: Alessandra Bianchi, "The Matchmaker," Inc. (September 1995), pp. 58–65.*

Every Business Needs a Plan

Successful small business owners know where they want to go and find a way to get there. To see their dreams of owning a business become a reality, they know they must plan each step along the way. Starting a business is like going on vacation—you do not reach your destination by accident. Whether you want to hike through Denali National Park in Alaska, or sell frozen yogurt to tourists in Miami, you need a map and adequate provisions.

The Plan

business plan A document describing a business that is used to test the feasibility of a business idea, to raise capital, and to serve as a roadmap for future operations.

A **business plan** is a written document that demonstrates persuasively that enough products or services can be sold at a profit to become a viable business. Planning is an essential ingredient for any successful business. While we all create mental plans, those thoughts need to be committed to writing before starting a business.[1] Planning can help find omissions and flaws in our ideas by allowing other people to critically review and analyze our plans.

A business plan gives the reader the *what, when, where, why,* and *how* your business will accomplish its objectives and tells *who* will be involved in running it. When planning, you need to define the goals of your business, determine the actions that need to be taken to accomplish them, gather and commit the resources needed, and aim for well-defined targets. A business plan can be the difference between running a business proactively and reactively. When NASA launched Apollo 7, the first manned spacecraft to land on the moon, they didn't aim at the moon. They pointed the rocket to the point in space where the moon would be, considering the time needed to get there.[2]

The Purpose

The three primary reasons for writing business plans are to aid you in determining the feasibility of your business idea, to attract capital for starting up, and to provide direction for your business after it is in operation.

Attracting Capital. Almost all startups must secure capital from bankers or investors. One of the first questions a banker or investor will ask when approached about participating in a business is "Where is your plan?" You need to appreciate the bankers' position. They have to be accountable to depositors for the money entrusted to their care. Bankers, in general, are financially conservative, so before they risk their capital, they want assurance that you are knowledgeable and realistic in your projections. Therefore, a complete business plan is needed before you can raise any significant capital. Your business plan will show that you know what you are doing and have thought through the problems and opportunities.[3]

Small Business IN THE Service Industry

Sunny Drewel of St. Louis, Missouri used her well-researched and well-written business plan to help line up financing for her new business, Linen & Lace. Linen & Lace is a mail-order catalog business in which Drewel sells unique imported and domestic linen and lace products. Twice a year, a full-color catalog containing 30 pages (or even more!) of pictures of the company's elegant products is sent to a mailing list that now numbers around 375,000 names. Currently, Linen & Lace's annual sales are approaching $1.5 million. But Drewel's business is thriving because she thoroughly researched her market, customers, and product, and formulated a well-written business plan. *Source: Claire Buhl, "Captivated By Lace," Nation's Business (October 1995), p. 16.*

Providing Direction. Business plans should provide a roadmap for future operation. You have heard the clichés, "can't see the forest for the trees" and "it is difficult to remember your initial objective was to drain the swamp when you are up to your hips in alligators." These illustrations apply to starting a small business in that so much of your time can be filled with immediate problems (management by spot-fire—paying attention to latest dilemma to flare up) that you have trouble concentrating on the overall needs of the business. By having a roadmap to refer to, you are more likely to stay on course.

Proving Feasibility. Writing a business plan is one of the best ways to prevent costly oversight. Committing your ideas to paper forces you to look critically at your means, goals, and expectations. Many people thinking of starting a small business get caught up in the excitement and emotions of the process. It is a truly exciting time! Unfortunately, business decisions based purely on emotion are often not the best long-term choice.

Wanting to have a business does not mean that a market exists to support your desire. You may love boats and want to build a business around them, but if you live 100 miles from the nearest body of water and are unwilling to move, it is unlikely that you can create a viable boat business. Successful entrepreneur Norm Brodsky states, "The initial goal of every business is to survive long enough to see whether or not the business is viable—no matter what type of business, or how much capital you have. You never know for sure if a business is viable until you do it in the real world."[4] Writing your plan can help remove strong personal emotions from the decision-making process. You need to be passionate about the business you are in, but emotion must be balanced and tempered with logic and rationality.

Global Small Business

Two individuals who understood the need to be logical and rational in their business are Jordan Levy and Ronald Schreiber. Their first business was Software Distribution Services, which they built into the premier distributor of personal computer software. They eventually sold that company for $10 million in 1986. They started Upgrade Corporation of America (UCA), based in Buffalo, New York, in 1990. UCA contracts with software makers to handle software upgrades and customer service complaints. As UCA grew, Levy and Schreiber knew it was critically important to have competent employees. So, as new employees were hired, they looked for people who would fit the business several years down the road, rather than hiring just for their present needs—even if it meant paying higher salaries. Both Levy and Schreiber knew they wanted UCA to continue growing and thus approached planning for growth logically and rationally. The company's growth efforts were focused on the increasing global demand for computers and software. Levy and Schreiber got their foot in the door of the global market by joining together as partners with Alexander & Lord, a subsidiary of Softbank, the Japanese high-tech giant. Their new company, UCA&L, hopes to generate $300 million in annual sales. *Source: Duncan Maxwell Anderson, "Profitable Headaches," Success (November 1995), p. 14.*

The Practice: Guidelines for Writing a Business Plan

No rigid formula for writing business plans exists that would fit every new business. Plans are unique to each business situation. Still, general guidelines should be followed.

Consider Your Audience. You need to show the benefit of your business to your reader. Investors want their money to go into market-driven businesses, which satisfy wants and needs of customers, rather than technology-driven ones, which focus more on the product or service being made than what people want.[5]

Keep it Brief. Your business plan should be long enough to cover all major issues facing the business, yet not look like a copy of *War and Peace.* Your final plan should be complete yet concise. Including financial projections and appendices, your plan should be less than 40 pages long. Your first draft will probably be longer, but you can sharpen your ideas by editing to 40 pages or less.

Point of View. Try to write your business plan in the third person (do not use "I" or "we"). This helps maintain objectivity by removing your personal emotions from the writing process.

Create a Professional Image. The overall appearance should be professional and attractive but not extravagant. Having your document laser printed on white paper, with colored stock cover, dividers, and spiral binding is fine. Think of the message your business plan will send to bankers and investors: having it bound in leather with gold leaf trimmed pages is not a good sign. Does it appear that you really need the money or will spend it wisely? Conversely, what might they think of a business plan scratched out on a Big Chief tablet with a crayon? Would it look like you were really serious about your business?

As you write the first draft of your plan, have several people who are not involved in your business read your work to get their initial reactions. Do they quickly grasp the essence of your proposal? Are they excited about your idea? Do they exclaim, "Wow"? Getting feedback while you are still writing the plan can help you refine your work and get the reader to say "Wow!"

Free or inexpensive business planning assistance is available to entrepreneurs from such sources as Small Business Development Centers.

Where to Get Help. Who should write the business plan for your proposed venture? You should! The person who is best qualified and who receives the most benefit from the planning process is the person who is going to implement the plan. It is *your* business and it needs to be *your* plan. With that stated, can you get aid in writing the plan? Of course, you can and should get help if you need it. You can get assistance in writing your business plan from:

- One of the many guides written on business plans, such as Andy Bangs's *Business Planning Guide,* Upstart Publishing
- Small Business Administration pamphlets
- Your area Small Business Development Center
- Your local Chamber of Commerce
- A college or university near you

Detailed information on these and other sources of information to help the small business owner is included in Appendix A.

Computer software is available to perform many functions of our daily lives. We can balance our checkbooks or design our dream house. While software packages can make our lives easier, you need to be careful in not using them to generate a "cookie-cutter" business plan. Filling in a few blanks on a master document does not produce a workable business plan any more than a paint-by-number kit produces art. Because your business will be different from others, you need to emphasize *your* competitive advantage and show *your* objectives.

This is not to imply that you should not use word processing, spreadsheets, or graphics packages to produce your plan. You should because they can be extremely helpful. This caveat is against "canned" business plans. Writing a business plan is as much an art as it is a science.

Manager's Notebook

Fast Track to Venture Capital

Daniel Lubin is a financier with D. H. Blair & Co., a New York investment banking firm that provides funding for new businesses. Each year D. H. Blair & Co. receives 3,000 business plans and Lubin reads most of them. What is the first thing he looks for in a plan? A lie or bad information—a reason to throw it out. The sheer number of plans requires Lubin to spend about as much time with each plan as you hope your next visit to the dentist lasts.

When asked for an example of a plan that sent him scrambling for the company checkbook, Lubin holds up Pierce Lowrey Jr.'s plan for Imtech, a startup that provides mailroom, work processing, printing, and other information-output services for large corporations. Lowrey's plan eventually won him $4.5 million in an initial public offering backed by Blair. The high points of his plan are summarized:

- *Executive summary.* In very few words, Lowrey hit three points that made the venture capitalists (VCs) sit up and take notice immediately. First, Lowrey showed that the company had a critical proprietary edge that no other company held. Second, his financial goals were attractive—break even in the first 18 months with a 20 percent return on investment. Finally, Lowrey displayed his proven track record. Management experience is the most important factor to most VCs. Lowrey had started ten other successful businesses within 15 years, the last of which was sold to NCR Corp.

- *Analysis of the competition.* Even though the industry was young, Lowrey identified and discussed three competitors. His thorough, realistic investigation of the market impressed Blair that Lowrey, not his competitors, had the edge.

- *Information about management.* The longest section of Lowrey's plan—five pages. Lowrey showed that his skills as CEO would complement the rest of the management team. Even though not all of Imtech's key slots were filled, Lowrey included a detailed job description for each position.

- *Financial projections.* Venture capitalists are suspicious of projections that appear "juiced up" or not grounded in reality. A red flag is an income statement that shows steady, even growth on every line—an indicator that a software program, not an in-depth analysis, was driving the numbers. Lowrey's financials contained appropriate footnotes and the assumptions that the numbers rested upon.

Writing plans for one year into the future is difficult—planning five years out is almost impossible. While venture capitalists want plans to be as realistic as possible, few hold entrepreneurs accountable to their initial plan. Lowrey's plan, however, has shown uncanny accuracy. His projected third year sales were $27 million—actual sales came in at $25 million. A good plan.

Source: Adapted from Ellyn Spragins, "Venture Capital Express," pp. 159–160. Adapted with permission, Inc. *magazine. November 1990. © 1990, Goldhirsh Group, Inc., 38 Commercial Wharf, Boston, MA 02110.*

Good, Bad, and Ugly Business Plans

In their jobs, Russ Marquart, a loan officer at a bank, and Rayanna Anderson, a small business consultant, are constantly examining business plans. A discussion with them about good and poor business plans reveals that they've seen the gamut from excellent to just plain awful! Marquart and Anderson shared some information about what they've seen in business plans over the years. Let's look at selected pages from two specific examples of business plans—one well written and one that needs a lot of revision. (Needless to say, the poorly written business plan has been altered to protect the identity of the writer.)

Company A. King's Medical Company of Hudson, Ohio, was started by Albert Van Kirk in 1981. Today Van Kirk's business, with 32 employees, leases costly medical equipment to physicians'

groups. As the company grew, Van Kirk and Bill Patton, the company's planning "guru," recognized the need to develop a comprehensive plan for the company that would provide the basis for the day-to-day operational plans. Selected pages from that plan follow in Figure 4-1a.

Company B. Jay's Quarterback Club was the idea for a sports bar and restaurant in Norcross, Georgia. When Jay M. went looking for financing of his idea, however, he found that potential investors and lenders were reluctant to loan him the startup capital. A close look at his business plan reveals mistakes that might explain their reluctance. Selected pages from that plan follow in Figure 4-1b.

Sources: Leslie Brokaw, "The Secrets of Great Planning," Inc. (October 1992), pp. 151–157; and interviews with Rayanna Anderson, Small Business Development Center, Southwest Missouri State University, Springfield, Missouri, and Russ Marquart, Assistant Vice President, Empire Bank, Springfield, Missouri.

Business Plan Contents

A business plan should be tailored to fit your particular business. Write the plan yourself even if you seek assistance from lawyers, accountants, or consultants. In 40 pages or less, the plan should present your strengths clearly and in a logical order.

While a plan's contents vary from business to business, its structure is fairly standardized. Your plan should contain as many of the following sections as appropriate for your type of venture.[6]

Cover Page

The cover page should include the name of the business, its address and phone number, and the date the plan was issued. If this information is overlooked, you have a problem if a potential investor tries to reach you to ask additional questions (or send a check).

KNOW YOUR BUSINESS — AND WRITE YOUR KNOWLEDGE DOWN
THIS SHEET SUMMARIZES THE PROCESS BY WHICH KING'S
MEDICAL CREATES ITS OVERALL STRATEGIC PLAN, FROM
WHICH A NUMBER OF DEPARTMENT- AND EMPLOYEE-SPECIFIC
PLANS FOLLOW. MUCH OF THE PROCESS HINGES ON AN
ASSESSMENT OF THE COMPANY, ITS PLACE IN THE MARKET AND
ITS GOALS. THE QUESTIONS ARE FUNDAMENTAL: WHAT BUSINESS
ARE YOU IN? WHAT'S UNIQUE ABOUT YOUR COMPANY? HOW WILL
YOU BE DIFFERENT IN FOUR YEARS?

Strategic Planning:
Overview

PROCESS

Step 1
Identify the major elements of the business environment in which your organization has operated over the previous two to three years;

Step 2
Describe the mission of the organization in terms of its nature and function for the next two to three years;

Step 3
Explain the critical internal and external forces that will impact the mission of the organization;

Step 4
Identify the basic driving force that will serve as the basis for directing the organization in the future;

Step 5
Develop a set of long-term objectives that will identify what the organization will become in the future; and,

Step 6
Outline a general plan of action which defines the logistical, financial, and personnel factors to integrate the long-term objectives into the total organization.

FIGURE 4-1a
A professional-looking report, with sound financial projections, is essential to prospective business owners. Of the hundreds of loan proposals that an investor or banker must sort through each year, only a fraction will be funded.
Source: Leslie Brokaw, "The Secrets of Great Planning," Inc. (October 1992), pp. 151–157; Mary Coulter, interview with Rayanna Anderson, Small Business Development Center, Southwest Missouri State University, Missouri, October 1995; Mary Coulter, interview with Russ Marquart, Assistant Vice President, Empire Bank, Springfield, Missouri, October 1995.

Table of Contents

You want the business plan to be as easy to read as possible. An orderly table of contents will allow the reader to turn directly to the sections desired.

Executive Summary

executive summary A condensed abstract of a business plan used to spark the reader's interest in the business and to highlight crucial information.

The **executive summary** gives a one- to two-page overview of your entire plan. This is the most important section of the plan because readers do not want to wade through 35 to 40 pages to get the essential facts. If you do not capture the reader's attention here, she is certainly not likely to read the rest of the plan.

(text continues on p. 103)

Long-Term Objective: 2.0 King's Medical Company will have a marketing strategy which can be implemented in a range of settings by the fourth quarter of 1988.

Measurable Outcome	Primary Responsibility	Needed Resources	Start	Complete	Review Action & Date
2.1 hire staff member to administer the marketing function in KMC related to fee-for-service sites	A. VanKirk	$28,000.00	1/88	3/88	Oral Report to Directors by 4/22/88
2.2 train new hire for marketing function related to fee-for-service	A. VanKirk C. Gray	40 hrs.	4/88	6/88	Training Log on file by 6/30/88
2.3 make two site visits to current hospitals using fee-for-service	C. Gray New Hire	24 hrs.	4/88	6/88	Call Reports by 5/30/88
2.4 prepare preliminary marketing strategy plan for review by A. VanKirk	New Hire A. VanKirk	120 hrs.	4/88	9/88	Draft Document by 8/15/88
2.5 finalize marketing strategy plan with action steps and time table	New Hire	40 hrs.	10/88	12/88	Market Strategy Plan by 12/15/88

MAKE PROJECT GOALS – AND DEADLINES – CLEAR
THIS WAS THE ACTION PLAN FOR KING'S MEDICAL'S LONG-TERM OBJECTIVE NUMBER TWO, WHICH WAS TO BOOST MARKETING CAPABILITY. CRITICAL TO THE EFFECTIVENESS OF THE ACTION PLANS IS HOW THEY CLEARLY ESTABLISH WHAT THE AIM IS, WHO'S TO BE HELD ACCOUNTABLE, WHAT THE STEPS WILL COST, AND HOW TO KNOW WHEN THEY'RE COMPLETED.

KEEP TRACK OF THE BIG PICTURE
THE PORTION OF THE MASTER PLAN SHOWN HERE TRACKS COMPANY ACTIVITY THROUGH A SEVEN-MONTH WINDOW OF TIME. THE DASHED LINES INDICATE THAT DISCUSSION, PREPARATION, OR FOLLOW-UP CONNECTED WITH A SPECIFIC TASK IS UNDER WAY. THE SOLID BARS INDICATE THAT THE TASK IS ACTUALLY BEING EXECUTED.

King's Medical Company
RSMA 1992 – MASTER PLAN

PLAN COMPONENTS	JUL	AUG	SEP	OCT	NOV	DEC	JAN
1.0 Over-All Plan							
Objectives With Measurable Outcomes and Rationales							
2.0 Marketing Plan							
Materials and Strategies (Before, During, After)							
3.0 Staffing Plan							
Who and When							
4.0 Travel/Arrangements Plan							
How and Where							
5.0 Training/Orientation Plan							
Expectations and Skills							
6.0 Follow-Up Plan							
Prospect, Qualify, and Close							
7.0 Budget and Budget Narrative							
Costs and Written Rationale/Explanation							
8.0 Building/Production Plan							
Pricing, Production Schedule, and Placement							
9.0 Evaluation Plan							
Feedback and Accomplishment of Objectives							

7/10/92

Figure continues on p. 102

King's Medical Company

1992 STAFFING PLAN

Three targets in the Company's strategic plan provide specific direction for operational decisions related to staffing. First, the plan calls for the increase of new MRI fee-for-service accounts. Second, we are committed to providing our value-added services to new and existing MRI accounts. Third, we will develop new business opportunities to complement our core business. The success of the Company's personnel in achieving all three targets requires the addition of new personnel.

The Board of Directors ordered a hiring freeze during the first half of 1992. Although hiring was frozen, the Company continued its success in gaining new business. The following pages outline the staff needs, the financial requirements for each position, and the preliminary time frame for hiring the identified positions. Fourteen new hires have been identified by division heads.

The financial implications of the new positions are outlined below.

Total Cash Requirements With Maximum Bonuses	$222,177
Total Cash Requirements With Minimum Bonuses	$208,157
Total Cash Requirements Without Bonuses	$185,194
Additional Fixed Cost For New Personnel Per Month (Average For Six Months)	$30,866

INTEGRATE PLANS THROUGHOUT THE COMPANY
SPECIFIC PLANS FOR STAFFING EACH DIVISION (SUCH AS THE ONE BELOW) ARE FORMED WITH AN EYE TOWARD ANTICIPATED NEEDS ARISING FROM THE COMPANY'S GOALS. THE COMPANY-WIDE STAFFING PLAN (ABOVE) ALSO MESHES WITH THE COMPANY'S GOALS, BUT IT INCORPORATES THE PLANS OF EACH DIVISION AS WELL. THE PLANS KNIT THE COMPANY TOGETHER.

King's Medical Company

DIVISION COMPONENTS FOR A STAFFING PLAN

Need #1: Support Staff People - The Division's eight personnel work without the services and benefit of a support staff person. Call reports must be farmed to Betty and Janet. Maintaining the data base on individual accounts must be done by the Marketing Specialists. Editing of reports, direct mail pieces, etc. are done by the person who wrote the original piece. Time must be taken away from the Marketing Specialists' work to have them do the labeling, stuffing, and postage of direct mail such as case studies, announcements, etc. The need is great.

	Position	Resource Requirements	Implementation Schedule
#1	Support Staff Person (Marketing Account Managers) (NEW HIRE)	$10,850: Sal/Ben	June 1, 1992
#2	Support Staff Person (MRI Account Managers) (NEW HIRE)	$4,650: Sal/Ben	October 1, 1992
#3			
#4			
#5			

JAY'S QUARTERBACK ~~CULB~~ CLUB

Proposed Business

My idea is to open a bar/restaurant that have a sports theme. Sports are big business right now and the timing is perfect. I think that people are really interested in sports and will be willing to pay good money for this type of dining experience. People eat out a lot and my business will give them another place to spend their money.

Marketing Research and Marketing Plan

I've done some research in the community and haven't seen any restaurant or bar like Jay's Quarterback Club. Since there's nobody else doing this type of business, I won't have no direct competition. So marketing expenses will be minimal. Perhaps I'll run some newspaper advertisements and put out coupons iif I need to when sales aren't enough to help me pay the expenses.

Operations Plan

As soon as I get word on my financing, I'll start looking for an appropriate location for my business. If I can't find something that fits my needs, I'll just build one. I've been checking into suppliers for food and the other materials I'll need. I feel confident that I can dedvelop good contacts and have reliable sources.

As far as employees goes, with the level of business that I know we can accomplish in the first few months of operations, I will be hiring 4 additional employees: cook, bartender, and 2 waitpersons. This will leave me free to do the scheduling, ordering, and managing.

Sales Projections

I've worked in restaurants in the past and have a lot of experience there so I believe that my bar/restaurant can make lots of money. I believe that my first year's sales will be $500,000 and expenses will be $410,000. That means I'll make $90,000. I intend to have several cost controls but, still it's really hard to tell exactly what my expenses will be, though. In the second year, because we'll be familiar to the customer, I know we can increase sales by 20% for total revenue of $510,000. I think I can hold my expenses constant at $90,000.

Conclusion

Since I've had a lot of experience working in restaurants, I am positive that I can make this venture work. The theme will be unique and there's not anyone else doing this, so there shouldn't be any problem attracting paying customers. If you'd like more information, I'd be happy to share my idea for Jay's Quarterback Club with you in person. Just call me at my home number. Thanks for your consideration.

FIGURE 4-1b

The executive summary should include:

- *Company information.* What product or service you provide, your competitive advantage, when the company was formed, your company objectives, the background of you and your management team.
- *Market opportunity.* The expected size and growth rate of your market, your expected market share, and any relevant industry trends.
- *Financial data.* Include financial forecasts for the first three years of operations, equity investment desired, and long-term loans that will be needed.

A Financial Workout That Builds Market Strength

For Caroline Sanchez Crozier, 1993 winner of the SBA Small Business Person of the Year for Illinois, business plans are more than a useless and painful exercise demanded by bankers. Crozier believes that business plans are important because of "the process of analyzing the effectiveness of your financial and marketing strategies. The plan itself is outmoded by the time it is written."

The owner of Computer Services & Consulting, a $2 million company founded in 1987, Crozier learned the art of writing business plans from a Chicago support group called the Women's Business Development Center (WBDC). Hedy Ratner, the WBDC's director, says "Entre-preneurs should be able to answer highly technical financial questions *and* broader marketing questions."

The WBDC plays devil's advocate with prospective business owners' plans in order to strengthen them and prepare the writers for rigorous examination by lenders and other perils of the real world. When you can answer tough questions like how to lower your breakeven point or how long your competitors can cut prices, Crozier says you are ready to succeed. The WBDC is something like an athletic coach pushing players through hard practice routines so they will be ready when the real game begins.

Source: Adapted from J. A. Fraser, "Plans That Ask, What If?", Inc. (August 1993), p. 35.

This is a lot to condense to two pages, but remember the concise executive summary that Pierce Lowrey, Jr. used in his plan for Imtech. (See Manager's Notebook p. 98.) If you truly understand something, you can explain it simply.

Although the executive summary is the first section of the plan, it should be written last. You are condensing what you have already written into the summary, not expanding the summary to fill the plan. A hint for writing the executive summary is: As you compose all the other sections of the plan, highlight a few key sentences that are important enough to include in your executive summary. To see examples of executive summaries, refer to the two complete plans included in Appendix A. One plan is written for a retail business, the other is for a service operation.

Company and Industry

In this section you should describe the background of your company, your choice of legal business form, and the reasons for the company's establishment. How did your company get to the point at which it is today? Give company history by going into some detail describing what your business does and how it satisfies customer's needs. How did you choose and develop your products or services to be sold? Don't be afraid to describe any setbacks or missteps you have taken along the way in forming your business. They represent reality and leaving them

Computer Applications

Even though "canned" business planning programs cannot produce a business plan that is perfect for every business, they can provide a starting point for a business plan that, with fine tuning, does capture the unique qualities of your company. Their main advantage is that they provide an easy-to-follow model. Their biggest drawback is that their final output typically is not terribly distinctive.

If you decide that you want to start off writing your business plan using one of these software programs, one to consider is called Business Plan Writer by Graphite Software of Rockville, Maryland. This program, which is accompanied by a manual and a booklet called *101 Tips for a Winning Business Plan*, takes you through a description of your company, products, and services. Next it asks you to develop a marketing plan, including a competitive analysis. Finally, in the financial analysis section, you are asked to project sales for the next five years, set up balance sheets, income statements, and profit projections. By providing a general outline rather than a prefabricated format, the Graphite program encourages a measure of creativity in writing the business plan.

Another software program is available from *Nation's Business* magazine called Bizplan Builder. It provides 90 pages of typed and formatted word processing and spreadsheet files, in which the user has only to plug in the requested information. While it is more structured and complete than the Graphite software, it allows for less in the way of individuality.

Sources: Dennis James, "Think Big," Success (October 1995), pp. 55–57; and Nation's Business order form.

out could make your plan and projections look "too good to be true" to lenders or investors.

You should also describe the industry you operate within. One helpful way to draw the line between what and who to include in your industry is to consider possible substitutes that your customers have for your product. If you own a business that sells ice cream, do your customers view frozen yogurt or custard as a possible substitute for your ice cream? If so, you should consider businesses that sell these substitutes as part of your industry. What competitive reactions and industrywide trends can you identify? Who are the major players in your industry? Have any businesses recently entered or exited? Why did they leave?

Products or Services

Once you have given the background of your company, you can go into detail describing your product or service. How is your product or service different than those currently on the market? Are there any other uses for your product that could increase current sales? Include drawings or photos if appropriate. Describe any patents or trademarks that you hold, since these give you a proprietary position that can be defended. Describe your competitive advantage. What sets your product or service apart as better than the competition?

What is your product's potential for growth? How do you intend to manage your product or service through the product life cycle? Can you expand the product line or develop related products? This gives you a chance to discuss potential product lines as well as current ones.

Entering the Internet

How can you use the Internet or World Wide Web to help you better define your product or service? As the number of companies with sites on the Web continues to grow, there's a wide amount of information about specific types of products currently available. Depending on your specific area of interest, you might find a group of individuals who share that interest and that you can "talk" to as a member of what's called a *chat group*. The best approach to finding information about specific products or groups is to use one of the Web search tools such as Yahoo, Lycos, or WebCrawler and do a keyword or topic search.

If you access the Internet or the Web through one of the proprietary online services, you can plug into any of their small business forums and get information on your potential product. For instance, on America Online's Small Business Center, entrepreneurs share ideas and experiences using either real-time chat groups or message boards. You can also download business-related software, read various business publications, get stock quotes, and access resources such as the American Institute for Small Businesses and the Small Business Administration. Prodigy offers Prodigy for Business, where you can find business articles and information about American companies, obtain expert business advice and members' experience and advice, and download letters and business forms. The other three "big" online services—CompuServe, GEnie, and Delphi—have similar information resources for the small business owner.

There are three additional specific Web sites that might be helpful as you attempt to describe your product or service. The National Technology Transfer Center home page, the U.S. Patent and Trademark Office home page, and the U.S. Department of Commerce Information Locator Service (CILS). The NTTC connects private-sector businesses with various branches of the federal lab system to help commercialize government-developed technologies. This service is a wonderful source for technological companies looking for new sources of commercial product ideas. At the U.S. Patent and Trademark Office home page, you can download publications, speeches, and press releases. The U.S. Department of Commerce Information Locator Service accesses various Department of Commerce databases for specific information. You might try this Web site if you have a specific question about a product or service. The addresses for these three home pages are shown below.

National Technology Transfer Center (http://iridium.nttc.edu/nttc.html)
U.S. Patent and Trademark Office (http://www.uspto.gov)
Commerce Information Locator Service (http://www.doc.gov/inquery/cils.html)

Sources: "Good Question!," Inc. (October 1995), p. 16; and Jenny C. McCune and Leslie Jay, "The Source," Success (October 1995), pp. 43–48.

Marketing Research and Evaluation

Evidence that a market exists for your business is much more convincing than an unsubstantiated claim or guesswork. Present the facts you have gathered on the size and nature of your markets. An investor will want to know if a large enough market exists and if you can be competitive in that market. State market size in dollars and units. Give your sales forecast by estimating from your marketing research how many units and dollars worth of your product you expect to sell in a given time period. That sales forecast becomes the basis for projecting many of your financial statements. Indicate your primary and secondary sources of data and the methods you used to estimate total market size and your market share.

Markets.   You must identify your target markets and then concentrate your marketing efforts on these key areas. These markets must have some commonly identifiable need that you can satisfy. What do the people who buy your product have in common with each other? There could be a demographic characteristic (for example, 18- to 25-year old females), a psychographic variable (similar lifestyles, usage rate of product, or degree of loyalty), a geographic variable (anyone who lives within a five-mile radius of your business), or other variable used to segment your markets. Describe actual customers who have expressed a desire to buy your product. What trends do you expect to affect your markets?

Market Trends.   Markets and consumer tastes change so you will need to explain how you will assess your customers' needs over time. A danger of segmentation and target marketing is the belief that those segments and markets will stay the same. Identify how you will continue to evaluate consumer needs so you can improve your market lines and aid new-product development.

Competition.   Among three or four primary competitors, identify the price leader, the quality leader, and the service leader. Realistically discuss the strengths and weaknesses of each. Compare your products or services with competitors on the basis of price, product performance, and other attributes.

This section offers a good opportunity to include the SWOT analysis you completed in the strategic planning chapter (Chapter 3). Identify the strengths and weaknesses of your business and the opportunities and threats that exist outside your business.

Market Share.   Since you have identified the size of your market and your competitors, you can estimate the market share you intend to gain. Market share refers to your sales in relation to the total industry sales expressed as a percentage. It can effectively be shown and explained using a pie chart.

Your job in writing the marketing research section of your business plan is to convince the reader that a large enough market exists for your product for you to achieve your projected sales forecasts.

Marketing Plan

Your marketing plan shows how you intend to reach your sales forecast. You should start by explaining your overall marketing strategy by identifying your potential markets and deciding the best ways to reach them. Include your marketing objectives (what you want to achieve) and the strategies you will use to accomplish these objectives.

Pricing.   Your pricing policy is one of the most important decisions you will have to make. The price must be "right" to penetrate the market, to maintain your market position, and especially to make profits. Compare your pricing policies with the competitors you identified earlier. Explain how your gross margin will allow you to make a profit after covering all expenses. Many poeple go into business with the intent of charging lower prices than the competition. If this is your goal, explain how you can do this and still make a profit: through greater efficiency in manufacturing or distributing the product, through lower labor costs, lower overhead, or whatever allows you to undercut the competition's price.

You should discuss the relationship between your price, your market share, and your profits. For example, by charging a higher price than the competition you may reduce your sales volume, but hold a higher gross margin and increase the bottom line.

Promotion.   How will you attract the attention of and communicate with your potential customers? For industrial products you might use trade shows and advertise in trade magazines, direct mail, or promotional brochures. For consumer products describe your advertising and promotional campaigns. You should also give the advertising schedule and costs involved. Examples of advertising or brochures may be included in the appendix of the business plan.

Place.   Describe how you intend to sell and distribute your products. Will you use your own sales force or independent sales representatives or distributors? If you will hire your own sales force, describe how it will be structured, the sales expected per salesperson per year, and the pay structure. Your own sales force will concentrate more on your products by selling them exclusively. If you will use sales representatives, describe how they will be selected, the territories they will cover, and rates they will charge. Independent sales representatives will also be handling other products and lines than just your own, but they are much less expensive for you since they are not your employees. Your place strategy describes the level of coverage (local, regional, or national) you will use initially and as your business grows. It includes the channels of distribution you will use to get and to sell products.

Service Policies.   If you sell a product that may require service, such as cameras, copy machines, or bicycles, describe your service and warranty policies. These policies can be important in the customer's decision-making process. How will you handle customer service problems? Describe the terms and types of warranties offered. Explain whether you will provide service via your own service department, subcontract out the service work, or return products to the factory. Also state whether service is intended to be a profit center or a breakeven operation.

Manufacturing and Operations Plan

The manufacturing and operations plan will stress elements related to your business's production. It will outline your needs in terms of facilities, location, space requirements, capital equipment, labor force, inventory control, and purchasing. Stress the areas most relevant to your type of business. For instance, if you are starting a manufacturing business, outline the production processes and your control systems for inventory, purchasing, and production. The business plan for a service business should focus on your location, overhead, and labor force productivity.

Geographic Location.   Describe your planned location and its advantages and disadvantages in terms of wage rates, unionization, labor pool, proximity to customers and suppliers, types of transportation available, tax rates, utility costs, and zoning. Again, you should stress the features most relevant to your business. Proximity to customers is especially important to a service business, while access to transportation will be of greater concern to a manufacturing business.

Facilities.   What kind of facilities does your business need? Discuss your requirements for floor space (including offices, sales room, manufacturing plant space, and storage areas), parking, loading areas, and special equipment. Will you rent, lease, or purchase these facilities? How long will they remain adequate: One year? Three years? Is expansion possible?

Make or Buy Policy.   In a manufacturing business, you must decide what you will produce and what you will purchase as components to be assembled into the finished product. This is called the make or buy decision. Many factors go into this decision (see Chapter 15). In your business plan, you should justify the advantages of your policy. Describe potential subcontractors and suppliers.

Control Systems.   What is your approach to controlling quality, inventory, and production? How will you measure your progress toward the goals you have set for your business?

Labor Force.   At the location you have selected, is there a sufficient quantity of adequately skilled people in the local labor force to meet your needs? What kinds of training will you need to provide? Can you afford to offer this training and still remain competitive? Training can be one of those hidden costs that can turn a profit into a loss.

Management Team

A good management team is the key to transforming your vision into a successful business. Show how your team is balanced in technical skills (possessing the knowledge specific to your type of business), business skills (the ability to successfully run a business), and experience. As in building any team, the skills and talents of your management team need to complement one another. Include a job description for each management position and specify the key people who will fill these slots. Can you show how their skills complement each other? Have these individuals worked together before? An organizational chart can be included in the appendix of your plan to graphically show how these positions fit together. Résumés for each key manager should also be included in the appendix.

A successful management team unites people with complementary business knowledge, technical skills, and life experience.

State how your key managers will be compensated. Your chances of obtaining financing are very slim unless the managers are willing to accept substantially less than their market value for salary while the business is getting started. Managers must be committed to putting as many proceeds as possible back into the business.

Discuss the management training your key people have had and may still need. Be as specific as possible on the cost, type, and availability of this management or technical traning.

Like your managers, you may need professional assistance at times. Identify other people with whom you will work, including a lawyer, a certified public accountant, an insurance agent, and a banker. Identify contacts you have supporting you in these areas.

Timeline

Outline the interrelationship and timing of the major events planned for your venture. In addition to helping you calculate your business needs and minimize risk, the timeline is also an indicator to investors that you have thoroughly researched potential problems and are aware of deadlines. Keep in mind that people tend to underestimate the time needed to complete projects. Your time schedule should be realistic and attainable.

Critical Risks and Assumptions

All business plans contain implicit assumptions, such as how your business will operate, what economic conditions will be, and how you will react in different situations. Identification and discussion of any potentially major trends, problems, or risks you think you may encounter will show the reader that you are in touch with reality. These risks and assumptions could relate to your industry, markets, company, or personnel.

This section gives you a place to establish alternate plans in case the unexpected happens. If potential investors discover unstated negative factors after the fact, they can quickly question the credibility of you and the business. Too many businesses are started with only a Plan A and no thought to what if X, Y, or Z happens.[7] Possible contingencies you should anticipate are:

- *Unreliable sales forecasts.* What will you do if your market does not develop as quickly as you predicted, or conversely, if your market develops too quickly? Each situation creates problems. Sales that are too low cause serious financial problems. Sales that are too high can cause bottlenecks in production, difficulties in purchasing enough products from vendors or suppliers, trouble hiring and scheduling employees, or dissatisfied customers who must wait longer than they expected for your product or service.
- *Competitors' ability to underprice or to make your product obsolete.*
- *Unfavorable industrywide trends.* Not long ago businesses that produced asbestos made up a thriving industry supplying products for automotive and building construction firms. Then reports linking asbestos with cancer drastically affected the demand for that product and virtually eliminated the industry.
- *Appropriately trained workers not as available as predicted.*
- *Erratic supply of products or raw material.*
- Any one of the 10,000 other things you didn't expect.

Benefits to Community

Your new business will have an impact on many other people beside yourself. Describe the potential benefits to the community that the formation of your business could provide.

- *Economic development:* Number of jobs created (total and skilled), purchase of supplies from local businesses, the multiplier effect (which shows the number of hands that new dollars brought into the community pass through before exiting).
- *Community development:* Providing needed goods or services, improving physical assets or the appearance of the community, contributing to a community's standard of living.
- *Human development:* Providing new technical skills or other training, opportunities for career advancement, developing management or leadership skills, offering attractive wages, other types of individual growth.

Financial Plan

Your financial plan is where you demonstrate that all the information from previous sections like marketing, operations, sales, and strategies can all come together to form a viable, profitable business. Potential investors will closely scrutinize the financial section of your plan to ensure it is feasible before they become involved. Projections should be your best estimates of future operations. Your financial plan should include the following statements (existing businesses will need historical statements and pro forma projections, while startups will only have projections):

- Sources and uses of capital (initial and projected)
- Cash flow projections for three years
- Balance sheets for three years
- Profit and loss statements for three years
- Breakeven analysis

We will discuss how to prepare these documents in later chapters. (See Chapter 11 for breakeven analysis, Chapter 17 for cash flow projections, balance sheets, and profit and loss statements, and Chapter 18 for sources and uses of capital.) With the financial statements, you need to show conclusions and important points such as how much equity and how much debt are included, the highest amount of cash needed, and how long the payback period for loans is expected to be.

Sources and Uses of Funds. This simple form shows where your money is coming from and how you are spending it. (See Figure 4-2.)

Cash Flow. The most important financial statement for a small business is the **cash flow statement** because if you run out of cash you are out of business. A cash flow statement shows you that from your opening cash balance you add all the money that comes into your business for a given time period (week, month, quarter), then you subtract all the money you spend for the same time period. The result is your closing cash balance, which becomes your opening balance for the next time period. (See Figure 4-3.)

You should project a cash flow statement by month for the first year of operation and by quarter for the second and third years. Cash flow shows you what the highest amount of working capital will be. This can be especially critical if your sales are seasonal in nature or cyclical.

sources and uses of funds A financial document used by start-up businesses that shows where capital comes from and what it will be used for.

cash flow statement A financial document which shows the amount of money a business has on hand at the beginning of a time period, receipts coming into the business, and money going out of the business during the same period.

FIGURE 4-2
The Sources and Uses of Funds Worksheet
A sources and uses of funds sheet shows where money comes from and what it is used for.

Sources of Funds:
    Debt:
        Term loans $_____
        Refinancing of old debt   _____
        Lines of credit
            Line 1   _____
            Line 2   _____
        Mortgage   _____
    Equity:
        Investments   _____

                                                                    Total Sources: $_____

Uses of Funds:
    Property $_____
    Inventory   _____
    Equipment (itemize)
                                              _____
                                              _____
                                              _____
    Working capital   _____
    Cash reserve   _____

                                                                    Total Uses: $_____

balance sheet A financial document that shows the assets, liabilities, and owner's equity for a business.

Balance Sheet. The **balance sheet** shows all the assets *owned* by your business and the liabilities, or what is *owed* against those assets. The difference between the two is what the company has *earned*, or the net worth of the business, which is also called capital. From the balance sheet, bankers and investors will calculate some key ratios, such as debt to equity and current ratio (see Chapter 17) to help determine the financial health of your business. You need to prepare balance sheets ending each of the first three years of operation. (See Figure 4-4.)

FIGURE 4-3
Sample Components of a Cash Flow Statement
A cash flow statement shows you how money enters and exits your business.

Opening cash balance
    Add: Cash receipts
           Collection of accounts receivable
           New loans or investment
           Other sources of cash
                Total receipts
    Less: Utilities
           Salaries
           Office supplies
           Accounts payable
           Leased equipment
           Sales expenses
           Loan payments
           General expenses
                Total disbursements
Cash increase (or decrease)
Closing cash balance

FIGURE 4-4
Balance Sheet
A balance sheet shows what you own and who you owe.

For year ended [month] [day], [year]

	YEAR 1	YEAR 2	YEAR 3
Current Assets			
Cash	$_____	$_____	$_____
Accounts receivable	_____	_____	_____
Inventory	_____	_____	_____
Supplies	_____	_____	_____
Prepaid expenses	_____	_____	_____
Fixed Assets			
Real estate	_____	_____	_____
Equipment	_____	_____	_____
Fixtures and			
leasehold improvements	_____	_____	_____
Vehicles	_____	_____	_____
Other Assets			
License	_____	_____	_____
Goodwill	_____	_____	_____
TOTAL ASSETS	$_____	$_____	$_____
Current Liabilities			
Accounts payable	_____	_____	_____
Notes payable	_____	_____	_____
(due within 1 year)			
Accrued expenses	_____	_____	_____
Taxes owed	_____	_____	_____
Long-term Liabilities			
Notes payable	_____	_____	_____
(due after 1 year)			
Bank loans	_____		
TOTAL LIABILITIES	$_____	$_____	$_____
NET WORTH	$_____	$_____	$_____
(ASSETS MINUS LIABILITIES)			

Profit and Loss Statement. Don't expect your **profit and loss statement** to be a finely honed, 100 percent accurate projection of the future. Your objective is to come up with as close an approximation as possible of what your sales revenues and expenses will be. In making your projections, it is helpful to break sales down by product line (or services) and to determine a best-case scenario, a worst-case scenario, and a most likely scenario somewhere between the two extremes.[8]

Start with the left column to show what your sales and expenses would be under the worst of conditions. (See Figure 4-5.) Assume that you have difficulty getting products, that the weather is terrible, that your salespeople are out spending all their time playing golf instead of selling, that the state highway department closes the road that runs in front of your only location for repairs. Imagine that anything bad that can happen, will. Now, in the right column, make projections as if everything goes exactly your way. What would your sales and expenses be if customers with cash in their hands are waiting in line outside your door every morning at opening time, if suppliers rearrange their schedules so you never run out of stock, and if competitors all close their doors for a month of

profit and loss statement A financial document that shows sales revenues, expenses, and net profit or loss.

FIGURE 4-5
Profit and Loss Projection
Projecting the best and the worst that could happen helps you calculate what your profits or losses are likely to be.

	Low	Most likely	High
SALES:			
Product/service line 1	$_____	$_____	$_____
Product/service line 2	_____	_____	_____
Product/service line 3	_____	_____	_____
Product/service line 4	_____	_____	_____
TOTAL SALES REVENUE	_____	_____	_____
Cost of Goods Sold:			
Product/service line 1	_____	_____	_____
Product/service line 2	_____	_____	_____
Product/service line 3	_____	_____	_____
Product/service line 4	_____	_____	_____
TOTAL COST OF GOODS SOLD	$_____	$_____	$_____
GROSS PROFIT			
EXPENSES:			
Variable:			
Payroll	$_____	$_____	$_____
Sales commission	_____	_____	_____
Freight and delivery	_____	_____	_____
Travel and entertainment	_____	_____	_____
Semivariable:			
Advertising/promotion	_____	_____	_____
FICA/payroll tax	_____	_____	_____
Supplies	_____	_____	_____
Telephone	_____	_____	_____
Fixed:			
Rent	_____	_____	_____
Utilities	_____	_____	_____
Property taxes	_____	_____	_____
Dues and subscriptions	_____	_____	_____
TOTAL EXPENSES	_____	_____	_____
Profit before depreciation	_____	_____	_____
Depreciation	_____	_____	_____
NET PROFIT	$_____	$_____	$_____

Note: Expense items for your business will vary from these three categories. For illustration purposes only.
Source: Adapted from David H. Bangs, Jr. Financial Troubleshooting, An Action Plan for Money Management in the Small Business, p. 49. Used with permission: © 1992 by Upstart Publishing Company, Inc. Published by Upstart Publishing Co., a division of Dearborn Financial Publishing Inc./Chicago. All rights reserved.

vacation just as you are beginning operations. This is a lot more fun, but not any more likely to happen than the first scenario, although either could happen. Your most realistic estimate will fall between the two in the center column.

Question and test your projections. Is there enough demand for you to reach your sales goal? Do you have enough space, equipment, and employees to reach your sales goal? Break your sales down into number of units, then the number of units bought per customer, and then the number of units sold per day.[9] When viewed this way, you may find that every person in town would have to buy eight bagels per day, 365 days per year, for you to achieve your sales projections for your proposed bagel shop. Obviously, you would need to revise

FIGURE 4-6
Breakeven Analysis
At what point will you make money?

1. Total sales $ _____
2. Fixed costs $ _____
3. Gross margin $ _____
4. Gross margin as a percent of sales   _____ %
   (line 3 \ line 1)
5. Breakeven sales $ _____
   (line 2 \ line 4)
6. Profit goal $ _____
7. Sales required to achieve profit goal $ _____
   [(line 2 + line 6) \ line 4]

your goal, expand your menu, do more to control your expenses, or convince people to eat more bagels than is humanly possible for your business to succeed.

Breakeven Analysis.   How many units (or dollars worth) of your products or service will have to be sold to cover your costs? A breakeven analysis will give you a sales projection of how many units or dollars need to be sold to reach your **breakeven point,** that is, the point at which you are neither making nor losing money. (See Figure 4-6.) (See also Chapter 11.)

> **breakeven point** The point at which sales and costs are equal and a business is neither making nor losing money.

To reinforce your financial projections, you may want to compare them to industry averages for your chosen industry. *Robert Morris Associates Annual Statement* publishes an annual index showing industry averages of key manufacturing, wholesale, and retail business groups. Compare your projected financial ratios with industry averages to give the reader an established benchmark. (See Chapter 17.)

Appendix

Supplemental information and documents not crucial to the plan, but of potential interest to the reader, are gathered in the appendix. Résumés of owners and principal managers, advertising samples, brochures, or any related information can be included. Different types of information such as résumés, advertising samples, organization chart, and floorplan should each be given a separate appendix labeled with successive letters of the alphabet (Appendix A, Appendix B, and so on). Be sure to identify each appendix in your table of contents (for example, "Appendix A: Advertising Samples").

Review Process

Writing a business plan is a project that involves a long series of interrelated steps. Beginning with your idea for a business, you want to determine its feasibility through the creation of your business plan. The technique illustrated in Figure 4-7 will allow you to identify the steps you need to take in writing your plan. Steps connected by lines show that lower-numbered steps need to be completed before moving on to higher-numbered ones. Steps that are parallel show that these take place simultaneously. For example, steps 6 through 10 can be com-

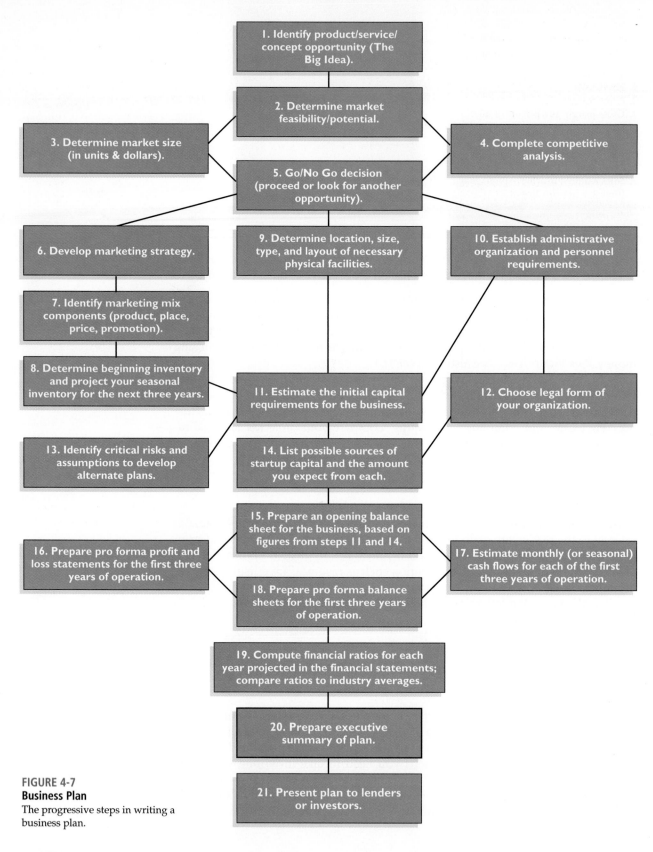

FIGURE 4-7
Business Plan
The progressive steps in writing a
business plan.

Manager's Notebook

How Does Your Plan Rate?

On the following checklist, take the perspective of a potential lender or investor in rating your own plan. Rate each section with an A through F grad-ing scale, with A being the highest or best grade. Would you want to invest *your* money in a business that does not earn an "A" in as many categories as possible? Use your rating to identify areas that can be improved.

	GRADE	MODEL (A+) PLAN
BUSINESS DESCRIPTION		
Company	_____	Simply explained and feasible.
Industry	_____	Growing in market niches that are presently unsatisfied.
Products	_____	Proprietary position (quality exceeds customer's expectations).
Services	_____	Described clearly. Service level exceeds customer expectations.
Previous success	_____	Business has past record of success.
Competitive advantage	_____	Identified and sustainable.
Risks turned into opportunities	_____	Risks identified and shown how minimized.
Orientation of business	_____	Market oriented, not product oriented.
MARKETING		
Target market(s)	_____	Clearly identified.
Size of target market(s)	_____	Large enough to support viable business.
User benefits identified	_____	Benefit to customers clearly shown.
MANAGEMENT TEAM		
Experience of team	_____	Successful previous experience in similar business.
Key managers identified	_____	Managers with complementary skills on team.
FINANCIAL PLAN		
Projections	_____	Realistic and supported.
Rate of return	_____	Exceptionally high. Loans can be paid back in less than one year.
Participation by owner	_____	Owner(s) has significant personal investment.
Participation by others	_____	Other investors already involved.
PLAN PACKAGING		
Appearance	_____	Professional, laser printed, bound, no spelling or grammatical errors.
Executive summary	_____	Concise description of business that prompts reader to say "Wow!"
Body of plan	_____	Sections of plan appropriate and complete.
Appendices	_____	Appropriate supporting documentation.
Plan standardized or custom	_____	Plan custom written for specific business. Not "canned."

pleted at the same time and all must be accomplished before you can estimate how much capital you need in step 11.

Like any project involving a number of complex steps and calculations, your business plan should be carefully reviewed and revised before you present it to potential investors. After you have written your plan, rate it yourself as lenders and investors will evaluate it. (See Manager's Notebook: How Does Your Plan Rate?)

Business Plan Mistakes

We can often learn from the mistakes of others. Writing business plans is no exception. Bankers and investors who view hundreds of business plans a year look for reasons to reject proposed plans. This practice helps them to weed out potentially unworthy investments and to identify the likely winners—the most organized, focused, and realistic proposals.

Your business plan says a lot about your level of financial and professional knowledge. How can you keep investors focused on your ideas while keeping your plan out of the "reject" pile? It helps to avoid the most common errors:

- *Submitting a "rough copy."* Your plan should be a cleanly typed copy without coffee stains and scratched-out words. If you have not worked your idea out completely enough to present a plan you are proud of, why should the investor take you seriously?
- *Depending on outdated financial information or industry comparisons.* It is important to be as current as possible to convince the investor that you are a realistic planner.
- *Making unsubstantiated assumptions.* Explain how and why you reach your conclusions at any point in the plan.
- *Being overly optimistic.* Too much "blue sky and rainbows" will lead the investor to wonder if your plan is realistic. Describe potential pitfalls also, and how you would cope with them.
- *Misunderstanding financial information.* Even if you get help from an accountant in preparing your financials, be sure you understand and can interpret what they say.
- *Ignoring the macroenvironment.* How will competitors react to your business? What other economic factors are likely to change? Considering the business climate and environment will help demonstrate the breadth of your understanding.
- *Having no personal equity in the company.* If you are not willing to risk your own money in the venture, why should the investor? A vested interest in the business will help to convince potential lenders that you will work as hard as possible to make the business succeed.

Source: Adapted from J. T. Broome, Jr., "How to Write a Business Plan," Nation's Business (February 1993), pp. 29–30.

Summary

Now that you have read the chapter, a summary of the objectives are:

■ *The importance of the business plan.*

Business plans are important: (a) to raise capital, (b) to provide a roadmap for future operations, and (c) to prevent oversight.

■ *The components of a business plan.*

The major components of a business plan include: cover page, table of contents, executive summary, company and industry, products or services, marketing research and evaluation, marketing plan, manufacturing and operation plan, management team, timeline, critical risks and assumptions, benefits to community, financial plan, and appendix.

■ *What NOT to do when writing a business plan.*

When writing your business plan do *not:* submit a rough copy, depend on outdated data, make unsubstantiated assumptions, be unrealistic, misunderstand your own financial information, forget factors outside your business, or hold your own money back.

■ *Where to get help in writing a business plan.*

You can get assistance in writing your plan from (a) a business planning guide, (b) Small Business Administration pamphlets, (c) your area Small Business Development Center, (d) your local Chamber of Commerce, (e) a college or university near you.

Questions for Review and Discussion

1. Why wouldn't a 100-page business plan be four times better than a 25-page business plan? *25-40 pages should be adeq.*
2. Should you write a business plan even if you do not need outside financing? Why or why not?
3. Who should write the business plan? *Entre. / assist. from att., acct., consult.*
4. If successful companies like Pizza Hut have been started without business plan, why does the author claim they are so important?
5. Why do entrepreneurs have trouble remaining objective when writing their business plans? *Dreams may blur reality*
6. Why do some prospective business owners refuse to plan?
7. Why is the executive summary the most important section of the business plan? *Essential facts — essence of plan*
8. Talk to the owner of a small business. Did he or she write a business plan? A strategic plan? If they received any assistance, where did they get it?

Critical Incident

Select one of the four startup companies described next to complete the questions at the end of the exercise.

Company A. Salad in a bag, sold in the produce section of supermarkets. Now that's an idea whose time has come! Busy, time-starved consumers will like the convenience of washed and premade salads. And they'll particularly appreciate the fact that they're not only getting something fast, they're getting something healthy. Fresh Express International of Salinas, California sees fresh bagged salads as a prime business opportunity.

Company B. Taking aerial photographs for a living isn't for the timid of heart—or stomach. Fickle weather conditions (particularly in Milwaukee, Wisconsin), strict insurance requirements, and soaring fuel costs are just a few of the variables that Skypix has to deal with. Yet the demand—both commercial and individual—for custom aerial photographs is strong and growing.

Company C.   Sassy Scents is not only the name but an apt description of this San Antonio-based business. Sassy Scents manufactures and markets home fragrance products including potpourri, wax chips, candles, and incense. The company intends to break into the intensely competitive gift market by taking on some of the industry's biggest and best-known competitors such as Claire Burke and Aromatics. You wouldn't really expect a business that calls itself "sassy" to be timid, now would you?!

Company D.   Mail Boxes Etc. is a fast-growing franchise operation that provides many types of services (copying, delivery, mailboxes, and so on) for customers. One of its franchises has asked to open a location in the student union at the University of Michigan. Students on a college campus seem like a prime market for this type of franchise. But are they?

Questions

1. Write an executive summary for the company you choose. (You should refer to the section beginning on page 100 to refresh your memory of the executive summary contents.)

2. Break into small groups (three or four per group) comprising students who selected the same company. Each student will write a brief business plan outline in addition to the executive summary and will take turns presenting them to the rest of the group as if they were potential financial lenders. Present your plan in the most positive light so the "lenders" will react favorably toward your business. Meanwhile, the financial lenders will look for holes in your business plan, so be sure to cover all the areas.

Take it to the Net

We invite you to visit the Hatten page on the Prentice Hall Web site at: http://www.prenhall.com/~hattensb for this chapter's World Wide Web exercise.

VIDEO CASE
Beer Battle

BREWPUBS, SMALL BARS OR restaurants that brew their own beer in small batches (known as micro-brewing), are gaining in popularity. More and more beer drinkers are preferring to quaff the full-bodied, fresh flavor of micro-brews rather than the bland beers produced for the masses by large American breweries. In fact, beer drinkers appear to be willing to pay more for fresh taste and higher quality, because the average brewpub micro-brew costs about 60 percent more than does a mass produced beer.

Large breweries are trying to counter the trend toward micro-brews by imitating them. Anheuser-Busch, Coors, and Miller have all released brands of beer that appear to be made by small breweries. Why? Because overall domestic beer sales are flat, but sales of micro-brews are gathering a good head and are growing by an average of 40 percent per year. That approximately four new brewpubs open in the United States every week just underscores the surging popularity of micro-brewed beer. *Source: Adapted from* The Wall Street Journal Report, *Show #670, July 29, 1995.*

Discussion Questions

- Do you see franchising as a possible extension of the brewpub concept? Why or why not?
- Assume you are starting a brewpub after you graduate. What factors would be most important to your new venture?
- How does the success of micro-brew sales illustrate the advantages that small businesses often have over large ones?

Chapter Focus

After reading this chapter, you should be able to:

- Establish what a franchise is and how it operates.
- Articulate the difference between product (or trade name) franchises and business-format franchises.
- Compare the advantages and disadvantages of franchising.
- Appreciate the relationship between franchisor and franchisee.
- Explain how to evaluate a potential franchise.
- Explore franchising in the international marketplace.

5 Franchising

THE BUSTLING NEON COMMERCIALISM of any large American shopping mall seems an unlikely outlet for a product created amid the rural charm of Pennsylvania's Amish farmland. Yet that product, a soft pretzel, made by a company called Auntie Anne's, is taking the nation's malls by storm. Headquartered in Lancaster County, Pennsylvania, Auntie Anne's is a fast-growing treats franchise that sells freshly made, delicious soft pretzels. Anne Beiler, who was raised in this Amish area, founded the company in 1988 when she began making soft pretzels to replace a pizza business she had managed at an Amish farmer's market. Business was so brisk that Beiler expanded first from one to two booths and then began refining her pretzel recipe. Like many successful businesses, chance played an important role in the company's history. When a supplier inadvertently delivered the wrong ingredients, Beiler added them to her original pretzel recipe, and the mix-up ended up making the pretzels taste better!

The first thing you notice about an Auntie Anne's franchise

location is its delightful smell, which Sean Kelly, director of marketing for the parent company, laughingly refers to as the "sweet smell of success." Because the bulk of the stores' sales is to impulse shoppers, the aroma of freshly baked pretzels is an important sales tool. Franchisees also use free product sample distribution throughout the malls, frequent-user programs, and brochures (extolling everything from the way the pretzels are made to their health benefits to suggested dip recipes) to market the products effectively. The company has since branched into selling related merchandise, primarily coffee mugs designed with traditional Amish quilt patterns and tumblers decorated with artwork about Lancaster County.

At the beginning of 1996, Auntie Anne's had over 300 units in its franchise chain. The majority of these were franchise operations located in shopping mall food courts, although the parent company owns and operates some of its own stores. Auntie Anne's has successfully developed an extensive franchise organization which has attracted individual franchisees. In this chapter, you will learn about the process of franchising, including the different types of franchising systems, the advantages and disadvantages of franchises, and how to go about selecting a franchise. Maybe you too will one day savor the sweet smell of success in a franchised business! *Source: Milford Prewitt, "Auntie Anne's Promo Showcases Sweet Smell of Success," Nation's Restaurant News, February 27, 1995, pp. 12+.*

About Franchising

franchise A contractual license to operate an individually owned business as part of a larger chain.

franchisor The parent company that develops a product or business process and sells the rights to franchisees.

franchisee The small business person who purchases the franchise in order to sell the product or service of the franchisor.

A **franchise** is an agreement that binds a **franchisor** (a parent company of the product, service, or method) with a **franchisee** (a small business that pays fees and royalties for exclusive rights to local distribution of the product or service). Through the franchise agreement, the franchisee gains the benefit of the parent company's expertise, experience, management systems, marketing, and financial help. Franchisors benefit by expanding their operations by building a base of franchisees rather than using their own capital and resources.

Background

Franchises have experienced growth since the 1950s. However, contrary to popular belief, they did not originate with McDonald's. They have existed since the early 1800s.

In the 1830s, Cyrus McCormick was making reapers and Isaac Singer began manufacturing sewing machines. As America's economic system was beginning to shift from being based on agriculture and small business to an economy based on industry and big business, business methods needed to change also. Early manufacturers also had to provide distribution and were faced with the choice of setting up a company-owned system or developing contracts with independent firms to represent them. The choice was not easy. Direct ownership guaranteed complete control and ensured quality levels of service. On the other hand, direct ownership was expensive and difficult to manage. McCormick and Singer were two of the first to use agents in building sales networks quickly at little cost to themselves.[1] This use of exclusive agents laid the groundwork for today's franchising.

Franchising Today

Franchising dominates the fast-food, automobile, and lodging segments of the U.S. economy.

Today franchising is represented in almost every industry. About 12 percent of all U.S. businesses are franchised and interest in international franchising is growing quickly. In 1992, franchised businesses had annual sales of $803 billion and employed 8 million people.[2] Most of these franchises are in the retail sector where sales reached $615 billion or 34 percent of total U.S. retail sales (see Figure 5-1).[3]

While the number of franchises has been increasing since the 1950s, the 1980s were a real boom period. Franchise sales in 1980 were $336 billion. Sales jumped to $714 billion in 1990 for a 112 percent increase. Figure 5-2 shows the growth of franchises in terms of number of establishments and sales.

Franchising Systems

The two types of franchises are *product* (or *trade name*) *franchises* and *business-format franchises*. These two forms are used by producers, wholesalers, and retailers to distribute goods and services to consumers and other businesses.

Product (or Trade Name) Franchising. Product franchising allows the franchisee (or dealer) to buy products from the franchisor (or supplier) or to license the use of its trade name. This approach typically connects a single manufacturer with many dealers. The idea is to make products available to consumers in a specific geographic region through exclusive dealers. Soft-drink bottlers and gasoline stations use this type of franchising. Auto manufacturers also use this system to make their cars, service, and parts available. Your local Chevrolet dealer, for instance, has full use of the Chevrolet trade name, brand names (like Corvette), and logos (like the bow tie symbol) to promote the dealership in your area. Product franchisors regulate their franchisees' locations to avoid excessive competition between them. Chevrolet would not allow a new dealership that sells its products across the street from your established local dealer.

product (trade name) franchise A type of franchise in which the franchisee agrees to purchase the products of the franchisor or to use the franchisor's name.

Franchises
40.9% of total U.S. retail sales
$803.2 Billion in 1992

FIGURE 5-1
Franchise Generated Revenue
Franchised businesses account for 40.9% of all U.S. retail sales. By the year 2000, franchise sales could reach $1 trillion.
Source: Franchise Fact Sheet, International Franchise Association, June 5, 1995.

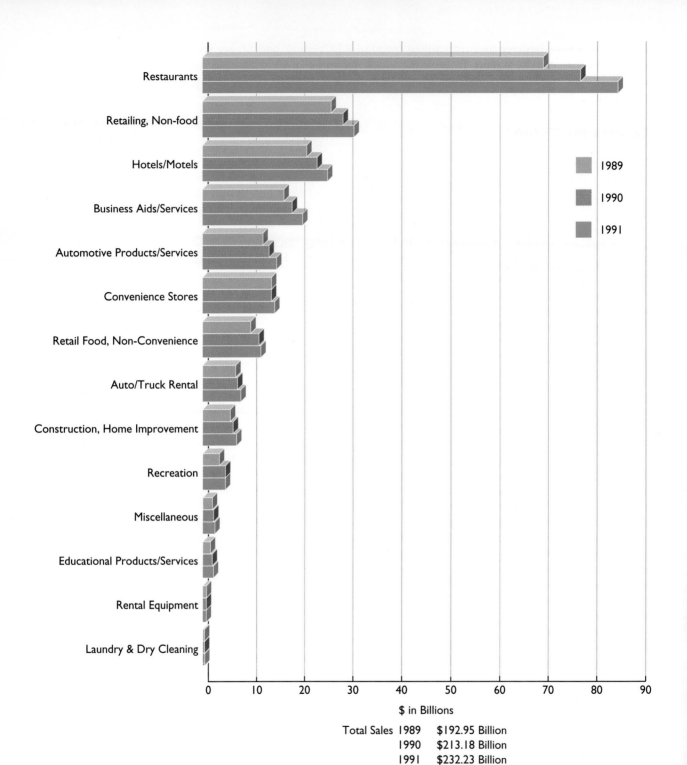

FIGURE 5-2
Business Format Franchise Sales by Business Category
Business format franchise sales growth from 1989 to 1991.
Source: Franchise Fact Sheet, *International Franchise Association, June 5, 1995.*

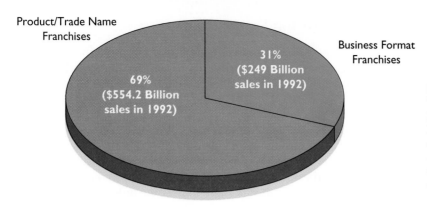

Product/Trade Name Franchises

Business Format Franchises

69%
($554.2 Billion sales in 1992)

31%
($249 Billion sales in 1992)

FIGURE 5-3
Types of Franchises
In 1992, Product/Trade Name Franchises accounted for 69% of all franchise sales.
Source: Franchise Fact Sheet, *International Franchise Association, June 5, 1995.*

Business-Format Franchising.   Business-format franchising is more of a *turnkey* approach to franchising. This means that the franchisee purchases not only the franchisor's product to sell, but also the entire way of doing business including operation procedures, marketing packages, physical building and equipment, and full business services. Business-format franchising is commonly used in fast-food restaurants and lodging establishments, such as hotel and motel chains. Figure 5-3 compares the growth of both types of franchises.

business-format franchise
A type of franchise in which the franchisee adopts the franchisor's entire method of operation.

Why Open a Franchise?

If you are considering the purchase of a franchise, you should compare its advantages and disadvantages to those of starting a new business or buying an existing nonfranchised business (see Chapters 6 and 7). You should also determine if the unique characteristics of franchising fit your personal needs and desires. Some small business owners would rather assume the risk and expense of starting an independent business than have to follow someone else's policies and procedures. Others prefer the advantages that a franchise's proven system can provide. Sometimes it makes sense not to reinvent the wheel. (See Table 5-1.)

TABLE 5 ▪ 1   The Advantages and Disadvantages of Franchising

FRANCHISEE'S PERSPECTIVE	FRANCHISOR'S PERSPECTIVE
Advantages	
1. proven product or service	1. expansion with limited capital
2. marketing expertise	2. multiple sources of capital
3. technical and managerial assistance	3. controlled expansion
4. opportunity to learn business	4. motivated franchisees
5. quality control standards	
6. ease of entry	
7. opportunity for growth	
Disadvantages	
1. fees and profit sharing	1. maintaining control
2. restrictions of freedom	2. sharing profit with franchisees
3. overdependence	3. potential for disputes with
4. unsatisfied expectations	franchisees
5. termination of the agreement	
6. performance of other franchisees	

Advantages to the Franchisee

For the franchisee, there are seven major advantages of franchising: proven product or service, marketing expertise, technical and managerial assistance, an opportunity to learn the business, quality control standards, ease of entry, and opportunity for growth.[4]

Product Readiness.   The advantage of selling a proven product or service is the greatest benefit to a franchisee. Customers are aware of the product, they know the name, and what to expect. For example, travelers may not know anything about the Ramada Inn in Colorado Springs, but they know of Ramada's reputation and are more likely to stay there than some independent, unknown motel.

Marketing Expertise.   Franchisors spend millions of dollars on national or regional advertising to help build an image that independent businesses could not afford. Franchisors also develop print, broadcast, and point-of-purchase advertising. Local franchisees do share in these advertising costs, usually based on their gross revenues.

Professional Guidance.   A franchise can provide a source of managerial and technical assistance not available to an independent business. You can benefit from the accumulated years of experience and knowledge of the franchisor. Most franchisors provide training, both as preparation for running the business and as instruction after the business is going. This training can allow a person without prior experience to be successful in owning a franchise. A good franchisor is available to provide day-to-day assistance and to give you someone to turn to when a crisis arises. In addition, franchisees can receive a great deal of technical assistance, such as store layout and design, location, purchasing, and equipment.

Opportunity to Learn.   While it is not usually advisable to go into a business in an unfamiliar field, franchising can provide an opportunity to be successful doing exactly that. This can be helpful for a mid-career change of direction. In fact, some franchisors prefer their franchisees not to have experience in that particular field. These franchisors would prefer to train from scratch, so there are no bad habits to break.

Recognized Standards.   Franchisors impose quality standards for franchisees to follow, a feature that might not seem advantageous at first. If independence is your motive for self-employment, why would you want to meet standards set by someone else? The benefit, though, is that the practice ensures consistency to customers. Consumers can walk into a McDonald's anywhere in the world and know what to expect. A franchisor's quality control regulations help franchisees to maintain high standards of cleanliness, service, and productivity. As a franchisee, you will benefit from standardized quality control because if another franchisee in your organization provides inferior service, it will affect attitudes toward *your* business.

Efficiency.   Because of increased efficiency, a franchise can sometimes be started and operated with less capital than it takes to start an independent business. Franchisors have already been through the learning curve and worked most of the bugs out of the process. Inventory needs like what to stock and what will sell quickly are known before you open the doors, so you won't be wasting money on equipment, inventory, or supplies that you don't need. Many franchisors often provide financial resources for startup and working capital for inventory.

Potential for Business Growth.   If you are successful with a franchise, you will often have the opportunity to multiply that success by expanding to other franchises in other locations. Most franchisors have provisions to open other territories.

Franchising can increase your chances of success in business and provide many things you might not otherwise have access to. These seven advantages have one theme in common—the opportunity to benefit from someone else's experience. You have the chance to learn from someone else's mistakes.

Disadvantages to the Franchisee

There are drawbacks to franchising also. You must give up some control, some decision-making power, and some freedom. The disadvantages to the franchisee include: fees and profit sharing, restrictions of freedom, overdependence, unsatisfied expectations, termination of the agreement, and performance of other franchisees.

Cost of Franchise.   The services, assistance, and assurance in buying a franchise come at a price. Every franchisor will charge a fee and/or a specified percentage of sales revenue. (See Table 5-2.) The disadvantage to the franchisees is that they are usually required to raise most of the capital before they begin operations. The total investment can range from $500 for a windshield repair franchise to $3 million for Applebee's Neighborhood Grill & Bar.

TABLE 5 ▪ 2   Getting In

FRANCHISE	FRANCHISE FEE	START-UP COSTS	ROYALTY
Gingiss Formalwear	to $15K	$103K–$200K	0.5%–6%
Maaco Auto Painting & Bodyworks	$30K	$155K	8%
Meineke Discount Mufflers	$22.5K	$93K	7%
Jazzercise, Inc.	$650	$1.3K–$16.8K	to 20%
Cost Cutters Family Hair Care	$19.5K	$48K–$93K	6%
Signs First	$15K	$50K	6%
Big Apple Bagels	$18.5K	$150K–$180K	5%
Rocky Mountain Chocolate Factory	$19.5K	$94K–$194K	5%
KFC	$25K	$125K	4%
Mrs. Fields Cookies	$25K	$151K–$215K	6%
Dunkin' Donuts	$40K	$181K–$255K	4.9%
Burger King	$40K	$247K–$1.3M	3.5%
Baskin-Robbins	to $15K	$42K–$370K	0.5–1%
Taco John's	$19.5K	$273K–$551K	4%
Subway	$10K	$55.7K–$141K	8%
Godfather's Pizza	$7.5K–$15K	$64K–$276K	5%
Super 8 Motels	$20K+	$300K–$2.5M	4%
Merry Maids	$13K–$21K	$8.3K–$16K	5%–7%
Play It Again Sports	$25K	$134K–$205K	5%
Together Dating Service	$50K–$200K	$38K–$127K	8%

Source: "17th Annual Franchise 500," Entrepreneur, January 1996, pp. 214–311.

These fees and percentages may begin to seem excessive after you have been in business for a while and you see their impact on your bottom line. It is not uncommon for franchisees to be grateful for the assistance a franchisor provides in starting the business, only to become frustrated by the royalties paid a few years later.

Restrictions on Freedom or Creativity. Restrictions on freedom may be a problem for some franchisees. This is especially true since most people open their own businesses because of a desire for independence. Franchises have policies and procedures that must be followed to maintain the agreement. The size of your market will be limited by territorial restrictions. You may feel that some products, promotions, or policies may not be appropriate for your area, but you have little recourse after the franchise agreement has been signed.

Risk of Fraud or Misunderstanding. Less than scrupulous franchisors have been known to mislead potential franchisees with promises that are not delivered. To avoid being taken by fraudulent franchises, be sure to consult an attorney and talk with as many current franchisees as possible. Do not think that because the agreement looks standard that you should not understand every section, especially the fine print.

Problems of Termination or Transfer. Difficulty in terminating the franchise agreement or having it terminated against your will can be a disadvantage to the franchisee. Before entering into the franchise, you should understand the section of the agreement that describes how you can get out of the agreement. For instance, what if you want to transfer your rights to a family member, or sell the franchise to someone else, or otherwise terminate your agreement? What provisions does the contract make for you to renew the agreement? Most franchise agreements are made for a specific period of time—typically between 5 and 20 years. Some may be renewed for perpetuity if both parties agree. Otherwise, franchise renewal must be considered by both sides when the term of the agreement expires. Check the agreement to see if the franchisee has a right of first refusal, which means that the franchisee must decline to continue the agreement before the franchisor can offer the franchise to someone else. Check to see if the franchisor must provide "just cause" for termination or must give a definite reason why the agreement is not continued.

Poor Performance of Other Franchisees. Poor performance on the part of other franchisees can lead to problems for you. If the franchisor tolerates substandard performance, a few franchisees can seriously affect the sales of many others. Customers view franchises as an entire unit because the implicit message from franchises is that "we are all alike"—good or bad. If customers are treated unsatisfactorily in one location, they are likely to believe the same treatment will occur elsewhere.

Advantages to the Franchisor

Now let's look at franchising from the franchisor's perspective. Franchisors also face advantages and disadvantages. The positive aspects include decreased capital investment when compared with forming so many outlets independently, multiple sources of capital coming into their business, expansion of the business

Once Burned . . .

After fighting fires with the New Orleans Fire Department for 25 years and making it to district chief, the last way Delo Breckenridge expected to get burned was by an unscrupulous franchisor. In fact, he was "taken to the cleaners"—literally—to the tune of $40,000.

The franchise operation Breckenridge signed on with, Automated Micro Dry Cleaning Centers, sold a system whereby customers were to drop off clothes to be drycleaned into a sorting machine located in an office building storefront. There the clothes were to be retrieved by a worker, cleaned, and then returned to the original location. When he picked up his or her clothes, the customer would pay with a credit card swiped through a machine. "It was supposed to work kind of like a jukebox," Breckenridge says. Yet when he went to California for a demonstration, the model didn't work. Breckenridge knows that he should have backed out at that point, but a franchise salesman kept calling him a "wussy," and the insult worked: Breckenridge sunk his money into the system.

Breckenridge has received absolutely nothing in return for his investment except letters from the franchisor stating, in effect, that there were problems with the machines, that the company was out of money, and asking him to send more. And Breckenridge wasn't alone in this nightmare. Nineteen other franchisees were also suckered in. He laments, "It's kind of like getting a new car and wrecking it the first day without having any insurance. I'll be paying $600 a month on my bank loan for the next five years."

It might seem that Breckenridge must have been some sort of ignorant fool to have gotten duped like this—but his background indicates otherwise. Not only is he an expert in his profession, he graduated from Louisiana State University with a degree in economics. His father was a lawyer and his mother was a respected journalist for the New Orleans *Times-Picayune* newspaper. His lesson: he now wishes he had contacted other franchisees and talked to them before signing on.

Thoroughly researching a potential franchise, particularly one that is newly established or unfamiliar to you, and doggedly asking questions until you get the information you need to make an intelligent decision is just smart business. And, as Breckenridge now admits, you must never let someone use insults to push you into making a bad decision.

Source: Andrew Serwer, "Trouble in Franchise Nation," Fortune, March 6, 1995, pp. 115–129.

happening much faster than if they were in business alone, and the synergy created by a group of motivated franchisees.

Expansion with Smaller Capital Investment. From the perspective of the franchisor, the biggest advantage of offering franchises is the expansion of its distribution sources with limited equity investments. The franchise fees from franchisees provide capital to the franchisor, rather than having to borrow from lenders or attract outside investors. For a business with limited capital, franchising may be the only viable way to expand by providing franchisees an opportunity to share the financial burden for all to succeed.

Multiple Sources of Revenue. Franchisors often have several sources of revenue built into franchise agreements. These sources include the franchise fee, which is paid when the agreement is signed, a percentage of the franchise monthly gross operating revenues, and revenue from selling the necessary products and supplies to the franchisees. For example, a fast-food restaurant can have a franchise fee of up to $200,000, pay 3 percent to 8 percent of monthly gross sales as a royalty fee, and be required to purchase all food items (from hamburger to condiments), office supplies, and restaurant supplies (napkins, coffee filters, paper cups) from the franchisor.

Controlled Expansion. When compared with the expansion of a corporate chain, expanding via franchising can be accomplished with a simpler management structure. Very rapid growth of a corporation can be more of a problem than an opportunity if the growth outpaces central management's capacity to control and monitor it. When this happens, problems with inconsistency, communications, and especially cash flow generally appear. While franchisors still face these problems to some degree, the franchise network reduces them. Mrs. Fields' Cookies is an example of a company that expanded very quickly—opening 225 new stores between 1985 and 1988—and refused to franchise at the start so control over the whole business, each location, and each cookie would not be lost. The company began offering franchises in 1991, but not until the reluctance to yield some control and franchise had built large amounts of debt. In 1993 Fields had to exchange ownership of 80 percent of the company to lenders to write off $94 million of debt.[5]

Motivated Franchisees. Since franchisees own their own businesses, they are almost always more highly motivated to make it succeed than an employee working for someone else. Franchisees have a direct personal interest in the entire operation so they are inspired to perform and create positive synergy within the franchise.

Bulk Purchasing. Centralized purchasing of products and supplies allows franchisors to take advantage of volume discounts, since they are buying for all the franchise locations. This can increase profit margins and hold down costs for franchisees.

Disadvantages to the Franchisor

Problems exist in every method of business and franchising is no exception. Maintaining control is the biggest disadvantage to franchisors. Others are profit sharing and potential disputes with franchisees.

Loss of Control. Franchisees who do not maintain their businesses not only reflect poorly on the other franchisees, but on the franchisor also. While the franchisor does control the organization to the limit of the franchise agreement, franchisees are still independent businesspeople. After the franchise agreement has been signed, the franchisor must get permission from franchisees before any products or services are changed, added, or eliminated. Permission is often negotiated individually. This makes adapting products to meet changing needs of customers very difficult for the franchisor, especially if a wide variety of consumer tastes are being served over a large geographic area.

One way franchisors have dealt with this problem is by establishing some company-owned units. Since these are not independently owned businesses, the franchisor can test market new products, services, and procedures in them. This can give the franchisor a way to track and respond to changing customer needs and to use as examples when negotiating with franchisees.

Profit Sharing. If franchisees expect (and are able) to recover their initial investment within two or three years, they could be yielding 30 percent to 50 percent return on investment. This can provide motivation for the franchisees, but it is also profit the franchisor is not making with a company-owned unit.

Franchisee Disputes. Friction between franchisees and franchisors may arise over such issues as payment of fees, expansion, and hours of operation. These potential conflicts point to the importance of communication between both sides and having a clearly written franchise agreement.

Selecting a Franchise

Choosing the right franchise is a serious decision. Investing in a franchise represents a big commitment of time and money. Determine what you need in a business and evaluate what several different franchises can offer you and your customers.

Evaluate Your Needs

The choice of which franchise to buy is not an easy one. You need to find a franchise opportunity that matches your interests, skills, and needs. Ask yourself the following questions to help determine whether or not franchising is the route to small business ownership for you.

- How much equity capital will you need to purchase the franchise and operate it until your income equals your expenses? Where are you going to get it?
- Are you prepared to give up some independence of action to secure the advantages offered by the franchise?
- Do you really believe you have the innate ability, training, and experience to work smoothly and profitably with the franchisor, your employees, and your customers?
- Are you ready to make a long-term commitment to working with this franchisor, offering its product or service to your public?[6]

Do Your Research

Inc., Nation's Business, The Wall Street Journal, Success, and *Entrepreneur* are general business periodicals that contain advertising and articles related to franchising. Trade journals and magazines that specialize in franchising are *Franchise, Franchising Opportunities World,* and *Quarterly Franchising World.* The Department of Commerce publishes *Franchise Opportunities Handbook* annually, which gives you an idea of requirements, expectations, and assistance for each franchise. Table 5-3 shows examples of franchise descriptions from this handbook.

Trade associations can be valuable sources of information when you are investigating franchise opportunities. The major trade association of franchising is the International Franchise Association (IFA), which is made up of 850 franchise companies. The IFA is a leading source of information for franchisors and franchisees offering publications on industrywide data as well as company-specific information. You can contact the IFA for information at 1350 New York Avenue NW, Suite 900, Washington, DC 20005-4709, (202) 628-8000.

TABLE 5 ▪ 3 Franchise Info

MCDONALD'S CORPORATION
Kroc Drive
Oakbrook, Illinois 60521
Licensing Department

Description of Operation: McDonald's Corporation operates and directs a successful nationwide chain of quick service restaurants serving a moderately priced menu. Emphasis is on quick, efficient service, high quality food, and cleanliness. The standard menu consists of hamburgers, cheeseburgers, fish sandwiches, French fries, apple pie, shakes, breakfast menu, and assorted beverages.
Number of Franchisees: Over 2,000 in the United States
In Business Since: 1955
Equity Capital Needed: Varies.
Conventional Franchise: 40 percent of total cost (approximately $610,000), which must be from personal unencumbered funds to lease a new restaurant; approximately $40,000 to lease an existing restaurant.
Business Facilities Lease: $66,000 from nonborrowed funds.
Financial Assistance Available: None
Training Provided: Prospective franchisees are required to complete a structured training program that includes approximately 18–24 months of in-store training (on a part-time basis) and 5 weeks of classroom training.
Managerial Assistance Available: Operations, training, maintenance, accounting and equipment manuals provided. Company makes available promotional advertising material plus field representative consultation and assistance.
Information Submitted: April 1990

DUDS 'N SUDS
CLEAN DUDS INC.
3401 101st Street, Suite E
Des Moines, Iowa 50322
Philip G. Akin

Description of Operation: Self-serve laundry, snack bar, and cleaning services. We call it "Good, Clean, Fun." A full service laundry that is energy efficient and also has a soda fountain that serves pop, coffee and even beer. It also has a big screen TV, pool table and video games. Approximately 3,000 square feet.
Number of Franchisees: 85 in 27 States
In Business Since: 1983
Equity Capital Needed: $60,000; total system price $80,000
Financial Assistance Available: We have a loan guide and loan proposal that we present to financial institutions. We also work with the SBA. Limited financial assistance available. Equipment lease programs.
Training Provided: On-site training in store during the opening. Also a week training prior to opening at Des Moines, Iowa. Also operations manuals and instructional video tapes are provided.
Managerial Assistance Available: Full promotional and management support, manuals, design and layout of store, all signage, video tapes, financial evaluations, inspections, maintenance program, regional and national franchisor meetings.

FANTASTIC SAM'S, THE ORIGINAL FAMILY HAIRCUTTERS
3180 Old Getwell Road
P. O. Box 18845
Memphis, Tennessee 38181-0845
Sam M. Ross, Chairman of the Board
George H. Carnall II, President

Description of Operation: The company sells licenses for Fantastic Sam's, the Original Family Haircutters, a unique retail haircare establishment oriented to the demands, pocketbooks and convenience of all American families.
Number of Franchisees: Over 2,200 stores in 45 States and 4 countries.
In Business Since: 1974
Equity Capital Needed: (1) One Fantastic Sam's store– $58,700–$120,500, which includes the license fee and all amounts to open that store. (2) Regional license to sell and provide service to Fantastic Sam's licensees with that region— $25,000–$300,000.
Financial Assistance Available: The company provides payment terms on initial product inventory and will finance shop equipment to qualified licensees.
Training Provided: The company provides training classes for all licensees, their shop managers, hairstylists and staff members in the company's training facilities. Further, experienced trainers assist all of the licensees in their store openings, provide seminars around the country and Canada, conduct in-store consultation and training, and provide a complete technical training program.
Managerial Assistance Available: In-store seminars and regional seminars are provided to all licensees and their store managers. Additionally, week long managment classes and daily training classes for all licensees and their store managers are scheduled regularly at the training facilities of the company.
Information Submitted: May 1990

DENNY'S INC.
P. O. Box 25320
Santa Ana, California 92799-5320
Director of Franchise Development

Description of Operation: Full service family restaurants.
Number of Franchisees: 200 plus
In Business Since: 1953
Equity Capital Needed: Franchise fee: $35,000
Financial Assistance Available: None
Training Provided: Store opening, 1 week prior to opening and 2 weeks after.
Managerial Assistance Available: Manager training 4 weeks.
Information Submitted: April 1990

ATHLETIC ATTIC MARKETING, INC.
dba ATHLETIC LADY
P. O. Box 14503
Gainesville, Florida 32604
C. J. Collins, Director of Franchise Sales

Description of Operation: A retail sporting goods operation specializing in the sale of women's fashion active wear and footwear (aerobic, tennis, running, swimming, etc.).

Number of Franchisees: 5 in Georgia, Florida, and North Carolina.

In Business Since: Athletic Attic—1974—started franchising Athletic Lady in 1983

Equity Capital Needed: $15,000 for initial fee. $125,000 to $175,000 total investment. Minimum $45,000 cash required.

Financial Assistance Available: No financial assistance is provided by franchisor. However, all necessary information for loan application is available.

Training Provided: Training program includes 1 week of classroom instruction in all aspects of store operation and 1 week of in-store instruction at franchisor's training store.

Managerial Assistance Available: Assistance includes, but is not limited to, the following: site selection, lease negotiations, store design, basic construction drawings, product mix assistance, opening suppliers accounts, accounting systems, inventory systems, on-site opening assistance, complete operations manual, advertising manual, local advertising materials, national advertising and publicity support, monthly management and newsletters, annual sales meetings.

Information Submitted: May 1990

TCBY ENTERPRISES, INC.
dba "TCBY" YOGURT
1100 TCBY Tower
425 West Capitol Avenue
Little Rock, Arkansas 72201
Herren Hickinbotham, President
Roger Harrod, Vice President,
    Franchise Sales

Description of Operation: Frozen yogurt and yogurt related treats.

Number of Franchisees: Over 1,700 locations from coast to coast and in Canada, the Bahamas, Taiwan, Malaysia, Singapore, and Japan.

In Business Since: 1981

Equity Capital Needed: $102,000–$182,000

Financial Assistance Available: No financing available on first two stores.

Training Provided: 10 day intensive training program at home office (personnel, accounting, operations) and 1 week in-store training at time of opening.

Managerial Assistance Available: Ongoing assistance available in all phases of operations is provided. Services include site approval, store design, complete manuals of operations, approved suppliers and equipment packages. Additionally, field supervisors make periodic in-store inspections to monitor store appearance and quality control and offer ongoing support.

Information Submitted: April 1990

DOMINO'S PIZZA, INC.
3001 Earhart Road
P. O. Box 997
Ann Arbor, Michigan 48105
Deborah S. Sargent, National Director of
    Franchise Services

Description of Operation: Pizza carry-out and delivery service.

Number of Franchisees: Approximately 1,000 in the United States and 19 foreign countries.

In Business Since: 1960

Equity Capital Needed: $83,000 to $194,000.

Financial Assistance Available: Domino's Pizza does not directly provide financing but can refer to lending institutions who will consider providing financing to qualified franchisees.

Training Provided: Potential franchisees must complete the company's current training program, which shall consist of both in-store training and classroom instruction.

Managerial Assistance Available: Domino's Pizza only franchises to internal people, and the kinds and duration of managerial and technical assistance provided by the company are set forth in the franchise agreement.

Information Submitted: May 1990

SUPER 8 MOTELS, INC.
1910 8th Avenue, NE
Aberdeen, South Dakota 57402-4090
Loren Steele, President

Description of Operation: Super 8 Motels, Inc., is a franchise of "Economy Motels" which offer a full size room with free color TV, direct dial phones and attractive decor.

Number of Franchisees: 672 plus 41 company-owned.

In Business Since: 1972

Equity Capital Needed: $150,000 to $1,000,000 depending on size of motel and arrangements with lender.

Financial Assistance Available: Will assist franchisee in seeking mortgage financing.

Training Provided: Complete management training program is provided, including training films, classroom study, examinations, and on-the-job training.

Managerial Assistance Available: Day-to-day managerial, advertising and accounting services provided. Complete front office procedures and accounting systems are included.

Information Submitted: June 1990

Source: U.S. Dept. of Commerce, Franchise Opportunities Handbook *(Washington: U.S. Government Printing Office 1991).*

Manager's Notebook

From the Horse's Mouth

A good place to get information about a particular franchise is from the people currently running one. Try asking the following questions to get the straight scoop:

- What does the business cost to operate on a monthly basis?
- How long did it take to break even?
- How profitable is the franchise?
- How much does the company charge for advertising fees? (Be careful if this number is more than 1 percent to 3 percent of gross sales.)
- Does the money go toward ads in the local market or mainly toward building the parent company's national image? (You should expect about 50 percent to benefit the franchisee.)
- How many units have failed?
- How rapid is unit turnover?
- How many stores does the parent company own? (About 25 percent is acceptable. Too many could weaken franchisee bargaining power, too few could indicate a weak system.)
- Would you buy the franchise again? (The bottom line)

Source: Laurel Allison Touby, "Should You Buy a Franchise?" Working Woman (October 1991), pp. 68–69.

The American Franchise Association (AFA) based in Chicago and the American Association of Franchisees and Dealers (AAFD) headquartered in San Diego are trade associations that provide information and services, represent the interests of members, and were formed to help negotiate better terms and conditions from franchisors. The AAFD has developed a Franchisee Bill of Rights as a code of ethical business conduct for franchised businesses.[7] Women in Franchising Inc. (WIF), also located in Chicago, (312) 431-1467, specializes in training women and minorities for advancement in franchising.[8]

When you have a general idea of the franchise you are interested in, contact the company for a copy of its disclosure statement. Before you sign the required contracts with a chosen franchisor, talk to current and former franchisees. They can provide priceless information that you could not learn anywhere else.

Once you have found a franchise you would consider (or possibly a few to choose from), consider your opportunity by asking yourself the following questions about the franchise.

- Did your lawyer approve the franchise contract you are considering after he or she studied it paragraph by paragraph?
- Does the franchise call upon you to take any steps which are, according to your lawyer, unwise or illegal in your state, county, or city?
- Does the franchise give you an exclusive territory for the length of the franchise or can the franchisor sell a second or third franchise in your territory?

- Is the franchisor connected in any way with any other franchise company handling similar merchandise or services? If so, what is your protection against this second franchisor organization?
- Under what circumstances can you terminate the franchise contract and at what cost to you, if you decide for any reason at all that you wish to cancel it?
- If you sell your franchise, will you be compensated for your goodwill or will the goodwill you have built into the business be lost by you?

Evaluate what the franchisor will offer you and your customers by asking the following questions about the franchisor.

- How many years has the firm offering you a franchise been in operation?
- Has it a reputation for honesty and fair dealing among the local firms holding its franchise?
- Has the franchisor shown you any certified figures indicating exact net profits of one or more going firms which you personally checked with the franchisee(s)?
- Will the firm assist you with:
  A management training program?   Capital?
  An employee training program?   Credit?
  A public relations program?   Merchandise ideas?
- Will the firm help you find a good location for your new business?
- Is the franchising firm adequately financed so that it can carry out its stated plan of financial assistance and expansion?
- Is the franchisor a one-person company or a corporation with an experienced management trained in depth (so that there would always be an experienced person at its head)?
- Exactly what can the franchisor do for you that you cannot do for yourself?
- Has the franchisor investigated you carefully enough to assure itself that you can successfully operate one of its franchises at a profit to both of you?
- Does your state have a law regulating the sale of franchises and has the franchisor complied with the law?

Analyze the Market

What do you know about your market, the people buying your product or service? In answering the following questions, determine if a franchise is the best way to match what the franchisor has to offer with your skills and your customers' needs.

1. Have you made any study to determine whether the product or service that you propose to sell under franchise has a market in your territory at the prices you will have to charge?
2. Will the population in your proposed territory increase, remain static, or decrease over the next five years?
3. Will the product or service you are considering be in greater demand, about the same, or less demand five years from now?

Entering the Internet

Y ou're already well aware of the vast information and research possibilities available on the Internet and the World Wide Web. To initiate research on a potential franchise, try searching keywords or topics using any of the Web search tools such as Yahoo, Lycos, or WebCrawler (described in Chapter 3). In Yahoo, under the Business and Economy category/Small Business Information, you'll also find a link to additional franchise information called FranNet. FranNet (address: http://www.frannet.com) can provide you with information to help you select the right franchise. Franchise Handbook On-Line is a comprehensive franchise directory devoted to providing useful information about franchising opportunities and franchising companies. Franchise Handbook On-Line address is: http://www.franchise1.com. Additional information on franchises can be found by doing a key word search using "franchise" on any of the popular search engines.

You might also want to check out the Better Business Bureau's Web site (found at: http://www.bbb.org/bbb). At this site, you'll find a publications directory, membership list, and contact information for Better Business Bureaus nationwide. You can also access the bureau's newsletter, check the scam alerts, and even file a complaint online. Another source of franchise information is the Institute of Management and Administration's page, which provides links to hundreds of other business sites, including many industry-specific resources (address:http://ioma.com/ioma). *Sources: Jenny McCune and Leslie Jay, "The Source," Success (October 1995), pp. 43–48; and Phaedra Hise, "Click Here for Business Help," Inc. (November 1995), p. 101.*

4. What competition already exists in your territory for the product or service you contemplate selling?
   a. Nonfranchise firms?
   b. Franchise firms?

Disclosure Statements

disclosure statement Information that franchisors are required to provide to potential franchisees.

Franchisors are required by the Federal Trade Commission (FTC) to provide **disclosure statements** to prospective or actual franchisees. Comparing disclosure statements from each franchise you are considering will help you identify risks, fees, benefits, and restrictions involved. Disclosure statements identify and provide information on 20 items. (See Figure 5-4.)

The franchisor. Information identifying the franchisor and its affiliates and describing their business experience.

Business experience of the franchisor. Information identifying and describing the business experience of each of the franchisor's officers, directors, and management personnel responsible for franchise services, training, and other aspects of the franchises in the franchise program.

Litigation. A description of the lawsuits in which the franchisor and its officers, directors, and management personnel have been involved.

Sell Ice Cream in Alaska? Yeah, Right.

Some good ideas may not always appear so good at first glance, a point that Julia and Eric Henderson will tell you. The success of their Baskin-Robbins ice-cream store in Wasilla, Alaska seems to defy logic. The Hendersons don't know why their Alaskan neighbors like ice cream so much, even when the mercury in the thermometer takes a nose-dive—but apparently they do. Julia thinks all the snow reminds people of ice cream. Since there is not much to do in the winter if you don't ski, the shop gives the people in the town of 4,000 a place to socialize.

Eric is the principal in the local middle school. Julia ran a restaurant with her sister before deciding she wanted to open a BR. "Initially, Baskin-Robbins was skeptical about selling ice cream to Alaskans," Eric says. But demographic research showed serious growth potential. Wasilla has twice as many kindergartners and first-graders than high school seniors. That statistic showed the Hendersons that there was a real potential for growth. It was also a good indicator of their target market—kids everywhere love ice cream, no matter what the temperature. Revenue for the first six months of operation was projected to be $250,000, 72 percent above initial expectations.

Source: Adapted from Meg Whittemore, "Winds of Change in Franchising," Nation's Business (January 1994), pp. 49–55

Bankruptcy. Information about any previous bankruptcies in which the franchisor and its officers, director, and management personnel have been involved in the past 15 years.

Initial fee. Information about the initial franchise fee and other initial payments that are required to obtain the franchise. The franchisor must also tell how your fee will be used and whether you must pay in one lump sum or if you can pay in installments. If every franchisee does not pay the same amount, the franchisor must describe the formula for calculating the initial fee.

Other fees. A description of the continuing payments franchisees are required to make after the franchise opens and the conditions to receive refunds.

Estimate of total initial investment. The franchisor must provide a high-range and a low-range estimate of your startup costs. Included expenses would cover real estate, equipment and other fixed assets, inventory, deposits, and working capital.

Purchase obligations. Information about any restrictions on the quality of goods and services used in the franchise and where they may be purchased, including restrictions requiring purchases from the franchisor or its affiliates.

Financial assistance available. Terms and conditions of any assistance available from the franchisor or its affiliates in financing the purchase of the franchise.

Product or service restrictions. A description of restrictions on the goods or services franchisees are permitted to sell. This could include whether you are required to carry the franchisor's full line of products or if you can supplement them with other products.

TABLE OF CONTENTS

Section

1. Franchisor and Any Predecessors
2. Identity and Business Experience of Persons Affiliated with the Franchisor
3. Litigation
4. Bankruptcy
5. Developer's/Franchisee's Initial Franchise Fee or Other Initial Payment
6. Other Fees
7. Franchisee's Initial Investment
8. Obligation of Franchisee to Purchase or Lease from Designated Sources
9. Obligations of Franchisee to Purchase or Lease in Accordance with Specifications or from Approved Suppliers
10. Financing Arrangements
11. Obligations of the Franchisor: Other Supervision, Assistance or Services
12. Exclusive Area or Territory
13. Trademarks, Tradenames, and Service Marks
14. Patents and Copyrights
15. Obligation of Franchisee to Participate in the Actual Operation of the Business
16. Restrictions on Goods and Services Offered by Developer/Franchisee
17. Renewal, Termination, Repurchase, Modification, and Assignment of the Franchise Agreement and Related Information
18. Arrangements with Public Figures
19. Statement of per Franchise Average Gross Sales and Ranges of Gross Sales for the Year Ended Month, Day, Year
20. Other Franchises of the Franchisor
21. Financial Statements
22. Contracts

EXHIBIT A	Franchise Agreement
EXHIBIT B	Area Development Agreement
EXHIBIT C	Preliminary Agreement
EXHIBIT D	Royalty Incentive Rider
EXHIBIT E	Disclosure Acknowledgment Statement
EXHIBIT F	List of Franchisees as of Month, Day, Year
EXHIBIT G	List of Franchisees Who Have Ceased Doing Business in the One (1) Year Period Immediately Preceding Month, Day, Year
EXHIBIT H	Financial Statements of Franchisor

FIGURE 5-4
Franchise Disclosure Statement
The table of contents from a disclosure statement includes information about the franchisor. The entire document can be several hundred pages long. As a prospective franchisee, you would want to read the document carefully and to consult a lawyer to review the Franchise Agreement.

Exclusive territory. A description of any territorial protection or restrictions on the customers with whom the franchisee may deal. Recently franchisees of Subway Sandwiches have alleged that the franchisor has placed franchises too close together and overlapped territories.[9] This practice cuts into the sales volume and market size of individual stores.

Renewal, termination, or assignment of franchise agreement. A description of the conditions under which the franchise may be repurchased or refused renewal by the franchisor, transferred to a third party by the franchisee, and terminated or modified by either party.

Training provided. A description of the training program provided to franchisees including location, length and content of training, cost of program, who pays for travel and lodging, and any additional or refresher courses available.

Public figure arrangements. A disclosure of any involvement by celebrities or public figures in promoting the franchise. If celebrities are involved, you need

Small Business IN THE Service Industry

Providing excellent training in all areas of operating a franchise is not only one of the benefits of franchising, it's an absolute necessity for both franchisor and franchisee to succeed. For a service franchise, training in outstanding customer service is one of the most important topics to be covered. American Leak Detection is a company which looks for leaks of any type in businesses and homes and corrects them. When the company, based in Palm Springs, California, began franchising in the mid-1980s, founder and president Dick Rennick recognized how important it was to provide franchisees with a strong program of customer service training. "We're a lot more high tech than baking a cookie. We have to make sure the customer is treated properly." The company's training program for franchisees is intense. It's six weeks long, 50 hours a week. And during five of those weeks new franchisees are out in the field actually going to job sites around the country. This hands-on training is followed by a 90-day home-study program. The benefit of this type of extensive customer service training is the payoff in satisfied customers whose demands for the services provided by American Leak Detection continue to grow. *Source: Echo Montgomery Garrett, "Why Franchising Works: Training and Support,"* Inc. *(September 1995), pp. 88–95.*

to be told if they are involved in actual management and how they are being compensated.

Site selection. A description of any assistance in selecting a site for the franchise that will be provided by the franchisor. Some franchises like McDonald's

Computer Applications

Many franchisors utilize technology to help support their franchisees. Take, for instance, American Leak Detection of Palm Springs, California, which looks for leaks of any type in businesses and homes and corrects them. The company maintains a database on unusual jobs done by its franchisees so it can immediately refer a franchisee to someone who has experience with a specific or unique type of problem. Franchise operations Fastsigns and PostNet both use electronic mail (e-mail) to provide their franchisees with instant access to franchise headquarters for seeking help and advice. People at headquarters use e-mail to keep franchisees up-to date on the latest technology that could help them run their businesses more efficiently and effectively.

Source: Echo Montgomery Garrett, "Why Franchising Works: Training and Support," Inc. *(September 1995), pp. 88–95.*

complete all site analysis and make all location decisions without input from franchisees. Others give franchisees complete discretion in site selection.

Information about franchisees. You will receive information about the present number of franchises; the number of new franchises projected; how many have been terminated, chose not to renew, or repurchased. Franchisors must give you the names, addresses, and phone numbers of all franchisees located in your state—contact several of them.

Franchisor financial statements. The audited financial statements of the franchisors are included to show you the financial condition of the company.

Personal participation of franchisees. A description of the extent to which franchisees must personally participate in the operation of the franchise. Some permit franchisees to own the franchise, yet hire a manager to run the business. Others require franchisees to be personally involved.

Earning capacity. A complete statement of the basis for any earnings claims made to the franchisee, including the percentage of existing franchises that have actually achieved the results that are claimed. Franchisors do not have to make any projections of what a franchisee may earn, but if they do, they must also describe the basis and assumptions used to make claims.

Use of intellectual property. The franchisor must describe your use of its trademarks, trade names, logos, or other symbols. You should receive full use of them since they are a lot of the value of a franchise.[10]

The FTC revised the Uniform Franchise Offering Circular (UFOC) in the spring of 1994. The changes were made to replace much of the "legalese" wording of disclosure statements with plain English and to provide more standardized information for comparing franchises.[11]

The Franchise Agreement

franchise agreement The legal contract which binds both parties involved in the franchise.

The **franchise agreement** is a document that spells out the rights and obligations of both parties in a franchise. It is a contract defining the precise, detailed conditions of the legal relationship between the franchisee and the franchisor. Its length, terms, and complexity will vary from one franchise and industry to another in order to maintain the delicate balance of power between franchisees and franchisors.[12] It may or may not be possible for you to negotiate the contents of the contract, depending on how long the franchisor has been established and the current market conditions.

You should remember that the franchisor wrote the contract and most of the conditions contained in it are weighted in the franchisor's favor. Read it carefully yourself, but never sign a franchise agreement without getting your lawyer's opinion. Some of the most important topics that you should understand in franchise agreements are fees to be paid, how the agreement can be terminated or renewed, and your rights to exclusive territory.

franchise fee The one-time payment made to become a franchisee.

royalty fee The ongoing payments that franchisees pay to franchisors—usually a percentage of gross sales.

Franchise, Royalty, and Advertising Fees. The **franchise fee** is the amount of money you have to pay to become a franchisee. Some agreements require you to have a percentage of the total franchise fee from a nonborrowed source, meaning you can't borrow it. Agreements may or may not allow you to form a corporation to avoid personal liability.

Royalty fees are usually a percentage of gross sales that you pay to the franchisor. Remember that royalties are calculated from gross sales, not from

M anager's Notebook

Communication Is the Key

The franchisor-franchisee relationship is unique in the world of business. Jan Kirkham and Timothy McGowan of Management 2000, a franchise consulting firm, have examined hundreds of franchises at every stage of development and have concluded that most problems between franchisors and franchisees result from misunderstandings about their relationship. Often neither fully understands what is expected of the other. They recommend that franchisors communicate the following points to franchisees:

- Unit-to-unit consistency is imperative to the success of franchising. Each franchise must look, act, and feel like all the others to the customers. Lack of consistency dilutes the investment made by all franchisees in the system because uniformity is a large part of what they are buying.

- Franchisees are not competitors, even if they are located in the same market. All parties involved in the agreement need to work as a team to develop the franchise name. An advantage that franchises have over independent businesses is the *synergy* that is created in a strong franchise system. Synergy exists when the total output is greater than the sum of the individual inputs; that is, 2 + 2 = 5.

- The franchisor and franchisee have an interdependent relationship. Each side must accept responsibility and accountability for the success of the system. The franchisor is not responsible to make the franchisee successful. Effort and trust must flow in both directions.

- The franchisee must understand the purpose of the initial franchise fee and the ongoing royalty fees. The initial franchise fee protects the franchisee by covering the expenses of selecting quality franchisees, training and support of franchisees prior to opening, covering costs of developing and organizing the franchise and related systems, paying for trademark and trade name registration and protection, and ensuring compliance with various laws. The royalty fees are paid from revenue generated because the use of the franchisor's brand name attracts customers and the operating system gets customers to come back, while the support services provided by the franchisor help the franchisee acquire and develop the ability to use the brand name and operating system to get and keep customers.

Source: Adapted from Jan Kirkham and Timothy McGowan, "Strengthening and Supporting the Franchise System," The Franchising Handbook (New York: AMACOM American Management Association, 1993), p. 297.

profits. If your business generates $350,000 of sales and the royalty fee is 8 percent, you have to pay $28,000 to the franchisor whether you make a profit or not. And you still have all your other operating expenses to cover.

When comparing two franchises, look at the combination of franchise fees and royalties. For example, franchise X charges $25,000 for the franchise fee and 10 percent royalty (not including advertising fees), and franchise Y charges $37,500 franchise fee with 5 percent royalty (no advertising fees either). Assume that gross sales for each franchise would be $250,000 per year. The total fee you would pay for either would be $50,000 for the first year. But for each year after the first, you would pay $25,000 ($250,000 × 10%) with franchise X, and only half that with franchise Y ($250,000 × 5%).

If the franchise agreement requires you to pay advertising fees, you want to be sure that a portion of the fee goes to local advertising in your area. If you operate a franchise on the outer geographic fringe of the franchise's operations, the franchisor could spend all of your advertising dollars where there is a greater concentration of other franchises, but none of *your* customers.

When it comes to total fees in franchising, you generally get what you pay for and if a deal looks too good to be true (unlimited potential earnings with no risk), it probably is.[13]

Termination of the Franchise Agreement. The agreement should state how you as the franchisee may lose your franchise rights. Also described should be the franchisee's obligations if you choose to terminate the agreement. Make sure the franchisor must have to show "good cause" to terminate the agreement. Since some states require this clause, it means there must be a good reason to discontinue the deal.

Terms and Renewal of Agreement. This section identifies how long the agreement is in effect and the renewal process. Most franchises run from five to fifteen years. Will you have to pay a renewal fee, or possibly worse, negotiate a whole new franchise agreement? Since fees and royalties are generally higher for well-established franchises, your royalties and fees would probably go up if you have to sign a new agreement in ten years from now.

Exclusive Territory. You need to know the geographical size of the territory and the exclusive rights the franchisee would have. Franchisors may identify how many franchises a territory can support without oversaturation and issue that many, regardless of specific locations. Rights of first refusal, advertising restrictions, and performance quotas for the territory are addressed in this section.[14]

This issue led Allen Whitehead to eventually sue the company he had once loved—McDonald's. Whitehead was proud of his McDonald's located in a low-income area of Hartford in 1983. The enterprise was an immediate hit with sales jumping well above the national average to a peak of $2.3 million by 1986. Then in 1987 McDonald's opened another site 2.5 miles away from Whitehead's location, and four more nearby soon after. Whitehead's sales fell to $1.5 million annually. What upsets Whitehead the most is that he did not have an opportunity to purchase the new location on what he considered to be reasonable terms. Now he advises new franchisees, "Remember the franchisor is in the business of maximizing his revenues, even if that means saturating your market with competing stores."[15]

In reviewing the franchise opportunity, a potential franchisee should gather and verify the accuracy of the information included in the franchise agreement and all other information provided by the franchisor. This process is called **due diligence.** It means doing your homework and investigating the franchise on your own, rather than accepting everything the franchisor says at face value. This is a big commitment—investigate. Some information you can find yourself, some you will need professional assistance to gather and interpret.

due diligence The process of thoroughly investigating the accuracy of information before signing a franchise (or any other) agreement.

Get Professional Advice

Consult a lawyer and a CPA *before* you sign any franchise agreement. Ask your accountant to read the financial data in the company's disclosure statements to determine if the franchisor would be able to meet its obligation to you if you buy

Cookie Cutter Franchising

If one franchise is good, then two must be better, three would be great, and so on . . . Right? Maybe. That's the way Richard Schuman thinks and he is not alone. Schuman is the area representative for 28 MotoPhoto franchises in the Washington, DC area. Schuman is practicing what is called *multiple-unit franchising* (MUF). MUF is an increasing trend in franchising as a way for franchisees to own or manage more than one franchise unit.

For franchisors, multiple-unit franchising is a way to expand efficiently and rapidly on a domestic or global scale. Many franchise companies have some kind of MUF program, of which there are three basic types:

1. *Area Developers*. Under this type of MUF, franchisees have the right to open and operate outlets within a specified geographical area. They do not sell franchises or offer direct support (the franchisors still do that). Their job is to sell new franchises and open a target number of new stores within a specified time.

2. *Subfranchisors*. Subfranchisors provide the same services as area developers, plus they sell franchises and provide management and other support to franchisees. Individual franchisees deal directly with the franchisor after signing the franchise agreement. In return for their services, the subfranchisors get a percentage of the franchise fee and of the royalty fees.

3. *Area Representatives*. This type of MUF places the area representative as a liaison between the franchisee and the franchisor. The area rep provides all the support and duties of the franchisor for a percentage of each franchise's fees and royalties. Individual franchisees do not deal directly with the franchisor, but with their area representative.

MotoPhoto has been selling its photo-finishing franchise territories to area representatives like Schuman since 1982. Their nine area reps oversee 329 franchises in the United States. Sales for 1992 were $101 million. Michael Adler, president of MotoPhoto, states that area reps give franchisees "on-the-ground contact from the corporate office" when problems arise. MotoPhoto area representatives feel that they can handle those problems more efficiently, since they know their specific areas better than someone in headquarters and because they have a direct financial interest in the success of their franchisees.

Source: Adapted from Meg Whittemore and Robert Perry, "Multiple-Unit Franchising," Nation's Business (July 1993), pp. 53–55.

a franchise. Then ask a lawyer who is familiar with franchise law to inform you of all of your rights and obligations contained in the franchise agreement—it *is* negotiable, but you have to push. Query your lawyer about any state or local laws that would affect your franchise. The cost of consulting professionals is small compared to the amount of time and money you will invest in a franchise. Do not assume that the disclosure statement tells you everything you need to know about the franchise. That is not the intent of the document.

International Franchising

Overseas franchising has become a major activity for U.S. companies faced with constantly increasing levels of domestic competition. Companies like KFC, Pizza Hut, and Taco Bell are signing almost no new franchises but are still rapidly adding foreign operations.[16]

In contrast to the comment of Allen Whitehead, McDonald's franchisee quoted in the previous section, Ray Kroc, who built McDonald's into a franchise giant once said, "Saturation is for sponges." What Kroc is saying is that by expanding less crowded or underserved markets, you can increase sales and profits.

Canada is a growing market for U.S. franchises because it is close and its markets are similar. With the passage of the North America Free Trade Agreement (NAFTA), franchise opportunities in Mexico are expected to increase. For example, TCBY Enterprises is quickly opening stores in Mexico after the agreement ended the 20 percent import duty on yogurt going into Mexico.[17] European (both Eastern and Western) and Pacific Rim countries (especially Taiwan, Thailand, Indonesia, and Singapore) are also attractive for franchise expansion. (See Figure 5-5.) When expanding abroad, franchisors must be sensitive to the demographic, economic, cultural, and legal climates of the host country.[18]

FIGURE 5-5
International Franchising
More U.S. franchisors are attracted to foreign markets to increase their sales and profits.
Source: Franchising in the Economy, *International Franchise Association, Washington, D.C., 1990, p. 99.*

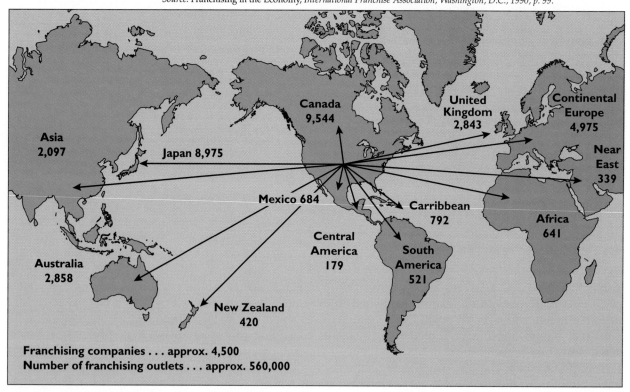

Global Small Business

The prospects for franchising on a global basis seem great. But tapping into this vast potential market means understanding how to establish units in unfamiliar locations with different laws, customs, and cultures thousands of miles away. One person facing that challenge is Terry Shores, president of Chico's Tacos, based in Temecula, California. In October 1995, he opened his first overseas store in Cairo, Egypt. Shores's approach to entering the new and unfamiliar market is one used by the vast majority of U.S. franchisors. He found and trained a "master franchisee" in Egypt who was an experienced businessperson, had access to needed capital, and who also thoroughly understood the local laws and marketplace. This master franchisee then bought the rights to develop Chico's Tacos units in that country. By using this approach, Shores assured himself of having someone in charge who was familiar both with his product and operations and the local market, and someone who was committed to seeing the venture succeed. As the prospects for growth and profits continue to escalate, we're going to see more and more franchisors move into overseas markets. *Sources: "Franchising Systems Around the Globe: A Status Report,"* Journal of Small Business Management *(April 1995), pp. 80–87; Mary E. Tomzack, "Ripe New Markets,"* Success *(April 1995), pp. 73–77; and Roberta Maynard, "Why Franchisors Look Abroad,"* Nation's Business *(October 1995), pp. 65–72.*

Summary

◼ What *franchising* is and how it operates.

Franchising is a legal agreement that allows a franchisee to use a product, service, or method of the franchisor in exchange for fees and royalties. A franchisee is an independent businessperson who agrees to operate under the policies and procedures set up by the franchisor.

◼ The difference between product (or trade name) franchises and business-format franchises.

Product or trade name franchises allow the franchisee to purchase the right to use the trade name of the manufacturer, and to buy or sell the manufacturer's products. Business-format franchises allow the franchisee to duplicate the franchisor's way of doing business.

◼ The advantages and disadvantages of franchising.

Five major advantages of franchising exist for the franchisee: proven product or service, technical or managerial assistance, less operating capital needed, quality control standards, and opportunity for growth. The primary disadvantages to the franchisee include: fees and profit sharing, restrictions of freedom, overdependence, unsatisfied expectations, termination of the agreement, and performance of other franchisees.

◼ The franchisor–franchisee relationship.

For a franchise to be successful, unit-to-unit consistency of quality is essential. If one franchisee is lax in standards, all other franchisees and the franchisor can be damaged. Franchisees are not competitors, but all franchisees and the franchisor are a team. Franchisors and franchisees are mutually dependent upon each other and if they work together, all can benefit.

■ Evaluating the franchise opportunity.

When evaluating a franchise opportunity, send for a copy of the company's disclosure statement (the company is required to send it to you), research the company through business periodicals, talk to current and former franchisees, and check with the International Franchise Association.

■ Franchising in the international marketplace.

Franchises are rapidly exploring international expansion when faced with saturated domestic markets. Foreign markets are often less crowded and underserved.

Questions for Review and Discussion

1. What is the difference between a franchise, a franchisee, and a franchisor?
2. How would you explain the difference between franchises and other forms of business ownership?
3. Why would you prefer to buy a franchise rather than start a new business or buy an existing business?
4. Why is franchising important in today's economy?
5. What is the difference between product or trade name franchises and business-format franchises? Give an example for each that has not been cited in the text.
6. Since you have read about entrepreneurship in Chapter 2, would you consider someone who buys a franchise an entrepreneur? Explain your answer.
7. What is the biggest advantage and the biggest disadvantage of franchising? Justify your answer.
8. What do you expect to get in return for paying a franchise fee?
9. What is a royalty fee?
10. Is the disclosure statement the *only* source of information you need to check out a potential franchise? Why or why not?
11. In reading topics included in a franchise agreement, who do you think controls most of the power in a franchise, the franchisee or the franchisor? Explain.
12. What are the potential sources of conflict between franchisees and franchisors?
13. You are worried that someone else will buy a specific franchise in your area before you do. Would it be alright to sign the franchise agreement before talking to your lawyer or accountant if you intend to meet with them later? Explain.
14. If you are the franchisee of a book store and you are offered twice the business's book value, should you or the franchisor collect the additional money? Take a position and justify it.
15. What do you think will be the growth areas (in products, services, and geographical areas) for franchises in the near future?

Critical Incident

Say you're convinced that purchasing a franchise is your method of choice for becoming a small business owner. Before you jump in, though, you'd better do your homework. For this exercise, we'll first present some basic information about two possible franchise operations. Then it's your turn!

Snip 'N Clip (SNC Franchise Corporation). This franchisor began business in 1958 and started franchising in 1985. Its business is providing all kinds of hair care procedures. There are 84 locations throughout the United States, 43 of which are owned by franchisees. The initial franchise fee is $10,000 and total investment ranges from $50,950 to $58,450. The company doesn't offer financing.

Applebee's Neighborhood Grill & Bar (Applebee's International Inc.). This franchisor began business in 1987 and started franchising in 1988. Applebee's is a full-service restaurant and bar. There are 603 locations globally, of which 486 are owned by franchisees. The initial franchise fee is $35,000 with total investment forecasted from $1,700,000 to $3,100,000. The company doesn't offer financing.
Sources: "The 6th Annual Franchise Gold 100," Success (November 1995), pp. 87–119.

Questions

1. Of the two franchises presented, draft a business plan outline for the one that you would be interested in.
2. Divide the class into teams to discuss the merits and potential drawbacks of each of these franchises.

Take it to the Net

We invite you to visit the Hatten page on the Prentice Hall Web site at: http://www.prenhall.com/~hattensb for this chapter's World Wide Web exercise.

Chapter Focus

After reading this chapter, you should be able to:

- Compare the advantages and disadvantages of buying an existing business.
- Propose ways of locating a suitable business for sale.
- Determine why a business would be sold.
- Identify ways to measure the condition of a business.
- Differentiate tangible and nontangible assets and assess the value of each.
- Calculate the price to pay for a business.
- Describe what makes a family business different from other types of business.

6 Taking Over an Existing Business

HIS TRAINING AT A MILITARY intelligence school in the 1970s and a three-year stint as a military attaché (or spy) prepared Don Logan well for entrepreneurial life. The three ways he learned to get information—through elicitation, observation, and penetration—were indispensable to him once he decided to go into business for himself by buying an established company.

The company Logan bought, Trinity Communications, was originally the corporate communications department of The New England Insurance Company (TNE), and Logan was department head. In fact, Logan had built the department into a company model, overseeing the computerization of all systems, instituting time reports and detailed financial analyses, and arranging training for employees in public speaking, business fundamentals, and other fields. In July 1992, TNE asked Logan and other department heads to find ways to cut costs and reduce overhead. Realizing that the company would just as soon sell his division as keep it, he decided to take it off their hands.

With the full approval of his employer, Logan began conducting research on how he might operate the department as an independent company.

Despite his intimate familiarity with the department's operations, Logan had to do just as much research as any other would-be entrepreneur who wanted to buy a business. After all, he'd be leaving the security and comfort of the corporate cocoon and facing the world alone. That's where his intelligence training came in. Logan attacked the situation like a military assignment.

To elicit information from the various corporate units he had done business with, Logan used his best spy techniques. "Elicitation," Logan says, "is simply getting information out of people without them knowing you're trying to get it." He asked managers about their problems and whether they thought an outside firm could help them with solutions.

Next he engaged in reconnaissance—gathering information by observation. He found a small company nearby that had also started as a corporate spin off. Logan spent several days talking with the individual who oversaw that effort and got his advice and suggestions.

Now Logan was ready to penetrate. Working with a corporate ally—his boss, TNE's senior marketing officer—Logan decided that the key to a successful launch was to create a business plan "that would enable the new entity to be in business instantly." He developed a proposal that demonstrated the economic viability of the breakaway company, Trinity Communications, and also showed TNE how it would realize cost savings with no loss of quality. The mission was successful and Logan purchased the breakaway company.

Trinity Communications has been operating as an independent company since January 1, 1993. Its revenues in 1993 were $3.5 million with pretax profits of $700,000. In 1994, revenues had increased to $4.5 million with pretax profits of $1 million. And 1995 revenues were projected at $5.3 million. Trinity has also moved out of its corporate parent's shadow. TNE business accounted for 75 percent of Trinity's business in 1993, half of its revenues in 1994, and should be only around 25 percent of 1995 revenues. But, as Dan Logan will readily tell you, he had to do his homework before even thinking about acquiring and running his own business. *Source: Alessandra Bianchi, "Breaking Away," Inc. (November 1995), pp. 36–41.*

The Business Buyout Alternative

Say you are a prospective small business owner. You possess the necessary personal qualities, managerial ability, and capital to run a business, but you have not decided on the approach you should take to get into business. If you are not inheriting a family business, then you have three choices to getting started: You may buy out an existing establishment, acquire a franchised business, or start a new firm yourself. This chapter will discuss the many factors to be considered in buying an existing business and taking over a family business.

Advantages of Buying a Business

The opportunity to buy a firm already in operation appears attractive for a number of reasons. Like a franchise, it offers a way to avoid some beginner's hazards.[1] The existing firm is already functioning—maybe even a proven success. Many of the typical serious problems should either have been avoided or corrected by now. It appears to be like a ship after its "shakedown cruise," a new automobile after the usual small adjustments have been made, or a computer program that has been "debugged."

Buying an existing business is becoming a more popular way for people to own a small business. In 1993, over 250,000 businesses valued at less than $5 million each changed hands.[2]

There are several advantages to buying an existing business when compared with the other methods of getting into business. Since customers are used to doing business with the company at its present address, they are likely to continue doing so once you take over. If the business has been making money, you will break even sooner than if you start your own business from the ground up. Your planning for an ongoing business can be based on actual historical figures, rather than relying on projections as with a startup. Your inventory, equipment, and suppliers are already in place, managed by employees who already know how to keep the business going. Financing may be available from the owner. If the timing of the deal occurs when you are ready to buy a business and the owner needs to sell for a legitimate reason, you may get a bargain. (See Table 6-1.)

Disadvantages of Buying a Business

Or is this business that you are considering, in fact, more like a used car that is a "lemon?" Most people do not sell their cars until they feel they need considerable mechanical attention. Is the same true when selling businesses?

There are disadvantages to buying an existing business as a way to become your own boss. The image of the business already exists and it is difficult to

Existing businesses must be scrutinized carefully to determine if they are a worthy investment of your time and money.

TABLE 6 ▪ 1   The Advantages and Disadvantages of Buying a Business

ADVANTAGES	DISADVANTAGES
1. Customers familiar with location	1. Image difficult to change
2. Planning can be based on known historical data	2. Employees may be ones whom you would not choose
3. Established customer base at present location	3. Business may not have operated the way you like and could be difficult to change
4. Supplier relationships already in place	4. Possible obsolete inventory and equipment
5. Inventory and equipment in place	5. The business's location may be undesirable—or a good location may be about to become not so good
6. Experienced employees	6. Potential liability for past business contracts
7. Possible owner financing	7. Financing costs could drain your cash flow and threaten the business's survival

R eality Check

Entrepreneurs Who Don't Start at the Beginning

A new facet of entrepreneurship is evolving as the current generation of entrepreneurs is looking to buy rather than start companies.

Clay Teramo has been starting and selling businesses since he founded Computer Media Technology, Inc. (CMT) in 1984. Selling magnetic recording media for computers, CMT grew so quickly it made the *Inc.* 500 two years in a row. Teramo found the startup to be both scary and thrilling. But once the company was established, he found running it to be boring. Teramo looked for a buyer. He stated, "The business was just perking along wonderfully, and if I were 50 years old, that's where I'd want to be. But I'm only 31—I want the juice, I want to build again. The fun part for me is to start something new." Teramo's intent is to become a buyout entrepreneur—find a business, make it successful, then find someone to buy it.

Phillip Harris, Dorothy Serdenis, and H. Michael Stevens are all buyout entrepreneurs who specialize in purchasing existing businesses. Let's look at their backgrounds, what they consider their ideal purchase, businesses they would consider, what they would pay, where they get financing, and opportunities they have spotted.

Phillip H. Harris, 47. Career Highlights: Xerox, 14 years; Wang, 5 years

Ideal Acquisition: An industrial products distributor or light manufacturer that needs sales and marketing expertise, with at least $10 million in sales.

Would Look At: Any industrial products company ("I don't know anything about consumer goods").

Willing To Pay: Up to five times earnings before interest and taxes.

Primary Source of Equity: Hambro International Venture Fund.

change. The employees who come with the business may not be the ones whom you would choose to hire. The previous owners have established precedents that may be difficult to change. The way the business operates may be outmoded. The inventory or equipment may be outdated. The purchase price may create a burden on future cash flow and profitability. You may pay too much for the business due to misrepresentation or inaccurate appraisal. The business's facilities or location may not be the best. You may be held liable for contracts left over from previous owners.

How Do You Find A Business For Sale?

If you have decided that you are interested in purchasing an existing business and have narrowed your choices down to a few types of businesses to consider, how do you locate one to buy? Perhaps you are currently employed by a small business. Is there a chance that it may be available some time soon? Since you know the inner workings of the business, it might be a good place to start. Newspaper advertising is a traditional place for someone who is actively trying to sell a business to start. Don't stop your quest with the newspaper, however, because many good opportunities don't get advertised. Word of mouth through friends

Opportunity Spotted: "A lot of low-tech companies aren't well managed and don't understand marketing. They don't employ multiple distribution channels or costing methods that allow them to look at profits by channel. Most of the owners don't even have a computer on their desks. Good management, marketing, systems—that's the value I can bring."

Dorothy Serdenis, 45. Career Highlights: Municipal government, 10 years; Merrill Lynch, 10 years

Ideal Acquisition: "Anything really—provided the challenges were interesting and the personal chemistry was right."

Would Look At: Retail businesses; manufacturers of retail products with $50 million in sales.

Willing To Pay: Up to $10 million.

Primary Source of Equity: Savings; other private investors.

Opportunity Spotted: "I want a business where I can see real value. For instance, as the population ages there will be a greater need for products and services that help older people. That's going to create a demand for businesses in health care, for instance. As a buyer, you can see the trend and you can see real value."

H. Michael Stevens, 39. Career Highlights: IBM, 2 years; Summa Four Inc., a startup telecommunications company, 7 years

Ideal Acquisition: Family-owned light manufacturing company, $3 million to $20 million in sales.

Would Look At: Corporate subsidiaries.

Willing To Pay: Three to six times pretax earnings, up to $20 million.

Primary Source of Equity: Investment partnership.

Opportunity Spotted: "Family-owned companies frequently haven't reached their potential. The owners have been taking a lot of money out; now they're getting on, and they don't want to risk their capital base to take the company to the next stage. They usually have good management. But they just don't have the horsepower to tackle that next step."

Source: John Case, "Buy Now—Avoid the Rush," Inc. (February 1991), pp. 36–45.

and family may turn up businesses that don't appear to be available through formal channels.

People who counsel small businesses on a regular basis, such as bankers, lawyers, accountants, and Small Business Administration representatives, can be good sources of finding firms for sale. Real estate brokers often have listings for business opportunities which include real estate and buildings.

Don't overlook a direct approach to finding a business. If you have been a regular customer of an establishment and have an attraction to it, why not politely ask the owner if he or she has ever thought of selling it? The timing may be perfect if the owner is considering a move to another part of the country or is exploring another new business. Perhaps this is an unlikely way to find a business, but what do you have to lose by asking?

Nearly every city has one or more **business brokers.** Most inspect and appraise a business establishment offered for sale before listing and advertising it. Some also assist a buyer in financing the purchase, but not all of them will provide you with the same level of service. A few will work very hard for you in trying to find a business that matches your talents and needs. Most will tell you what is available at the moment, but not much more than that. Some will do you more harm than good. Remember, business brokers normally receive their commission from the seller, so their loyalty is to the seller—not to you.

business broker A business which brings sellers of their businesses together with potential buyers.

Don't overlook the direct approach to finding a business for sale. If you are attracted to a business where you have been a customer, why not politely ask the owner if he or she has thought of selling?

Unfortunately for prospective buyers, however, something approaching a "business opportunities racket" has developed in many cities—the practice of selling unprofitable businesses to unwary buyers who are usually inexperienced in running a business. The ruse is most common in the retail field, where a single business unit can wreck a dozen or more owners through successive sales and re-sales to a steady stream of newcomers, each confident that he or she can succeed where others have failed. Naturally, the brokers who promote these sales make more commission the more frequently the business changes hands. Check with bankers, accountants, or other businesspeople who have used the broker in the past for recommendations. You need to be on guard to keep from being included among that group immortalized by the late P. T. Barnum, who said, "There's a sucker born every minute."

Brokers take classes and pass examinations to become certified business intermediaries (CBI). To find a reliable business broker, contact the International Business Brokers Association (118 Silver Hill Road, Concord, MA 01742, (508) 369-5254).

Entering the Internet

To examine the ins and outs of buying an existing business, there are a couple of unique information sources on the Internet that you might find useful. One of these is the World M&A Network (found at: http://raptor.cqi.com/MandA/). This site contains hundreds of listings of companies for sale, possible merger candidates, and corporate buyers. (The only possible drawback is that this network focuses on mid-sized companies.) Another source is the National SBDC (Small Business Development Center) Research Network (found at http://www.smallbiz.sunycentral.edu/). This site provides information to Small Business Development Centers about small business and entrepreneurial opportunities. And don't forget to link to the Better Business Bureau (http://www.bbb.org/bbb) to check the business scams that are currently described.

What Do You Look for in a Business?

To successfully analyze the value of any business, you should have enough experience to recognize specific details that are most relevant in this type of business. You need enough knowledge to take information provided by sales, personnel, or financial records and evaluate the past performance of the business and predict probable future developments. You need objectivity in order to avoid excess enthusiasm that might blind you to the facts. Don't let emotions cloud your decisions.

At a minimum, you should ask the following questions to gather information about the business you consider buying:

- How long has the business existed?
    Who founded it?
    How many owners has it had?
    Why have others sold out?

Manager's Notebook

Look Before You Leap

Businesses constantly change hands and have for hundreds of years. But the process of buying a business is no less confusing now than it ever has been. The following steps are a compilation of answers from experts in the business-selling world to questions like: How do I find the right company? How much should I pay for it? What should I watch for? The common thread that runs through the comments is that business buyers rarely think hard enough about the *real* personal and professional questions that they should be asking. The outcome of their search ends up focusing on timing and opportunity (read–"luck") instead of a clear understanding of the role the business will play in their life.

1. Make sure you shouldn't be starting a company instead of buying an existing business.
2. Determine the kind of business you want and whether you're capable of running it.
3. Consider the lifestyle involved in running your own business.
4. Consider the location. Where in the world, country, state, and town do you want to be for a long time?
5. After you've determined the kind of business you're after, find the right company.
6. Have lenders lined up in advance.
7. Choose the right seller. (If it's so great, why does the owner want out?)
8. Do research *before* setting the initial price.
9. Make sure your letter of intent is specific.
10. Don't skimp on due diligence.
11. Be skeptical.
12. Don't forget to assess the employees.
13. Make sure the final price reflects the real value.

Source: Jay Finegan, "The Insider's Guide," Inc. (October 1991), pp. 27–36.

- What is the profit record?
  Is profit increasing or decreasing?
  What are the true reasons for the increase or the decrease?
- What is the condition of the inventory?
  Are the goods new or obsolete?
- Is the equipment in good condition?
  Who owns it?
  Are there liens against any of it?
  How does it compare with competitors' equipment?
- How long does the lease run?
  Is it a satisfactory lease?
  What are its conditions?
  Can it be renewed?
- Are there dependable sources of supply?
  Are any franchises or other special arrangements expiring soon?
- What about present and future competition?
  Are new competitors or substitute materials or methods visible on the horizon?

- What is the condition of the area around the business?
  Are traffic routes or parking regulations likely to change?
- Does the present owner have family, religious, social, or political connections that have been important to the success of the business?
- Why does the present owner want to sell?
  Where will he or she go?
  What is he or she going to do?
  What do people (customers, suppliers, local citizens) think of the present owner and of the business?
- Are personnel satisfactory?
  Are key people willing to remain?
- How does this business, in its present condition, compare with one that you could start and develop yourself in a reasonable amount of time?[3]

General Considerations

If you aspire to entrepreneurship by buying out an existing business, do not be rushed into a deal. Talk with the firm's banker and verify account balances with its major customers and creditors. Be sure you get any verbal understanding in writing from the seller.

Put the earnest money in escrow with a reputable third party. Before an agreement to purchase is signed, have all papers checked by your accountant and attorney.

If the business you are buying involves inventory, you need to be familiar with the bulk sales provisions of the Uniform Commercial Code. The law varies from state to state, but it generally requires a seller to provide a list of all business creditors and amounts due to each buyer. Then you as the buyer must notify each creditor that the business is changing hands. This protects you from claims against the merchandise previously purchased.

Why Is the Business Being Sold?

When the owner of a business decides to sell it, the reasons the owner tells prospective buyers may be somewhat different from those known to the business community, and both of these may be somewhat different from the actual facts. There are just as many factors that could contribute to the sale of a business as there are reasons for business liquidations. Be careful: Business owners who are aware of future problems (such as losing a contract for a strong line of merchandise, or who know of a new law that will affect the business unfavorably) may not tell you all that they know. (As a prospective buyer, a discussion with the firm's customers and suppliers is recommended. Check with city planners about proposed changes in streets or routing of transportation lines that might have a serious effect upon the business in the near future.)

Although anyone can be misled or defrauded, a savvy business buyer with "business sense" will rely on his ability to analyze the market, judge the competitive situation, and estimate the profits that could be made from the business rather than rely upon the present owner's reasons for selling. These "reasons" are often too hard to verify.

Financial Condition

A study of the financial statements of the business will reveal how consistently the business has rewarded its previous owner's efforts. As a prospective purchaser, you must answer several questions. Will this income be satisfactory to you and your family? If it is not, could that income be increased? You will want to compare the firm's operating ratios with industry averages in order to detect where costs could be reduced or more money is needed.

The seller's books alone should not be taken as proof of stated sales or profits. You should also inspect bank deposits for at least five years or for as long as the business has been operated by the present owner.

When analyzing the financial statements of the business, don't rely strictly on the most recent year of operation. Profits can be artificially pumped up and expenses cut temporarily for almost every business. Check to see if the business employs the same number of people as in previous years, since most businesses can operate shorthanded for a while to cut labor expenses. Maintenance on equipment, vehicles, or the building can be cut to increase short-term profit figures. Profits that show on the books may also be overstated by insufficient write-off of bad debts, inventory shortages and obsolescence, and underdepreciation of the firm's fixed assets.

Ask to see the owner's tax returns. This shouldn't be a problem if everything is legitimate. Compare bills and receipts with sales tax receipts. Reconcile past purchases with sales and markup claimed. Make certain all back taxes have been paid. Make sure that interest payments and other current obligations are not in arrears.

Realize that the financial information that you need to analyze the business is sensitive information to the seller, especially if you two do not know each other. You can decrease the seller's suspicions about your using this information to aid a competing business or some other improper use by writing a letter of confidentiality.

Independent Audit. Before any serious discussion of purchasing a business occurs, an independent audit should be conducted. This will identify the condition of the financial statements. You will want to know if the business's accounting practices are legitimate, and if its valuation of inventory, equipment, and real estate is realistic.

Even audited statements need some subjective interpretation. For example, owners may underreport their income for tax reasons. A family member may be on the payroll and paid a salary although unneeded by the business. Business owners who use a company car or a credit card for nonbusiness purposes also misrepresent their business expenses.

The Profit Trend. Financial records of the business can tell you whether sales volume is increasing or decreasing. If it is going up, which departments or product lines account for the increased volume? Did the increased volume lead to increased profitability? Many businesses have failed by concentrating on selling volume goods at such low margins that making net profits was impossible.

If the sales volume is decreasing, is it due to the business's failure to keep up with competition or its inability to adjust to changing times? Or is the decline simply due to a lack of effective marketing?[4]

Interpret net profit of the business you are considering in terms of the amount of capital investment you will have to make in the business as well as

Manager's Notebook

Letter of Confidentiality

Houston Polson, CEO
Polson Product Company

Dear Mr. Polson:

It was a pleasure to talk with you last week concerning the possible purchase of your produce business. Our conversation has brought my interest in your business to the point that I would like to examine your financial records for the past five years. With the company records I also wish to see tax returns filed for that period of time.

I realize that this information is confidential in nature and that you are concerned about improper use of these records. I assure you that I re-quest this information strictly for the purpose of making a purchase decision regarding your business and the terms of the deal. The only persons I will disclose this confidential information to are my spouse, my attorney, and my accountant. I will obtain signed confidentiality statements from them before showing them your records.

I will return all of your records, including any copies made, within two weeks of their delivery to me. Thank you for your trust. I will not violate it and I look forward to continuing our business transaction.

Sincerely,
Dallas Green

---

sales volume. In other words, a $5,000 annual net profit from a business that requires a $10,000 investment and sales of $20,000 is much more attractive than a business that generates the same profit but requires a $100,000 investment and sales of $200,000.

The Expense Ratios. Industry averages comparing expenses to sales exist for every size and type of business. Industrywide expense ratios are calculated by most trade associations, many commercial banks, accounting firms, university bureaus of business research, and firms like Dun & Bradstreet and Robert Morris Associates.

For example, Robert Morris Associates (RMA) publishes industry averages for 392 specific types of businesses (by SIC number) in manufacturing, whole-sale, retail, and service sectors in *RMA Annual Statement Studies.*[5] Comparisons are made by percentages of assets, liabilities, and income data. RMA also provides industry averages of 16 common financial ratios such as current ratio, quick ratio, sales/working capital, and sales/receivables. (These and other financial ratios are explained further in Chapter 17.)

Imagine you are interested in buying a health club. The location is good, the advertising has caught your attention for several months, and the equipment is state of the art. You are very excited about the possibilities and are now looking over the financial statements. You divide the total current assets by the total current liabilities to calculate the club's current ratio. You get a current ratio of 0.5, knowing this figure shows the ability of a business to meet its current obligations. You want to get an idea of the management performance so you divide the profit before taxes by total assets and multiply by 100 (to convert to a percentage). This computation gives you 4.8 percent. You ask yourself, "Is a current ratio of 0.5 and an operating ratio of 4.8 percent good or bad for a health club?" They could be either. You need something to compare them with to tell you if they are in line. You go to the library at nearby Wassamatta U. to compare your figures to RMA industry averages. You look in the RMA reports under Service-Physical Fitness Facilities (SIC #7991) and find the median current ratio is listed at 0.9 and the median percentage profit before taxes/total assets is 7.5 percent. Your figures are well below industry average, so you decide you need to dig deeper to find why such large deviations exist between the business you are interested in buying and the average for other similar-sized businesses in the health club industry.

Operating ratios are standards or guides for comparison. Their effective use depends on your ability to identify problems that exist and change conditions that have caused any ratios to be appreciably below the standard.

Other Measures of Financial Health. Profit ratios are excellent indicators of a business's worth, but you should also examine other aspects of its financial health. A complete financial health examination consists of the calculation and interpretation of a variety of other financial ratios in addition to those relating to profit. Of particular interest to you and your accountant will be:

1. The working capital and the cash flow of the business: Is there enough to adequately keep the business going?
2. The relationship between the firm's fixed assets and the owner's tangible net worth.
3. The firm's debt load or leverage.

What Are You Buying?

When buying an existing business, the value of that business comes from what the business owns (its assets and what it earns), its cash flow, and the factors that make the business unique, such as the risk involved. (See Figure 6-1.)

FIGURE 6-1
What Should You Pay?
The price you offer for a business should begin with adding the value of tangible and intangible assets with the profit potential of the business.

Tangible Assets

tangible assets Assets that a business owns which can be seen and examined.

The **tangible assets** of a business, like inventory, equipment, and buildings, are generally easier to place a fair market value upon than intangible assets such as trade names, customer lists, and goodwill.

If the firm is selling its accounts receivable, you should determine how many of these are collectible and discount them accordingly. Receivables that are 120 days or older are not worth as much as those less than 30 days old because the odds are greater that you will not collect them. This is called *aging accounts receivable*. Of the other tangible assets of a business up for sale, inventories and equipment should be examined most closely because they are most likely to be outdated and therefore worth less than the seller is asking.

Manager's Notebook

The Declining Value of Aging Accounts Receivable

Accounts receivable represent cash that's owed to you. However, all accounts receivable are not equal! Those which have been owed to you the longest are worth the least because they are the least likely to be collected. In other words, the longer it takes someone to pay his account, the more likely it is that he is not ever going to pay it. Therefore, in valuing a business for sale, the cash value of long overdue accounts needs to be reduced to reflect the odds that they're not going to be paid. This process is called *aging accounts receivable*. Let's look at a simple example.

Determining how much to reduce the value of old accounts should be based on the debtor company's past payment trends. In the hypothetical example of a company we'll call Fabio's Floral Wholesalers, let's say that accounts receivable 30 days and under have a 100 percent likelihood of being paid. Those accounts 31 days to 60 days old have had a 70 percent probability of being paid, those 61 days to 90 days old have had a 50 percent probability, and those over 90 days have had

a 25 percent probability of being paid. Keep in mind that these percentages were determined by looking at the company's accounts receivable history—a fair and logical request to make of the business owner. Now let's see how the valuation process works.

ACCOUNTS RECEIVABLE	PROBABILITY %	BOOK VALUE	AGED VALUE
30 days and under	100%	$ 75,000	$ 75,000
31–60 days	70%	$ 50,000	$ 35,000
61–90 days	50%	$ 30,000	$ 15,000
Over 90 days	25%	$ 30,000	$ 7,500
Total Value		$185,000	$132,500

You can see by this simple example that there's a significant difference in the aged value and the book value of the accounts receivable: $52,500! So when you're buying an existing business, play it smart and be sure to value accounts receivable accurately.

Sources: R. Lawrence Nicholson, "Aging Criteria Help Reduce Accounts Receivable," Healthcare Financial Management (June 1984), pp. 56–58; and Calvin D. Byl, "Reporting Accounts Receivable to Management," Business Credit (October 1994), pp. 43–44.

The Inventory. Inventory needs to be timely, fresh, and well balanced. An indicator that the business has been well managed is an inventory of goods that people want, provided in the proper sizes, designs, and colors, and priced to fit the local buying power and purchasing habits.

Your biggest concern about inventory is that you are not buying "dead" stock (merchandise that has no, or very little, value) that the seller has listed as being worth its original value. The loss in value of dead stock should be to the original buyer, and you must be sure that the loss is not passed on to you as part of the sale.

The Equipment. It is important that a business be equipped with current, usable machines and equipment. Book value for electronic office equipment, especially computers, becomes outdated quickly.[6] A cash register designed for the book-keeping requirements of a generation ago will not record the information now required for tax reporting or scan UPC codes for efficient inventory control.

Often the usefulness of the firm's equipment was outlived long ago, and its value depreciated. The owner has delayed so long in replacing equipment that it has no trade-in value, and without this discount the owner finds the prices of new equipment to be exorbitant. This reason alone could lead to the decision to sell the business. Anything the owner makes on the fixtures and equipment is now clear profit, an extra bonus on his period of operation.

Intangible Assets

Businesses are also made up of **intangible assets** that may have real value to the purchaser. Among these are goodwill; preferred merchandise lines; favorable leases and other advantageous contracts; and patents, copyrights, and trademarks.

intangible assets Assets that have value to a business but are not visible.

Goodwill. **Goodwill** is an intangible asset that enables a business to earn a profit in excess of the normal rate of return earned by other businesses of the same kind. Few businesses that are for sale have much goodwill value.

goodwill The intangible asset that allows businesses to earn a higher return than a comparable business might generate with the same tangible assets.

We all know businesses in existence for years that have not established enough goodwill for the average customer to see the business as being "special." If strong competition existed, such companies would have been driven out of business long ago. From a consumer preference standpoint, they are at the bottom of the scale. This public attitude cannot be changed quickly. A good name can be ruined in far less time than it takes to improve a bad one.

A successful business has goodwill as an asset. Taking over a popular business brings with it public acceptance that has been built up over a period of many years, which is naturally valuable to the new owner.

Leases and Other Contracts. A lease on a favorable location is a valuable business asset. If the selling firm possesses a lease on its building, or if it has any unfulfilled sales contracts, you should determine if the lease and other contracts are transferable to you or if they must be renegotiated.

Patents, Copyrights, and Trademarks. Intellectual property can also be a valuable intangible asset. Protection of your machine, process, or a combination of the two against unauthorized use or infringement lasts for only a limited period of time, after which they are open to use by others. Thus, it is important for the prospective buyer of an existing business to determine precisely when the firm's patent rights expire and to value these rights based on the time remaining.

Copyrights offer the best protection for books, periodicals, materials prepared for oral presentation, advertising copy, pictorial illustrations, commercial prints or labels, and similar intellectual property. Unlike patent rights, copyrights are renewable.

Registered trademarks provide offensive rights against unauthorized use or infringement of a symbol, such as the Mercedes-Benz star or McDonald's arches, used in marketing goods. The function of trademarks is to identify specific products, and create and maintain a demand for those products. Since trademark protection lasts as long as the trademark is in continuous use, you should consider its value when purchasing a business that owns a trademark.

Personnel

When purchasing a business, the people working there must be considered just as important as profits and production. Retention of certain key people will keep a successful business going. New employees rarely come in as properly trained and steady workers. To help you estimate expenses related to finding, hiring, and training new employees, you will want to know if there are enough qualified people presently employed. Will any of these people depart with the previous owner? Are there any key individuals who may be unwilling or unable to continue working for you? The loss of a key person or two in a small business can have a serious impact on future earnings.

The Seller's Personal Plans

As a prospective purchaser of an existing business, you should not feel that all sellers of businesses have questionable ethical and moral principles. Just remember that "Let the buyer beware" has been a reliable maxim for years. There are laws against fraud and misrepresentation, but intent to defraud is usually very difficult to prove in court.

Reduce risk by writing protective clauses into contracts of sale, such as a **noncompetitive clause** in which the seller promises not to enter the same kind of business as a competitor within a specified geographical area for a reasonable number of years. If the seller resists agreeing to such a clause, it may be a signal that she intends to enter into a similar business in the future.

noncompetitive clause A provision often included in a contract to purchase a business which restricts the seller from entering the same type of business within a specified area for a certain amount of time.

How Much Should You Pay?

Even if you do not plan to buy an existing business, the methods of evaluating one will be useful in appraising the success of any firm.

When you make a substantial financial investment in a business, you should expect to receive personal satisfaction as well as an adequate living. A business bought at the wrong price, at the wrong time, or in the wrong place can cost you and your family more than the dollars invested and lost. After you have thoroughly investigated the business, weighed the information collected, and decided that the business will satisfy your expectations, a price must be agreed upon.

Determining the purchase price for a business involves several important factors: (1) valuation of the firm's tangible net assets, (2) valuation of the firm's intangible assets, especially any goodwill that has been built, (3) expected future

Tire Kicking for Beginners

In 1987 Lauren Karpinski, then the director of international trade and customs for accounting firm Arthur Andersen, faced a tough choice: to accept a transfer from her Orlando office or stay close to her family. Family ties won. "But I told my husband," she recalls, "that if I were going to leave a perfect job, I wanted to buy a business." Her second requirement was to buy it fast—within six weeks, while still on her employer's payroll.

So began the nightmare for the Karpinskis, who spent $750,000 to buy a Port Canaveral marina that was probably worth no more than $550,000. Their biggest error: they relied on financial numbers that were incomplete, vague, and in some cases downright inaccurate. Although Dolphin's Leap Marina is profitable today, with about $800,000 in annual revenues, the Karpinskis' experience provides a casebook lesson in how *not* to evaluate a possible purchase.

Karpinski admits that, despite her accounting-firm background, she was naïve, largely because she was so eager to do a deal. "We were given a compilation on an accountant's letterhead," she explains. (A compilation is simply a list of sales and other business results, without any elaborative information such as footnotes or accountants' opinions about the reliability of the numbers. A more thorough analysis—a limited financial review—applies generally accepted accounting standards. A full audit includes tests of the accuracy of line items such as inventory.)

The couple was easily satisfied, though, since the compilation "showed the correct trends," Karpinski recalls. But she concedes that "we didn't realize that the categories on the list were much too general—and that all kinds of numbers were combined to hide losses." Case in point: beer, bait, and tackle were listed on a single line, even though the margins and buying patterns for each were wildly different.

Also, the list of the marina's assets was inaccurate—and what's more, the Karpinskis didn't receive the list until the close. That left them with no time to physically verify the accuracy of asset valuations, which the couple never considered doing in any case. "There were items that didn't even belong to the marina. They belonged to vendors," Karpinski says. Other items were overvalued. One painful example: a compressor valued at more than $1,000 was a hollow shell. Worse: the Karpinskis relied on a *single* appraisal, which had valued the marina on its sales potential, not on realities such as current sales.

Karpinski's advice to others? "Insist on at least a limited financial review and sit down with the company's accountant to make sure you understand every single line. If you can't talk to the accountant, don't do the deal."

She also urges that you "request a full list of assets *prior* to the closing and verify all important items. Make sure assets exist, that they don't belong to anyone else, that they work, and that they're worth what you're told they're worth." And she recommends obtaining at least two appraisals, reflecting more than one appraisal method.

Source: Jill Andresky Fraser, ed., "Tire Kicking for Beginners," p. 173, adapted with permission, Inc. *magazine, December 1993. © 1993 By Goldhirsh Group, Inc.*

earnings, (4) the market demand for the particular type of business, and (5) the general condition of the business (including completeness and accuracy of the records, employee esprit de corps, and physical condition of facilities).[7]

Approaches to valuing a business that focus on the value of the business's assets are called **balance sheet methods of valuation.** These are most

balance sheet method of business valuation A method of determining the value of a business based on the worth of its assets.

When Marilyn Marks spearheaded a buyout of Dorsey Trailers, Inc., a maker of specialized refrigerator, dump, and parcel truck trailers, in 1987, she knew she was getting into a "macho" business. But that wasn't the hard part of her decision—putting a value on the business was. The trailer business had lost $2.4 million in 1986, but in 1984, it had earned $11 million. So Marks knew that it had profit potential. But how does one translate that knowledge into a reasonable offer? Marks used a team of advisers to establish the business's value and to help prepare her bid for the company. Her final and successful offer was a $25 million bid that put her in the title role of Dorsey Trailers chairman. By 1995, the company's revenues reached approximately $230 million. *Source: Randall Lane, "Don't Mess with Marilyn," Forbes, December 4, 1995, pp. 106–110.*

income statement method of business valuation A method of determining the value of a business based on its profit potential.

appropriate for businesses that primarily generate earnings from their assets rather than from the contributions of their employees. Approaches that focus more on the profits or cash flow a business generates are called **income statement methods of valuation.**

What Are the Tangible Assets Worth?

As stated earlier, the worth of tangible assets is what the balance sheet method of valuation seeks to establish. Their value is determined according to:

Book value—what the asset originally cost or what it is worth from an accounting viewpoint; the amount shown on the books as representing the asset's value as a part of the firm's worth.

Replacement value—what it would cost to buy the same materials, merchandise, or machinery today; relative availability and desirability of new items must be considered.

Liquidation value—how much the seller could get for this business, or any part of it, if it were placed on the open market.

There are significant differences in these three approaches in determining value. Book value may not hold up in the marketplace. Buildings and equipment may not be correctly depreciated, while land may have appreciated. Replacement value may not be a reliable figure because of opportunities to buy used equipment. Replacement value is significant as a measure of value only as a comparison to what it would cost to start your own business.

Liquidation value is the most realistic approach in determining the value of tangible assets to the buyer of a business. This value may represent the lowest figure that the seller would be willing to accept.

You have to determine the value of the following physical assets before serious bargaining can begin:

1. Cost of the inventory adjusted for slow-moving or dead stock
2. Cost of the equipment less depreciation

Computer Applications

Needless to say, there are numerous computer software programs on the market that can help make the job of valuing a business a little easier. However, keep in mind that like any software program, the information you get out is only as good as the information you put in. With this caveat in mind, let's look at the two methods of valuation and selected computer software to help you perform that task.

The **balance sheet method of valuation** focuses attention on the *value of the business's assets.* Value is defined as the fair market value, which financial experts say is the "price at which the business would sell in an arm's-length exchange between an informed buyer and informed seller, neither of whom are under any duress to make the transaction." Using the balance sheet valuation approach, fair market value would be the value placed on the tangible assets of the business. Using any spreadsheet program such as Microsoft's Excel, Lotus 1-2-3, or Novell's Quattro Pro, you could perform simple calculations and analyze the differences in book value, replacement value, and liquidation value. Actually, because you're typically dealing with a limited set of numbers, you could also do the same analysis using a calculator.

However, the real power of spreadsheets is exploited when using the other approach to valuation—the **income statement method of valuation.** Here fair market value is calculated from *forecasted profits or cash flow.* This task is made much simpler by using a spreadsheet program. The three most popular—Excel, Lotus 1-2-3, and Quattro Pro—are designed to help make number crunching easy yet thorough. Each of these programs does essentially the same types of analysis and forecasting, and each has its vocal advocates. When you're ready to use a spreadsheet, you'll probably want to talk to people you know and trust who use spreadsheets and ask them for their particular favorite. Another type of software program that you might consider using to help forecast sales is called Forecast Pro by Business Forecast Systems of Belmont, Massachusetts. Although its primary use is helping managers working in organizations to forecast sales, it could also be used to calculate future sales projections as part of a business valuation.

Sources: Ripley Hatch and Jon Pepper, "How to Buy Business Software," Nation's Business (June 1994), pp. 20–28; Alison L. Sprout, "Surprise! Software to Help You Manage," Fortune, April 17, 1995, pp. 197–201; and Bruce Lane and David Forman, "What Is It Worth?" Beverage World (May 1995), pp. 64–66.

3. Supplies
4. Accounts receivable less bad debts
5. Market value of the building

Don't make an offer for a business based on the seller's asking price. You may feel as if you got a real bargain if you talk the seller down to half of what the seller is asking—but half may still be twice as much as the business is worth.[8]

What Are the Intangible Assets Worth?

An established business may be worth more than the sum of its physical assets and its owner is likely to be unwilling to sell for liquidation value alone. The value of a business's intangible assets is difficult to determine. Intangible assets are the product of a firm's past earnings and they are the basis on which its earnings are projected.

Goodwill is the term used to describe the difference between the purchase price of a company and the net value of the tangible assets. Goodwill is the most difficult asset to set a value upon that the seller will think is fair. It includes intangible but very real assets with real value to the prospective purchaser. Goodwill can be regarded as: (1) compensation to the owner for her losses on beginner's mistakes you might have made if you started from scratch, and (2) payment for the privilege of carrying on an established and profitable business.[9] It should be small enough to be made up from profits within a reasonably short period.

What is goodwill worth? To determine a company's goodwill, you can start by using the income statement method of valuation. To do this you should capitalize your projected future earnings at an assumed rate of interest that would be in excess of the "normal" return (earnings adjusted to remove any unusual occurrences like a lawsuit settlement or a one-time gain from the sale of real estate) in that type and size of business. The capitalization rate is a figure assigned to show the risk and expected growth rate associated with future earnings.

For example, suppose that the liquidation value of the firm's tangible net assets is $224,000 and that the normal before-tax rate of return on the owner's investment in this business is 15 percent, or $33,600 per year. We will assume that the actual profit during the past few years has averaged $83,600, *exclusive of the present owner's salary* (which may have been overstated or understated).

From the profit, we will deduct a reasonable salary for the owner or manager—what he or she might earn by managing this type of business for someone else. If we assume a going-rate annual salary of $40,000, then the excess profit to be capitalized (that is, the amount of profit based on goodwill) is $10,000 ($83,600 minus $40,000 salary minus a normal profit of $33,600).

The rate of capitalization is negotiated by the buyer and the seller of the business. The capitalization rate should be appropriate to the risk taken. The more certain you are of the estimated profits, the more you will pay for goodwill. The less certain you are—the higher you perceive your risk to be—the less you will pay.

If you assume a 25 percent rate of return on estimated earnings coming from goodwill, then the value of the intangible assets is $10,000 ÷ 0.25, or $40,000. Usually this relationship is expressed as a ratio or multiplier of "four times (excess) earnings." You would expect to recover the amount invested in goodwill in no more than four years.

When you put these two figures together, you come up with an offering price of $264,000 for the business—net tangible assets of $224,000 at liquidation value plus goodwill valued at $40,000. The calculations for this price are shown in Table 6-2.

If the average annual net earnings of the business before subtracting the owner's salary (line 4) was $73,600 or less, then there would be no goodwill value. Even though the business may have existed for a long time, the earnings would be less than you could earn through outside investment. In that case, your price would be determined by capitalizing the average annual profit (net earnings minus all expenses and owner's salary) by the normal or expected rate of return on investment in this business. For example:

$$\$73,600 - \$40,000 = \$33,600 = \text{Profit}$$

$$\$33,600 \div 0.15 = \$224,000 = \text{Offering Price}$$

TABLE 6-2 Calculating the Purchase Price of an Existing Business

1. Adjusted value of tangible net worth		$224,000
2. Earning power at 15%	$33,600	
3. Reasonable salary for owner or manager	40,000	
	$73,600	
4. Average annual net earnings before subtracting owner's salary	83,600	
5. Extra earning power of business (line 4 − total of lines 2 and 3)	$10,000	
6. Value of intangibles, using four-year profit figure for moderately well-established firm (4 × line 5)		40,000
7. Offering price (line 1 + line 6)		$264,000

Valuing goodwill is a highly subjective process. The value of intangible assets comes down to what *you* think they are worth and what you are willing to pay. You will need to negotiate with the seller to reach a consensus.

Buying Your Business

To complete the purchase of your business, you need to negotiate the terms of the deal and prepare for the closing.

The Terms of the Sale

After agreeing on a price for the business, the terms of sale need to be negotiated. Few buyers are able to raise the funds required to pay cash for a business. A lump-sum payment may be in neither the buyer's nor the seller's best interests for tax reasons, unless the seller intends to reinvest in another business. Paying in installments is often the most practical solution.

By building installment payments into your cash flow projection, you should be assured that the business can be paid for out of earnings. Installments assure the seller that his investment in the business will be returned on a tax-deferred basis, as opposed to paying all taxes at one time with a lump-sum payment.

A seller may need to take steps to make the business more affordable. One way to do this is known as *thinning the assets.* The seller can adjust the assets to be more manageable for the new owner in one or more of the following ways:

- Separate real estate ownership from business ownership. The new owner leases rather than purchases the building. The buyer has less to borrow and the seller receives a steady rental income.
- Lease equipment and/or fixtures in the same manner as real estate.
- Sell off excess inventories.
- Factor accounts receivable, or carry the old accounts.

Closing the Deal

When you and the seller have reached an agreement on the sale of the business, several conditions must be met to ensure a smooth, legal transaction. Closing can be handled by either using a settlement attorney or an escrow settlement.

A settlement attorney acts as a neutral party to draw up the necessary documents and represents both the buyer and the seller. Both parties meet with the settlement attorney at the agreed upon closing date to sign the papers after all the conditions of the sale have been met, such as financing being secured by the buyer and a search completed to determine if any liens against the business's assets exist.

In an escrow settlement, the buyer deposits the money and the seller provides the bill of sale and other documents to an escrow agent. You can find an escrow agent at most financial institutions like banks and trusts that have escrow departments or through an escrow company. The escrow agent holds the funds and documents until proof is shown that all conditions of the sale are completed. When the conditions are met, the escrow agent releases the funds and documents to the rightful owners.

Global Small Business

Buying an existing business can be a complicated and nerve-wracking adventure. And, the adventure becomes even more complex and frustrating if the business you're looking at is in a foreign market. One way that many small business owners who want to go global are approaching this issue is by joining with, or even acquiring, a foreign partner or distributor. However, this approach too has its drawbacks. If the partner you select is incompetent, it could ruin your company's reputation quickly. Take, for instance, WIN Laboratories, Ltd. of Manassas, Virginia. In early 1995 it had dissolved its partnership with a Chilean distributor because of customs delays and poor sales. Looking back, WIN's director of business development says that they should have done a lot more examination of potential partners. In fact, before jumping into a similar type of arrangement in Brazil and Mexico, they'll research the situation thoroughly. *Source: Amy Barrett, "It's A Small (Business) World," Business Week, April 17, 1995, pp. 96–101.*

Taking Over a Family Business

A fourth route into small business (besides starting from scratch, buying an existing business, or franchising) is taking over a family business. This alternative offers unique opportunities and risks.

What Is Different about Family Businesses?

Family businesses are characterized by two or more members of the same family who control, are directly involved in, and own a majority of the business. Family businesses make up 80 percent of all businesses in the United States and comprise nearly 50 percent of the nation's GNP.[10] Family businesses are obviously an important part of our economy, but what makes them different than nonfamily businesses? Two factors are: (1) the complex interrelationships of family members interacting with each other and interacting with the business, and (2) the intricate succession planning needed.

Family Business Perspectives

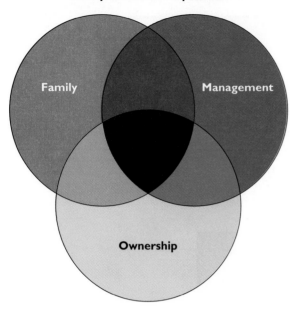

FIGURE 6-2
Family Business Perspectives
The family business owner views the business and what goes on within it from three different but overlapping perspectives.

Complex Interrelationships

When you run a family business, you have three overlapping perspectives of its operation. (See Figure 6-2.)[11] For example, suppose a family member needs a job. From the family perspective, you would see this is an opportunity to help one of your own. From the ownership perspective, you might be concerned about the effect of a new hire on profits. From a management perspective, you would be concerned about how this hire would affect nonfamily employees.

Everyone involved in a family business will have a different perspective, depending on each one's position within the business. The successful leader of this business must maintain all three perspectives simultaneously.

Planning Succession

Many entrepreneurs dream of the time they are able to "pass the torch" of their successful business on to their children. Unfortunately, many factors such as jealousy, lack of interest, or ineptitude can cause the flame to go out.

If the potential successor wants to take over the family business, he must gain acceptance and trust within the organization. (See Figure 6-3.) When a family member enters the business, he is usually not immediately accepted by nonfamily employees. This skepticism increases when that person moves up to a leadership position within the business. The successor must earn credibility by showing that he is capable of running the business. Only after being accepted and earning credibility will the new manager have legitimate power and become successful as the new leader.[12]

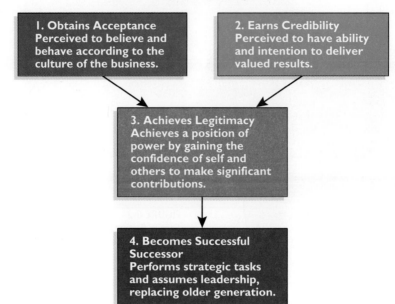

Succession Model of Family Business

1. Obtains Acceptance Perceived to believe and behave according to the culture of the business.

2. Earns Credibility Perceived to have ability and intention to deliver valued results.

3. Achieves Legitimacy Achieves a position of power by gaining the confidence of self and others to make significant contributions.

4. Becomes Successful Successor Performs strategic tasks and assumes leadership, replacing older generation.

FIGURE 6-3
Succession Model of Family Business
Passing ownership of a family business is a difficult process. The successor must earn the trust of employees before becoming a successful leader.

General Family Business Policies

Since family businesses have unique situations and problems, they need a set of policies to deal with such situations that are not needed in other types of businesses. David Bork, a family business consultant, makes the following suggestions as part of a family employment policy. A set of policies such as these can help prevent problems like animosity from nonfamily employees, which can decrease their motivation and productivity.

- When hiring family members, they must meet the same criteria as nonfamily employees.
- In performance reviews, family members must meet the same standards as nonfamily employees.
- Family members should be supervised by nonfamily employees when possible.
- If family members are under age 30, they are only eligible for "temporary" employment (less than one year).
- No family member may stay in an entry-level position permanently.
- All positions will be compensated at fair market value.
- For family members to seek permanent employment, they must have at least five years' experience outside the company. Family members must prove their worth to another employer to be useful here.[13]

Summary

■ The reasons for which a business owner might wish to sell out.

There are as many reasons for selling a business as there are businesses to sell. As a prospective buyer, you must learn to cut through what is said to determine the realities of a situation. You must develop an ability to analyze a market and estimate potential profits and worth.

■ The means of measuring a business's condition.

Profitability, profit trends, comparison of operating ratios to industry standards, and total asset worth are all measures of the financial health of a business.

■ The difference between tangible and nontangible assets.

Tangible assets are those that cast a shadow. Real estate, inventory, and equipment are important tangible assets. Nontangible assets, while unseen, are no less valuable. Goodwill, merchandise franchises, leases and contracts, and patents, copyrights, and trademarks are examples.

■ The price to pay for a business.

The offering price to pay for a business is calculated by adding the adjusted value of tangible assets with the value of intangible assets (including goodwill, if appropriate).

■ What makes family businesses different from other types of businesses?

The two primary differences between family businesses and other businesses are: (a) the complex interrelationships among family members and their interaction in the business, and (b) the intricate succession planning needed.

Questions for Review and Discussion

1. What are some arguments for buying an established business rather than starting one yourself?
2. In buying an established business, what questions should you ask about it? From whom might you seek information about the business?
3. Identify and discuss some of the more important factors to consider in appraising a business.
4. Which is more important in appraising a business—profitability or return on investment? Discuss.
5. Should one ever consider purchasing a presently unsuccessful business (that is, a business with relatively low—or no—profits)? Explain.
6. What factors warrant special attention in appraising a firm's (a) inventory? (b) equipment? and (c) accounts receivable?
7. What should a prospective buyer know about the seller's inventory sources and other resource contacts? How is this information obtained?
8. Does competition help or hurt a business? Explain.
9. Discuss the ways in which the tangible assets of a business may be valued. What is the most realistic approach to true value? Why?
10. What is goodwill and how may its value be determined?
11. How can a buyer determine the rate of return to use in evaluating the worth of a business?
12. What is an installment sale? What are its advantages to the buyer of a business? To the seller of a business?

mK, bus, more affordable
- sep. real Est, ownership
  From Bus, ownership
- lease Eq. access chnge
  sell off access chnge

13. What is meant by *thinning the assets?* Cite examples.
14. Discuss the advantages of dealing through a business broker. What precautions should one take when dealing with a business broker?
15. Say that you are analyzing the financial records of the business you have been thinking about buying. You discover that although the firm has excellent current and quick asset ratios by industry standards (current assets are higher than current liabilities), its cash if low and it hasn't paid its bills on time. What might have caused this? Would this influence your decision to buy the business?

Critical Incident

Masters of Music (MM) is a retail music store located in South Bend, Indiana. At its two locations, one which is downtown and the other in the Heritage Mall, MM sells musical instruments, sheet music, and musical accessories. It also provides music lessons—piano and guitar—for school-age students and for adults. Michele Smith has owned the business for 20 years and wants to sell out so she can retire to "someplace warm." This type of business is exactly what you've been looking for, but you want to make sure you pay a fair market price for it. Smith has provided you with the financial information you requested. (See the Income Statements on this page and the Balance Sheets on page 175.)

Income Statements for Masters of Music

	1990	1991	1992	1993	1994
Revenues:					
Retail Sales	1,500,000	1,200,000	1,500,000	1,550,000	1,720,000
Music lessons	78,000	80,000	80,000	83,000	82,000
Total revenue	1,578,000	1,280,000	1,580,000	1,633,000	1,802,000
Expenses:					
Costs of goods sold	780,000	830,000	860,000	875,000	927,000
Salaries and wages	120,000	125,000	138,000	140,000	157,000
Other operating expenses	145,000	157,000	160,000	172,000	175,000
Marketing expenses	57,000	65,000	72,000	83,000	90,000
Other expenses (including insurance, interest, etc.)	55,000	50,000	63,000	70,000	78,000
Income before taxes	421,000	53,000	287,000	293,000	375,000
Income taxes (33%)	138,930	17,490	94,710	96,690	123,750
Net income	282,070	35,510	192,290	196,310	251,250

Balance Sheets for Masters of Music

	1990	1991	1992	1993	1994
Assets:					
Cash	105,000	65,000	93,000	98,000	117,000
Accounts Receivable	39,800	49,000	43,700	45,000	50,200
Inventory	947,000	986,000	993,000	1,200,000	1,205,000
Building	542,000	542,000	542,000	542,000	542,000
Furniture fixtures	213,000	213,000	233,000	249,000	252,000
Less accumulated depreciation	87,000	79,200	73,000	68,000	67,100
Total Assets	1,759,800	1,775,800	1,831,700	2,066,000	2,099,100
Liabilities:					
Accounts payable	32,000	43,000	30,000	35,000	28,000
Line of credit	500,000	500,000	530,000	550,000	550,000
Roosevelt Federal	151,000	149,000	176,000	180,000	185,000
Sales tax payable	45,000	36,000	45,000	46,500	51,600
Other payables	17,000	28,000	28,000	30,000	31,500
Total Current Liabilities	745,000	756,000	809,000	841,500	846,100
Long-term notes/leases	375,000	375,000	343,000	343,000	343,000
Total Liabilities	1,120,000	1,131,000	1,152,000	1,184,500	1,189,100
Stockholder's Equity:					
30,000 shares at $15/share	450,000	450,000	450,000	450,000	450,000
Retained Earnings	189,800	194,800	229,700	431,500	460,000
Total Liabilities and Stockholder's Equity	1,759,800	1,775,800	1,831,700	2,066,000	2,099,100

Questions

1. Calculate a range of values for Masters of Music. Use both the balance sheet method of valuation and the income statement method. Be sure to note your assumptions on your valuations.

2. Students are to break into groups of four, with each group divided into pairs. One pair will act as sellers and the other pair will act as buyers, for which each pair will set their own value for Masters of Music. Negotiate a sale for the company. Be prepared to justify your estimation of value.

Take it to the Net

We invite you to visit the Hatten page on the Prentice Hall Web site at: http://www.prenhall.com/~hattensb for this chapter's World Wide Web exercise.

Chapter Focus

After reading this chapter, you should be able to:

- Evaluate the advantages of starting a business from scratch.
- Discuss the common characteristics of fast-growth companies.
- Examine business ideas in the context of changing windows of opportunity.
- Suggest sources of business ideas.
- Demonstrate the importance of customer service.

7 Starting a New Business

TUCKER

N 1977 BRIAN MAXWELL was ranked third in the world in marathon running with a personal best of 2:14:43. Despite his efforts and training, a sensitive stomach prevented him from improving on his 2:14. If he ate anything before a race, he would get digestive problems and cramps during the race. Yet if he did not eat anything, he had no energy left for the final miles.

Out of frustration with his condition, Maxwell, aided by biochemist and runner, Bill Vaughan, sought to create a high-energy, easily digestible food bar for athletes. The pair first began experimenting with different grains, proteins, textures, and flavors. They were making progress when, after two years of tests, they were joined by Jennifer Biddulph, a runner and student majoring in food science. For three more years the group would make up batches at home and product-test them at races every weekend.

In February 1986, Maxwell and Biddulph took a big jump toward turning a hobby into a business. With their combined life savings (the couple married in 1988), they contracted a single production run of 40,000 PowerBars. Word-of-mouth promotion spread quickly through the close-knit running and cycling community. Mail-order sales in 1987 were $400,000. PowerBar's marketing philosophy was, and still is, "We have a good product that works. All we have to do is get athletes to try it." Maxwell and Biddulph spent half of their promotion budget on direct marketing—sponsoring events and giving away bars at road races "at 7:00 A.M. in the rain," as Maxwell put it. The other half of the budget went for simple print and broadcast advertisements produced by Maxwell and Biddulph. It worked. Between 1987 and 1991, sales grew 6,915 percent(!), from $400,000 to $6.7 million. PowerFoods, the company's name, ranked twenty-second on the 1992 *Inc.* list of the 500 fastest-growing companies in America. By 1993, revenue was up to nearly $14 million.

Although few young companies have such extraordinary success, PowerFoods' founders are not unlike many entrepreneurs. A need in their lives motivated them to find a solution. That solution also satisfied a need in other people's lives. The initial focus was not on creating a business. That was more of a by-product—a means to an end. Their focus was to simply solve a problem.

Can you identify some problem or need that exists? Can you come up with a solution to that problem or need? Do you have the perseverance to stay focused and follow through? If you answer "yes" to these three questions, you are well on your way to starting a successful business. *Source: Adapted from Bob Wischnia, "PowerPlay," Runner's World (June 1994), pp. 90–95.*

About Startups

Starting a business from the ground up is more difficult than buying an existing business or a franchise because nothing is in place. There is also more risk involved. However, to many people the process of taking an idea through all the steps, time, money, and energy needed to become a viable business is the essence of entrepreneurship. The period in which you create a brand new business is an *exciting* time.

Do you want to be totally independent at work? If so, you may be ready to start your own business.

Do you think you would like to be totally independent? Can you set up an accounting system readable to you and acceptable to your bank and the Internal Revenue Service? Can you come up with a promotional campaign that will get you noticed? Can you find sources of products, components, or distribution? Can you find employees with the right skills your business will need? If so, you may be ready to start your own business.

Advantages of Starting from Scratch

When you begin a business from scratch, you have freedom to mold your new creation into whatever you feel is appropriate. Other advantages of starting from scratch include the ability to create your own distinctive competitive advantage. Many entrepreneurs thrive on the challenge of beginning a new enterprise. You

"The great thing about being your own boss is that you can work whenever you want — as long as you always want to work."

By Patrick Hardin. From Management Review (February 1994), p. 61.

can feel pride when creating something that did not exist before and in accomplishing your own goals. The fact that the business is all new can be an advantage in itself—there is no carryover baggage of someone else's mistakes, location, employees, or products. You establish your own image.

Disadvantages of Starting from Scratch

The risk of failure is higher with startups than with purchasing existing businesses or franchises. You may have trouble identifying market needs in your area that you are able to satisfy. You have to inform people that your business exists—it can be tough to get noticed. You have to deal with thousands of details that you did not foresee from how to choose the right vendors to where to put the coffee pot to where to find motivated employees.

Types of New Businesses

No matter what type of business you are starting, your most important resource is your time. Nothing happens until you make it happen. You have to create and build upon the enthusiasm that will attract others to your idea and your business. In the beginning, the only thing you have is your vision and only you will be responsible for its success.

As the service industry plays an ever greater role in the U.S. economy, startup businesses become more popular. The reason? Service businesses tend to be more **labor intensive,** as opposed to manufacturing businesses, which are more **capital intensive.**

Start by finding out all you can about your industry and trade area from

labor-intensive business A business that is more dependent on the services of people than on money and equipment.

capital-intensive business A business that depends greatly upon equipment and capital for its operations.

Small Business
IN THE Service Industry

The labor-intensive nature of service businesses is evident in the company that brothers James and Peter Kovolsky started in Charlotte, North Carolina. James had worked his way through college putting together unassembled manufactured products for people. He could—and did—construct just about anything—bicycles, toys, bookshelves, office furniture, you name it. When James and Peter were both laid off from their sales jobs in 1991, they decided to start their own business, Frustration Solvers, that would take advantage of their skills and allay people's fear of those three simple words: "Some Assembly Required." They've since developed close relationships with stores that sell toys, office furniture, lawn and garden supplies, sporting goods, and home-improvement goods. The stores do not pay the brothers directly, but allow their salespeople to give Frustration Solvers' phone number to customers. Obviously, the brothers have identified a true market niche because company revenues have tripled every year since 1992, reaching over $1 million in 1995. The Kovolsky brothers are considering franchising or seeking investors to help fund the company's growth. Says James, "The business is out there. We've got retailers calling us from other states." By identifying a critical customer need, the Kovolskys started a profitable service business. *Source: Dorothy Elizabeth Brooks, "Putting It All Together," Nation's Business (September 1995), p. 16.*

books, newsletters, trade publications, magazines, organizations, and people already in business. After all your questions and investigation, if you are ready for the challenge, you will find several possible routes in starting your business.

Let's look at a few of those routes that people take aside from the typical goal of a low-growth, stable startup, which provides the small business owner a comfortable, modest living.

Home-based Businesses

home-based business A popular type of business which operates from the owner's home, rather than a separate location.

The fastest-growing segment of business startups comprises those operated out of people's homes. In 1992, the number of **home-based businesses** hit the 12 million mark and 39 million people do at least some of their work from their residence.[1] About 30 percent of home-based businesses deal with financial or computer-related services. Two reasons stand out as advantages of this type of business: schedule flexibility and low overhead.

Technology has had a lot to do with making this trend possible. Notebook computers, wireless modems and fax, cellular phones, and laser printers contribute to the flexibility with quality results from working at home. The idea is becoming more widely accepted.

Meg Gottemoller left her position as a vice president of Chase Manhattan Bank in New York to start her own communications and training consultancy. Martha Gay runs her own corporate research business from her home in Fort Washington, PA.[2] Both of these businesses are successful because they take advantage of *corporate outsourcing*. As larger companies reduce the size of their work force, they must not contract out work that was once done by their own workers. This outsourcing provides many opportunities for small businesses. (See Chapter 1.)

Starting a Business on the Side

Many people start businesses while keeping their regular jobs. While it is often not recommended as a way to enter business, the Bureau of Labor Statistics estimates that just over 600,000 people did so in 1991.[3] Working a full-time job while getting a business going may require superhuman organizational skills and discipline, yet there can be advantages. A transitional period can allow you to test the waters without complete immersion in the marketplace. You can also prepare yourself psychologically, experientially, and financially so when—or if—you leave your job, you will have a running start. Before taking this route, however, you should be absolutely clear on your company's moonlighting policy and avoid doing anything that might resemble a conflict of interest. Moonlighting policies could include not starting an identical business or soliciting current customers.

Fast-growth Startups

Not every new business can be or desires to be a hypergrowth company like PowerFoods, with its nearly 7,000 percent growth rate, as we saw in the chapter opener. But *Inc.* magazine compiled its own database on these businesses with those of government agencies, university researchers, and independent research firms. From these data, *Inc.* identified characteristics and patterns of similarity these fast-growth companies shared:

1. *They rely on team efforts.* In contrast with low-growth firms, most fast-growth companies are started by partnerships. In an increasingly complex and competitive environment, teams can deal with a much wider range of problems than an individual operating alone. One half of the fast-growth CEOs owned less than 50 percent of their businesses' equity.

2. *They're headed by people who know their line of work.* A majority of high-growth CEOs had at least ten years of experience in the industry. This contrasts with just a few years of prior experience for owners of low-growth companies.

3. *They're headed by people who have started other businesses.* Research shows that 63 percent of the founders of high-growth companies had started other companies, and 23 percent had started three or more. This compares to only 20 percent of all business owners who had been self-employed previously.

4. *They're headed by men.* The number of firms owned by women increased twice as fast as all businesses did in the 1980s. But 93 percent of fast-growth companies have male CEOs. This does not suggest inferior female management by any means. Possible explanations could be that women as a group have not yet gained the business experience needed to form fast-growth firms, or that rapid growth has not been a primary goal of women CEOs.

5. *They're disproportionately manufacturers, and they're high tech.* Of the fast-start companies, 47 percent label themselves "high tech." While manufacturing firms make up only 3 percent of all U.S. businesses, they represent 27 percent of the *Inc.* 500. Services make up a full 56 percent, which is another indicator of the importance of the service sector in our economy.

6. *They're better financed—but not by much.* This factor is harder to measure because of the subjectivity in determining what is "well financed." The

Manager's Notebook

Information Technology: Your Silent Partner

Information technology (IT) is rapidly changing the way organizations large and small are doing business. As costs have continued to decrease and the capabilities increased, small business owners and managers are wholeheartedly embracing the benefits offered by information technology. In fact, results from a recent survey of small business owners showed the overwhelming majority of them felt that information technology was a critical or important factor in helping them work faster and smarter. Significantly, the annual growth rate of small businesses ranking technology as extremely important was an impressive 27.8 percent. (See Figure 7-1.)

Information technology gives you a competitive advantage in starting a small business. In fact, a high-tech office is becoming more of a necessity than a luxury for the small business owner. IT can increase your productivity when resources are stretched tightly.

A growing amount of computer hardware and software is being designed for small businesses. You can find software to help you with all facets of planning for your business, provide you with legal advice, or furnish your business with order forms, invoices, business letters, and other forms to run your business on computer disk. Hardware that combines printer, copier, fax, and scanner functions into one machine affordable to small businesses can hold down your equipment costs. Computer on-line services can open access to new customers, investors, and information to small businesses.

Deborah Doelker's company, Doelker Inc., publishes reports on African safari tours. Before 1991, she did most of the office work by hand. After she invested $2,500 in a computer system, she was able to handle more work, and sales increased from $500,000 to $800,000 per year.

As you're organizing your startup, you might find IT useful in different areas of your business. Let's take a closer look at what IT can do for you.

- *Simplify your organizational structure.* Computers linked in networks allow information to be shared simultaneously and instantly among employees. The result is that employees anywhere can easily access information about marketing, sales, finances, operations, or whatever else they might need to do their jobs properly. For instance, you might decide to use an electronic mail system in your small business to communicate both internally and externally. This type of communication creates a much more open organizational structure since you, your employees, customers, and others can freely communicate.

- *Make operations more efficient and effective.* IT can help your startup run more efficiently and effectively whether you have a manufacturing or a service business. For instance, computer inventory systems can help a small manufacturer keep close tabs on the amount and type of inventory in the warehouse. Or, if you're a retail firm, you might use a point-of-sale system to calculate daily sales, control inventory, and read product bar codes as customers check out. For instance, Katie Patterson of Irving, Texas, uses a complete point-of-sale system at her bakery store to help her track sales and estimate demand for holidays such as Valentine's Day and Christmas. A personal information management system can help you manage time—your most valuable asset. Programs such as Desk-Top Set will allow you to print your itinerary for the day, week, or month. It can also let you make phone calls from your computer. A modem on your computer can connect you to on-line services such as Prodigy, America Online, or CompuServe and provide access to the Internet. These services allow you to gather market research or correspond with other people in your life of business, customers, or vendors.

- *Limit the number of employees.* IT enables many small businesses to operate with fewer full-time employees and to utilize freelancers or part-timers as needed for certain projects or tasks. At Rickard Associates of Hopewell, New Jersey, for instance, owner Wendy Rickard publishes magazines and marketing materials with the help of one full-time assistant and a part-time employee. However, she also utilizes freelance artists and editors across the United States, and she is able to communicate with them via the Internet and America Online. Her small business operates just as effectively as if these people were physically in the office.

- *Enhance new-product development.* Many small businesses live and die by their adeptness at developing new products. IT can play a role through capabilities such as computer-aided design (CAD) software programs, in which product designs are developed and manipulated on the computer screen before a physical model is built. Computer information systems that funnel customer comments about current and future products to product designers can also be useful.

- *Enhance customer service.* This is another area in which IT can have a major impact. For instance, as stated earlier, your business might utilize electronic mail (e-mail) to communicate with customers. Or your business might establish a presence on the Internet or World Wide Web, where you communicate with potential customers or even market products through your site (called a home page). And desktop publishing packages can provide your small business with a way to cost-effectively design attractive marketing pieces, customer newsletters, or catalogs. Another IT application that can enhance customer service is a customer database with which you can keep track of customer names, addresses, phone numbers, recent order history, special orders, and so forth. For example, Gary L. Mead of Lompoc, California, owns a pizza parlor called Mi Amore Pizza & Pasta. He's able to compete with the likes of Pizza Hut, Domino's, and Little Caesar's because he uses database and direct-marketing technologies to personalize his marketing efforts. Of course, telephones are critical for your business operation, but electronic mail (e-mail) can free you from the phone, because communications can be stored if you are not available to talk on the phone. A wireless modem in your laptop computer allows you to transmit or receive e-mail while you are on the go.

Sources: Thomas A. Stewart, "Managing in a Wired Company," *Fortune, July 11, 1994, pp. 44–56;* Ira Sager, "The Great Equalizer," Business Week, *Special Bonus Issue, 1994, pp. 100–107;* Gary McWilliams, "Mom and Pop Go High Tech," Business Week, *November 21, 1994, pp. 82–90;* Bronwyn Fryer, "How to Succeed With Software," Working Woman *(November 1995), pp. 55–60;* Gary McWilliams, "Small Fry Go Online," Business Week, *November 20, 1995, pp. 158–164;* and Timothy O'Brien, "The Electronic Edge," The Wall Street Journal Report—Small Business, *October 15, 1993, p. R12.*

Census Bureau shows that 30 percent of all businesses were started with less than $5,000—only 22 percent of the newest *Inc.* 500 began with less than $5,000. One third of all businesses were started with less than $50,000 compared to one-half of the *Inc.* companies with that amount. The high-growth companies had a little more money, but not much (because many were manufacturing firms, which tend to *need* more capital).

7. *Their markets are not just local.* Small businesses are becoming more global in the 1990s. Successful companies are expanding their horizons. A majority get more than half of their revenue outside their home region, and a third are international players. They are looking for **strategic alliances** also. One third have agreements with large companies, which expand their markets.[4]

strategic alliance A partnership between two businesses that join forces to produce a product or serve a market that neither could do alone. Often used as a means to enter a foreign market.

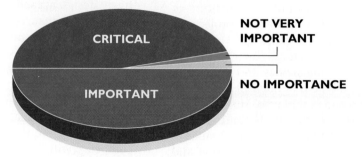

SMALL BUSINESS IS BIG ON TECHNOLOGY

It's ready to invest...

How small-business owners rate information technology as a factor in making them work faster and smarter

CRITICAL

NOT VERY IMPORTANT

IMPORTANT

NO IMPORTANCE

FIGURE 7-1
Small Business is Big on Technology
Source: Gary McWilliams, "Mom and Pop Go High Tech," Business Week, *November 21, 1994, p. 82.*

...and gets a big payoff

Annual growth rate of small businesses that rank technology as extremely important: 27.8%

Computer Applications

A startup business provides the perfect opportunity for a small business person to jump on the information superhighway and to fashion a business which utilizes the power of computers and information to compete profitably in the global marketplace of the twenty-first century. What types of computer applications would such an investment in the future require? Industry experts make three suggestions as to how small companies can invest to enhance current communications while planning for future opportunities. One suggestion is to link your computers into a network and install some type of electronic-mail system. This will allow easier and quicker communication both internally and externally.

Second, learn to explore the opportunities offered by the Internet and the World Wide Web. To do so requires computer modem connections and Web browser software. Finally, keep adaptability and compatibility in mind when purchasing any computer products or service. Many of the technical and ethical standards for a global information superhighway are still being developed. That means you might want to stick with known companies when purchasing computer hardware or software or, at the very least, to carefully investigate any computer hardware and software investing dollars in a product.

Source: Albert G. Holzinger, "The Virtual Future," Nation's Business *(May 1995), pp. 45–47.*

Evaluating Potential Startups

The first thing you need to start your own business is an idea. But not every idea is a viable business opportunity. You must be able to turn this idea into a profitable business. How do you tell an idea from an opportunity? Where do people come up with viable business ideas that are opportunities?

Business Ideas

While there is no shortage of ideas for new and improved products and services, there is a difference between ideas and opportunities. But are they all business opportunities? Harvard business professor Jeffry Timmons states that a business opportunity has the qualities of being attractive, durable, and timely and is anchored in a product or service that creates or adds value for its buyer or end user.[5] Many ideas for new products and businesses do not add value for customers or users. Maybe the time for the idea has yet to come, or maybe it has already past.

Consider the idea for a new device for removing the crown caps that were common on bottles of soft drinks for many years. You could concoct an exotic and ingenious tool that would be technically feasible to produce, but is there an opportunity to build a business from it? Not since soft-drink and beer companies switched to resealable bottles and screw-off tops to solve the same consumer problem that your invention does.[6] Good idea—no opportunity.

An idea that is too far ahead of the market can be just as bad as one too far behind consumer desires. In 1987 Jerry Kaplan left his job as a software writer for Lotus Development to start Go Computers because he thought the world was ready for portable pen-based computers. He had some big-time backing from IBM and AT&T, who pitched in $75 million to help with startup. He had a vision of salespeople, lawyers, insurance adjusters, and millions of other people writing away on Go computers as if they were paper. Unfortunately, consumers did not find computers that could recognize their handwriting and turn it into print—a tool that they need—eight years later, they still don't. Even with a great idea, a talented leader, and strong financial backing, Go Computers sold only 20,000 units and lasted only three years—it was ahead of its market. Kaplan believes that "A new class of computing devices will come into being . . . it's just a question of when."[7] A startup, even one with substantial resources, can't wait for technology or markets to catch up with an idea.

You have probably heard of the term **window of opportunity**. These windows constantly open and close (sometimes rapidly) as the market for that product (*product* means either goods or services) or business changes. Products go through stages of introduction, growth, maturity, and decline in the **product life cycle.** During the introduction stage, the window of opportunity is wide open because there is little or no competition. As products progress through this cycle, competition increases, consumer expectations are higher, and profit margins are lower so the window of opportunity is not open as wide. (See Figure 7-2.)

Optimally, you want to get through while the window is still opening—if the opportunity is the right one for you. To tell if you should pursue an opportunity, ask yourself the following questions about your business idea:

- Does your idea solve a consumer want or need? This can give you insight on current and future demand.

window of opportunity A period of time in which an opportunity is available.

product life cycle Stages that products in a marketplace pass through over time.

Manager's Notebook

Next Time, I Would . . .

Asked what they would do differently if they could start their businesses all over again, veteran entrepreneurs gave the following advice.

Ready, Fire, Aim Kenneth Heller of Nu Tech Environmental Corp., which works with odor-control technology for municipal waste facilities and food processing businesses, would understand his market better. "When you have a technology, that's not enough. You also need to know how to sell to potential buyers of the product." Heller wasted two years cold-calling on a wide variety of companies, until he started focusing his efforts on companies with a well-defined use for his product.

Friends and Business Don't Mix Management consultant Craig Dreilinger found that "friendships aren't good for business" when he hired two friends for well-paying consulting jobs even when better talent was available. Luckily for Dreilinger, an understanding client explained to him, "You have to focus on our interests, not your friends' interests." Now he makes business decisions based on what his clients and his business need.

Go For It March Nathanson of Falcon Holding Group would have given more equity or taken more debt to expand the cable television system of his company. He feels that he was not aggressive enough in expanding during the early years of his business. Even though Nathanson created one of the largest cable systems in the country, he feels that Falcon would be in a better position now if it were bigger.

You Deserve a Break When Rachelle Nacht founded her mortgage-brokerage firm, Mortgage Match Inc., she wanted to "conquer the world," she says. So she worked 20-hour days and gave up her private life for three years. Now she wishes she would have hired a sales manager and slowed her pace, so she wouldn't have sacrificed those years.

Put Your Eggs in More Than One Basket Steve Brown started his Fortune Group International by training people to work in the real estate industry. But when the real estate market fell in the early 1980s, his company slumped with it. Had he diversified into "every type" of industry, the company could have better withstood fluctuations of the real estate market.

Source: Timothy O'Brien, Brent Bowers & John Emshwiller, "Twenty-Twenty Hindsight," The Wall Street Journal Report—Small Business, October 15, 1993, p. R4.

- If there is a demand, are there enough people who will buy your product to support a business? How much competition for that demand exists?
- Can this idea be turned into a *profitable* business?
- Do you have the skills needed to take advantage of this opportunity? Why hasn't anyone else done it? If others have, what happened to them?[8]

In the idea stage of your thinking (before you actually pursue an opportunity), discuss your idea with a wide variety of people to get feedback. While praise may make you feel good at this stage, what you really need is people who can look for objectivity, possible flaws, and point out the shortcomings of your idea.

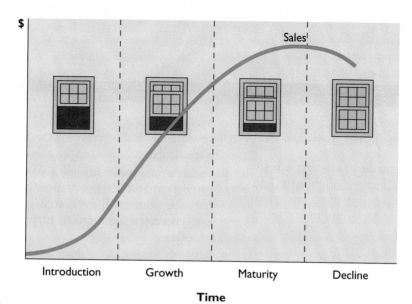

FIGURE 7-2
Windows of Opportunity at Stages of the Product Life Cycle

The final answer to whether your idea is an opportunity that you should follow or not will come from a combination of research and intuition. Both are valuable management tools, but don't rely exclusively on either. Although research has kept some good ideas from becoming products or businesses, it has kept many more bad ones from turning into losing propositions. Do your homework; thoroughly investigate your possibilities. But don't get "analysis paralysis," which prevents you from acting because you think you need more testing or questioning while the window of opportunity closes. Managerial decision making is as much an art as it is a science. There are times you have to make decisions without having every last shred of evidence possible. Get all the information that is practical, but also listen to your gut instincts.

Where Business Ideas Come From

The National Federation of Independent Business reports that prior work experience generates a majority of ideas for new businesses for both men and women, although it is a more common source for men. Women look slightly more to hobbies and personal interests for ideas for their businesses. (See Figure 7-3.)

Prior Work Experience. Experience can be a wonderful teacher. Working for someone else in your area of interest can help you to avoid many errors and begin to build competitive advantages. It gives you the chance to ask, "What would I do differently, if I ran this business?"

One startup may even lead to another. Seeing opportunities for new ventures after starting the first is known as the **corridor principle**.[9] Entrepreneurs start second, third, and succeeding businesses as they move down new venture corridors that did not open to them until they got into business. As we saw with fast-growth startups, 63 percent of fast-growth CEOs had started other companies in the past suggesting that one idea really does lead to another.

Research by Karl Vesper of the University of Washington shows that big ideas occur to small business owners almost twice as often after the business is already running than before it begins.[10] This illustrates that experience pays off whether you are working for someone else or for yourself.

corridor principle Opportunities that become available to an entrepreneur only after the entrepreneur has started a business.

M anager's Notebook

Fatal Flaws

Many mistakes that are made in starting a business can be overcome. In fact we often learn and grow through our mistakes. But there are a few mistakes that usually lead to failure of a startup business:

- *Very small or very large market for the product.* A market that is too small will not produce the profit needed for the business to survive or to grow. Markets that are too large will not be satisfied by a small startup business and may attract large competitors with the resources to capture the needed market share.

- *Overpowering competition and high cost of entry.* Invading the territory of an existing and very strong competitor is extremely dangerous, especially if the capital investment required is high. Delorean Motor Company failed because it lacked the resources to compete with established sports car manufacturers. It also violated the first fatal flaw by targeting a very small market: affluent people who owned

several cars but who were first-time buyers of a sports car.

- *Inability to expand beyond a one-product company.* Demand for every product eventually fades. If your business is based on one product, you have nowhere to turn if it becomes obsolete.

- *Inability to provide a product at a competitive cost.* You have to make a profit to stay in business. Small businesses' profit margins are squeezed to nonexistence if they must hold down prices to maintain market share while facing expenses that are higher than competitors' because of their small volume.

- *Lack of influence and control over product development and component prices.* If the product you provide consists largely of component parts made by someone else, you cannot control the destiny of your own business.

Source: Jeffry Timmons, Daniel Muzyka, Howard Stevenson, and William Bygrave, "Opportunity Recognition: The Core of Entrepreneurship," Frontiers of Entrepreneurship Research, 1987, pp. 109–123.

FIGURE 7-3
Sources of New Business Ideas Among Men and Women
Prior work experience is the most common source of ideas for new businesses for both men and women.
Arnold C. Cooper et al., New Business in America, *1990, NFIB Foundation/VISA Business Card Primer, as shown in William Q. Dennis, Jr.,* A Small Business Primer, *1993, National Federation of Independent Business, p. 17.*

Sources of New Business Ideas Among Men and Women

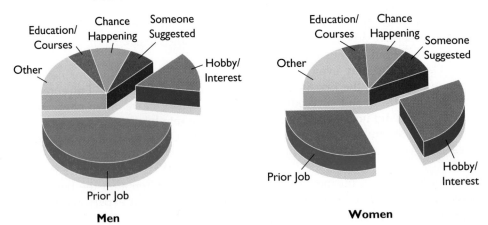

Men

Women

Reality Check

A Natural Talent for Business

A small paper bag filled with brown cotton seeds and lint gave Sally Fox the inspiration to start her own business. In 1982 Fox was working for a California cotton breeder, studying insect-killing bacteria, when she chanced upon the bag of cotton seeds and lint. The breeder had planned to study the insect resistance of the naturally colored brown cotton but never got around to it. The seeds gave Fox an idea. An accomplished hand-spinner and weaver, she thought that other hobbyists who hand-spun their yarn might pay more for the natural undyed, brown cotton. So Fox took some of the seeds and planted them in six plastic pots in her mother's backyard in Menlo Park. Little did she know that her seeds would eventually sprout a business that grossed $5 million in annual revenues.

Once the business was off and running, the path wasn't easy—Fox had to overcome several obstacles. First, she had to find a way to produce seeds that would yield consistently colored cotton with fibers long enough to be easily spun into yarn. Next she had to scramble to locate alternate growers when her request to the Acala Cotton Board, a San Joaquin Valley industry group, denied her permission to commission valley farmers to grow 2,000 acres of her cotton so she could fulfill a $4 million order from a Japanese mill. Finally, she had to finesse the move of her company's headquarters to Arizona following another battle with the Acala Cotton Board. The company, Natural Cotton Colours, Inc., is now based in Wickenburg, Arizona. Fox's experience in the field (literally!) gave her the knowledge she needed to start her business and then to cultivate it into becoming a real success story.

Source: Suzanne Oliver, "Seeds of Success," Forbes, August 15, 1994, pp. 98–100.

Hobbies and Avocations. Turning what you do for pleasure into a part-time or full-time business is a possibility that you should consider. It helps ensure that your business will be one that you enjoy and understand. If you enjoy fishing, could there be an opportunity for you to use your skills to become a guide? If you love pets, could you channel your affections into a dog grooming, or a pet-sitting business?

Andy Zimmerman loves music, stereo equipment, and making deals. Zimmerman breaks many of the "rules" of retailing in turning his audiophile skills into a part-time business. He only opens his discount stereo store on Thursday evenings and all day Saturday. He concentrates the whole business toward restricted hours and customers tolerate them because of great deals. The store specializes in blemished products, floor models, discontinued merchandise, and used equipment. Zimmerman's hobby expects revenues of $650,000 in 1994.[11]

Chance Happening or Serendipity. Serendipity means finding something valuable that you were not looking for. Sometimes business opportunities come to you unexpectedly. The ability to recognize them takes an open mind, flexibility, a sense of adventure, and good business sense.

Dorothy Noe, who ran an antique shop, was initially disappointed that her customers were less interested in her merchandise than in the frilly curtains that

Hung Van Thai has struggled to make his entrepreneurial ideas work in a very tough environment—Communist Vietnam. Thai started his first two private businesses successfully, only to have the government take them away. The first was a soap manufacturing operation that had sales of $5,000 a day, half of which was net profit. But government authorities shut down his operations because he was undercutting the state-owned soap producers. After that, Thai started his second business making plastic slippers. Again, because of his success, he attracted government attention. But this time, Thai offered to turn his business into a state-owned facility if the government would leave him alone, and his offer was accepted. In the late 1980s, as the Vietnamese government began easing up on economic controls, Thai saw his chance to once again start his own private company. His third startup, Hunsan Co., a manufacturer and retailer of sports shoes, has since thrived. Hunsan achieved $12 million in sales in 1994. And Thai hopes to become a viable player in the intensely competitive global shoe industry. He's living proof that the corridor principle—whereby one business naturally leads to another—is alive and well in the global marketplace. *Source: Neil A. Martin, "Invincible Spirit,"* Success *(October 1994), p. 24.*

Antique dealer Dorothy Noe recognized that her customers were more eager to buy her decor—frilly curtains—than her merchandise. Undaunted, Noe started a new business selling curtains. Annual sales have reached $10 million.

decorated the store windows. After numerous customers had stated "I'll pay whatever for them," she gave in and started a curtain business called Dorothy's Ruffled Originals. A production problem existed since Dorothy hated to sew. She solved that by forming a cottage industry of local seamstresses to begin sewing her elaborate curtains. Dorothy got her curtains hung in doctors' offices, restaurants, and businesses all over Wilmington, NC. From 1975 to 1993 Dorothy's Ruffled Originals has grown to a business selling $10 million worth of home decor products.[12]

Brother and sister Ethan and Abby Margalith had to borrow a truck in the summer of 1973 to move a few things to a local swap meet. Both were just out of high school and out of work. While driving the truck to the swap meet, they realized that moving could be their summer job. Their first truck was a 1944 weapons carrier they got for free by rescuing it from a mudslide. Starving Student Moving Company became the low-priced alternative to other movers with full uniforms and high prices. The Margaliths used their sense of humor in their advertising—one ad stated that they offered "24-hour service for lease breakers." Even without knowing what they were doing, they had more business than they could handle. Ethan has stated that it wasn't until he got to law school that he realized he and his sister were really running a business. He finished law school but decided that the moving business is fun, exciting, and profitable so he stayed in business with his sister. By 1992, Starving Students had 14 locations in five states with combined revenues of $15 million—and it started by digging a truck out of the mud![13]

Getting Started

Most of the topics involved in starting your own business are covered in detail in other sections or entire chapters of this book. Let's look at what else is needed to get a business off the ground.

Riding on Air

While getting ready to visit a friend's son in the hospital, Dan Pharo was inflating a Mylar balloon as a gift. In his haste, he overinflated the balloon and the side seam blew. Before he repaired the seam, Pharo, who had designed balloons in his art studio, had an idea. Why not put the toy truck he had as another gift inside the balloon before fixing the seam? His gift within a gift was a hit. The boy was so fascinated he didn't want to open it. Everyone who saw it was intrigued.

Pharo decided to patent his invention and to set up a company to market it. The Puff Pac Industries began selling its inflatable gift wrap in 1988 distributing the wrap through gift stores and shopping center kiosks across the United States and Canada. In 1989, Pharo made an innovation that could turn his novelty into something far more promising. He found a way to heat seal a polyethylene bag within a Mylar bag. This allowed him to suspend an object in midair. This whole new type of packaging promised to help reduce packaging waste, which accounts for 30 percent of landfill space by volume. Pharo estimated he could reduce the amount of packaging trash by 90 percent. However, Pharo recognized that he was better at generating ideas than running a company of the magnitude that Puff Pac might become. Recruiting top-flight talent was easy for a company with his potential.

Setting up operations turned from problem to nightmare. Puff Pac needed specialized machinery to move sheets of film along a conveyor at precise speeds and heat seal the plastics together. Such machinery would cost about $500,000—but it didn't exist yet and had to be made. In the meantime, production was done by hand while the machinery was produced. This caused a lot of problems. Setbacks in production caused tremendous backorders. Pharo stated, "The minute you don't deliver product, the sales reps don't even know your name." Finally, the corner was turned, production came up to speed, and revenue was covering expenses. Sales for 1992 were projected at $16.5 million, of which half was gift wrap and half was industrial bags. Despite all the problems Pharo went through, he remains optimistic about the future of the company.

Source: Jay Finegan, "Packing Them In," Inc. (February 1992), pp. 90–96.

What Do You Do First?

You must first decide that you want to work for yourself rather than for someone else. You need to generate a number of ideas for a new product or service that people will buy until you come up with the right opportunity that matches your skills and interests.

Whether you are starting a business because you have a product or service that is new to the world or because your product or service is not available locally, you have to get past the questions: "Is there a need for this business?" "Is this business needed here?" "Is it needed now?" These questions address the most critical concern in getting a business off the ground—the feasibility of your idea. Owning a business is a dream of many Americans, but there is usually a gap between that dream and bringing it to reality. Careful planning is needed to bridge that gap.

The Importance of Planning to a Startup

Before you begin your business, you should start by writing a comprehensive business plan. (See Chapter 4.) A business plan not only helps you determine the direction of your business and keeps you on track after it opens, it will be required if you need to borrow money to start your business. It shows your banker that you have seriously evaluated the business opportunity and how you will be able to pay back the loan.

In addition to writing your business plan, you will need to decide and record other important steps in starting your business, primarily:

- *Market analysis.* For your small business to be successful, you have to get to know your market by gathering and analyzing facts about your customers to determine the demand for your product. Market analysis takes time and effort, but it does not have to be statistically complex or expensive. Who will buy your product? What do your customers have in common with each other? Where do they live? How much will they spend?

- *Competitive analysis.* Your business needs a competitive advantage that separates it from competitors. Before you can develop your own "uniqueness," you need to know what other businesses do and how they are perceived.

  An exercise to help you remove some of the subjectivity of the competitive analysis process begins with you identifying four of your direct competitors. Then set up a grid on which you will rank your business with your competitors.

- *Startup Costs.* How much money will you need to start your business? Before you can seek funding, you need to itemize what your expenses will be. (See Figure 7-4.) Although some of these expenses will be ongoing, others will be incurred only when you start business. There will be many expenses that you do not expect; therefore, add 10 percent to your subtotal to help offset them.

FIGURE 7-4
How Much Money Will You Need?

Expense	Estimated Cost
Capital equipment	_____
	_____
	_____
	_____
Beginning inventory	_____
Legal fees	_____
Accounting fees	_____
Licenses and permits	_____
Remodeling and decorating	_____
Deposits (utilities, telephone)	_____
Advertising (preopening)	_____
Insurance	_____
Startup supplies	_____
Cash reserve (petty cash, credit accounts)	_____
Other expenses:	_____
	_____
	_____
	_____
Subtotal startup expenses:	$_____
Add 10% safety factor:	_____
TOTAL STARTUP EXPENSES	$_____

Entering the Internet

Don't forget to check the Internet for help in starting your business! At a site called Galaxy, Business and Commerce, you can access a listing with several options on various topics appropriate for startup businesses. (See addresses that follow for all sites mentioned here.) From the Small Business Administration's menu, you can access the topic areas "How to Start a Home-Based Business" and "How to Start a Small Business." Another source for startup information could be found at a site called Entrepreneurs on the Web, which lists several research categories such as Entrepreneur's Exchange, the Internet Business Center, or The Global Trade Center. At Yahoo's site called Business and Economy: Small Business Information, you'll find links to useful sources such as Best Businesses to Start, Complete Gameplan for Starting and Operating a Home Business, Entrepreneur Guides, Entrepreneur Resource Center, and WomenBiz. Finally, you might want to use a keyword or topic search using any of the Web search tools introduced in earlier chapters to get more specific information in your particular areas of interest.

Web Address for Galaxy, Business and Commerce
http://www.galaxy.einet.com

Web Address for SBA:
gopher://www.sbaonline.sba.gov

Web Address for Entrepreneurs on the Web:
http://www.eotw.com//EOTW.html

Web Address for Yahoo's Business and Economy: Small Business Information
http://www.yahoo.com

Capital equipment assets have a life of more than one year. Computers, office equipment, fixtures, and furniture are examples of capital equipment. List the equipment you need with the rest of your startup costs. Beware of the temptation to buy the newest, most expensive, or fastest equipment available before you open your doors. You don't have any revenue yet and more small businesses have failed due to lack of sales than from lack of expensive "goodies." Is good used equipment available? Should you lease rather than buy it? If sales do materialize, you can replace used equipment with new from actual profits.

- *The legal form of your business.* As discussed in Chapter 2, when starting a business you need to consider the appropriate legal form of business. Your decision will be based on tax considerations, personal liability, and cost and ease of organizing.

- *The location of your business.* Consider how important the location of your business is to your customers. (See Chapter 8.) If customers come to your business, your location decision is critical. If your business comes to them, or if you don't meet with them face to face, location is a less critical decision.

- *Your marketing plan.* The marketing decisions you need to make before you open your business include who your customers are, how you will reach

Manager's Notebook

Startup Myths and Realities

The human mind has a remarkable ability to rationalize just about anything. If we want to do something, we can often tell ourselves something that sounds right—whether it is reality or not. Dave Kansas identified the following myths which may add some perspective to starting a business.

Myth 1: I'm Smart—I Can Just Wing It *Reality:* Face it—you need a plan. One of the few things that a group of small business lenders, advisors, and consultants would agree on is the need for a business plan. New York business consultant Jim Gabe reminds us that "an entrepreneur's perception isn't always in step with reality."

Myth 2: I Can Do It on a Shoestring *Reality:* While no one ever has *enough* money, having too *little* can be doom. Thomas Dandrige of State University of New York at Albany states, "People forget that most businesses require a great deal of spending before they can begin to develop cash flow." Having money is not as important to a business as having a product that people want, but you have to have enough money for you and the company to survive until it can support itself.

Myth 3: No Sweat, I Have a Great Idea *Reality:* According to William E. Dunn of University of Pennsylvania's Wharton School, "About 5 percent of the success equation is having a good idea." Great ideas are an important start for businesses, but ideas alone won't get you far. You also need the resources, skills, and products to make a business.

Myth 4: I've Got Nothing Better to Do *Reality:* You cannot start a successful small business halfheartedly. Starting a business because you have been laid off your job and just need something to do is not a good idea. The level of commitment associated with making a quick buck is a long way from the reality needed for success in starting a new business.

Myth 5: Maybe Starting a Business Will Help Our Marriage *Reality:* A risky bet. The stress involved in starting a business can amplify marital weaknesses. Marriage counselors advise people not to start businesses until they are emotionally stable. The distraction of personal problems takes away from your ability to concentrate on your new business.

Myth 6: A Bad Economy Will Mean Fewer Competitors *Reality:* Maybe, but it can also make the survivors more fierce competitors. Bank loans and customers with money may be more difficult to find.

Myth 7: I'm Mad as Hell and I'm Not Going to Take It Anymore *Reality:* The frustration that you have built up with your current job can be a good rationale for starting your own business, if your anger is focused on positive outcomes. Anger in general won't get you ahead. W. L. Gore was a frustrated chemist with Du Pont Co. because he didn't think Teflon was being used to its potential. He quit to start his own business, W. L. Gore & Associates. The company grew to $1 billion annual revenue from Gore-Tex, the Teflon-based waterproof fabric.

Myth 8: If I Can't Think of Anything Else, I'll Open a Bar *Reality:* Despite common opinion, restaurants and bars are not easy businesses to start or run. The rationale that everyone likes to eat and drink does not hold up. Having dined out regularly or bellied up to a bar does not qualify as experience in this business. Dunn advises, "You have to know customers and know how to solve their problems. You have to be better and cheaper to get their business."

Source: Dave Kansas, "Don't Believe It," The Wall Street Journal Report—Small Business, October 15, 1993, p. R8. Reprinted by permission of the Wall Street Journal © 1993 Dow Jones & Company, Inc. All rights reserved worldwide.

your potential customers, what you will sell them, where it will be available, and how much it will cost. (See Chapter 10.)

Some aspects of starting your business are not included in the business plan. Now let's look at what your business will focus on, how you will approach customer service, the licenses you will need to acquire, and the taxes you must withhold to begin business.

How Will You Compete?

Before you begin your small business, consider what you want to be known for. Since no business can be all things to all people, you need to realize what your customers value and strive to exceed their expectations. For instance, if your customers value low price, you must set up your business to cut costs wherever possible so you can keep your prices low. If your customers value convenience, you need to set up your business with a focus on providing speed and ease for them. In providing value to your customers, we can identify three disciplines on which companies compete: operational excellence, product leadership, and customer intimacy.[14] In choosing to focus on one of these disciplines, you are not abandoning the other two. Instead you are defining your position in consumers' minds. Visualize your choice of discipline by picturing each as a mountain on which you choose to compete by raising the expectation level of customers in that area. (See Figure 7-5.) By becoming a leader in that discipline, you are better able to defend against competing companies below you.

Companies that pursue **operational excellence** know that their customers value low price and concentrate on the efficiency of their operations to hold down costs. They don't have the very best products or cutting-edge innovations. They strive to offer good products at the lowest price possible. Dell Computer is an example of a company that competes on operational excellence.

Companies that are **product leaders** constantly innovate to make the best products available even better. This kind of commitment to quality is not inexpensive, but product leaders know that price is not the most important factor to their customers. New Balance athletic shoes are known for their technical excellence, not for their inexpensive price or their customer service.

Companies that focus on developing **customer intimacy** are not looking for a one-time sale. They seek to build a long-term, close working relationship with their customers. Their customers want to be treated as if they are the company's

operational excellence Creates a competitive advantage by holding down costs to provide customers the lowest-priced products.

product leadership Creates a competitive advantage based on providing the highest quality products possible.

customer intimacy Creates a competitive advantage by maintaining a long-term relationship with customers through superior service.

On Which Mountain Will You Compete?

FIGURE 7-5
On Which Mountain Will You Compete?
When setting up your small business, you must decide how you will satisfy your customers. Do you need to offer them the best product, the best price, or the best service?

only customer. The Lands' End operator you speak with on the telephone sees records of clothing sizes, styles, and colors from your previous orders as soon as you call. Customer-intimate companies offer specific rather than general solutions to their customers' problems.

Customer Service

Your business relationship with your customers does not end with the sale of your product or service. Increasing your level of customer service and adopting professional standards are critical, especially in an industry where all competitors appear to be the same. Satisfying the customer is not a means to achieve a goal, *it is the goal.* Customer service can be your competitive advantage.

The importance of a startup business providing an emphasis on the highest-quality customer service cannot be overstated. Evidence of this statement can be seen in examining the finalists of the 1993 Ernst & Young Entrepreneur of the Year Award. Although the industries represented were diverse (construction, alternative energy products, wholesale distribution, body art, baked goods, and DNA research marketing), there were common threads.[15] These entrepreneurs are in business for the "long haul" rather than the "quick buck." An emphasis on customer service can be the focus of any type of business.

When her father suddenly became ill, Deborah Silverberg took over the family's commercial floor contracting business, AnchorMann Enterprises of St. Louis, MO. Despite a recession, she increased the size of the business tenfold—basically starting the business all over again. She expanded service to other cities and bought out a competitor. For Silverberg, making customers happy is an essential part of her strategy for success. As one of the only companies in the flooring industry with its own maintenance department, AnchorMann Enterprises is able to offer longer warranties on its products than its competitors. Silverberg admits that this advantage is "not mindboggling. But it's unique enough to get people to do business with us rather than the competition."[16]

Licenses, Permits, and Regulations

If your business has no employees, you have fewer legal requirements to meet. First, let's look at the common requirements for all businesses. You need to file your business name with the secretary of state of the state in which you are forming your business. This is to make sure that the name you have chosen for your business is not registered by another company. If it is, you will have to find another name for your business.

You must obtain the appropriate local licenses from the city hall and county clerk's office before you start your business. Find out if you can operate your business in the location you have picked by checking local zoning ordinances. You may need a special permit for certain types of businesses. For example, if your business handles processed food, it must pass a local health department inspection.

Most states collect sales tax on tangible property sold. If your state does, you must apply for a state sales tax identification number to use when paying the sales taxes you collect. Contact the Department of Revenue in your state for information regarding your requirements. Many types of businesspeople like accountants, electricians, motor vehicle dealers, cosmetologists, and securities dealers require specific licenses. These licenses are obtained from the state agency that oversees that type of business. Contact the Department of Revenue for details.

Very few small businesses are likely to need any type of federal permit or license to operate. If you will produce alcohol, firearms, tobacco products, meat products, or give investment advice, contact an attorney regarding regulations.

Taxes

When your business begins operations, you must make advance payments of your estimated federal (and possibly state) income taxes. Individual tax payments are due in four quarterly installments—on the 15th day of April, June, September, and January. It is important for you to remember to set money aside from your revenues so it will be available when your quarterly taxes are due. The Internal Revenue Service is not known for its sense of humor if funds are not available.

If your business is a sole proprietorship, you report your self-employment income on Schedule SE of IRS Form 1040, and any income or loss on Schedule C of IRS Form 1040. A partnership reports partnership income on IRS Form 1065 and each partner reports his or her individual share on Schedule SE and Schedule E. Corporations file tax returns on IRS Form 1120. Any payment you make over $600 for items like rent, interest, or services from independent contractors must be shown on Form 1096, and copies of Form 1099 sent to the people you paid.

When you begin employing other people, you become an agent of the U.S. government and must begin collecting income and social security taxes. You must get a federal Employer Identification Number, which identifies your business for all tax purposes. Your local IRS office will supply you with a business tax kit with all the necessary forms. You withhold 7.51 percent of an employee's wages for social security tax and you must pay a matching 7.51 percent employer's social security tax. Pay both halves of the tax quarterly with your payroll tax return.

If a person provides services to your business but is not an employee, they are considered to be **independent contractors.** Since independent contractors are considered to be self-employed, you do not have to withhold social security tax, federal or state income taxes, or unemployment taxes from their earnings—an obvious advantage to you. Because of the advantage of classifying a person as an independent contractor rather than an employee, the IRS imposes stiff penalties on businesses that improperly treat employees as independent contractors.

independent contractor Persons who are not employed by a business, and unlike employees, are not eligible for benefit packages.

You must deposit a percentage of each employee's earnings for federal and state unemployment tax with a federal tax deposit coupon. The federal unemployment tax rate is 6.2 percent of the first $7,000 per employee, but a credit of up to 5.4 percent is allowed for state unemployment tax. In reality, only 0.8 percent goes to federal tax. The state rate you pay depends on the amount of claims filed by former employees. The more claims, the higher your unemployment tax within certain limits.

Summary

■ The advantages of starting a business from scratch.

When starting a business from scratch, the small business owner is free to establish a distinct competitive advantage. There are no negative images or prior mistakes to overcome as may occur when purchasing an existing business. The creation of a new business builds pride of ownership.

■ The common characteristics of fast-growth companies.

Companies developed with the intent of fast growth are generally led by teams of people with experience starting that type of business (usually high-tech manufacturing). They are well financed and constantly look to expand into new markets.

■ How business ideas are realized in the context of changing windows of opportunity.

When a new product idea is introduced to the market, the window of opportunity is open widest (assuming it is a product that people want and will buy) because little competition exists. As a product progresses through the product life cycle, the window of opportunity closes as more competition enters the market and demand declines.

■ Sources of business ideas.

Most people get ideas for new businesses from prior employment. Turning a hobby or outside interest into a business is also common. Ideas may come from suggestions of other people or spring from information gained while taking a class. Sometimes business ideas occur unexpectedly by chance.

■ The importance of customer service.

Providing customers with outstanding service during and after the sale of a product shows that a business cares about the customer's needs. Customer service is the basis for establishing a long term relationship with customers.

Questions for Review and Discussion

1. Compare and contrast the advantages and disadvantages of starting a business from the ground up. Be sure to include the different types of businesses in your analysis. *challenge, molding vs. higher risk, Est. mkt.*

2. Define a "hypergrowth" company and evaluate the reasons for their phenomenal rate of growth. What are the most valid explanations for the rate of success found in these companies? *high growth (p. 181)*

3. Explain the concept "window of opportunity" as it relates to new starts in business from idea conception through the final decision about whether or not to turn the idea into a reality. *Time for idea to wk.*

4. Entrepreneurs get their ideas for business startups from various sources. Elaborate on these sources and give an analysis of which ones are the most reliable indicators for the new business owner with regard to future success.

5. Once a decision has been made to start up a new business, give some examples of things the new entrepreneur should immediately investigate in order to ensure to the maximum extent possible that the business will "get off the ground."

6. Is a business plan really necessary even for a very small startup business? *yes*

How much market analysis and competitive analysis should the new entrepreneur conduct prior to startup? *Ident. Costs, risk + projections*

7. What are some of the tangible resources that the new entrepreneur might need in order to go into business initially? What are some options for obtaining capital for a business that is brand new and therefore has no financial history? *Eg., Supp., Inv., facil.*

8. After startup, what is the *single* most important tool the small business owner has at his or her disposal for ensuring the success of the business and why it is so crucial? *Keeping hus, updated as mgt, tool*

9. What are some examples of consumer preferences and values? What are some examples of things the new business owner can do to ensure capturing some of the market for the good or service being produced?

10. Discuss the legal ramifications of starting your own business. Where should the new entrepreneur go to get information and advice regarding laws that govern the type of business that is being promoted?

Critical Incident

Todd Holmes and Louis Amoroso enjoy going out to a bar and having a beer. In 1990, they noticed a trend—beer drinkers like trying out different high-quality, regional beers. Research into industry statistics disclosed the same trend. Since 1988, overall beer consumption had been flat, but the combined volume of 460 U.S. microbrewers had grown an average of 46 percent a year. So the 24-year-old pals put their heads together to find a way they could tap into this trend, and came up with two prospects. But they weren't sure of the approach they wanted to take. The first prospect was that they could start their own microbrewery—a small, regional brewery producing fewer than 15,000 barrels a year. As a manufacturer, they'd make their own regional beer and market it. Or they might try a different approach by acting as a distributor. Here their idea was to set up a beer-of-the-month club that would send subscribers a different regional beer every month. What do *you* think about these two startups that Holmes and Amoroso could pursue to take advantage of this market trend? *Source: James M. Clash, "Beer Bash," Forbes, December 5, 1994, pp. 66–69; and "Beer Across America," Success (September 1995), p. 34.*

Questions

1. Draft a proposal for the startup business in this example which you feel has the greatest potential. Be sure to consider all the aspects of being a manufacturer or being a distributor.

2. Working together in teams of two or three individuals, discuss the relative merits of each of Holmes's and Amoroso's possibilities. Develop a bulleted list of pros and cons for each approach.

Take it to the Net

We invite you to visit the Hatten page on the Prentice Hall Web site at: http://www.prenhall.com/~hattensb for this chapter's World Wide Web exercise.

Chapter Focus

After reading this chapter, you should be able to:

- Determine factors in selecting a region or state in which to locate your business.
- Calculate the sales conversion index to compare location sites within the city.
- Explore the central issues of choosing a particular site.
- Compare the three basic types of locations.
- Present the circumstances under which leasing or buying a building is an appropriate choice.
- Explain the types of layout you may choose.

8 Site Selection and Layout

PIZZA HUT, KFC, OLIVE GARDEN, and other restaurant chains are not using their stomachs anymore. Restaurants not interested in stomachs? Actually, they are still interested in stomachs, more precisely, they are not depending on "gut feelings" as much anymore—at least when it comes to choosing a restaurant location. Market saturation and soaring real estate prices have increased the stakes in choosing a location for all types of restaurants. As a result, managers are turning to more dependable and sophisticated decision-making tools in choosing locations. They are combining demographics, psychographics, census figures, and computerized sales projections in selecting future sites.

Restaurant chains like Pizza Hut are using all kinds of information tools to help them move into more nontraditional locations. New Pizza Hut operations—whether franchised or company owned—aren't likely to be found only in the traditional stand-alone, red-roofed buildings of the past. Instead you'll also see them branching out with small delivery units without seating, with stand-alone kiosks

201

in shopping malls, and with locations in college cafeterias. Pizza Hut says that their company's standard trade area has been shrinking as more smaller-sized, delivery-only and take-out units are built. A Pizza Hut unit can operate within a very small trade area if the population is concentrated. For instance, in New York City, a unit may be dedicated to only one office or apartment building. In fact, you may even have a small Pizza Hut operation somewhere on your campus.

How do business owners make these location decisions? Restaurant chain executives who consult databases built from ZIP+4 codes can find out a lot more than just the income and education levels of people in a general area. Indeed, they can now find out which households own dogs, which households drive vehicles of what make and year—even where those households are located to within 250 feet! But even if your small business isn't part of a large chain of restaurants or retailers, the more you know about the people in your market, the better your odds of selecting the "right" location. *Kevin Farrell, "Risky Business Sites and Saturation,"* Restaurant Business, *July 1, 1991, p. 74.*

Locating for the Long Run

Selecting a location for your business is one of the most important decisions you will make as a small business owner. While not every business depends on foot traffic for its customers, just about any business can pick a poor location for one reason or another. For example, retail businesses need to be easily accessible to their consumers. A company which produces concrete blocks for construction must be located in an area that frequently uses that type of building material if it is to keep down transportation costs. Manufacturing businesses need to consider locating near their workers, sources of raw materials, and transportation outlets.

People do not tend to go out of their way to find a business. Although Ralph Waldo Emerson had great literary success when he wrote, "If a man can make a better mousetrap than his neighbor, though he builds his house in the woods, the world will make a beaten path to his door," it's best not to take his advice literally when selecting a location for your business.

This chapter will follow the building location process from broadest decisions (selecting a state or region) to narrowest (designing a layout of your facilities). The four essential questions you need to ask are:

1. What region of the country would be best for your business?
2. What state within that region satisfies your needs?
3. What city within that region will best suit you?
4. What specific site within that city will accommodate your business?

Don't automatically jump to the fourth question. By beginning the site selection process broadly and then narrowing your choices down, you can choose a location that meets the needs of your target market and is near other businesses that are complementary to yours. (See Figure 8-1.)

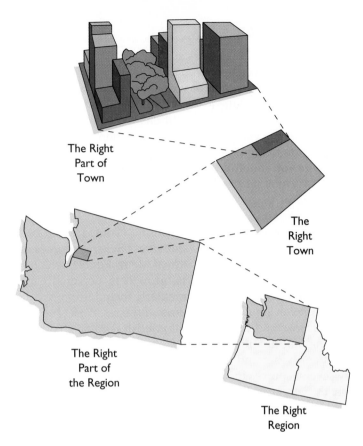

The Right
Part of
Town

The
Right
Town

The Right
Part of
the Region

The Right
Region

FIGURE 8-1
Identification of Regional and Local Markets
Choosing the right location for your business may be a process of narrowing down the region, state, city, and neighborhood that are right for you.

What to Evaluate

To analyze a potential location for your business, you will want to consider the specific needs of your business in conjunction with your personal preferences. Establish the criteria that are essential to your success first. Then list those that are desirable but not mandatory. Examples of criteria include:

Price and availability of land and water

Quality and quantity of labor pool

Access to your customers

Proximity of suppliers

Access to transportation (air, highway, rail)

Location of competition

Public attitudes toward new business

Laws, regulations, and taxes

Your personal preference of where to live

Financial incentives provided (tax breaks, bond issues, guaranteed loans)

Quality of schools

Quality of life (crime rate, recreation opportunities, housing, cost of living, cultural activities)

State Selection

Most small business owners start and operate their businesses in the area where they currently live. However, there are people who are anxious to relocate to another part of the country (or world) to run their small business.

The United States is a collection of local and regional markets rather than one big market. Business conditions vary from place to place. Economic booms and recessions vary from region to region.[1] Markets and people's tastes vary from region to region as well, and these regional differences may have an impact on where you should locate your business. For example, your recipe for deep pan pizza may not set your business apart from the competition in Chicago where that style of pizza is very popular. But it may make your business unique in Flagstaff, Arizona, or Biloxi, Mississippi.

Where do you find information to compare and contrast the economic performance of regions, states, and cities? Several sources are available. Every year *Inc.* magazine publishes its annual Metro Report, which ranks job growth, population growth, business starts, growth in personal earnings, and employment pool data. *Fortune* magazine regularly includes information on regional and state economies in its *Fortune* Forecast. *Business Week, Forbes, The Wall Street Journal, Entrepreneur,* and *USA Today* all publish regular accounts of current regional and national information. The U.S. Census Bureau gathers data by geographic region every ten years and maintains an extensive database. Census data are reported by several sources including the *Survey of Buying Power,* which is published annually by *Sales and Marketing Management* (SMM).

The *SMM Survey of Buying Power* combines data on population, income, and retail sales for nine regions within the United States. The survey assigns a weight to each factor to calculate a buying power index (BPI) so that different markets can be compared (see Table 8-1 for an example of the Mountain Region). The BPI allows you to compare any city, county, or state to the United States as a whole (U.S. = 100).[2]

Another figure useful in helping you determine a location for your business is the **effective buying index (EBI).** The EBI takes the census's figures for personal income and subtracts all personal taxes and deductions that are charged in each area. This shows what is known as disposable personal income, or money that people have left over after taxes. This figure is especially useful if your business is based on a product or service that is more of a luxury than a necessity. You would want to locate a business that sells luxury goods in an area with a high EBI since a higher disposable income means that more people in that area are available to buy your goods.

effective buying index (EBI) The amount of personal income after taxes and deductions made by people in a specific geographic area.

Your location decision will depend on criteria that you establish yourself. However, some trends among entrepreneurs are noticeable. Economic consultant David Birch has noticed that fast-growing companies tend to locate in "nice places to live," even if the cost is higher.[3] Birch's top five states for entrepreneurs are:

1. Hawaii
2. Nevada
3. Georgia
4. Utah
5. North Carolina

TABLE 8 ▪ 1 Regional and State Summaries of Population, Effective Buying Income, and Retail Sales

1995 REGIONAL AND STATE SUMMARIES OF POPULATION

S&MM ESTIMATES: 1/1/95

REGION State	Total Population (Thousands)	% Of U.S.	Median Age of Population	Population by Age Group					Households (Thousands)	% Of U.S.
				0–17 years (Thousands)	18–24 years (Thousands)	25–34 years (Thousands)	35–49 years (Thousands)	50 & Over (Thousands)		
MOUNTAIN	**15,476.5**	**5.9023**	**32.7**	**4,453.8**	**1,424.8**	**2,420.3**	**3,524.6**	**3,653.0**	**5,717.6**	**5.9207**
Arizona	4,144.7	1.5807	33.4	1,128.6	395.5	650.8	896.6	1,073.2	1,552.8	1.6080
Colorado	3,715.9	1.4171	33.5	985.9	338.2	627.4	939.8	824.6	1,453.3	1.5049
Idaho	1,149.8	.4385	32.7	355.4	97.4	158.9	256.4	281.7	414.5	.4292
Montana	863.3	.3292	35.1	241.6	67.7	120.6	203.3	230.1	332.5	.3443
Nevada	1,518.5	.5791	34.5	381.2	135.9	254.2	368.8	378.4	585.9	.6067
New Mexico	1,672.9	.6380	32.2	501.3	150.2	257.0	373.3	391.1	599.8	.6211
Utah	1,932.2	.7369	26.8	715.2	201.3	279.9	371.5	364.3	599.0	.6203
Wyoming	479.2	.1828	32.9	144.6	38.6	71.5	114.9	109.6	179.8	.1862
TOTAL UNITED STATES	**262,213.3**	**100.0000**	**34.1**	**68,229.8**	**25,340.4**	**41,315.9**	**59,631.6**	**67,695.6**	**96,571.0**	**100.0000**

1995 REGIONAL AND STATE SUMMARIES OF EFFECTIVE BUYING INCOME

S&MM ESTIMATES: 1/1/95

REGION State	1994 Total EBI ($000)	% Of U.S.	Per Capita EBI	Average Household EBI	Median Household EBI	Population by Age Group				
						Under $10,000 (Thousands)	$10,000 $19,000 (Thousands)	$20,000 $34,000 (Thousands)	$35,000 $49,999 (Thousands)	$50,000 & Over (Thousands)
MOUNTAIN	**238,152,965**	**5.3685**	**15,388**	**41,653**	**34,116**	**631.5**	**930.3**	**1,373.8**	**1,117.1**	**1,664.9**
Arizona	61,017,989	1.3755	14,722	39,295	31,521	195.5	274.8	389.4	295.0	398.1
Colorado	64,774,974	1.4602	17,432	44,571	36,770	143.3	216.0	331.3	281.5	481.2
Idaho	16,639,002	.3751	14,471	40,142	33,052	42.4	71.1	106.9	83.8	110.3
Montana	13,014,010	.2933	15,075	39,140	31,959	40.6	59.9	81.2	63.3	87.5
Nevada	26,269,994	.5922	17,300	44,837	36,713	53.2	85.8	139.1	120.6	187.2
New Mexico	22,642,998	.5104	13,535	37,751	30,032	88.6	110.1	144.8	107.1	149.2
Utah	26,008,997	.5863	13,461	43,421	37,524	49.6	84.9	141.4	130.5	192.6
Wyoming	7,785,001	.1755	16,246	43,298	36,686	18.3	27.7	39.7	35.3	58.8
TOTAL UNITED STATES	**4,436,178,724**	**100.0000**	**16,918**	**45,937**	**37,070**	**10,732.0**	**14,188.2**	**20,695.3**	**18,014.6**	**32,940.9**

1995 REGIONAL AND STATE SUMMARIES OF RETAIL SALES

S&MM ESTIMATES: 1/1/95

REGION State	1994 Total Retail Sale ($000)	% Of U.S.	Per Household Retail Sales	Retail Sales by Store Group						Sales/Advertising Indexes		
				Food ($000)	Eating & Drinking Places ($000)	General Merchandise ($000)	Furniture/ Home Furnish. Appliance ($000)	Automotive ($000)	Drug ($000)	Sales Activity	Buying Power	Quality
MOUNTAIN	**137,910,310**	**6.1532**	**24,120**	**27,964,128**	**17,376,273**	**17,168,697**	**8,404,934**	**29,780,080**	**3,005,104**	**104**	**5.7107**	**97**
Arizona	36,516,933	1.6293	23,517	7,603,512	4,628,690	4,664,866	2,094,558	7,934,094	1,065,743	103	1.4927	94
Colorado	35,669,581	1.5915	24,544	6,893,576	4,672,220	4,394,160	2,434,067	7,568,099	553,993	112	1.4910	105
Idaho	10,489,397	.4680	25,306	2,211,328	1,128,760	1,177,636	623,988	2,643,563	214,823	107	.4156	95
Montana	7,591,809	.3388	22,833	1,535,335	1,026,955	865,984	426,581	1,680,098	159,238	103	.3141	95
Nevada	14,897,617	.6646	25,427	3,038,920	1,899,494	1,872,121	875,640	2,941,217	367,181	115	.6114	106
New Mexico	14,092,171	.6287	23,495	2,741,327	1,871,332	1,803,864	773,102	2,915,267	377,432	99	.5714	90
Utah	14,267,538	.6366	23,819	3,109,818	1,589,619	1,834,457	1,001,058	3,173,218	205,235	86	.6315	86
Wyoming	4,385,264	.1957	24,390	830,312	559,203	555,609	175,940	924,524	61,459	107	.1830	100
TOTAL UNITED STATES	**2,241,319,080**	**100.0000**	**23,209**	**406,017,508**	**229,542,193**	**285,351,264**	**125,302,413**	**521,583,362**	**84,203,636**	**100**	**100.0000**	**100**

Source: 1995 Survey of Buying Power, Sales & Marketing Management, *pp. B-2, B-3, B-4.*

The six-state Rocky Mountain region—Colorado, Idaho, Montana, Nevada, Utah, and Wyoming—has grown economically much faster than the economy of the United States as a whole.[4] All six rank among the top 11 states for employment growth. Building permits rose by at least 40 percent in 1992 compared to 15.9 percent nationally. Attractive tax rates, reasonable government regulations and cost of living, high quality of life and available telecommunications combine to make this the fastest growing economic area of the country.

Once again, be warned to do your homework in advance. Do not assume that every state is looking for economic expansion and new businesses. For instance, while Utah actively pursues businesses to locate there, neighboring New Mexico is much less interested in rapid growth.[5]

City Selection

To most businesses, what is going on in our city or state is more important to us than what goes on in the $5 trillion U.S. economy.[6] The economic condition of a particular city, state, or region is often much different than the national situation.

Let's look at the Fort Collins–Loveland metropolitan area of Colorado as an example of the specific demographic information available from the annual *SMM Survey of Buying Power.* (See Table 8-2.) You can compare population by age groups, retail sales by type of store, and percentages of effective buying income to other cities that you are also considering for your business location.

In 1987 a Canadian company that makes city buses, New Flyer Industries Ltd., built a new plant outside of Oakland, California to be near a major customer.[7] But productivity at the plant was not what the company had hoped and the expense of transporting its finished buses became a problem as their customer base increased. Admitting that the California location had been a mistake, New Flyer decided to close the plant and set up operations elsewhere. The company selected Grand Forks, North Dakota, where rent cost them $7,000 per month compared to $23,000 per month in Oakland, and where average wages were just under $8 per hour instead of the $12 to $13 per hour paid in California. Company president Guy Johnson stated that employee attitude was one of the largest benefits of the move, with a productivity increase of 25 percent.

If your business is involved in retail or service sales, a technique for comparing different locations based on residents' ability to convert personal income into retail purchases is the sales conversion index (SCI).[8] This index allows small business managers to analyze a market area in relation to a benchmark area with similar income and nonretail spending characteristics. You can even examine specific categories of retail activity. The SCI measures the strength of the retail sector by calculating **inshopping,** which occurs when consumers come from outside the local market area to shop. A city with a weaker retail sector experiences **outshopping,** or consumers going outside the community to shop.

inshopping The effect of more consumers coming into a town to purchase goods than leave it to buy the same product.

outshopping The effect of more consumers leaving a town to purchase goods than enter it to buy the same product.

Because it takes only a simple calculation of readily available secondary data, any business can use the SCI. The data can be found in the *Sales and Marketing Management's Survey of Buying Power.* (See Table 8-2.) To make the calculation, you need to begin with the following data:

- Total retail sales from the retail trade area(s) being examined (called the *subject area*)
- Retail sales for an appropriate *benchmark* unit.
- Retail sales for the subject and benchmark areas in each of the product categories.
- Effective buying income (EBI) for the subject and benchmark areas. EBI is personal income minus personal tax and nontax payments.

Calculating the SCI takes five steps:

TABLE 8 ▪ 2   Population, EBI, and Retail Sales for Fort Collins, Colorado

COLORADO

S&MM ESTIMATES: 1/1/95

POPULATION

METRO AREA County City	Total Population (Thousands)	% Of U.S.	Median Age Of Pop.	% of Population by Age Group				House-holds (Thousands)
				18–24 Years	25–34 Years	35–49 Years	50 & Over	
FORT COLLINS-								
LOVELAND	**216.0**	**.0824**	**32.0**	**12.9**	**16.4**	**24.7**	**20.3**	**82.0**
Larimer	216.0	.0824	32.0	12.9	16.4	24.7	20.3	82.0
• Fort Collins	101.7	.0388	28.5	20.5	18.3	22.2	16.0	39.3
• Loveland	44.7	.0170	34.2	7.1	15.2	24.7	24.1	17.0
SUBURBAN TOTAL	69.6	.0266	36.3	5.5	14.4	28.2	24.4	25.7

RETAIL SALES BY STORE GROUP

METRO AREA County City	Total Retail Sales ($000)	Food ($000)	Eating & Drinking Places ($000)	General Mdse. ($000)	Furniture/ Furnish. Appliance ($000)	Auto-motive ($000)	Drug ($000)
FORT COLLINS-							
LOVELAND	**2,145,070**	**348,377**	**256,790**	**358,100**	**149,181**	**419,451**	**32,610**
Larimer	2,145,070	348,377	256,790	358,100	149,181	419,451	32,610
• Fort Collins	1,395,698	222,454	169,618	225,410	114,678	274,502	19,998
• Loveland	538,071	99,191	50,496	126,254	19,949	125,354	9,785
SUBURBAN TOTAL	211,301	26,732	36,676	6,436	14,554	19,595	2,827

EFFECTIVE BUYING INCOME

METRO AREA County City	Total EBI ($000)	Median Hsld. EBI	% of Hslds. by EBI Group: (A) $10,000–$19,999 (B) $20,000–$34,999 (C) $35,000–$49,999 (D) $50,000 & Over				Buying Power Index
			A	B	C	D	
FORT COLLINS-							
LOVELAND	**3,467,143**	**35,288**	**16.0**	**23.3**	**18.6**	**31.7**	**.0843**
Larimer	3,467,143	35,288	16.0	23.3	18.6	31.7	.0843
• Fort Collins	1,576,827	32,505	17.8	21.8	17.0	29.7	.0442
• Loveland	694,442	36,687	15.4	24.4	22.5	30.1	.0184
SUBURBAN TOTAL	1,195,874	38,304	13.5	24.8	18.9	35.7	.0217

Source: 1995 Survey of Buying Power, Sales & Marketing Management, *pp. C-21, C-23.*

1. Determine the metropolitan area, city in metropolitan area, or county to be examined (the subject area).
2. Establish the benchmark area to use for comparison.
3. Divide retail sales by the EBI for both the trade area and the benchmark area. This provides conversion factors.

$$\text{Conversion factor} = \frac{\text{Total retail sales}}{\text{Effective buying income}}$$

4. Divide the subject area's conversion factor by the benchmark area's conversion factor after both are expressed as a percentage of EBI. The figure is the sales conversion index (SCI).

$$SCI = \frac{\text{Conversion factor for subject area}}{\text{Conversion factor for benchmark area}} \times 100$$

5. Calculate SCI for each of the retail categories from the *Survey of Buying Power:* food, eating and drinking places, general merchandise, automotive, drugs, and furniture, furnishings, and appliances.

An SCI above 100 indicates inshopping. The higher the SCI, the more desirable the location. An SCI below 100 suggests outshopping. The lower the number, the less desirable the location.

Using the data from Table 8-2, let's calculate the SCI for Fort Collins, Colorado, using Larimer County as a benchmark.

$$\text{Fort Collins conversion factor} = \frac{1,395,698}{1,576,827} = 0.88$$

$$\text{Larimer County conversion factor} = \frac{2,145,070}{3,467,143} = 0.62$$

$$\text{Fort Collins SCI} = \frac{0.88}{0.62} \times 100 = 141.94$$

Since the sales conversion index for Fort Collins is well above 100, you can conclude that it enjoys substantial inshopping. In Table 8-3 we calculate SCI by retail group for Fort Collins by using data from Table 8-2.

When using Larimer County as a benchmark, Fort Collins is an attractive location for all store groups. The SCI shows that eating and drinking and the fur-

TABLE 8 ▪ 3   Sales Conversion Index (SCI) for Fort Collins, Colorado

FORT COLLINS	TOTAL RETAIL SALES ($000s)	EBI ($000s)	CONVERSION FACTOR	SCI
	1,395,698	1,576,827	0.88	142
By store group				
Food	222,454	1,576,827	0.14	140
Eating/Drinking	169,618	1,576,827	0.11	157
General Merchandise	225,410	1,576,827	0.14	140
Furniture/Appliances	114,678	1,576,827	0.07	175
Automotive	274,502	1,576,827	0.17	142
Drugs	19,998	1,576,827	0.01	100
Benchmark				
Larimer County	2,145,070	3,467,143	0.62	
By store group				
Food	348,377	3,467,143	0.10	
Eating/Drinking	256,790	3,467,143	0.07	
General Merchandise	358,100	3,467,143	0.10	
Furniture/Appliances	149,181	3,467,143	0.04	
Automotive	419,451	3,467,143	0.12	
Drugs	32,610	3,467,143	0.01	

Source: 1995 *Survey of Buying Power,* Sales & Marketing Management, *pp. C-21, C-23.*

niture, furnishings, and appliances categories are especially prone to inshopping. You could use the same process to compare Fort Collins with Cheyenne, Wyoming or Colorado Springs, Colorado, or other similar locations.

Site Selection

While the total makeup of the U.S. marketplace is diverse and complex, neighborhoods tend to be just the opposite. People are generally more comfortable in areas where people like themselves live. The cliché "opposites attract" doesn't usually hold true in neighborhoods, where residents tend to be very much alike. The reasons for this demographic fact can be a matter of practicality as much as preference. People of similar income can afford similarly priced houses, which are generally built in the same area. Neighborhoods also tend to contain clusters of similar age groups, religious groups, families, and cultural groups. These factors distinguish one neighborhood from another. They are, therefore, important to consider in locating your business.

To distinguish different neighborhood types, Claritas Corp. has created a database program called PRIZM™ (Potential Rating Index for Zip Marketers).[9] For a neighborhood to be classified by the PRIZM program, it must be different enough from all others to be a separate segment and it must contain enough people to be worthwhile to businesses. By using the ZIP+4 codes combined with demographic data from the census, nationwide consumer surveys, and hundreds of interviews, PRIZM creates an accurate geodemographic segmentation system. Each of the 62 neighborhood types is ranked in socioeconomic order and is identified by a group identifier, an ID number, and a nickname. (See Table 8-4.)

Site Questions

Choosing the correct site involves answering many questions about each location being considered. You must find the right kind of site for your business. It must be accessible to your customers and vendors, and it must satisfy all legal requirements and economic needs of your business.

Type of Site
- Is the site located near target markets?
- Is the type of building appropriate for your business?
- What is the site's age and condition?
- How large is the trade area?
- Will adjacent businesses complement or compete with your firm?

Accessibility
- How are road patterns and conditions?
- Do any natural or artificial barriers obstruct access to the site?
- Does the site have good visibility?
- Is traffic flow too high or too low?
- Is the entrance or exit to parking convenient?
- Is parking adequate?
- Is the site accessible by mass transit?
- Can vendor deliveries be made easily?

Computer Applications

People Who Need People:
Mapping Out Success

Geographic Information Systems (GIS). The business community is turning more and more to geographic information systems (GIS) to analyze the demographics of target markets, choose new retail site locations, and optimize distribution routes.

GIS enthusiasts predict that the use of digital mapping (in which maps are recorded on computer disks) will increase as companies recognize the importance of visualizing information in accurate, flexible ways. There is a variety of geodemographic segmentation systems on the market in various price ranges. Geodemographic segmentation systems start with millions of raw statistics on individuals and then on the basis of these statistics, divide the nation's households into groups based on similarities. (The process is much like biologists dividing things into orders, families, genuses, and so on.) The various systems differ in the data they use, the number of segments they can configure, the base level of geography on which they're built, and the way they describe or name segments.

What are some of the more commonly used geodemographic segmentation systems? One desktop mapping and GIS program, ArcView, integrates map data, spreadsheets, business graphics, multimedia, large relational databases, and word processing in a single program. It allows you to see neighborhoods on a map and the concentration of demographic characteristics (age, income, and so on) of your target markets within each neighborhood. ACORN is available from CACI Marketing Systems of Arlington, Virginia. It divides over 220,000 census block groups into 40 clusters based on 61 characteristics (such as income, age, household type, types of cars owned, home value, and preferred radio formats). Another of these systems is ClusterPLUS 2000 from Strategic Mapping Inc. of Stamford, Connecticut.

ClusterPLUS identifies a larger number of clusters (60 broad ones and 450 very specific ones). The PRIZM system, available from Claritas of Alexandria, Virginia, classifies every U.S. neighborhood into one of 62 different types of clusters. (See p. 212.)

Most GIS applications are available on CD-ROM from many vendors, including the U.S. government's Topographically Integrated Geographic Encoding and Referencing (TIGER), which includes precise maps down to individual streets for any town in the United States.

Large companies like Levi Strauss Co. make the most of geodemographic data (such as that generated by the PRIZM™ software) by comparing it to the company's own shipment data. This market analysis helps Levi's managers to determine the best merchandise mix for stores in specific areas.

Because all these systems provide a vast amount of information, they're not cheap. A complete geodemographic system can cost from $30,000 to $75,000 on an annual basis with data upgrades—an amount that's undoubtedly beyond the financial resources of most small businesses. But there are less expensive alternatives available that let you manipulate data from your personal computer and that will provide you with basic site information that you can use. One is called First Street, which has a list price of $1,995 and is available from Wessex Inc. of Winnetka, Illinois. First Street consists of 17 CD-ROM disks. Eleven of these disks contain the U.S. Census Bureau's TIGER 92 files. The remaining six CDs hold 3,000 demographic variables which are broken down at the block-group level. Essentially First Street provides the same type of information available in the more expensive geodemographic systems, but you have to manipulate the data yourself instead of paying for that to be done.

Another option would be the $395 Maptitude 3.0 by Caliper Corporation of Newton, Massachusetts. This package contains mapping software, geographic information system, analysis tools, and a geographic and demographic database. Finally, MapInfo Corporation's MapInfo is another choice. This product is priced higher than Maptitude, but it's one of the best-selling geographic mapping software programs on the market. It provides many of the same features as First Street. However, a key factor to remember about any of these software tools, costly or inexpensive, is that they are just that—tools. You'll still have to correctly interpret and use the information in planning your location.

Sources: Susan Mitchell, "Birds of a Feather," American Demographics (February 1995), pp. 40–48; Jon Goss, "We Know Who You Are and We Know Where You Live . . . ", Economic Geography (April 1995), pp. 171–198; John Taschek, "First St. Helps Users Map Out Business Plan," PC Week, May 1, 1995, p. 69; Bruce Brown, "First St.: The Road to Demographics," PC Magazine (July 1995), p. 48; Evelyn Gilbert, "Desktop Mapping Software Gaining Popularity," National Underwriter, August 28, 1995, pp. 8+; Bruce Brown, "Maptitude: Mapping Software with Low Hurdles," PC Magazine, September 12, 1995, p. 56; and Maryfran Johnson, "GIS Popularity Growing," Computer World, March 22, 1993, pp. 41–42.

Reality Check

Just Like Being There

Even small businesses can tap into the information power provided in these geographic information systems.

Take, for instance, Whiteco Outdoor of Merrillville, Indiana, a business that owns and operates 20,000 billboards nationwide and generates over $100 million in revenues annually. Getting prospective clients to invest in billboard advertising at a particular site used to mean taking a paper map of the area where the prospect did business, painstakingly placing colored dots indicating the location of the proposed billboards, and then trying to get the client to understand how this billboard placed in a certain location would be a great place to advertise. Any changes meant physically constructing new maps and spending more time explaining. The process was labor intensive, frustrating, and time-consuming.

Whiteco decided to invest in a geographic information system (GIS) that contained standardized digital maps of every area where it had billboards. Now every billboard the company owns is pinpointed exactly using the Global Positioning System. Photographs of each billboard and its location are stored on compact disks. The company is even adding other data such as traffic flow patterns. Prospects are now shown brilliantly colored computer-generated maps with the billboard locations clearly marked. They even get a recent photograph of the site and data on traffic flow. Any changes can be illustrated instantly on a computer screen. The power of a GIS has clearly helped Whiteco Outdoor capitalize on its numerous sites.

Source: Srikumar S. Rao, "Corporate Treasure Maps," Financial World, June 20, 1995, pp. 61–66.

TABLE 8 - 4 PRIZM Neighborhood Types

CLUSTER NAME	MEDIAN INCOME	MEDIAN HOME VALUE	% COLLEGE GRADUATES	% U.S. HOUSEHOLDS
Top 10				
Blue Blood Estates	$70,307	$200,000+	50.7%	1.1%
America's wealthiest neighborhoods. Include suburban homes and one in ten is a millionaire.				
Money and Brains	45,798	150,755	45.5	0.9
Posh big-city enclaves of townhouses, condos, and apartments.				
Furs and Station Wagons	50,086	132,725	38.1	3.2
New money in metropolitan bedroom suburbs.				
Urban Gold Coast	36,838	200,000+	50.5	0.5
Upscale urban high-rise districts.				
Pools and Patios	35,895	99,702	28.2	3.4
Older, upper-middle class, suburban communities.				
Two More Rungs	31,263	117,012	28.3	0.7
Comfortable multiethnic suburbs.				
Young Influentials	30,398	106,332	36	2.9
Yuppie, fringe-city condo and apartment developments.				
Young Suburbia	38,582	93,281	23.8	5.3
Child-rearing, outlying suburbs.				
God's Country	36,728	99,418	25.8	2.7
Upscale frontier boomtowns.				
Blue-Chip Blues	32,218	72,563	13.1	6.0
The wealthiest blue-collar suburbs.				
Bottom 10				
Norma Rae-Ville	18,559	36,556	9.6	2.3
Lower-middle class milltowns and industrial suburbs, primarily in the South.				
Smalltown Downtown	17,206	42,225	10	2.5
Inner-city districts of small industrial cities.				
Grain Belt	21,698	45,852	8.4	1.3
The nation's most sparsely populated rural communities.				
Heavy Industry	18,325	39,537	6.5	2.8
Lower-working-class districts in the nation's older industrial cities.				
Share Croppers	16,854	33,917	7.1	4.0
Primarily southern hamlets devoted to farming and light industry.				
Downtown Dixie-Style	15,204	35,301	10.7	3.4
Aging, predominantly black neighborhoods, typically in southern cities.				
Hispanic Mix	16,270	49,533	6.8	1.9
America's Hispanic barrios.				
Tobacco Roads	13,227	27,143	7.3	1.2
Predominantly black farm communities throughout the South.				
Hard Scrabble	12,874	27,651	6.5	1.5
The nation's poorest rural settlements.				
Public Assistance	10,804	28,340	6.3	3.1
America's inner-city ghettos.				

Source: Compiled from Michael Weiss, The Clustering of America *(New York: Harper & Row Publishers, 1988) (based on 1987 census data).*

Legal Considerations

- Is zoning compatible with your firm?
- Does the building meet building codes?
- Will your external signs be compatible with zoning ordinances?
- Can you get any special licenses you will need (such as a liquor license)?

Economic Factors

- How much are occupancy costs?
- Are amenities worth the cost?
- How much will leasehold improvements and other one-time costs be?

Traffic Flow

The number of cars and pedestrians passing a site strongly affects its potential retail sales. If you are a retailer, you need to determine if the type and amount of traffic are sufficient for your business. Fast-food franchises have precise specifications on number count of vehicles traveling at specified speeds in each direction as part of their location analysis. State highway departments can usually provide statistics on traffic counts for most public roads.

Type of traffic is important because you don't receive any particular benefit if the people passing your business are not likely to stop. For example, suppose you are comparing two locations for your upscale jewelry store—one in a central business district and the other in a small shopping center with other specialty stores in an exclusive neighborhood. Total volume of traffic by the central business district location will be higher, but you will enjoy more of the right type of traffic for your store at the small shopping center.

Other businesses in the area will affect the type of traffic. This explains why you will often see automotive dealerships clustered together. The synergy created from several similar businesses located together can be very beneficial with customers coming to a specific area to "shop around" before buying. Your chances of attracting customers in the market for an auto will be much greater in a location with complementary competition than if your location is isolated.

The volume of automobile and foot traffic, the speed of vehicles, and the presence of turn lanes and parking are factors to consider when choosing a location for a retail or service business.

Reality Check

Coffee, Tea—or Crab Ashtray?

It sounded like a dream come true: a new retail store in a prime location with nonstop customer traffic. And for Melissa Fulton, president and CEO of Celebrate Maryland! that dream became reality. Fulton was already operating two thriving stores in historic Maryland towns—their merchandise includes state souvenirs—when the opportunity came for her to establish a new location at the busy airport. She opened a 700-square-foot store in the Baltimore-Washington International Airport in September 1995. This location, although desirable, has meant some additional challenges. One is that her employees have needed to be superefficient in stocking merchandise and ringing up sales since most airport customers are in a hurry. But, Fulton says, she wouldn't dream of giving up this location.

Source: Roberta Maynard, "The Lure of Locating in the Fast Lane," Nation's Business (December 1995), p. 12.

Going Global

If you are considering expanding your operations into another country, you need information on the location of your foreign project. You can get background information and opinions on foreign locations from magazines and newspapers at your local library. Keep in mind that all local Chambers of Commerce and economic development groups exist to promote their area, not to criticize it, if you receive information from them. The American Management Association and the American Marketing Association (and other organizations) sponsor seminars on opportunities and problems in foreign operations.[10] The U.S. Department of State can be very helpful in telling you about political developments, local customs and differences, and economic issues in specific countries.

In addition to doing your research, it is very important that you get to know the area personally before you establish operations abroad. Visit potential sites, meet with others in business there, and locate your distribution sources before you consider setting up business in another country.

Location Types

Service and retail businesses have three basic choices for types of locations: central business districts (CBDs), shopping centers, and stand-alone locations. Let's look at them now.

Central Business Districts

The central business district (CBD) is usually the oldest section of a city. While urban blight caused many businesses to desert CBDs in favor of the suburbs, many other CBDs have undergone a gentrification process. This means that old buildings have been restored or razed and replaced with new offices, retail shops, or housing. This planning and development, such as Denver's Larimer Square or Chicago's Water Tower Place, have recreated some of the best and most expensive locations for many types of retailers.

The advantages of locating in a CBD are that your customers generally will have access to public transportation, to a variety of images, prices, and services and to many other businesses. The disadvantages can include parking availability that is usually very tight and expensive, traffic congestion, possible high crime rate, older buildings, and disparity between neighborhoods, in which one block can be upscale while the next is run down.

Shopping Centers

anchor store A large retail store which attracts people to shop at malls.

While concentrated shopping areas have existed for centuries, the last four decades have witnessed the "malling of America." Shopping centers and malls are centrally owned or managed, have balanced store offerings, and have their own parking facilities. **Anchor stores** are major department stores that draw people into the shopping center.

Over the last several decades shoppers have come to demand the convenience of shopping centers. People living in the suburbs want to be able to drive to a location where they can park easily and find a wide variety of goods and services. Shopping centers have also gone through an evolutionary process, tending

Entering the Internet

Finding information on the Internet to help you make intelligent location decisions about global markets is fairly easy. The U.S. government has created Web sites for various governmental agencies that can provide the small business person with appropriate information. For instance, the Central Intelligence Agency server provides access to the latest edition of the *CIA World Factbook,* which includes information about every country in the world, with details such as geography, climate, terrain, natural resources, religions, languages, and so forth.

Another good source for governmental information can be found at the University of Missouri, St. Louis gopher. (A gopher is, very simply, an Internet program that organizes a site's files and other resources into layers of file directories. It enables you to access those directories by pointing to them and clicking or by entering the file's number when prompted. Gophers are extremely popular on the Internet because of this ease of use.) The UMSL gopher offers a veritable treasure trove of federal information including state profiles prepared by the Small Business Administration, and such major U.S. government publications as the *U.S. Industrial Outlook,* the *Occupational Outlook Handbook,* and the *International Business Practices Guide.* You can download (copy onto your computer files or print on your printer) these and other publications, for free, from this gopher site. It can be time-consuming, but it's easy if you follow the simple instructions.

In addition, there are some Web sites devoted to specific geographic locations that you might want to access once you've narrowed your selection decision. For instance, you can access information about Vietnam, Latin America, China, The European Commission, and Russia and Eastern Europe at the following addresses:

Web address for Central Intelligence Agency: http://www.odic.gov

Address for University of Missouri, St. Louis Gopher
 gopher: umslva.umsl.edu Path: *The Library/Government Information*

Address for selected global locations:
Vietnam—http://www.govietnam.com
Latin America—http://lanic.utexas.edu/
China—http://www.yahoo.com/Regional/Countries/China/Business
European Commission—http://www.cec.lu/welcome.html
Russia/Eastern Europe—http://www.pitt.edu/~cjp/rees.html

toward larger centers offering more variety, wider selections, and more entertainment. Have mega-malls like the West Edmonton Mall or the Mall of America gone too far in this evolutionary process? Have they reached the point of being "too big"? Ultimately, the consumer market will decide.

Advantages that shopping centers can offer to your business, compared to a CBD, include heavy traffic drawn by the wide variety of products available, closeness to population centers, cooperative planning and cost sharing, access to highways, ample parking, lower crime rate, and a clean, neat environment.

A disadvantage of locating within a shopping center is the inflexibility of your store hours. If the center is open from 9 a.m. to 10 p.m., you can't open your store from noon until midnight. Your rent is often higher than in an outside location. The central management of the shopping center may restrict the merchandise you sell. Your operations are limited, membership is required in the center's merchant organization, and you face the possibility of having too much competition. Smaller stores may be dominated by anchor stores.

Shopping centers will continue to evolve rapidly. Aging centers are being renovated. As shoppers become more dependent on malls and shopping centers to supply their needs, more service-oriented businesses, such as banks, health clinics, day care centers, and insurance offices, will be located in malls.

Stand-alone Locations

Drawing in and keeping customers are difficult tasks, especially if you choose a freestanding, or stand-alone, location. With a freestanding location your business must be the customers' destination point. Therefore, your competitive advantage must be made very clear to them. You must have unique merchandise, large selections, low prices, exceptional service, or special promotions to get them in.

Some advantages of stand-alone locations include the freedom to set your own hours and operate the way you choose. You may have no direct competition nearby. More parking may be available, and rent may be lower than what you would pay at a shopping center.

The disadvantages of having your business in a stand-alone location include the loss of synergy that can be created when the right combination of businesses is located together. You have to increase your advertising and promotion

Reality Check

Site-seeing Help

What are the three most important aspects of real estate? Location, location, and location! That oft-repeated adage is especially true in choosing a site for your retail business. In an age of specialization, site selection specialists are now available to assist in the process. Sexter Marston, owner of Retail Site Selectors of Minneapolis, helps store owners find, evaluate, and negotiate the best deal possible for the best site possible.

A good site selection specialist is attuned to the real estate market in your area, possesses sharp negotiating skills, and knows the legal ins and outs of real estate contracts. He should also be able to evaluate market data based on your needs. If you decide to hire a site selection expert, be sure that he understands the intricacies of your particular business and industry. "Selecting a consultant is like hiring an employee," Marston suggests. "Don't be afraid to check references and interview the prospective site selection consultant to ensure that he or she will save you, not cost you, money."

Source: Adapted from Richard Maturi, "Site-seers," Entrepreneur (January 1994), pp. 282–284.

spending to get customers in your door. You can't share operating costs with other businesses. You may have to build rather than rent.

If the goods or services that you offer are destination-oriented products (like health clubs, convenience stores, or wholesale clubs), a freestanding location may be the right choice for your business.

Service Locations

With some exceptions, the location decision for service businesses is just as important to businesses selling tangible products. If your service business is visited by the customer, location is critical. Services tend to be hard to *differentiate*—to show how one is different from another. People will certainly not go out of their way if they think there is very little difference between services. So car washes, video rental stores, dry cleaners, and similar services must be *very* careful about the convenience of their locations. With service businesses that visit the customer (like plumbers, landscapers, and carpet cleaners), location is not critical.

Incubators

In the early 1980s, government agencies, universities, and private business groups began creating business incubators to help new businesses get started in their area. Today there are several hundred incubators operating in the United States and the number is growing. Incubators offer entrepreneurs rent below market prices, along with services and equipment that are difficult for startup businesses to provide on their own. Incubators encourage entrepreneurship, which contributes to economic development. Businesses are not allowed to take advantage of these benefits indefinitely, and they must "graduate" to outside locations as they grow.

Choosing an incubator as your starting location can help you through the first months when your new business is the most fragile. A major advantage of incubators is the lower than market rent they charge. Other benefits include:

Support services. Incubators typically make copy machines, computers, fax machines, and other equipment available for their tenants to share. These items can improve your productivity as a young business, but they would cost a lot of money if you had to buy them. In an incubator you can have access to such equipment and pay only when and if you use it. Receptionists, secretarial support, and shipping and receiving services are also available on a shared basis, so you don't have to add to your payroll.

Professional assistance. Incubators often negotiate reduced rates with needed professionals like accountants and lawyers. Incubators also offer training in cash flow management, marketing practices, obtaining financing, and other areas.

Networking. Incubators can put you in contact with other local businesses. A "family" atmosphere often develops between businesses located in incubators because all are at about the same stage of development. This atmosphere usually leads to esprit de corps between tenants.

Financing. Incubators often have financial assistance available or have access to other funding sources like revolving loan funds, which can provide loans at less than market rates.[11]

An incubator is an attractive place to start a new small business. It offers support services and equipment such as photocopiers, fax machines, and computers, which young businesses often cannot afford by themselves.

Layout and Design

After you have selected a site, you need to lay out the interior of your business. If yours is a type of business that customers visit, most of your management decisions will be directed toward getting customers into your business to spend money. No matter what type of business you run, this is where the activity happens. How your location is laid out and designed is important because it affects the image and productivity of your business.

Legal Requirements

The Americans with Disabilities Act (ADA) of 1990 requires businesses to be accessible to disabled customers and employees, with businesses with over 14 employees required to accommodate disabled job candidates in hiring. (See also Chapter 19.) This law affects the way every business operates. Buildings constructed after January 26, 1993 must meet stricter requirements than those built earlier.

Some ADA requirements for customer accommodation include:

- Access ramps must be built where floor level changes more than one-half of an inch.
- Elevators are required in buildings of three stories or more and in buildings with more than 3,000 square feet of floor space per story.
- Checkout aisles must be at least 36 inches wide.
- Carpets of accessible routes must be less than one-half inch in pile.
- Toilet facilities, water fountains, and telephones must be accessible to people in wheelchairs.
- Self-service shelves, counters, and bars must be accessible to people in wheelchairs and to the visually impaired.[12]

Retail

The layout of your retail store helps create the image that people have of your business. It is important to display merchandise in an attractive, logical arrangement to maximize your sales and to make shopping as convenient as possible for your customers.

Three types of layouts are commonly used in retail stores in various combinations. The simplest type is the **free-flow** layout, which works well with smaller stores such as boutiques that sell only one type of merchandise. (See Figure 8-2.) As there is no established traffic pattern, customers are encouraged to browse.

A **grid layout** establishes a geometric grid by placing counters and fixtures at right angles in long rows. (See Figure 8-3.) It effectively displays a large amount of merchandise with tall shelves and many shelf facings. Supermarkets and drugstores tend to be set up with this layout because it suits customers who wish to shop the entire store by moving up and down alternate aisles. But if customers can't see over fixtures or if they want only one or two specific items, they may find this layout frustrating.

The **loop layout** has gained popularity since the early 1980s as a tool for increasing retail sales productivity. (See Figure 8-4.) The loop sets up a major aisle that leads customers from the entrance, through the store, and back to the check-

free-flow layout A type of layout used by small retail stores which encourages customers to wander and browse through the store.

grid layout A type of layout used by retail stores to move customers past merchandise arranged on rows of shelves or fixtures.

loop layout A type of retail layout with a predominant aisle running through the store which quickly leads customers to their desired department.

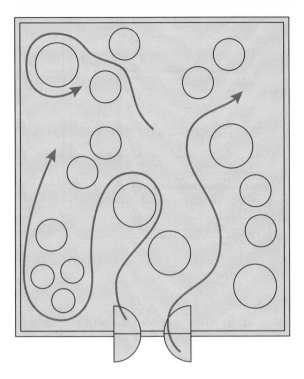

FIGURE 8-2
The Free-flow Layout
The free-flow layout encourages shoppers to browse.

out counter. Customers are led efficiently through the store in order to expose them to the greatest amount of merchandise. Yet they still have the freedom to browse or cross-shop. This layout is especially good for businesses that sell a wide variety of merchandise because customers can be routed quickly from one department of merchandise to another.

Service

Service businesses that customers visit, such as beauty shops or restaurants, need to be concerned about how their layout affects their customers' convenience and the business's work flow. The image of these service businesses is just as affected by layout as the image of retail stores is. Speed of service becomes more critical

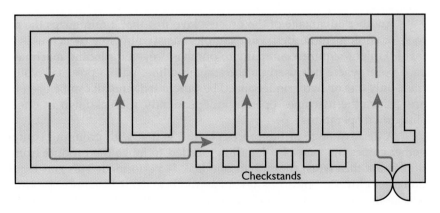

FIGURE 8-3
The Grid Layout
The grid layout routes customers up and down aisles to expose them to a large quantity of merchandise.

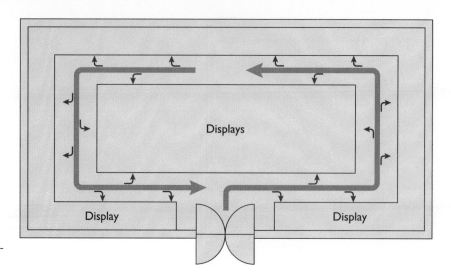

every year. Consider the decreasing amount of time needed for photo finishing—from one week, to two days, to one hour, to while you wait. Layout is critical to maintaining the speed and efficiency of service providers.

Manufacturing

The layout of a manufacturing business is arranged to provide a smooth flow of work. The specific layout of your plant will depend on the type of product you make, the type of production process you use, the space you have available, and other factors such as volume of goods and amount of worker interaction needed. There are three basic types of manufacturing layouts, which may be combined as needed.

process layout A way to arrange a manufacturing business by placing all comparable equipment together in the same area.

Process Layout. With the **process layout,** all similar equipment or workers are grouped together so that the goods being produced move around the plant. (See Figure 8-5.) This layout is common in small manufacturers because of the flexibility it allows. The product being made can be changed quickly. An example of the process layout can be seen in a small machine shop, in which all the grinders would be in one area, all the drills would be in another, and all the lathes would be in a third. Restaurant kitchens commonly use this type of layout also with the refrigerators in one place, the ovens in another, and a food preparation area elsewhere.

Another advantage of the process layout is that it minimizes the amount of tools or equipment needed. For example, an assembly line (which uses a product layout) might require a company to purchase several grinding machines, one for each point where it is used on the assembly line. With a process layout, by contrast, only one or two grinders need be purchased, and all can be used in the one area. Since the machines operate independently, a breakdown in one does not shut down operations.

A disadvantage of the process layout is that with grouping equipment together comes the increased handling needed to move the product from one station to another when more than one task is performed. This can require additional employees. Since this layout is more general in nature, producing long runs of the same product would be less efficient than the product layout.

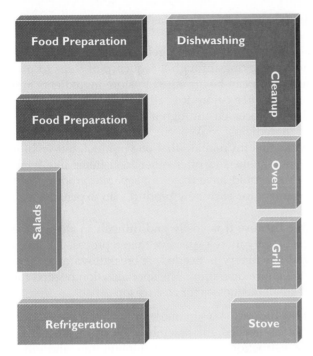

FIGURE 8-5
Process Layout in a Restaurant Kitchen
In a process layout, similar equipment is grouped together in areas to complete specified tasks.

Product Layout. With a **product layout,** you arrange workers, equipment, and activities needed to produce a single product in a particular sequence of steps. (See Figure 8-6.) Using a product layout is best when you are producing many standardized products or using specialized equipment. Auto assembly lines, textile mills, and other continuous-flow assembly lines in which raw material enters one end of the line and finished products exit the other end are examples of a product

product layout A way to arrange a manufacturing business by placing equipment in an assembly line.

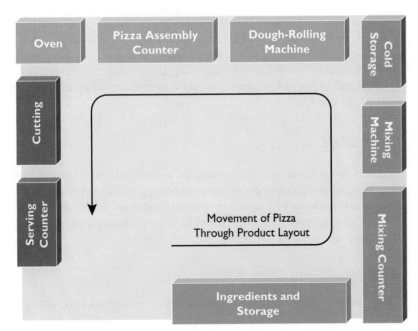

FIGURE 8-6
Product Layout in a Pizza Kitchen
In a product layout, workers, equipment, and activities are laid out according to the sequence of steps needed to make the product.

layout. Material handling costs can be decreased and tasks can often be mechanically simplified so that skilled labor is not needed.

A restaurant that specializes in a product like bagels, pizzas, or cookies can make use of the product layout by moving through a sequence of steps to prepare the finished product. The kitchen can be arranged to store ingredients and mix the dough at one end of the counter before it is all moved to cold storage. Then batches can be removed and processed through a dough-rolling machine, prepared and mixed with other ingredients, cooked, cut, and served in an assembly-line fashion. The layout works fine for making that one product, but what if you would want to diversify your menu and offer other food items like hamburgers, French fries, or tacos? You would have to set up separate product lines with new ovens, stoves, and counters for each new product—an expensive way to expand a menu.

Product layout is inflexible because it is costly and difficult to change the product that is being made. It is usually more expensive than a process layout to set up because more specialized machinery is needed. A breakdown anywhere along the line can shut down the entire operation. The specialization needed for product layout eliminates most small businesses for cost reasons.

fixed layout A type of layout for a manufacturing business in which the product stays stationary while workers and equipment are brought to it.

Fixed Layout.   In a fixed layout the product stays in one spot to which equipment, material, and labor are brought as needed for assembly. Types of businesses using this layout are building construction, aircraft and shipbuilding, and other large, immovable product production.

Home Office

Home-based businesses are becoming increasingly common as more people set up operations in their homes. The primary layout consideration for designing this type of space is to be sure that it is separate from all other home functions. If you don't do this, the IRS will not allow deductions for home-office expenses.[13] A home office may not also be used as a den or guest bedroom if it is to be considered as a tax deduction.

You must make sure that it is legal to operate a home-based business where you live. Some communities have adopted tough restrictions, such as not allowing a home office even for work you bring home from your "real" office. More typical concerns involve complying with zoning regulations that govern parking, signage, and types of businesses allowed in residential areas. Check with your local zoning board.

Buy, Build, or Lease?

You have three choices of ownership of your location: leasing a facility, building your own, or purchasing an existing building. In this section, we will discuss the relative advantages of leasing or purchasing your building. (In Chapter 17, Financial Management, we will compare the advantages of leasing versus buying the equipment needed to operate your business.)

Leasing

A lease is basically a long-term agreement to rent a building, equipment, or other asset. The biggest advantage of leasing is the amount of cash you free up for other purposes. Not only do you avoid a large initial cash outlay through leasing, you also reduce your risk during the startup period. Once your business is established, your needs may change. A lease can give you the flexibility to move to a bigger, better, or more suitable location in the future.

A disadvantage of a lease is that it may prevent you from altering a building to fit your needs. You also do not have long-term assurance that you can stay in a location. The owner may decide not to renew your lease at the end of the term or may increase your rent payments. Leased space in shopping centers commonly requires a monthly fee based on square feet, plus a percentage of gross sales.

Review any lease with your lawyer before signing it. This is true of any legal document, but with a lease there is a tendency to think, "These forms are pretty much standard." Remember who drew up the document—the lessor. Whom do you think the conditions of the lease will favor? Not you, as the lessee. You may need to negotiate the provisions of the lease, or *escape clauses*. These can allow you to terminate the lease if your circumstances drastically change. You will also want to consider the lease's renewal options. Will it allow you to remain in the same location at the end of the lease period? **Leasehold improvements** are important considerations to negotiate. These are the improvements you make to the property, such as upgrading lighting or plumbing, installing drop ceilings, building walls, or making other changes to the property. Of course, you cannot take these improvements with you when you leave so try to negotiate rent payments in exchange for them. These are just a few factors you need to negotiate *before* signing a lease. Get all agreements in writing.

leasehold improvements Changes which make a property more valuable, such as painting, adding shelves, or new lighting.

Purchasing Your Building

The decision to buy a building can be a difficult one. Ownership increases your up-front expenses and the amount of capital you need. The major expense of purchasing and remodeling can drain already stretched resources from other business needs.

With ownership, you gain the freedom of customizing the property any way you want. You know what your payments will be. At the same time, you are tied down to that location much more if you own rather than rent the property. Tax considerations enter the picture. While lease payments are deductible business expenses, only depreciation on the building is deductible if you own it. Finally, the value of your investment is subject to the whims of the local real estate market. The value may appreciate or depreciate for reasons that have nothing to do with your own efforts. In the end, the choice comes down to economics and flexibility. Since most entrepreneurs are in business because of what they make or sell and not in the "brick and mortar" business of real estate speculation, a majority will choose leasing.

New Construction

Building a new facility to meet your own specifications may be necessary if your business has unique needs or if existing facilities are not located where you need them, which may be the case in some high-growth areas.

As with buying an existing property, building greatly increases your fixed expenses. Will your revenue increase enough to cover these additional expenses? Building a new facility may enable you to incorporate new technology or

Manager's Notebook

Before You Sign on the Dotted Line

The best way to avoid disputes between landlords and tenants is for both parties to understand the lease agreement *before* it is signed. Since a lease will legally bind you for a long period of time, you should have the following questions answered to your satisfaction when you enter the deal.

1. *How long will the lease run?* The length of most leases is negotiable, with three to ten years being typical. In the past, landlords wanted the lease term to be as long as possible to hold down their vacancy rates. Now in areas where vacant office space is at a premium, many businesses often want long leases as a hedge against rising prices. For example, in New York City, an office tower charges $60 per square foot for rent while only five years earlier the same offices rented for $16 per square foot.

2. *How much is the rent?* Be sure you know the dollar amount per square foot of space that the rent is based on for any location you consider. Be sure you know how much you are paying for different kinds of space—you don't want to pay the same dollar amount for productive office space as you do for space like lobbies, hallways, mechanical areas, and bathrooms.

   There are at least five types of leases, which calculate rent differently—though they are all based on square feet. The first is called a **gross lease,** which is a flat monthly amount paid by the tenant. The landlord pays all building operating expenses like taxes, insurance, and repairs. Utility bills may or may not be included. The second type is called a **net lease** in which the tenants pay some or all real estate taxes above their base rent. The **Net-net lease** includes insurance on top of base rent

and taxes. The fourth type is called *net-net-net* or **triple net lease.** It requires tenants to pay not only the base rent, taxes, and insurance, but also to pay other operating expenses related to the building, such as repairs and maintenance. The final type is called a **percentage lease.** Common in shopping centers or other buildings that include many different businesses, it requires tenants to pay a base rent plus a percentage of gross income.

3. *How much will the rent go up?* To protect against inflation, most landlords include an **escalation clause** in leases, which allows them to adjust rent according to the consumer price index (CPI), or some other scale. You should not agree to pay the full CPI increase, especially if you are already paying part of the building operating expenses.

4. *Can you sublease?* There are many reasons that you may not be able to stay in a location for the stated duration of the lease, including at the extremes a failure of your business or being so successful that you need to move to a larger space. If you must move, can you rent your space to another tenant who meets the same standards that the landlord applies to all other tenants?

5. *Can you renew?* Unless a clause is written into your lease that guarantees you the first rights to your space at the end to the lease term, the landlord has no legal obligation to continue it. A formula for determining the new rent payment may be included in the renewal clause, or you may pay current market rate.

6. *What happens if your landlord goes broke?* A *recognition* or *nondisturbance clause* can protect you from being forced out or into a new lease should the property change ownership.

7. *Who is responsible for insurance?* Landlords should be expected to carry a comprehensive policy on the building that includes casualty insurance on the structure and liability cover-

age for all public areas like hallways and elevators. Building owners can require tenants to buy liability and content insurance.

8. *What building services do you get?* Your lease should state the specific services you can expect to receive, including any electricity use limits, cleaning schedules, and heating, ventilation, and air conditioning (HVAC). Note that unlike residential rents, commercial space does not usually come with 24-hour HVAC service (Monday through Friday from 8 A.M. to 5 P.M. and Saturday 8 A.M. to 1 P.M. is normal). This could produce some hot or cold working conditions if you work at other hours.

9. *Who else can move in?* Clauses can be written into leases that restrict direct competitors, or businesses that are exceptionally noisy or otherwise disruptive to others, from locating in adjoining spaces. Remember that such restrictions can become a problem to you if you need to sublease.

10. *Who pays for improvements?* Construction and remodeling become expensive quickly. While you are usually allowed to make leasehold improvements, the building owner does not always have to pay for them. Improvements are an area wide open to negotiation in leases—make sure agreements are in writing.

Source: Adapted from Robert Cunningham, "Ten Questions to Ask Before You Sign a Lease," Inc. Magazine Guide to Small Business Success, *1993 supplement issue.*

---

gross lease A lease in which the monthly payment made by the tenant remains the same and the landlord pays the operating expenses of the building.

net lease A lease in which the tenant pays a base monthly rent plus some or all real estate taxes of the building.

net-net lease A lease in which the tenant pays a base monthly rent plus real estate taxes and insurance on the building.

triple-net lease A lease in which the tenant pays a base monthly rent plus real estate taxes, insurance, and any other operating expense incurred for the building.

percentage lease A lease in which the tenant pays a base monthly rent plus a percentage of their gross revenue.

escalation clause A lease which varies according to the amount of inflation in the economy.

Global Small Business

Rostislav Ordovsky-Tanaevsky Blanco, a native of Venezuela, chose his father's homeland, the former Soviet Union, as the location for his chain of photo retail stores and restaurants. He's been called crazy by others, but Ordovsky-Tanaevsky has had the last laugh on those naysayers. His business, Rostik International, had 1994 revenues in excess of $100 million and employed about 6,000 people. He's become Moscow's leading restaurateur with a number of hamburger joints, pizzerias, New York-style delis, and theme restaurants. Achieving this level of success hasn't been easy. Site selection of any type is fraught with risks. But when you add in the uncertainties of a newly democratized society, you've increased the challenges. However, Ordovsky-Tanaevsky is a perfect example of how a global small business owner can bridge the uncertainties and develop successful businesses in locations where others fear to tread. *Source: Niklas von Dachne, "Ears to the Ground,"* Success *(December 1995), p. 14.*

features that will lower your operating costs compared to an older, existing building. Look at your *total* costs over the long term in making this decision.

Summary

■ The crucial factors important in selecting a region or state in which to locate your business.

In deciding where to locate your business you should consider the price and availability of land and water, the labor pool you can hire from, accessibility to customers and suppliers, closeness of competition, adequacy of transportation, public attitude toward new business, taxes and regulations, your personal preference about where you want to live, financial incentives offered, and the quality of life available.

■ How to calculate the sales conversion index to compare location sites for a business.

A city's sales conversion index (SCI) is calculated from *Survey of Buying Power* data to determine the amount of inshopping for a city compared to another benchmark location. Begin by determining a conversion factor for the considered city and the benchmark area by dividing total retail sales by the effective buying income for each place. Then divide the chosen city's conversion factor by the benchmark conversion factor. An SCI above 100 indicates inshopping, or that more people come to that town to buy your type of product than go elsewhere.

■ The central issues in choosing a particular site.

The correct site for your business comes from answering specific questions related to matching the needs of your business with the type of site, accessibility, legal considerations, and economic factors.

■ The three basic types of locations.

The three types of location you may choose are central business districts, shopping centers, and stand-alone locations. The central business district for most cities and towns includes the original "downtown" area, so it is usually the oldest section of the area. Shopping centers can range from small, ten-store strip malls which serve a neighborhood to very large regional malls which draw customers from hundreds of miles. A stand-alone location places your business apart from other businesses.

■ Circumstances which make leasing or buying a building appropriate choices.

When deciding whether to lease or to buy a building, you need to consider how long the building will be suitable for your business and whether you can afford to tie up your capital that could be used for other purposes. Before leasing you need to carefully examine the terms and conditions of the lease before signing it.

■ The types of layout you may choose.

For retail businesses, a free-flow layout encourages customers to wander and browse through the store. A grid layout moves customers up and down rows of shelves and fixtures. A loop layout features a wide central aisle which leads customers quickly from one department to another. For manufacturing businesses, a process layout groups all similar equipment and jobs together. A process layout provides flexibility needed by many small manufacturers. A product layout arranges equipment and workers in a series to produce products in a continuous flow. With a fixed layout, the product being made stays in one place, while equipment, materials, and labor are brought to it.

Questions for Review and Discussion

[handwritten: target mkt.]

1. Why should the small business owner consider demographics of an area when choosing a location for opening a new business? Name some sources of demographic information that are valuable tools to use in this evaluation. *[handwritten: Geog. diff. syst. (p.210)]*

2. When choosing a location for a new business what are the most important criteria for the entrepreneur to consider? Explain the connection between type of business and location. *[handwritten: – type of Bus.]* *[handwritten: convenience crit.]*

3. Why would a small business flourish in one area of the United States but fail in another region?

4. What is the sales conversion index (SCI) and why should the small business owner become familiar with the way it is calculated and the information to be obtained from it? *[handwritten: Customers tendencies to purchase, The higher, the better]*

5. Explain the importance of knowing the legal requirements of an area before attempting to open a small business. *[handwritten: Zoning & tax regs. (Sales, etc.)]*

6. What are some considerations that should be taken into account by the entrepreneur if business is to be conducted in a foreign market? *[handwritten: Does mkt. exist? Culture?]*

7. What are the three location types and their sub-categories? Give an example of a type of small business that would have the greatest chance of succeeding in each location type. State your reason for selecting that particular business type by giving specific advantages.

8. What is the ADA and what is its impact on the small business owner's site layout and design plan? *[handwritten: Elevators, ramps, shelving, wide aisles]*

9. What are the main types of layout plans and what should the entrepreneur focus on when designing the layout plan for a new business?

10. Compare and contrast the advantages and/or disadvantages of buying, building or leasing space for a small business. *[handwritten: – don't have to move but $ are tied up]* *[handwritten: same as purch. frees up whg, Cap, vs. terms of lease]*

Critical Incident

Once you have chosen your location site, designing an effective and efficient layout for your business is the next important step. And it's important to keep in mind the legal requirements, as well as what is the best flow for your business. Read through the following descriptions of three small businesses and answer the questions at the end.

Sam's Suitables. Sam's Suitables is a specialty retail shop that will be selling suits, sportscoats, shirts, slacks, and clothing accessories for big and tall men. Sam has found an ideal location in a strip shopping mall that has heavy traffic flow. The only challenge is that the store is fairly small (1,500 square feet) and Sam must provide display areas, dressing rooms, cash register checkout, storage and other backstore areas, in addition to an attractively designed front window to draw customers.

Diane's Delectables. Ahhhh . . . the fresh aroma of bread, cookies, and other pastries being baked. Diane's Delectables is opening a store that will make and bake the goodies as well as sell them to the public. In addition, Diane wants to have a limited number of tables and chairs so that customers can sit and enjoy pastries and beverages (coffee, juices, and sodas) before taking a bagful of goodies to go. The bake shop has 900 square feet and is located on a busy downtown street with numerous office buildings.

Cathy's Crafts. Cathy's Crafts is a highly successful wood crafts business. Cathy has "carved" a lucrative niche for her hand-wrought products, which include items such as small shelves, picture frames, and wood cut-outs (bunnies, Santa Clauses, roosters, cows, and so on). Each product in these lines is carefully cut (using state-of-the-art wood-cutting machines), meticulously sanded, and then either stained or painted. Then the finished products are ready to be prepared for shipping. Cathy's business has outgrown its present location and she's found an ideal building (5,000 square feet of space) that's close to other light manufacturers.

Questions

1. Choose one of the businesses and draw a layout for it that you think would be efficient and effective. Think of the legal requirements that might impact the business. As part of your drawing, be sure to include a listing of the necessary equipment.

2. Divide into teams of two to three students and make a list of the important factors that would influence the layout for one of these businesses. Then, keeping those factors in mind, discuss sites in your community that would be appropriate for it. (If you happen to be in a large city, narrow your site selection to a radius of 5 miles from your campus.)

Take it to the Net

We invite you to visit the Hatten page on the Prentice Hall Web site at: http://www.prenhall.com/~hattensb for this chapter's World Wide Web exercise.

VIDEO CASE
Stealth Marketing

ARKETING IS THE BUSINESS OF building images, but appearances can be deceiving. While many small businesses are trying to appear larger than they really are to assure customers that their needs will be served, many large businesses are now trying to appear small.

For example, Origins, which appears to be a small, environment-friendly bath oil, perfume, and cosmetics company, is actually owned entirely by Estee Lauder—a $2.9 billion firm. Tobacco giant R. J. Reynolds created The Moonlight Tobacco Company for the same reason that General Motors started its Saturn division and that Miller Brewing Company formed Plank Road Brewery: so they would look like small businesses. This practice is called stealth marketing.

Why would large corporations seemingly abandon the images they have worked so hard to create? Because customers are rejecting old, established brands in favor of appealing upstarts. *Source: Adapted from* The Wall Street Journal Report, *Show #679, Oct. 1, 1995.*

Discussion Questions

• Describe how the large corporations in the video are altering each of the four P's of their marketing mix to appear small.

• What dangers do these corporations face by practicing stealth marketing?

Chapter Focus

After reading this chapter, you should be able to:

- Define competitive advantage.
- Demonstrate the importance and benefits of having a competitive advantage.
- Describe three ways to create a competitive advantage for your business.
- Explain the purpose of the marketing research process and the steps involved in putting it into practice.
- Illustrate what marketing research can do for your small business.

9 Competitive Advantage and Marketing Research

AVID GUIDRY OF MARRERRO, Louisiana understands the importance of combining competitive advantage and marketing research in business. Because of this, he's been able to build a company with annual revenues of around $1.8 million and which continues to grow despite an unstable business environment.

Guidry's company, Guico Machine Works, specializes in the contract manufacturing of precision machine parts. It has developed a competitive advantage by providing quality products and service to its customers in the defense and oil industries. Guidry, an oil industry technician, started Guico with his brother John in 1982. "I kept seeing equipment that was down because they couldn't find spare parts for it," Guidry recalls of his decision to enter the business. Like many new businesses, Guico struggled at first, but by 1986 it employed nine people.

The collapse of oil prices, however, dealt Guico its first severe blow by its impact on the company's oil industry and customers. Guico suffered another hit when the space shuttle *Challenger* exploded and the shuttle program was put on hold, suspending the company's contracts in the aerospace industry. Guidry recalls that he lost 80 to 85 percent of his business in one three-month period. His brother John left the company as well. However, Guidry was confident that his company's products were both needed by customers and better than those of his competitors.

Guidry decided to look to other geographic markets for potential customers. A rebound in the oil industry, he reasoned, might be a long time in coming. So he targeted the northern part of the United States and decided to investigate Philadelphia, taking advantage of cheap air travel that was then available. From the Philadelphia Chamber of Commerce he received a list of manufacturers with more than 500 employees and help in picking out which companies to visit. His market research paid off. Within two years, Guico was shipping 70 percent of its business outside Louisiana. And that was just the start of Guico's rebound. Guidry says, "We've never slid back since 1988. It's been constant growth." *Source: Michael Barrier, "Precision-Tooled Ambition," reprinted by permission,* Nation's Business *(December 1995), pp. 14–16. © 1995, U.S. Chamber of Commerce.*

Competitive Advantage

If you were forced to condense the description of your business down to *one* thing that is most important; to count on *one* finger what makes you successful; to identify *one* factor that sets your business apart from all other similar businesses, you would recognize your **competitive advantage.**

competitive advantage The facet of a business that it does better than all of its competitors.

Definition of Competitive Advantage

A competitive advantage is the aspect of your business that gives you an edge over your competitors. Your strategic plan (discussed in Chapter 3) helps you identify and establish a competitive advantage by analyzing different environments, studying your competition, and choosing appropriate strategies. Advantages you have over your competitors could include price, product features and functions, time of delivery (if speed is important to customers), place of business (if being located near customers is needed), and public perception (the positive image your business projects).[1] Remember, a competitive advantage must be sustainable. If competitors can easily copy it, it is not a true competitive advantage.

Three core ideas are valuable in defining your competitive advantage. First, keep in mind that any advantage is relative, not absolute. What matters in customers' minds is not the absolute performance of your product or service, but its performance compared to competing products. For example, no toothpaste can make teeth turn a pure white, but you could build an advantage if you developed a toothpaste that gets teeth noticeably whiter than competing toothpastes.

Second, you should strive for multiple types of competitive advantage. Doing more than one thing better than others will increase the chances that you can maintain an advantage over a longer period of time.

Third, remember that areas of competition change over time. Customers' tastes and priorities change as products and processes for making them evolve, as the availability of substitute products changes, and for a variety of other reasons which can affect your competitive advantage. For example, consumers used to compare watches on their ability to keep time accurately. But the introduction of the quartz watch changed customer priorities. The cheapest quartz watch in the display case kept time more accurately than the most expensive mechanical watch, so the differentiating factors for watches are now styles (types of watch faces) and features (built-in calculators, stopwatches, and television remote controls).[2]

One of the leading researchers and writers on the topic of competitive advantage is Michael Porter, professor at Harvard Business School. Porter identified five basic forces of competition that exist within every industry. Analyzing these forces for your chosen industry can help you determine the attractiveness of the industry and the prospects for earning a return on your investment. (See Figure 9-1.)

> *Competitive advantage must be defined from the customer's perspective. A brand of tight-fitting jeans may prove popular among the young and slim, while losing market share among the not-so-young and not-so-slim.*

Reality Check

Show 'Em What You Can Do

For three generations, Bissett Nursery had been in the business of growing shrubs, trees, and plants for landscape contractors to use for building projects. Sounds like a business without many ways to create a competitive advantage, right? Maybe not.

During the construction boom years of the 1980s on New York's Long Island, landscape contractors didn't need to make a presentation to clients to make sales—they just needed to show up. Then the recession of the early 1990s made high-end residential customers more demanding and tightfisted. Showing customers pictures of plants and shrubs in books, walking them through nurseries, and drawing and redrawing blueprints were not enough to sell a job. Customers had trouble picturing what their finished lawn would look like.

Bissett Nursery created its competitive advantage by solving that problem. Using electronic imaging, the Bissetts could take a 35mm photograph of a home or business to be landscaped, scan it into their computer, and use their database of plant, tree, and shrub images to create a dazzling computer-generated picture of how the property could look. They might even redraw the scene to add gazebos, waterfalls, ponds, or rocks to propose highly imaginative projects. The results of the Bissetts' marketing tool have been impressive. Since 1982, their customer base has gone from 600 to 7,500.

Bissett Nursery provides an example of how a business can take existing tools (computers, scanners, imaging software, and so on) and apply them intelligently to create a powerful marketing tool for themselves—and an appreciable benefit for their customers.

Source: Adapted from Donna Fenn, "Picture This," Inc. (February 1994), pp. 66–71.

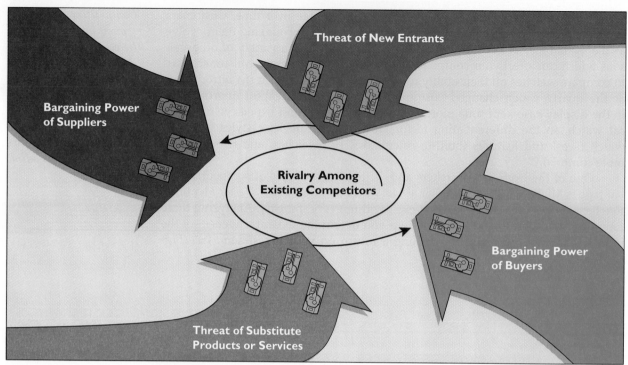

FIGURE 9-1

The Five Forces for Competition

The interplay of competitive forces helps to determine which products and companies succeed in the marketplace—and those which don't.

Source: Michael Porter, "Know Your Place," Inc., September 1991, p. 91.

The *degree of rivalry among existing competitors* refers to how passively or aggressively the businesses within an industry compete with each other. If they consistently attack one another, the attractiveness of the industry is reduced because the potential to make a profit is decreased. For example, compare the airline industry, whose strong rivalries produce low profits, with the packaged consumer goods industry, where companies try to attract different groups of customers.

The *threat of new entrants* is a function of how easily other businesses can enter your market, which keeps prices and profits down. If a certain type of food, like Cajun bagels, becomes popular, very little prevents new bakeries from opening or converting to produce this popular item. Low barriers to entry reduce profitability for incumbents.

The *bargaining power of suppliers* affects the price you will have to pay to produce your goods. If the supplies in question are commodities carried by several companies, suppliers will have little power to raise the prices they charge. If you only have one or two choices of vendors, or if you require very specialized goods, you may have to pay what the suppliers ask.

The *bargaining power of buyers* affects how much latitude you have in changing your prices. The more choices of substitutes your buyers have, the more power they have to influence your prices or the extent of services you must provide to keep their business.

The *threat of substitute products or services* is determined by the options your customers have when buying your product or service. The greater the number of substitutes available, the more your profit margin can be squeezed. Overnight delivery services must consider the threat of fax machines and e-mail, even though they are entirely different ways to transmit messages.

There are five fatal flaws associated with applying strategic thinking to specific competitive situations. These flaws are:

- *Misreading industry attractiveness.* The highest-tech, highest-glamour, fastest-growing field may not be the best for making a profit because of its attractiveness to competition.
- *Failure to identify a true competitive advantage.* Imitation can put you in the middle of the pack. Being different from competitors is both risky and hard.
- *Pursuing a competitive advantage that is not sustainable.* Porter recommends that if small businesses cannot sustain an advantage, the owner should view the business as a short-term investment rather than an ongoing enterprise. This business philosophy might be stated as, "Get in, grow, and get out."
- *Compromising a strategy in order to grow faster.* If you are fortunate enough to identify a significant competitive advantage, don't give it up in order to become more like your larger competitors. Remember what made you successful in the first place.
- *Not making your strategy explicit or not communicating it to your employees.* Writing your strategy down and discussing it with your key people sets up an atmosphere for everyone in your organization to move toward a common goal. Each of your employees makes decisions every day. If your overall strategy is to offer products at the lowest possible cost, decisions by everyone in your business need to reinforce that goal.[3]

While defining competitive advantage is fairly simple and understandable, measuring it is not. This is because it is relative to your competitors—who are constantly trying to improve at the same time you are. Despite its dynamic and relative nature, though, the importance of competitive advantage cannot be overlooked.

Importance of Competitive Advantage

Having a competitive advantage is critical: Your business must do *something* better than others or it is not needed. In order to cope with a quickly changing competitive environment, small businesses need to be market driven.[4] Part of becoming market driven includes closely monitoring changing customer wants and needs, determining how those changes affect customer satisfaction, and developing strategies to gain an edge.

Porter states that competitive advantage as a core of small business strategy is critical because small businesses cannot rely on the inertia of the marketplace for their survival.[5] When running a small business, you cannot solve problems by throwing money at them—you need to see your competitive environment with crystal clarity, then identify and secure a position you can defend.

In developing your competitive advantage, you will make decisions under conditions of uncertainty. This is the art, rather than the science, of marketing decision making. In his book *Marketing Mistakes*, Robert Hartley notes that we can

On-line Grocery Shopping

Peapod Inc. is taking advantage of the information superhighway to take customers' grocery orders and then make deliveries to approximately 7,000 customers in San Francisco and Chicago. Attention to detail is allowing Peapod to thrive in a market in which several national on-line shopping services have floundered.

Customers order groceries from Peapod via personal computer, telephone, or fax. Peapod's competitive advantage is their software. Customers shop using current, not estimated, prices. They can browse electronic "aisles" such as "Ethnic Foods." They can choose a specific grocery category, brand, or size. Customers can rank items, isolate specials, and use coupons.

Peapod employees pick out the grocery items ordered and they receive bonuses for filling orders perfectly. Peapod's revenues have increased from startup in 1991 to an estimated $15 million in 1994. Currently Peapod works only with Jewel Food Stores in Chicago and Safeway stores in San Francisco, but it is planning expansion into other cities.

To emphasize the importance of customer service, all Peapod employees (including software programmers and managers) start as shoppers and delivery people.

Source: Adapted from Barbara Marsh, "Peapod's On-Line Grocery Service Checks Out Success," The Wall Street Journal, June 30, 1994, p. B2.

seldom predict with any exactitude the reactions of consumers or the countermoves and retaliations of competitors.[6]

While it may be easy to play "Monday Morning Quarterback," or view mistakes with 20-20 hindsight, we can learn lessons from others' mistakes, especially when looking for a competitive advantage. It seems safe to say that no one ever set out to design a bad product or start a business that would fail. But what seems to be a good idea for a competitive advantage may often not be, for one reason or another.

The lack, or loss, of competitive advantage exists in every size business. Apple Computer, which began small, has fought to maintain the competitive advantage of ease of use. In 1983, Apple tried to break into the business market for personal computers with the Lisa. While that computer was easy to use and had nice graphics, its advantages were not noticed by the business community because of its limited software and expensive price tag ($10,000).[7] Similar problems (performance below customer expectations and high price) plagued Apple's Newton MessagePad when it came out in 1993. Occasionally, competitive advantages are gained well after a product is introduced. For instance, the unsuccessful Lisa evolved into the Macintosh, one of the world's most popular models.

In the late 1970s and early 1980s, videodisks tried to break into the fledgling videocassette market. Videocassettes quickly won the battle in the marketplace for one simple reason: their advantage of being able to record programs, even though recording accounts for a small percentage of VCR use.[8]

Just being the first product in the market may be all the competitive advantage that you need. Despite the advantages of being quicker and easier to use, the Dvorak keyboard has not made a dent in the traditional "qwerty" keyboard market for typewriters and computers. The reason? Once people learn to type on one layout, they don't want to relearn how to type—even on a better keyboard.[9]

The list of products and businesses that have failed to gain a competitive advantage is long and distinguished. Entrants include Ford's Edsel (a car with lots of innovations—and lots more problems), Du Pont's Corfam (synthetic leather), Nutrasweet's Simplesse (edible fat substitute), and R. J. Reynolds' Premier (cigarettes that didn't burn or smoke).[10]

Benefits of Competitive Advantage

Gaining a competitive advantage can help you establish a self-sustaining position in the marketplace. Whether your edge comes from external factors such as luck or the failure of a competitor, or internal factors such as exceptional skills or superior resources, it can set up a cycle of success. (See Figure 9-2.)[11]

Because of your competitive advantage, your customers will be more satisfied with your business than with your competitors'. You will, therefore, gain market share. Increased market share translates into larger sales and profits, which in turn give you more resources for improving your products, facilities, and human resources—all of which allow you to improve your competitive advantage. Businesses that don't gain competitive advantages, therefore, lose out in this cycle. Their customers receive less value and are less satisfied. Their market share, sales volume, and profit fall. Without profits, they have fewer resources to reinvest in the business so positioning is difficult to maintain. The gap between follower and leader grows wider.

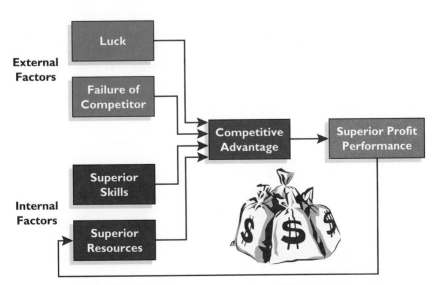

FIGURE 9-2
Competitive Advantage Cycle
However it is created, a competitive advantage will increase your profit margins, providing more resources for your small business to use to strengthen itself.
Source: John Czepiel, Competitive Marketing Strategy, *(Englewood Cliffs, NJ; Prentice Hall 1992) p. 41.*

Timing Is Everything

Twenty years ago, Robert Beaumont had a product with a competitive advantage. Unfortunately, it was one that customers did not want enough to buy the product, so his company didn't survive. In 1974, people told Beaumont that he was 20 years too early with the idea for his electric vehicle (EV), the CitiCar. After CitiCar went bankrupt in the mid-1970s, Beaumont waited for the right time to reenter the EV market.

Beaumont improved on his original advantage and was ready to try again. By 1994, industry experts thought Beaumont had the first sporty, competitively priced EV that would sell. Beaumont's new company is Renaissance Cars. Renaissance's convertible model, the Tropicana Roadster, features an aluminum chassis and a plastic body. It will go up to 80 miles on a single charge and cruises at 60 miles per hour. The $12,900 price tag competitively prices it with conventional gas-powered autos.

Having a competitive advantage is not enough. Sometimes you have to have it at the right time also. Innovation is important in creating advantages, but you can't be successful unless there is a demand for your product.

Source: Adapted from Alessandra Bianchi, "Start-Ups: Charged Up: Electric Vehicles," Inc. (May 1994), pp. 36–37.

How to Create Competitive Advantage

Michael Porter has identified three generic competitive strategies by which a business can gain a competitive advantage: lower cost, differentiation, and focus strategies.[12] Focus strategies means aiming at a narrow segment of a market. By

Global Small Business

Small businesses can also find it difficult to compete against foreign competition, particularly when it comes to sales price. However, by developing a competitive advantage based on a variable other than price you can overcome even this challenge. Take, for instance, Lyon's Designs of Salt Lake City, Utah, which designs, manufactures, and sells gifts and novelties. The retail gift industry is fickle and tricky to compete in. To survive, suppliers must constantly provide new designs at attractive prices. Paul Lyon, founder and owner of Lyon's Designs, knew that he couldn't compete with Taiwanese designers and manufacturers on price. It made more sense for him to work closely with foreign suppliers than to compete head-on, so he decided to establish a close manufacturing relationship with a limited number of factory owners in the Far East. Most of Lyon Designs' products now come from this region. To further cement his company's relationships, Lyon invited two Taiwanese factory owners to go camping in the Utah mountains. (When he asked a third Taiwanese to visit the United States, the man accepted but said, "Promise you won't take me camping!") Through its owner's ingenuity, Lyon's Designs has created a competitive advantage based on its global manufacturing relationships. *Source: Robert A. Mamis, "Second-Time Smart," Inc. 500, October 17, 1995, pp. 47–50.*

definition, all small businesses concentrate on niches or narrow market segments, so let's concentrate on the first two strategies.

You must find a way to lower costs if you intend to compete primarily on price. If you try to compete on price without obtaining a cost advantage, you are headed for trouble. This advantage can come from reduced labor costs, less expensive raw materials or supplies, more efficient distribution, or any number of other factors.

A competitive advantage based on differentiation means that your product or service is different from your competitors'. Its value is that you can show customers why your difference is *better,* not just cheaper. In this way, differentiation can effectively remove direct competition. For example, when a mass merchandiser like Wal-Mart or Target enters a town, small retailers are not necessarily run out of business. Studies that measure the impact of Wal-Mart on local retailers in Iowa have shown that as long as the small retail stores stock different merchandise than Wal-Mart, they actually benefit due to the increased number of shoppers coming into town. Small stores have to differentiate rather than trying to compete head-to-head against the giants.[13]

Reality Check

Staying Ahead of the Game

Getting and keeping a competitive advantage can be a challenge—especially in the intensely competitive CD-ROM publishing field where price plays an important role in enticing customers to buy. However, Quantum Axcess of Columbus, Ohio, has succeeded in maintaining its advantage—low prices—by minimizing its costs. Co-owners Stephan Smith, Gregory Pruden, and Kim Keiser have kept costs down by keeping the number of employees low even as sales have increased. Sales of $3 million were expected for 1995—and that was with six employees. In the coming years, Smith, Pruden, and Keiser plan to manage with fewer than ten employees while continuing to grow. Still, they know that keeping costs low isn't enough to ensure survival of their business, they must also satisfy customers' wants and needs. Quantum serves its niche so well that one of its CD-ROMs, Wire Head, was voted "Best CD in 1994" by *PC World* magazine.

Small businesses can also create a competitive advantage through a strategy of differentiation. Oakley Inc., the Irvine, California, sunglass and goggle manufacturer known for its exclusive, fashionable, and expensive products, epitomizes successful product differentiation. Oakley models sell for anywhere from $40 to $225 a pair—for a product made from plastic, carbon fiber, and other inexpensive materials. (It's been estimated that a $100 pair of Oakley Blades costs about $15 to manufacture). Yet customers snap them up because celebrities such as Michael Jordan, Andre Agassi, and Cal Ripken, Jr. wear them. Even Phil Knight, CEO of Nike, is rarely photographed without his signature pair of Oakleys.

Sources: Reed Abelson, "A Solid Bet or Just the Current Fashion Fad?" The New York Times, August 6, 1995, p. B11; Josh McHugh, "Who's Hiding behind those Shades?" Forbes, October 23, 1995, pp. 66–70; and Heather Page, "Game Time," Entrepreneur (October 1995), pp. 106–108.

Manager's Notebook

Competing on Intangibles

Many businesses operating in today's Information Age are built upon intangible services and assets, such as expertise in gathering, analyzing, and transmitting information. The competitive advantages of businesses that work in intangibles are inherently different from those of producers of tangible goods like automobiles, furniture, or typewriters. A few decades ago, when U.S. businesses were concerned primarily with manufacturing products, such advantages were easy to quantify. The success factors for businesses to compete in the twenty-first century are difficult (or impossible) to quantify, but just as important to have. Following are examples of ways for information-based businesses to create competitive advantages.

- *Generate passion.* A recent study showed that only 23 percent of U.S. workers surveyed were currently working to their full potential. About 44 percent stated that they only put out enough effort to keep their jobs. Three-fourths said they could do their jobs significantly more effectively than they do now. Think of the effect of these attitudes on productivity. What can you do to build a bond between your business and your employees so they care about what happens to the business and your customers? An orientation toward long-term outcomes rather than short-term actions is a start. Giving people a reason to feel pride in their work, that they are making a real contribution, and that the results of their efforts matter shows employees that they are important.
- *Constantly reinvent yourself.* If you want the people in your company to be innovative, you have to reward new ideas rather than stifle them with politics and protocol. Creativity is important in maintaining a sustainable competitive advantage—and it must be nurtured. You will encourage more ideas by looking for the good in them rather than automatically shooting them down.
- *Build concentration and focus.* Everyone in your business should know the direction and priorities of your business. If your people don't know the mission of your business, don't expect them to be passionate enough about the company to make personal sacrifices when needed.
- *Devote yourself to service excellence.* Traditional accounting systems do not show the true costs or benefits of long-term customer relations that are developed through providing excellent service. For example, they do not show the cumulative cash flows that you build by doing business with the same customer over a long period of time. Each sale is not an isolated event, it is an investment in future business. You can develop a competitive advantage by treating customers well to encourage future business.
- *Adapt to change.* Rapidly increasing changes at work and home mean that advantages can be quickly lost without the ability to adapt. Change needs to become part of your and your employees' mind set. Be prepared to adjust your product offerings, the services you provide, or your organizational structure to take advantage of new opportunities.

Source: Adapted from Frank Sonnenberg, "The Age of Intangibles," pp. 48–53. Reprinted by permission of the publisher from Management Review (*January 1994*), ©1994 American Management Association, New York. All rights Reserved.

An advantage does not have to be in the product itself. It can come from anything your business does—including distribution. In his autobiography *Iacocca*, Lee Iacocca stated that "The company with the best distribution system and the best service will win all the marbles—because you can't keep an advantage in other areas for long."[14]

To create a sustainable competitive advantage, your strategy needs a combination of methods to continuously differentiate your product and to improve it in areas that make a meaningful difference to your customers.[15] But how can you keep up with the changing tastes and preferences of your customers? There are so many questions about your customers you must try to answer. The products and services that people like and dislike at any particular time are shaped by hundreds of influences, many of which can't be identified. You need to gather facts about your markets in an objective and orderly manner. Marketing research is a way to answer questions about your customers' changing wants and needs to help you create and hold onto your competitive advantage.

Marketing Research

One of the major advantages that small businesses have over large businesses is close customer contact. Although this closeness can help you maintain your competitive advantage, you will also need a certain amount of ongoing **market research** to stay closely tuned to your market. If you are starting a new business, you will need market research even more.

marketing research The process of gathering information that will link consumers to marketers in order to improve marketing efforts.

Larry Read conducts the marketing research for Oil Changers, his chain of oil and filter quick-change shops, where you might expect—on the road. Read originally considered buying Jiffy Lube locations, but he was not satisfied with the answers he received about pricing, profit margins, and growth. That led him to spend a year on the road from California to Florida talking to owners of small, independent oil-change centers. The information he gathered was used to start Oil Changers in 1986. He continues to spend about $60,000 per year on at least ten trips across the country to see what is going on firsthand. The information paid off—Oil Changer annual growth rate was 367 percent from 1986 to 1990.[16]

The American Marketing Association defines marketing research as the function that links the consumer, customer, and public to the marketer through information. That information can be used to identify and define marketing opportunities and problems; to generate, refine, and evaluate marketing actions; to monitor marketing performance; and to improve understanding of marketing as a process.[17]

Not all marketing research conducted by small businesses is formal and intense. Most small business owners want to get information as quickly and as inexpensively as possible. (See Figure 9-3.) One survey showed that most spend between one and six months and less than $1,000 conducting market research on the last product or service they launched.

Marketing research can be as simple as trash and peanuts—literally. Owners of small restaurants often inspect outgoing waste to see what customers leave on their plates uneaten. Why? Because customers may order a dish like crayfish and pineapple pizza for the novelty, but if most don't actually eat it, it should be taken off the menu. One creative discount merchant conducted an in-store marketing research project using peanuts. During a three-day promotion, customers were given all the roasted peanuts in a shell they could eat while in the store. At

Manager's Notebook

"Yeah, Whaddya Want?" The Small Business and Customer Service

Think of the numerous small businesses you've frequented. No doubt, you will remember some because of the outstanding treatment you received, while others will bring to mind their absolutely awful service. What characterized those with great customer service? What did the others do wrong? And, more importantly, how can your small business develop a competitive advantage by providing outstanding customer service? Let's look at specific suggestions for making sure your small business is customer oriented.

Know your customers' likes and dislikes. One of the unique advantages of the small business is its ability to personalize its products and services. Knowing what individual customers appreciate and what they want to avoid, and keeping track of this information, can add up to one of those "intangible differences" that create a competitive advantage. For instance, Katherine Barchetti of Pittsburgh has been called one of the best retailers in America by industry experts. Her two small specialty shops offering high-fashion merchandise generate annual revenues of around $720 per square foot compared to a national average of $262. How does she do it? One of the keys to Barchetti's success is the fact that she keeps tabs on her customers, recording their names, likes and dislikes, sizes, and so on in a computer database. When a customer comes into the store, a salesperson quickly scans the computer before suggesting possible purchases.

Provide customers with something extra. Customers like to feel that they are getting a good value for the dollars they spend, and providing them with a little something extra—it doesn't have to expensive—can help convey that perception. Again, this is something a small business can do that larger businesses often won't take the time to do. For instance, at a butcher shop, the owner distributes recipes for different ways of cooking various cuts of meats. Not only do customers feel as if they're getting that "something extra," the owner is actually encouraging sales of products. A small Mexican restaurant provides breath mints at the end of the meal—giving customers a little "something" to combat the spicy aftertaste. A small business that recharges laser printer cartridges sticks a few pieces of gum and candy in the package for customers. There are many different things you can do as a small business owner or manager, when it comes to providing excellent customer service. Be as creative as possible—put yourself in your customer's shoes. What little extra can you provide to get that customer to come back again and again?

Train employees in the concept of customer service. You need to communicate your expectations of customer service to any employee who will be in contact with your customers. Whether it's the person taking customer orders over the phone, the repair person out on service calls, or even you, the owner, all employees need to know how to treat customers. Typically, excellent customer service means treating customers with respect and courtesy and taking care of their needs. *That* is what customers remember, particularly when it's absent! For instance, an experience at a small photo shop in Baltimore illustrates the wrong way to treat the customer. When a customer went in to pick up her order, she was presented with a double set of prints although she had ordered only a single set. When the customer objected, the owner argued with her, then grabbed the photos back and proceeded to drop the duplicates in the trash can one by one. Obviously, not a good way to keep a customer!

Communicate frequently with customers. Customers like to feel that they're important to and appreciated by the businesses they patronize. Most small business owners convey this feeling through the frequent face-to-face contact and personal conversations that their business affords. In addition, you can also publish information about your business. It doesn't have to be something expensive. It can be as simple as a flyer or a newsletter mailed to your customers or provided at the checkout. A hobby shop posts flyers around the store announcing meets and competitions for race car enthusiasts. A locally owned franchise of Wild Birds Unlimited sends out a quarterly newsletter with information for seasonal bird feeding, coupons, and suggestions for gift giving. Bruno's, an Italian bakery in New York City, distributes a newsletter that offers holiday recipes, advertises seasonal specials, and provides other news. (One issue explained what a "caper" is—the flower of a wild Mediterranean shrub, *Capparis spinosa*.) Again, there are numbers of ways that you can

communicate with your customers to let them know they're important to you—and to keep them interested in your business. What a wonderful way to create a competitive advantage!

Stay focused on providing excellent customer service. Amid the day-to-day hassles of running a small business, it's easy to lose sight of the fact that customers are your bread and butter. But you should always remember the importance of keeping customers happy. Some small businesses provide recognition—plaques, pins, certificates, and so forth—to employees who exemplify excellent customer service. Others have regular training sessions on how to treat customers and solve problems that inevitably arise. Whatever your approach, the key is to remain focused on providing the best service you can.

FIGURE 9-3
Market Research Expenditures
Small businesses often spend less than $5,000, and less than six months, gathering market research for new products.
Source: Survey of 173 CEOs, 57 percent from companies with sales of $10 million or less, by Inc. and The Executive Committee, San Diego, 1992. Susan Greco, "Sales & Marketing," Inc., July 1992, p. 118.

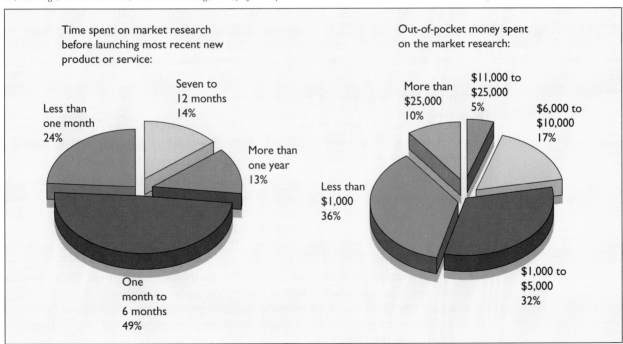

Grassroots Marketing Research

Cathy Schnaubelt Rogers, CEO of Schnaubelt Shorts, takes a pragmatic approach to marketing research—she asks women what they want. Rogers's company produces cycling clothing for women. She found that many older riders and casual bikers were not able to get what they wanted to wear from bicycle shops, so she put together a cross-country sounding board.

Rogers started out by identifying the eight states with the most female bicyclists and handpicked a "leader" from each one. Then each of her eight leaders selected ten other women from a wide range of cycling interests. Some are weekend dirt bikers, some are racers, some are casual riders. Rogers then met each of the 80 women in person. After the initial feedback meeting, she sent them mail surveys about her products' fit, color, and durability every few months. The $500 Rogers spends on each mailing (including samples, postage, and tabulation) is cheap feedback to get from the people who are using her products.

Source: Adapted from Susan Greco "Riding on Real Feedback," Inc. (January 1994), p. 95.

One creative merchant conducted a secret marketing survey by giving his customers roasted peanuts. The piles of empty hulls on the floor showed him how people had moved through the store—and which displays had attracted the most attention.

the end of each day, the empty hulls on the floor provided information about traffic patterns of people moving through the store. Piles of shells in front of displays showed the merchandise that was attracting particular interest.[18]

A large factor looms as a reason for an increase in the amount of time and money small businesses should spend on market research: changing conditions. Because many markets and demographics change quickly, the businesses which emerge as winners are those that are *proactive* rather than *reactive*. Marketing research can give you information on what your customers are going to want as opposed to historical data which tell you what they used to want.

Marketing Research Process

The marketing research process follows five basic steps: identifying the problem, developing a plan, collecting the data, analyzing the data, and drawing conclusions. (See Figure 9-4.)

Identify the Problem. The most difficult, and most important, part of the research process is the first step—identifying the problem. You must have a clearly stated, concisely worded problem in order to generate usable information. Many people (novice and experienced researchers alike) have trouble with this step because they confuse problems with symptoms. If there is an underlying reason for what you have identified, it is a symptom and not the problem itself.

For example, if you go to a physician complaining of a fever, the physician could prescribe medication that would bring your fever down. But that would not cure you. There is an infection or another problem that is causing your fever to be high. Your physician will search until the problem is found and then fix it—not just mask the symptom.

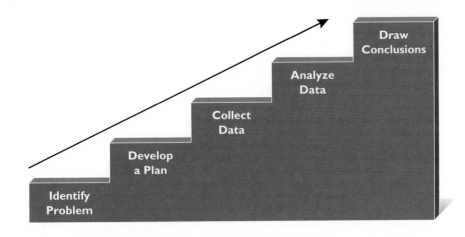

FIGURE 9-4
Marketing Research Process
Conducting research on your markets involves a logical five-step process.

Would declining sales in your small business be a problem or a symptom? A drop in your sales revenue would be like the fever—it is a symptom. While the symptom itself is not pleasant to experience, there is an underlying reason causing it to occur. That is what you would want to try to uncover with your research. Has the competition increased? Do your salespeople need retraining? Have your customers' tastes changed?

Your marketing problem does not always have to be something that is wrong. You can use marketing research to find real problems or to identify new opportunities. Whatever your goal, your ability to complete this first step of the research process is important in guiding the rest of your research efforts.

Planning Marketing Research. Marketing research is often expensive, but a plan of how you will conduct your research project can help keep costs down. Before you start, you must separate what is "critical to know" from what would be "nice to know." Your next step is to design a way to address the problem, or answer the question that you have identified concerning your business. You can do it yourself and you should keep it as simple as possible.

In planning your marketing research project you need to:

- Identify the types of information that you need.
- Identify primary and secondary sources of data.
- Select a sample that represents the population you are studying.
- Select a research method and measurement technique (phone survey, focus group, and so on) to answer your research question.

In conducting research for your small business, you should choose a method that provides enough reliable data for you to make a decision with confidence. The method you choose must also use your limited time, money, and personnel efficiently.

Collecting Data. After you have identified the research problem and laid out a plan, you are ready to gather data. While it sounds simple, do not get this order reversed. A common research error is to begin the process by gathering data and then trying to figure out what the information means and where to go with it— putting the cart before the horse. Determine what you need, then go get it. There are two basic types of data you may seek—secondary and primary.[19]

Secondary Data. Secondary sources of data are those which already exist, having been gathered for some other purpose. You should check secondary sources first because they are less expensive than conducting your own study. You may be able to solve your problem without an extended primary search.

The good news about **secondary data** is that the amount of available data is considerable. The bad news, however, is that that mountain of information can be overwhelming.

A good place to begin your search of secondary data is your local library. Computerized CD-ROM databases such as ProQuest or ABI Inform allow you to enter key terms into the program and receive titles, abstracts, and entire articles from journals and periodicals immediately. The *Government Printing Office Monthly Catalog* contains report references from many government agencies that may help you, such as the Department of Commerce and the Small Business Administration. The Department of Commerce also publishes *Selected Publications to Aid Business and Industry.* Check the *Encyclopedia of Associations* for the thousands of trade, professional, technical, and industrial associations that exist. These associations compile information that can be very relevant to your business.

You can get data on your personal computer from on-line computer services such as CompuServe. Dow Jones, publisher of *The Wall Street Journal,* offers Dow Jones News/Retrieval®. This service can help you scan the newspaper's daily Enterprise column, which is devoted to topics on small business. The SBA provides 24-hour access to information on services it provides, to publications, training, and other programs, and to trade fairs, through its electronic bulletin board *SBA On-line.* Using a computer modem, dial 1-800-697-INFO.

If you have an aversion to libraries or a computer phobia, there is an alternative to aid your research. *Information brokers* are companies that are expert

secondary data Marketing data that has been gathered, tabulated, and made available by an outside source.

Entering the Internet

One of the best sources for demographic information can be found at the Census Bureau's Home Page on the Internet and World Wide Web. Here you'll find such information as social and economic indicators (income, business failures, poverty levels, and so forth) for each state. You can also access County Business Patterns, which contain state- and county-level data on employment and payroll figures, and types and numbers of establishments. Another source is the SBA Online Gopher service. It includes a document entitled "Knowing Your Market," which contains suggested sources and questions to ask in learning about your market. Finally, you might want to query the U.S. Department of Commerce's Commerce Information Locator Service with specific questions you have about geographic areas, target markets, or customer groups. Type in the keywords and see what comes up.

Web Address for Census Bureau
http://www.census.gov

Web Address for SBA Online
Gopher://www.sbaonline.sba.gov:70/11/Business-Development/General-
  Information-And-Publications

Web Address for U.S. Department of Commerce
http://www.doc.gov/inquery/cils.html

gatherers of competitive information.[20] Rates and specialties of these businesses vary. Examples include DataSerch of Fort Wayne, Indiana, whose 1992 average rate was $60 per hour with an average project cost of $120. Its specialties include competitor intelligence, plastics, and the former Soviet states. InfoQuest of Portland, Oregon, charged $60 to $75 per hour in 1992 with an average project cost of $120 to $225. To find an information broker near you, contact the Association of Independent Information Professionals (AIIP), or the *Burkwell Directory of Information Brokers.*[21]

Potential problems with secondary data are that they may not be specific or detailed enough for your purpose or that they may be obsolete. In either case you will need to gather your own primary data.

Primary Data. **Primary data** are qualitative or quantitative data that you collect yourself for your specific purpose. Both types of data have their advocates and critics, but either type can provide valuable information if collected and analyzed correctly.

primary data Marketing data that a business collects for its own specific purposes.

Qualitative data refer to research findings that cannot be analyzed statistically. Qualitative data are useful if you are looking for open-minded responses to probing questions, not yes-or-no answers.[22] These can be obtained through personal interviews or focus groups (groups of six to ten people), which provide considerable depth of information from each person. Qualitative data do not lend themselves to statistical analysis. They help you look for trends in answers or to obtain specific or detailed responses to your questions.

Quantitative data are structured to analyze and report numbers to help you explain relationships between variables and to see frequency of occurrences. Quantitative data are useful in providing information on large groups of people. Their less-probing questions yield results that can be analyzed statistically to show causation.

Telephone interviewing, personal interviewing, and mail surveys are common methods small businesses use in gathering both types of primary data. Since the questionnaire is such a common small business research tool, the following advice is offered to increase its usefulness and the readers' response rate:

- Try to make the questionnaire visually attractive and fun to answer. This will help to keep it from ending up in the recipient's wastebasket.
- Try to structure possible responses. Instead of asking "What do you think of our product?" list answers like reliability, quality, and price for respondents to check.
- Don't ask for more than most people remember. Annoying questions, like asking for the number of lightbulbs a business uses in a year, can end the response.
- Don't have more than 20 words per question. People lose interest quickly if questions are too long.
- Be as specific and unambiguous as possible.
- Include a cover letter explaining the reason for the questionnaire. Say "thank you."
- Include a self-addressed, stamped return envelope to increase the response rate.
- Include a return date. A reasonable deadline will increase the number of responses and will let you know how long to wait before tallying the results.[23]

Other techniques of primary data collection for small businesses are limited only by your imagination. The automobile license plates of many states show the county where the vehicle is registered. You can get an idea of where your customers live by taking notes of the license plates in your parking lot. This information can help you determine where to aim your advertising. You can use the same technique by spending some time in your competitor's parking lot. Telephone numbers can also tell you where customers live. You can get this information from sales slips, credit slips, or checks.

By running "lucky draw" contests, you can get a lot of information about your customers. Have customers fill out cards with name and address to win a prize if their name is drawn from the box. You can plot these addresses on a local map to see your trade area for the price of a small give-away prize.[24]

Computer Applications

What software programs are available to help analyze data? Some database programs can also be used to analyze qualitative information. Or, if your data are quantitative, you can use statistical analysis programs to analyze your numbers.

Let's look first at database management programs that can analyze information. To use these programs you must have information on your customers or potential customers in a database. Knowledge-SEEKER, by Angoss Software of Toronto, Canada, is a fairly sophisticated program that reads and draws conclusions from your database. It's relatively inexpensive (DOS-based, $799 and Windows-based, $899) and easy to use. Even lower-priced programs include DBMS/COPY by Conceptual Software Inc. of Houston, Texas. This program features over 100 math and trigonometry functions for transforming data in any combination. It also allows data to be moved between many different program formats (such as databases, spreadsheets, statistics packages, and so forth). And its companion product, Data Muncher, provides sophisticated cross-tabular analyses.

DBMS/COPY retails for $295. Finally, you might try Data Pivot by Brio Technology (retail, $299). This program can create reports while its multidimensional spreadsheet allows you to rotate, reorganize, or pivot data to suit your particular needs.

Among statistical analysis software are two very popular programs that you can use for analyzing marketing research data. One is Mathcad by MathSoft. This program facilitates algebraic and statistical analysis and provides elementary calculation features as well. Its ability to integrate calculations, graphics, and text would be convenient for generating reports. Two other programs that provide statistical analysis and quantitative modeling features are SPSS and SPSS/PC+ by SPSS Inc. of Chicago, Illinois. The SPSS software provides the highest power, most available analytical procedures, largest variable ability, and most complete menus of all the software programs cited here.

Sources: Alistair Davidson and Sharon Weller-Cody, "Software Tools for the Strategic Manager," Planning Review *(April 1995), pp. 32–35; and* Campus Computing Sourcebook *(Fall 1995), pp. 65 and 73.*

Advertisements that provide coded coupons or phrases customers can use to get a discount in your broadcast advertising can help you determine the effectiveness and reach of your ads.

Data Analysis. Basically, data analysis is the process of determining what the responses to your research mean. Once data have been collected, they must be analyzed and translated into usable information. Your first step is to clean the data. This includes removing all questionnaires or other forms that are unusable because they are incomplete or unreadable. Depending on the instrument or methodology used to gather data, you need to code and examine the data to identify trends and develop insights. (An exhaustive description of data analysis is not appropriate for this text. For details of this process, refer to a source such as *Marketing Research: An Applied Orientation* by Malhotra.)

If you collected quantitative data, several software programs exist to aid you in "number crunching" and in transforming data into charts and graphs that make interpretation easier.

Presenting the Data and Making Decisions. Marketing research that does not lead to some type of action is useless. Your research needs to aid you in making management decisions. Should you expand into a new geographic area? Should you change your product line? Should you change your business hours?

Conclusions based on your data analysis may be obvious. Data may fall out in such a way that you can see exactly what you need to do next to answer the research problem identified in step 1.

Marketing research can provide you with information that will allow you to be proactive. This is important because, as a small business owner, deciding what you need to do in the future is much more important than knowing what has happened in the past.

Limitations of Marketing Research

As important as marketing research can be for small businesses, it should be used with caution. Marketing research can provide you with a picture of what people currently know and expect from products or services, but it has limited ability to indicate what people will want in the future. Relying on marketing research exclusively for your marketing strategy and new product ideas is like driving a car while only watching the rear-view mirror.[25]

As noted in Chapter 1, small businesses provide many of the most innovative products that we use. Our economy and consumers depend on a stream of such innovations as fax machines, CD-ROMs, and mini-vans, but innovation does not come from marketing research. Peter Drucker notes that although the fax machine was designed and developed by U.S. companies, no U.S. companies began producing fax machines for domestic consumption because marketing research indicated that there would be no demand for such a product.

When asking about a product that does not yet exist, Drucker says all you can do is ask people "Would you buy a telephone accessory that costs upwards of $1,500 and enables you to send, for one dollar a page, the same letter the post office delivers for 25 cents?" The average consumer predictably said "no".[26] Hal Sperlich designed the concept of the mini-van while he was working for Ford, but when Ford didn't believe a market existed for such a vehicle (based on its historical marketing research), he switched to Chrysler. Sperlich says, "In ten years of developing the mini-van, we never once got a letter from a housewife

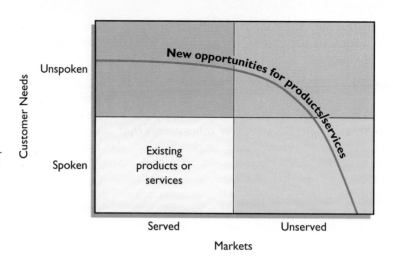

FIGURE 9-5
Matrix of Customer Needs and Types
Marketing research is most effective when used to evaluate existing products which satisfy known needs that customers can talk about.
Gary Hameland and C. K. Prahaled, "Seeing the Future First," Fortune, September 5, 1994, pp. 64–70.

asking us to invent one. To the skeptics, that proved there wasn't a market out there."[27]

While marketing research is good for fine tuning concepts for known products, customers don't have the foresight to ask for what they don't know about or know they need. As one axis of Figure 9-5 shows, there are two types of customer needs: those that they can tell you about and those that they have without realizing they have them. How many people were asking for cellular telephones, MTV, or compact disk players ten years ago? The other axis of Figure 9-5 shows that there are two types of markets or customers for any given business: those served by the company's existing products and those not yet served—the company's potential customers. Marketing research can tell us the most about the spoken needs of a served market, but a lot of room for growth exists in exploring the three other sectors. When you are driving a car, you need to check the rear-view mirror occasionally, just as you should check your current and past markets with marketing research. But the ideal is to concentrate on defining markets rather than reacting to them. An entrepreneur must go beyond what marketing research can tell.

Summary

■ The definition of competitive advantage.

A competitive advantage is what a business does better than all of its competitors. It can be built on any facet of a business including price, location of the business, product features, or customer perception of the business. A competitive advantage must be sustainable. Competitive advantages are relative, not absolute. Having more than one base for your competitive advantage increases your chances for success. Bases for competition, along with customer tastes and preferences, change over time.

■ The importance and benefits of having a competitive advantage.

If a business does not have a competitive advantage—if it does not do something better than competitors—that business is not needed and will not survive. Having a competitive advantage can set up a self-sustaining cycle of success in which higher profit margins are generated that can provide you superior resources and allow you to increase your competitive advantage.

■ The three ways to create a competitive advantage.

A business can build a competitive advantage by using a low cost, a differentiation, or a focus strategy. The only way for a business to successfully compete on price is to adopt a low cost strategy. Differentiation builds competitive advantage by showing customers important differences, benefits, and product uses among competing products. Differentiation is the way businesses avoid competing on price alone. Focus strategies involve concentrating on narrow segments of a market, which provides an advantage for all small businesses.

■ The purpose of the marketing research process, and the steps involved in putting it into practice.

Marketing research provides information about the people who are buying the products of a business. Conditions change and the owner of a business must know about those changes in order to be proactive and maintain a competitive advantage. The steps of the marketing research process include: problem identification, development of a plan, data collection, data analysis, and drawing conclusions.

■ What marketing research can do for your small business.

Marketing research can provide valuable information regarding people's current tastes, preferences, and expectations. It is useful in fine-tuning products which already exist for markets that are already known. Marketing research is of limited use for markets which do not exist yet, or for needs which customers do not realize they have.

Questions for Review and Discussion

1. Why is competitive advantage such an important concept for the small business owner to understand? Define competitive advantage and how it relates to the strategic plan for the business.

2. Explain Porter's concept of the forces of competition. What does Porter mean when he states that small businesses can't rely on the inertia of the marketplace? Why is that important?

3. Define and elaborate on the five fatal flaws that can occur when strategic thinking is applied to specific competitive situations.

4. How does the entrepreneur create competitive advantage and how is it measured?

5. The lack of loss of competitive advantage is not limited to small businesses. Elaborate on some failures that have been produced by large corporations. Give your opinion as to why the products failed to gain a competitive advantage.

6. What is the significance of marketing research to the small business owner? How is marketing research defined and what degree of complexity is necessary in the research plan for it to be valid?

7. Explain the marketing research process from a small business owner's perspective when she is trying to assess competitive advantage.

8. What types of data should be collected and analyzed in order to get a clear picture of the market for the good or service being produced?

9. Name some sources of information that are valuable to the entrepreneur who is designing a marketing research plan to analyze competitive advantage. *trade assoc., internet, SBA, st. gvt.*

10. What are some of the limitations of marketing research? What can be done to offset these limitations by the entrepreneur?

Critical Incident

Marketing research is an important tool for small business owners and managers. Knowing what to ask and how to ask it are important skills. The three businesses described here all need help in terms of performing marketing research. Read through the scenarios and then answer the questions.

Vitalink. During the late 1980s, the federal government proposed more stringent controls of drugs in nursing homes. Sensing an opportunity, Donna DeNardo established Vitalink to provide this service. She describes her company as "basically a hospital pharmacy, but we're not in the hospital basement." The company provides drugs and recordkeeping services to nursing homes. As the population of the United States continues to age, you'd think Vitalink's revenues would be increasing. However, revenues have not increased as fast as DeNardo would like. She'd like to find out possible reasons for this situation.

Klutz Press. The company isn't anything like its name implies. Klutz Press is a successful publisher of interactive multimedia children's books, covering diverse topics from clay modeling to knot tying to map reading. The company has published 45 titles and sells nearly 5 million books a year to the tune of $25 million. Its books are unique because, in addition to their durable cardboard pages, they are accompanied by "equipment" that lets readers experience what they read. For instance, the company's *Braids and Bows* book comes with the hair ribbons and ties to actually make braids and bows. The *Cat's Cradle* book comes with a tie-dyed loop of string so kids can try out the string figures illustrated in the book. But Klutz Press wants to expand into Europe. Marketing research could help answer its questions about that move.

Westec Security. Westec Security Inc. is one of the largest full-service security firms in the United States with more than 60,000 monitored clients and revenues of around $80 million. The company provides clients with an in-house security system and employees who patrol clients' neighborhoods. Because excellent service is extremely important for getting and keeping customers in this type of industry, Westec wants to survey its customers to get their feedback about the service being provided. *Sources: Nancy Rotenier, "Drug Runner," Forbes, October 23, 1995, p. 332, Steven B. Kaufman, "A 'Klutz' Who Knows Kids," Nation's Business (May 1995), pp. 14–15; and Thomas Rollins and Dennis Buster, "Westec Guards Its Competitive Edge," Personnel Journal (August 1995), pp. 84–88.*

Questions

1. Select one of the three businesses described. State what you think the research problem is. Then develop five survey questions that you think would help answer the question posed in the research problem.

2. Divide into student groups with others in the class who selected the same business you did. (Aim for five to eight people per group.) After discussing your proposed research problems, select the five survey questions that you think would best answer the research problem. Be prepared to present your group's work to the class.

Take it to the Net

We invite you to visit the Hatten page on the Prentice Hall Web site at: http://www.prenhall.com/~hattensb for this chapter's World Wide Web exercise.

Chapter Focus

After reading this chapter, you should be able to:

- Describe the evolution of business philosophies.
- Explain the need for market segmentation and its process.
- Describe the "Black Box" model of consumer behavior.
- Identify the five forms that a product can take.
- Explore how "efficiencies" affect channels of distribution.
- Outline how small businesses put together a promotion mix.
- Identify the possible objectives of advertising.
- List the seven steps in personal selling.

10

Marketing for Small Business

WHAT WOULD YOU DO IF YOU owned a Colorado ski area close to a major resort like Aspen but which had only 450 acres, poor public access, little name recognition, and which was losing about $2 million annually? That was the situation facing Crested Butte owners "Bo" Calloway and Ralph Walton in the early 1980s. Their solution? An innovative, aggressive ad campaign—and it worked. In a decade in which 25 percent of all ski areas closed, Crested Butte's $2 million loss became a $1.5 million annual profit, thanks to smart marketing.

Here's how it worked: Calloway and Walton hired a team of talented marketers to bring attention to Crested Butte's "funky" character and "real West" setting. Ad themes like "Heaven Forbid We Should Ever Become Like Aspen or Vail" and "Crested Butte—What Aspen Used to Be and Vail Never Was" promoted Crested Butte's differences from the major competitors as positive attractions. The partners also added skiable acres—mostly expert terrain. This too was promoted as differentiation: "Extreme Skiing—Not Extreme Pricing."

They improved access to the remote location by guaranteeing American Airlines a profit if it offered direct flights from major cities to nearby Gunnison.

Still, Crested Butte was losing money between Thanksgiving and Christmas, so marketing manager John Norton came up with a novel offer—free skiing between the holidays. Local hotels and restaurants voluntarily gave the resort some of the revenue from customers who came to ski free. Bookings jumped to (and exceeded) capacity, and everyone profited.

Such innovations at Crested Butte have provided capital to install new lifts, to expand terrain, and to improve services. Crested Butte is an example of a niche player that understands what its customers want, what its competitive advantages are, and how to go up against very large, very well known, deep-pocketed competitors. *Source: Marj Charlier, "How an Obscure Ski Hill Carved a Niche Among Resorts,"* The Wall Street Journal, *January 20, 1994, p. B1–B2.*

Small Business Marketing

What do you think of when you hear the term *marketing?* Do you think of selling or advertising? Probably, but marketing is actually much more than just selling or advertising. Marketing involves all the activities needed to get a product from the producer to the ultimate consumer. Management guru Peter Drucker stated that businesses have two—and only two—basic functions: marketing and innovation. These are the only things a business does that produce results, everything else is really a "cost."[1] This is just as true for the one-person kiosk as it is for the largest corporate giant.

Of course, some selling will always be necessary, but the goal of marketing is to make selling superfluous.[2] A truly customer-driven company understands what consumers want in a product and provides it so that its products sell themselves. Of course, this is not easy. To paraphrase President Lyndon Johnson, doing the right thing is easy. Knowing the right thing to do is tough.

The Marketing Concept

Many businesses operate today with a customer-driven philosophy. They want to find out what their customers want and then provide that good or service. This philosophy is called the **marketing concept.**

marketing concept The philosophy of a business in which the wants and needs of customers are determined before goods and services are produced.

Businesses have not always concentrated their efforts on what the market wants. Before the Industrial Revolution and mass production, nearly all a business owner needed to be concerned about was making products. Demand exceeded supply for most goods like boots, clothing, or saddles. People had to have these products, so about all a business had to do was to make them. This philosophy—in which companies concentrate their efforts on the product being made—is now called the **production concept** of business.

production concept The philosophy of a business that concentrates more on the product the business makes than on customer needs.

After the mid-1800s, when mass production and mass distribution became possible for manufactured products, supply began to exceed demand. Some selling was needed, but the emphasis was still on producing goods. World War II temporarily shifted resources from consumer markets to the military. But after the war, when those resources were returned to the consumer market, businesses were producing at capacity and many new businesses were started. Managers found that they could no longer wait for consumers to come to them in order to sell all they could make. Although these companies still emphasized making products, they now had to convince people to buy *their* products, which inaugurated the *selling concept* of business.

Early in the 1960s many businesses began to adopt the marketing concept. According to this view, the customer is the center of a business's attention. It involves finding out what your customers want and need and then offering products to satisfy those desires.

The essence of the marketing concept is to first find out what customers want and then supply it. It is a practice of world-class businesses.

World-Class Marketing

If you take the marketing concept another step beyond production and apply it to the internal operation of a business, it is the basis of total quality management (TQM). TQM is defined as the process of meeting the wants and needs of internal

Reality Check

Marketing Concept— Give 'em What They Want

Scott MacHardy and Mark Lane don't know exactly why their customers buy so many T-shirts with off-color messages, but they do know about the marketing concept. MacHardy and Lane know what their customers want and make a product to satisfy them.

MacHardy and Lane met while they were both students at the University of New Hampshire working for a company called Coed Sportswear, which made T-shirts bearing (or bare-ing) the "Coed Naked" logo. The owner of the company ran into financial and legal trouble and the two students were in danger of losing their jobs. So MacHardy and Lane approached a bank and, with the help of a silent partner, were able to purchase the company. They had seen the success the products enjoyed on their own campus and were sure that success could be duplicated elsewhere. "Out of 10,000 students, almost 9,000 had one of these shirts," said MacHardy.

Production began in MacHardy's garage in

1991. Within 60 days, a sales representative working along the East Coast had lined up 500 new accounts. The partners realized the importance of satisfying retailers selling their shirts and offered 24-hour shipping and no minimum number of shirts that could be ordered. This innovative approach allowed small businesses to stock all of their designs without carrying a tremendous inventory. Within four years, more than 10,000 retailers around the world carried the Coed Naked line and annual sales now top $25 million. Not bad for two college students making a $15,000 investment.

To keep their core target market of unpredictable teenagers happy, MacHardy and Lane are constantly looking for outrageous new slogans. The partners employ 60 young people who are encouraged to submit marketing or new product ideas. Recent additions include "I Own the Zone" and "Just Hafta."

Source: Tom Stein, "Scoring With Sportswear," Success (September 1995), p. 31.

and external customers by developing and providing them with high-quality, high-value, want-satisfying products.[3] Businesses of all sizes are facing increasingly tougher world-class competition, which calls for **world-class marketing** (WCM). WCM combines the basics of TQM with the best marketing practices:

world-class marketing The practice of satisfying the internal and external customers of a business.

- An **external customer orientation.** Everyone in the organization concentrating on customer wants; the marketing concept.
- An **internal customer orientation.** Hiring, training, motivating, rewarding, and empowering employees to provide world-class service including continuous training to maintain world-class standards.
- A **total quality orientation.** Putting the 14 points of TQM into practice. (See pages 359–360.)
- A **goal orientation.** Measuring results to ensure that the organization is meeting goals previously established.
- A **societal orientation.** Recognizing that your business has an impact on other stakeholders such as suppliers, dealers, community leaders, government agencies, stockholders, and the environment.[4]

The role of marketing in small and large businesses continues to change. Marketing must be used not only to bring in customers but also to build alliances and long-term relationships with customers. Businesses that adopt this long-term view could be furthering the evolution of the marketing concept into what may become known as the *customer concept*.[5]

Marketing Strategies for Small Business

marketing strategy What the marketing efforts of a business are intended to accomplish and how the business will achieve its goals.

Your **marketing strategy** should be decided in the early stages of operating your business. It should state *what* you intend to accomplish and *how* you intend to accomplish it. The marketing section of the business plan is a good place for the small business owner to identify marketing strategies. Any potential investor will carefully inspect how you have laid out the marketing action that will drive your business.

A good marketing strategy will help you to be proactive, not reactive, in running your business. You can enhance your marketing plan by:

- Watching and understanding trends in your customers, suppliers, demographics, and technology
- Having a vision that provides direction for your business
- Having an adaptable, flexible organization.[6]

The National Retail Federation recognized James Baum as 1993 Small Store Retailer of the Year largely because he did these three things in forming a strategy for his small department store in Morris, Illinois. Baum was faced with a difficult situation. He knew he had to eliminate the store's fabric department for the sake of his business's survival. The difficulty came from the fact that the business had been started by his family 114 years before as a fabric store. But in cutting the company's tie with its historical roots and replacing fabrics with women's sportswear, sales eventually doubled the previous best year of fabric sales.[7] With a marketing plan to provide an understanding of his customers' changing tastes, a vision where his business needed to go, and a mechanism to change it, Baum was able to take his business to the next level.

Small businesses in the service industries must pay special attention to marketing. When their service is one which customers could perform themselves, such as lawn mowing, a marketing strategy is critical. It is also often more difficult to differentiate or establish a brand image with services than with tangible products. Can the average car owner tell the difference between automatic transmissions that have been rebuilt by different shops? Probably not. A marketing strategy that communicates the benefits that consumers receive is crucial. However comprehensive or simple your marketing plan, it should include a description of your marketing objectives, sales forecast, target markets, and marketing mix.[8]

Global Small Business

With respect to global markets, it is just as important to craft an appropriate marketing strategy. And the number of small business owners and managers going global is surging. One survey by Arthur Anderson & Company and National Small Business United found that 20 percent of the 750 companies surveyed (all with 500 employees or less) exported products and services during 1994. That was up from 16 percent in 1993 and 11 percent in 1992. One small business that has made the leap is Preco Industries of Kansas City, Missouri, a manufacturer of automated die cutting and stamping equipment. With annual sales of around $12 million, Preco sells 32 percent of its equipment overseas. It has been able to market overseas successfully by preparing thoroughly before entering any of its global markets, adapting to the country's culture, and making a firm commitment to its global ventures. It maintains its position by responding immediately to problems and challenges, being realistic about expectations, and by nurturing relationships within the country. *Source: Amy Barrett, "It's a Small (Business) World," Business Week, April 17, 1995, pp. 96–101; and Judith Ferlig, "Small World," Ingram's (June 1995), pp. 53+.*

Setting Marketing Objectives

Your marketing objectives define the goals of your plans. They can be broken into two groups: marketing performance objectives and marketing support objectives.[9] *Marketing performance objectives* are specific, quantifiable outcomes such as sales revenue, market share, and profit. *Marketing support objectives* are what you must accomplish before your performance objectives can be accomplished, such as educating customers about your products, building awareness, and creating image.

Like any goal you want to accomplish in business, marketing objectives need to be: (1) measurable, (2) action oriented by identifying what needs to be done, and (3) time specific by targeting a date or time for achievement.

Developing a Sales Forecast

sales forecast The quantity of products a business plans to sell during a future time period.

Your marketing plan should include a **sales forecast** in which you predict your future sales in dollars and in units—in other words, what your "top line" will be. Forecasting is difficult, but it will help you establish more accurate goals and objectives. Your sales forecast will have an impact on all sections of your marketing plan, including appropriate channels of distribution, sales force requirements, advertising and sales promotions budgets, and the effects of price changes.

There are two basic ways to forecast sales: *build-up methods* and *break-down methods*. With a build-up method, you identify as many target markets as possible and predict the sales to each group. Then you combine the predictions for a total sales forecast.

When using a break-down method, you begin with an estimate of the total market potential, an entire industry for example. This figure is broken down into forecasts of smaller units until you reach an estimate of how large a market you will reach and how many sales you will make.

Identifying Target Markets

target market A group of people with a common want or need which your business can satisfy, who are able to purchase your product and who are more likely to buy from your business.

Market segmentation is the process of dividing the total market for a product into identifiable groups, or **target markets,** with a common want or need that your business can satisfy. These target markets are important to your business because they are the people who are more likely to be your customers. They are the people toward whom you direct your marketing efforts. Identifying and concentrating on target markets can help prevent you from getting caught in the trap of trying to be everything to everyone—you can't do it.[10]

When asked about their target markets, many small business owners will respond, "We don't have specific target markets, we will sell to anyone who comes in the door." Of course, you sell to anyone who wants your product, but that is not the point of segmenting target markets. See the Reality Check on page 261 for an example of a business that turned target marketing into increased profit.

A market for your business must have:

1. A need that your products can satisfy.
2. Enough people to generate profit for your business.
3. Possession of, and willingness to spend, enough money to generate profit for your business.

segmentation variables Characteristics or ways to group people which make them more likely to purchase a product.

To identify the most attractive target markets for your business, you should look for characteristics that affect the buying behavior of the people. Does where they live influence whether or not they buy your product? Does income, gender, age, or lifestyle matter? Do they seek a different benefit from the product than other groups do? These differences, called **segmentation variables,** can be based on geographic, demographic, or psychographic differences, or on differences in benefits received.

Not every way to segment a market is equally useful for every business. For example, if males and females react to the marketing efforts of your business in the same way, then segmenting by gender is not the best way to identify a target market for your business. When segmenting target markets, keep in mind the

Reality Check

Aiming at the Right Target (Market)

Like many small business owners, Mac McConnell thought that price was the main competitive concern of his Plantation, Florida, business, Artful Framer Gallery—that is, until he polled 300 of his customers. Over a six-week period, he asked his walk-in customers to fill out a one-page survey. They answered questions about who they were, where they lived, how they heard about the business, and how they rated the store.

McConnell was shocked by his customers' priorities. They had listed quality as their first priority, and uniqueness as their second. Price was at the bottom of the list. Fortunately for McConnell, his concentration on price had not undermined the quality of his work, and 85 percent of his customers rated his framing service as excellent. As a result of his survey, McConnell did some business reinvention to better serve the target market that he now had identified:

- **Upscaling merchandise.** Customer response about quality gave McConnell the courage to drop the bottom-end merchandise. He improved customers' options by increasing the number of samples he kept on hand to 1800. Museum-quality framing became the standard.

- **Revamping customer service.** McConnell learned that word-of-mouth advertising brought in a third of his customers. He added a lifetime guarantee on all work, follow-up calls after purchase, and more notice if orders were going to be delayed, all in an effort to give customers more to tell their friends.

- **Upgrading sales training.** Salespeople were trained in a consultative approach and paid salary plus commission since they would be selling up-scale merchandise.

A year after making the changes, the average sale increased from $67 to $167. Total sales have tripled in four years and net profits are up 26 percent.

Source: Susan Greco, "Targeting Your Best Customer," Inc. (December 1992), p. 25.

---

reason for grouping people is to predict behavior—especially the behavior of buying from you.

A caveat for the future—segmenting and targeting may not always be enough. The most common marketing strategy in the 1960s was **mass marketing,** or selling single products to large groups of people. Then in the 1970s, **market segmentation** was used. Businesses took segmentation a step further in the 1980s with specialized **niche marketing,** which involves concentrating marketing efforts toward smaller target markets. The next step in market evolution for the 1990s has been **individualized marketing,** or customizing each product to suit the needs of individual customers. These trends in marketing techniques do not mean that businesses need to throw out every technique that has been used in the past. Rather, these trends indicate that businesses may need to add another tool to their marketing toolbox.

Two factors leading to more individualized marketing are clutter and technology. Clutter in traditional media channels (newspaper, direct mail, television,

mass marketing Treating entire populations of people as potential customers for specific products.

market segmentation Breaking down populations of people into groups, or target markets.

niche marketing Segmenting populations of people into smaller target markets.

individualized marketing Adjusting the marketing mix of a business to treat individual persons as separate target markets.

Entering the Internet

Can the Internet help you obtain specific information about your target market? Yes! And a good place to start is at the Small Business Administration home page. Here, under the category of Business Development/General Information and Publications, you'll find a couple of files worth reading. One is called "Knowing Your Market" and the other is "Marketing Strategies for the Growing Business." Each provides basic background information on marketing topics for small business managers and owners.

When you're ready for more specific information on markets, check out the Census Bureau's World Wide Web site. Here you'll find specific information by state and county regarding county business patterns and census information for a specific county. So as you're researching the viability of a target market, you can check for the number and types of businesses already operating and also the demographic characteristics of that location's population. The Census Bureau is also fine tuning its TIGER map service, which provides census maps including: street-level detail for the entire United States, counties and states for the entire United States, cartographic design, and many other features. However, be aware that this site can be slow in creating the maps because of the amount of data that must be transmitted.

Small Business Administration home page: http://www.sbaonline.sba.gov
Census Bureau: http://www.census.gov
  Specific country: http:///www.census.gov/
  TIGER map service: http://tiger.census.gov

radio) has reached a point that "shotgun" approaches of the same message directed to no one in particular do not stand out. Consider that the average American household has access to 22 television channels and spends 50.8 hours per week watching them.[11] The American public has over 11,500 different magazines to choose from. Then add all the radio stations, the catalogs, and the direct mail consumers receive daily and you begin to understand how consumers are bombarded by advertising. An individualized message to segments in need of your product has a better chance of being heard above the noise.

Technology is also allowing us to conduct more individualized marketing by allowing us to track our customers with more precision.

Individualized marketing, if taken to an extreme, could mean treating each person as a separate market (offering different products, different advertising, and different channels to each). While this may not be practical, technology has made it possible.

Consumer Behavior

While market segmentation and target marketing tell you *who* may buy your products, it is also essential to your small business marketing efforts to understand consumer behavior—*why* those people buy.

Information on consumer behavior comes from several fields, including psychology, sociology, biology, and other professions which try to explain why people do what they do. In running a small business, the behavior we are interested in is why people purchase products. We will start with a stimulus-response

R eality Check

Target Markets of One

Several popular marketing terms like *database marketing*, *relationship marketing*, and *one-to-one marketing* are adding up to the same thing—collecting mountains of information on customers and storing it in a computer, using that information to predict how they are likely to buy, and customizing a marketing message to encourage them to do so. Database marketing can allow businesses to tailor their services to the point that each customer can comprise an individual target market. Big companies use database marketing to appear small. Small companies can use it to look big and well organized.

Since 1984, Pizza Hut franchises have entered all of the phone orders they receive into a database, creating profiles of about 9 million customers. Now each franchise in the chain can use those profiles to get a relevant message to the right customers. For instance, people who usually order thick-crust pizza are mailed coupons for thick-crust pizza. People who order their pizza Neapolitan style get a coupon for that. When the

company introduced the giant 1-foot by 2-foot Bigfoot pizza, coupons were sent to people willing to try new foods. Customers who have not bought pizza for a while are offered big discounts. As a result of initiating these precision marketing techniques, Pizza Hut's earnings have increased 25 percent.

The cost of database marketing is dropping rapidly. Even a small business on a tight budget can creatively use databases to help individualize their service. For instance, with the purchase of the right computer equipment, a small business can track its own customers over time. Or to create or expand a list of potential customers, the business owner can purchase a database from an existing business in the same industry.

Source: Adapted from Susan Greco, "The Road to One-to-One Marketing," Inc. (October 1995), pp. 56–66. Jonathan Berry, John Verity, Kathleen Kerwin, and Gail DeGeorge, "DataBase Marketing," Business Week, September 5, 1994, pp. 56–62; and Zachary Schiller, "How to Get Close to Your Customers," Business Week, Enterprise edition 1993, pp. 42–45.

---

model of consumer behavior called the "Black Box" model. (See Figure 10-1.)[12] This model is based on the work of psychologist Kurt Lewin, who studied how a person's behavior is determined or affected by the interactions of personal influences like inner needs, thoughts, and beliefs and a variety of external environmental forces.

The title "Black Box" is appropriate because it represents what goes on in the customer's mind that remains hidden from businesspeople. We can see the external factors that go in and the responses that come out, but we can't see the internal influences or the decision-making process.

As a small business owner, closeness to your customers is an advantage in understanding the internal influences that are going on in customers' minds. Their beliefs, attitudes, values, and motives and their perceptions of your products are critical to your success.

A small business owner needs to be aware of the steps of the mental decision-making process that consumers use in satisfying their needs. We all use them, even if we are not conscious of every step. Most people do not usually buy products just for the sake of buying. What consumers buy is the solution to some

The Fine Art of Selling Novelties

Terry Watanabe, owner of Oriental Trading Company in Omaha, Nebraska, has made his money selling yo-yos, costumes, whoopee cushions, and other outrageous and amusing things. From the company's slick and colorful catalog, you can purchase four dozen Groucho glasses (with big nose and mustache attached) for $4.80. Or you might settle on 144 two-inch plastic spiders for $1. Watanabe said, "What this company really comes down to is getting a package and opening a box of fun." But, as fun as Oriental Trading Company's products might be, it takes its marketing very seriously. It's as sophisticated as a mail-order business can be. The company tracks its 4 million customers by what, when, where, and how much they bought, and mails future catalogs accordingly. For instance, if you ordered a dozen friendship bracelets with a religious saying imprinted on them, you'll get future catalogs with extra pages of religious and inspirational products. Or, if you once bought Oriental's nutty, cheap products but stopped, you'll get a catalog from Terry's Village, a more expensive giftware catalog (also part of Oriental Trading Company). Watanabe knows that in order to provide good service to customers, the company needs to be great at marketing also!

Source: John R. Hayes, "Fun by the Gross," Forbes, April 24, 1995, pp. 80–84.

FIGURE 10-1
The Black Box Model of Consumer Behavior
Many internal and external factors influence consumer behavior.
Source: Warren Keegan, Sandra Moriarty, & Thomas Duncan, Marketing. *Englewood Cliffs, NJ: Prentice Hall, 1992, p. 193.*

External Factors

STIMULI → **TRANSFORMER** → **RESPONSES**

Marketing Mix
• Product
• Price
• Place
• Promotion

Other
• Demographic
• Economic
• Situational
• Social
• Lifestyle

Black Box (Buyer's Mind)

Internal Influences
• Beliefs/Attitudes/Values
• Learning
• Motives/Needs
• Perception
• Personality
• Lifestyle

Decision-Making Process
• Problem solving
• Information search
• Alternate evaluation
• Purchase
• Postpurchase evaluation

Purchase
• Product
• Brand
• Source
• Amount
• Method of Payment

No Purchase

problem or need in their lives. *Problem recognition* occurs when we are motivated to reduce a difference between our current and desired states of affairs. For example, consider a young couple expecting their first child who realize they do not have a way to record events for future memories—they have recognized a problem. Now they begin the second step in the decision-making process—an *information search*. What products exist that can solve the problem identified in the first step? This search will usually lead consumers to read advertising, magazine articles, and ratings like *Consumer Reports.* They also talk with salespeople, friends, and family members to learn more about products that will satisfy their needs.

These information searches usually turn up several possible solutions, which lead the consumer to the third step—an *evaluation of alternatives.* The parents-to-be need a camera to capture little junior for posterity, but the choices between a 35mm (SLR or point-and-shoot), or a camcorder (VHS, compact VHS, or 8mm) leave them with five alternatives to evaluate. As a small business owner, you enter the customers' decision-making process by being in their **evoked set** of product alternatives that come to mind when considering a purchase. For example, if you need a pair of shoes, how many businesses that sell shoes come to mind quickly? Those stores are your evoked set for shoes. If your business does not come into the customers' mind as a possible solution to their problem, you can't sell them anything. The purpose of most advertising is to get products into a customer's evoked set.

evoked set The group of brands or businesses that come to a customer's mind when he or she thinks of a type of product.

The most attractive alternative usually leads consumers to the fourth step, which is *purchase,* but many factors that you don't know about can alter this decision. For example, the attitudes of other people can influence the purchase decision. If the prospective parents intended to buy a specific camera and learned that friends had trouble with that model, their decision to purchase would probably be changed.

Finally, the *postpurchase evaluation* occurs when the consumer uses the product and decides about his level of satisfaction, which will affect your repeat sales. **Cognitive dissonance,** which is the internal conflict we feel after making a decision, is a normal part of the process. If the parents in our example purchased a 35mm SLR camera, you might expect them to later think about the motion and sound that they could have received from a camcorder. Marketers try to reduce cognitive dissonance with return policies, warranties, and assurance that the customer made the right choice.

cognitive dissonance The remorse that buyers feel after making a major purchase.

Using Your Marketing Mix

Your **marketing mix** consists of the variables that you can control in bringing your product or service to your target market. Think of them as the tools you have available to use. The marketing mix is also referred to as the "Four Ps": product, place, price, and promotion. You must offer the *product* (including both goods and services) that your target market wants or needs. *Place* refers to the channel(s) of distribution you choose. Your *price* must make your product attractive and still allow you to make a profit. *Promotion* is the means you use to communicate with your target market. Pricing is covered in Chapter 11, while the other three variables are discussed in the remainder of this chapter.

marketing mix The factors that a business can change in selling products to customers—product, place, price, and promotion.

Furniture (assembled, not delivered) — Clothing — Automobile — Fast Food — Vacation Package — Fine Dining — Advertising — Education — Lawn Mowing

FIGURE 10-2
Spectrum of Goods and Services
What most small businesses sell is a combination of goods *and* services.

Product

The product is at the heart of your marketing mix. Remember that product means tangible goods, intangible services, or a combination of these. (See Figure 10-2.) Hiring someone to mow your lawn is an example of the service end of the goods and services spectrum. Here you don't receive a tangible good. A tangible good would be the purchase of a chair that is finished, assembled, but not delivered. Thus, no services were purchased. Many businesses offer a combination of goods and services. Restaurants, for instance, provide both goods (food and drink) and service (preparation and delivery).

When determining your product strategy, it is useful to think about different levels of product satisfaction. Products are the "bundle of satisfaction" that consumers receive in exchange for their money. (See Figure 10-3.)

The most basic level of product satisfaction is its **core benefit.** The core benefit is the fundamental reason people buy products. For an automobile, the core benefit that customers purchase is transportation from point A to point B. With a hotel room, the core benefit is a night's sleep. People don't buy drills—what they really buy is holes.

The next level of product satisfaction is the **generic product.** For an automobile, the generic product is the steel, plastic, and glass. For the hotel, the building, the front desk, and the rooms represent the generic products.

FIGURE 10-3
Levels of Products
The benefits that consumers receive from products are represented by different product levels.

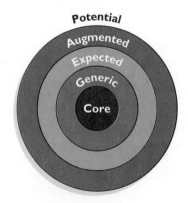

Potential
Augmented
Expected
Generic
Core

The third level of product satisfaction is the **expected product,** which includes the set of attributes and conditions that consumers assume will be present. U.S. consumers expect comfortable seats, responsive handling, and easy starting from their cars. A hotel guest expects clean sheets, soap, towels, relative quiet, and indoor plumbing.

The **augmented product,** the fourth level of product satisfaction, is all the additional services and benefits that can distinguish your business. For example, multidisk CD players, satellite-linked navigational systems in autos, and express checkout and health-club facilities in hotels are product augmentations. Augmentations represent the sizzle that you sell along with the steak. The problem with product augmentations is they soon become expected. When you have raised your costs and prices by adding augmentations, you open the door for competitors to come in and offer more of a generic product at a lower price. That's how the Motel 6 franchises became so successful—by offering a plain room for a low price when competitors were adding amenities which raised their cost structure and prices.

The fifth and final level is the **potential product.** This includes product evolutions to come. Not long ago, CD-ROM was a potential product for personal computers. It soon became a product augmentation, and quickly after that, expected.

Developing New Products. Part of a marketer's job is managing products through the stages of their life cycle. (See Figure 7-2, page 187.) Trends like increased global competition and quickly changing customer needs have shortened product life cycles and increased the need for new products.[13]

As a company's current products enter the stages of late maturity and decline, they need to be replaced with new ones in demand. What is new? Good question. Marketing consultants Booz, Allen & Hamilton group new products into six categories:

- *New-to-the-world products:* Products that have not been seen before, which result in entirely new markets. Ken Fischer developed and patented a marine paint that the U.S. Navy uses to keep its ships free of barnacles. The paint is made from a mixture of epoxy and cayenne peppers. Fischer came up with the idea for the paint after blistering his mouth on a Tabasco-covered deviled egg. He decided that animals would react the same way. He was right.[14]
- *New product lines:* Products that exist but are new to your type of business. For example, the addition of a coffee bar to your bookstore would be taking on a new product line.
- *Additions to existing product lines:* Products that are extensions of what you already sell. For example, creating Jell-O Gelatin Pops from existing Jell-O Pudding Pops.
- *Improvements in, revisions of, or new uses for existing products:* Increase the value or satisfaction of your current product. Take the example of WD-40 spray lubricant. Although it was originally developed to prevent rust by displacing water, so many new uses have been found for it that the WD-40 Company holds an annual "Invent Your Own Use" contest. Besides quieting squeaky hinges and freeing zippers, the product also removes gum stuck in hair or carpet and sticky labels from glass, plastic, and metal. The

Denver fire department even used WD-40 to free a nude burglary suspect who got stuck while attempting to enter a restaurant through an exhaust vent.

- *Repositioning:* Changing the perception that customers have of your product rather than changing the product. John Sundet, owner of SnowRunner, makes recreational snow skates, which are like ski boots with short runners attached. Sundet wanted a new image for his three-year-old company. A Minneapolis-based consulting firm, Nametag, helped him come up with the name Sled Dogs™, since *dogs* are a slang term for feet and sleds are fun in the snow. The new name has created a new image for the product by opening up promotional phrases like "Unleash Yourself," "Join the Pack," "You're Not an Indoor Animal," and "Sled Dogs Obey Your Every Command."[15]

- *Cost reductions:* Products that provide value and performance similar to existing products but at a lower cost. For example, food stands that sell hamburgers and hot dogs offer products similar to the big-name fast-food franchises[16] but at a lower price, thus enticing customers with their cost advantage.

Of course, there is increased risk in new products. How many new products can you remember seeing on the shelves at the grocery store in the last year? Ten? Fifty? One hundred? Now think of how many of those you chose to adopt. However many you remember, it was surely far below the 15,401 new food products and 2,863 nonfood items introduced in 1991![17] Many of those new products did not survive. Despite the risk, innovation is the key to success. Innovation is part of being proactive in the marketplace.

Packaging. Think of packaging as the last 5 seconds of marketing. But packaging provides more than just a wrapper around your product, it can add value that benefits both you and your customers. Good packaging can make handling or storage more convenient. It can reduce spoilage or damage. Packaging can be beneficial to your customers by making the product more identifiable and, therefore, easier to find on a crowded shelf.

Small Business IN THE Service Industry

Recognizing a customer need for new service products and acting on it can be the impetus to starting a new small business. Tom Christopher first spotted a demand for same-day delivery services while employed at a large transportation company. A customer came in asking to rush a package from Nashville, Tennessee, to Arlington, Texas. When his boss refused, Christopher volunteered to make the delivery on his own time for the price of a tank of gas for his Cessna 310 airplane. Eventually, Christopher decided to go into business himself to offer the service. His business, Kitty Hawk Group, Inc., has since grown from being just a freight forwarder to a full-fledged air-freight carrier. In fact, his freight service company now has a fleet of 21 planes to service customer needs. *Source: Christopher Caggiano, "Fleet Delivery," Inc. (August 1995), p. 36.*

Marketing by Brand: Vermont Milk Producers

If you make a premium product, you can charge a premium price. We see that rule in every product line from cars to wristwatches to clothing. You can name brands from each of these categories that people will buy because they recognize that brand as being better. But some products are considered to be commodities—meaning that *all* brands are alike. Everyone knows that the only way to compete in commodities is on price, right? And what would you consider the ultimate commodity—milk, maybe?

Well, Steven Judge started Vermont Milk Producers (VMP) to create a *premium brand of milk* called Vermont Family Farms. The idea was to produce milk that not only tasted better, but that also helped to increase income for small family farms that otherwise have trouble being profitable. The big question: Would consumers buy a half gallon of premium milk that cost $.49 more than store brands? (And how could a product like milk be differentiated from other brands? VMP targets northeastern metropolitan areas, where Judge expects the target market to be well-educated, environmentally concerned parents. The packaging for VMP milk boldly explains the product's differences (or promised differences). They are that:

1. The milk is superior, better tasting, and usually fresher than competing milk.
2. The cows that produce the milk are treated humanely.
3. The farmers who supply the milk will manage the land as a living resource vital to the survival of our planet.

The ten dairy farmers who make up the marketing group (with up to 75 expected within six years) are trying to take back some of the marketing functions that farmers have turned over to intermediaries for years. These farmers are the owners of VMP—each with a 100-share stake.

To stand out in a dairy case filled with white-on-white cartons, VMP containers show green grass and blue sky, with cows grazing in the foreground, and a red barn, a windmill, and rolling hills in the background. The red and orange logo is eyecatching and suggests old-fashioned quality.

VMP faces an uphill battle to create a "brand" of milk to justify a higher price. But that is just what Frank Perdue did with chicken, so it is possible. The price a product brings depends on many factors. What do you think is the biggest challenge facing VMP?

Source: Elizabeth Conlin, "Milking the Profits," Inc. (July 1993), pp. 92–98.

Packaging can help create a new product or market. Chesebrough-Ponds didn't change the formula of nail polish with its Polishing Pen, but the changed packaging has made the product very successful. Inspired by the Magic Marker, Chesebrough-Ponds developed what amounts to nail polish in a pen.[18]

Place

Of the Four Ps of the marketing mix, place (or distribution) is especially significant for your small business because an effective distribution system can make or save a small business just as much money as a hot advertising campaign can

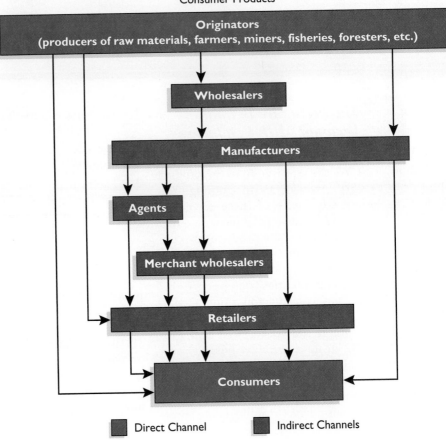

Consumer Products

FIGURE 10-4
The Channels of Distribution
Channels of distribution are systems through which products flow from producers to consumers.

distribution channel The series of intermediaries a product passes through when going from producer to consumer.

generate. In fact, distribution is about the last real bastion for cost savings—as techniques for tracking and individualizing promotion improve, as manufacturing becomes more and more efficient, and as employee productivity rises. Your choice of **distribution channel** is especially important when entering international markets, where you are not likely to have as many options for distribution as in the U.S. market.

In marketing, distribution has two meanings: the physical transportation of products from one place to the next, and the relationships between intermediaries who move the products—otherwise called the channels of distribution.

There are two types of distribution channels: direct and indirect. (See Figure 10-4.) With a **direct channel,** products and services go directly from the producer to the consumer. For example, when you buy sweet potatoes and corn at a farmers' market, or a pair of sandals directly from the artisan who made them, those are examples of sales through a direct channel. Other examples are buying seconds and overruns from factory outlets or through catalog sales managed by the manufacturer. **Indirect channels** are so called because the products pass through various intermediaries before reaching the consumer. Small businesses that use more than one channel (such as a swim suit producer selling to an intermediary like a retail chain and directly to consumers via catalog sales) is said to use **dual distribution.**

Intermediaries include the following:

Agents—Agents bring buyers and sellers together and facilitate the exchange. They may be called manufacturer's agents, selling agents, or sales representatives.

Brokers—Brokers represent clients who buy or sell specialized goods or seasonal products. Neither brokers nor agents take title to the goods sold.

Wholesalers—Wholesalers buy products in bulk from producers in order to resell them to other wholesalers or to retailers. Wholesalers take title to goods and usually take possession.

Retailers—Retailers sell products to the ultimate consumer. Retailers take title and possession of the goods they distribute.

The key word for evaluating a channel of distribution is *efficiency*—getting products to target markets in the fastest, least expensive way possible. Did you realize that about three-fourths of the money spent on food goes to distribution?

Does adding intermediaries to the channel of distribution increase the cost of getting the product to the consumer? Or does "doing away with the middleman" always mean a savings to consumers? While the latter has become a marketing cliché, it is not always true. Adding intermediaries can *decrease* the price to the consumer if each intermediary increases the efficiency of the channel. You can do away with the middleman, but you can't replace his function. *Someone* still has to do the job.

For example, if your business needs one-half of a truck load of supplies every month from your main supplier 400 miles away, should you buy your own truck or have the supplies shipped via a **common carrier** (a trucking company that hauls products for hire)? If that were the only time you need a truck, of course it would be chapter to have the supplies shipped even though it adds an intermediary to your channel of distribution. If you do away with the middleman—in this case the trucking company—you must replace his function by buying your own truck, paying a driver, maintaining the vehicle, filing paperwork, and so on. The question here is not *whether* the functions of an intermediary are performed, the question is *who* performs them.

You need to be prepared to revise the way you get your products to consumers because the efficiency of channels can change. Currently the fastest growing distribution systems involve nonstore marketing, including vending machines, telemarketing, and direct mail. Sometimes a break from the industry norm can create a competitive advantage for your business. When Michael Dell started Dell computer, he eliminated all the usual intermediaries found in the personal computer market. Dell advertised and sold directly to consumers. This distribution strategy shot Dell Computer into the *Fortune* 500.

Efficiencies in channels of distribution not only allow small businesses to offer goods more efficiently (and therefore more profitably), they also provide opportunities for starting new businesses. If you establish a firm that will increase the efficiency of an existing channel, you are providing a needed service, which is the basis for a good business.

Price

The third P of the marketing mix is price. If you do everything else in your business correctly, your business can fail if you price your products incorrectly. Pricing is a delicate balance between keeping prices low enough to push sales up and keeping them high enough to make a profit.

While price may be the easiest of the Four Ps to change, there are dangers involved with movement of your prices either up or down. In Chapter 11, we will discuss how to establish well-planned pricing strategies and policies to avoid dangers and ensure a profit.

Promotion

The goal of a company's promotional efforts is to communicate with target markets. There are four major tools to use in developing a *promotional mix:* advertising, sales promotion, personal selling, and public relations. The weight you choose to place on each of these tools will depend on your type of business.

Advertising. Advertising is a way to bring attention to your product or business by publishing or broadcasting a message to the public through various media. Your choices of media include:

Print media: Newspapers, magazines, direct mail, Yellow Pages
Broadcast media: Radio, television, or computer billboards
Outdoor: Billboards, or posters placed on public or other transportation.

The habits of your target market will affect your choice of advertising media. For example, if your target market is teenagers, radio and television would be the most appropriate choices. The nature of your product will also help to determine the media. Does advertising for your product need to include color, sound, or motion to make it more attractive? The cost of your advertising is another important factor in choosing a media. You should look at the total dollar amount an ad costs and the cost per thousand people exposed to the message.

Advertising is critical, but there are some real downsides to it, including slow feedback, expense, difficulty in cutting through clutter, and difficulty in creating a personalized message. Choosing the medium for your message is important (see the following Manager's Notebook for the advantages and disadvantages of each medium).

Many small businesses determine how much to spend on advertising by allocating a percentage of their total sales revenues. This percentage varies considerably by type of business. (See Table 10-1.)

Advertising Objectives. Different types of advertisements help to accomplish different objectives. You may be trying to:

- **Inform** your audience of the existence of your business, your competitive advantage, or product features and benefits.
- **Persuade** people to take an immediate action—such as buying your product!

Manager's Notebook

Which Advertising Medium Should You Use?

Advertising Medium (with percentage of total media dollars spent)

Newspaper (23.2%)

ADVANTAGES	LIMITATIONS
Flexible; timely; covers local markets well; believable (because people read newspapers to get information); relatively inexpensive; can use color, coupons, or inserts.	Short life of ad; number of ads per newspaper causes clutter; poor photo reproduction; low pass-along value (meaning that newspapers are rarely read by more than one person).

Magazine (5.3%)

ADVANTAGES	LIMITATIONS
Target markets can be selected geographically and demographically; long life since magazines are often passed along; high-quality reproduction.	Long lead time needed in purchasing ad; no guarantee of placement within magazine; higher relative cost than other print media.

Television (22.2%)

ADVANTAGES	LIMITATIONS
Reaches large audience; combines sight, sound, and motion; perceived to be prestige medium.	High absolute cost; several ads run together increases clutter and decreases impact; short exposure time.

Outdoor (0.8%)

ADVANTAGES	LIMITATIONS
High repeat exposure, low cost, and little competition.	Limited amount of message due to exposure time to ad, little selectivity of target market.

Direct Mail (19.8%)

ADVANTAGES	LIMITATIONS
Can be targeted very specifically; message can be personalized; less space limitations than other media.	Perceived as "junk mail"; relative high cost; mailing lists expensive and often inaccurate.

Yellow Pages

ADVANTAGES	LIMITATIONS
People viewing ad are likely to be interested buyers, relatively inexpensive, effectiveness of ad easy to measure.	All your competitors listed in same place, easy to ignore small ads, may need to be listed in several sections.

Radio (6.9%)

ADVANTAGES	LIMITATIONS
Can be targeted to specific audience; low relative cost; short lead time so ads can be developed quickly.	People are often involved with other activities and do not pay full attention to ad; people cannot refer back to ad; competition for best time slots.

Computer Bulletin Boards

ADVANTAGES	LIMITATIONS
Good selectivity of target markets, inexpensive.	Often negative reaction to advertising on computer networks, uncertainty of number of people reached.

Source: Alexander Hiam and Charles Schewe, The Portable MBA in Marketing, (New York: John Wiley & Sons, 1992) p. 365.

TABLE 10 ▪ 1   Ad Dollars Spent by Business Type

INDUSTRY	AD DOLLARS AS PERCENT OF SALES[a]
Air cond, heating, refrig equip	1.5
Air transport, scheduled	1.8
Apparel and other finished products	2.9
Beverages	9.5
Bolt, nut, screw, rivets, washers	0.9
Bottled and canned soft drinks, water	2.9
Can/frozen preserved, fruit, veg	6.9
Carpets and rugs	0.7
Catalog, mail-order houses	5.7
Computer and office equipment	1.2
Cutlery hand tools, general hardware	10.9
Educational services	5.0
Electronic computers	5.1
Games, toys, child vehicles—except dolls	14.2
Groceries and related products—wholesale	1.5
Grocery stores	1.3
Guided missiles and space vehicles	5.3
Hospitals	5.0
Industrial inorganic chemicals	16.5
Investment advice	8.6
Iron and steel foundries	1.2
Lawn, garden tractors, equipment	4.0
Lumber and other building material—retail	1.8
Membership sport and rec clubs	11.0
Motion picture, videotape distributors	13.0
Perfume, cosmetic	10.4
Phono records, audio tape disc	8.3
Prepackaged software	4.8
Radio, TV consumer electronic stores	5.3
Retail stores, all	5.8
Security brokers and dealers	3.1
Sugar and confectionary prods	10.6
Women's clothing stores	2.7

[a] Ad dollars as percent of sales = Ad expenditures/net sales.

Source: Alexander Hiam and Charles Schewe, The Portable MBA in Marketing (New York: John Wiley & Sons, 1992), p. 365.

- **Remind people** that your business or product still exists. Get them to remember what they received from your business in the past—so that it remains in their evoked set.
- **Change perception** of your business rather than trying to sell specific products. This is generally called **institutional advertising** and it aims to build goodwill rather than to make an immediate sale.

While these are broad objectives that you may try to achieve with your advertising, creating effective advertisements is both a science and an art. Creativity, humor, and excitement can help break through the clutter or crowding of media. These traits, however, can also hide the real message of your ad. Communicating your message clearly while catching the viewer's attention is a tough balance to achieve. Common strategies that you might choose to achieve your advertising objectives include:

- **Testimonials.** Using an authority to present your message. Athletes and movie stars attract attention, but their public image can change rapidly and must be consistent with that of your business.

- **Humor.** Humor can get attention, but be careful who the brunt of the humor is or you could offend some group and generate negative publicity for your business. Advertising history is also full of some very funny ads that did not generate a single dollar of additional revenue.

- **Sensual or sexual messages.** A common cliché says "sex sells." Sex is certainly used in a lot of ads, but research shows it is not an effective way to get a message across. Like humor, using sex to get attention is worthless if people don't get what you are trying to say.

- **Comparative messages.** Naming competitors in your advertising is legal and quite common. It can be a very powerful way to position your product in the customer's mind against another known entity. This gives the potential customer a reference point, but it also gives your competitor free exposure.

- **Slice-of-life messages.** These messages may use a popular song or a brief scene from life to position your product. Music is a great way mentally to transport people back to another time in their lives. Nostalgia can help create a brand identity for your product.

- **Fantasy messages.** These messages stress the ideal self-image of the buyer. What you are trying to do is link a product with a desirable person or situation. This is what almost every beer or soft drink commercial is attempting. The message is "drink this liquid and you will be beautiful, popular, and desirable." Right.[19]

How do you tell if your advertising works? A common complaint among advertisers runs, "I know that half of my advertising dollars are wasted, I just don't know which half." Measuring the effectiveness of your advertising is difficult. Is the cost of producing and running the ad justified with increased sales and profit? A few techniques might help you find out:

- *Response tracking.* Using coded or dated coupons can let you compare different media, such as redemption rate of coupons in newspapers versus flyers handed out on the street.

- *Split ads.* Another way to compare the effectiveness of various media is to use split ads. You can code two different ads, different media, or broadcast times to see which produces greater response.

- *In-store opinions.* You can ask in-store customers where they heard of your business, what they think, what you are doing right, and why they buy from you rather than from a competitor.

- *Telephone surveys.* Make random phone calls with numbers from customer files. Ask customers if they have seen your advertising and what they think of it.

- *Statement questionnaires.* Drop a brief questionnaire in the monthly bills you send out to ask customers if they are satisfied with the product or service and how they found out about it.

Advertising Development. Most small business owners plan their own advertising programs, which is usually more appropriate for them than hiring a professional producer. Even if you choose to use an advertising agency, you should still be in active control of your advertising campaign. Remember, you cannot afford to buy a solution to every problem you will face. This is true with your advertising. Spending money will not automatically get you better advertising. As Paul Hawkin said, "The major problem affecting businesses, large or small, is a lack of *imagination*, not a lack of capital."[20] Don't let money replace creativity.

When Ben Cohen and Jerry Greenfield started Ben and Jerry's Ice Cream, they couldn't afford to buy an image as Häagen-Dazs, or its knockoff Frusen Glädjé, did. Their message was unpretentious and "down home." That image became their biggest asset. Their packaging and advertising with their pictures on the top and a Vermont cow on the side represented their product—natural and honest.

A common problem among self-produced advertisements is that business owners try to cram too much into them. Their reasoning is: "This space costs a lot of money, so I am going to use every minuscule part of it." The result is usually an ad that is busy, unattractive, and uninteresting. Simplicity should be the rule here. White space draws the reader's attention. The same principle applies to package design: It doesn't have to tell the consumer everything.

Even though self-produced ads are appropriate for many small businesses, owners should at least investigate the options and promotions that outside professional advertising services make available.

Advertising Agencies. To mount an effective campaign, you may want to consider consulting an advertising agency. These businesses can help you by conducting preliminary studies, developing an advertising plan, creating advertisements, selecting the appropriate media, evaluating the effectiveness of the advertising, and conducting ad follow-up.

A small agency that specializes in and understands your type of business may be a better choice for a small business than a large agency.[21] Ask your friends and colleagues for recommendations and get samples of the agency's work before signing a contract. Remember that fees are often negotiable, so flexibility may exist in the agency's fees.

Media Agencies. You can create your own advertising and hire a media buyer to coordinate the purchase of print space or broadcast time for your ads. Why would you choose to use a media buyer? If you have identified your specific target market, a media buyer can help coordinate your media mix to reach that market. Suppose you had designed a new line of blue jeans targeted toward urban females from 13 to 17 years old. A media buyer can tell you in which magazine, radio station, or television show to advertise.

Art and Graphic Design Services. If you design your own ads and write your own copy but lack the artistic skills needed to produce the final piece of art or film, an

Computer Applications

With the wide range of hardware and software available today, you can turn out advertising and marketing materials like a pro. Desktop publishing is just what it says it is. It allows you to publish professional-looking materials from your own personal computer and printer. Whether you're using an Apple or an IBM compatible computer, there is a variety of software programs that can help you get great-looking results.

While some word processing programs such as Microsoft Word or WordPerfect allow you to create attractively designed documents, specific desktop publishing software helps you produce documents with impressive layouts and graphics, giving you many more options than simple word processing software. It helps you publish materials that incorporate text, graphics, clip art, pagination, and background grids, among other elements.

The most popular desktop publishing software is Microsoft's Publisher. Publisher is an inexpensive option (with a suggested retail price of $99.95) that lets you create simple brochures, product flyers, business cards, labels, calendars, and newsletters. It is easy to insert text and graphics into the program's ready-made templates. Publisher walks users through the process, using "Page Wizards"—visual cues on screen—which ask you to "fill in the blank"—it's that simple.

If you want to invest a little more in your desktop publishing system, or if you think that you might be creating marketing materials (such as flyers, newsletters, or product information sheets) that are longer than ten pages, you can consider higher-end desktop publishing software. QuarkXPress and Aldus PageMaker, for instance, feature a design layout program, Adobe Photoshop provides a photo manager, while Aldus FreeHand allows you to create special graphics or icons. However, these programs aren't inexpensive, and they aren't recommended for a desktop publishing novice.

Keep in mind that you can hire graphic design firms to do this type of work if you lack the time or desire to do it yourself. But if you're willing to give desktop publishing a try, you might look for courses that are offered on the topic or call the National Association of Desktop Publishers at 508-887-7900 for more information.

Sources: Jane Applegate, "Entrepreneurs Offer Some Low-Cost But Provocative Ideas on Marketing," Los Angeles Times, January 31, 1995, p. D3; Jane Applegate, "Small Businesses Can Market Themselves Inexpensively," Kansas City Business Journal, February 12–23, 1995, p. 15; Leon Erlanger, "Small-Office Software: The Essentials," PC Magazine, June 13, 1995, pp. 120–121; Joseph F. Schuler, Jr., "The Perfect Presentation," Nation's Business (September 1995), pp. 46–47; Merlisa Lawrence Corbett, "Choosing the Right Publisher," Block Enterprise (October 1995), pp. 48–50; and Robert Sentinery, "How to Get Great Design With Desktop Publishing," Folio: The Magazine for Magazine Management, Special Sourcebook Issue, 1996, pp. 211–214.

art service can do this for you. Like the art director in an advertising agency, this service needs to work closely with the person writing your copy to coordinate the message.

Other Sources. Radio and television studios, newspapers, and magazines with whom you contract to run your advertising can also produce ads for you. Their services generally cost less than those of an advertising agency.

Personal Selling. Personal selling involves a personal presentation by a salesperson for the purpose of making sales and building relationships with customers. There are many products not large enough, complex enough, or differentiated enough to need personal selling, but for those products that are, it is the best way to complete the purchase (close the deal).[22] Through personal selling, you are trying to accomplish three things: to identify customer needs, to match those needs with your products, and to show the customers the match between their need and your product.

Personal selling, though costly, can be closely tailored to customer needs—making it an effective way to close a sale.

Cost is the biggest drawback to personal selling. When you calculate what it costs for a salesperson to contact each prospect, it is much more expensive than the cost per person for advertising. The average cost of a sales call is over $225.[23] Salespeople have gained a poor reputation because of the high-pressure tactics and questionable ethics of a few of them. The biggest advantage of using personal selling is the flexibility of the presentation that is possible. A trained salesperson can tailor a presentation to the prospect around:

Features—what the product is.

Advantages—why the product is better than alternatives.

Benefits—what the product will do for the customer.

Customer expectations are rising. A good product at a fair price, offered by a well-trained sales staff, backed by a responsive customer service department is just the starting point in a competitive marketplace. For your business to stand out, its products need to be tailored to the particular needs of your customers. George Robinson, CEO of Robinson Brick Co. in Denver, Colorado said, "A lot of competitors still think they're selling just bricks. We hope they keep thinking that way." Robinson Brick has changed its way of thinking about bricks as commodities to unique products. It offers extras that are unexpected in brick production, such as 68 colors, state-of-the-art same-day delivery and responsive field service.[24]

The steps in the personal selling process are as follows:

Preapproach	Before meeting with the prospective customer, a salesperson must acquire knowledge about the product, and perhaps about the customer and his business.
Approach	Upon first meeting the customer, the salesperson tries to establish a rapport with him. People seldom buy from someone they don't trust, so a successful salesperson must first earn a customer's trust.
Questioning	To find out what is important to the customer, the salesperson will try to define his needs as early in the process as possible.
Demonstration	The salesperson shows how the product will solve the customer's problem and meet his needs.
Handling objections	An effective salesperson will listen to what the customer is really saying. An objection shows that the customer is

	interested but needs more information. Would you raise objections to a salesperson if you are not really interested in a product? No, you would probably just walk away.
Closing the deal	When she senses that the customer is ready to buy, the salesperson should ask for the sale. Many sales are lost when a customer is ready to buy, but the salesperson continues to sell.[25]
Suggestion selling and follow-up	Suggestion selling means recommending products that are complementary to those just sold. Following up with a phone call after the sale builds upon the rapport established in the approach and works toward a long-term relationship between the customer and the business.

Public Relations (PR). Public relations involves promotional activities designed to build and sustain goodwill between a business and its customers, employees, suppliers, investors, government agencies, and the general public.[26] **Publicity** is

Manager's Notebook

Road Warriors

Personal selling is an effective way to move products. It is also expensive and time-consuming. Bob Crawford, CEO of Brook Furniture Rental, spends 50 percent of his time on the road with salespeople, going to conferences, chamber of commerce meetings, and showrooms.

Crawford is emphatic about the importance of business travel. "It's real hard to listen and get the full content, unless you see the person, feel his or her presence," he said. "A telephone gives you only diluted communications with customers."

To make the best use of your time on the road gathering useful information and capitalizing on it at home, Crawford recommends:

- Make sure the office can do without you. You must delegate tasks and invest in hiring and training team members.
- Commit to the time needed. Scheduling takes discipline.
- Let others tell you where you're needed. Crawford gets input from regional managers about traveling with salespeople.
- Talk about your objectives with your salespeople.
- Pump every meeting for industry information. People at most meetings become obsessed with getting their own messages out. Listen to what is going on elsewhere.

Source: Leslie Brokaw, "Road Warriors," Inc. (March 1992), pp. 44–50.

M anager's Notebook

Global Marketing Primer

This chapter has made it clear what the marketing concept is and what it means for small businesses. Being a customer-driven small business in global markets is just as important, although it will require you to consider many other issues. The world may indeed be at your feet, but you don't want to stumble and fall as a result of poor marketing. Let's look at specific topics as they apply to global marketing efforts.

Developing a Sales Forecast. While forecasting can be a difficult procedure for domestic markets, developing sales forecasts for foreign markets just takes extra effort. Since reliable historical data of industry and product sales are often unavailable, particularly in lesser-developed countries, you'll have to be creative in finding the desired statistics. The United Nations and other international trade agencies often have information on broad sales trends that you can use to roughly estimate product demand. Many foreign governments are encouraging economic trade and may be able to provide you with selected information.

In the absence of reliable information, you might want to use a technique that estimates sales demand by analogy. This technique assumes that product demand develops in a similar fashion in all countries as comparable economic development occurs. So, for instance, if you know that demand for Product X (let's say it's carbonated cola beverages) increases a certain amount each time that personal disposable income increases, then you can use that same analogy for the new foreign market you're looking at. But keep in mind that estimating sales by analogy is not a perfect approach. It can be useful where other sales data are limited.

The best approach for collecting data for sales forecasts is to research the market directly by doing surveys or interviews. However, this type of marketing research is expensive and typically beyond the reach of many small businesses.

Identifying Target Markets. Global markets are not equally desirable. How can you identify a good prospect for your small business's product or service? You should start by establishing criteria to screen potential markets such as sales potential and current and potential competitors. Other criteria might be market readiness (determining whether consumers have the necessary education and technology to use the product or service, whether they can easily obtain it, and whether they can afford it at a price which will allow your business to make a profit) and country characteristics (political stability, economic vitality, cultural constraints, and geographical features).

Consumer Behavior. What, how, when, where, and why people "consume" products and services is a function of their country's culture. Since culture influences the way we think, dress, eat, speak, and act, you need to understand the cultural beliefs of the markets you're hoping to enter. You don't want to make the mistake of missing sales trends or offending potential consumers by not understanding and respecting cultural differences.

How can you find out about another culture? Read, study, and ask questions. Read books and magazines about different countries—including the travel section of your newspaper and even novels or biographies. Consult an atlas. Study demographics and other data about a specific country in an encyclopedia or from business literature. Talk to people who have visited or lived in that region and ask them about their experience. When it comes to learning about another land, let your curiosity be your guide!

Packaging. The type and amount of packaging that you use in a foreign market is influenced by cultural, legal, and financial constraints. For instance, Germany has very strict laws that regulate the amount and type of packaging materials that businesses can use. In other countries, certain colors should be avoided. In Latin America, for example, you'd want to avoid black and purple for most products, since they are associated with the Catholic lenten season and are therefore considered not conducive to sales. Financial considerations may play a role in packaging decisions as language and graphics may need to be changed for export to various countries.

Advertising.   Advertising can be an important part of your foreign marketing program. However, your advertising should be both culturally sensitive and legally acceptable. You should understand the culture well enough to know what types of images are appropriate and what types are not. Plus, translations can create unexpected problems that you should be alert to. For instance, a company marketing tomato paste in the Middle East discovered that the phrase "tomato paste" translates as "tomato glue" in Arabic—which hardly made their product sound edible! The type

of advertising you select will depend on the availability of media (television, radio, newspaper, and so on) in the country as well as the amount of money you have to spend.

Public Relations.   Many of the PR activities typical in the United States aren't as common in foreign countries. However, as you become more familiar with the customs, laws, and language of your new market, you might decide to try some of the PR activities listed in Table 10-2, keeping in mind what's acceptable and what's not. After all, you don't want to end up with negative publicity and undo what you've worked so hard to achieve.

Sources: Donald A. Ball and Wendell H. McCulloch, Jr., International Business *(Homewood, Illinois: BPI/Irwin), 1990; and Philip R. Cateora,* International Marketing *(Homewood, Illinois: Irwin), 1993.*

an aspect of PR consisting of any message about your company communicated through the mass media that you do *not* pay for. Generally, PR works by generating publicity.

Public relations involves a variety of communication formats including company publications such as newsletters, annual reports and bulletins, public speaking, lobbying, and the mass media. Each format can have an appropriate use and benefit to the marketing effort of your company. Table 10-2 shows some PR activities, their target audience, and their impact on your business.

TABLE 10 ▪ 2   The Relationship Between Marketing and Public Relations

TARGET	PR ACTIVITIES	BENEFITS TO MARKETING
Customers	Press releases Event sponsorship	Increase name awareness Increase credibility
Employees	Newsletters Social activities	Improve communications to decrease absenteeism and product defects Increase morale
Suppliers	Articles in trade publications Promotional incentives	Improve image Improve delivery schedule
General Public	News releases Plant tours Support for community activities	Attract better employees Improve image to customers Improve local relations
Government	Lobbying Direct mail Personal calls	Favorable legislation Less regulation

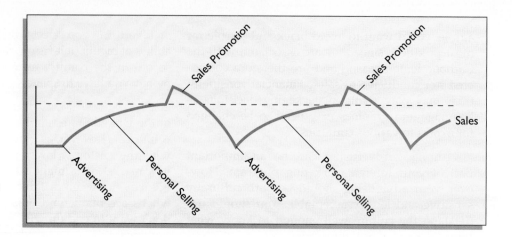

FIGURE 10-5
Short-term Ratchet Effect of Sales Promotion
When used with advertising and personal selling, sales promotion can give a short-term boost to sales.

Sales Promotions. Any activity that stimulates sales and is not strictly advertising or personal selling is called a sales promotion. Special in-store displays, free samples, contests, trade show booths, and the distribution of coupons, premiums, and rebates are examples of sales promotions. These activities enhance but do not replace your advertising or personal selling efforts.[27] They are most effective when used in intervals, since customer response decreases over time as customers become familiar with the promotions.

Advertising and personal selling are used on a continuous basis, while sales promotions are intermittent. A strategy that combines all three can produce a *ratchet effect* on sales. (See Figure 10-5.) Advertising is used to increase customer interest while personal selling is used to increase sales. Sales promotions at the point of purchase are usually used to increase sales over a short period of time.

The Promotional Mix. In deciding how to combine each of your four tools into a promotional mix, you need to consider when each type of promotion may be appropriate. On one hand, advertising reaches so many people that it is good for creating awareness, but its power to stimulate action decreases quickly. Personal selling, on the other hand, is the most effective tool for building customer desire for the product and prompting customers to take action. But since it requires one-on-one contact, it is less useful in creating awareness. Sales promotions are most effective with customers who are already interested in the product, but who may need prompting to make the purchase. Public relations builds awareness, though it results in few immediate sales.

Summary

■ The evolution of business philosophies.

A business using the production concept concentrates more on the product being made than the desires of its customers. Under the selling concept, a business still focuses on its products but strives to convince customers to buy its products rather than those of competitors. A business using the marketing concept finds out what customers want and then produces that product. The customer concept could become the view of a long-term relationship between business and customer.

■ The need for market segmentation and its process.

Market segmentation is needed because no business can be everything to everyone. Segmenting involves breaking down populations into target markets that have a common want or need which the business can satisfy. Target markets are the focus of a company's marketing efforts.

■ The "Black Box" model of consumer behavior.

The "Black Box" model explains consumer behavior because it illustrates that marketers can see the external stimuli that consumers are exposed to, such as different marketing mixes and differences between individuals. Marketers can also see consumer responses of purchasing or not purchasing products. What marketers cannot see is what goes on within the "black box" of the consumer's mind.

■ The five forms that a product can take.

The five forms of a product are the core benefit, the generic product, the expected product, the augmented product, and the potential product. The core benefit represents the value a customer gets from a product. The generic product is the simplest components that a product is made from. The expected product represents the characteristics that customers expect to find in a product. The augmented product contains the characteristics of a product that are over and above what customers expect to find.

■ The potential product represents what future generations of the product can become.

How efficiencies affect channels of distribution. The purpose of a channel of distribution is to get a product from a producer to consumers as quickly and cheaply as possible. Since distribution represents such a large portion of the price of many products, the channel that is most efficient will help to keep costs down.

■ How small businesses put together a promotional mix.

A promotional mix is the combination of advertising, personal selling, sales promotion, and public relations that best communicates the message of a small business to its customers.

■ Possible advertising objectives.

Through advertising, a small business may try to *educate* customers about the business or its products, *persuade* customers to buy, *keep customers thinking about* what the business or product can do for them, or to *create a public image* of the business by building goodwill.

■ The seven steps in personal selling.

The seven steps of personal selling include the preapproach, the approach, questioning, demonstration, handling objections, closing the deal, and suggestion selling and follow-up.

Questions for Review and Discussion

1. What factors should be considered when a small business owner decides to advertise?
2. How has television affected the marketing concept? How has the internet?
3. A good marketing strategy will help you be proactive, not reactive in running your business. Give examples that would illustrate this point.
4. Do service professionals such as surgeons, orthodontists, lawyers, and investment counselors need a marketing strategy? Why or why not?
5. Discuss the difference between the build-up method and the break-down method of sales forecasting. Give examples. *Ident. target m/cts.* *Set Sales goal*
   - Est. tot. mkt.
   + Est. mkt. share
6. Give examples (different from those in the text) of a product and its target market for each of the following marketing strategies:
   mass marketing *- fast-food*
   market segmentation *- gourmet Coffee Shops*
   niche marketing *- Ethnic food*
   individual marketing *- Customized home decor.*
7. Identify and discuss new uses for existing products that you currently use.
8. Discuss the personality traits that a good salesperson should have. What traits would detract from the personal selling process? *prod, Knowl., Communic., Empathy*
9. Explain the ratchet effect on sales. *Cumul. Effect of adv., Selling Promot.*
10. How would promotional mix decisions change for a small business expanding to a foreign market?

Critical Incident

Developing an effective marketing strategy can be tough. But without it, a small business will be fighting for survival. Read through the following two examples and answer the questions at the end.

DAPAT Pharmaceuticals. DAPAT is a small manufacturer of external analgesics (pain relievers) based in Nashville, Tennessee. Its main product, called Dr.'s Cream, faced this marketing challenge: In competition with much larger makers of over-the-counter remedies (such as Ben Gay), it had to find some ways to attract customers despite a small advertising budget.

Macromedia, Inc. Macromedia, Inc. is also in a highly competitive field—software publishing. The company makes graphic arts software tools for graphic designers, CD-ROM developers, and people who need to make "flashy" presentations. Macromedia's products are technologically "spiffy," but technology alone won't sell the product.

Questions

1. Working in teams of no more than three, choose one of the two examples to work on. Develop a comprehensive marketing strategy for the company and the product. Be specific in defining the product, place, price, and promotion aspects.

2. Once your team has developed its marketing strategy, find another team in the class who has worked on the same example. Take turns presenting your information to each other.

Take it to the Net

We invite you to visit the Hatten page on the Prentice Hall Web site at: http://www.prenhall.com/~hattensb for this chapter's World Wide Web exercise.

Chapter Focus

After reading this chapter, you should be able to:

- Establish the three main considerations in setting a price for a product.
- Explain breakeven analysis and why it is important in pricing in a small business.
- Present examples of customer-oriented and internal-oriented pricing.
- Describe why and how small businesses extend credit.
- Demonstrate the importance of having a collection system.

11 Pricing and Credit Policies

HOMAS LAM UNDERSTANDS how important it is for a small business to balance pricing and demand. After immigrating to the United States from Hong Kong in 1969, Lam's first job—picking cucumbers in Oxnard, California—enabled him to learn the business side of growing and selling vegetables from older Asian growers. After attending college, Lam became the sales manager for an Oxnard vegetable wholesaler, Seaboard Produce, selling vegetables to Chinatown wholesalers in New York City.

A telephone call one night from a regular customer who had a problem got Lam to thinking about the way his company's vegetables were packaged and priced. "We used to ship the broccoli whole, bound in rubber bands, but Chinese restaurants use only the tops. Send them ten boxes of broccoli, ten boxes of garbage go on the street," Lam said. And hauling away garbage is expensive, especially in New York. Lam's brainstorm was for Seaboard to ship only the broccoli crowns (the edible top part, without the stem) at a higher price than for the whole plant. Lam discovered he could charge about 30 percent more for a box of broccoli crowns than for a box of whole broccoli.

In 1986, Lam left Seaboard to start his own company growing and wholesaling his own brand of fresh vegetables, Ho Choy—meaning "Good Luck". His business grew quickly and Lam soon had to establish contracts with other vegetable packers to ship broccoli crowns. However, Lam soon learned another important lesson in pricing: greater volume isn't always profitable. At Ho Choy's sales peak of $25 million in 1992, Lam was losing money as competition increased and as costs outstripped profits. So Lam cut back by cutting his sales staff in half. He decreased his reliance on mass-market vegetables like broccoli and began experimenting with more specialized crops like choy sum and yu choi, which faced less competition from the big growers. Despite the reduced sales volume, profits have grown. How much? "At $25 million a year, I lost money," Lam noted. "This year, at $11 million to $13 million, we'll be profitable."

Lam's experience illustrates that pricing and quantity are important parts of the marketing mix. Establishing the right price for your goods or services at an appropriate level of production is critical. In this chapter, we'll describe the factors that should be considered in setting prices, as well as how to establish credit policies. *Source: Steve Kichen, and others, "The Best Small Companies," Forbes, November 6, 1995, pp. 237–238.*

Economics of Pricing

In the previous chapter, we discussed two Ps of the marketing mix (product and promotion). Later, in Chapter 16, we will look at place (or distribution). In this chapter, we will investigate the third component of the marketing mix, which is price. We will consider why price is one of the most flexible components of a business's marketing mix, factors that must be considered in setting prices, strategies related to pricing, and the use of credit in buying and selling.

We deal with prices every day. The coins you exchanged for a cup of coffee on the way to class, the tuition paid for the semester, and the money you earn from a job all represent a form of price for goods and services.

The Price Component of Your Marketing Mix

Price is the amount of money charged for a product. It represents what the consumer considers the *value* of the product to be. The value of a product depends on the benefits received compared with the monetary cost. As stated in the previous chapter in the discussion of personal selling, people actually buy benefits—they buy what a product will do for them. If consumers bought on price alone, then no Cadillac convertibles, Curtis Mathis televisions, or Godiva chocolates would ever be sold because less expensive substitutes exist. People buy premium products such as these because they perceive higher benefits and increased quality that delivers value despite the higher cost. Typical consumers do not want the *cheapest* product available—they want the *best* product for the most reasonable price.

Price is different from the other three components of the marketing mix because the product, place, and promotion all add value to the customer and costs to your business. Pricing lets you recover those costs. While the "right" price is actually more of a range between what the market would bear and what the product costs, many elements enter into the pricing decision. For example, the image of your business or product has an impact on the price you can charge.

Even though the pricing decision is critical to the success of a business, many small business owners make pricing decisions poorly. Total reliance on "gut feeling" is inappropriate, but so is complete reliance on accounting costs that ignore what is going on in the marketplace—what the competition is doing and what customers demand.

Three important economic factors have an impact on what you can charge for your products: competition, customer demand, and costs. Let's take a closer look at how these forces can affect your small business.

> *Your total costs represent the minimum price you can charge for your goods or services. If you cannot cover your costs and make a profit, you will not stay in business.*

Competition

Your competitors will play a big part in determining the success of your pricing strategy. The number of competitors and their proximity to your business influence what you can charge for your products because they represent substitute choices to your customers. The more direct competition your business faces, the less control you have over your prices. Direct competition makes product differentiation necessary—to compete on points other than price.

Proximity of competition can be a factor in pricing for many small businesses. The closer the competition, the more influence it will have on your pricing. For example, if two service stations located across the street from each other had a price difference of 10 cents per gallon of gasoline, to which one would customers go? The same price difference between stations several miles apart may not make as dramatic an impact.

The type of products sold will have an impact on price competition. If you run a video rental business, then other video rental places are not your only competition. So are movie theaters, athletic events, or even the opera. Don't think of being in the video rental business—think of being in the entertainment business because you are competing for entertainment dollars. Therefore, you should monitor not only what other video rental places are charging, but also what indirect, or alternative, entertainment charges.

More small businesses are facing competition from large chains like Wal-Mart and K mart coming to town. Can small businesses compete with gigantic discount stores? Of course they can. The key is flexibility. In this situation, you probably can't compete on price for identical items. The discounters have economy-of-scale advantages from mass purchasing and distribution that can knock you out of a head-to-head price war over identical products.

Wal-Mart provides a formidable opponent to many small businesses. Its distribution system is state of the art in efficiency, linking manufacturers directly to individual stores. Its shrinkage (loss from theft and damaged goods) target is 1 percent.[1] Most retailers average 3 percent to 5 percent. Wal-Mart spends only about 0.5 percent of sales on advertising, relying on word of mouth, compared with major competitors, which spend about 2 percent on advertising. Wal-Mart's success is directly related to its efficiency, which goes straight to the bottom line.

To survive in an industry dominated by giants, don't compete directly—differentiate. *Offer your customers value—the best quality and service for their money.*

In 1992, Wal-Mart held a gross margin of 22 percent, compared with Sears's 30 percent. But Wal-Mart yielded a 4 percent net profit margin—nearly doubling Sears. Tough competition, but you *can* compete.

Ken Stone, professor of economics at Iowa State University, has studied the impact of Wal-Mart on rural economies and small businesses. For a small business to compete with Wal-Mart (and other major retailers), Stone recommends:

- Don't compete directly—differentiate.
- Specialize—carry harder-to-get and better-quality goods.
- Emphasize customer service.
- Extend your hours.
- Advertise more—not just products, but also your business. (See Chapter 10, p. 272, on institutional advertising.)
- Work together with other small businesses.[2]

In preparation for Wal-Mart's move to Bath, Maine, Jayne Palmer took steps to ready her business, Gediman's Appliance. She increased advertising by 30 percent. She added a computer to track her inventory and linked it into General Electric Credit so she could order directly with better credit terms. She extended the store's hours. She offered more credit to her customers. She built a television viewing room with space for children to play on the floor. Finally, she cut the low-end appliances from her inventory to avoid competing directly with Wal-Mart on those items.[3]

Demand

The second economic factor that affects the price you can charge for your products is demand—how many people want to buy how much of your product. Each price you may choose for a product will be accompanied by a different level of demand. The number of units people will buy at different prices is called the

Small Business IN THE Service Industry

Although it seems like the big retailers have all the ammunition for competing in the marketplace, small business owners and managers are finding that they *can* fight back. For instance, look at what's happened in the gardening industry. As sales revenues have "blossomed," competition in the gardening industry has intensified. While large discount chains such as Wal-Mart and home improvement centers such as Lowes and Home Depot may have lured away many customers with low prices, small nurseries like John Darin's English Gardens in Detroit have prospered by offering high quality, a wide selection of products, and specialized advice. In fact, Darin has been able to turn his exceptional customer service into a profitable sideline. Customers who want more than a few words of advice and a wide variety of unusual plants can hire his landscaping service to tackle any gardening or landscaping project. English Gardens' annual revenues now exceed $15 million. It is definitely possible for a small business to prosper even in an intensely competitive market. *Source: Gayle Sato Stodder, "Green Thumbs,"* Entrepreneur *(November 1995), pp. 100–105.*

demand curve (even though in economics terms a curve is often a straight line. (See Figure 11-1.) The slope of that curve is called the *elasticity of demand.*

Price elasticity is the effect that price changes have on sales. The elasticity of demand for a product indicates how price sensitive the market is. **Price elastic** demand means a *price-sensitive* market. **Price inelastic** demand means the market is *not price sensitive.*[4]

If sales rise or fall more than prices rise or fall in percentage terms, demand for your product is **price elastic.** For example, assume that the demand for your computer software is elastic. (See Figure 11-1.) If you drop your price by 5 percent, you would expect sales to increase by more than 5 percent. Restaurant usage, personal computers, and airline travel all tend to have elastic demand.

If sales rise or fall less than prices rise or fall in percentage terms, demand for your product is **price inelastic.** You would expect the change in demand to be small after a change in your price. (See Figure 11-1.) A physician who increases the price of a medical procedure by 10 percent can expect the demand for that procedure to change by less than 10 percent. Health care is price inelastic (at least without government intervention). Both staple necessities and luxury goods tend to have inelastic demand. If you absolutely have to have a product or service, you are less sensitive to price. If a product is truly a luxury, price becomes less of a concern.

Three factors influence the price elasticity of demand for a product:

1. *Product substitutes:* The more alternatives that exist, the more price elastic a product tends to be.
2. *Necessity of the product:* Necessary and luxury goods tend to be price inelastic.
3. *The significance of the purchase to the consumer's total budget:* Cars and houses are elastic. Food and clothing are more inelastic.[5]

The theory of the elasticity of demand is important to small business owners because it shows how price sensitive their customers are when setting prices.

demand curve The number of units of a product people would be willing to purchase at different price levels.

price elastic Products for which customers are price sensitive.

price inelastic Products for which customers are not sensitive about the price.

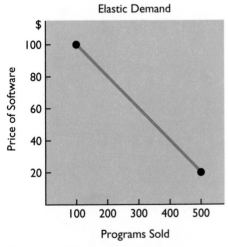

Elastic Demand

When demand for a product is elastic, as with computer software, a decrease in price will cause an increase in demand.

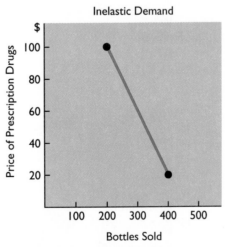

Inelastic Demand

When demand for a product is inelastic, as with prescription drugs, a change in price will have little effect on the quantity demanded.

FIGURE 11-1
Demand Curves

How easily your customers can do without your product or use something else in its place will affect what you can charge. Marketing research can tell you about the demand and elasticity for your product.

Costs

Earlier it was stated that the "right" price is actually a range of possible prices. What your competition charges and what consumers are willing to pay set the ceiling of your price range. Your costs establish the floor of your price range. If you cannot cover your costs and make a profit, you will not stay in business.

fixed costs Costs that do not change with the number of sales made.

variable costs Costs that change in direct proportion with sales.

Your total costs fall into two general categories: **fixed costs** and **variable costs.**

$$\text{Total costs} = \text{fixed costs} + \text{variable costs}$$

Fixed costs remain constant, no matter how many goods you sell. In the short run, your fixed costs are the same whether you sell a million units or none at all. Costs like rent, property taxes, and utilities are fixed. **Variable costs** rise and fall in direct proportion to sales. Sales commissions, material, and labor tend to be variable costs.

break-even point The point at which the total costs equal the total revenue and the business neither makes nor loses money.

By using these three cost figures in a **break-even analysis,** you can try to find the volume of sales you will need to cover your total costs.[6] Your **break-even point** in sales volume is the point at which your total revenue equals total costs. Calculating your break-even point will allow you to set your prices above your total costs, creating profit.

Figure 11-2 is an example of a break-even graph. First notice the fixed cost line runs horizontally because fixed costs don't change with sales volume. The

FIGURE 11-2
Break-even Analysis
When the price of a compact disk is $13, the break-even point would be reached when 50 CDs were sold and $650 of revenue generated.

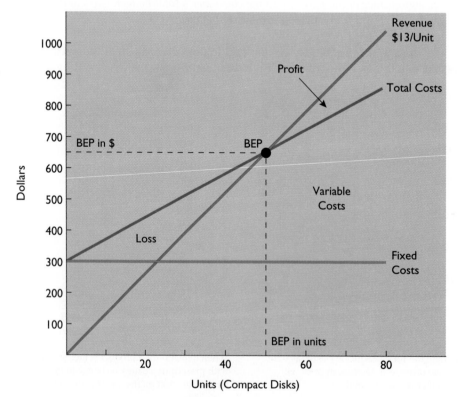

total cost line begins where the fixed cost line meets the y-axis of the graph show-ing that your total costs are your fixed costs when you haven't sold anything. To-tal costs rise from that point at an angle as variable costs and sales increase. The area between the total cost line and the fixed cost line represents your variable costs. The revenue line represents the number of units you will sell at any given price level—the demand curve for your product. The point at which the revenue line meets the total cost line is your break-even point (BEP). The area above the BEP between the revenue and total cost lines shows profit. The area below the BEP between the revenue and total cost lines represents loss.

The slope and shape of the revenue line for your business will vary depend-ing on your customer demand. The information to draw this line can come either from sales history or, if hard data are not available, from your personal best "guesstimate" of how much people will buy. You can also plot other revenue lines based on different selling prices. The revenue line in Figure 11-2 is based on product sales. Let's use the example of compact disks (CDs) selling for $13 each. You can also find your BEP for units with the following formula:

$$BEP(units) = \frac{\text{total fixed costs}}{\text{unit price} - \text{average variable cost}}$$

where average variable cost = total variable cost/quantity. Using the data from Figure 11-2, we could calculate the break-even point in units for a new CD of Christmas songs from Hatten and His Yodeling Goats. Total fixed costs to pro-duce this musical masterpiece are $300. Variable costs run $7.00 per unit. When charging $13 per CD, we would have to sell 50 CDs to break even on the venture. (Would 50 people pay $13 to hear yodeling goats or should Hatten keep his day job?)

$$BEP(units) = \frac{300}{13 - 7} = 50$$

In order to calculate our break-even point in dollars, we need to find the average variable cost of our product. This is done by taking the total variable cost (350) and dividing by the quantity (50). 350/50 = 7. The following formula is used to calculate the BEP in dollars:

$$BEP(dollars) = \frac{\text{total fixed costs}}{1 - \dfrac{\text{average variable cost}}{\text{unit price}}}$$

To find the BEP in dollars for our struggling musician's CD example, we would find that at $13 per CD, the break-even point would be $650.

$$BEP(dollars) = \frac{300}{1 - \dfrac{7}{13}} = 650$$

What would happen to our BEP in dollars and BEP in units if we would change the selling price to $20 each or to $11 each? At $20 per CD, we would break even at only $400 in sales. At $11 per CD, we would break even at $880. Figure 11-3 il-lustrates what happens at different price levels.

Break-even analysis is a useful tool in giving you a guideline for price set-ting. It can help you see how different volume levels will affect costs and profits. But in reality, lines rarely run perfectly straight indefinitely. The usefulness of

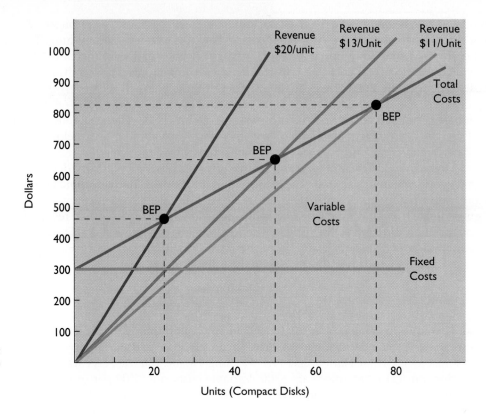

FIGURE 11-3
How Price Changes Affect the Break-even Point
When the price of a compact disk is changed to $11 or $20 the break-even point also changes.

your analysis depends on the quality of your data. The most valuable information for figuring your BEP is the demand for your products at each price level, which is difficult to predict with precision.

Another use for break-even analysis is to tell you how many units you need to sell to earn your desired return. If Hatten and His Yodeling Goats wanted a return of $1,000, how many units would need to be sold?

$$\text{Target return} = \frac{\text{total fixed cost} + \text{desired profit}}{\text{unit price} - \text{average variable cost}}$$

$$\$1,000 \text{ return} = \frac{300 + 1,000}{13 - 7} = 217 \text{ units}$$

When the sales price is $13 per CD, 217 CDs would have to be sold to generate a return of $1,000.

Price-setting Techniques

After taking competition, consumer demand, and your costs into consideration, you have made a start toward establishing your "right" price. You have a feel of what the price floor and price ceiling might be, but the price you finally choose will depend on the objectives and strategies you choose to pursue—what you are trying to accomplish in your business. Pricing strategies fall into two broad categories: customer oriented and internal oriented.

Manager's Notebook

Cost-cutting Strategies

To run a profitable small business, cutting costs is as important as increasing sales, especially during difficult economic times like recessions. Cost reduction is often a matter of making many little cuts rather than one or two major ones. Strategies for trimming fat from your company include:

- **Trim Your Payroll.** Laying off employees is no one's favorite activity but sometimes it must be done. Labor costs can represent 20 percent to 30 percent of a small business's total expenses.

- **Evaluate Attrition.** As workers leave your business, evaluate whether you need to hire a replacement or if the job can be restructured so someone else in the company can assume the duties. Some employees are made happier by adding more variety to their jobs.

- **Watch Supplies and Inventory.** These two areas can almost always be a source of savings. Don't reorder items that haven't sold quickly enough. You don't have to go so far as rationing pens and pencils, but you probably can cut supplies.

- **Shop Around for Suppliers.** Get competitive bids for merchandise. By letting your current supplier know that you will be shopping for bids, you can probably sit down and negotiate new terms.

- **Do Things Really Have To Be There Overnight?** Sending items via express mail is expensive—there is a large difference between first-class mail (32¢) and overnight delivery ($20). Use express mail as a last resort.

- **Make Sure Your Advertising Works.** Ask customers where they learned about your business. Cut back on advertising that is not bringing in customers. Maybe you just need one Yellow Pages listing rather than multiple listings.

- **Set Limits on Travel and Entertainment.** Authorize only those trips that bring in money. Stipulate that you and employees must travel coach and take advantage of airline discounts for weekend stays. Rent compact or subcompact cars.

Source: Michelle Singletary, "Trimming the Fat," Black Enterprise (June 1991), pp. 246–250.

Customer-oriented Pricing Strategies

Customer-oriented pricing strategies focus on target markets and factors that affect the demand for products. Strategies that are consumer oriented include: skimming, penetration, and psychological pricing.

Your pricing objectives may be to:

- Increase sales.
- Increase traffic in your store.
- Discourage competitors from entering your market.

To accomplish these objectives and gain rapid market share, **penetration pricing** is the most appropriate strategy. Penetration pricing is setting prices below what you might expect in order to encourage customers to initially try your product. This strategy is effective in keeping competition from entering the

penetration pricing Setting the price of a new product lower than expected in order to gain fast market share.

Don't Give Away the Farm with Special Offers

Businesses with new products often use *seeding*, or giving away products to select people so they will spread the word. Approach Software influenced people to try its database software program without completely giving up sales.

Competing databases sold for as much as $799 when Approach brought out Approach 1.0 for Windows with a $149 limited time offer. Why $149, instead of $99, or even $49? Wouldn't a lower price reach more people? Research by Approach's marketing director Jaleh Bisharat showed that it is possible for prices to be *too* low. Bisharat tested price points of $99, $129, $149, and $199 to 50,000 prospects from five different mailing lists. Surprisingly, demand was almost as high at $149 as at $129.

CEO Kevin Harvey said, "We never could have guessed the price-sensitivity curve if we hadn't tested it." Why sell for $20 below the price people are willing to pay? After the introductory period, it was much easier to move up to the full retail price.

Penetration pricing is a good technique for introducing a new product, but Approach Software shows that penetration prices can be set too low. Don't leave too much money on the table.

Source: Susan Greco, "Smart Use of 'Special Offers,'" Inc. (February 1993), p. 23.

---

market for your product. Thus, by making less profit on each unit and removing the incentive for competition to enter, you are building a long-term position in the market.

Your pricing objectives may be to:

- Maximize short- or long-run profit.
- Recover product development costs quickly.

price skimming Setting the price of a new product higher than expected in order to recover development costs.

If these are your objectives and if you have a truly unique product, a strategy of **price skimming** may be appropriate. Price skimming is setting your price high when you feel that customers are relatively price insensitive, or when there is little competition for consumers to compare prices against. Skimming helps recover high development costs, so businesses with new-to-the-world inventions often use this strategy. Home electronics are often introduced using a skimming strategy. Think of the price declines in personal computers, cellular phones, and VCRs. These products usually have high development costs and have unit costs that fall as production increases. Of course, consumers have to be willing to pay a premium to be willing to be one of the first to own these new products. Skimming is not a long-term strategy. Eventually, competition forces prices down.

Your pricing objectives may be to:

- Stabilize market prices.
- Establish your company's position in the market.
- Build an image for your business or product.
- Develop a reputation for being fair with suppliers and customers.

To accomplish these objectives, you may employ one of the **psychological pricing** strategies. Psychological pricing aims to influence the consumer's reaction toward prices of products. Several strategies are included under psychological pricing including *prestige pricing, odd pricing,* and *reference pricing.*

People often equate quality with price, a belief that has led to a practice called **prestige pricing.** Prestige pricing is especially effective with goods whose quality is difficult to determine by inspection or for products that consumers have little solid information about. Products as diverse as jewelry, perfume, beer, and smoke detectors, or the services of law firms, can all be prestige priced.

In an experiment at Stanford University, graduate students were given three unmarked bottles of beer. One bottle had a dime taped to it, one had nothing, and to get the third required payment of a dime. The students did not know that the beer in all three bottles was identical. The "premium" beer (the one with the dime) won the taste test. Some students even said the "discount" beer made them ill. Price does affect the image of a product.

psychological pricing Setting the price of a product in a way to alter its perception to customers.

Reality Check

To Live with Everyday Low Prices

Most marketers advise that a business of any size cannot compete solely on price anymore because today's customers want more than just a good price. They want pampering service, rapid delivery, and high quality. But some small businesses like Jan Bell Marketing believe you can compete on price alone, you just have to be smart about it. If you want to compete on price, price must drive every decision you make.

For example, you have to keep your prices consistent—changing your prices often confuses your customers. If you run sales or rebates, you condition people to wait for the sale or rebate to buy (ask the auto makers or the commercial airlines).

Jan Bell Marketing produces and distributes jewelry under private labels to wholesale clubs, such as Sam's Club and Pace Membership Warehouse. Bell does not depend on one big factor to allow it to sell gold chains and earrings, tennis bracelets, and rings for a third of the price competitors charge. Jan Bell Marketing finds at least one small way to cut costs at every step of the process.

Jan Bell Marketing competes on price by:

- **Allowing price to govern everything.** Jan Bell Marketing buys in bulk. It does not advertise, selling only to retailers who operate on low margin.

- **Subcontracting wherever possible.** Jan Bell Marketing contracts out most of its assembly work to decrease fixed costs.

- **Knowing its costs.** Jan Bell Marketing produces a portion of all its product lines so it knows exactly what its costs should really be.

- **Not getting fancy.** To compete on price, you can't have inventory laying around. All Jan Bell Marketing's lines are designed to move *quickly.*

Source: Paul Brown, "How to Compete on Price," Inc. (May 1990), p. 105.

We are more likely to see goods priced at $4.98, $17.89, or $49.95 than at $5.00, $18.00, or $50.00—this is **odd pricing**. Research has yet to prove a positive effect of odd pricing, but proponents believe that consumers see $99.99 as a better deal than $100. Sales of some products seem to benefit from **even pricing** if you are trying to convey the image of quality. For example, pricing a diamond ring at $18,000 gives the appearance of being above squabbling over loose change.

Reference pricing is common in retailing goods that consumers have an idea what the price of the product "should be" and they have a "usual" price for that item in mind.

If your customers are price sensitive to comparison prices of competing items, you may choose to use **price lining.** An example of price lining would be a men's clothing store that has ties at three different price points, such as $24.95, $33.95, and $44.95.

price lining Grouping product prices into ranges, such as low, medium, and high-priced items.

Internal-oriented Pricing Strategies

Pricing strategies that are internal oriented are based on your business's financial needs and costs rather than on the needs or wants of your target markets. Be careful if you use these strategies that you don't price your products out of the marketplace. Remember that consumers don't care what your costs are, they care about the value they receive. Internal-oriented strategies include: cost-plus pricing and target-return pricing.

Cost-plus Pricing. Probably the most common form of pricing is adding a specified percentage, a fixed fee, or **markup** to the cost of the item. While this type of pricing has always been common in retailing and wholesaling, manufacturers also use this relatively simple approach. Markup can be based on either *selling price* or *cost* and it is important to distinguish between the two.

markup The amount added to the cost of a product in setting the final price. It can be based on selling price or on cost.

For example, if an item cost $1 and the selling price is $1.50, the **markup on selling price** is 33.3 percent. Fifty cents is one-third of $1.50. However, using the same figures, the **markup on cost** is 50 percent. Fifty cents is one-half of $1.00. Markup based on cost makes your markup appear higher, even though the amounts are exactly the same. Most businesses base markup on selling price.

Effective use of markup depends on your ability to calculate the *profit margin* you need to cover costs. Formulas useful in calculating markup include:

$$\text{Selling price} = \text{cost} + \text{markup}$$

$$\text{Markup} = \text{selling price} - \text{cost}$$

$$\text{Cost} = \text{selling price} - \text{markup}$$

Target-return Pricing. If you have accurate information on how many units you will sell and what your fixed and variable costs will be, target-return pricing will allow you to set your selling price to produce a given rate of return. To calculate a target-return price, add your fixed costs and the dollar amount you wish to make, divide by the number of units you intend to sell, and then add the variable cost of your product.

$$\text{Target return price} = \frac{\text{fixed costs} + \text{target return}}{\text{unit sales}} + \text{variable cost}$$

For example, say demand for your product is 5,000 units. To meet this demand, you need a target return of $100,000 while your fixed costs are $200,000 and your variable costs run $50 per unit. Using this strategy, your price would be:

$$\frac{\$200,000 + \$100,000}{5,000} + 50 = \$60 + \$50$$

$$= \$110 = \text{your selling price}$$

Creativity in Pricing

The importance of being proactive and creative in running your business is a theme that runs through this book. The need for creativity may apply to pricing also. The key to creativity is breaking out of thought processes that keep you in ruts like: "That's not the way it's done in my type of business." To be creative in your pricing, look at techniques and practices of pricing used in different types of businesses and ask yourself, "How can that be applied to my business?" To begin this process, look at Table 11-1, the "Creative Pricing Primer" compiled by Michael Mondello of Celestial Seasonings.[7] Take note of how each approach could apply to your business.

TABLE 11 ▪ 1   Creative Pricing Primer

PRICING APPROACH	HOW IT WORKS	EXAMPLE
1. Bundling or unbundling	Sell products or services together as packages or break them apart and price accordingly.	Season tickets; stereo equipment; car rentals charging for air-conditioning.
2. Time-period pricing	Adjust price, up or down, during specific times to spur or acknowledge changes in demand.	Off-season travel fares (to build demand); peak-period fees on bank ATMs (to shift demand).
3. Trial pricing	Make it easy and lower the risk for a customer to try out what you sell.	Three-month health-club starter memberships; low, nonrefundable "preview fees" on training videos.
4. Image pricing	Sometimes the customer wants to pay more, so you price accordingly.	Most expensive hotel room in a city; a private-label vitamin's raising price to increase unit sales by signaling quality to shoppers.
5. Accounting-system pricing	Structure price to make it more salable within a business's buying systems.	Bill in phases so no single invoice exceeds an authorization threshold; classify elements so pieces get charged to other line items.
6. Value-added price packages	Include free "value-added" services to appeal to bargain shoppers, without lowering price.	A magazine's offering advertisers free merchandising tie-ins when they buy ad space at rate-card prices.
7. Pay-one-price	Unlimited use or unlimited amount of a service or product, for one set fee.	Amusement parks; office-copier contracts; salad bars.
8. Constant promotional pricing	Although a "regular" price exists, no one ever pays it.	Consumer-electronics retailers' always matching "lowest price" in town; always offering one pizza free when customer buys one at regular price.

table continues on following page

TABLE 11 ▪ 1   Creative Pricing Primer (Continued)

PRICING APPROACH	HOW IT WORKS	EXAMPLE
9. Price = performance	Amount customers pay is determined by the performance or value they receive.	Money managers' being paid profits; offering a career-transition guide for $80 and allowing buyers to ask for <u>any</u> amount refunded after use.
10. Change the standard	Rather than adjust price, adjust the standard to make your price seem different (and better).	A magazine clearinghouse's selling a $20 subscription for "four payments of only $4.99."
11. Shift costs to your customer	Pass on ancillary costs directly to your customer, and do not include those costs in your price.	A consulting firm's charging a fee and then rebilling all mail, phone, and travel costs directly to client.
12. Variable pricing tied to a creative variable	Set up a "price per" pricing schedule tied to a related variable.	Children's haircuts at 10¢ per inch of the child's height; marina space billed at $25 per foot for a boat.
13. Different names for different price segments	Sell essentially the same product, under different names, to appeal to different price segments.	Separate model numbers or variations of the same TV for discounters, department stores, and electronics stores.
14. Captive pricing	Lock in your customer by selling the system cheap, and then profit by selling high-margin consumables.	The classic example: selling razors at cost, with all the margin made on razor-blade sales.
15. Product-line pricing	Establish a range of price points within your line. Structure the prices to encourage customers to buy your highest-profit product or service.	Luxury-car lines (high-end models enhance prestige of entire line but are priced to encourage sale of more profitable low end).
16. Differential pricing	Charge each customer or each customer segment what each will pay.	In new-car sales, a deal for every buyer; Colorado lift tickets sold locally at a discount, at full price for fly-ins.
17. Quality discount	Set up a standard pricing practice, which can be done several ways.	Per-unit discount on <u>all</u> units, as with article reprints; discounts only on the units above a certain level, as with record clubs.
18. Fixed, then variable	Institute a "just-to-get-started" charge, followed by a variable charge.	Taxi fares; phone services tied to usage.
19. "Don't break that price point!"	Price just below important thresholds for the buyer, to give a perception of lower price.	Charging $499 for a suit; $195,000 instead of $200,000 for a design project.

NOTE: Once you've been creative, make sure you're covered. The most important aspect of any pricing approach is that it is legal and ethical. Check with counsel.

Source: Michael Mondello, "Naming Your Price." Adapted with permission, Inc. *magazine, July, 1982, p. 82.* © *by Goldhirsh Group, Inc., 38 Commercial Wharf, Boston, MA 02110.*

Credit Policies

After establishing your pricing practices comes an even more important task: deciding how you will get customers to pay for their purchase! Payment methods include cash, check, or credit.

Of course, accepting only cash really cuts down on those bad debts. But the trend is toward consumers carrying *less* cash, not more, so a cash-only policy will probably keep many customers from buying who would like to purchase with another form of payment. Most small businesses accept checks with adequate identification such as a phone number and driver's license number in case the bank returns the check for insufficient funds. For bookkeeping purposes, checks are treated the same as cash and actually make bank deposits easier.

The main reasons for your small business to extend credit are to make sales that you would not have otherwise made and to increase the volume and frequency of sales to existing customers.

Types of Credit

Credit is broken down into two basic categories: **consumer credit** offered to the ultimate consumers by retailers in exchange for goods and services, and **trade credit** which is the sales terms that one business extends to another for purchasing goods.

Should you extend credit to your customers? Good question. Do your competitors? Will your sales increase enough to pay finance charges? Will sales increase enough to cover the bad debts you will incur? Can you extend credit and still maintain a positive cash flow? Will credit sales smooth out fluctuations in sales volume?

Consumer Credit. You have several choices of ways to extend credit to your customers. You can carry the debt yourself, you can rely on a financial institution like a bank to loan money to your customers, or you can accept credit cards.

If you wish to carry the debt yourself, you can set up an **open charge account** for customers. Customers take possession of the goods and you bill them. Invoices are usually sent out to customers monthly. You can encourage them to pay early by offering cash discounts or punish late payment with finance charges. Open accounts must be managed carefully. As we will see in Chapter 17, open accounts can absolutely kill cash flow and drain the life out of your business.

An **installment account** is frequently offered to customers purchasing big-ticket items (like autos, boats, and appliances). Customers rarely have the cash up front to pay for such items. With an installment account consumers make a down payment and then make monthly payments on the unpaid balance plus interest for an extended period of time. This type of financing is not quite as dangerous as the open account because you usually have the product to use for collateral. Generally, small businesses exist to sell their products and financial institutions are in business to sell money—let them handle installment loans.

You may extend a **line of credit** to your customers. This operates like a revolving credit account: You approve credit purchases for your customer up to a certain dollar limit. Lines of credit allow customers to buy goods without a new credit check for each purchase. Finance charges are paid on the unpaid balance monthly. Extending lines of credit can simplify the amount of paper in your credit application process since a new application is not required for each purchase. This type of financing allows you to control the total amount of credit you extend.

To avoid the expense and inconvenience of maintaining your own accounts receivable, you can rely on credit cards as your source of consumer credit. Consumers' use of cash and checks is decreasing as a percentage of total consumer

consumer credit Credit extended to customers for the purchase of products.
trade credit Credit extended from one business to another.

Entering the Internet

On-line Credit Checks: It's a snap to find information about the creditworthiness of customers and suppliers on the Internet and through computer and other services. However, before trying this, you might want to use the Net to do some background reading about effective pricing and credit decisions. The U.S. Small Business Administration's site is a good place to start, especially in the General Information and Publications section. There you'll find a file on "How to Price Your Products and Services" and another on "Pricing Your Products." In addition, you might find useful information in "Financial Management for the Growing Business" and "Cash Flow Analysis."

Once you're familiar with the ins and outs of pricing and credit, you're ready to begin conducting your credit checks. Where to start? Databases are available to help you look into a customer's financial past to determine the would-be customers who might have trouble paying you. You can instantly find out about any tax liens, bankruptcies, court judgments, payment history, financial data and analysis, company background, public filings, and other information. Data are available for each geographical zone in the country.

Prentice Hall Online, offered by Prentice Hall Legal and Financial Services (a subsidiary of the company which published this textbook), can connect your business via modem to more than 250 million public records in 35 states. The service costs $300 per quarter for up to 60 searches. Subscribing to it could be money well spent if you are concerned about the creditworthiness of potential customers.

For business credit requests, the Yahoo Web search site lists several merchant credit services that you can access through the Web links capability. Just point your mouse to the one you want to investigate and click. Also, Dun & Bradstreet provides a free search of millions of U.S. companies. Then, for a nominal fee, you can receive a Business Background Report that lists important credit information about the company you're investigating.

For about $300 per year, you can join the National Association of Credit Management, a membership organization which researches and reports on many small firms that are often overlooked by larger credit agencies. As a member you can get a comprehensive report on a particular firm from the database, which includes about 6.5 million firms.

SBA General Information and Publications: http://www.sbaonline.sba.gov

Yahoo Web search site: http://www.yahoo.com/Business_and_Economy/Companies/Financial_Services/Credit/Merchant_Services

Dun & Bradstreet: http://www.dbisna.com/

Sources: Timothy O'Brien, "Customer Credit Records Become Required Reading," The Wall Street Journal, July 13, 1993, p. B1, and "On-line Checks on Customers," Inc. (December 1993), p. 169.

spending while the use of credit and debit cards is skyrocketing. Consumers still use cash and checks for about 67 percent of all payments made outside the home.[8] Credit card use is expected to account for 50 percent of all transactions by the year 2000. (See Figure 11-4.)

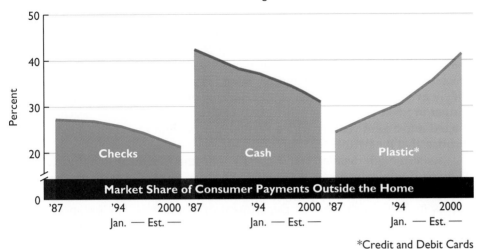

Cards are Clobbering Checks and Cash

FIGURE 11-4
How Do Consumers Pay?
Consumers are using more
credit cards than cash or
checks to purchase products.
Business Week, February 14, 1994,
p. 105.

In development now are plastic cards with microchips that handle purchasing transactions called Smart Cards. They could have the effect of putting a personal computer in consumers' pockets. Other changes in plastic money include more use of debit cards, which deduct purchases directly from checking accounts electronically.[9] Increased use of debit cards can be good news for the small business owner because the fees that businesses pay for accepting debit cards are usually lower than for credit cards.

New types of money transactions are changing the way we do business. The cafeteria and vending machines at the Chase Manhattan Bank Metrotech Center in Brooklyn, New York, take only prepaid cards. You can't pay with cash.

Convenience for customers comes at a price, however. Businesses have to pay a percentage of each sale to the credit card company handling the sale. While card companies offer discount rates for small businesses, transaction and statement fees increase the amount you will pay. The percentage most small businesses pay to MasterCard and Visa varies according to the number of transactions made, but most small businesses are charged between 1.5 percent to 3 percent.[10] The Discover Card's stated rates are 1 percent to 2.5 percent, while American Express discounts small business rates to 3.5 percent. Total fees, including sales percentages and transaction and statement fees, can run as high as 6 percent.

Trade Credit. If you can purchase goods and services and be allowed to take 30, 60, or 90 days to pay for them, you have essentially obtained a loan of 30 to 90 days. Many new businesses can take advantage of trade credit even when no other form of financing is available. Be warned that habitual late payment or nonpayment may cause your suppliers to cut off your trade credit and place your business on COD—cash on delivery.

Trade credit can be offered in several forms: extended payment periods and terms, goods offered on consignment, payment not required until sold, or seasonal dating, which means that suppliers ship goods before the purchaser's peak selling season and do not require payment until after the peak season. Credit

Global Small Business

The challenges of establishing viable credit policies are magnified if and when you decide to take your small business global. Even with the vast economic potential of global markets, you still need to make sure that your customers can pay for their purchases. What makes the process difficult is that credit and payment history information typically isn't as widely available as it is in the United States. For instance, Brian Zimbler, a law partner in a San Francisco law firm, tells of one of his small business clients who entered into a joint venture with a Russian partner and found out, much to their surprise, that the partner was part of the Russian Mafia.

Even though detailed credit checks and other payment investigations can be difficult to obtain, a small business owner can, with a little effort, find information to evaluate the creditworthiness of potential customers. A good place to start is to check with the U.S. Department of Commerce. For instance, if your business is looking at the Russian market, the department has a service called the Business Information Service for the Newly Independent States (BISNIS) which offers broad advice for doing business in Russia. Other possibilities include contacting industry trade associations or your local chamber of commerce for assistance and advice. *Source: Armin A. Brott, "How to Avoid Bear Traps," Nation's Business (September 1993), pp. 49–50; and Paul J. Mignini, Jr., "The Globalization of Credit," Business Credit (April 1994), p. 3.*

lines are popular ways for you to receive trade credit from your suppliers. Suppliers offer trade credit to get new customers. A survey by the National Federation of Independent Business found that about 75 percent of small businesses use lines of credit for working capital.[11]

Controlling Credit Accounts

If you don't collect on sales, they aren't sales. If you extend credit to customers, you need an accounts receivable system to keep cash flowing into your business. A very easy trap that growing new businesses fall into is the thought, "Get the sales now, work on improving profit margins later."[12] This trap is especially serious for service businesses whose largest expense is labor, which must be paid when the service is provided. Manufacturers also suffer from slow collection due to the long time lag between purchasing raw material, labor, and inventory and the actual sale of the product.

Western Machine & Chrome Inc. was a small machine shop that was at risk in 1989 when its overdue accounts stretched from 90 to 120 days.[13] CEO Alvin Bennett and bookkeeper JoAnne Wheeler revised the old collection system into one that identifies bills deserving immediate attention. Western Machine has so many different kinds of customers over a wide geographical area, the system had to be simple and concise. They produce one report for every different industry showing details about customer invoices.

The system allows them to manage time and money by asking the right questions: "Which invoices present the biggest cash flow problems? Which aging bills are really not problems? Which present the biggest risk of not being paid?" (See Figure 11-5.)

JoAnne Wheeler explains how the system works:

REPORT TYPE

This report is a sample of the type that my assistants—two full-timers and one part-timer—and I use. I've designed it specially to make it easy for each clerk to keep track of his or her collection responsibilities. It also helps me evaluate each person's collection performance. There's a second type of report that I compile to keep the rest of our employees aware of every overdue account.

CLIENT TYPE

This page covers only our lumber clients. We follow different collection strategies with each sector. With municipalities, for example, we concentrate on making sure our paperwork is in order. We don't hound government agencies. They'll pay eventually—we just don't know when. But we aggressively pursue overdue lumber accounts, concentrating on the biggest amounts first because those have the largest effect on our cash flow. Farmers' invoices are generally smaller, so we go after the oldest bills first. They're the toughest to collect.

CLIENT

I don't alphabetize client names or list them numerically. I list customers with the largest and oldest outstanding balances at the top of each page, and those with the smallest and newest unpaid bills at the bottom. There's no confusion about which ones are most important to keep after.

INTEREST

It really pays to stay on top of your interest charges, and every month I mail our late payers separate invoices for interest fees. Collection clerks sometimes want to offer an incentive to get a very old bill paid. They can use the interest assessment listed on the form to help make a deal. And, if a case goes to court, we have complete records of our activities to support our claim.

TOTAL DUE

Most accounts-receivable forms list this number on the right side of the page, but I'm convinced that people pay the most attention to details listed on the left. So I emphasize the total due and the oldest invoices. If the "current" column gets overlooked, because of its position on the page, that's much less worrisome than if the "over 120 days" number gets skipped.

LAST ACTION

I wish we had more room to record a description of the last action, because there are often so many details to keep track of. But to expand this column, I would have had to switch to a larger piece of paper, instead of using one that's 8¹/₂ by 11 inches, and that would have taken up too much desk space and been more difficult to manage. So we simply use the back of the form when our follow-up activities get complicated.

SECURITY INDICATORS

An effective accounts-receivable form reports the good as well as the bad. We include the security-indicators column to show clerks which accounts have an additional measure of security, such as a personal guarantee, a letter of credit, a standby letter of credit, or collateral. I flag an unusually good relationship with a company's accounts-payable clerks, too. If we have no reason to worry about a particular bill, that helps our clerks decide whether to devote their collection efforts elsewhere.

PROBLEM INDICATORS

I've devised a code to highlight possible danger signs. These are the problem indicators: *P* stands for past problems. *I* indicates invoices paid out of order. *B* means broke agreement. *C* is changes in payment practices. *M* indicates changes in major management or other critical personnel. *L*, the biggie, means total due is at or exceeds credit limit. These codes tell us which bills are crucial for us to collect quickly.

CLERK'S INITIALS

No accounts-receivable clerk wants the recognition of having the worst or the most outstanding accounts!

TOTALS AND PERCENTAGES

Calculating the dollar totals and the percentages is the most time-consuming part of preparing the forms every week, but it's so valuable. It reminds us that credit and collections are an aggregate issue. We have to keep track of the larger picture, even while we're pursuing individual accounts. These figures provide a fast and easy measure of improvement.

FIGURE 11-5
Bill Collection System

Jill Andresky Fraser, "The Outstanding Bill Collection System." Adapted with permission, Inc. *magazine, May 1993, pp. 94–95. © 1993, Goldhirsh Group, Inc.*

Accounts Aging
Report Type: CONFIDENTIAL
Client Type: Lumber

Client	Total Due	Over 120	90– 119	60– 89	30– 59	Current	Clerk Init.	P/I	Secu	Date/last Action
										1/5 referred To attorney
ABC Lumber	12,197.22	11,497.22	172.98			190.94	PB	PB		1/5 Call Talked
XY Mill	931.57	931.57					SS	C	C	12/5 Call Talked To atty w/o
Workers Inc.	9653	9653				137.47				12/5 Call w/Tor
Overseas LBR	18,285.51	18,285.51				149.17	PB	L	R	12/5 Call w/Tor
Workers Inc.	350.19	350.19				18,285.51				12/5 Call w/Tor
Jackson Inc.	11,779.10					53.30	JW	C	C	Cash AP clerk
River Mill						176.48	PB			12/5
Dollars Total	64,730.49	11,492.10		98,006		124,041.84	298,811.66	691		
Percentage	1.00	17.5	1.51			1.81				

Collecting Overdue Bills

Bill collecting is never fun, but it is critical for small businesses. Paul Mignini, Jr., president of the National Association of Credit Management, said that you will often hear customers' excuses like, "Times are tough, we're having a hard time making it." You should acknowledge their difficulty by saying, "I know times are tough. Let's get this settled before other bills get in the way." The longer bills go unpaid, the lower your chances are of collecting. (See Figure 11-6.)

Begin your collection process by telephone if you don't receive a check after 30 days. Create a sense of urgency that the bill must be paid. Try to get a commitment for a certain amount by a specific day, like $100 by the 25th. That puts the burden on the customer. If repeated calls lead you to believe that the customer is playing games, with little intention of paying what he owes, you have five choices: a letter service, an attorney, small claims court, a collection agency, or writing it off. Always remain professional and try to stay on friendly terms. You can say something like, "I really busted my tail to get the delivery to you on time. Will you please help us serve other customers by sending a check?"

To help collections, pay attention to your invoices and credit applications. Always print your late service charges on your invoices. Include a venue provision on your invoices if you are selling goods out of state so any court case concerning the sale will be heard in a court of your choice. State the specific number of days a customer has to notify you of any problems with the shipment.

On your credit application form, ask customers to sign a release that authorizes creditors to disclose relevant information. This will help you to spot credit problems in advance.

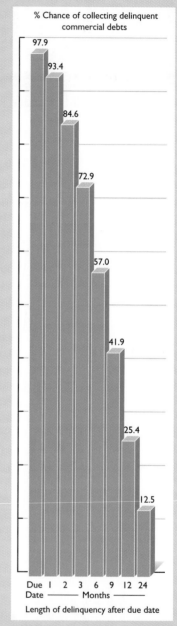

% Chance of collecting delinquent commercial debts

97.9 — 93.4 — 84.6 — 72.9 — 57.0 — 41.9 — 25.4 — 12.5

| Due Date | 1 | 2 | 3 | 6 | 9 | 12 | 24 |

Months

Length of delinquency after due date

FIGURE 11-6

Source: Adapted from Jill Andresky Fraser, "Improve Invoices and Credit Forms," Inc. (November 1992), p. 139; Eugene Carlson, "Collecting Overdue Bills Involves Walking Delicate Line," The Wall Street Journal, October 10, 1990, p. B2; Jill Andresky Fraser, "Never Say Die," adapted with permission Inc. magazine, October 1993, p. 44. © 1993 by Goldhirsh Group, Inc.

Computer Applications

How can you make the arduous and often unpleasant task of collecting overdue bills more manageable? Help is as close as your nearest computer keyboard—**if** you have a good billing software program! Identifying overdue bills and following up to get payment as soon as possible can be automated using billing software that's relatively easy to use. One program packed with features is M.Y.O.B. Accounting (its initials stand for Mind Your Own Business and is available from Bestware at 800-322-6962). It's easy to set up and use and comes with more than 100 templates for different types of businesses. This program uses flowcharts for entering invoices and customer payments. However, it's designed more as a total accounting package rather than simply as billing software.

What are some stand-alone billing software programs? One is The Invoice Store (DOS-based) that's primarily for product-based, not service, businesses. It focuses on inventory management and shipping records and can create customized reports to track a customer's payment history. It's available from Software Store Products (800-232-8561). Another popular program is MyAdvancedInvoices & Estimates (Windows and Macintosh versions) by MySoftware Company (800-325-3508). This program is easy to use and focuses specifically on invoicing and payment tracking. Another billing program designed for Macintosh users is OnAccount (White Crow Software: 802-658-1270). This program lets users dress up invoices with artwork, but it uses balance-forward accounting—in which payments are recorded against client account totals. This approach means that you won't be able to match payments to individual invoices.

As with any software program the key is to identify your needs and then the best software to address those needs. With the wide variety of programs available, keeping on top of overdue accounts doesn't have to be a dreaded task.

Summary

■ The three main considerations that relate to pricing.

The economic factors that have the largest influence on pricing are the price charged by competitors, the amount of customer demand for your product, and the cost incurred in producing, purchasing, and selling your products.

■ What break-even analysis is and its importance in pricing.

The value of break-even analysis is to ensure that your prices are set above your total costs in order to make a profit. Break-even analysis is also useful in estimating what demand for a product is likely to be at different price levels. Finally, break-even analysis is useful to show how many units need to be sold to generate a target dollar return.

■ Examples of customer-oriented and internal-oriented pricing.

Customer-oriented price strategies, like penetration pricing, skimming, and psychological pricing, are based on the wants and needs of your target customers and how many units of your product they will buy. Internal-oriented pricing involves setting your prices according to your own financial needs.

■ Why and how small businesses extend credit.

Small businesses extend credit to their customers in order to increase sales that would not have been made without credit, and to increase the volume and frequency of sales to existing customers. Credit is extended through open charge accounts, installment accounts, lines of credit, and acceptance of credit cards.

■ The importance of having a collection system.

Credit collection systems are important because sales are not sales until you get paid. Making sales but not collecting increases your accounts receivable. A buildup of accounts receivable causes a negative cash flow, which can spell the end of your business.

Questions for Review and Discussion

1. What strategies should be considered if a small business is setting prices for a product that is to be exported? How are these strategies different from those used in a domestic market?

2. What advantages and disadvantages are involved for a small business offering sales on credit?

3. Discuss the different impressions a consumer has between a product that is "inexpensive" and one that is "cheap." *assoc. w/ Qual.*

4. As the owner of a small, hometown drugstore, how would you prepare for a Wal-Mart being built in your area? *differentiate & deepen prod line*

5. Is demand for the following products elastic or inelastic?
   Guess? jeans *inel*
   generic corn flakes *inel*
   used Dodge Caravan *El*
   new Dodge Caravan *El*
   filling a cavity in a tooth *inel*
   automobile insurance *inel*
   automobile oil change *El*
   health club membership *El*
   a hair cut *El*

6. What can happen if the price of a product does not fit with the three other "p's" of the marketing mix?

7. Nestle' gave away candy bars on college campuses and issued coupons for free candy bars in newspapers to launch its new Lion bar. How could these practices affect the price strategy of the new candy bar?

8. Should a small business owner's judgment be used to determine prices, since so many mathematical techniques have been developed for that purpose?

9. Discuss the difference between price and value. *# vs. what get for #*

10. Discuss the importance of remaining professional and friendly when trying to collect an unpaid bill.

Critical Incident

Kadali Brothers Coffee Company. Mark Overly's Kadali Brothers Coffee has been voted as having the best espresso in Alaska. Based in Anchorage, Alaska, Overly has built the once tiny coffee roasting and supply business into a multi-million-dollar venture. Kadali Brothers had projected sales of $4.2 million in 1995. Overly traces his company's success to the quality of his product and service.

Tenth Planet. With a name like "Tenth Planet," you're sure to get attention. CEO Cheryl Vedoe has just seen her company's first product—a set of books, blocks, and CD-ROMs designed to acquaint school children in kindergarten through second grade with the basics of geometry—go on sale. But how can a company make money supplying a product to cash-short schools? Because most public schools have invested in computers, Vedoe's company is confident it can persuade these schools to buy its products and put those computers to good use.

Questions

1. Working in teams (no more than three on a team, please) use Table 11-1, to propose at least three different alternative pricing strategies for each of the small businesses just described. Think carefully about your suggestions.

2. Develop an appropriate credit policy for each of these small businesses. Be specific in defining what factors you're going to use to influence your decision about whether or not to extend credit.

Take it to the Net

We invite you to visit the Hatten page on the Prentice Hall Web site at: http://www.prenhall.com/~hattensb for this chapter's World Wide Web exercise.

Chapter Focus

After reading this chapter, you should be able to:

- List the components of an international business plan.
- Analyze the advantages and disadvantages of exporting for small businesses.
- Enumerate the five ways for small businesses to conduct international trade.
- Explain how small businesses can manage their finances in international trade.
- Articulate the cultural and economic challenges of international small business activity.

12

Global Small Business

ENDY WIGTIL DOESN'T SELL her toy creations in other countries just for fun. She exports for the survival of her company, Barnyard Babies, which makes cloth toys that children color themselves. In 1993, export sales were the difference in her profit margin that put the business in the black.

For some time when Wigtil started trying to export, she found agents tentative about taking new products. Now, she said "There are more intermediaries out there looking for American products." She explains the increased interest as partly due to other countries' improving economies, providing more discretionary income for people to buy products like hers.

Wigtil's first international orders came by accident from stop-by sales at a trade show. Those few international sales helped Wigtil recognize that while the U.S. toy market is crowded with competitors, many other unsaturated markets exist. Now she has regular accounts in Japan, France, and Canada. Soon she will expand to Brazil, and she has her eye on the former Soviet countries.

Several developments have created tremendous opportunities for small exporters like Wigtil, including: NAFTA (the North American Free Trade Agreement), the declining value of the dollar compared to foreign currencies, new foreign markets opening or expanding (China, Vietnam, the Czech Republic, and Argentina, for example), and finally, the promise of GATT (the General Agreement on Tariffs and Trade) to reduce or eliminate tariffs among its 117 participating countries.

Opportunities for small businesses selling their products in other countries have never been better. Engaging in business abroad may be intimidating at first, and may require a business to make some changes, but no business is too small to become a global player. *Source: Roberta Maynard, "A Good Time to Export?" Nation's Business (May 1994), pp. 22–32.*

Preparing to Go Global

The size of a business does not determine its ability to enter global markets but it may influence the number and scale of markets a business can enter.

When most people think of international business, they envision large, multinational corporations with operations all over the globe. A common conclusion is that small- and medium-sized businesses are at a disadvantage in their ability to compete internationally. Actually, research shows that the size of a business is not a barrier to entry into international markets, it only limits the number of markets you can serve.[1] Having improper strategies, negative attitudes toward expansion abroad, or lack of experience may keep businesses out of the international game, but size does not have to be a factor. In fact, the same competitive advantages— your unique skills, talents, and products—that have made your business successful in local markets may create the same advantage in foreign markets.

Growth of Global Business

Not only can small businesses succesfully compete in other countries, they are increasing their export rate much faster than large businesses. (See Figure 12-1.) A study showed that 11 percent of small businesses exported goods and services to other countries in 1992. By 1993, the total had grown to 16 percent, and by 1994, 20 percent were exporting. (See Figure 12-2.)[2]

"The bigger the world economy, the more powerful its smallest players," stated John Naisbitt, author of *Megatrends* and *Global Paradox*.[3] The world is integrating economically, and as it does there will be more and smaller component parts. Market niches will become smaller, and this is good news for small businesses. "Success in seizing market niches has to do with swiftness to market and innovation, which small companies can do so well," added Naisbitt.[4]

International Business Plan

To navigate these shifting international tides, you will, of course, need a business plan. As we discussed in Chapter 4, a solid business plan is behind most successful small businesses. Adding the following information to your basic business plan will help you analyze your ability to go international and chart the course to follow:

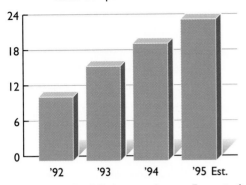

Small Companies Go Global . . .

Percent of Small Businesses that are Exporting*

*Companies with Fewer than 500 Employees

FIGURE 12-1
Small Business Exporters
The percentage of companies with less than 500 employees that have begun exporting has nearly doubled since 1992. *Amy Barrett, "It's a Small (Business) World," p. 96.* Reprinted from April 17, 1995 issue of Business Week by special permission, © 1995 by the McGraw-Hill Companies.

- Your commitment to international trade.
- Your export pricing strategy.
- Your reason for exporting.
- The most attractive potential export markets and customers.
- Your methods of entering foreign markets.
- Exporting costs and projected revenues.
- Your financing alternatives to allow you to export.
- Any legal requirements you need to meet.
- The transportation method that would be most appropriate.
- Any overseas partnership contacts and foreign investment capabilities.[5]

One expert recommends that an international business plan should include both market entrance and exit approaches because markets that are hard to leave can drain export sales profit.[6]

If you conclude from your planning that you should proceed with your expansion into other countries, you have four basic choices: exporting, licensing

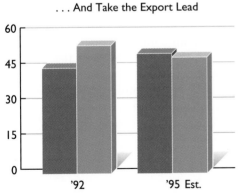

. . . And Take the Export Lead

Percentage of Total Manufactured U.S. Exports

■ By Small Business
■ By Big Business

FIGURE 12-2
Small Business Exporters
Percentage of exported products manufactured by small business and big business. *Amy Barrett, "It's a Small (Business) World," p. 97.* Reprinted from April 17, 1995 issue of Business Week by special permission, © 1995 by the McGraw-Hill Companies.

R eality Check

Just Do It

You hear a lot about barriers that keep small businesses with few resources from entering foreign markets. Jeffrey Ake, vice president of sales and marketing at Electronic Liquid Fillers (ELF), which makes liquid-packaging equipment, thinks the biggest barrier is not expertise, finance, or culture—it's psychology. Ake says that once you have made the decision that you want to sell in overseas markets, everything else will fall into place.

ELF had the typical problems that most small businesses face when considering international expansion—no expertise, no line of credit, and a location in the industrially depressed Rustbelt. But ELF's sales rose from $150,000 in 1988 to $6 million in 1992 due to entering international markets. This gain represented half of its total sales and all of its growth. Here's the advice Ake gives on getting started:

- Name someone—probably yourself, but maybe your top sales or marketing person—to be the international tiger.
- Announce to the world that your company's products exist and are available for purchase.
- Get yourself over there and sell.
- Stick to what you know works.
- Strongly consider raising your prices.
- Let the experts lead you through the details of processing the order.
- Once you get an order, service it.
- Keep your initial market-entry costs low, low, low.

Source: Jeffrey Ake, "Easier Done Than Said," Inc. (February 1993), pp. 96–99.

your product, establishing a joint venture, and setting up operations in the other country. Each of these options represents an increased level of commitment on your part, so let's look at your options in that order.

Exporting

exporting Selling goods or services in a foreign country.

Exporting is defined as selling in another country the goods or services that you offer domestically. It is the most common way for small businesses to operate in other countries.[7] Of all the ways to conduct business internationally that we are considering in this chapter, exporting provides the lowest levels of risk and investment, increasing your chances of being profitable.

The Small Business Administration (SBA) has identified advantages and disadvantages of exporting. *Advantages* of exporting include:

- Increased total sales and profits.
- Access to a share of the global market.
- Reduced dependence on your existing markets.
- Enhanced domestic competitiveness.
- A chance to exploit your technology and know-how in places where they are needed.
- Realization of the sales potential of existing products and extension of the product life cycle.

- Stabilization of seasonal market fluctuations.
- Opportunity to sell excess production capacity.
- Chance to gain information about foreign competition.[8]

Disadvantages to exporting revolve around the additional responsibilities and obligations your business may incur. You may be required to:

- Develop new promotional material suitable for foreign customers.
- Forego short-term profits in the interest of long-term gains.
- Incur added administrative costs.
- Allocate funds and personnel for travel.
- Wait longer for payments than with your domestic accounts.
- Modify your product or packaging.
- Acquire additional financing.
- Obtain special export licenses.[9]

Only you can decide if the disadvantages of global expansion outweigh the advantages. The timing of entering a foreign market may not be right or you may be short on cash to fund the expansion at this point. But there are no solid rules of international expansion. Some businesses go abroad before selling *anything* at home. For instance, Ray Ciliv and Robin Hillyard, founders of NovaSoft Systems software company, were down to their last $250 when the stock market crashed in 1987. The only thing they had going for them was their company's product—the latest technology in computer-based engineering document management systems. Without the resources for marketing in the United States and no chance of attracting outside capital, their next step was unique—they decided to sell their software overseas to prove it was good and then let sales momentum bring it back to the United States. They started in Italy, then Germany, Venezuela, Belgium, Israel, and Japan, all *before* beginning distribution in the United States in 1991.[10]

If you decide that exporting is right for your business, you have two methods that you can use: indirect and direct exporting. Whether you choose to use intermediaries is the primary difference between the two.

Indirect Exporting

The simplest and perhaps most cost-effective way for a small business to export is to hire an export service company to market products abroad.[11] This method minimizes the financial and personnel resources needed to promote international sales. Using an intermediary reduces your risks and can help you learn the exporting process. Even if you start using indirect exporting, you may choose to set up an international sales staff once you develop the capital and expertise.

Of course, the fee charged by an export service company will reduce your profit margin, but the increased sales should offset this disadvantage. A more dangerous disadvantage is that you lose control by operating through an intermediary. Your company name and image is in the hands of the exporting intermediary. Finally, the price the ultimate consumer pays may be increased by using intermediaries. You should negotiate what all costs, fees, and final price will be up front in the contract.

There are several kinds of intermediaries for you to consider. Agents and brokers, export management companies (EMCs) and export trade companies (ETCs), ETC cooperatives, foreign trade companies, and piggyback exporting are all domestic-based intermediaries. Foreign-based intermediaries include foreign distributors and foreign agents.

Agents and Brokers. Both agents and brokers will put your company in touch with foreign buyers. They set up the deal, but they don't buy the products from you. They can also provide consultation on shipping, packaging, and documentation.

Export Management Companies (EMCs). EMCs provide a much fuller range of services than agents or brokers, but they still do not take title to your goods. EMCs act as your own export department, conducting marketing research, arranging financing and distribution channels, attending trade shows, and handling logistics. EMCs will even use your company letterhead in all correspondence and provide customer support after a sale. EMCs are a good option for small businesses new to international trade.

Export Trade Companies (ETCs). ETCs perform many of the same functions as export management companies, but they generally take title of your goods and pay you directly. ETCs operate individually and also join together to form cooperative groups of companies selling similar products.

Reality Check

Sporting a Global Look

Drew Pearson's name is instantly recognized by many sports fans worldwide. As an all-pro wide receiver with the Dallas Cowboys, Pearson's NFL career was cut short by an automobile accident in 1984. When his next job, as a broadcaster for CBS, didn't provide him the fulfillment he was looking for, Pearson hooked up with two long-time friends to start a sports apparel business. Drew Pearson Companies (DPC), with its 175 employees, has become a leading maker of sports caps and one of the most successful minority-owned businesses in the United States. Gross sales in 1993 reached $78 million and DPC was named 1994 company of the year by *Black Enterprise* magazine.

Today the company concentrates on headwear and has more than 40 licenses with major sports leagues, entertainment entities, and black colleges and universities. Its caps feature the logos of teams like the Dallas Cowboys and the Orlando Magic, as well as cartoon characters like Bugs Bunny. Known for its innovative designs, DPC's hats are marketed with trendy names such as Jagged Edge, The Claw, and Super Highway. Says one sportswear buyer for a leading retail sports apparel chain, "It's the flair and style that goes into every cap that makes DPC popular among the hotly contested preteen and teen market." DPC hats are starting to sell well in Europe, Australia, South America, and even China. And Drew Pearson isn't content to stay still. He's betting on continued international growth for his company.

Source: J. Tol Broome, Jr., "Locker Room to Board Room," Nation's Business *(October 1995), pp. 13–14.*

Piggyback Exporting. If you can find another company that is already exporting, you may be able to make a piggyback arrangement to take advantage of the international connections the other company has already established. If your products do not directly compete with the other company's products, they may simply add your product line to their own.

Foreign-based Distributors or Agents. Using a distributor or an agent that is based in the foreign country, rather than one based in the United States, can provide the advantage of cultural and local knowledge that you may not be able to get elsewhere.

George Grumbles, president of Universal Data Systems, has been exporting electronic equipment for over 20 years. He believes in building groups of local distributors in his foreign markets. Grumbles said, "You have to work through nationals [residents of the foreign country]. If you send U.S. folks into a foreign country, you have to expect it will take a couple of years for them to find their way around. Instead, you should find people who are embedded in the local economy."[12]

Foreign agents do the same jobs overseas that manufacturer's representatives do in the United States. Agents work on commission within their sales region of specific countries. Local laws and customs vary greatly between countries, so you must be clear on what you can expect an agent to legally do. Some countries go to extremes in protecting their citizens from foreign companies.

Foreign distributors may sell on a commission basis or buy your goods directly. You and the distributor should work together to produce your marketing materials since translating your packaging and promotional material into another language can be a problem.

Direct Exporting

With direct exporting, you do not use any intermediaries as with indirect exporting. If you choose to use direct exporting as your method of selling your products in other lands, you have more control over the exporting process, greater potential profit, and direct contact with your customers. A point you must remember when considering any channel of distribution is that you can do away with the intermediary but someone has to perform this function. If you choose not to use an intermediary for your exporting, then *you* have to perform those duties. You have to choose the target countries, arrange the most efficient channel of distribution, and market your product in the foreign country. Direct exporting is therefore riskier, more expensive, and more difficult than indirect exporting, but since you pay less service fees or commissions, your potential profit could also be greater.

In direct exporting, one approach could be the use of **sales representatives** who sell your products and other (noncompeting) products on a commission basis. You may choose to use a **distributor,** or to sell **directly to the final consumer.**

Selling your product in other countries may be a logical extension of your domestic business. Many business executives say that exporting is essentially no different from expanding into a new market in your own country. Of course, operating in other countries can create unique challenges, but first you have to go back to basics. You have to do your market research to determine who will buy your product and where they are. You have to determine your channels of distribution and your prices. Remembering these basics may take some of the intimidation out of "going international."

Identifying Potential Export Markets

Successful marketing depends on your knowledge of the people and places with which you are dealing. In addition to marketing research you would conduct locally, marketing research in the international sector needs to include the following activities:

Find Countries with Attractive, Penetrable Markets. Sometimes the largest trading partners of the United States may not be the best countries for you or your products. For example, Harden Wiedemann of Assurance Medical Inc., a provider of alcohol and drug-testing services, was surfing around on the Internet one day when

Reality Check

Bagels To Go—A Long Way

Many small business owners think their business is too small to export products. But Jerry Shapiro, president of Petrofsky's International, thinks that the success of small businesses trying to break into the trade game has more to do with courage than size.

Petrofsky's began as a family owned neighborhood bakery in St. Louis that developed a way to quick-freeze uncooked bagel dough as a way to let bakers take weekends off. Next they expanded by selling to supermarkets that would prepare and package the bagels as their store brand. Petrofsky's increasing success with this product led it to build a new factory with a production capacity of 1.5 million bagels per day. As a way to spread increased overhead over a larger market, Petrofsky's began to consider exporting.

In 1985, Shapiro attended a trade show in Japan where he passed out 8,000 sample bagels. He also observed local customs and test-marketed his bagels to find out if any changes would be needed to sell the bagels in that country. (He found that softer and larger bagels sold best.) But

when Petrofsky's made the decision to export, Japanese food inspectors refused to allow the bagel dough into the country because of the "active bacteria" in the dough. Of course, that bacteria was yeast, which makes bread and bagels rise. To solve the entry problem, Shapiro joined forces with Itochu, a large Japanese trading company. Itochu used its local influence to get Petrofsky's product certified.

By 1993, Petrofsky's annual revenues were up to $12 million, with $1.5 million representing international sales. Not bad for a company that started as a neighborhood bakery! In 1994, the company opened its own retail bagel stores in Tokyo to complement its wholesale business.

Shapiro has learned that choosing the right partner is a critical decision when entering foreign markets. When he tried to expand into Europe, he says, he chose the wrong person—neither side trusted the other completely. After finally terminating that relationship, Petrofsky's found itself three years behind schedule for its European expansion.

Source: Adapted from Rob Norton, "Strategies for the New Export Boom," Fortune, August 22, 1994, pp. 124–130.

he stumbled upon information about growing alcohol-related problems in Argentina. A little more investigation revealed a sizable opportunity for his company.

Most small businesses begin their search for market information from U.S. government sources. The Department of Commerce's *National Trade Data Bank (NTDB)* is a rich source of information. Available at federal libraries on CD-ROM, the NTDB contains more than 100,000 documents on export promotion and international economic information.[13] With the *Automated Trade Locator Assistance System (SBAtlas)* the SBA provides current market information to small businesses on foreign markets where their products are being bought and sold and on which countries comprise the largest markets. SBAtlas is available at your local SBA office.

Canada, Japan, and Mexico top the list of importers of products made in the United States. (See Figure 12-3.) More detailed information on foreign markets for small businesses is available through sources like *Inc.* magazine's Going Global series. (See Figures 12-4, 12-5, and 12-6.)

Define Export Markets that Match Your Product.   After you have identified potential countries, you must find out if a need exists there that you can satisfy. You should ask yourself:

- How does the quality of products in the foreign country compare with your products?
- Will your prices be competitive?
- Can you segment customers?
- Are there political risks in the country you are considering?

Entering the Internet

The Internet and World Wide Web are a veritable treasure trove of information on different countries and doing business with these countries. The National Trade Data Bank is a one-stop source for export promotion and international trade data collected by various U.S. government agencies. However, be aware that a fee is charged for accessing information from this site. You could also try any of the Web search engines (such as Yahoo, WebCrawler, Lycos, and others, as described in Entering the Internet in earlier chapters) to find relevant business information on a specific country. Also, the U.S. Council for International Business provides broad information on international business topics. You can, however, also access specific country Web sites. For instance, if you're interested in Russian and Eastern European countries, try Russian and East European Studies Business and Economic Resources. The Pacific Region Forum on Business and Management Communication provides information on Pacific Rim (Asian) countries. Other Web addresses for specific countries are listed in the Internet section in Chapter 8.

National Trade Data Bank: http://www.stat-usa.gov/

Russian and East European Studies Business and Economic Resource: http://www.pitt.edu/~cjp/rsecon.html/

Pacific Region Forum on Business and Management Communication: gopher://hoshi.cic.sfu.ca/11/dlam/business/forum/

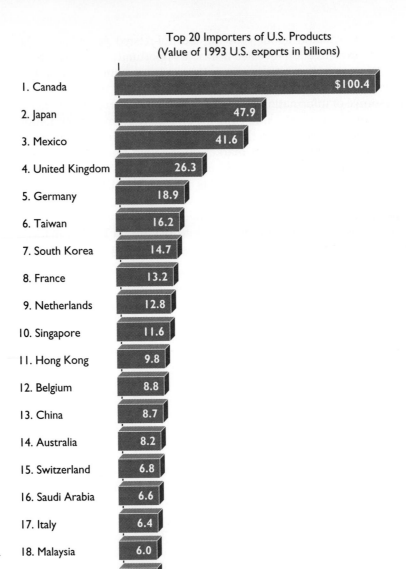

Top 20 Importers of U.S. Products
(Value of 1993 U.S. exports in billions)

1. Canada — $100.4
2. Japan — 47.9
3. Mexico — 41.6
4. United Kingdom — 26.3
5. Germany — 18.9
6. Taiwan — 16.2
7. South Korea — 14.7
8. France — 13.2
9. Netherlands — 12.8
10. Singapore — 11.6
11. Hong Kong — 9.8
12. Belgium — 8.8
13. China — 8.7
14. Australia — 8.2
15. Switzerland — 6.8
16. Saudi Arabia — 6.6
17. Italy — 6.4
18. Malaysia — 6.0
19. Brazil — 6.0
20. Venezuela — 4.5

U.S. exports in 1993 totaled $464 billion

FIGURE 12-3
Top 20 Importers of U.S. Products
U.S. exports in 1993 were valued at $464 billion.
Source: Roberta Maynard, "A Good Time To Export," Reprinted by permission, Nation's Business *(May 1994) p. 23. © 1994, U.S. Chamber of Commerce.*

- Will your products need any modifications?
- Will tariffs or nontariff barriers (restrictions or quotas) prevent your entry into the market?

The Department of Commerce and the Small Business Administration produce various publications and reports to help provide this information. The Department of State gathers information on foreign markets through consulates and embassies. Foreign affiliates of the U.S. Chamber of Commerce, called *American Chambers of Commerce (AmChams),* also collect and disseminate information.

Export Product Classification. To be able to gather data from government sources about markets for your product you need to know their classification number or

MEXICO AT A GLANCE

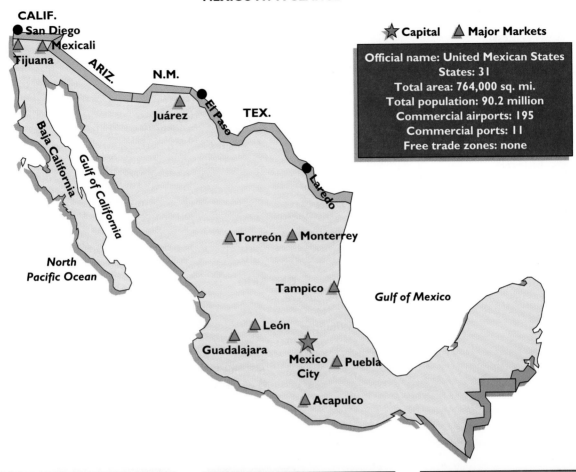

★ Capital   ▲ Major Markets

Official name: United Mexican States
States: 31
Total area: 764,000 sq. mi.
Total population: 90.2 million
Commercial airports: 195
Commercial ports: 11
Free trade zones: none

Business Pulse Rates	
Imports from U.S.	$40.6b
% Change ('91–92)	+21.9%
Exports to U.S.	$35.2b
% Change ('91–92)	+12.8%
Exchange rate (N$/US$)	N$3.12
GDP ('92)	$317.0b
'93 Growth (projected)	2.8%
Unemployment (1 Q. '93)	7.5%
Avg. min. wage (US$/day)	$4.30
Organized labor	35%
Taxes—Corporate rate	35%
VAT (general rate)	10%
Inflation (% change in CPI)	11.9%

Sources: U.S. Embassy (Mexico City), U.S. Department of Commerce

Mexico's World Ranking	
U.S. trading partner	3rd
Air traffic (no. passengers)	7th
Population	10th
Area	12th
Natural gas	6th
Oil reserves	7th
Mining	9th
Agriculture	11th
Manufacturing	13th
GDP	15th

Source: Mexican Investment Board

Major Markets (population)	
Mexico City	20.2 million
Guadalajara	3.3 million
Monterrey	2.8 million
Puebla	776,000
Juárez	720,000
León	708,000
Tijuana	640,000
Acapulco	505,000
Torreón	476,000
Tampico	450,000
Mexicali	433,000

FIGURE 12-4
Mexico at a Glance

CANADA AT A GLANCE

★ Major metropolitan areas (pop. 600,000+)
▲ Manufacturing Center

Economy's Pulse Rates	
GDP ('92)	US$612.3b
'93 Growth (projected)	2.8%
Inflation (CPI)	2.1%
Prime rate	6.25%
Exports to U.S.	US$101.2b
Imports from U.S.	US$96.5b
% Change ('91-92)	9.3%
Exchange Rate	US$1=C$1.246
Goods & Svcs. Tax (GST)	7%
Sales taxes (provincial)	8%-9%*
Unemployment	11%
Unionized labor	31%
Average hourly wage	C$14.72*

*Average; varies by province   Sources: Statistics Canada, Inc.

Prospects by Province

Ontario (pop. 10.1M)
  3.0% growth   consumer spending lags
Quebec (pop. 6.9M)
  3.6% growth   construction weak
British Columbia (pop. 3.3M)
  3.7% growth   mining slow
Alberta (pop. 2.5M)
  4.6% growth   farm income down
Manitoba (pop. 1.1M)
  2.5% growth   construction sluggish
Saskatchewan (pop. 989,000)
  3.2% growth   construction dip, farm income dive
Nova Scotia (pop. 900,000)
  1.7% growth   13.1% jobless
New Brunswick (pop. 724,000)
  2.6% growth   services & fishing down
Newfoundland (pop. 568,000)
  2.1% growth   20.9% jobless
Prince Edward Island (pop. 130,000)
  2.3% growth   17.2% unemployment

Sources: The Conference Board of Canada

FIGURE 12-5
Canada at a Glance

Adapted with permission, Inc., *magazine, 1993.* © 1993 by Gold-hirsh Group, Inc., 38 Commercial Wharf, Boston, MA 02110.

JAPAN AT A GLANCE

Prefecture (states): 47
Total area: 145,856 sq. mi.
Total population: 124.5 million
Commercial airports: 131
Commercial ports: 18
Free trade zones: none

Business Pulse Rates	
Imports from U.S.	$48.1b
% Change ('92–93)	+0.01%
Exports to U.S.	$101.9b
% Change ('92–93)	+4.6%
Exchange rate (¥/US$)	107
January '93 rate (¥/US$)	125
GDP ('92)	$2,891.3b
'93 Growth (projected)	0.2%
Inflation (% change in CPI)	1.1%
Unemployment	2.1%
Organized labor	27%

Sources: Japan Economic Institute, U.S. Department of State

Top 10 Manufacturing Companies (No. of employees)		
Hitachi	290,800	[2]*
Matsushita Electric	198,300	[3]
Toshiba	142,000	[5]
Nissan Motor	129,500	[4]
Fujitsu	115,000	[11]
NEC	114,600	[7]
Toyota Motor	96,800	[1]
Sony	95,600	[10]
Bridgestone	95,300	[16]
Mitsubishi Electric	89,100	[8]

Source: MITI   *Rank by total sales

Major Markets (1 million+ population)	
Tokyo	8.5 million
Yokohama	3.2 million
Osaka	2.5 million
Nagoya	2.1 million
Sapporo	1.7 million
Kobe	1.4 million
Kyoto	1.4 million
Fukuoka	1.2 million
Kawasaki	1.2 million
Hiroshima	1.1 million
Kitakyushu	1.0 million

Source: Japan Ministry of Home Affairs

FIGURE 12-6
Japan at a Glance

numbers. The U.S. government classifies products by a system called the *Standard Industrial Classification (SIC)*. The *Standard International Trade Classification (SITC)* number assigned to your products will help you find data from international organizations. To export, all documentation will need to contain your products *Harmonized System (HS)* classification number.

Importing

When your small business is importing rather than exporting, the major focus of your activities shifts from supplying to sourcing. You need to identify markets making products that you see a demand for domestically.

Factors to consider when choosing a foreign supplier include its reliability in having products available for you, the consistency of product or service quality, and the delivery time needed to get products to you. A bank subsidiary office, and the embassy of the supplier's home country are sources for this information.

As an importer, you must comply with the regulations and trade barriers of both the foreign country and the United States. You must make sure that your product can legally cross national borders. For example, cigars made in Cuba cannot be imported into the United States because of an embargo against that country. The United States also has import quotas that limit the amount of products like steel and beef that can be brought in. The intent of such quotas is to protect domestic industries and jobs, although their results are not completely positive. Debate over trade restrictions are, and will be for years, a topic of political discussion. You should try to stay as current as possible on trade and tariff regulations if you are involved in global trade.

Establishing Business in Another Country

A vast majority of small business activity in the international market will be conducted via importing and exporting. Still, for the experienced, visionary, and adventurous businessperson, other options exist which represent an even greater

 Global Small Business

Anthony Raissen knew from personal experience that he needed a product that could cleanse his breath, especially after eating the spicy foods that he loved. And it's a problem faced by many people. Yet he found gum, mints, candies, and other breath aids didn't do the job. These products tended to mask the bad breath as opposed to eliminating it. During a trip to his native South Africa, Raissen was introduced to a group of chemists who had developed a formula of parsley seed oil and sunflower oil that worked like magic on the bad breath problem. Raissen bought the rights to the formula and returned to the United States to form BreathAsure, Inc. of Calabasas, California. Selling this product, Raissen's company has achieved annual sales revenues of nearly $18 million. In fact, responding to consumer demand, the company released in late 1995 Pure Breath, a version of the original BreathAsure product designed for dogs and cats—another obvious target market for this imported formula. *Source: Tom Stein, "The Sweet Smell of Success," Success (December 1995), p. 23.*

Computer Applications

Many small business owners and managers faced with the prospect of completing all the documentation necessary for operating a successful exporting/importing business would just throw up their hands in frustration. The paperwork involved can seem overwhelming. However, there are software packages to help make the process more tolerable. These programs are not inexpensive, but if you're intending to make a major commitment to global exports and imports, the cost would be well worth it in terms of time and energy—and frustration—saved.

One of the best programs is the EMS-2000 (Version 4.0 for Windows) available from Export Software International (ESI) of Reston, Virginia (703-648-9256). This package offers international businesses a virtually paperless export office. The EMS-2000 produces commercial invoices, packing lists, export summaries for the U.S. Shippers Export Declaration form, bills of lading, and certificates of origin. This information can be transmitted via fax or e-mail to almost any worldwide location that has a fax machine or computer. The drawback is that the system starts at $40,000, but keep in mind it's a complete source for helping you deal with export/import paperwork.

Another product is called EX-TRA, developed by Syntra Ltd. of New York (212-714-0440). This package starts at $25,000 and it can automate your exporting function all the way from initial quotation to invoicing to shipping. Finally, one lower-priced program you might check into is XDOC from Seattle-based Interactive Designs Inc. (800-863-0389). Its cost is $495 for a single user, $995 for a network of four users, and $100 for each additional user. Although its features aren't as extensive as the higher-priced software, XDOC creates basic export documents and just might be the thing for smaller businesses starting out in global markets.

Sources: Joe Dysart, "Export Documentation: Bringing It All Back Home," Distribution (May 1994), pp. 46–49; and Rhonda Reynolds, "Managing Traffic Overseas," Black Enterprise, (February 1995), pp. 52–54.

commitment to global trade. Small businesses can license their products or services, form joint ventures or strategic alliances, or even set up their own operations to conduct business in other countries.

International Licensing

As an exporter, you can stop exporting at anytime you wish. However, other forms of international business represent a larger commitment on your part. The next level of commitment in international business above exporting is **licensing.** As a licenser you are contractually obligated to another business for a period of time.

Licensing is a way to enter foreign markets by assigning the rights to your patents, trademarks, copyrights, processes, or products to another company in exchange for a fee or royalty. The two biggest advantages of licensing are speed of entry and cost. You can enter a foreign market quickly for virtually no capital. Licensing is similar to franchising domestically. Licensing agreements are generally written to endure for a specified period of time. A disadvantage of licensing is that your licensee may become your competitor after the agreement expires if it continues to use your licensed process without paying you for it.

licensing The agreement that allows one business to sell the rights to use a business process or product to another business in a foreign country.

International Joint Ventures and Strategic Alliances

joint venture An agreement in which two businesses form a temporary partnership to produce a product or service a market that neither could satisfy alone.

A foreign **joint venture** is a partnership between your business and a business in another country. As with any partnership, choosing the right partner is critical to the success of the venture. Each of you need to bring something (products, knowledge, channel of distribution, access to a market, or other quality) to the venture that the other would not have alone.

Partnerships of *any* type can be difficult (see Chapter 2). Joint ventures are often costly failures. A study by Columbia University shows a success rate of only 43 percent, with an average life span of 3.5 years.[14] Despite the difficulties, joint ventures and strategic alliances are and will be needed to be competitive globally. Finding a local partner is the only way to enter some countries.

Following are seven advantages that often work in combination to improve your chances of forming a successful joint venture:

- Penetrating protected markets.
- Entering heavily concentrated industries.
- Lowering production costs.
- Sharing risks and high R&D costs.
- Preventing competitive alliances.
- Maximizing marketing and distribution channels.
- Gaining leverage over a supplier and strategic knowledge of a supplier's products.[15]

strategic alliance A partnership between two businesses (often in different countries) that is more informal than a joint venture.

Strategic alliances are not exactly the same as joint ventures.[16] Lorraine Segil, of the Lared Group, specializes in establishing strategic alliances, helping to match small organizations with large ones through a chain of contacts in the United States, Europe, the United Kingdom, and Australia. The match is often made between a large well-established company abroad that needs fresh ideas and products. Since many entrepreneurial firms have just that but only limited capital, the result is often a profitable alliance for both.

Direct Investment

direct investment Establishing a permanent location in a foreign country.

Once you have established your international operations, you may choose to set up a permanent location in another country. Opening an office, factory, or store in a foreign land is the highest level of international commitment you can make. Small businesses rarely start out their global experience this way. Exporting, licensing, or joint ventures are much more common vehicles.

Mechanisms for Going Global

Once you decide to enter the international trade game, you face challenges such as how to finance your expansion, how to pay your debts and get paid, and where to find information and assistance.

International Finance

Selling overseas is only half the challenge; the other half is finding the money to fill the order.[17] Working capital may be needed for your new transaction level. Options for additional sources of capital include: conventional financing, venture capital from investor groups, and prepayment or down payment from overseas buyers. To start looking for export financing, contact:

The Export-Import Bank (Eximbank). The Eximbank is an independent federal agency with a program that covers 100 percent of working capital for a commercial loan. It also offers export credit insurance to protect exporters in case a foreign buyer defaults on payment. To get information on the Eximbank's programs, call (800) 424-5201.

The Small Business Administration. The SBA has several financial services for exporters, including an international trade loan program for short-term financing, and the 7(a) business loan guarantee program for medium-term working capital and long-term fixed-asset financing. The SBA's free booklet on export finance is titled *Bankable Deals*.

A problem for most small businesses is that of getting paid. Most small businesses do not have the financial resources to carry excessive accounts receivable, which can be amplified by selling in other countries. In the United States, the average number of days needed to collect accounts receivable is 42. That's quite a while for a small business to have money outstanding, but the international branch of the National Association of Credit Management says there are countries that average much longer. (See Table 12-1.)[18]

Managing International Accounts

Your primary financial concern as a global operator should be to ensure that you get paid in full and on time. Keep in mind that your foreign buyers will be concerned about receiving products on time that meet their specifications. Thus, terms of payment must be agreed upon in advance in a way that satisfies both parties.

The primary methods of paying for international transactions follow, ranked from most secure for the exporter at the top of the list to least secure at the bottom:

Payment in Advance. Requiring clients to pay in advance provides the least risk to you, but unless you have an extremely specialized product, the buyer can probably get a better deal from someone else. Still, it is reasonable to negotiate partial payment and/or progress payments.

Letter of Credit. A letter of credit is an internationally recognized instrument issued by a bank on behalf of its client, the purchaser. It is a guarantee that the bank will pay the seller if the conditions specified are fulfilled.

Documentary Collection (Drafts). Drafts are documents which require the buyer to pay the seller the face amount either when the product arrives (called a sight draft) or at a specified time in the future (called a time draft). Since title does not pass until the draft is paid, both parties are protected. Drafts involve a certain amount of risk but are cheaper for the purchaser than letters of credit.

TABLE 12 ▪ 1   We'll Get Paid When???

COUNTRY	AVERAGE DAYS OUTSTANDING
Iran	310
Syria	175
Kenya	143
Ethiopia	138
Argentina	121
Uruguay	120
Tunisia	116
Chile	109
Ecuador	107
Cameroon	106
Morocco	105
Algeria	103

Source: Jill Andresky Fraser, "How Bad Can Collections Get?" Inc., March 1993, p. 94.

Consignment.   Selling on consignment means that you advance your product to an intermediary who tries to sell it to the final user. If you sell on consignment, you don't get paid until the intermediary sells the product. Consignment is risky because there is no way of knowing when, if ever, the goods will be sold.

Open Account.   While commonly used in selling products in the United States, delivering goods before payment is required is very risky for international sales. If the creditworthiness of the buyers, or the political and economic stability of their country, are questionable, you stand to lose your entire investment, possibly without recourse.[19]

Countertrade and Barter

A problem encountered in trading with many economically emerging countries (such as many Eastern European and former Soviet countries) is that their currency is virtually worthless outside their borders. A solution to this problem may be **countertrade.** While countertrade takes several forms, it is basically substituting a product for money as part of the transaction. While countertrade is not often a long-term solution, it may be a tool to make deals that could not be made otherwise.[20]

countertrade The completion of a business deal without the use of money as a means of exchange. Barter is a common form of countertrade.

The most common form of countertrade that small businesses can use is **barter.**[21] This type of trading has existed throughout history. In countertrade, some creativity may be needed to find a business that has complementary needs. Pepsico arranged creative trades within the former Soviet Union by trading soft drinks for vodka. The vodka was worth much more on the open market than the ruble and was much easier to sell. You may make deals just as creatively.

The key to making money in countertrade is to have somewhere to sell the goods you get in trade. Swapping your product for something you can't get rid of is no bargain.

Information Assistance

In addition to the information assistance cited throughout the chapter, help is available from your state export office (it may be listed under your state economic development office). The AT&T Export Hotline (800-872-9767) is a good

Changes Here + There = International Opportunity

Small businesses must often react to volatile external changes—changes beyond their control that may threaten the way they have done business. Highly regulated businesses, like those producing medical supplies, have enjoyed relative stability and predictability for some time. But it is dangerous to think that a stable environment will stay the same forever.

Integrated Surgical Systems (ISS) Inc. manufactures the Robodoc surgical-assistant system, a 3-D computer imaging and robotic arm which helps surgeons plan and perform total hip replacements. When ISS began producing medical devices in 1990, approval from the U.S. Food and Drug Administration (FDA) took two to four years. While that may seem like a long time for a startup to wait to bring a product to market, ISS knew about it and planned for it. Because technologically innovative firms like ISS expect a high rate of return, investors are willing to underwrite them, anticipating certain delays. ISS planned to introduce products in the United States and then distribute them in Europe and the Far East.

Events over the next two years, however, dramatically altered ISS's plans. A new commissioner took over the FDA, and some well-publicized problems with medical devices (such as heart valves and breast implants) led to changes in the FDA's approval process. The approval process became much longer and the environment was changing. ISS, which had initially planned on a three-year approval process, was now facing a best-case scenario of six years.

ISS's reaction? Radically reevaluate and change its rollout strategy for new products. ISS decided to introduce the new product in Europe first, then the Far East, and ultimately bring it to the United States. ISS became an international business much sooner than expected because other countries offered less stringent approval procedures. Today, this strategy is not uncommon for medical-device firms.

ISS is another example of a small business that has successfully responded to an unexpectedly changing environment. Small businesses need to respond to market demands and conditions.

Source: Bela Musits, "When Big Changes Happen to Small Companies," Inc. (August 1994), pp. 27–28.

"fax-back" service to provide demographics, industry reports that assess market conditions, competition, and the best sales opportunities for countries of your choice.[22]

One of the best one-stop sources of addresses, telephone numbers, fax numbers, and office names for global assistance is a book copublished by the SBA and AT&T titled *Breaking Into the Trade Game: A Small Business Guide to Exporting*. This book also includes a step-by-step guide for developing your international business plan.

The International Challenge

Success for many small businesses will increasingly depend on some degree of sales to markets in other countries. Global business presents quite a few challenges, but then, most entrepreneurs thrive on challenge. There are no hard and fast rules for going global, and space does not permit coverage of every situation you may face, but some issues you need to be aware of are cultural differences, global trading regions (especially NAFTA), GATT, and ISO 9000 quality certification.

Understanding Other Cultures

When marketing your product globally, you must think and act globally. This means you need to be sensitive to cultural beliefs that vary from country to country. Every culture has different accepted norms and ways of doing business. Not understanding and not following these norms can lead to embarrassment for you at the least, to completely blowing your deal at the worst. In the United States a pat on the back says "attaboy," while in Japan it is a sign of disrespect. Nodding your head means "no" in Bulgaria, and shaking your head side to side means "yes," the opposite of American customs.[23]

Training employees you send overseas can help them adjust to cultural differences so they can perform their jobs better.[24] There are several types of programs available that provide cross-cultural training beyond training in foreign language. These global training programs generally involve six overlapping categories: cultural awareness, multicultural communication, country-specific training, executive development, language courses, and host-country work force training.[25]

Customs like gift giving are important to understand. Gifts from business partners are expected in some cultures, but they are considered offensive in others. Should you present the gift on the first meeting or afterward? In public or private? To whom? What kind of gift is appropriate? In Japan, gifts are exchanged to symbolize the depth and strength of a business relationship.[26] When dealing with a Japanese business, the first meeting is the appropriate time for exchanging gifts; if you are presented with a gift, you are expected to respond with one in return. By contrast, gifts are rarely exchanged in Germany, Belgium, or the United Kingdom.

Exchanging business cards is no big deal, right? Wrong. Taking someone's card and immediately putting it in your pocket is considered very rude in Japan. You should carefully look at the card, observe the title and organization, acknowledge with a nod, and make a relevant comment or question. Even presenting your business card has a proper protocol in Japan or South Korea. You should use both hands and present the card so the other person can read it. If English is not the primary language, you should print the native language on the reverse side.

Language is another obvious problem. You cannot depend on what you might think of as "easy" transitions. In England, what they call a "lorry," "petrol," and "biscuits" are what Americans call a truck, gasoline, and a cookie. A rule of thumb to try to follow in international business is to conduct business in the buyer's language.

You are not expected to speak another language like a local, but making an attempt to learn some of the language can be a sign of good faith. Most trade specialists recommend that you employ a professional translator for written communication and absolutely have one available when you travel for face-to-face meetings.[27]

Trade experts at Moran, Stahl & Boyer International, an international consulting firm, said that culture has two components: surface culture (fads, styles,

Manager's Notebook

Goals for Globetrotters

We continue to emphasize the importance of understanding other cultures before jumping into the global marketplace. If you want your small business to be successful in another country, you'd better do your homework first! There's a lot of available information about cultural aspects, but it's going to take effort on your part to locate and digest the information. Here are some hints.

Find Out All You Can About the Culture of the Country You're Looking At. The most important cultural factors you'll want to look at include: language, religion, education, and social systems. Ask questions such as:

- How do these factors differ from my home country—what I'm most familiar with?

- How does my business or product name translate into the language? (This could affect brand-name usage, advertising, and other promotions.)

- What are the recognized religious holidays and customs? (They could affect when, where, and how you conduct business.)

- What is the average educational level of your potential customers? (This could impact the type of employee training needed or packaging and advertising decisions.)

- What are the accepted and practiced social rituals, customs and behaviors? (These could influence many different business decisions.)

And just where can you find this information? First of all, there are numerous books and other publications on cultural customs and the differences among countries. A trip to your local library can provide a wealth of sources. You could also contact international business professors or foreign language professors at a local college.

These individuals are typically highly knowledgeable about cultural factors, or at the very least, they can point you toward other information. If you know someone who has traveled to or lived in the country you're investigating, most certainly talk to that person. Such firsthand knowledge is invaluable. Another source for information would be the U.S. Department of Commerce, which has a number of programs and services for companies interested in doing business in other countries.

Enroll in a Cross-Cultural Training Course. The first place to look for a cross-cultural training course would be at a local college or university. If there's no program of this type provided there, check with your local chamber of commerce or local Small Business Administration office. These local offices might offer a course or might be able to steer you to one that's conveniently located. If these approaches yield nothing, you could always enroll in a training course offered by professional training companies. These professional courses are generally going to cost more than university or locally sponsored courses, but in return you'll be getting specific and intense training. Some selected courses and training companies include: Global Interface Skills Training offered by Moran, Stahl & Boyer International; Going Global offered by ITAP International; and Global Perspectives by Lawton International. For more information about professional global training programs, contact the American Society for Training and Development (703-683-8129).

Sources: Philip R. Cateora, International Marketing, *8th ed. (Homewood, Illinois: Richard D. Irwin, Inc.), 1993; Sylvia Odenwald, "A Guide for Global Training,"* Training and Development *(July 1993), pp. 22–31; and Mark Mendenhall, Betty Jane Punnett, and David Ricks,* Global Management *(Cambridge, Massachusetts: Blackwell Publishers), 1995.*

food, and holidays) and deep culture (norms, attitudes, values and beliefs). According to the tip-of-the iceberg concept, only 10 percent to 15 percent of a region's culture is visible. (See Figure 12-7.)[28] This means you must look below the surface to identify forces that truly drive a culture.

You can see that the cultural aspects of international business are very complicated and confusing, but their importance cannot be overstated. Doing your homework can prevent serious mistakes.

International Trading Regions

Since World War II, a major development in the world economy has been the creation of regional trade associations—the European Economic Community, the Association of Southeast Asian Nations, and the alliance created by the North American Free Trade Agreement.

Since World War II, a major development in the world economy has been the creation of regional trade groupings. That trend has accelerated in recent years. A trade region is established through agreements to create economic and political ties between nations usually located within a close geographical area. These agreements reduce trade barriers between countries within the region and standardize barriers with countries outside the region. They also intend to increase competition within them so that inefficient nationalized companies or monopolies lose their protective walls and are forced to come up to speed. Table 12-2 identifies major trading regions and the member countries.

What effect do world regions have on you and your small business? The passage of the North American Free Trade Agreement (NAFTA) was intended to open markets and to reduce barriers for you to send your products to Mexico

FIGURE 12-7
The Cultural Iceberg
Many important cultural factors are not easily seen.
Source: Kevin Walsh, "How To Negotiate European Style, Journal of European Business, *(July/August 1993). Reprinted by permission of Faulkner & Gray.*

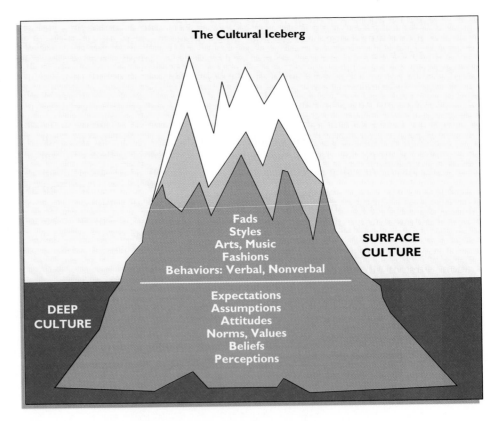

The Cultural Iceberg

Fads
Styles
Arts, Music
Fashions
Behaviors: Verbal, Nonverbal

SURFACE CULTURE

DEEP CULTURE

Expectations
Assumptions
Attitudes
Norms, Values
Beliefs
Perceptions

Recognizing an increasing shift in attitudes—part of that "deep" culture—in favor of community planning and environmental protection was a key to the global success now enjoyed by Sheily Brady. As president of Brady and Associates, a small landscape architecture firm located in Berkeley, California, she fueled her company's push into the Asian market during travels to Vietnam and China. There she met with government officials regarding urban design and environmental planning services. Brady had recognized the fact that these geographic regions had just finished a decade of unbridled and largely unrestricted economic and development growth. And she knew public and governmental officials' opinions were changing toward the use of community planning to help manage growth. Brady was able to capitalize on her assessment of the cultural change and establish a solid foothold in this market. *Source: Roberta Maynard, "Trade Tide Rises Across the Pacific," Nation's Business (November 1995), pp. 52–56.*

and Canada. Regional agreements also change your strategy for dealing with businesses in those countries. For example, since the European Community (EC) has higher tariffs and barriers for products coming from countries outside the region than for products that come from within, it may make sense for you to establish operations in an EC country if you intend to do a lot of business there. Then you can sell in any of the 12 member nations under reduced barriers.

TABLE 12 ▪ 2   Major Regional Trade Associations

North American Free Trade Agreement (NAFTA):
   United States, Canada, Mexico
European Community (EC):
   Belgium, Denmark, France, Germany, Greece, Ireland, Italy, Luxembourg, Netherlands, Portugal, Spain, United Kingdom
European Free Trade Association (EFTA):
   Austria, Finland, Iceland, Norway, Sweden, Switzerland
Latin American Integration Association (LAIA):
   Argentina, Bolivia, Brazil, Chile, Columbia, Ecuador, Mexico, Paraguay, Peru, Uruguay, Venezuela
Andean Common Market (ANCOM):
   Bolivia, Columbia, Ecuador, Peru, Venezuela
Central American Common Market (CACM):
   Costa Rica, El Salvador, Guatemala, Honduras, Nicaragua
Association of Southeast Asian Nations (ASEAN):
   Brunei, Indonesia, Malaysia, Philippines, Singapore, Thailand

NAFTA. In 1993, Congress passed the North American Free Trade Agreement joining Canada, Mexico, and the United States in a free trade area. One of the primary goals of NAFTA is to eliminate tariffs and nontariff barriers between the United States, Canada, and Mexico on nearly all qualifying goods by the year 2003.[29]

A key word here is *qualifying.* Products will qualify for tariff elimination if they **originate,** as defined in article 401 of NAFTA, in one of the three countries. For example, products that are made in Japan and are shipped through Mexico cannot enter the United States under preferential NAFTA duty rates. First, you need to determine if your products are **originating goods.** There are four primary ways for goods to qualify:

- Goods **wholly obtained or produced** in a NAFTA country
- Goods made up entirely of **components and materials** that qualify
- Goods that are **specifically cited** in an article of the agreement (very few products are cited)
- Goods that are covered under **specific rules of origin** for that product, as listed in NAFTA Annex 401. This is the most common way to qualify.[30]

Your products need to be assigned a harmonized system (HS) number. The harmonized system classifies products so their chapter, heading, and subheading numbers are identical for all three countries. For example:

Chapter 95 . . . . Toys, games, and sports requisites
Heading 95.04 . . . . .Table or parlor games
Subheading 9504.20 . . . . Articles for billiards and acc.
Tariff item 9504.20.21. . . . . Billiard tables

Once you have determined the HS number for your products, you can find the specific NAFTA rule of origin that applies. Some specific rules of origin will call for additional requirements. Usually this is a test of the product's **regional value content (RVC),** which means that a certain percentage of the product's value has to originate in a NAFTA country. For example, if the rule specifies that a good must have at least 65 percent RVC, then you need to demonstrate that at least 65 percent of the good's value originated in either Canada, the United States, or Mexico.

If your products do qualify as originating goods, you need to complete a **certificate of origin** for each product. The importer of your products must have a valid certificate to claim preferential tariff treatment. The certificate of origin shows names and addresses of the importer and the exporter, a description of the goods, the HS number, the preference criteria (how it qualified), the producer, the net cost, and the country of origin.

Don't be intimidated by the documentation process required by NAFTA. Assistance at every step of the process is available. David Hirschmann, director of Latin American affairs for the U.S. Chamber of Commerce, said, "Small business should benefit the most, not just because tariffs will be lifted, but because there will be fair and reliable rules. Products won't be held up at the border for ten days because of costly, confusing regulations."[31]

For help in determining a product's HS number, exporters can call the Census Bureau Foreign Trade division (301-763-5210) or contact your Commerce Department district office. The Commerce Department's Industrial Trade Staff

(202-482-5675) can determine the tariff rate and phase-out schedule for specific products. To understand NAFTA rules of origin and other important provisions, exporters should obtain a copy of the NAFTA agreement, available from the Government Printing Office (202-783-3238). U.S. Customs has set up a help desk for assistance on how NAFTA affects a wide variety of issues (202-927-0097). The Trade Information Center (TIC) is a convenient first stop for new exporters offering information on the export process (800-USA-TRADE). Finally, companies new to exporting should buy a copy of *A Basic Guide to Exporting* from the Government Printing Office.[32]

GATT—General Agreement on Trade and Tariffs.   The first global tariff agreement began in 1947 with the General Agreement on Tariffs and Trade (GATT). The agreement, which originally included the United States and 22 other countries, has grown to include 117 member countries that represent over 90 percent of world trade. Since GATT's inception, it has gone through eight "rounds" of negotiations or meeting sites. The latest series of negotiations, called the Uruguay Round, lasted from 1986 until 1994. One of its provisions was to create a successor to GATT, called the World Trade Organization, which has broader authority over services and agricultural products.

"GATT has created a safer, more stable environment in which to do business. Smaller companies without the resources to protect themselves in international markets will feel safer," said Mike Van Horn, president of Pacific Rim Consortium, a consulting firm that helps American businesses enter Asian-Pacific markets.[33]

ISO 9000

Quality is not just a concern among American managers who have adopted total quality management (TQM). It is also an international issue. The International Standards Organization, based in Europe, has established quality standards to show industrial customers that manufacturers' *methods* of product development and achieving quality standards are designed to assure quality.[34] The intent of ISO standards is to minimize the need for on-site visits by vendors to make sure their suppliers are producing quality products.

The process of getting your business ISO certified is time-consuming, complex, and expensive. The procedure works like this: After you document all the steps of your operations that ensure the quality of goods and services, an auditing firm visits your company to conduct a process audit and a financial audit to determine whether or not you pass. Two follow-up audits per year are required to maintain certification.

Why would a small business bother? Lori Sweningson, owner of Job Boss Software, is taking her company through the ISO certification process because she wants to sell software in Europe. Sweningson has budgeted $30,000 to $50,000 for consultant and auditor fees to get certified.[35] The payoff is expected to be the marketing tool of being ISO certified. She believes that ISO certification will soon be the minimum requirement for many international sales.

Currently, large businesses and divisions of major corporations are the ones getting ISO certified and small manufacturers are quickly following. Free information packets are available from the American Society of Quality Control (800-248-1946) or the American National Standards Institute (212-642-4900). We will revisit the topic of ISO 9000 in more depth in Chapter 15.

Summary

■ The components of an international business plan.

In addition to your domestic business plan, you need to include how you intend to enter foreign markets, which markets are the best opportunity for your business, projected costs and revenues, any contacts you have in overseas partnerships or foreign investment, and any legal requirements or restrictions you must consider.

■ The advantages and disadvantages of exporting for small businesses.

The advantages of exporting are that it offers you a way to increase sales and profits, increase your market share, reduce your dependence on existing markets, increase your competitiveness in domestic markets, satisfy a demand for your products abroad, extend your product's life cycle, stabilize seasonal sales fluctuations, sell excess production capacity, and learn about foreign competition.
The disadvantages of exporting are the expense of changing your products and promotional material, the increased costs that cut into short-term profit, time needed to receive payment which may be longer than domestic accounts, the need for additional financing, and the increased paperwork involved.

■ The five ways for small businesses to conduct international trade.

The five methods for small businesses to conduct international business are importing, exporting, licensing, joint ventures, and direct investment.

■ How small businesses can manage their finances in international trade.

In managing your finances for international trade, you must plan how to raise additional funds and how to get paid. Funding can come from your current commercial bank, the Eximbank, or with assistance from the SBA. Methods for payment include payment in advance, by letters of credit, by draft, on consignment, and by open account.

■ The challenges of international small business activity.

Some of the challenges you will face when going global include learning and adapting to cultural differences, dealing with provisions of trade regions and agreements like NAFTA and GATT, and assuring the quality of your products to customers who are not familiar with you or your business through international standards such as ISO 9000.

Questions for Review and Discussion

1. Discuss the difference between, and the advantages and disadvantages of indirect and direct exporting.
2. What is the advantage of a strategic alliance over direct investment when entering a foreign market?
3. What information should a small business owner gather before deciding to export products?

4. Why is finding financial assistance for international expansion more difficult than for domestic?

5. Why would a small business choose to license its products in other countries?

6. Choose three foreign markets and find the customs and courtesies for greetings in those countries (possibly using the Internet as a source).

7. Imagine that you own a small manufacturing business—identify the product that you produce and a foreign market that appears to be an opportunity. What country would pose a bigger risk?

8. Name a form of countertrade and when it would be appropriate to use.

9. Discuss the differences and similarities between domestic- and foreign-based intermediaries.

10. What does the Eximbank do for potential exporters? for importers?

Critical Incident

Roberto and Efrain Rodriguez have run a neon and electrical signage business in Miami since 1985. Recently, they've developed a lucrative sideline selling brightly colored neon lighting kits for cars and other vehicles. This sideline business—Motion Neon, Inc.—has reached sales levels of $2 million. However, with the passage of NAFTA, the two brothers see a lot of potential and want to expand their business into Mexico, where they think consumers will be attracted to the bright and colorful neon accessories. They've collected several pieces of information already: The main language spoken in the country is Spanish. The major religions are Protestant and Roman Catholic. Mexico's culture is characterized by a heavy dependence on family structures and community, high emphasis on titles, rank, and status, and strong emphasis on the acquisition of material goods. Economic and other trade information can be found in Figure 12-4. Oh, and one final thing, the value of the peso has been on a wild ride, reflecting the uncertainty of the economic stability of the country.

Questions

1. Working in pairs, make a list of additional information that you think the Rodriguez brothers will need before expanding their business into Mexico and why you think they need this information. Also try to indicate where you think they could find this information.

2. Assume that the Rodriguez brothers have decided to expand into Mexico by licensing their product name and technology to a business based in Mexico City. And they need to select that business—a critical decision. Using the cultural and economic information presented here, role play an interview between the Rodriguezes and a potential licensee.

Take it to the Net

We invite you to visit the Hatten page on the Prentice Hall Web site at: http://www.prenhall.com/~hattensb for this chapter's World Wide Web exercise.

VIDEO CASE
Super Supermarket

EGMANS DID NOT BEGIN AS a super supermarket chain. But this family-run business has expanded from delivering groceries with a horse and cart, to operating 50 supermarkets throughout New York and Pennsylvania. The growth of Wegmans is unique because many family-owned businesses succumb to internal management problems long before they achieve Wegmans' level of success.

Although some Wegmans stores are over 110,000 square feet and include day care, a pharmacy, video rentals, film developing, dry-cleaning, and a restaurant, they still offer customer service as if they were a small business. Competitors and executives from other industries travel to Wegmans' headquarters from all over the world to see first-hand how Wegmans is able to offer such amazing service and still keep prices competitive. *(Source: Adapted from* The Wall Street Journal Report, *Show #641, Jan. 7, 1995)*

Discussion Questions

- The point was made in the video that the biggest mistake Wegmans could make would be a too-rapid expansion and loss of management controls. How can a business grow too rapidly? What type of controls could they lose?
- What human resource management practices can you see Wegmans using to keep employees from joining unions?
- What type of layout does Wegmans use?

Chapter Focus

After reading this chapter, you should be able to:

- Describe the functions and activities of managing a small business.
- Explain the stages of growth and their consequences on your business.
- Discuss the significance of leadership to small business.
- Explain the importance of motivation in small business.
- Compare the positive and negative aspects of total quality management (TQM) for small business.

13 Professional Small Business Management

S CEO OF VECTRA MARKETING Services, Craig Taylor is just as competitive as he was when he was captain of the Ohio State basketball team. He sees his employees as teammates and thinks of business as a game. When everyone is on the same team, information should be shared about *why* people have to perform on their jobs. Taylor is among the ranks of small business owners who are helping transform American management, focusing on teamwork rather than individual effort.

Business can be seen as a game because *everyone* in a company, not just the key executives, has a stake in the business's succeeding, profiting, and growing. Everyone's livelihood is at risk if the company loses. This perspective is different than the traditional approach to management, which reacts to business problems like weak cash flow or low profit margins with memos, meetings, and orders. Instead, the game players set up a game with rules that everyone understands, offering some kind of payoff when the problem is solved and the game won.

At the end of 1992, Taylor gave his 54 employees two choices for the next year's bonus plan. They could take a 5 percent raise and be given the chance to share a $200,000 bonus pool if targets were met. Or they could forego the raise and have a chance at a $400,000 pool. Bonuses in this latter case would be tied to hitting four targets: sales, operating expenses, inventory accuracy, and the current ratio. Employees voted 48 to 6 to go for the option with no guaranteed raise, bigger bonus pool, and nothing if the goals were not hit. At the end of the game, goals for inventory accuracy and sales were hit, so employees shared only half of the bonus pool. Still, most did better than if they had gone for the raise. For 1994, targets were adjusted and the game was started over. If employees win the game, bonuses could add 15 percent to 20 percent to their earnings.

If you are like Nancy Cohen of Published Image, a newsletter and publishing company, and don't care for the term *game*, fine—call it something else. But Cohen's company still has teams and captains, coaches (not managers), and scoreboards (for teams to monitor progress). Since changing to this way of doing business (that is, teams with bonuses tied to sales and quality that allow players to "win" up to 40 percent over their base pay), Published Image's earnings are up 35 percent and customer satisfaction is up 78 percent.

A game approach to managing a small business appears to change the company in two important ways. First, instead of different parts of the business engaged in internal rivalry, everyone is on the same team—against the competition. Second, people not only help set their own goals, they can see how they are doing and what needs to be done to win. *Source: Adapted from John Case, "Games Companies Play," with permission of Inc. magazine, October 1994, pp. 46–56. © 1994 by Goldhirsh Group, Inc.*

Managing Small Business

Businesses of every size must be managed or they will cease to exist. While there are many similarities between managing a large business and a small one, significant differences exist also. Managing a small business is a complex job. You have to perform many activities well without the resources of your large competitors. The expectations of customers, associates, and employees are raising to the point that small businesses can rarely survive without understanding the tools and practices of professional management. In this chapter we will investigate the processes of managing a growing business, of leading people, and of facing concerns of a small business owner.

The Four Functions of Management

The functions of management are generally accepted to be planning, organizing, leading, and controlling a company. To an extent, these are the broad functions that a manager performs whether she is in charge of a large or a small operation, of a for-profit or a nonprofit organization, or of a retail, service, or manufacturing business. These four functions are *continuous* and *interrelated*. (See Figure 13-1.) Managers do each of them all the time. You don't have the luxury of getting out of bed in the morning and saying, "I think I am going to just organize today." Rather you will have to do some planning, some organizing, a lot of leading, and some controlling every day.

These four functions are interrelated in that there is a progressive cycle to their achievement. Planning begins the process as the manager determines what to do. Organizing involves assembling the resources (financial, human, or material) to accomplish the plan. Leading is the process of getting the most output possible from those resources. Controlling is comparing what was initially planned with what was actually accomplished. If a deviation exists between what was planned and what was done (which is almost always the case), a new plan is needed and the cycle begins again.

What Managers Do

Management is getting things done through people. When running a small business, you will have to spend a certain amount of time performing the actual duties and daily tasks of the business—probably more during the early stages in the life of the business and less later. You must decide where to strike the balance between doing and managing. This doesn't mean that managers don't "do" anything. It means that the time that you spend on the daily tasks like selling, or writing new software, or cleaning machinery is time that you are not managing. Those tasks have to be done, and the small business owner is usually the one who has to do them, but managing a business is more than a collection of tasks.

First-time managers and business owners often think of management as doing the job they have previously done, only with more power and control. Rather, to use an analogy of an orchestra, a novice business owner or manager must move from being a musician who concentrates on playing one instrument to being the conductor who brings the talents of each musician together and knows every instrument.[1]

While the four functions described previously are as generally true today as they were in 1916 when first articulated by Henri Fayol, there is more to describing what managers *do*. Henry Mintzberg has gone to considerable depth in searching for descriptions of how managers spend their time.[2]

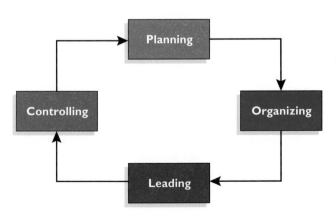

FIGURE 13-1
The Four Functions of Management
The functions of managing a business are continuous and interrelated.

First, rather than being reflective, systematic planners, managers tend to work at an unrelenting pace on a wide variety of activities that are brief and have little continuity. The front-line managers in Mintzberg's study averaged 583 activities per eight-hour day—one every 48 seconds. Half of CEOs' activities lasted less than nine minutes and only 10 percent took longer than one hour.

Second, rather than managers having no regular duties to perform, Mintzberg found that they spend a lot of time on regular duties, such as performing rituals and ceremonies, negotiating, and dealing with the external environment. Managers must receive visitors, take care of customers, and preside at Christmas parties and other rituals and ceremonies that are part of their job, whether the business is large or small.

Third, even though management is often viewed as a technological science, information processing and decision making remain locked in the manager's brains. Managers are people who depend on judgment and intuition more than technology. Computers are important for the business's specialized work, but managers still greatly depend on word-of-mouth information for almost all their decisions. A manager's job is complex, difficult, and as much an art as a science.

Mintzberg suggests several important skills a manager needs to plan, organize, lead, and control.[3] A small business manager needs to:

- Develop relationships with peers
- Carry out negotiations
- Motivate subordinates
- Resolve conflicts
- Establish information networks and then disseminate information
- Make decisions in conditions of extreme ambiguity in allocating resources
- Most important, a manager must be willing to continually learn on the job.

effectiveness Actions that achieve your goals.

As a manager, you must use your resources *efficiently* and *effectively*. The difference is more than an exercise in semantics. **Effectiveness** means achieving your stated goals. Having a helicopter fly you everywhere you go (across town to meetings, to the grocery store, to a ballgame) is an effective way to travel. You get where you intend to go. But with the reality of limited resources, effectiveness alone is not enough.

efficiency The accomplishment of goals while making the best use of available resources.

Efficiency, by contrast, involves accomplishing goals and tasks while making the best use of the resources required. In running a small business, you have to get the job done, but you have to contain costs also. Wasting your limited resources—for instance, on helicopter rides—even though you accomplish your goals will lead to bankruptcy just as fast as if you were not making sales. A small business manager must balance effectiveness and efficiency to be competitive.

Growth

Growth is a natural, and usually desirable, consequence of being in business. Growth of your business can be seen in several forms, but not necessarily all at once. We see it in revenues, total sales, number of customers, number of employees, products offered, and facilities needed. It is something to be expected and planned for as your business evolves, but it should not be an end in itself.

Global Small Business

Katherine Allen of Springfield, Missouri, runs a company that specializes in oil-cleanup products and services. She estimates that half of her company's nearly $4 million in annual sales comes from exports to locations ranging from Singapore to São Paulo. Because her business is in a field traditionally dominated by men, she's had to expend significant time and energy building this global business. She says, however, that her company's success in global markets is due to her efforts to understand her markets and her customers. This type of knowledge is invaluable for any small business owner wanting to expand into global markets. *Source: Amy Barrett, "It's a Small [Business] World," Business Week, April 17, 1995, pp. 96–101.*

Growth brings change to what your business needs and does, but bigger is not necessarily better. A sunflower is not better than a violet.

As your business makes upward progress, you will experience "growing pains" like people do as they move through childhood, adolescence, and adulthood. Signals of growing pains can be jobs that are not delivered on time, costs that rise out of control, or feelings that chaos is reigning. Such signals can indicate that your business has grown to a point where your staff or operating structure can't match the rising demands. Breakdowns in customer service and product quality soon follow.[4] Managing growth is a difficult part of managing a small business because of the transitions needed as your business passes from one stage to another.

The Growing Firm

When a business grows in size by increasing its number of employees and its volume of sales, the way in which it is managed must also change. As it evolves from a bare-bones startup to an expanded, mature firm, there are roughly four stages that it may pass through. Naturally, not all small businesses are the same size at startup, nor do they all seek to achieve the same level of growth in maturity. Yet these four stages provide a way to understand the changing needs of your business.

In the first or **solo stage,** the owner runs the business by herself. (See Figure 13-2.) While not every business begins as one individual running (and being) the entire business, it is not uncommon. In fact, technology is making the solo type of business much more common than ever. (See Reality Check, "Flying Solo," in Chapter 1.) Personal computers connected via modems and networks have allowed the creation of electronic cottage industries out of peoples' homes. So while some people intentionally keep their businesses at the solo stage, it represents the first stage of growth.

A business enters the **second stage** of growth when other people are hired. Now the entrepreneur is no longer just responsible for her own efforts. Management begins because the entrepreneur must now get work done through other people rather than trying to accomplish everything that needs to be done alone.

When the business grows to the point that employees operate within several departments, the entrepreneur must either become a professional manager

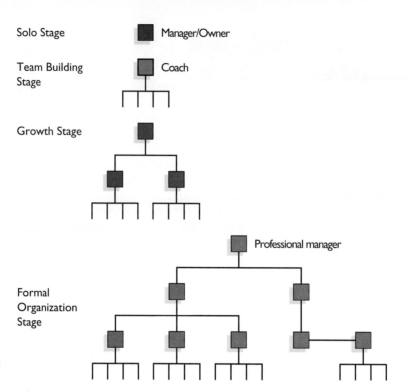

Solo Stage — Manager/Owner

Team Building Stage — Coach

Growth Stage

Professional manager

Formal Organization Stage

FIGURE 13-2
Stages of Business Growth
Businesses tend to evolve through four stages as they grow from single-person firms to full-fledged businesses.

or hire managerial expertise. **Stage three** occurs when a level of supervision is added. At this point the entrepreneur is performing less of the daily production herself and may not be in direct contact with part of the company's efforts. The small business owner must turn loose more of the "doing" and assume more of the "managing." Turning loose in this way can be hard.

Carey Stacy began Dialogos International Corp., a foreign-language service company, as a solo business. The business prospered and more teachers and staff were added, but Dialogos was typical of a business whose growth potential was stunted because it was dependent on one key individual—Stacy, the owner. Until Stacy was elected president of the National Association of Women Business owners (NAWBO), she was a very hands-on owner. But because of the extensive travel she undertook for NAWBO, jobs were being lost waiting on Stacy's desk for her to return and make a decision. Stacy realized that she simply had to turn over the day-to-day decisions of Dialogos to employees. Although she didn't realize it at the time, she was creating a management system that functioned no matter who was staffing it—a key to growing a successful business. It turned out to be the best thing that could have happened to her and her business.

In the fourth **formal organization stage,** the business has grown to include multiple departments managed by numerous supervisors. As with the preceding stages, the owner is still the "head honcho" here, but now his responsibilities are more conceptual than technical in nature. That is, rather than focusing on daily operations—making and selling the product or service—he will more exclusively focus on managing the bigger picture—through long-range planning and overseeing supervisors, for instance. The business now needs someone to establish policies, handbooks, job descriptions, training, and budgets, and the owner will now assume those executive duties. In this stage, the entrepreneur must either go through the difficult metamorphosis of becoming a professional manager, hire someone else to run the business and step out of the way, or sell the firm.

None of these four stages is inherently better or worse than the others. Competitive advantage can be drawn from the speed and adaptability of a solo business or from the muscle achieved from growing a larger organization. Problems occur at every stage also, but their magnitude is intensified when growth occurs too rapidly. Cash flow can turn negative, quality can suffer, and employees can lose the vision of the business. Growth has to be managed, and it is not a heresy to try to limit the size of your business.[5]

Transition to Professional Management

The transition from entrepreneur to professional manager is difficult because the same skills or characteristics that were needed to establish and run the business in the startup phase are not the same skills needed to manage a larger business.[6] The transition from an entrepreneurial style of running a business to a managerial approach can be complicated by factors such as:

1. A highly centralized decision-making system in which few or none of the business decisions are made by employees.
2. An overdependence on one or two key individuals with little delegation.
3. An entrepreneur's inadequate repertoire of managerial skills and training in all areas of the business.
4. A paternalistic atmosphere within the company which leads to employees' reluctance to act without clearance from the entrepreneur.[7]

In one study, 121 CEOs of *Inc.* 500 firms were asked about their most significant problem during their first year of operation and during a later period when their business grew rapidly. (See Table 13-1.)[8] Their responses provide practical insight to the differences in problems faced during those two periods of business development.

Note that problems associated with securing external financing and product development declined in the growth period. At the same time problems related

TABLE 13 ▪ 1   What's Bugging You?

	STARTUP	GROWTH
Obtain external financing	17%	1%
Internal financial management	16%	22%
Sales and marketing	38%	23%
Product development	5%	2%
Production and operations management	4%	8%
General management	11%	14%
Human resource management	5%	17%
Economic environment	3%	2%
Regulatory environment	1%	8%

Source: David Terpstra and Philip Olson, "Entrepreneurial Startup and Growth: A Classification of Problems," Entrepreneurship Theory and Practice *(Spring 1993), pp. 5–20. Reprinted with permission.*

Gotta Go Pro

Changes in almost every industry, from bookstores to funeral parlors, require running your business more professionally than has been possible for most "Mom and Pop" operations in the past.

In the spring of 1986, bookseller David Schwartz was preparing for a morning meeting with his banker, Bill Pattenson. He figured they would simply go over a few numbers—no big deal. Schwartz and his new partner, Avin Domnitz, knew that their business, Harry W. Schwartz Bookshops, was turning around. The year before, their six bookstores had lost $300,000, but currently they were close to breaking even. They had reduced their bank debt by over $100,000 and had missed no monthly payments. Unfortunately, Pattenson did not see the future for Harry W. Schwartz Bookshops to be anything rosy.

Pattenson recognized that the book industry was changing and growing and that Schwartz was not keeping pace. Waldenbooks, B. Dalton, and Barnes and Noble had spread across the country bringing sophisticated merchandising and computerized inventory and financial controls to an industry once dominated by small independent stores. Pattenson dissected the company's inventory turnover, salaries, expenses, and advertising. The banker leaned forward and asked the partners, "So when are you closing the company?" Hardly a simple review of numbers—rather, a wake-up call.

David Schwartz's father had started Harry W. Schwartz Bookshops in 1927. Though David grew up with the business and had been in charge since 1972, he didn't realize, until confronted by Pattenson, that he was "totally unlettered in the business part of my profession." Schwartz stated, "I knew how to buy books from the sales reps, and I knew how to sell them to people. And I knew nothing about the business in between."

If Schwartz and Domnitz did not become professional managers soon, they would be out of business. The partners took 10 percent pay cuts, required employees pay for half of their health insurance costs, and required any purchases to be cleared through Domnitz, among other changes. In the transition to becoming professional managers, the partners realized they could no longer rely on intuition about ordering, hiring, and spending. They had to master the numbers of the business and "start doing structured, formal financial planning."

Before the meeting with Pattenson, for example, inventory turnover was below twice a year—well below industry standards. If Schwartz thought he would sell ten copies of a book, he would order ten copies and carry them until they finally sold. By ordering in smaller batches and tracking numbers with a computerized inventory system, inventory turnover rose to 2.8 in 1987, 3.2 in 1988, and 3.7 in 1989. Many other changes were made in the transition from a sleepy little father and son book business into a professionally run company. As Domnitz says, "We have to be the best retailers in the marketplace. We have to know our systems, our numbers, everything there is to know about this business. We have to bring people into our stores. We need this to be the most attractive, most well-stocked, best-serviced, most value-oriented, most selection-driven experience that anyone could possibly have."

Competition from larger players like Wal-Mart, Home Depot, Waldenbooks, and Toys "R" Us means that thousands of independent businesses, like Schwartz's, must come up to speed to survive.

Source: Adapted from Tom Ehrenfeld, "The New and Improved American Small Business," pp. 34–45, adapted with permission, Inc. *magazine, January 1995. © 1995 by Goldhirsh Group, Inc.*

to internal financial management, sales and marketing, human resource management, and government regulation problems increased significantly.

A recent *Inc.* article identified attributes that distinguish professionally managed small businesses. To achieve professional standards you should:

Be automated. Computers can efficiently track items like inventory, expenses, and customers; use technology wisely.

Be competitive. Being small no longer means you will have less competition—you have to produce quality.

Be resourceful. There is no shortage of services available to tap for assistance and tools you may lack.

Be planned. Sophisticated marketing information like demographic mapping is no longer affordable by only the largest businesses.

Be experienced. More "corporate refugees" are starting small businesses with incredible links, talent, and management experience.

Small businesses can no longer operate unmolested in anonymity. Competition raises standards. As one small business owner put it, "Running a business is like playing a video game. You work and scramble to reach the next level only to find out that the game speeds up and everything gets even harder."

Computer Applications

As you make the transition to more professional management, one tool that you might find extremely useful is the form of communication called e-mail. Just exactly what is e-mail? The name stands for "electronic mail." It's made possible by computers' ability to be linked together by computer networks or by telephone lines. E-mail software allows users to communicate with fellow employees as well as with people outside the business.

Your e-mail system may be furnished by your on-line access provider (a company such as America OnLine, Compuserve, or Prodigy). These providers typically charge a monthly service fee and an on-line charge that depends on how long you use it. You might instead decide that a LAN-based system (Local Area Network) is what your business needs. Some software programs de-

signed for LAN-based e-mail systems are Lotus cc: Mail, Microsoft Mail, and Wordperfect Symmetry. The typical cost for a LAN-based system is $40 to $100 per user for software. But keep in mind that these LAN-based systems are for internal use only. If you want to communicate via e-mail with persons outside your business, you're going to require the services of an on-line access provider.

Some companies have started using their World Wide Web home pages for communicating information and exchanging ideas. These sites will typically offer internal publications (such as newsletters, announcements, and so forth) posted on the Web page. However, employees can also interact and discuss issues via the Web page. And customers can also use the Web site to leave comments or suggestions.

Balance: A Manager's Goal

One goal you will want to achieve as your business grows is to maintain a balance between retaining the innovation and flexibility of an entrepreneur and the administrative skill of a manager. Stevenson and Gumpert illustrate these two opposing points of view as follows:

A manager with an **entrepreneurial focus** is one who would ask:

Where is the opportunity?

How do I capitalize on it?

What resources do I need?

How do I gain control over them?

What structure is best?

A manager with an **administrative focus** is one who would ask:

What sources do I control?

What structure determines our organization's relationship to its market?

How can I minimize the impact of others on my ability to perform?

What opportunity is appropriate?[9]

Manager's Notebook

Self-help Source Book

Your small business is flourishing. Sales revenues are increasing steadily. The excitement of running a growing business is contagious. However, you recognize that with growth comes the need for more sophisticated administrative management systems than what you've been using. Where can you find this type of management assistance? Let's look at some possible sources.

Local SBA Office. If there is one located nearby, your local SBA office can be an appropriate place to obtain information on how to develop and implement management systems. These offices offer a variety of pamphlets and brochures to assist you with practically any facet of managing your small business. Also SBA employees are typically good sources of information and can often direct you to additional sources of assistance. If

there's not an SBA office nearby, you can access SBA on the Internet (http://www.sbaonline.gov/) or you can call their toll-free telephone number (800-ASKSBA or 800-827-5722). As with any government agency, however, funding for continued services is subject to change.

Service Corps of Retired Executives (SCORE). Another source of assistance is SCORE, whose members have, on average, 35 years of business expertise. They are a good source of advice and counseling. The national SCORE office can be reached at 800-634-0245.

Local Chamber of Commerce Office. Another good source for advice and assistance is your local chamber of commerce. Many chambers recognize how important small businesses are to the economic vitality of a community. For that reason, they often provide small business management workshops, seminars, or short courses. Many also have management literature available that small business persons can take. In addition, chamber employees might be able to provide assistance or provide you with the names of individuals who can assist you with management issues.

Local Colleges or Universities. You can usually request management assistance and advice from business professors at nearby colleges or universities. For instance, you might be able to persuade a management professor to use your small business as a class project. In this way, you could obtain a wide variety of ideas and advice from the students for next-to-nothing (maybe a pizza party for the students would be your out-of-pocket cost).

Or you might want to enroll in a short-term class or seminar that's offered on campus or a satellite location. These courses are typically inexpensive and oriented to small business persons by providing specific and practical information.

Colleges and universities are where you'll find Small Business Institute (SBI) programs. The SBI program, sponsored by the SBA, pairs small companies with business schools. To locate an SBI program near you, call the Small Business Advancement National Center (501-450-5377).

You might also find that your local college or university has a Small Business Development Center (SBDC) program. This program provides management assistance, counseling, training, and research results to current and potential small business owners. These centers offer one-on-one counseling in easily accessible locations and typically at no charge. Many SBDCs also offer workshops for a minimal fee.

Local Bank or Financial Lender. If you have an established relationship with a local bank or financial institution, ask what types of management assistance are offered. Often lenders want to "protect" their investment in small businesses and will provide seminars, newsletters, pamphlets, or workshops on various topics of interest.

Industry Trade Associations. Many industry trade associations will provide member businesses with low-cost information and advice. If you belong to your industry trade association, be sure to check on the availability of such assistance.

Consultants. We can't forget to mention that you might choose to hire a consultant to help your company with the challenges associated with growth. The advantage is that a consultant will tailor suggestions to your particular business. But the drawback is that consultants are normally more expensive than any of the other listed sources of management assistance. If you decide that what your business really needs is a consultant, you can obtain names from your chamber of commerce, bank, industry trade association, or from other referrals. If you do choose to work with a consultant, be sure to identify specifically what the consultant will be doing, the costs, and the time frame.

Leadership in Action

Small businesses need managers who are also leaders because building an organization requires every employee to contribute to productivity and efficiently use every resource. Owners of small businesses must be very visible leaders since they work closely with their people. Jim Schindler, CEO of ESKCO Inc., says that leaders of small businesses are building a different foundation than their counterparts in large organizations. "[The small business owner's] character, his vision, what he brings to the equation has a lot more direct impact."[10]

Jim Kouzes, president of Tom Peters Group/Learning Systems, says that the foundation of small business leadership is credibility. He summed up his concept with one sentence: "If people don't believe in the messenger, they won't

Leadership abilities are crucial for small business owners because they work so closely with people—employees, vendors, and customers.

management The processes of planning, organizing, leading, and controlling resources in order to achieve the goal of an organization.

believe in the message."[11] How do you build credibility? Kouzes prescribes an acronym—DWWSWWD (Do What We Say We Will Do).

A lot of literature on **management** is devoted to an ongoing debate over management versus leadership. The debate began with a now-famous statement from professor Warren Bennis: "American businesses are overmanaged and underled."[12] Management has been depicted as unimaginative, problem solving, controlling, rigid, analytical, and orderly, while leadership is seen as visionary, passionate, creative, flexible, and charismatic.[13] Are these labels useful when running a business? Not really, for running a small business takes a combination of *both* qualities. Vision without analysis produces chaos, and structure without passion produces rigid complacency. Leadership is the inspirational part of the many things a manager must do—along with an amount of planning, directing, and controlling.

leadership The process of directing and influencing the actions of members within a group.

Leadership Skills

The magazine *Management Review* conducted a study to determine the attributes that business leaders will need for the year 2000. Its findings included:

Vision. Having a mental picture of where the company is going will always be an important part of leadership. It also means describing that vision to others so everyone is headed in the same direction. A person with a vision that can't be put into action is a dreamer, not a leader.

Manager's Notebook

Six Styles of Entrepreneurial Management

There is more than just one right way to run a new, entrepreneurial business. Contrary to much management literature and many consultants, *any* of the many ways to run a business can work. The key is to recognize *your* style and match your strategy to your business goals.

To help business owners get a handle on the different management types, Merrell and Sedgwick identified six entrepreneurial styles. Three are individual oriented and three are team oriented. Merrill and Sedgwick call the individual styles the Classic, the Coordinator, and the Craftsman. The team styles are called Employee Teams, Small Partnerships, and Big-Team Ventures.

Classic. Sue Scott of Primal Lite practices a Classic management style. Scott is involved in every aspect and every decision of the business. Many people are reluctant to admit they are Classics because of criticism for not delegating. Actually, this is a very legitimate way to run your business. Scott recognizes that the Classic style limits the size of her operation. The main problem with this style is not its lack of delegation, but when Classics delude themselves that they are using a team approach. Delegating is fine, not delegating is fine, but don't pretend to delegate because no one will be happy.

Coordinator. As a Coordinator, you can build a good-sized business without a single employee—also called a *virtual corporation*. You can farm out everything from accounting, to sales, to manufacturing. Do what you enjoy or what you do well. Will Hills sees himself as a Coordinator of Craftsmen in his custom furniture business, Limitless Design. Hills realized that having employees meant overhead, while hiring contractors only when he had a job for them gave him larger capacity without full-time responsibility.

Craftsman. The Craftsman is the opposite of the Coordinator because he does everything himself. Stanley Herz runs his own executive-search firm. Since his is such a personal service business, he feels that doing it all will keep him from having to compromise quality. There are many advantages to doing everything yourself—no payroll taxes, no unions, no worker's compensation insurance, no hiring or firing. If you opt for a single-person business, you must first ask yourself how big you want the business to become. Since you will do it all, you may want to consider doing away with parts of the business that you dislike.

The Entrepreneur + Employee Team. This style gives the entrepreneur both control and the ability to grow. Authority can be delegated to key employees while final control is retained by the entrepreneur. Katharine Paine, CEO of Delahaye Group, is a self-proclaimed Classic entrepreneur who has empowered her people to create a consensus-driven team. In return, Paine has received more free time and higher profits.

Small Partnership. Entrepreneurs in Small Partnerships give up more control than those in other styles. When you start a business with two or three other equal owners, you have to share both tactical and strategic decisions with your partners. *Inside-outside partnerships* are a good way to split the turf. Inside partners are in charge of the inside tasks like operations and administration. The outside partners handle sales and marketing.

Big-Team Venture. Some business opportunities with rapid growth possibilities require substantial capital, resources, and a hot-shot team to take advantage or competition will take market share. Several owners are needed from the start, so setting up Big-Team Ventures is no time to scrimp. Terry Tognietti is part of the Big Team running Drypers (#1 on 1993 *Inc.* 500 list of fastest-growing U.S. companies). Five partners make up the executive team, each with complete responsibility for a business function. Tognietti said, "The critical challenge is to preserve individual accountability. All team members need to know exactly what they are expected to deliver. If you've got thin skin, you're going to have a tough time here. We think the critique makes each of us smarter and makes the company better."

Source: Excerpted by permission, from The New Venture Handbook, © 1993, Ronald E. Merrill et al. Published by AMACOM, a division of American Management Assoc. All rights reserved.

Integrity. Leaders must have inner strength and demonstrate honest behavior in all situations. People will not follow a leader who lacks integrity unless they are moved by fear. Leaders need a dedication to doing what they know is right.

Trust. The bond between leaders and followers must run in both directions. Leaders need to be able to trust their people and at the same time they themselves must be trustworthy.

Commitment. Loyalty to one's company is more precarious in today's climate of economic uncertainty. With this being the case, leaders must be seen as even more caring. Passion for what is good for the business *and* for the workers can't be faked.

Creative Ability. Good leadership involves creating something that didn't exist before. A person must have a positive mindset to see creative opportunities and different ways to do things.

Toughness. Often a manager is aware of the difficult choices or changes that must be made for the health of the business but is unable to make them. This indecisiveness is often perceived as lack of leadership. A leader needs a certain amount of toughness to make unpopular decisions or to stand against the majority. A successful leader can set high standards and not be willing to compromise them.

Communication. Constant communication is needed for a leader to not only find out what is going on but to let others know.

The Ability to Take Action. Small business leaders must realize that without action, all these attributes are merely academic rhetoric. These attributes need to be consistently practiced to be effective. Leadership is easy to talk about but a challenge to demonstrate.[14]

Delegation

delegation Granting authority and responsibility for a specific task to another member of an organization. Empowerment to accomplish a task effectively.

By delegating authority and responsibility, a manager gives employees the power to act and make decisions. **Delegation** allows the manager freedom from making every decision that has to be made, giving him time to concentrate on more important matters. Delegation also empowers employees, meaning that it increases employees' involvement in their work. By giving employees authority and responsibility, they are held more accountable for their own actions. Delegation allows managers to maximize the efforts and talents of everyone in the company.

While delegation may be an important part of management, many small business owners are either unwilling or unable to do it for several reasons. For entrepreneurs who have started a business, giving up control is difficult. Owners often know the business more thoroughly than anyone else and feel like they *have* to make all the decisions in order to protect the business. They may feel that subordinates are unwilling or unable to accept responsibility. In reality, this attitude may become a self-fulfilling prophecy. If employees' attempts to take responsibility or to show initiative are squelched too often, they will either stop trying or leave the business. Some small business owners simply misunderstand the meaning of management. These managers want to get the job done right by doing it themselves. That is a commendable attitude, but it can be counterproductive to being an effective manager—someone who needs to get things done through people.

Delegation is not the same as abdication. Nor is empowering people the same as instituting a pure democracy, where you simply count votes and the majority rules. In using delegation and empowerment, an effective leader is trying to encourage participation and to take advantage of shared knowledge so everyone can contribute. Consensus can't always be reached, so sometimes the leader has to make a decision and go with it.

When you assign tasks, make sure you clarify exactly what is expected, when the job should be done, the performance level expected, and how much discretion is allowed. Your employees need feedback control for their own sake and for yours. Controls help monitor employees' progress by letting them know how they are doing and serving to prevent mistakes before they happen.

Motivating Employees

motivation The forces that act on or within a person which cause the person to behave in a specific manner.

The word *motivation* comes from the Latin *movere*, which means "to move." For our purposes **motivation** is the reason an individual takes an action in satisfying some need. It answers the question, "Why do people behave the way they do?"

Flexible and Focused Managing

Tomina Edmark started TopsyTail Co. believing two things strongly: (1) Her hairstyling gadget would be a major success, and (2) her company would not turn into a big business of "suits" for her to manage. A one-time sales representative for IBM, Edmark had seen time and effort wasted on meetings, office politics, and trying to keep everyone happy. "In my own business," Edmark said, "I wanted to spend my time doing business rather than managing people."

Edmark has successfully met her own challenge. She has created an $80 million business and after three years has just hired her second employee. How can three people run the kind of volume that would normally require at least 50 full-time employees? By outsourcing. Edmark set up a network of 20 vendors who manufacture the products, sell them, distribute them, and service the accounts. She started with very little capital—the $25,000 severance pay she received from IBM. Hardly enough to purchase the tooling and injection molding needed to make TopsyTails. Outsourcing has allowed her to be flexible and stay focused on the important parts of controlling her business.

Just because TopsyTail depends so heavily on outsourcing does not mean that it does not require management. Edmark retains control of the business by staying on top of new-product development and marketing strategy. These two functions are the heart of a fast-growing company.

Although the company started with only one product, growth has been aided through new products. The My Pretty TopsyTail doll that comes with a miniature version of the tool has become a rapid success. Edmark has come up with another hair-styling gizmo: a line of hair jewelry, and a book showing examples of hair styles that can be done using the TopsyTail.

A concern about outsourcing is that you will lose control of quality and delivery if you don't manufacture and distribute yourself. Edmark insists this is not the case, noting that if vendors do not perform to her satisfaction, they can be replaced. All contracts contain performance clauses that lay out minimum performance standards and time constraints.

Managing TopsyTail has been less stressful than Edmark's corporate life at IBM. She is in control and sets her own schedule. She hired her first employee, George Asmus, chief financial officer, when she reached 1 million unit sales, and hired the second, Elisabeth Cater, marketing director, a year later.

Source: Echo Montgomery Garrett, "Innovation + Outsourcing = Big Success," Management Review *(September 1994), pp. 17–20.*

As a small business manager you will be interested in how to motivate employees to perform.

Motivation Theories. Some people say that one person cannot motivate another, that one can only create an environment for self-motivation. Still, many theories on motivation exist. Although a thorough examination of each of them is not appropriate for this text, you are encouraged to revisit any principles of management or organizational behavior text for more depth of coverage.

A small business owner can benefit from a knowledge of how to apply motivation theory. One of the best known is **Maslow's hierarchy of needs.** Psychologist Abraham Maslow stated that people have in common a set of universal needs occurring in order of importance. The lowest-level needs are *physiological* (food, water, air, sleep, sex, and so on). *Safety and security* needs are the next level, followed by *social* needs, *esteem* needs, and the highest-level needs of *self-actualization*.

As a small business owner you should understand that these needs do not occur in a rigid order. People will be at different levels of needs at different times—sometimes simultaneously—so a variety of ways to motivate their behavior is needed. The use of money to motivate is often misunderstood, especially in terms of Maslow's hierarchy. Money is generally seen as providing for basic physiological needs and not important to the higher-level needs. But money is actually a motivator because it buys the time and resources needed for self-actualization.

The biggest contribution of Maslow's theory to motivating employees is its recognition that people have needs that "pop-up" and require attention until satisfied. If a lower-level need pops up for an employee, he or she will not be able to concentrate on a higher-level need until the lower-level need is fulfilled. For example, if an employee receives a phone call from a school nurse informing the employee that his second grade child had an accident and broke her arm on the playground, a safety need has popped up. This employee will probably not be very productive on the job until he can be sure the situation is under control, either by going to the school in person or by making other arrangements. Any effort to interfere with his handling of this need will create frustration and antagonism, which will undermine your employee's motivation and damage his attitude toward work.[15]

Another important motivational theory is **Herzberg's motivation-hygiene theory.** This theory is important to the small business owner because it recognizes that factors producing job *satisfaction* are not the same as factors producing job *dissatisfaction*. Herzberg called things that cause people to feel good about their job *motivators* and things that cause people to feel bad about their job *hygiene* factors. By eliminating hygiene factors on the job (like unfair or inadequate company policies), you may create contentment among employees but will not necessarily motivate them to excel. (See Figure 13-3.) For you to truly motivate your people, you need to create an opportunity for them to achieve.

Look at the factors listed in Figure 13-3 that cause satisfaction on the job: achievement, recognition, the work itself, and responsibility. These provide intrinsic rewards to people. The practical application of Herzberg's theory gives a small business manager some direction in keeping employees satisfied on the job. Satisfaction may not translate directly into motivation, but it is a significant component in keeping employees on the job.

Motivation Techniques. A key to motivating the employees of your small business is to know what is important to them. For instance, if you provide a motivational reward that they do not want, it is a kind of inadvertent punishment. Say you promise a "sweet year-end bonus" for the top performer for the month of December. You will probably set up healthy competition that increases morale and achievement. But if your sweet bonus turns out to be a fruitcake—and your employees don't care for fruitcake—don't expect your next incentive to be motivational.

Bill Mork is the owner of Modern of Marshfield, a furniture maker located in Marshfield, Wisconsin. Mork followed the popular advice of using recognition instead of cash to reward participants in his new employee-suggestion program.

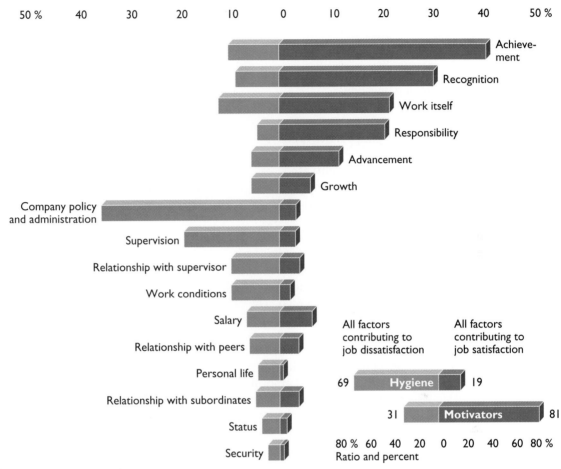

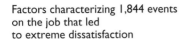

FIGURE 13-3
Job Satisfiers and Dissatisfiers
The factors or experiences that cause people to feel satisfied with their jobs *(motivators)* are distinctly different from those that create job dissatisfaction *(hygiene factors)*. This chart records factors affecting job attitudes as reported in 12 investigations.
Source: Reprinted by permission of Harvard Business Review. *An exhibit from "One More Time: How Do You Motivate Employees?" by Frederick Herzberg, September/October 1987, p. 112. © 1987 by the President & Fellows of Harvard College; All rights reserved.*

From the suggestions received, Mork and other managers picked a "colleague of the month," who was awarded with a special parking space and a big handshake in front of all the gathered employees. The number of suggestions that came in was underwhelming. One winner pleaded not to be chosen again to avoid embarrassment and being called a brownnose by coworkers.

As a result, Mork changed the whole program and added cash bonuses at each step. For any cost-saving suggestion made by an employee that was implemented by the company, the employee was given a bonus worth 10 percent of the estimated savings. An additional 10 percent of the savings was added to a fund

Can You Motivate?

To determine how effective you are at motivating, ask yourself the following questions:

Do you know what motivates each of the people who report to you?

To what extent are they motivated by money?

To what extent are they motivated by recognition?

To what extent are they motivated by opportunity for growth?

Have you done anything in the last week that was intended to motivate someone else?

Have you done anything lately that would undermine an employee's motivation—such as embarrass or criticize an employee in front of others?

Have you praised anyone today?

---

to be split by all suggestion makers at the end of the year. Anyone who had contributed a suggestion was eligible for prize drawings whether or not the suggestion was implemented. The "colleague of the month" is now chosen by previous winners rather than by managers.

Since the program was revised Modern's sales have almost doubled. Each year Mork pays out $10,000 in rewards for the 1,200 suggestions submitted by 100 employees. While this may sound like a lot of money, Mork estimates savings to be five times that amount. Employees have a very different attitude toward the program since bonus checks have been added.[16] This example provides evidence toward that long-asked management question: Does money motivate? Apparently, at a very visceral level, the answer is yes.

Motivation Myths. While theories of motivation help managers to understand what drives employees, there are so many theories that confusion exists about what does and does not motivate people. Examples of misconceptions include:

- *All employees need external motivation.* Some employees have such a strong internal drive that external techniques will not increase their motivation—but they still need your support, backing, and guidance.

- *Some employees don't need any motivation.* Since motivation is the force that prompts every action—we all have to have motivation, it just comes from different sources.

- *Attempts to motivate always increase performance and productivity.* If our attempts to motivate involve incentives that employees do not desire, they can decrease performance. We can also increase happiness and morale without seeing an increase in productivity.

- *Money always motivates people.* Base salary is generally not a long-term motivator. A person who receives a raise may work harder temporarily but soon rationalize, "I'm *still* getting paid less than I'm worth," and return to his previous level of productivity.

- *Intrinsic rewards provide more motivation than money.* As seen in the Bill Mork example, money—as a one-time bonus—*does* motivate at a visceral level.
- *Fear is the best motivator.* Workers who are afraid of a boss will work hard in the boss's presence, but may not have the best interests of the business in mind. The best workers will also be looking for another job—so fear may drive out the very people the business needs the most.
- *Satisfied workers are always productive.* Happy people do not *necessarily* produce more. The goal of employee motivation is not to create a country-club or amusement-park atmosphere. The goal is to get everyone in the company to maximize their efforts in order to increase their contribution (and earnings).
- *This generation of workers is less motivated than the last.* Most generations think this of the following generation. While members of the so-called Generation X have been mislabeled as "slackers," they have already produced notable entrepreneurs, including many who have been used as examples throughout this book.

Total Quality Small Business Management

So much has been written over the past few years about quality and quality management that definitions have blurred and debate has increased over their meaning and worth. Total quality management (TQM) is a philosophy of management focusing on problem solving and control. It was *not* intended to be a panacea or a cure-all. TQM is based on the writings of W. Edwards Deming, who helped ingrain and teach the concept of quality to Japanese manufacturing managers after World War II.

As outlined by Deming, the fourteen points which serve as the foundation of TQM are:

1. *Constant purpose toward improvement.* The quality-centered business should aim to remain competitive, provide jobs, and stay in business—not just make money in the short run.
2. *Adopt the new philosophy.* Change comes from leadership. Western management must learn responsibility and not continue to tolerate inferior workmanship or service.
3. *Stop depending on mass inspection to ensure quality.* Quality products and services are built correctly from the beginning. Inspection only tells you what should be thrown out or reworked.
4. *Stop awarding business on the basis of price tag alone.* Rather than supporting inferior products by buying on price alone, minimize total cost by building long-term relationships of loyalty and trust with suppliers.
5. *Constantly improve the system of production and service.* Improvement does not start and stop. By always looking for ways to get better, you increase productivity and lower costs.
6. *Train everyone.* All workers need to learn how to do their job properly from the time they start.
7. *Institute leadership.* Leading is not just giving orders and applying punishment. Leading is helping, guiding, and teaching.

8. *Drive out fear.* People cannot perform at their best without feeling secure to ask questions or point out problems.

9. *Break down barriers between departments.* Different parts of the business should view competitors outside the business as the competition, not each other. All need to be part of the same team.

10. *Eliminate slogans, exhortations, and targets that demand zero defects.* These create adversarial relationships. Address quality and productivity problems by correcting the system, rather than by badgering the work force.

11. *Eliminate numerical quotas.* Deming states that numerical programs like management by objectives (MBO) draw attention to numbers rather than quality.

12. *Remove barriers to pride in workmanship.* When employees (either salaried or hourly workers) feel that they are being judged or graded, they don't reach their potential.

13. *Start a vigorous program of education and self-improvement.* Continuous improvement must come from greater knowledge, so new methods of teamwork, processes, and techniques need to be taught.

14. *Put everyone to work on the transformation.* Transformation of a company to carry out the mission of quality takes every person in the organization. A few people, or even most of the people can't do it—transformation is everyone's job.[17]

TQM is not just a set of tools and techniques a business can pick up and use—it involves a change in the way of thinking about how the business is run. When so much attention is given to a topic, there is a danger of it becoming perceived as the latest management fad, buzzword, or quick-cure-for-what-ails-American-business. But if a small business owner has realistic expectations of what TQM is and what it can do, and if he is committed to involving every aspect of the business to produce a quality product or service, the philosophy can work. For TQM to have a positive impact, managers need to understand basic principles. They must:

1. Strive to do work right the first time
2. Be customer-centered
3. Know that continuous improvement is a way of life
4. Build teamwork and empowerment.[18]

How can TQM programs and a company's quest for quality be criticized? Few would argue against quality, so the answer to that key question lies in making sure that the quality offered is the quality that customers want.[19] Of course, quality should be the focus of a business's operations, but programs can become so cumbersome they replace the real reason a company is in business.[20]

Varian Associates Inc. makes scientific equipment in California's Silicon Valley. From the beginning of the total quality movement in the mid-1980s, Varian was on the bandwagon. One thousand of its managers went through a four-day quality course, work teams were set up, and cycle times were discussed. They even had a mascot—Koala T, a manager dressed up in a koala bear suit who handed out quality homilies in the lunchroom. As a result, Varian's on-time delivery for the vacuum system department improved from 42 percent to 92 percent, while the service department for radiation equipment ranked first in the industry for speed of customer visits.

Varian appeared to be on top of the quality world, but not *everything* was improving. The people in the vacuum system department were so obsessed with meeting production schedules they didn't return customers' phone calls. The service people in the radiation repair unit were working so quickly to meet their self-imposed targets they would rush from one job to the next without ever talking to or explaining things to the customers. "Quality" was up, but everything else was down. Sales grew only 3 percent, and profit went from $39 million in 1989 to a $4.1 millon loss in 1990.

A concerted push for quality can come from the best of intentions yet still be misguided. TQM programs can turn into expensive exercises that raise costs (therefore reducing profits) without creating anything of real benefit to the customer. Deming stated, "The trouble with Total Quality Management—failure of TQM, you call it—is that there is no such thing. It is a buzzword. I have never used the term, as it carries no meaning."[21]

Management guru Tom Peters cites three reasons for the failure of TQM. First, to be done right, quality must be a way of life, not a program. Second, the essence of offering quality is the belief in the abilities of your front-line employees—the people who meet your customers. Third, many quality programs are internally focused, not customer focused.[22]

Lifeline Systems Inc. is a Massachusetts company that makes a home personal-response system to summon emergency aid when the owner pushes a button. Quality is a serious topic for a product that *must* work every time. Lifeline overhauled operations in 1987 to improve its quality, products, and systems. It realized improvements in productivity and waste reduction, but eventually sales dipped. John Gugliotta, vice president of operations, realized that continuous improvement in quality and productivity must be supported with increased sales.[23] The quality of Lifeline's process—it reduced wastefulness, for instance—was meaningless to customers and thus did not pay off in increased sales, profit, or market share. Quality in unneeded areas creates additional expense and wastes effort.[24] Because of the experience of companies like Lifeline, successful total quality management is evolving into *return on quality (ROQ)*, which emphasizes that quality improvements must be ones that customers want and that will have a positive financial impact.

Special Management Concerns

Beyond the standard functions of management lie many other duties and responsibilities. Besides running your business, you also have personal, family, and social activities to tend to. You must be a good manager of time and be able to keep stress at acceptable levels.

Time Management

Management is the *effective* and *efficient* use of resources. What is a small business owner's most precious and most limited resource? Time. No one seems to have enough of it, yet everyone has the same amount—24 hours per day, 168 hours per week, 8760 hours per year. You can't store it, rent it, horde it, sell it, or buy any more of it. So you had better use it wisely.

You can't store, horde, or buy time—so you had better use it wisely!

Few of us use time as effectively or as efficiently as possible. The key to effective time management for a small business owner is investing time in what is important in life—including the business. This assumes that the small business owner knows what her priorities are—making time management a goal-oriented activity. To be an effective time manager, you must prioritize what needs to be accomplished in any given day.

Indicators of possible time management problems are if you:

1. Are frequently late for or forget meetings and appointments
2. Are consistently behind in responsibilities
3. Don't have enough time for basics—eating, sleeping, family
4. Are constantly working and still miss deadlines
5. Are often fatigued, both mentally and physically.

How can you determine your effectiveness in using your time? A good starting point is to conduct a *time audit.* A time audit makes as much sense as conducting a financial audit, but few small business managers can account for their minutes as precisely as they can their dollars. Why? They don't have time to conduct a time audit!

Begin your time audit by keeping a log to record your activities. Break days down into 15-minute intervals and keep track of what you do for about two weeks. When the log is complete, you can analyze how you have spent your time. Then you can prioritize activities according to their importance. Did you accomplish your most urgent needs? Which activities were a waste of time and could be eliminated? In the end, the time audit should help you set daily goals on a regular basis.

After you conduct your time audit, some additional tips are:

Make a to-do list. Write down and rank by importance what you want to accomplish each day. The return you receive will be many times greater than the small amount of time you invest.

Eliminate time wasters. Combine similar tasks and eliminate unnecessary ones.

Remember Parkinson's Law. "Work expands to fill the time available." If you schedule too much time to accomplish something, you'll probably set a pace to take that amount of time.

Know when you are most productive. We all have a daily cycle. Some of us are "morning people." Some are "night owls." Schedule your work so you handle your most demanding problems when you are at your best.

Stress Management

stress Emotional states that occur in response to demands, which may come from internal or external sources.

One of the most ambiguous words in the English language is **stress.** There are almost as many interpretations of the term as there are people who use it. Common usage leads us to think of stress as a negative thing, as if it were something to be avoided. The stress response is actually the unconscious preparation to fight or flee that a person experiences when faced with a demand. The negative side of stress, called **distress,** entails unfavorable psychological, physical, or behavioral consequences that may or may not result from stressful incidents.

distress The negative consequences and components of stress.

For a situation to create distress for a person, two conditions are necessary: its outcome must be uncertain and it must be a matter of importance to the person. Very few (if any) small businesses are "sure things" guaranteed to produce the outcome that the owner desires. Since small businesses are almost always the sole means of support for their owners, saying they are important to the owners is not an understatement. Therefore, both conditions causing distress exist in running a small business.

Other sources of stress that small business owners encounter are role conflicts, task overload, and role ambiguity. *Role conflict* exists when we are faced with a situation that presents divergent role expectations. For example, a two-day business trip to meet with a potential client could help you land a large new account and be very profitable for your business. But say the only days the trip can be made would mean that you miss your second-grader's school play—creating role conflict for you. The desire to attend both the meeting and the play—to be both a focused entrepreneur and a loving parent—creates a stressful internal conflict.

Task overload is another common source of stress for a small business owner. More is expected of you than time permits—a common scenario in a small business. Unfinished work can be a sign of overload. In a business climate that calls for leaner organizations, work can pile up and more work taken on before existing jobs are finished. Unfinished work creates a tension and uneasiness. If the pattern continues of taking on more and more, eventually an accumulation of unfinished work produces stress and decreases performance.

Role ambiguity occurs when you are not entirely sure what you should do in a situation. Owning a small business generally means you don't have anyone to consult when problems arise and you will have to make decisions on a wide variety of topics. Some people have higher tolerance or preference for ambiguity than others, but it is still stress producing.

Stress is cumulative—it builds up. Sales declining at the business, a key employee being unhappy, a child having discipline problems, and the transmission going out of the family car all combine to form a lot of stress. Individual stressors that could be handled by themselves may combine and become overwhelming.

Stress cannot, and should not, be eliminated from everyday life but it must be managed. General recommendations for controlling your stress level include:

Preventative Stress Management. Attempt to modify, reduce, or eliminate the source of distress. Any changes you can make in your schedule or role as business owner can help prevent distress from building to a dangerous level.

Relaxation Techniques. A few minutes of concentrated relaxation will prevent a buildup of distress. Practice a five-step relaxation exercise. First, sit in a comfortable position in a quiet location. Loosen any tight clothing. Second, close your eyes and assume a passive, peaceful attitude. Third, relax your muscles as much as possible—beginning with your feet and continuing to your head—and keep them relaxed. Fourth, slowly breathe through your nose and develop a quiet rhythm of breathing. After each exhale, quietly say "one" to yourself. Fifth, continue relaxing muscles and concentrate on breathing for 10 to 20 minutes. Open your eyes occasionally to check the time. It will take practice for you to learn to ignore distracting thoughts during relaxation, but soon this exercise can help you reduce stress.[25]

Social Support Systems. Working in an environment that provides social and emotional support can help us deal with distress. Relationships within the workplace, family, church, and clubs provide emotional backing, information, modeling, and feedback.

Small Business
IN THE **Service Industry**

Running a successful small business can be stressful. So, how would you like to run a business that does one-third of its revenues in just 20 days during December? Talk about a service nightmare waiting to happen! How could you get and keep good employees, never knowing from month to month if you would have the revenue to pay them?

That's the challenge that caterer Ruth Meric of Houston faced. She's met the challenge by finding creative ways to expand her catering business and even out cash flow by sponsoring off-season activities. For instance, she has begun providing diet planning and kitchen design advice. And she has inaugurated "Evening with the Chef" parties in which guests participate in preparing a meal, learning cooking techniques and tips, and then enjoying the "fruits" of their labors. Meric said, "Instead of having a seasonal business that had trouble retaining employees and meeting its bills during slow times, we now have a company that makes the most of its resources—particularly the experience and talents of its employees—and can accommodate even more growth." *Source: Ruth Meric, "Cooking Up New Revenues,"* Nation's Business *(February 1996), p. 6.*

Physical Exercise. A person's physical condition affects his response in stressful situations. Aerobically fit people have more efficient cardiovascular systems and better nervous system interaction, which allows them to deal with and recover from stressful events more quickly.[26]

Stress can increase performance and quality of life if it is controlled. Many articles and books have been written on the subject of stress control so comprehensive coverage is beyond the scope of this section.

Summary

■ The functions and activities of managing a small business.

Managers plan, organize, lead, and control. To accomplish these functions, they perform many activities such as developing relationships, negotiating, motivating, resolving conflicts, establishing information networks, making decisions, and continually learning.

■ The stages of growth and their consequences on your business.

In the earliest stage of many businesses, the entrepreneur acts alone. Many entrepreneurs even prefer to keep their businesses as one-person organizations. In the second growth stage employees are added, so the entrepreneur often acts as a coach in getting work accomplished through other people. In stage three, a new layer of supervision is added, so the entrepreneur does not directly control all the people or activities of the business. In the fourth or formal organization stage, the entrepreneur must transform herself into a professional manager in order to run a complex business.

■ The significance of leadership to small business.

Leadership means inspiring other people to accomplish what needs to be done.

Entering the Internet

Stressed out? You can also find relief on the Internet. As we've shown already, there is a lot of information out there on the Net to help you manage your small business. But all work and no play makes a dull entrepreneur. So here are some "fun" sites that you might try!

A Web site that provides current weather maps and movies can be found at **http://wxweb.msu.edu/weather/**. Or stop at the Discovery Channel Online for some diversion at **http://www.discovery.com**. Check out the intriguing on-line experiment called Ferndale at **http://www.ferndale.com**. Another fun site, particularly for college students, goes by the unusual name of FishNet and can be found at **http://www.jayi.com/sbi/Open.html**. Go see what "fish" they've caught in their net!

If you're into music, a couple of fun sites are the Rock and Roll Hall of Fame at **http://www.rockhall.com** and HitsWorld at **http://hitsworld.com**. Need a good joke to tell someone? Visit the self-proclaimed Biggest List of Humor Sites on the Web at **http://www.yahoo.com/entertainment/humor_jokes_and_fun/ index.html**. You'll find a "funny" for every occasion, and even some that aren't so funny! Speaking of funnies, what listing of stress relievers would be complete without our favorite man at work—Dilbert. You can find him at **http://www.unitedmedia.com/comics/dilbert/**.

If you're looking for games on the Web, you're also in luck. Check out any of the following: TicTacToe, at **http://www.bu.edu/Games/tictactoe/**; a game of Scrabble, **http://www.yak.net/kablooey/scrabble.html**; or if you're looking for something more challenging, check out the 3-D riddles at **http://cvs.anu.edu.au/ andy/rid/riddle.html**. Finally, one very cool site is the one maintained by the Levi's people. Check it out at **http://www.levi.com**.

Hopefully, there's something in this list that will help you temporarily get your mind off work. But, don't forget, you do have a business to run!

Leadership is part of a manager's job in providing the vision, passion, and creativity needed for the business to succeed.

■ The importance of motivation in small business.

Since management is getting things done through people, a small business manager must be able to motivate employees. The manager must therefore understand employees' behavior and what is important to them. Maslow's and Herzberg's theories provide small business managers with a framework for understanding motivation.

■ The positive and negative aspects of total quality management to small business.

A small business manager can use Deming's fourteen points to focus on problem solving, control, and quality. If a small business manager adopts the way of thinking and running a business that is the heart of TQM, a constantly improving company can be operated. If TQM is approached as an internally focused program that raises costs without improving the quality of features that are important to customers, it may fail.

Questions for Review and Discussion

1. Give examples of efficiency and effectiveness in managing your everyday life.
2. Discuss some of the skills or characteristics that are needed by a manager in the start-up phase of a business that differ from those needed later to manage a larger, established firm.
3. Study the six styles of entrepreneurial management. Which one best describes you? Explain. Do you recognize a different style in managers you have worked for in the past?
4. What is motivation? Can managers really motivate employees?
5. How can TQM programs and a company's quest for quality be criticized? Elaborate on this question.
6. Are you a good manager of time in your personal life? How will this affect your ability to manage your time as a business owner?
7. Give examples of stress and distress.
8. How can the owner of a small business apply Maslow's hierarchy of needs to working with employees?
9. What are positive and negative aspects of delegation?
10. As a business owner, in which of the leadership skills discussed in the text are you weakest? How could you help yourself improve in this area? How could others help you? Which is your strongest skill?

Critical Incident

Chadwick's Manufacturing. It's a situation that no one ever likes to face, and a common one at large companies and small. Yet it seems to have a more profound impact for small businesses because of their size. The death of a popular and well-liked coworker can be devastating on workers' morale. At Chadwick's Manufacturing in Minot, North Dakota, employees were understandably upset over the unexpected death of the company's plant manager, who was well liked and respected by the 35 employees. In the month after his death, productivity was well below previous levels. As one employee was overheard saying, "It's hard for me to accept Roy's death. What's the use in working so hard when tomorrow I could be gone?" In such a situation, how can employees mourn the loss, and have their enthusiasm and motivation reignited?

Wizards of the Coast. Wizard's best-known product, "Magic: The Gathering," is selling like hotcakes. Magic is a popular fantasy game designed for teens. Although the company keeps its financial figures a close secret, industry experts estimate that the company's sales totaled $50 million in 1994 and probably doubled that in 1995. With that type of incredible growth comes management challenges. How can employee enthusiasm and motivation be maintained in the light of such growth rates?

Questions

1. Write a plan outlining how you would confront the employee motivation challenges presented in each of these situations. Focus on possible reactions of employees, alternative plans, and best- and worst-case scenarios.

2. Pretend you're the new plant manager hired to fill Roy's position at Chadwick's Manufacturing. Role play your first meeting with all the plant employees. Then role play a meeting between yourself and one of the employees one-on-one.

3. Pretend you're the supervisor of five software designers at Wizards of the Coast. Role play a meeting between yourself and these designers over a looming deadline for a game update. Then pretend you're Peter Adkison, Wizard's founder and CEO. Role play a motivational speech you're going to make at the company's annual employee retreat.

Take it to the Net

We invite you to visit the Hatten page on the Prentice Hall Web site at: http://www.prenhall.com/~hattensb for this chapter's World Wide Web exercise.

Chapter Focus

After reading this chapter you should be able to:

- Define the job analysis process and the function of job description and job specifications.
- Evaluate the advantages and disadvantages of five sources of employee recruitment.
- Describe the three steps of employee selection.
- Discuss the need for employee training and the six methods of doing so.
- Explain the three components of a compensation plan and the variable elements of a benefits system.
- Profile an effective sequence for disciplining and terminating an employee.

14

Human Resource Management

I N A SMALL BUSINESS, the repercussions from hiring an incompatible employee can be devastating and demoralizing. Just ask Jody Wright, president of Motherwear, a $5 million-a-year catalog company based in Northampton, Massachusetts. She faced that situation early in her company's history. The person she had hired had an impressive résumé, the job interview was a smashing success, and a job offer was made and accepted. However, it wasn't long before Wright discovered that the rest of the work team couldn't get along with the new employee. Since that disastrous hire, Wright has taken a new approach to bringing employees on board. She now allows her employees to interview and hire the individuals they'll be working with. In fact, more than 60 percent of Motherwear's 40-member staff have been hired that way. The disadvantage to this approach is that a consensus must be reached by the work team doing the hiring, and that can take up to two or three weeks. But, as Wright says, "Integrating the person into the job takes less time. Everybody has already bought in." But Wright doesn't use this open approach with every human resource decision. In fact, she still uses a mostly traditional process for promoting employees in that the manager makes the yes-or-no promotion decision. *Source: Donna Fenn, "Employees Take Charge," adapted with permission,* Inc. *magazine, October 1995, p. 111. © 1995 by Goldhirsh Group, Inc.*

Getting the Right Employees

Are human resource issues important to small businesses? Can small business owners afford the time and cost of developing formal recruitment, selection, training, and benefits programs? Perhaps the more appropriate question is: "Can small business owners afford *not* to spend the time and money on such programs?" In today's marketplace, one of the most valuable resources and competitive advantages a small business has is its employees.

According to a recent Roper Organization study, small business owners reported that their biggest problems were finding competent workers and motivating them to perform.[1] Part of the problem in finding employees is the cost involved. According to the Families and Work Institute, a nonprofit research group in New York, hiring and training costs to replace a nonmanagerial employee typically average 75 percent of a year's pay.[2] To make matters worse, 50 percent of all new hires last an average of only six months in their new positions.[3] As alarming as these figures are, they do not include other potential costs such as defending against charges of discrimination, the loss of customer satisfaction, low employee morale, or wrongful discharge suits. Once you find people to hire, you must find ways to retain and motivate your work force, which costs money. These costs may also be high as you increasingly implement various employee incentive and benefit plans.

All told, the costs and risks associated with human resource issues are too great for any company to ignore. Small business owners need to realize that their most valuable assets walk out the door at closing time.

The Recruitment Process

The recruitment process involves attracting talented individuals to your company. To achieve this goal, you must be able to (1) define the positions to be filled and (2) state the qualifications needed to perform them successfully. This requires that you conduct a job analysis, prepare a job description, identify a list of job specifications, and identify alternative sources of employees.

Job Analysis

job analysis The process of gathering all of the information about a particular job, including a job description and a job specification.

The **job analysis** indicates what is done on the job, how it is done, who does it, and to what degree. It is the foundation upon which all other human resource activities are based and, if necessary, defended in court. While no single job analysis technique has been endorsed by the courts or the Equal Employment Opportunity Commission (EEOC), both entities urge, and in some cases require, that the information from a job analysis be used to ensure equal employment opportunity.

The first step in completing the job analysis is to gain the support and co-operation of employees, since they often know best what the job involves. Next you must identify the jobs to be analyzed. Generally, the amount of time and money you have available, and the importance of the particular job to the company's overall success, will determine the order and the number of jobs you will analyze.

Step three involves identifying the job analysis technique or techniques you will use to obtain information about each job. While numerous techniques exist, for reasons of cost, ease of use, and time savings, the most commonly used technique is the questionnaire. Job analysis questionnaires typically seek to identify the following: identification facts about the job, skill requirements, job responsibilities, effort demanded, and working conditions. (See Figure 14-1.)

Once you have analyzed your jobs, you are ready to prepare the job description and job specifications.

Job Description

The purpose of the **job description** is to identify the duties, tasks, and responsibilities of the position. While a standard format for the job description (increasingly being termed the *position description*) does not exist, it is generally agreed that one should include:

job description A written description of a nonmanagement position, which covers the title, duties, and responsibilities involved for the job.

- **A job identification section.** The job title, location or department within the company, and date of origin should be included in this introductory section. This section might also include the job code, salary range, pay classification, and analyst's name.
- **A job summary.** This summary should outline the jobholder's responsibilities, the scope of authority, and superiors to whom the jobholder is to report.
- **The *essential* duties to be performed by the jobholder.** While this list may contain both essential and nonessential duties, the Americans with Dis-

FIGURE 14-1
SBA Sample Job Analysis Questionnaire

Form 1	IDENTIFICATION FACTS

Job Title _____   Location _____
Other titles used _____   Number employed: M _____ F _____
Brief summary of nature or function of job* _____

Code number** _____
Salary range: Minimum _____ Maximum _____
   Average bonus or incentive payment _____
Working hours: Shift: _____ From _____ To _____
   Overtime: _____never _____ seldom _____ frequent; average hours per week: _____
Misc. _____

*A 1-sentence description, to give a general idea of job.
**Job definition (from the Dictionary of Occupational Titles; your local State Employment Service Office can be helpful).

Form 2   SKILL REQUIREMENTS

Educational Requirements   (general education—grade or years)
    Grammar   High   Business
    School _____   School _____   School _____   College _____
    Specific education for job _____

Job Experience:
    Previous experience required: None _____
        Acceptable type and length _____
    Average length of time with organization _____
    Previous jobs normally held_____
    Next job in line of promotion _____
Relation to Other Jobs: Contacts regularly as part of job:
    Within the Company _____   Outside the Company _____
    _____   _____

Exercises Supervision Over:
    Position of individual: _____
    Subject of supervision:_____
Is Supervised by: Position of individual   Subject of supervision
    Immediate supervisor _____   _____
    Others _____   _____

Job Duties:
    Regular:
        Before open for business _____
        During business hours _____
        After business hours _____
    Periodic (weekly or monthly):
        Performed on regular time _____
        Performed after hours _____
    Occasional: Performed on regular time _____
                  Performed after hours _____

Job Knowledge: Policies and Regulations:

    General   Special and Departmental
    _____   _____
    _____   Procedures and Methods
    _____   _____
    _____   _____
    _____   _____
Technical Information   Related Information

Use of equipment: Types of equipment: _____
    Special operations _____

FIGURE 14-1 (continued)

abilities Act requires that each be clearly identified, since employment decisions may be based upon only the essential components of the job. (See
Chapter 19.)

● **A list of tasks associated with each duty.** Task statements detail the logical
steps or activities needed to complete the overall duties. These statements
should focus on the outcomes or results rather than on the manner in which
they are performed. For example, a loading dock worker might "*move* 50-
pound boxes from the unloading dock to the warehouse," rather than "*lift*
and *carry* 50-pound boxes from the unloading dock to the warehouse."

Form 3 — RESPONSIBILITIES

Direction & Group Leadership:
None _____ Occasional _____ Frequent _____ Continual _____
Nature of responsibility_____

Business Operation:
None _____ Occasional _____ Frequent _____ Continual _____
Nature of responsibility_____

Care of Equipment:
None _____ Occasional _____ Frequent _____ Continual _____
Nature of responsibility_____

Safety and Health of Others:
None _____ Occasional _____ Frequent _____ Continual _____
Nature of responsibility_____

Contact with Public: None _____ Occasional _____ Frequent _____ Continual _____

Form 4 — EFFORT DEMAND

Physical Activities

____ Standing   ____ Turning   ____ Reaching   ____ Pushing   ____ Smelling
____ Walking   ____ Running   ____ Throwing   ____ Pulling   ____ Tasting
____ Balancing   ____ Stooping   ____ Lifting   ____ Fingering   ____ Hearing
____ Climbing   ____ Sitting   ____ Carrying   ____ Feeling   ____ Seeing

Worker Characteristics

____ Planning   ____ Talking   ____ Making decisions
____ Directing others   ____ Showing initiative   ____ Working rapidly
____ Writing   ____ Getting along with people
____ Showing enthusiasm   ____ Working at various tempos
____ Being well groomed   ____ Concentrating amid distractions
____ Controlling emotions   ____ Remembering names and faces
____ Using arithmetic   ____ Remembering details
____ Working accurately   ____ Examining and observing details
____ Discriminating colors   ____ Attending to many items

Form 5 — WORKING CONDITIONS

____ Inside   ____ Hot   ____ Dirty   ____ Inadequate light
____ Outside   ____ Cold   ____ Dusty   ____ Inadequate ventilation
____ Humid   ____ Dry   ____ Odors   ____ Working with others
____ Hazards   ____ Wet   ____ Noisy   ____ Working around others
____ High places   ____ Working alone
____ Change of temperature   ____ Working under pressure

Details of Working Conditions   (summary based on working conditions) _____
Details of Hazards _____
Permissible Handicaps: Limb _____   Hearing _____   Sight _____

GPO 908-656

Copies of this Aid are available free from field offices and Washington headquarters of the Small Business Administration. Aids may be condensed or reproduced. They may not be altered to imply approval by SBA of any private organization, product, or service. If any material is reused, credit to SBA will be appreciated. Use of funds for printing this publication approved by the Office of Management and Budget.

"Employees: How to Find and Pay Them," U.S. Small Business Administration; Personnel Management Publication number PM 2, 1992.

FIGURE 14-1 (continued)

- **Task statements.** Task statements help to identify the knowledge, skills, abilities, and educational levels needed to perform the job and to establish performance standards for the position. In addition, these statements are valuable in complying with various federal and state employment provisions.

General working conditions, travel requirements, equipment and tools used, and other job-related data may also be included in the job description. To preserve your status as an at-will employer, which gives you the right to discharge an employee for any reason, you may also add a general duty clause such as "and other duties as assigned," or write "representative tasks and duties" to indicate that your list is not comprehensive. Figure 14-2 shows an example of a typical job (position) description.

Job Specifications

job specification The identification of the knowledge, skills, abilities, and other characteristics an employee would need to perform the job.

Job specifications indicate the skills, abilities, knowledge, and other personal requirements a worker needs to successfully perform the job. In writing the specifications, care must be taken to ensure that the stated requirements are truly necessary for successful performance of the job. For example, stating that a college degree is a requirement for a given job may be difficult, if not impossible, to prove if questioned by an Equal Employment Opportunity representative. For this reason, you may wish to add a qualifier, such as "or equivalent," and limit specifications to those that are truly job related and necessary. Job specifications are often integrated into the job description, as shown in Figure 14-2.

FIGURE 14-2

Sample Job Description

Job Title: Word Processor
Department: Sales
Status: Nonexempt
Principal Position Objective: To enter documents into computer within deadlines at acceptable levels of accuracy.
Reporting Relationships: Reports to Office Manager. Completes work for personnel from all departments.
Qualifications:
- High school diploma or equivalent
- Type 75 words per minute error-free
- One year word processing experience or equivalent
- Working knowledge of WordPerfect for Windows
- Knowledge of proofreading symbols

Attendance Requirements: Normal office hours are 8 am to 5 pm, Monday through Friday.
Work Performed:
- Type letters, memos, reports, contracts, and other forms in text and graphical format using a variety of formats and layouts.
- Proofread own work in addition to documents produced by other word processors.
- Operate photocopy machine in producing hard copies and transparencies.
- Operate other office equipment such as fax, binding machine, and scanner.

Other Duties:
- Deliver documents as needed
- Occasional travel required

Finding Employees

You may recruit employees from a variety of sources. Each has advantages and disadvantages.

Advertising for Employees. Help-wanted ads placed in newspapers, trade publications, or storefronts generate a large number of responses, but generally the quality of applicants is not equal to that generated by other sources. Nevertheless, ads reach a wider, more diverse audience than other techniques, which may be needed to ensure equal opportunity representation or an adequate supply of employees with unique or specialized skills.

Employment Agencies. Located in all states and most large cities, government-funded employment agencies focus primarily on assisting blue- or pink-collar employees. On the positive side, they allow you to obtain screened applicants at no cost. On the negative side, the quality of applicant may not be equal to that generated by employee referrals.

Executive Recruiters (Head Hunters). These firms can be useful for small businesses looking for a key person or two rather than manual or lower-level positions that government agencies concentrate on. These firms search confidentially

Entering the Internet

Yes, it is possible for a small business owner to find employees on the Internet. Keep in mind that most of the Web sites that post job openings charge a fee (usually fairly low) for doing so. By charging a fee to employers, it's possible for job hunters to browse through job openings free of charge. One on-line job listing service that allows employers to target qualified applicants is JobTrak, a Los Angeles-based company. JobTrak connects companies with job openings to college students and alumni around the United States. So if an employer is looking, for example, for a computer science major from Stanford, the job posting is directed to only those candidates. Users of the service can target up to 300 campuses and pay as little as 60 cents per college for a two-to-four week posting. JobTrak is used by some 150,000 companies.

There's also the Online Career Center, which offers an Internet recruitment service. The Online Career Center was started around 1993 by six companies (Aetna, Alcoa, IBM, Eli Lilly, Monsanto, and Procter & Gamble). It now has 262 corporate members. The fee: $3,900 to join and $2,400 a year thereafter for the right to list available jobs. You might also want to check out E-Span's Interactive Employment Network. Or, if your small business has its own Web page, you can list job openings directly on it. However, you'd want to be sure that your job ad lists the necessary information to keep from being bombarded with inappropriate job candidates.

JobTrak: http://www.jobtrak.com

Online Career Center: http://www.occ.com

E-Span's Interactive Employment Network: http://www.espan.com

Sources: Tom Stein, "Find the Perfect Employee," Success (October 1995), p. 13; Donna Fenn, "Recruiting in Cyberspace," Inc. (November 1995), p. 93; and Marshall Loeb, "Getting Hired by Getting Wired," Fortune, November 13, 1995, p. 252.

> *Small business owners must realize that the single most valuable asset of a company is its employees.*

for people who are currently employed and not usually actively seeking another job. Their services can be expensive.

Employee Referrals. Since your employees know the skills and talents needed to work in your company, they can be a good source for finding people to fill slots. This inside-track approach to recruiting is not very costly and can generate qualified, highly motivated employees as long as your current employee morale is high and your work force is somewhat large and diversified. On the downside, an exclusive use of this source may perpetuate minority underrepresentation or create employee cliques. In cases where the referral is not hired or does not work out, the referring employee may become resentful.

Relatives and Friends. The advantage of hiring relatives or friends is that you generally know beforehand of their abilities, expertise, and personalities. However, no approach is more laden with long-term repercussions. The effects of a poor decision may be felt long after the desk has been cleared and the nameplate changed. According to Peter Drucker:

Family members working in the business must be at least as able and hardworking as any nonrelated employee.

Family-managed businesses, except perhaps for the very smallest ones, increasingly need to staff key positions with nonfamily professionals.

No matter how many family members are in a company's management, nor how effective they are, one top job must be filled by a nonrelative.

Before the situation becomes acute, the issue of management succession should be entrusted to someone who is neither part of the family nor part of the business.[4]

Global Small Business

Obviously, hiring employees in a foreign location presents special challenges. Unless you have a lot of firsthand knowledge about or experience in the country where you'll be hiring employees, you'd be wise to get assistance and advice from local experts. That's what Eli E. Hertz, founder of Hertz Computer Corporation in New York, did. In fact, when Hertz wanted to expand into Israel, he purchased a small distributor there to handle his computer equipment. Because of the nature of the business, potential employees would need technological as well as cultural understanding. Hertz felt that this was the best option for him in expanding into this market. *Source: Amy Barrett, "It's a Small [Business] World," Business Week, April 17, 1995, pp. 96–101.*

Selecting Employees

Once you have a pool of applicants from which to choose, you should match the applicants with the job requirements outlined in your job description and specifications. Three commonly used tools for selecting employees include the application form and résumé, the selection interview, and testing.

Application Forms and Résumés

Application forms and résumés contain essentially the same information. The difference between them is that applications are forms prepared by your company and résumés are personal profiles prepared by the candidates. Both contain the candidate's name, address, telephone number, education, work experience, and activities. The four purposes of the application form and the résumé are:

- To provide a record of the applicant's desire to obtain the position.
- To provide a profile of the applicant to be used during the interview.
- To provide a basic personnel record for the applicant who becomes an employee.
- To serve as a means of measuring the effectiveness of the selection process.

The application form need not be complex or long to achieve these objectives. It must, however, ask enough of the right questions to enable you to differentiate applicants on the basis of their knowledge, skills, and ability to perform the job. In addition, the application form should provide the names of potential references and furnish the applicant's permission for you to contact them to discuss the applicant's qualifications and prior job performance. Finally, it should include a notice that you are an at-will employer and may, therefore, discharge an employee for cause or no cause.

Time and money constraints will prevent you from interviewing every candidate. Applications and résumés give you a screening tool to decide whom to bring in for the next stage of the selection process—the interview.

Interviewing

Considered by many employers to be the most critical step in the selection process, the personal interview gives you a chance to learn more about the applicants, to resolve any conflicts or gaps in the information they provided, and to confirm or reject your initial impressions of them which you might have drawn from the application or résumé. The interview also gives you a chance to explain the job and company to the applicant.

To conduct an effective interview, you should:

Be Prepared. Start by thoroughly reviewing the job description and job specifications. You must know what your needs are before you can find a person to fulfill them. Next review the candidate's application form. Look for strengths and weaknesses, areas of conflict, and questions left unanswered or vaguely worded.

Set the Stage for the Interview. Arrange to hold the interview at a time and location demonstrating its importance. The location should provide privacy and comfort, and present the right image of your company. It should allow you to talk without interruptions. Taking telephone calls, answering employee questions, or working on another task while conducting the interview does little to ease the fears of the applicant and simply does not facilitate good communications or a good image.

Use a Structured Interview Format. Develop a set of questions to ask each candidate so you can compare their responses. Your job description and specifications should be the source for the majority of your questions. Such a format will allow you to collect a great deal of information quickly, to systematically cover all areas of concern, and to more easily compare candidates on the basis of similar information.

Use a Variety of Questioning Techniques. While closed-ended questions are appropriate when looking for a commitment or for verifying information, they are very limiting. Consequently, you should use open-ended or probing questions that are related to the job. For example, rather than asking, "Do you like working with figures?" you may wish to probe with the question: "What is it that you like about working with figures?" Open-ended, probing questions encourage the applicant to talk, providing you with a wealth of information and insight into the applicant's ability to communicate effectively.

No Matter the Type of Question, It Must be Job Related. The EEOC requires that all job interview questions be nondiscriminatory in nature. In other words, they must be devoid of reference to race, color, religion, sex, national origin, or disability, and they must be job related. You should be able to relate each interview question to one or more of the items on your job description or job specifications and to show how the information obtained from the questions will be used to differentiate candidates.

Keep Good Records Including Notes from the Interview. The EEOC construes any selection device as a test, and as is true of any test which results in underrepresentation of a protected group, the interview process must be validated. In the case of most small business owners, the problem is not one of questionable behavior or wrongdoing within this area, but one of inadequate documentation. You must be able to show that your decision to hire or not to hire was based upon a sound business reason or practice.

Testing

Employee testing has long been used by U.S. businesspeople to screen applicants. And, for the most part, prior to the 1971 Supreme Court *Griggs* v. *Duke Power Co.* decision, employers were fairly free to do as they pleased.[5] Today, however, employers must be able to prove that their tests and other selection criteria are valid predictors of job performance. This can be done, according to the Supreme Court and the Equal Opportunity Commission, through statistical or job-content analyses.

For small business owners, the prospect of statistically validating a test is generally far too time-consuming and expensive. Therefore, short of eliminating all tests, two options remain: purchasing preprinted tests from commercial vendors who have conducted the necessary standardization studies to ensure test reliability (although ultimate liability still rests with the employer) or using content-based tests. While not an absolute defense, you are more likely to be able to prove a test's validity if the test is a sample or measure of the actual work to be performed on the job. For example, if a clerk's job involves counting back change to customers, then asking an applicant to count back change as a test is probably content valid and its use is therefore permitted.

Regardless of the type of test used, in few cases should the results of a single test or indicator be used as the sole reason for hiring or not hiring an applicant. In addition, all test results should be kept strictly confidential and in a file other than the employee's personnel file. Commonly used tests include the following five options.

Achievement Tests. Achievement tests are given to measure the specific skills a person has attained as a result of his or her experiences or education. These tests are easy and inexpensive to administer and score. Proving validity and job-relatedness, however, is another matter. Therefore, you should have a very compelling business-related reason to justify their use during the selection process.

Performance (Ability) Tests. Performance tests are administered to assess the ability of the applicant to perform the job. The tests provide direct, observable evidence of performance. They are also easily administered, relate directly to the job, and are relatively inexpensive to conduct. Validity is generally not an overriding issue with performance testing.

Physical Examinations. Often considered the last step in the screening process, physical examinations are given to discover any physical or medical limitations which might prevent the applicant from performing the duties of the job.

The Americans with Disabilities Act (ADA) states that physical examinations may be given only after a conditional offer of employment and only if they are administered to all applicants in the particular job category.[6] In addition, you may not disqualify individuals as a result of such examinations unless the findings show that the person would pose a "direct threat" to the health and safety of others.[7] All medical findings must be kept apart from general personnel files and be made available to only selected company personnel on a need-to-know basis.

Drug Tests. Organizations are increasingly using drug tests for screening applicants. According to a 1994 survey, 64 percent of reporting firms administered drug tests as part of their health and safety programs.[8] While tests for illegal use of drugs are not considered tests under the ADA and are, therefore, not subject to its regulations, many state legislatures have imposed conditions under which drug tests may be administered, samples tested, and results used. Generally, to justify the cost and privacy concerns caused by these tests, you must be able to demonstrate a strong need for safety within your workplace or services.

Honesty Tests. The 1988 Employee Polygraph Protection Act essentially outlawed the use of voice stress analyzers and other devices in most business situations. As a result, employers have increasingly relied upon paper-and-pencil honesty tests. However, to date, these tests are suspect in terms of their validity, and the courts have yet to rule decisively on their use. Several congressional committees are also looking into restricting or outlawing their use as a preemployment tool. Unless one has an overriding reason—for example, unless the employee will have ready access to merchandise or money—the use of an honesty test is not recommended.

Temporary Employees and Employee Leasing

Many small business owners are recognizing the benefits of hiring temporary employees. In the past, agencies such as Kelly Services and Manpower, Inc. were generally called upon only when someone in the company went on vacation or demand suddenly exceeded capacity. Although these are still the most popular reasons for using temporary services, other reasons include the need to fill new or highly specialized positions, to ensure a full work force during periods of labor shortages, and to take advantage of the growing pool of workers who like the flexibility and challenge of working for multiple employers. Today temporary employees are being used by small and large businesses to perform tasks formerly done by permanent employees. According to the National Association of

Temporary Services, 1.5 million people are working as temporary employees within the United States.[9]

The employment costs of temporary employees are often lower than for those of permanent or full-time employees. The employment agency generally takes care of all federal and state reporting and record keeping requirements, thus lowering the company's overhead costs. In addition, training and other costs, such as workers' compensation, unemployment insurance, and fringe benefits are paid by the agency, not the company. Finally, once the job has been completed in the case of seasonal demands, temporary workers can be laid off quickly and with fewer concerns for wrongful discharge claims.

A relatively recent trend in human resource management (HRM) involves leasing employees. In this arrangement an employee leasing company becomes the legal employer, handling employee-related duties including recruiting, hiring, payroll tax paperwork, and provision of benefits. The handling of benefit packages, especially health insurance, is usually what makes employee leasing attractive to small businesses.[10] Since employees with an employee leasing company are part of a larger group than they would be with a small business, they can get insurance coverage that either is not available or prohibitively expensive. Cost savings of benefits and other HRM functions may outweigh the leasing fee, making leasing employees cheaper than hiring employees for small firms.

But cost is seldom the only factor in such decisions. Many business owners are understandably reluctant to turn over responsibility of their most important assets—employees—to an outside company. Before leasing employees, check with your lawyer and accountant for legal and tax implications. Make sure the benefits provided by the leasing company are better than those you currently offer. Check the financial stability of the leasing company by finding out the years it has been in business, its capitalization, and its credit rating. If the leasing company goes out of business, you will face the problems of rehiring all your employees and finding a new insurance carrier. If the leasing company does not pay its insurance premiums on time, your leased workers could be left without insurance. Finally, the leasing company sets its own personnel policies like performance appraisals and wage reviews—it does not administer yours. Make sure its policies are consistent with yours.[11]

Employee leasing may be a viable alternative for your small business if you can pick the right leasing company, but remember that you don't get anything for nothing. There are advantages and disadvantages. For assistance on choosing a leasing company, contact the National Staff Leasing Association, 1735 North Lynn Street, Suite 950, Arlington, VA 22209 (703-524-3636).[12]

Placing and Training Employees

employee orientation The process of helping new employees become familiar with an organization, their job, and the people they will work with.

Every employee, no matter how experienced, will need to be introduced to the methods and procedures of his job and to the rules of your company. This process of introduction is called **employee orientation.** Many organizations mistakenly leave orientation of new hires to coworkers on an informal, as-time-permits basis. Unfortunately, this casual approach often results in an incomplete orientation, and it cannot be formally documented in the event of a wrongful discharge claim. A formal orientation will, by contrast, ensure that the new hire is welcomed to the company in a positive, complete, and cost-effective manner.

The orientation should be comprehensive and spread over several days. The scope of topics should include both hard and soft issues. Hard issues, which are relatively easy to cover, include specifics such as how the job is to be performed, the company's policies and procedures, and a discussion of pay and fringe benefits practices. Soft issues might include the organization's interest in making a profit, producing a quality product, being socially responsible, and providing a safe, efficient, team-oriented work environment. These soft issues establish the tenor of the employment relationship and generally make the difference between an "acceptable" and a "good" employee. The sessions at which soft issues are discussed should be kept short, generally not exceeding two hours, and should be spread over several days if the employee is to truly learn and grow from the orientation experience.

An effective way to prioritize the order in which you present the orientation topics is to use a checklist. (See Figure 14-3.) When an employee reports to work for the first time, he has many needs, some of which are more immediately pressing than others. For example, the fear of not being at the right place at the right

FIGURE 14-3

Professional or Technical Employee Orientation Checklist

☐ Provide employee with job description for position.
☐ Explain specific requirements and expected accomplishments.
☐ Provide overview of the organization and mission of the department, its relationship to other departments, and the employee's role as it relates to the goals of the department.
☐ Introduce employee to department staff.
☐ Provide tour of facility and introduce employee to employees outside of the department.
☐ Review:
  - Working hours
  - Lunch period
  - Jury duty
  - Overtime
  - Probation period
  - Illnesses
  - Military obligation
  - Time and attendance reporting
  - Personal emergencies
  - Performance appraisals
☐ Review benefits:
  - Insurance (life, disability, medical, travel, accident, workers' compensation)
  - Tuition reimbursement
  - Holidays
  - Sick days
  - Vacation days
  - Career development
  - Employee assistance program
☐ Review paperwork for completeness:
  - Application
  - Signature on employment agreement
  - Personnel questionnaire
  - I.D. card
  - W-4 form
  - Sales forms
  - Insurance applications
☐ Provide employee with:
  - Employee handbook
  - "Where to Go" guide
  - Time card
  - Security procedures
  - Copy of newsletter
  - Building layout
  - Organization chart
  - History and product line
  - Telephone directory
  - Restaurant guide
☐ Make public announcement on bulletin board of new employee's name, position, and starting date.

Source: Excerpted by permission of the publisher, from "Effective Employee Orientation" by Linda A. Jerris ©1993 *AMACOM,* a division of *American Management Association.* All rights reserved.

time, or of saying the wrong thing to the wrong person generally far outweigh concerns over fringe benefits or the company's plan for future growth. Consequently, the order of the orientation presentation should be directed at fulfilling the most pressing needs first. We can organize orientation by need level, following Maslow's hierarchy. (See Chapter 13.) According to Maslow, human needs fall into five categories: physiological, safety, social, esteem, and self-actualization. These needs can generally be fulfilled through the following types of actions or discussions.

Physiological. Draw a flow chart of the employee's typical day. Start by discussing the time at which the employee should report to work; where she should park her car or how to access public transportation; the location of her office; and so on. Your goal is to give the employee time to set up shop and become comfortable with her new surroundings.

Safety. Review the company's employee handbook, procedures manual, safety and health guidelines, and benefits package with the employee. Your goal is to give the employee a sense of security by letting her know the dos and don'ts of the organization and the safeguards available in the event of illness, disability, or discharge.

Social. Introduce the employee to personnel outside her immediate work area; go over committee assignments; and inform her of special company events or days and other company traditions, norms, and standards. Your goal is to provide the employee with enough information so that she can interact comfortably with coworkers and others.

Esteem. Review the company's employee performance appraisal and promotional processes, training programs and procedures, and any employee assistance programs. Your goal is to reassure the employee that her sense of self-worth, and the respect of others toward her, are supported by your company.

Self-actualization. Discuss the company's past, present, and future plans and the employee's participation in its evolution, along with the opportunities for promotion and transfer within the company. Your goal is to instill within the employee the desire to achieve his fullest potential both as an individual and an employee.

Employee Training and Development

employee training A planned effort to teach employees more about their job in order to improve their performance and motivation.

An important means of motivating employees, often overlooked by managers, is **employee training** and development. Training involves increasing the employee's knowledge and skills to meet a specific job or company objectives. It is usually task and short-term oriented. Development, on the other hand, is more forward looking, providing the employee with the knowledge, skills, and abilities to accept a new and more challenging job assignment within the company.

A trained work force can give you a competitive advantage that, once gained, is not easily duplicated by competitors. That advantage can be maintained and enhanced through an ongoing training and development program. Training and development help to keep employees from becoming bored and unfulfilled and increases retention of qualified personnel. Not only are turnover costs reduced, but over a period of time, the overall level of employee morale is increased. Finally, training and development assure your firm a place in tomorrow's competitive environment. New employee skills and abilities will be

R eality Check

Personality Plus

Will Knecht, vice president of Wendell August Forge in Grove City, Pennsylvania, uses what some might consider an "unusual" approach to placing workers in the right job. He says, "A small business needs every tool available to help place people in the jobs they can do most effectively." Although he was skeptical at first about the value of personality testing, Knecht has used such testing for four years as an aid to making human resource decisions about hiring, promoting, and training. He is firmly convinced of its value.

Wendell August Forge, a family-owned business that crafts metal giftware such as platters, mugs, and pitchers, consists of a direct-mail business, two retail stores, and a production facility. Because the business requires a variety of workers such as artists, salespeople, customer-service representatives, and craftsmen, Knecht recognized

the need to be flexible in managing each worker. Keeping workplace friction low and productivity high were also important goals. Knecht said that the personality test results suggested the best way to manage each worker—indicating who likes close supervision and who doesn't, for example. The test Knecht uses is called the Predictive Index (PI) developed by Management Development Group, Inc. of Cleveland. It measures traits such as patience, independence, and exactitude. Although the company pays an annual fee (for instance, it's $2,400 for companies with up to 25 employees) for a one-time right per employee to use the test, Knecht feels it's money well spent. Even the company's managers take the test. And they're often surprised by its results!

Source: Roberta Maynard, "Match the Right Workers with the Right Jobs," Nation's Business (June 1994), p. 10.

Small Business IN THE Service Industry

It's particularly important for small businesses to employ individuals who are committed to providing outstanding customer service. This is particularly true for businesses where employee turnover can be extremely high, like in food retailing. William Brodbeck, president and CEO of Brodbeck Enterprises of Platteville, Wisconsin, preaches the importance of employee training and orientation for reducing employee turnover and thus being able to keep service high. His company owns and operates eight supermarkets where a highly systematic training program is in effect for new hires. The company's basic training and orientation session is six and one half hours long. Cashiers receive another 38 and one-half to 40 hours of training on top of that, deli employees get another 33 hours, and seafood workers an additional 47 and one-half hours of training. Brodbeck feels strongly that his company's commitment to training and orientation makes a difference in the customer service his supermarkets provide. Source: Frank Hammel, "Tackling Turnover," Supermarket Business (October 1995), pp. 103–108.

required as the business expands into new product lines, acquires new technologies, and strives to maintain or reach a higher level of customer service.

According to the American Society for Training and Development, despite an annual investment of $210 billion in worker training, of which American companies contribute $30 billion, 50 million workers need additional training just to perform their present jobs.[13] And by the year 2000, the Census Bureau estimates 65 percent of all jobs will require at least some special training and additional education beyond high school.[14] Employee training will not be an option but a competitive necessity in the future.

Ways to Train

Depending upon the objectives of our training program, there are several techniques available. Some of the more commonly used methods include lecture, conferences, programmed learning, role playing, job rotation, and correspondence courses.

Lecture. Lecturing involves one or more individuals communicating instructions or ideas to others. The technique is often used because of its low cost, the speed with which information can be covered, and the large number of individuals that can be accommodated. Employee participation is limited, however, and no allowance is made for individual employee differences.

Conferences. Also termed *group discussions,* this technique is similar to the lecture method except that employees are actively involved in the learning. While this technique produces more ideas than lecturing does, it also takes more time and limits the number of participants involved.

Programmed Learning. Programmed learning or instruction is achieved through a computer screen or printed text. The employee receives immediate feedback and learns at his or her own speed. This method is good for almost any type of training. However, outside materials must generally be purchased and the learner must be self-directed and motivated for this technique to be effective.

Role Playing. In this method, employees take on new roles within the company, acting out the situation as realistically as possible. If videotaped, playing back the situation allows for employee feedback and group discussions. Some employees find the technique threatening, and not all business situations lend themselves to this type of training.

Job Rotation. Job rotation allows employees to move from one job to another within the company. In addition to providing employees with a variety of job skills and knowledge, the technique also provides management with trained replacements in the event that one employee becomes ill or leaves the company. However, the technique does not generally provide in-depth, specialized training.

Correspondence Courses. This technique is especially useful for updating current knowledge and acquiring new information. Generally sponsored by a professional association or university, the employee receives prepackaged study materials to complete at her own pace. In addition to providing individualized learning, the technique is applicable to a variety of business topics. The employee must be motivated to learn, and course costs may be high.

Compensating Employees

Employees expect to be paid a fair and equitable wage. Determining what is fair and equitable is a challenging and ongoing task that involves primarily two components: wages and incentives.

Determining Wage Rates

Based upon the Fair Labor Standards Act (FLSA) of 1938, employees are classified as either exempt or nonexempt. Exempt employees are not covered by the major provisions of the FLSA, which controls minimum wage, overtime pay, child labor laws, and equal pay for equal work regulations. Most exempt employees are paid on a straight salary basis. Nonexempt employees, however, must be paid a minimum wage set by Congress (or your state government, if higher). These payments may be in the form of hourly wages, salary, piecework rates, or commissions.

Hourly Wages.   Most organizations pay their nonexempt employees an hourly wage (a set rate of pay for each hour worked).

All-Salaried Employees.   Some organizations are moving to an all-salaried work force. These companies pay both exempt and nonexempt employees a salary (a fixed sum of money). While still subject to FLSA provisions, this type of compensation plan removes the perceived inequity between the two "classes" of employees and fosters a greater esprit de corps.

Piecework Rates.   Unlike the salaried or hourly wage rates, the piecework rate is a pay-for-performance plan. Under a piecework rate, the employer pays an employee a set amount for each unit he produces. Some employers pay, as an incentive, a "premium" for units produced above a predetermined level of production. For example, an employee may receive $2 per unit for the first 40 units produced and $2.25 for any units above 40. Other plans may pay a straight rate for all units, say $2.15, once the standard output quota of 40 units has been surpassed.

Commissions.   Commissions are another type of pay for performance. Some jobs, especially those in sales, are not easily measured in units produced. Under a straight commission plan the employee's wages can be based solely upon his sales volume. Since employees often cannot control all of the external variables that affect sales, employers are increasingly paying on a base salary plus commission basis. Employees tend to favor this combination approach since they are provided with a degree of income security during slow sales periods.

Still other employers are allowing the employee to "draw" against future commissions. This means that the employee may draw an advance from the employer during a slow sales period, and repay the advance (draw) out of commissions earned during the remainder of the pay period or, in some cases, future pay periods. Such draws are particularly effective if sales fluctuate from month to month or from quarter to quarter.

Incentive Pay Programs

An incentive pay program is a reward system that ties performance to compensation. Two common types of incentive pay programs involve the awarding of bonuses and profit-sharing programs. **Bonuses** are generally awarded on a one-

bonus A one-time reward provided to an employee for exceeding a performance standard.

Wages and incentives—including health care and other benefits—are necessary to keep employees alive, healthy, and motivated.

time basis to reward employees for their high performance. They may be given to either an individual employee or a group of employees. Bonuses are frequently awarded when an employee meets objectives set for attendance, production, cost savings, quality, or performance.

To be an effective motivator, the bonus must be tied to a specific measure of performance. The reason for which the bonus is being awarded must be communicated to employees at the time they are informed that they will receive it. The bonus should be paid separately from the employee's regular paycheck to reinforce its specialness. In this way, the bonus is less likely to be viewed by employees as an extension of their regular salary and something to which they are automatically entitled.

profit-sharing program A plan in which employees receive additional compensation based on the profitability of the entire business.

Under most **profit-sharing plans,** employers make the same percentage of salary contributions to each worker's account on a semiannual or annual basis. The percentage of contributions varies according to the amount of profits earned, making the system highly flexible. Startup costs for a profit-sharing plan typically run about $2,000, with another $2,000 being incurred annually to administer the plan. Most employers believe these plans serve to motivate workers by giving them a sense of partnership with the employer. Profit-sharing plans are a mainstay of many small business owners' compensation plans. According to Mac McConnell, owner and president of Artful Framer Gallery, a $600,000 business with a staff of eight, "A company can never be too small to benefit from a well-designed profit-sharing plan."[15]

Benefits

benefit Part of an employee's compensation, in addition to wages and salaries.

An employee **benefit** consists of any supplement to wages and salaries. Health and life insurance, paid vacation time, pension and education plans, and discounts on company products are examples. The cost of offering and administering benefits has increased greatly—from 25.5 percent of total payroll in 1961 to 38 percent in 1992.[16] Often employees do not realize the market value and high cost of benefits.

According to a 1994 survey by the Employee Benefit Research Institute, Americans' satisfaction with their benefits packages is declining.[17] Only 56 percent of survey respondents said they were completely satisfied with their benefits package, down from a high of 70 percent satisfied in 1991. At the same time, the number of respondents satisfied with the level of benefits but who wanted a different mix of benefits increased to 27 percent in 1994, up from 15 percent in 1991. Health care coverage, vacation or other time off, and life insurance were the three areas in which most respondents wanted to see changes made.

With this increasing discontent and call for a new mix of benefits, the challenge for small business owners is to provide a mix of benefits that is affordable to employers and motivational to employees.

Flexible Benefit Packages. Because employees do not all have the same needs, a flexible (cafeteria) benefit package allows each employee to select the benefits that best suit his financial and lifestyle needs. Employees generally favor such plans due to their flexibility and pretax benefits.

Increasingly, flexible benefit packages not only provide employees with a choice or menu of benefits from which to choose, they also include choices between taxable and nontaxable benefits. Under these latter, IRS-approved plans, employees are allowed to purchase benefits with pretax dollars. In this way, they can reduce their taxable income while at the same time increasing their benefit options.

The advantages of flexible plans are not realized without additional costs. As the number and mix of benefits increase, so do administrative costs associated with activities such as record keeping, communications with employees, and compliance with government regulations. A second, but no less important, concern is that employees may select the wrong mix or types of benefits. Often employees do not worry about their benefits until they are actually needed, generally in response to a major illness or accident. Yet the law does not allow benefit choices to be changed during the plan year, so employees often find their benefit options do not match their immediate needs.

Health Insurance. One of the most common and valued employee benefits is health insurance. According to Dallas Salisbury, president of the Employee Benefit Research Institute, "There's no question that workers value health insurance benefits above all others."[18] In response, employers are increasingly providing employee health care coverage, although many are also opting for a copayment plan of some type. As of 1990, 69 percent of all small private employers provided some form of medical care coverage.[19]

In order to hold down the growing costs of health insurance, many small business owners are joining cooperative health maintenance organizations (HMOs) or preferred provider organizations (PPOs). Under an HMO system, a firm signs a contract with an approved health maintenance organization which agrees to provide health and medical services to its employees. In return for the exclusive right to care for the firm's employees, the HMO offers its services at an adjusted rate. Unfortunately, employees often object to these plans since they are restricted to using the health care specialists employed or approved by the HMO. To overcome this objection, some companies are switching to preferred provider organizations (PPOs).

With a PPO, a firm or group of firms negotiates with doctors and hospitals to provide certain health care services for a favorable price. In turn, member firms then encourage their employees, through higher reimbursement payments, to use these "preferred" providers. Employees tend to favor PPOs since they have the opportunity or freedom to use the doctor of their choice.

Pension Plans. To assist employees in saving for their retirement needs, employers provide them with retirement plans. Pension plans present employees with an accumulated amount of money when they reach a set retirement age or when they are unable to continue working due to a disability. Five of the more common options are individual retirement accounts, simplified employee pension plans, salary-reduction simplified employee pension plans, 401(k) plans, and Keogh plans.

Individual Retirement Accounts. Individual retirement accounts (IRAs) allow employees to make tax-exempt contributions of up to $2,000 per year into their own account. In 1986, Congress revised the IRA's tax-exempt provisions. While interest earned on IRAs remains tax deferable, contributions are totally deductible from personal income taxes only if an individual earns less than $25,000 ($40,000 if married filing jointly) or if the individual is not covered by a company-sponsored pension plan. Eligible employees pay tax on the principal and accrued interest only when money is withdrawn. (There is a penalty for withdrawing funds before retirement.) As the name implies, IRAs are individual plans: contributions are at the discretion of the employee, not the employer. In addition to the obvious advantage of providing a retirement income, IRAs reduce eligible employees' current taxable income.

Simplified Employee Pension Plans. A simplified employee pension (SEP) plan is similar to an IRA but is only available to people who are self-employed or who work for small businesses which do not have a retirement plan. Those who are eligible may contribute up to 15 percent of their salary or $22,500 per year, whichever is less. There are few, if any, startup or administrative costs for the employer in establishing a SEP. (See Table 14-1.) In addition, there are no additional IRS reporting requirements for the employer, and she may change the percentage of salary contributions made from one year to the next. Employees are immediately vested (meaning that they are eligible to keep the employer's contribution without having to wait for a probationary period to end) and may withdraw funds from their accounts at any time (provided they are willing to pay income

TABLE 14 ▪ 1   Four Pension Plans for Small Business

PLAN NAME	BASIC DESCRIPTION	MAXIMUM ANNUAL CONTRIBUTION PER EMPLOYEE*	TYPICAL COST TO START**	ANNUAL ADMINISTRATIVE COSTS	ALLOWS VESTING AND LOANS	ADVANTAGES AND DRAWBACKS
Simplified Employee Pension (SEP)	Works like an IRA for each employee. Employer makes same percentage of salary contributions for each worker, but the percentage may vary from year to year.	15 percent of salary or $22,500, whichever is less.	None	$0 to $500	No	No annual IRS forms to file. SEPs provide immediate vesting of contributions. Most part-time workers are eligible for contributions.
Salary-Reduction Simplified Employee Pension (SAR-SEP)	As in a 401(k) plan, employees contribute pretax dollars to their own accounts, which in this case are IRAs. Employer may also contribute a percentage of salary to each worker.	Employee salary-reduction contribution may not exceed 15 percent of salary or $9,240, whichever is less. Employer may contribute up to 15 percent of each employee's salary or up to $22,500, whichever is less.	None	$0 to $1,000	No	No annual IRS forms to file, and employers aren't required to contribute. Administration is moderately complex. Can't be used by firms with more than 25 workers. Half of eligible workers are required to participate.
401(k)	Employees put pretax dollars into their accounts. Employers may contribute nothing, or match some or all of employee contribution.	Employee contributions may not exceed 15 percent of salary or $9,240, whichever is less. Employer may contribute up to 15 percent of each employee's salary or $22,500, whichever is less.	$1,000 to $4,500	$1,500 to $6,000	Yes	Permits hardship withdrawals. Administration is extremely complex. Requires strict compliance with government regulations. Rules limit contributions by highly paid employees.
Profit Sharing	Employer makes same percentage of salary contribution to each worker but may vary this percentage each year.	15 percent of salary or $22,500, whichever is less.	$0 to $2,000	$0 to $2,000	Yes	Employers have maximum flexibility in deciding how much or even whether to contribute each year. Annual IRS filing is required.

* Total contributions from employer and employee to a defined-contribution plan may not exceed $30,000 per year.

** Cost estimates are based on a company with 15 employees and $1 million in annual sales. Figures assume plans contain no special features that could boost costs. All expenses may be paid by employer or passed along to plan participants.

Source: Chart by Michael Rook. From Mary Rowland, "Pension Options for Small Firms," reprinted by permission, Nation's Business, *March 1994, p. 26. © 1994, U.S. Chamber of Commerce.*

tax on the principal plus early withdrawal penalties if under age 59½). In addition, any employee who has earned $396 or more in compensation, is 21 years of age, and has worked for the employer for at least three out of the last five years is covered. Thus, most part-time workers are eligible for SEP plans.

Salary-reduction Simplified Employee Pension Plans. Salary-reduction Simplified Employee Pension (SAR-SEP) plans are funded entirely by the employee through payroll deductions. In 1994, employees could elect to contribute up to $9,240 in pretax salary or 15 percent of salary, whichever was less.

Employers may, by setting up an employer-funded SEP for each employee, match the employees' contributions up to a combined employee-employer limit of 15 percent of each employee's salary or a combined total of $22,500, whichever is less. SAR-SEP plans are easy to set up and fairly inexpensive to administer. Only companies with fewer than 26 employees are permitted to establish SAR-SEPs and then only if half of all eligible workers participate in the plan.

As in the case of SEPs, SAR-SEPs are nonqualified plans and are therefore not protected from creditors in the event of bankruptcy. Because of this concern, many small business owners are establishing "qualified" (IRS-Department of Labor approved) 401(k) plans.

401(k) Plans. Named after Section 401(k) of the 1978 Revenue Act, 401(k) plans allow small businesses to establish payroll reduction plans that are more flexible and have greater tax advantages than an IRA. As was true of the foregoing plans, the amount deferred and any accumulated investment earnings are excluded from current income and are taxed only when distributed.

The contributory limits for 401(k) plans are the same as for SAR-SEP plans. (See Table 14-1.) While not required to do so, many employers match employees' contributions on a percentage basis. The most common match is 50 cents for each $1 contributed by the employee up to a cap of 5 percent or 6 percent of the employee's salary.[20] This 50 percent rate, according to a study by William Mercer, Inc., encourages almost as much employee participation as does a 100 percent match rate.[21] The funds are managed by a trustee overseeing the company's pension plans. In many cases, employees have the flexibility of selecting the investment vehicle for their investment or, in the case of mutual funds, switching from one fund to another. Employers may establish vesting requirements. Loans as well as hardship withdrawals are available from the plan.

On the downside, 401(k) plans are expensive to develop and administer since they require IRS approval and must meet Labor Department pension guidelines. In response, some mutual fund companies are beginning to offer 401(k) packages that fulfill the basic needs of investment options, administration, communication to employees, and compliance with government requirements specifically to small business customers.[22]

Keogh Plans. A Keogh plan is a special type of retirement account for self-employed individuals and their employees. Currently, a self-employed person may contribute the smaller of $30,000 or 20 percent of self-employment income to a qualified money-purchase Keogh plan for herself and the smaller of $30,000 or 25 percent of each employee's taxable compensation to an employee account. Contributions and accumulated investment earnings are tax exempt until the time of withdrawal.

Employers may, with IRS approval, establish various limitations and eligibility requirements for employee participation in these plans. However, once established, the employer is required to make yearly contributions at the stated contributory rate. As a qualified plan, Keogh plans require IRS approval resulting in startup costs which range from $1,000 to $4,500 while administrative costs may vary from $1,500 to $6,000 annually.

Child Care. As the number of dual-income families continues to increase and the concern over family values grows, more and more employees are looking to their employers for help. For example, a recent survey of employees showed that 68 percent of respondents said they would be willing to contribute to a benefit program that allowed them to set aside money before taxes to pay for health care or child care expenses.[23] Apparently, employers are listening, as nearly eight out of ten major U.S. employers now offer some form of child care assistance.[24] This aid takes many forms, of which the most common types are flexible work schedules, flexible spending accounts that allow workers to set aside a portion of their pre-tax earnings to pay for child care costs, resource and referral services, and, to a much lesser extent, company-sponsored day care centers. Employers who offer child care assistance generally do so for one or more of the following reasons: to accommodate employee requests, thus increasing employee morale; to retain high-performing employees; to improve recruiting efforts; to reduce employee absenteeism and tardiness; and to increase employee productivity.

Miscellaneous Benefits. The number and variety of employee benefits are limited only by the generosity of the employer and his ability to pay. As of 1991, benefits provided by firms with fewer than 100 workers represented 25.3 percent of total compensation, while those provided by firms with 500 or more workers amounted to 30.7 percent.[25] Table 14-2 summarizes the types of benefits provided by small private establishments as of 1990.

TABLE 14 ▪ 2   Benefits Provided by Small Private Employers[a]

EMPLOYEE BENEFIT PROGRAM	ALL EMPLOYEES	PROFESSIONAL, TECHNICAL, AND RELATED EMPLOYEES	CLERICAL AND SALES	PRODUCTION AND SERVICE
Paid				
Holidays	84%	95%	91%	75%
Vacations	88	94	93	83
Personal leave	11	17	13	7
Lunch period	8	7	7	8
Rest period	48	42	46	51
Funeral leave	47	57	54	38
Jury duty leave	54	72	62	43
Military leave	21	29	26	15
Sick leave	47	70	61	29
Maternity leave	2	3	3	1
Paternity leave	e	e	e	e
Unpaid				
Maternity leave	17	26	20	12
Paternity leave	8	13	8	5
Sickness and Accident Insurance	26	25	24	27
Wholly employer financed	17	14	15	19
Partly employer financed	9	10	10	9
Long-Term Disability Insurance	19	36	25	9
Wholly employer financed	16	30	21	8
Partly employer financed	3	5	4	2

TABLE 14 ▪ 2 Benefits Provided by Small Private Employers[a] (continued)

EMPLOYEE BENEFIT PROGRAM	ALL EMPLOYEES	PROFESSIONAL, TECHNICAL, AND RELATED EMPLOYEES	CLERICAL AND SALES	PRODUCTION AND SERVICE
Medical Care	69	82	75	60
Employee coverage				
wholly employer financed	40	46	40	37
partly employer financed	29	36	35	23
Family coverage				
wholly employer financed	22	23	22	22
partly employer financed	46	59	53	38
Dental Care	30	38	35	24
Employee coverage				
wholly employer financed	17	19	19	15
partly employer financed	12	18	18	8
Family coverage				
wholly employer financed	11	11	12	11
partly employer financed	19	27	23	13
Life Insurance	64	79	70	55
Wholly employer financed	53	69	60	43
Partly employer financed	11	11	10	11
Retirement[b]	42	49	47	37
Defined benefit pension	20	20	23	18
wholly employer financed	19	18	21	18
partly employer financed	1	2	1	1
Defined contribution[c]	31	40	36	24
wholly employer financed	16	19	17	15
partly employer financed	11	17	16	6
Capital Accumulation[d]	4	5	4	2
Wholly employer financed	1	2	2	1
Partly employer financed	2	3	3	2
Types of Defined Contribution Plans				
Savings and thrift	10	16	15	5
Deferred profit sharing	15	17	17	13
Employee stock ownership	1	1	1	e
Money purchase pension	6	9	6	6
Stock bonus	e	f	e	f
Stock Option	e	f	e	e
Stock Purchase	e	e	e	e
Cash Only Profit Sharing	e	f	e	f
Flexible Benefits Plans	1	3	2	1
Reimbursement Accounts	8	13	9	4

Source: U.S. Department of Labor, Bureau of Labor Statistics, Employee Benefits in Small Private Establishments, 1990 (Washington, DC: U.S. Government Printing Office, 1991).

[a] These tabulations provide representative data for 32 million full-time employees in private nonagricultural establishments with fewer than 100 employees. The survey was comprised primarily of small independent businesses, although about 25 percent of respondents were small establishments that were part of larger enterprises.

[b] Includes defined benefit pension plans and defined contribution retirement plans. Many employees participated in both types of plans. Does not include pension plans that are fully employee financed.

[c] Includes money purchase pension, profit-sharing, savings and thrift, stock bonus, and employee stock ownership plans in which employer contributions must remain in the participant's account until retirement age, death, disability, separation from service, age 59½, or hardship withdrawal.

[d] Includes plans in which participants may withdraw employer contributions from their accounts without regard to the conditions listed in footnote c.

[e] Less than 0.5 percent.

[f] No participants in the program.

Source: Joseph Placientini and Jill Foley, "Employer Spending for Benefits Remains Unchanged Relative to Total Compensation Between 1980 and 1990," EBRI Databook on Employee Benefits, 2e (Washington, DC: Employee Research Institute, 1992) pp. 52–53.

The Benefits of Education

It all started on a fishing trip with John Strazzanti, founder and president of Com-Corp Industries in Cleveland, his vice president of finance, David Wright, and Wright's son. Wright's son wanted to attend the University of Southern California but the Wright family had saved little money. That's when Strazzanti came up with the idea of providing low-interest educational loans for his employees' dependents.

Strazzanti, upon learning that other employees in his auto-parts manufacturing firm were experiencing similar concerns, called a company-wide meeting to announce the loan program. Employees liked the program, but they wanted to limit Com-Corp's risk. At their suggestion, four safeguards were built into the system. First, employees were eligible only after three years of employment. Second, the company would never have more than $40,000 outstanding in loans. Third, dependents would repay the loan at 3 percent annual interest over ten years. Fourth, the company could take legal action if it got burned, or if legal action would cost too much, it could recover any losses from the company's profit-sharing fund.

The program cost virtually nothing to set up, and Com-Corp believes it helps account for its low 2.5 percent annual turnover rate. When Wright's son graduated from USC, he was the program's first beneficiary. His sister started college shortly afterward.

Source: Adapted from Michael P. Cronin, "Managing People," Inc. (September 1993), p. 29.

When Problems Arise

While you can strive for harmony in the workplace, sometimes problems arise. When they do, you need policies laid out when discipline or dismissal of employees is necessary.

Disciplinary Measures

Discipline involves taking timely and appropriate actions to modify or correct the performance of an employee or group of employees. The purpose of discipline is to ensure that company rules and regulations are consistently followed for the well-being of both the company and its employees. A fair and just disciplinary procedure should be based upon the four following tenets.

The first of these principles is a comprehensive set of rules and regulations. Expressed in the form of an **employee handbook** or policy manual, these rules and regulations should inform employees of their rights and responsibilities in the employment relationship. To be effective, the rules and regulations must be up to date, easily understood, and, most importantly, communicated to employees. An effective way to achieve this latter goal is to go over the employee handbook during employee orientation and to have employees sign a statement acknowledging receipt of the document. (See the Manager's Notebook in Chapter 3, page 70, covering employee handbooks.)

employee handbook Written rules and regulations informing employees of their rights and responsibilities in the employment relationship.

A well-designed **performance appraisal** system is the second essential component. Not only does a sound performance appraisal process document the need for possible discipline, but it also affords management the opportunity to address problem areas before they become disciplinary concerns. In addition, a well-defined performance appraisal process will help to fulfill the third tenet, which is a system of progressive penalties.

Increasingly, managers are moving away from the "hot-stove" principle of discipline, in which discipline is immediate and of consistent intensity, to the **progressive approach,** in which discipline is incremental and increasingly forceful. Under most progressive systems, managers first issue an oral (informal)

performance appraisal
A process of evaluating an employee's job-related achievements.

progressive approach Discipline that is applied to employees in appropriately incremental, and increasingly forceful, measures.

M anager's Notebook

Productive Disciplinary Steps

- **Determine whether discipline is needed.** Is the problem an isolated incident or part of an ongoing pattern?

- **Have clear goals to discuss with the employee.** You should discuss the problem in specific terms. Indirect comments will not make your point clear. You must also state what you expect the employee to do. If the employee has no idea about your expectations after discussing a performance problem with you, the employee is likely to repeat past performance.

- **Talk about the problem in private.** Public reprimand is embarrassing for the employee and for everyone who witnesses it. If you chastise in public, you will not only lose trust and respect from that individual but also from those who observe the act.

- **Keep your cool.** A calm approach will keep a performance discussion more objective and prevent distraction by irrelevant problems.

- **Watch the timing of the meeting.** If the problem is not obvious and you schedule the meeting far in advance, the employee will spend time worrying about what is wrong.

On the other hand, if the problem is obvious, the meeting should be scheduled to give the employee plenty of time to prepare.

- **Prepare opening remarks.** Performance meetings will be more effective if you are confident in your opening remarks. Think them out in advance and rehearse them.

- **Get to the point.** Beating around the bush with small talk does more to increase the employee's anxiety level than to reduce it.

- **Allow two-way communication.** Make sure the disciplinary meeting is a discussion—not a lecture. You can get to the heart of the problem only if the employee is allowed to speak. Your intent is to arrive at a solution to a problem, not to scold the employee.

- **Establish a follow-up plan.** You and your employee need to agree to a follow-up plan to establish a time frame within which the employee's performance is to improve.

- **End on a positive note.** Highlight the employee's positive points so he will leave the meeting with a belief that you want him to succeed in the future.

Source: Adapted from D. Day, "Training 101: Help for Discipline Dodgers," Training and Development *(May 1993), pp. 19–22.*

reprimand, then a written warning (formal notice), followed by suspension, and finally, discharge. Arbitrators and the courts generally favor progressive discipline over that of the hot-stove approach, except in cases of gross misconduct, such as theft or assault, when immediate discharge is warranted.

The final component of an effective disciplinary program is an **appeal process.** The most common appeal process in nonunion companies is the open-door policy, a procedure whereby employees seek a review of the disciplinary decision at the next level of management. For such a process to be effective, it must involve a thorough and truly objective review of the facts of the case by an executive of higher rank than the supervisor who applied the discipline. Open-door policies are appropriate for companies with many employees and levels of management, but in the majority of small businesses the only level of management is you—the owner. If an employee feels unjustly treated and is not satisfied with your decision, his only recourse is through the courts.

appeal process A formal procedure allowing employees to seek review of disciplinary measure at a higher level of management.

Computer Applications

Computer software can help make the paperwork behind a good human resources management system seem less overwhelming and burdensome. For instance, performance appraisals are an important ingredient in compensating and developing good employees, yet the process is very time-consuming. But there are two software programs that can make it easier. The software Performance Now! by Knowledge Point (list price $129) asks users to rate employees on a scale of one to five for skills ranging from "takes responsibility for own actions" to "keeps on top of current developments in field." The computer program then generates descriptive text that supports that rating, prompting the user to add specific examples and even giving warnings when the ratings for different performance factors are inconsistent.

Another of these performance appraisal software tools is Employee Appraiser by Austin-Hayne (list price $129). Rather than taking a numerical rating approach, it provides sample text that the user can adjust to be more positive or negative using a "writing tuner" function. This program also includes extensive advice on how to improve performance between reviews. A third useful human resource management software program is ManagePro from Avantos Performance Systems Inc. (list price $240). This program combines traditional personal information manager (names, addresses, phone numbers, and so forth) capabilities, database functions, and some focused management tools. One of the unique features of ManagePro is its "expert system" with tips and techniques about planning, delegating, rewarding, and managing employees.

On the higher-priced end of human resource management software is a program called InCompliance by Decisis. Its $25,000 base price provides sound legal advice based on broad employment-law principles. Although it's expensive, it can save a lot of costly calls to legal experts.

Sources: Ripley Hatch and Jon Pepper, "How to Buy Business Software," Nation's Business *(June 1994), pp. 20–28; and Alison L. Sprout, "Surprise! Software to Help You Manage,"* Fortune, *April 17, 1995, pp. 197–201.*

Dismissing Employees

Since dismissing an employee is the most extreme step of discipline you can exercise, it must be taken with care. Your legitimate reasons for dismissing an employee may include unsatisfactory performance of the job or changing requirements of the job, which make the employee unqualified.

When it comes to discharging an employee, what you can and cannot do will be influenced to a large degree by two considerations. First, the decision to discharge an employee must be based upon a job-related reason or reasons, not on the basis of race, color, religion, sex, age, national origin, or disability. Second, your ability to legally discharge an employee and the manner in which you may do so will be highly dependent upon your at-will status. Over the past century, the prevailing law in the United States has been that unless an employment contract is signed, either the employer or the employee can terminate the employment relationship at will. Under the **at-will doctrine,** an employer has great leeway in discharging an employee in that he or she has the right to discharge the employee for a good reason, a bad reason, or no reason at all.

Within the past decade, however, the courts and some state legislatures have imposed one or more of the following restrictions upon at-will employers. Check the laws of your state to find which apply to your business.

at-will doctrine The legal restrictions on an employer's ability to discharge an employee without just cause.

Implied Contract. An employer may be restricted in discharging an employee if an implied contract exists as a result of written statements in the company's employment application, employment ads, employee handbook, and other company documents. Verbal statements by company representatives to employees may also erode an employer's at-will status, as may an employee's record of long-term employment with the firm.

Good Faith and Fair Dealing. This exception holds that the employer must have acted fairly and in good faith in discharging the employee. For example, an employee may not be fired simply because he is about to become vested in the company's pension plan.

Public Policy Exception. Under the public policy exception, employers may not discharge workers for exercising a statutory right such as filing a workers' compensation claim, or performing public service, such as serving on a jury. Nor may an employee be fired for refusing to break the law or to engage in conduct that is against one's beliefs, for example, refusing to falsify an employer's records to cover up possible misconduct on the part of the company.

In the event that a terminated employee seeks legal redress by filing a lawsuit against you, whether or not you have acted in a manner consistent with the at-will principle will be decided by a judge. In all cases, you should be able to provide evidence of *just cause* for the dismissal. Just cause generally implies due process and reasonability on the part of the employer. You are likely to have just cause if you can:

- Cite the specific work rule violation, and show that the employee had prior knowledge of the rule and the consequences of violating it.
- Show that the work rule was necessary for the efficient and safe operation of the company and was therefore a business necessity.
- Prove that you conducted a thorough and objective investigation of the violation and in the process afforded the employee the opportunity to present her side of the story.

Manager's Notebook

Firing an Employee

Despite the economic recovery, companies are continuing to use layoffs as a cost-cutting strategy. But even though firing employees is an all-too-common part of their duties, few managers handle the process well. That's because, whatever the facts of the dismissal, most managers feel bad about letting someone go. Ironically, expressing feelings of remorse can be cruel, because it gives the employee false hope. Instead, the best way to deal with the termination is to make it a quick, unambiguous act. Spell out exactly why you are letting the employee go, state clearly that the decision is final and explain the details of the company's notice policy or severance. Then ask the employee to leave by the end of the week, if possible (so his or her presence won't demoralize the rest of the staff), and to sign a letter of acknowledgment, which will make it more difficult for him or her to reopen the discussion—or sue. Above all, resist any attempts to turn the discussion into an argument. (The manager's words begin in red; the employee's begin in blue.)

Icebreaker. I'm sorry to have to give you some bad news: Your job here is being terminated. [*If for economic reasons:* I think you'll find the terms of the severance quite generous. I have also prepared a letter of reference, which I'll give you at the end of this meeting.]

Fired for Poor Performance. Please understand that this decision is final. You haven't made any real progress with the problems we discussed at your last two performance reviews. I'm sure you'll be able to put your skills to better use in a different position. If you'll sign this letter that says you understand our discussion, we can put this matter behind us.

Laid Off for Economic Reasons. Unfortunately, this decision is final. Please understand that it's purely an economic move and it's no reflection on your performance. I'll be happy to make that clear to any new employers you interview with. If you'll just sign this letter outlining what I've just said, we can get this unhappy business over with.

Gets Angry. You've got some nerve getting rid of me this way. This company might not be in such a mess if it didn't treat its employees so shabbily.

Gets Defensive. You're singling me out. I've performed as well as anyone else—better, in fact, considering the new accounts I just landed.

Gets Personal. How could you do this to me? We're friends. You've come over to my house for dinner. Isn't there something you can do?

Absorb Anger. I'm sorry to hear that you feel that way. Everyone here, including me, wanted to see your position work out. Unfortunately, it hasn't. Why don't you take a few minutes to look over this letter and then sign it.

Deflect Defense. As I've said, this is purely an economic decision. You were simply the last one hired. **OR:** Your skill in lining up new clients doesn't make up for your consistent problems with our existing accounts.

Deflect Guilt. I feel bad about this, but it is strictly a business decision. My personal feelings don't count. As your friend, I'll do everything I can to help you land another job. For now, though, I need you to take a look at this letter and then sign it.

Demands More Severance. I'm not going to sign anything until we talk about this severance package. It isn't nearly enough, considering how long I've worked here.

Threatens Legal Action. I'm not going to sign anything until I speak to my lawyer. I think there are some issues that I need to get some legal advice on.

Asks for Another Chance. Isn't there something I can do to reverse this decision? I need this job. I promise my work will improve. Please give me another chance.

End Discussion. You're welcome to discuss the severance offer with someone higher up, although I have to warn you that they're the ones who set the terms. **OR:** Of course. You have every right to speak with your attorney first. I'll hold on to the check and the paperwork until I hear from you. **OR:** I'm terribly sorry, but the decision really is final. [*Stand up.*] Good luck in the future.

Source: Stephen M. Pollan and Mark Levine, "Firing an Employee," Working Woman (August 1994), p. 55. Reprinted by permission of Stuart Krichevsky Literary Agency, Inc. © 1994 by Stephen M. Pollan and Mark Levine.

- Document that the employee was given the opportunity to improve or modify his performance (except in cases of gross misconduct or insubordination, when it is unnecessary).
- Show that there was sufficient evidence or proof of guilt to justify the actions taken.
- Show that you treated the employee in a manner consistent with past practices.
- Demonstrate that the disciplinary actions taken were fair and reasonable in view of the employee's work history.
- Document that the disciplinary action was reviewed by an independent party either within or outside the company prior to being implemented.

Summary

■ Define the job analysis process and the function of job descriptions and job specifications.

Job analysis is the process of determining the duties and skills required to do a job and the kind of person who should be hired to do it. A job description is part of the job analysis. It is a list of duties, responsibilities, and reporting relationships of a job. A job specification is another part of the job analysis. It identifies the education, skills, and personality that a person needs to have to be right for a job.

■ Evaluate the advantages and disadvantages of five sources of employee recruitment.

Help-wanted advertising reaches numerous potential applicants, but many of them will not be right for the job you are trying to fill. Employment agencies screen applicants for you so you do not have to deal with as many people. Those run by the government are usually appropriate only for positions requiring lower-level skills. Executive recruiters offer more expensive services but can help you find people with higher-level skills. Employee referrals are effective because your current employees know the skills and talents needed, but hiring in this manner can create cliques. It can also build resentment if the new hire does not work out. When hiring friends and relatives, you have the advantage of knowing their abilities and expertise, but personal relationships can be strained on the job.

■ Describe the three steps of employee selection.

When recruiting employees, you first need to generate a pool of applicants. In the selection process, you will try to narrow the applicant pool down to match the needs of your business with the skills of the person. Application forms and résumés, interviews, and testing are the three most common tools of selection.

■ Discuss the need for employee training and the six methods of doing so.

To become a better, more productive worker, every employee needs to have her knowledge and skills enhanced through training. Lectures, conferences, programmed learning, role playing, job rotation, and correspondence courses are six common techniques.

■ Identify the three components of a compensation plan and the ten variable elements of a benefits system.

Employees can be compensated for their efforts with hourly wages or salary, or on the basis of piecework or commission plans. Incentive pay programs are a way to motivate and reward employees above their base pay by paying bonuses or profit-sharing amounts. Common types of benefits, which are part of a compensation package, include flexible benefit plans, health insurance, paid vacation time, pension plans, educational programs/child care, and discounts on company products. The most common pension plans adopted by small businesses are the Individual Retirement Account (IRA), the Simplified Employee Pension (SEP) Plan, the Salary-Reduction Simplified Employee Pension Plan (SAR-SEP), the 401(k) Plan, and the Keogh Plan.

■ Profile an effective sequence for disciplining and terminating an employee.

The progressive disciplinary system, favored by many managers today, begins with an oral reprimand, followed by a written warning, suspension without pay, and finally, termination from the company.

Questions for Review and Discussion

1. What is the difference between a job analysis and a job description?
2. When would you, as a small business owner, prefer to receive a résumé rather than an application form?
3. How is the use of temporary employees different from employee leasing? What are the advantages and disadvantages of each?
4. What are the differences between hard and soft issues during a job orientation? Is one more important than the other?
5. List the advantages of a flexible benefit package to employees. To the employer.
6. Explain the four components to an effective disciplinary system.
7. Define "at-will" status.
8. Discuss three key pieces of legislation that are used to prevent job discrimination.
9. What factors influence the type and amount of employee benefits which a small business can offer?
10. Review the section on training new employees. Give examples of types of jobs that would best lend themselves to each training method.

Critical Incident

Magnet Inc. is the world's leading manufacturer of refrigerator magnets in the specialty advertising products industry. You've no doubt seen examples of their products—in fact, you may even have a few stuck on your refrigerator. Bill Wood is the founder and chairman of the company. The company is growing rapidly and Bill needs to hire a market research analyst to help him with marketing issues. Here's a copy of the job information that's been used in advertising the position.

Market Research Analyst

Individual with good marketing research and data analysis skills needed by fast-growing small company that specializes in making refrigerator magnets. College degree in marketing research desirable, but will look at individuals without degree who have at least 5 years' experience in a marketing research position. Skills in computer data entry and data analysis an absolute requirement. Must be willing to locate to small town in east-central Missouri. Salary is competitive and commensurate with education and experience.

The applicant pool has been narrowed down to the following three individuals. Information about the three applicants has been summarized from their job applications and résumés.

Flora Cheung. Flora is a recent graduate of a state university in California. Her undergraduate degree is in marketing research and she has participated in three marketing research projects for one of her professors while a student. Her grades are average (2.9 on a 4.0 scale) and she speaks French fluently.

Edward Fleck. Edward is a victim of corporate downsizing. He was employed for 22 years at Procter & Gamble, the last 7 years, in the marketing research department. He doesn't have a college degree, but his reference recommendations seem to be good. He's been out of work now for 19 months and really wants to find a job.

Bill Hampton. Bill has been out of school now for 5 years. He graduated from Howard University in Washington, D.C., with an undergraduate degree in business administration. Since graduating, Bill has had four different jobs. His latest job was in sales and he's tired of living out of a suitcase. He's proficient in computers.

Questions

1. Develop a job description and job specification for this marketing research analyst position.
2. Pair off in teams and discuss the three applicants. From the information provided, write down what you see as the pros and cons of each individual. Then develop questions that you would like to ask each individual during his or her interview.

Take it to the Net

 We invite you to visit the Hatten page on the Prentice Hall Web site at: http://www.prenhall.com/~hattensb for this chapter's World Wide Web exercise.

Chapter Focus

After reading this chapter, you should be able to:

- Describe the elements of an operating system.
- Explain how manufacturers and service providers use operations management.
- Describe how to measure productivity.
- Recount the four methods of scheduling operations.
- Explain the role of quality in operations management.
- Identify the three ways to control operations.

PUT A BAYSIDE ON IT!

Precision Gearheads for Servo and Stepper Motors

BAYSIDE
PRECISION GEARHEADS

BAYSIDE
PRECISION GEARHEADS

15 Operations Management

HEN HOWARD LIND AND Avi Telyas purchased Bayside Controls, a small, struggling gear-parts factory in Queens, New York, in 1986, the first thing they did was to adopt a new production process. This technique, which got its start in the Japanese auto industry, was called *cell manufacturing.*

At that time, practically no small companies employed cell manufacturing. Today about 40 percent of U.S. factories with fewer than 100 employees use some form of it, while 74 percent of large manufacturers use it. What makes this process unique is its use of small, self-directed teams—or cells—of employees who make the entire product. Gone is the traditional assembly line where each employee works on one small stage of production.

Bayside now operates four cells in which workers measure, cut, assemble, and clean gearheads that will be used in industrial motors. The process has led to empowerment of employees, productivity increases, and a decrease in production time. It has even enabled

Bayside to manufacture and deliver a custom-made gear overnight to handle an emergency for Ford. Since changing processes, the company's average production time has dropped from six weeks to two days while overall productivity has increased by 50 percent.

Cell manufacturing entails significant disadvantages also. Cost is the main one, as cell manufacturing is capital intensive. Bayside, for instance, has had to set up four separate manufacturing operations instead of just one. But for Bayside, the costs have paid off. When Lind and Telyas bought the company in 1986, annual revenues ran about $300,000. By 1993, after the switch, sales had grown to $7 million, and 1994 sales were projected at $11 million.

Will cell manufacturing become the production process of the future? *Adapted from: Stephanie Mehta, "Cell Manufacturing Gains Acceptance at Smaller Plants," The Wall Street Journal, September 15, 1994, p. B2.*

This chapter focuses on operations management (OM) and the processes associated with it. The function of operations management has evolved over the last few decades from a narrow view of production, inventory, and industrial management into a broader term that includes services. The management of production and operations is critical to all small businesses, not just those involved in manufacturing. Every business performs an operations function—the processes and procedures of converting labor, materials, money, and other resources into finished products or services.

How Do You Develop Operating Systems?

Operations management systems contain five basic elements: inputs, transformation processes, outputs, control systems, and feedback. These elements must be brought together and coordinated into a system to produce the product or service—the reason for the business to exist.

Inputs

inputs All the resources that go into a business.

The **inputs** in an operations management system include all physical and intangible resources that come into a business. **Raw materials** are needed as the thing to be transformed. A company which makes in-line skates, for instance, must have polymers, plastics, and metal. **Skills and knowledge** of the people within the organization are other inputs. A management consulting firm, for example, needs people with special expertise. The in-line skate manufacturer needs trained workers to fabricate the product. **Money, information,** and **energy** are all needed in varying degrees. Inputs are important to the quality of the finished product of the business. Remember the computer cliché "Garbage in—garbage out." You can't produce high-quality outputs from inferior inputs.

Transformation Processes

transformation process What a business does to add value to inputs in converting them to outputs.

Once we have identified the inputs of a business, we can look at the processes that are used to transform them into finished products. **Transformation processes** are the active practices—including concepts, procedures, and technologies—which are implemented to produce outputs. Dry cleaners, for instance, take soiled clothing (inputs) and use chemicals, equipment, and know-how to transform them into clean clothing (the outputs of the business).

Outputs

Outputs, the result of the transformation processes, are what your business produces. Outputs can be tangible, like a CD, or intangible, like a doctor's diagnosis.

Since a business's social responsibility has become an even more serious matter, along with product liability lawsuits and other forms of litigation, we need to consider *all* the outputs a business produces—not just the beneficial or intended ones. When we look at the big picture of the transformation process,

outputs The tangible or intangible products that a business produces.

FIGURE 15-1
Control Systems
Every type of business takes inputs and transforms them into outputs.

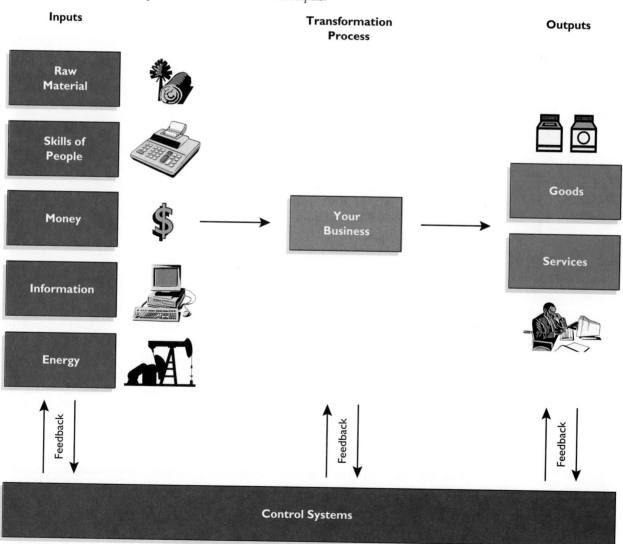

we see that employee accidents, consumer injuries, pollution, and waste are also outputs.

Control Systems

control systems The means to monitor input, transformation, and output in order to identify problems.

Control systems provide the means to monitor and correct problems or deviations when they occur in the operating system. Controls are integrated into all three stages—input, transformation, and output. (See Figure 15-1.) An example of a control system would be the use of electronic monitors in a manufacturing process to tell a machine operator that the product is not being made within the allowed size tolerance level. In service companies, employee behavior is part of the transformation process to be controlled. A bank manager, for instance, might hire people to pose as new bank customers and then report back to the manager on the quality of service they received from tellers or loan officers.

Feedback

feedback Communication tools to connect control systems to the processes of a business.

Feedback is the information that a manager receives in monitoring the operation system. It can be verbal, written, electronic, or observational. Feedback is the necessary communication that links a control system to the inputs, transformation, and outputs.

Types of Operations Management

Production broadly describes the creating that businesses of all types do in making goods and services. Computer hardware and software companies, health care providers, and farmers are all involved in production. **Manufacturing** is just one type of production. It is making goods as opposed to providing services or extracting natural resources. One of your highest priorities as a manager is to ensure that productivity remains high. **Productivity** is the measure of output per worker. It is important to measure productivity in order to control the amount of resources used to produce outputs.

Manufacturing Operations

Manufacturing businesses can be classified by the way they make goods and by the time used to create them. Goods and services can be made from analytic or synthetic systems using either continuous or intermittent processes.

Analytic systems reduce inputs into component parts to extract products. Auto salvage businesses buy vehicles from insurance companies or individuals to dismantle them for parts or scrap iron to sell. **Synthetic systems,** by contrast, combine inputs to create a finished product or change them into a different product. Restaurants take vegetables, fruits, grains, meats, seafood, music, lighting, furniture, paintings, and a variety of human talents to create and serve meals.

continuous process A production process which operates for long periods of time without interruption.
intermittent process A production process that operates in short cycles in order to change products.

Production by **continuous process** is accomplished over long periods of time. Production of the same, or very similar, products goes on uninterrupted for days, months, or years. Microbreweries or wine makers are examples of small businesses that produce goods via continuous process.

Production runs that use an **intermittent process** involve short cycles and frequent stops to change products. Small businesses using intermittent processes

Reality Check

Work Hard, Play Hard

At Alexander Doll Company in New York City, the Japanese principle of *kaizen*—or continuous improvement—is more than just child's play. As a manufacturer of collectible dolls, the company had gone into bankruptcy, and president Patricia Lewis was looking for a way to improve the firm's production efficiency and effectiveness. A consulting group, TBM Consulting Group, Inc. of Durham, North Carolina, felt that *kaizen* could turn the business around.

Implementing *kaizen* is a matter of evaluating the manufacturing system and involving employees in the search for greater efficiency and quality. At Alexander, operations were spread out over three floors, which wasted time and caused additional damage to the dolls. So TBM's first move was to set up a cross-functional team of ten Alexander employees charged with evaluating production line problems. The team observed 25 operations and measured each with a stopwatch. After this evaluation was complete, said William Schwartz, vice president of TBM and now a director at Alexander Dolls, "We physically moved the operation within the building and combined everything in one location on one floor. We started to flow the product so that each operation was carried out as each doll moved through the process."

As a result, the distance that each doll traveled from beginning to end of the process was reduced from 630 feet to 40 feet. The number of unfinished doll pieces shrank from 29,000 to 34 while the time required to complete a doll decreased from 90 *days* to 90 *minutes*. The square footage required for the production line went from 2,010 to 980. And productivity increased from 8 dolls per person per day to 25 dolls per person per day—a 212 percent improvement! Obviously, Alexander Doll Company wasn't just toying around with the Japanese principle of *kaizen*!

Source: Roberta Maynard, "A Company Is Turned Around Through Japanese Principles," Nation's Business (February 1996), p. 9.

---

are also called **job shops.** Custom printing shops and custom jewelry makers are examples.

Can small businesses compete in a manufacturing sector long associated with gigantic factories? Yes, primarily because automation makes **flexible production** possible. Computers assist small manufacturers in determining raw material needs, scheduling production runs, and designing new products. Automation allows the retooling of production machines in seconds rather than hours or days so shorter batches can be produced profitably. Machines can be programmed to perform many combinations of individual jobs and functions, rather than just one. With the help of computers, products and processes can be designed at the same time, rather than designing a product and then figuring out a way to make it.

Many small businesses are benefiting from the number of large businesses that are examining what they do best, determining that manufacturing is not exactly their strong suit, and farming out production to smaller specialty firms. For example, your new Dell computer did not come from a Dell computer factory—none exist. Dell concentrates on marketing, buying computer components from different companies and assembling them in a warehouse.[1] This type of flexible contract production opens many opportunities for entrepreneurs.

mass customization A production process that allows products to be produced specifically for individual customers.

Manufacturing is already evolving past flexible production, however, to **mass customization,** which means tailoring products to meet the needs of individual customers. An example of mass customization would see a customer in need of a new business suit stepping into a kiosklike device. An optical scanner would measure the customer's body. As soon as the choice of fabric and style are made, the order is beamed to the plant where lasers cut the material and it is sewn together. The suit is ready and shipped directly to the customer in a matter of days.[2]

Operations Management for Service Businesses

Do both service providers and product manufacturers need and use operations management? Yes, they do. Both take inputs and produce outputs through some type of transformation process. However, operations processes differ from one product and service to another, while some overlap. Manufacturers often offer repair services. Restaurants offer food products as well as services.

Traditionally, all service businesses have been seen as intermittent process businesses, since standardization didn't seem possible for businesses like hair salons, accounting firms, or auto service centers. But, in an effort to increase productivity, some service businesses are adopting continuous processes. For example, Merry Maids house cleaners, Jiffy Lube auto service, Fantastic Sam's family hair-cutting salons, and even chains of dentists located in malls are all using manufacturing techniques of continuous production.

Reality Check

Pass the Solder Please— Very Quickly

Robots are making their way into small businesses to increase productivity and hold down costs. For example, Engineering Concepts Unlimited (ECU), of Fishers, Indiana, makes electronic boards and controllers and sells about 5,000 units a year. The company uses robots to do the work of about 10 people.

Adam Suchko, CEO of ECU, stated that "When we started building these, you put the parts in the holes, you put the boards in a rack, flipped them over, and soldered the connections. One every three or four seconds." Suchko bought the company's first robot for $350 at an auction in 1989. It took two months to rebuild the robot and get it into the production loop. Once the robot came on-line, production increased tenfold. Suchko's robot could solder connections at a rate of hundreds of connections *per second.*

ECU now has four robots and the entire process can go for up to 50 hours at a time without people intervening. Suchko programs the robots to perform as many tasks as possible. Then he and his three employees "do whatever's left," like reloading parts into the machines, and making special adjustments.

Adapted from: John DeMott, "Look, World, No Hands!" Nation's Business (June 1994), pp. 41–42.

Computer Applications

Computer-aided design (CAD) software packages run the extremes. You can spend upwards of thousands and thousands of dollars for an extremely sophisticated software program and the hardware (computers, laser printers) to run it. If your technical design is complicated and if errors were costly, then it might pay to invest in such a system. Or you might even decide to hire someone outside the firm to handle that type of sophisticated product design demands.

However, if your design needs aren't quite that sophisticated, you might find some of the inexpensive CAD programs useful. For instance, Visio Corporation's Visio Technical 4.0 provides 57 templates and over 2,000 technically "Smart-Shapes." This program is ideal for creating two-dimensional drawings, technical schematics, and technical documentation and presentations. Another relatively simple CAD program is Micro Cadam 2-D. Engineers at Orbit Sprinklers in Bountiful, Utah, used this software to redesign their most popular selling product, a pop-up sprinkler head. Another relatively inexpensive CAD package is CAD/3X by IBMCAD, Inc. The software does many of the functions of more expensive CAD packages, such as dynamic highlighting, drag-and-drop features, and text capabilities.

Sources: Thomas Ehresman, "Low-Cost CAD Fills the Bill," Machine Design, August 24, 1995, pp. 148–149; "2-D CAD Quickens Sprinkler-Component Design," Design News, November 6, 1995, p. 35; and Melissa J. Perenson, "Technical Drawing Was Never This Fun," PC Magazine, November 7, 1995, pp. 61–62.

A notable difference between service and manufacturing operations is the amount of customer contact involved. Many services such as hair salons require the customer to be present for the operation to be performed. Consider the examples of product and service operations systems in Table 15-1.

TABLE 15 ▪ 1 Product and Service Operations Systems

INPUTS	TRANSFORMATION	OUTPUTS	FEEDBACK
Restaurant			
Food	Cooking	Meals	Leftovers
Hungry people	Serving	Satisfied people	Complaints
Equipment			
Labor			
Factory			
Machinery	Welding	Finished products	Defects
Skilled labor	Painting	Services	Returns
Raw material	Forming	Waste products	Market share
Engineering	Transporting		Complaints
Management			
Buildings			

What Is Productivity?

You read in Chapter 13 that as a manager, you are involved in planning, organizing, leading, and controlling. But how do you tell if and when you are reaching the goals you have set? You can measure and describe your success by your productivity or efficiency. As we noted on p. 404, **productivity** is the measure of output per worker. It can be described numerically as the ratio of inputs used to outputs produced, such as output per labor-hour. The higher the ratio, the more efficient your operating system. You should constantly look for ways to increase outputs while keeping inputs constant or to keep outputs constant while decreasing inputs.

productivity The measure of outputs according to the inputs needed to produce them. A way to determine the efficiency of a business.

Measurement of Productivity

Productivity can be measured for your entire business or for a specific portion of it. Since many inputs go into your business, the input you choose determines the specific measure of productivity. Total productivity can be determined by dividing total outputs by total inputs.

$$\text{Total productivity} = \frac{\text{outputs}}{\text{labor} + \text{capital} + \text{raw materials} + \text{all other inputs}}$$

If your software company sold $500,000 worth of software and used $100,000 in resources, your total productivity ratio would be 5. But you may not always want to consider all your inputs every time. For example, since materials may account for as much as 90 percent of operating costs in businesses that use little labor, materials productivity would be an important ratio for you to track.

$$\text{Materials productivity} = \frac{\text{outputs}}{\text{materials}}$$

If 4,000 pounds of sugar are used to produce 1,000 pounds of candy, the materials productivity is 1,000 divided by 4,000 = 0.25, which becomes a base figure for comparing increases or decreases in productivity. Stated simply, you can increase the productivity of your business by increasing outputs, decreasing inputs, or a combination of both. Most productivity improvements come from changing processes used by your business, from your employees accomplishing more, or from technology that speeds production.

Productivity ratios can be used to measure the efficiency of a new process. Say that you run a furniture shop whose productivity ratio is:

$$\frac{\text{Output}}{\text{input}} = \frac{\text{number of tables}}{\text{hours}} = \frac{100}{100} = 1$$

You have invented a new process that will save 20 percent on your labor costs. Now you can still produce the same number of tables (100), yet only take 80 hours to produce them. Your new productivity ratio is:

$$\text{New productivity ratio} = \frac{100}{80} = 1.25$$

Unfortunately, your new process ends up increasing defects in the tables. To correct these defects, you have to increase labor-hours to 120. Your productivity ratio is now:

$$\text{Corrected productivity ratio} = \frac{100}{120} = 0.833$$

Your corrected productivity ratio shows that it is back to the drawing board for your new process.

Service Productivity

Productivity in the U.S. service sector has been flat over the last decade with a growth rate averaging only 0.2 percent.[3] This statistic is even more significant when you remember that almost 80 percent of the U.S. work force is in the service sector.

Productivity in service-related businesses has not grown as rapidly as manufacturing businesses because service businesses are more labor intensive. Factories can substitute machines for people and increase output. Can service businesses do the same?

Actually, to some degree they can. Rick Smolan, president of Wildfire Communications, has developed an electronic device that can totally automate your telephone communications. By blending computer, telephone, and

Reality Check

Low Tech Is Still OK

Not all production in the 1990s is fully automated and assisted by high technology.

Andy Glanzman learned to make candles because he had to. Glanzman and his wife were caring for an elderly friend who happened to have no running water, heat, or electricity. Soon after dipping candles purely for function, Glanzman began forming and sculpting them with more artistic intent.

This led the Glanzmans to begin traveling the country selling the waxen sculptures. It didn't take long for them to find that they couldn't keep up with demand by relying on Andy to produce every candle himself by hand. The solution was to form Northern Lights Candles, hiring other artisans and teaching them his craft.

The intricate wax wizards, dragons, unicorns, cats, pigs, penguins, and lots of Santas (75 percent of revenues are realized in the Christmas season) are found in over 2,000 retail stores and in many mall kiosks. The company's emphasis is on developing new products and keeping overhead down. Since all the work is done by hand, the Glanzmans want to put as much money as possible in labor. Training for some of the complicated forms can take years. But the Glanzmans haven't exactly ignored distribution either. Besides their U.S. network, their sales reach England, Italy, Australia, Germany, and Japan.

Most of Northern Lights's creations cost around $20 each and company revenues have reached an incredible $4 million annually, even though every candle is made by hand.

Adapted from: Ben Fanton, "The Wizard of Wax," Nation's Business *(March 1994), pp. 14–15.*

Ergonomics is the key to worker productivity. Make sure that there is a healthy fit between people and equipment.

ergonomics The study of the interaction between people and machinery.

voice-recognition technology, Wildfire receives and directs calls wherever you are, takes messages, and maintains your calendar and Rolodex—and does it all by responding to your voice. Smolan and others who are always on the phone but rarely in an office use Wildfire in place of a personal secretary. "Secretarial work is just not good use of a human being," according to Smolan.[4]

Besides technological innovation, another key to productivity in a service business is making sure your employees are comfortable. **Ergonomics** studies the fit between people and machines. "The human body is simply not designed to sit. Yet between 70% to 75% of today's workforce is sitting and working on computers," said corporate ergonomist Rajendra Paul.[5] Lighting levels, furniture size and height, and the location of computers and telephones are important factors to consider in designing your work stations. With physical differences and varying needs of employees, you may need to consider chairs with adjustable armrests and footrests, keyboards and mousepads that adjust to the correct height and angle, and nonglare monitor screens.

Small Business
IN THE Service Industry

Management style, too, is another key factor in improving the quality and quantity of service workers' output. At Mountain Shadows Inc., in Escondido, California, owner H. Douglas Cook knew that keeping his employees' productivity high meant he had to stay out of the way and let his employees do their jobs. And Cook has a special interest in Mountain Shadows, a residential facility for the developmentally disabled, because not only is he its owner, but his son Brian is a resident there. The facility's 105 residents range in age from 7 to 63, and almost all of them use wheelchairs. Mountain Shadows is, by necessity, a highly labor-intensive operation. Yet Cook doesn't interfere with the 170 employees. Instead he has introduced an open management style that recognizes the importance of the employees. By doing so, he has dramatically reduced employee turnover, which in turn has increased his workers' efficiency. *Source: Michael Barrier, "You Have a Purpose in Life," Nation's Business (September 1995), pp. 13–14.*

What About Scheduling Operations?

Scheduling is a basic operations management activity for both manufacturing and service businesses which involves the timing of production. The purpose of scheduling is to put your plans into motion by describing what each worker has to do.

Scheduling is necessary to maximize levels of efficiency and customer service. For example, if a beauty shop schedules one haircut every 30 minutes, although each could actually be done in 20 minutes with no decrease in quality, the operator could be working one-third more efficiently. Three haircuts could be produced per hour rather than two. But a shop that schedules too much work cannot complete jobs on time, resulting in poor customer service and probably losing future business from customers aggravated by having to wait for their appointments. If you can schedule the exact amount of work to meet your customer demand at a given time, you will optimize your resources.

Scheduling Methods

Most business operations use forward scheduling, backward scheduling, or a combination of the two methods. With **forward scheduling,** materials and resources are allocated for production when the job order comes in. Any type of custom production in which the product changes or in which demand is unknown in advance needs forward scheduling. **Backward scheduling** involves arranging production activities around the due date for the product. You take the date the finished product must be delivered, then schedule in reverse order all material procurement and work to be done.

Henry L. Gantt devised a simple bar graph for scheduling work in any kind of operation. Developed in 1913, it still bears his name: the **Gantt chart.** This chart can be used to track the progress of work as a product makes its way through various departments. (See Figure 15-2.) It allows you to see the time required for each step and the current status of a job.

FIGURE 15-2
The Gantt Chart
Stages of work in building a house.

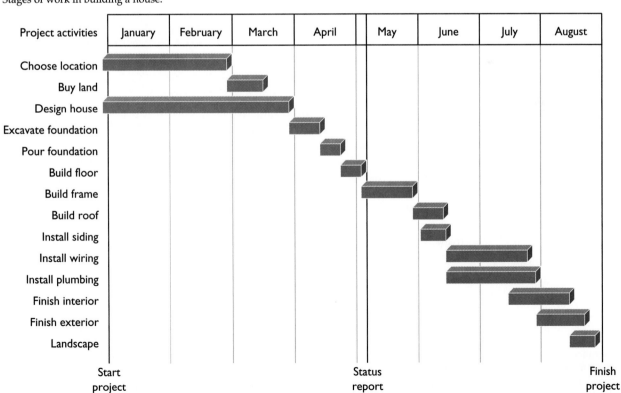

Routing

routing Information showing the steps required to produce a product.

Scheduling involves **routing,** sequencing, and dispatching the product through successive stages of production. Routing shows the detailed breakdown of information explaining how your product or service will be produced. **Routing sheets** are the paper copy, while **routing files** are the electronic versions of this information. Needed information could include tooling specifications and set-ups, number of workers or operators needed, the sequence in which steps are to be taken, and control tests to be performed.

Sequencing

sequencing The order in which the steps need to occur to produce a product.

Sequencing is the critical step of determining the order a job will go through your production system. Sequencing is most important when the job involves more than one department of your business, because a holdup in one department could cause idle time for another. Drafting a Gantt chart is a good way to track the flow of jobs between departments.

Dispatching

dispatching Allocating resources and beginning the steps to produce a product.

Dispatching is the act of releasing work to employees according to priorities you determined in planning the work sequence. Taxi companies often use *first-come, first-served* priority dispatching rules. A tailor may use an *earliest due date* rule, in which the order due first is dispatched first. A company which assumes that orders that will take the longest will be the largest (and most profitable) will use a *longest processing time* priority dispatching rule. Companies that make significant profit from handling charges and that reduce costs by completing more orders will use a *shortest processing time* priority dispatching rule.

Quality-Centered Management

There is no quality more important to businesses in the 1990s than just that—quality. Many U.S. businesses lost tremendous market share to foreign companies for one reason: They had not paid enough attention to quality. Now few industries and businesses, large or small, can afford *not* to focus their attention on quality.

To manage a small business centered on quality, you must keep two things in mind about what the word **quality** means. First, from the customers' perspective, quality is how well your product or service satisfies their needs. Second, from your business's standpoint, quality means how closely your product conforms to the standards you have set.

quality How well a good or service meets or exceeds customers' expectations, or the degree to which a product conforms to established tolerance standards.

Six Sigma in Small Business

A common way that companies measure the quality of a product is to keep close track of the **defect rate.** A defect rate is the number of goods produced that were out of the company's accepted **tolerance range**—the boundaries of acceptable quality. But how good is good enough? Is 99 out of 100 good enough? With a 1 percent defect rate, consider this: the U.S. Post Office would lose over 18,000 pieces of mail per hour!

tolerance range The boundaries a manager sets in determining the acceptable quality of a product.

How Good Is Good Enough?

If 99.9 percent accuracy were good enough:

- The Internal Revenue Service would lose 2 million documents per year.
- *Webster's Third International Dictionary of the English Language* would have 315 misspelled words.
- 12 newborn babies would go home with the wrong parents daily.
- 107 medical procedures would be performed incorrectly every day.
- 114,500 pairs of new shoes would be mismatched each year.

- 2,488,200 books would be printed each year with no words.
- Telephone companies would send 1,314 calls to the wrong number each minute.
- 5,517,200 cases of soft drinks would be made every year with no fizz.
- Two airplanes would crash at Chicago's O'Hare International Airport every day.
- 811,000 rolls of 35mm film would not take pictures each year.

From an office "pass around"

Perfection is not possible, but companies are striving for zero (or very near zero) defects. **Six sigma** is the term that has come to signify the quality movement, not just in manufacturing, but throughout entire organizations. In statistical terminology *sigma* denotes the standard deviation of a set of data. It indicates how all data points in a distribution vary from the mean (average) value. Table 15-2 shows different sigma levels and their corresponding defects per million.[6]

With a normal distribution, 99.73 percent of all the data points fall within three standard deviations (three sigma) of the mean. Pretty good, but that is just for one stage of the production process. Products that have to go through hundreds or thousands of stages could still come out with defects.

If you choose six-sigma defects as your production goal, you will have 99.99966 percent of your products within your specification limits—only 3.4 de-

six sigma The tolerance range in which only 3.4 defects per million are allowed.

TABLE 15 ▪ 2   Sigma Levels and Defect Rates

SIGMA LEVEL	DEFECTS PER MILLION
3.0	66,810.0
3.5	22,750.0
4.0	6,750.0
4.5	1,350.0
5.0	233.0
5.5	32.0
6.0	3.4

Manager's Notebook

Six Sigma at Work

Many businesses have set a goal of six-sigma quality in production. Just what *is* this strange phrase *six sigma* referring to?

Six sigma has to do with the concept of near-perfection in production, and was initially introduced by the well-known quality expert, Philip B. Crosby, in his book *Quality Is Free* (1979). Motorola Corporation then popularized six sigma in the mid-1980s as a way to measure the probability that companies can produce any given unit of a product (or service) with only 3.4 defects per million units or operations. Motorola's goal was to manufacture defect-free products and to eliminate defects throughout its organizational processes. A six-sigma rating, therefore, signifies "best-in-class" status.

What are the components of a six-sigma quality program? Let's take a closer look at the basic components and the activities and tools needed to practice them.

Basic Components. The basic components of a six-sigma program include the actual improvement process and quality measurement. The actual improvement process involves the following steps:

1. Define products and services by describing the actual products or services that are provided to customers.
2. Identify customer requirements for products or services by stating them in measurable terms.
3. Compare product with requirements by identifying gaps between what the customer expects and what she is actually receiving.
4. Describe the process by providing explicit details.
5. Improve the process by simplification and mistake-proofing.
6. Measure quality and productivity by establishing baseline values and then tracking improvement.

Those quality measurements should include: process mean and standard deviation, capability index, and defects per unit.

Quality Activities and Tools. The quality activities are ongoing management processes that businesses need to practice in a six-sigma program. These include participative management, short-cycle manufacturing, designing for manufacturing benchmarking, statistical process control, and supplier qualification. The improvement tools and analytical techniques include: flow charts, Pareto charts, histograms, cause-and-effect diagrams, and experimental design.

Small businesses which would like to achieve six-sigma status must work diligently to reduce and eliminate defects. The ultimate goals—improved manufacturing and increased customer satisfaction. It's not easy to achieve, but six sigma *can be* something more than just a strange phrase. It can provide a worthwhile target toward which to strive!

Sources: Fred R. McFadden, "Six-Sigma Quality Programs," Quality Progress (June 1993), pp. 37–42; J. P. Donlon, "The Six Sigma Encore," Chief Executive (November-December 1993), pp. 48–54; Gwen Fontenot, Ravi Behara, and Alicia Gresham, "Six Sigma in Customer Satisfaction," Quality Progress (December 1994), pp. 73–76; and Jim Carbone, "How AT&T Gets Six-Sigma Quality," Purchasing, January 12, 1995, pp. 52–53.

fects per million! Even if your product has to go through 100 different stages, the defect rate will still be only 3,390 defects per million.

The concept of six sigma is not limited to producing goods in your small business. You can also apply it to customer satisfaction in your service business. Consider a company with 1,000 customers and ten employees (or stages) that can

Entering the Internet

One thing that can be helpful to small business managers is seeing how others—particularly those who are the best in their field—do things. At the SBA Web site, you can access small business success stories. The files in this section include several success stories of small businesses that have received SBA assistance. You can read about the unique things these small businesses do and what makes them successful. In addition, you could do a keyword search of the various Web search browsers. For instance, a keyword search in Yahoo of *quality* uncovered links to quality certification sites, quality consultants, quality organizations (such as the American Society for Quality Control), and quality software.

SBA small business success stories: gopher://www.sbaonline.sba.gov

Yahoo keyword search ("quality"): http://www.yahoo.com/Business_and_Economy/Companies/Quality

affect customer satisfaction. The difference between three sigma (499 dissatisfied) and four sigma (60 dissatisfied) is 439 dissatisfied customers. That represents 44 percent of your entire customer base![7]

Quality Circles

A popular technique for improving quality is the use of **quality circles** to involve everyone within the organization in decisions that affect the business. Small groups of employees meet regularly to discuss, analyze, and recommend solutions to problems in their area after they receive training in problem solving, statistical techniques, and organizational behavior.

quality circles The use of small groups of employees to analyze products and processes in order to improve quality.

Global Small Business

Small manufacturers in Russia face many of the same operations challenges that their U.S. counterparts face. And they're addressing these challenges in much the same way. For instance, take Aktiv Ltd., a small commercial packaging manufacturer located outside of Moscow in Vladimir, Russia. Founders (and brothers) Pavil and Valery Snegiryov saw a huge opportunity in food packaging and they decided to act on it. They imported used packaging equipment from Germany and began producing Western-quality plastic vacuum-pressed packages, trays, and cups. Aktiv's emphasis on producing quality products led McDonald's Corporation to accept the company as one of its suppliers. In addition, Aktiv counts several Russian food companies as customers. So quality isn't just an American issue. It's an issue for small business owners and managers around the globe.

Source: Betsy McKay, "Small Manufacturers Emerging in Russia," The Wall Street Journal, November 10, 1995, p. A13.

Being One of the Best

Voted one of *Industry Week's* Best Plants of 1995, Symbiosis Corporation of Miami, Florida, embodies excellence in operations management. What does it do that's so outstanding? Several things. Symbiosis has been able to blend an aptitude for creative engineering, rapid product introduction, and adapting employees' hobbies to its job skills in an entrepreneurial environment where ideas flow freely and employees enjoy their managers' support.

Symbiosis was started in 1988 by two engineers who left their jobs with a medical device company to form a syringe-manufacturing business. Like many successful small businesses, Symbiosis was started in a garage on a shoestring budget. In 1992 it was acquired by American Home Products Corporation, and today it is a $50 million company that commands about 72 percent of the world market for disposable gastrointestinal biopsy forceps. Symbiosis also manufactures disposable laparoscopic scissors and other instruments used in abdominal surgery.

The idea for producing inexpensive, disposable surgical instruments grew out of one employee's fascination with model railroading. While pursuing his hobby, this employee had learned about investment casting, a technique traditionally used in jewelry making that can produce very small, but very precise, metal parts. Although making scale railroad models is a far cry from making surgical instruments, the skills acquired in following this hobby were beneficial in developing Symbiosis's manufacturing techniques. Other employees, who had hobbies such as watch repair, auto racing, and model airplane building, have transferred those skills to the company's manufacturing operations, much to the company's benefit.

What's it like to work at Symbiosis? In the manufacturing facility, production operations are grouped around *focused factory* teams, each of which is aligned with a major customer or product line. The company maintains extra tooling and workstation equipment in order to cope with dramatic growth spurts. The vice president of manufacturing stated, "We don't want to be in a situation where we have to wait to start up a second assembly line because of the lead time on tooling. To meet customer needs, I want to be able to turn on a line overnight." Needless to say, the corporate culture at Symbiosis discourages corporate bureaucracy and favors teamwork and open communications. In fact, President Bill Box says one of the company's hallmarks is its "freedom for independent action."

And what are its measures of success? In five years, productivity climbed 169 percent, while the cost per unit decreased by 29 percent. The manufacturing cycle time has been reduced by 50 percent as scrap and rework costs have been slashed by 64 percent. And on-time delivery is realized 100 percent of the time. With these impressive figures, it's not surprising that Symbiosis is regarded as running one of America's best plants!

Source: John H. Sheridan, "Symbiosis," Industry Week, October 16, 1995, pp. 55–56.

How Do You Control Operations?

The issue of quality affects the entire production process, so controls need to be built in at every stage. Feedforward quality control applies to your company's inputs. Concurrent quality control involves monitoring your transformation processes. Feedback quality control is inspecting your outputs.

Feedforward Quality Control

Control of quality begins by screening out inputs that are not good enough. Feedforward control depends strongly on the TQM principles that every employee is a quality inspector and is responsible for building better, long-term relationships with suppliers. When you have a long-term relationship with suppliers, they can help you achieve higher quality standards by continuously improving their products. Teamwork with your employees and cooperation with suppliers are keys to feedforward control.

Small businesses must monitor their productivity closely to stay competitive, to remain profitable.

Reality Check

"We're Moving Where . . . ?!"

For years Loranger Manufacturing Corp. existed peacefully in Warren, Michigan, making and supplying parts for Ford Motor Company. That changed in the summer of 1993, when George P. Loranger, owner and CEO, decided to follow Ford and move to Szekesfehervar, Hungary. His decision to relocate the entire operation was a gutsy move for a small business, to say the least, and one that illustrates the pressure on small businesses to maintain long-term vendor and customer relationships and to operate internationally.

International expansion is difficult for the largest businesses, and even harder for small businesses which usually have no such experience or teams of lawyers and experts to blaze a trail. In retrospect, Loranger calls the move "one big roller coaster ride." Some of Loranger's hurdles included negotiating terms for leasing a building on an abandoned Soviet military base (complete with 2,000 sheep to trim the front lawn); dealing with rapidly rising inflation and Hungary's nonconvertible currency; unfamiliarity with the local language; and the theft of telephone cables.

Why would Loranger make such a crazy move? The reason came down to his fear of losing Ford as the company's only customer. Ford rewarded such loyalty with a multiyear contract. The strategy is similar to a Japanese system called *keiretsu* in which Japanese companies take suppliers with them when they expand into other countries. The intent of *keiretsu* is to reduce startup costs, keep the quality level of goods consistent, help transfer technology between the companies, and produce a product more in line with the needs of the host country.

Loranger became interested in the idea of moving in 1987, when Ford began talking of new operations in Spain and Portugal. He initially envisioned relaxing in his spare time on sunny beaches. But Ford's decision to locate the new plant in Hungary put him far from the nearest beach. Risks like moving entire businesses to other countries are extreme but may be part of "the way business is done" as large and small businesses begin forging long-term, mutually beneficial relationships.

Source: Adapted from Dana Milbank, "It's Not Easy Being a Little Guy Overseas." Reprinted by permission of the Wall Street Journal, *September 15, 1994, p. A11. © 1994 Dow Jones Co., Inc. All rights reserved worldwide.*

Concurrent Quality Control

Concurrent control involves monitoring the quality of your work in progress. To facilitate this type of monitoring many small businesses are realizing the value of the international quality standards known as **ISO 9000** (pronounced ICE-oh 9000). The purpose of the ISO 9000 standards is to document, implement, and demonstrate the quality assurance systems used by companies that supply goods and services internationally.[8]

ISO 9000 The set of standards which certify that a business is using processes and principles in order to assure the production of quality products.

ISO standards do not address the quality of your specific products. Rather, they are a way to show your customers (whether consumers or other businesses) how you test your products, how your people are trained, how you keep records, and how you fix defects. ISO standards are more like generally accepted accounting principles (GAAP) than they are a spinoff of TQM.[9] Certification in the United States comes from the American National Standards Institute, 11 West 42nd Street, New York, New York 10035 (212-642-4900).

American Saw of East Longmeadow, Massachusetts, an 800-employee, family-owned business, was the first in its industry to receive ISO certification. Tim Berry, quality control manager, believes that because the company took the steps necessary to become certified, its product defects have decreased, communication has improved, and workplace accidents have been reduced.[10] More important, meeting the standards will ease entry into foreign markets and cut costs. Unfortunately, the up-front costs of certification can be high for small businesses. American Saw laid out $60,000 for outside consultants and registrars.

Richard Thompson of Caterpillar stated, "Today, having ISO 9000 is a competitive advantage. Tomorrow, it will be the ante to the global poker game."[11] Small businesses may find themselves between the proverbial rock and a hard place relating to certification and costs if the larger companies who buy their products require certification before they will purchase from the small business. Some suggestions for dealing with costs include:

Negotiate consultation prices. Different consultants and registrars charge different amounts. Consultation prices are on the way down so shop around, but be sure the consultant you select is familiar with your particular industry.

Request customer subsidies. If the company you are selling to is pushing its suppliers for certification, they may help you become certified. A primary customer of Griffith Rubber Mills of Portland, Oregon, paid the entire certification bill for them because they needed the technology.

Look for consultant alternatives. A local college may be able to help set up an ISO networking group.

Consider your need for full certification. You may be able to save money if it is more important to your suppliers for your business to meet ISO standards than to have the full certification.[12]

An important tool for monitoring the quality of product while it is being produced is **statistical process control (SPC).** SPC is the process of gathering, plotting, and analyzing data to indicate problems from a specified sample of products you make. Using statistical analysis, you can determine the probability of a deviation being a simple, random, unimportant variation or a sign that a problem exists in your production process that must be corrected.

statistical process control The use of statistical analysis to determine the probability of a variation in product being random or a problem.

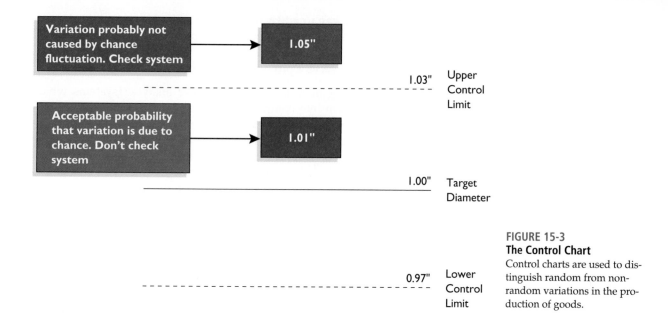

FIGURE 15-3
The Control Chart
Control charts are used to distinguish random from non-random variations in the production of goods.

For example, if you are producing titanium bars that need to be 1-inch in diameter, not every single bar will measure *exactly* 1 inch. You need to calculate the probabilities of various deviations occurring by chance alone or because of some problem. If a sample bar measures 1.01 inches, you wouldn't be too concerned since that amount of variation occurs by chance once in every 100 products. (See Figure 15-3.) But if a sample bar measures 1.05 inches, we know that the probability of that much variation occurring by chance is only one in 10,000. What now? A problem needs correction in your production process or more defective parts will be produced.

Feedback Quality Control

Inspecting and testing products after they are produced is called feedback quality control. Quality control inspectors may be used to check products. Rejected products will either be discarded, reworked, or recycled.

A problem with many types of product inspection is that the product can no longer be used. The product has to be cut up, taken apart, or disassembled to test and measure. However, nondestructive testing of several metal and plastic parts is being perfected by using laser ultrasound and other electromagnetic and acoustic-based methods.[13]

Summary

■ How to develop operating systems.

In developing a system for producing your product or service, your business takes inputs such as raw materials, skills, money, information, and energy and transforms them in some way to add value to product outputs. You need to receive feedback at every stage in order to control the process.

■ How manufacturers and service providers use operations management.

Operating systems used by manufacturers are either analytic (systems which take inputs and reduce them into component parts to produce outputs), or synthetic (systems which combine inputs in producing outputs). The processes manufacturers use are either continuous or intermittent. A continuous process is one that produces the same good without interruption for a long period of time. An intermittent process is one which is stopped with some frequency to change the products being made. Service businesses also take inputs and produce outputs through some transformation process. Most have used intermittent processes, but some have adopted continuous processes in order to increase productivity.

■ How to measure productivity.

The ratio of inputs used to produce outputs is called productivity. Productivity measures the efficiency of your entire business or any part of it. Productivity can be improved by changing processes used by your business, by getting your employees to accomplish more, or by using some type of technology that speeds production. To calculate productivity, simply divide outputs by inputs.

■ How to schedule operations.

Scheduling involves planning what work will need to be done and determining what resources you will need to produce your product or service. Forward scheduling is accomplished by having resources available and ready as customer orders come in. Backward scheduling is used when you plan a job around the date when the project must be done. Gantt charts are a useful backward scheduling tool.

■ Building quality into operations.

A company's tolerance range denotes the boundaries of acceptable quality. The defect rate indicates the number of products made that fall outside the tolerance range. Six sigma establishes a tolerance range of only 3.4 defects per million products produced. Statistical process control is a procedure used to determine the probability of a deviation being a simple, random, unimportant variation or a sign that a problem exists in your production process that must be corrected.

■ How to control operations.

Controlling operations is how you measure what is being accomplished in your business. Feedforward quality control applies to your company's inputs. Concurrent quality control involves monitoring your transformation processes. Feedback quality control is inspecting your outputs.

Questions for Review and Discussion

1. Discuss the elements of an operations management system. What would happen if the control system was not included? The feedback?
2. What is the difference between flexible production and mass customization?

3. Define productivity.

4. How can ergonomics be tied to productivity? To motivation? To Maslow's hierarchy?

5. Explain the difference between forward and backward scheduling.

6. Define "six sigma" both technically and how it is used as a business standard.

7. What type of small business would benefit from having ISO 9000 certification?

8. Give examples of products that would be suited to each of the dispatching rules.

Critical Incident

Easy Living and the Salute to the Performing Arts. Every year, Savannah, Georgia, salutes organizations involved with the performing arts with a formal dinner and dance. The Savannah Symphony, Southern Regional Opera, Savannah Ballet, Community Theatre Association, and Savannah Visual Artists Alliance are among the organizations honored. Your party planning service, Easy Living, has been awarded a contract to plan this year's Salute. You will be making all the arrangements for the food, drinks, entertainment, decorations, and advertising. In addition, you will have to coordinate the awards that are given to one person from each of the five community performing arts organizations. This year's Salute is planned for April 28.

Super Sack Manufacturing Corporation. At Super Sack Manufacturing Corporation in Savoy, Texas, employees are elated to learn that they've received a huge order from a large well-known animal feed producer. However, the order is for a product that they've never made before—a bag that has microscopic air holes so that air can circulate around the animal feed. The first order of 500,000 bags is due to the customer within three months, and the customer would like to approve the prototype before proceeding with actual production. Plant capacity is 25,000 bags per day.

Questions

1. Choose one of the businesses described and develop a Gantt chart timeline for it. Take into consideration the tasks that need to be done and the approximate amount of time that you think it will take to complete the task.

2. Divide into teams according to the business you've chosen. Compare your individual charts and come to a consensus about the most reasonable time frame and sequence of activities.

Take it to the Net

We invite you to visit the Hatten page on the Prentice Hall Web site at: http://www.prenhall.com/~hattensb for this chapter's World Wide Web exercise.

Chapter Focus

After reading this chapter, you should be able to:

- Outline the importance of purchasing and its procedures.
- Discuss the three main concerns in selecting a supplier.
- Calculate how much inventory you need and when.
- Describe the seven methods of inventory control.

16

Purchasing, Inventory Management, and Distribution

ELLING SNOW BOOTS IN AUGUST? That's what Richard Siegel does through his 15 Dunkirk Shoe stores located throughout New York and Massachusetts. Siegel runs sales before seasons in order to get important feedback directly from customers about the inventory he will need. Early information gives him a chance to make adjustments in colors, sizes, and styles when seasons are in full swing.

Siegel has learned a lot about inventory management, having grown up with a family-owned shoe business. One thing he remembers about his father's store was the quantity of unsold shoes that filled its basement. He traveled to shoe shows with his father where he saw other retailers scattering orders from booth to booth, often buying duplicate merchandise using no planned system. A common problem for small retailers, he realized, was their reliance on instinct for inventory management.

In his own business, Siegel devised an inventory system that went counter to that old "gut instinct" standard. "It's not necessary for each store to have a fully stocked inventory," he said, "just access to one." Siegel began transferring merchandise between stores. If one store ran out of a particular size or style, new stock would be sent from another store rather than being reordered from a manufacturer. Siegel kept close records of styles, sizes, colors, stores, and trends favored by his customers as a guide to what to keep in inventory.

The tactics on inventory control are critical to a small business because inventory is its most expensive asset—it *controls* the cash flow. Joseph Siegel (no relation to Richard), vice president of merchandising for the National Retail Federation, commented, "There are two things in life that improve with age, and inventory isn't one of them."

Richard Siegel's tight, smart inventory system produces impressive results—gross profit margins of at least 54 percent and inventory turnover four times a year. Siegel believes that if you watch what your customers buy, they will tell you what is right and wrong about your inventory. *Source: Adapted from Meg Whittemore, "When Not to Go with Your Gut," Nation's Business (December 1993), pp. 40–41.*

logistics The process of physically moving products and materials through production and distribution.

The process of moving raw materials, work-in-process inventory, and finished products through the business and distributing them to other businesses and consumers is called **logistics.** This chapter will examine purchasing and inventory control as part of your small business logistics.

Purchasing for Small Businesses

Your ability to offer quality goods at competitive prices depends on your purchasing skills. You need to seek the best value—the highest quality for the best price—for the goods, services, and equipment you purchase because that is exactly what your customers will be expecting when they purchase your products. Price is, therefore, only one of many factors to consider. You should also consider the consistency of your supplier's quality, their reliability in meeting delivery schedules, the payment terms available, product guarantees, merchandising assistance, emergency delivery and return policies, and other factors.

Purchasing Guidelines

Your purchasing skills greatly affect your company's profitability. Yet price is only one of many factors you must consider.

The following questions provide guidelines for evaluating your small business purchasing and inventory control:

- Are you using the proper sources of supply?
- Are you taking advantage of all purchase discounts?
- How do you determine minimum inventories and reorder points?
- Have you run out of raw materials or finished goods?
- What is the record of your current suppliers for quality, service, and price?
- Are you using minimum quantities or economic ordering quantities?
- What are your inventory holding costs?

- Do you know your optimum average inventory? Does it guide your purchasing policy?
- Could you improve your purchasing to increase profits?
- What is your inventory turnover ratio? How does it compare with the industry average?[1]

To illustrate the importance of purchasing to the profit of your small business, suppose your business spends $500,000 annually, has yearly sales of $1 million, and a profit margin of 10 percent or $100,000. If you were able to decrease the costs of your purchases by 3 percent, you would save $15,000—increasing your profits by 15 percent. To see the same profit increase through sales revenue, you would have to generate $150,000 additional sales, or a 15 percent increase. This means that a 3 percent savings on the cost of purchased items has the same impact on your bottom line as a 15 percent increase in sales.

Selecting Suppliers

Whom you buy from can be as important as what you buy. At the very least, supplier (or vendor) selection should be based on systematic analysis, not on guesswork or habit. Vendors are an important component of your operation.

Make or Buy Decision. A decision you must make in running your small manufacturing business is whether to produce your own parts and components or buy them from an outside source. It is called a *make or buy decision*. Much of the decision rests on the availability and quality of suppliers.

make or buy decision The choice of whether to purchase parts and components or to produce them.

The more specialized your needs or the more you need to hide design features, the more you may need to make your own parts. Standardized parts like bolts or standardized components like blower fans are generally better to buy than to make.

The make or buy decision is not limited to manufacturing operations or functions. Service and retail businesses need to consider whether or not to outsource such functions as janitorial or payroll services. You could either hire your own personnel for those services or hire another specialized business to produce them for you.

Investigating Potential Suppliers. Since the products you purchase become the products you sell, you want to be sure that you are dealing with the best suppliers available. But how do you do that? Tom Thornbury, CEO of Softub, a hot tub builder in California, asked that very question after his company had been burned by some bad vendors. His answer was to create a vendor audit team made up of ten employees from several areas of the business. The team spends from two hours to two days visiting and investigating the potential supplier.

Such thorough investigation is justified because companies like Softub are viewing their relationship with vendors as a long-term partnership. Since developing the audit team, product defects have dropped and vendor turnover has been cut in half. To help the audit team remember everything they want to look for, Softub developed a checklist. (See Figure 16-1.)[2]

Perhaps you could develop a checklist to evaluate your vendors. Factors you need to consider would include: product quality, location, services provided, and credit terms.

A serious question that a small business owner must answer is whether to use one supplier or multiple suppliers. It takes time to investigate and analyze

Manager's Notebook

Purchasing Basics

Whether you're purchasing inexpensive toilet paper for the employee bathroom or expensive components for your manufacturing process, you want to make good purchasing decisions—decisions that will get you the best possible product at the best possible price. To make your decisions wisely, it helps to know how the purchasing process *should* work. Let's look more closely at the steps in the purchasing process.

1. *Recognize, describe, and transmit the need.* If you're the only employee in your business, you'll have to rely on your own knowledge of your work processes to know **what** needs to be ordered and **when**. However, if your small business has other employees, you should train them to alert the person in charge of purchasing (yourself or another person whom you designate) of any needs. You'll probably want to use a purchase requisition form to standardize this process. A **purchase requisition** is simply a form that lists and describes the materials, supplies, or equipment that are needed. In addition, the purchase requisition should list the quantity needed, date required, estimated unit cost, budget account to be charged, and an authorized signature. Also this form should have at least two carbons: one for the person who does the purchasing and the other for the person requesting the items.

2. *Investigate and select supplier(s) and prepare a purchase order.* Once you know what's needed, you can begin to look for the best possible source(s) for obtaining the desired products. Since the text describes the factors you need to examine in selecting a supplier, let's concentrate on describing the purchase order.

    Once you've selected a supplier, you should prepare a serially numbered purchase order. In most instances, the **purchase order** becomes a legal contract document between you and the supplier, so you want to make sure you prepare it carefully. Be sure to specify quantity requirements, price, and delivery and shipping requirements accurately. If you have any quality specifications, these should also be described precisely. If you have any product drawings or other documents that relate to the order, these should be included, as well. If it's necessary for you to inspect sample products before an order is completed, be sure to specify what, when, and how much you want to sample. In other words, be sure to include all the data on your purchase order and word it so it's clear to both you and the supplier what the specifications and expectations are.

    You'll probably want to use a multipart purchase order form so that you and the supplier can keep track of the order coming in and being fulfilled. In fact, purchasing experts say that *seven* is the minimum number of copies you'd want on a purchase order form. Although you may consider this to be extreme, be sure that your purchase order form has enough copies so that both you and your supplier can keep track of the order.

3. *Follow up on the order.* Although the purchase order represents a legal offer to buy, no purchase contract exists until the seller accepts the buyer's offer. The supplier accepts by either filling the order or at the very least notifying the purchaser that the order is being filled. By **following up** on the order by mail, e-mail, fax, or phone call, you can keep on top of the status of your orders. If the goods you ordered are critically needed, the follow-up can be doubly important. (For important orders, you'll want to get written verification that your order was accepted.) Besides being a good way to keep on top of your purchasing activities, the follow-up also lets you maintain good relations with your suppliers.

4. *Receiving and inspecting the order.* Once the order is received, you should inspect it immediately to see if it's correct. The supplier should have enclosed a **packing slip** with the order that you can use to compare against your copy of the purchase order. You should check for quantity as well as quality of the goods. If you have someone other than yourself checking orders, you'll probably want to use a **receiving report form** that indicates what's included in the order—quantity and quality. And, in fact, even if you're the person who checks the order, it would be smart to have some way of noting the condition of the shipment just in case you need this information in the future. If the order is correct, it's ready to go into inventory or into use. However, if there's a problem with the order, you should contact the supplier immediately. Let the supplier know what the problem is and follow up with written **documentation** describing the

problem. The supplier will let you know the procedure for handling the incorrect order.

5. *Completing the order.* The order isn't complete until you've paid the **invoice**—a bill that should be included with the order or may even be sent later by the supplier—and prepared whatever accounting documents you need. Once you've done this, the purchasing process is complete.

Although the purchasing process as outlined here may seem burdensome and time consuming, keep in mind that being an effective and efficient purchaser makes an important difference in your small business!

Sources: Donald W. Dobler, David N. Burt, and Lamar Lee, Jr., Purchasing and Materials Management, *5/e (New York: McGraw-Hill, Inc.), 1990, pp. 50–64; and Barry Render and Jay Heizer,* Principles of Operations Management (*Upper Saddle River, NJ: Prentice Hall), 1995, pp. 406–415.*

several potential suppliers, so many businesses are working toward building long-term relationships with fewer suppliers and vendors. An advantage for buyer and seller when using a single source comes from a mutual dependence that benefits both companies. Another benefit of using a single source is the savings in decreased paperwork from dealing with only one other business.[3]

An advantage of multiple-source purchasing is the competition between vendors to decrease prices and improve services offered. A lack of this competition can be a disadvantage of single-source purchasing if your one supplier becomes complacent or is not able to provide the goods you need when you need them.

Managing Inventory

Before considering how much inventory is needed, we should investigate the meanings of the term **inventory**. Depending on the context, there are four common meanings of the term:

inventory Goods a business owns for the completion of future sales. Also the act of counting the goods held in stock.

- The monetary value of goods owned by a business at a given time. "We carry a $500,000 inventory."
- The number of units on hand at a given time. "We have 1,000 yo-yos in inventory."
- The process of measuring or counting goods. "We inventory the office supplies every month."
- The detailed list of goods. "I need to look at the inventory on the computer."

SOFTUB'S MANAGERS POINT OUT THE VIRTUES OF THEIR VENDOR CHECKLIST:

"We check how busy vendors are in relation to their size. Say they're using only an eighth of a building's footage. Why is it empty? Did they lose business? The ones we'll end up doing business with can answer easily. And if you notice they don't have the proper space, you'll want to know where they keep their material. Will they have to leave it outside in the rain? They might show you a fancy brochure, and you find they're operating out of five garages."

"We want to make sure a supplier's sales manager will work with its manufacturing people to meet our needs. When we hit a problem, the sales manager is our liaison. Does he have the influence to change schedules on the production line? Also, the vendor's ability to turn out a quality product is often reflected by the quality-control manager's experience. We want to know all about that."

"Once we went into a place where they said they made circuit boards, but they really specialized in making custom boards in very small volumes. We needed someone who could make thousands a month."

"When we get back to the office, we always check with other customers to ask if the supplier delivers on time or has quality problems."

Softub
VENDOR SURVEY FORM

REPORT BY: GARY ANDERSON

COMPANY NAME: ANY BOARD CO. **PROFILE** DATE: 12-14-93

ADDRESS:
MAIN ST.
ANYTOWN, USA 12345

TELEPHONE / FAX #: 800-555-5555
YEARS IN BUSINESS: 14
NUMBER OF EMPLOYEES: 170

SQUARE FOOTAGE OF BUILDING(S): 48,000 USA (60,000 IRELAND)
AGE OF BUILDING(S): 20 YRS
TYPE OF BUILDING(S): CONCRETE TILT-UP OPEN BEAM CEILING + IN GOOD CONDITION

PERSONNEL MET
CEO: JOHN G. DOE
PRESIDENT: AS ABOVE
SALES MANAGER: JACK B. DOE
SALES CONTACT: AS ABOVE
Q.C. MANAGER: JANE Q. PUBLIC
PRODUCTION MANAGER: JIM Z. SMITH
OTHERS: PRODUCT/ACCOUNT SPECIALIST

BUSINESS PROFILE
ANNUAL SALES IN DOLLARS: $10 MILLION
MAIN PRODUCT LINE: PRINTED CIRCUIT BOARDS
MINOR PRODUCT LINE: CABLE ASSEMBLIES
MAJOR CUSTOMERS: BENDIX, PACKARD BELL + GEORGIA PACIFIC

D & B REQUESTED: ☑ YES ☐ NO ☐ ATTACHED

Q.C. DEPARTMENT
EQUIPMENT CALIBRATED: ☑ YES ☐ NO
CALIBRATION TAGS IN PLACE: ☑ YES ☐ NO
TRAVELERS IN PLACE AT WORK STATIONS: ☑ YES ☐ NO
MILITARY OR ISO RATING: ISO 9000 U.L. F.C.C. C.S.A. F.D.A. T.U.V. (GERMANY)
TOTAL Q.C. EMPLOYEES: 8 + 1 MANAGER
GENERAL IMPRESSION: EXCELLENT, WELL LAID OUT, CALIBRATION EQUIPMENT IN GOOD SHAPE, INSPECTION LAB A-1 CONDITION AND STAFF IS VERY KNOWLEDGEABLE.

PRODUCTION

"We don't have the expertise, the manpower, or the time to look into every procedure. If a large company (or the military) has done an audit on the supplier and given it a rating, it gives us a good idea if that supplier has sound systems and procedures in place. Why not let the big company do the work for us?"

"Our impression of this supplier was really favorable, and we've learned from it, too. During our audit, we saw illustrated work instructions hanging in front of every station on the line. Each sheet had a checklist of things the operator was supposed to do. We started using similar instructions here. We asked the supplier to send one of its engineers to help us do it."

FIGURE 16-1 Vendor-audit Checklist Sample checklist, which Softub uses to analyze potential suppliers.

Source: Stephanie Gruner, "The Smart Vendor-audit Checklist." Adapted with permission, Inc. *magazine (April 1995), pp. 93–95. © 1995 by Goldhirsh Group, Inc.*

"We always request a Dun & Bradstreet report unless it's a mom-and-pop shop. Our chief financial officer also looks at the report. We want to know if the company owes more than it's worth. If it does, our finance department will call their finance people and ask more detailed questions."

"This company has the resources to make our product. But the 50% capacity would trigger us to check its financials and talk to its management, because it should be a little busier. We'd also ask how many shifts it's running, how many hours a day it's using certain machines, how many people it has now, and how many people it's had there before."

"If the place is messy and dirty, that's an indicator of the kind of service and product you're going to get. But if we see a board with tools hanging there so that when a tool is in use you see a black silhouette, that's a pretty good sign. It means people aren't wasting time looking for things, and they're probably not going to ship us a product with tie wraps in places where they don't belong."

"One big accident and a company can get sued and be out of business. Are first-aid charts posted on the walls? Are people wearing safety glasses? We want to know what a vendor is doing to prevent accidents. It's also a good indication of its management philosophy."

"International ratings are important because we sell our product overseas. If a vendor is already certified to sell in that country, we feel more confident that its product will pass inspection."

...ION AREA

CLEANLINESS:	_EXCELLENT_		
ORGANIZED:	_EXCELLENT_		
SQ. FOOTAGE:	_43,000 PROX_		
CAPACITY PERCENTAGE OF TOTAL PRODUCTION:	_50%_	☑ YES	☐ NO
SAFETY DEVICES IN PLACE:		☐ AVERAGE	☐ POOR
GENERAL SAFETY CONDITION:	☑ GOOD	☐ AVERAGE	☐ POOR
GENERAL EMPLOYEE DEMEANOR:	☑ GOOD	☐ AVERAGE	☐ POOR
EQUIPMENT CONDITION:	☑ GOOD	☑ YES	☐ NO
REGULAR MAINTENANCE SCHEDULES MAINTAINED:		☑ YES	☐ NO
DOES THE FACTORY APPEAR BUSY?:		☑ YES	☐ NO
IS THE EQUIPMENT RUNNING?:		☑ YES	☐ NO
ARE THERE STOCK PILES OF RAW MATERIAL?:		☑ YES	☐ NO
ARE THERE STOCK PILES OF FINISHED GOODS?:		☑ YES	
IS THE SHIPPING DOCK BUSY?:		☑ YES	

SUMMARY

HOW DOES VENDOR INTEND TO MEET OUR REQUIREMENTS?: _THEY WILL RAMP UP TO_
3 NEW EMPLOYEES AND 1 NEW FLOW SOLDER MACHINE..

OVERALL IMPRESSION: ☑ EXCELLENT ☐ GOOD ☐ AVERAGE ☐ POOR

SHOULD SOFTUB DO BUSINESS WITH THIS COMPANY?: _YES! NOTES:: 1). REVIEW D+B_
WITH FINANCE 2). REVIEW WITH MANAGEMENT + HAVE THEM VISIT ALSO.
3) MAKE FINAL DECISIONS AFTER REFERENCE CHECKS

VENDOR RATING

PLEASE CIRCLE ONE

1 - SHOULD NOT DO BUSINESS WITH
2 - CAUTION RATING
3 - AVERAGE
4 - GOOD RATING
5 - WORLD CLASS RATING

WHITE - PURCHASING   CANARY - Q.C.   PINK - OPERATIONS

"If a vendor is doing preventive maintenance, there are records we can see. If machines are down, it could cost a company hundreds of thousands of dollars a day. Good companies will monitor their machines religiously."

"The pink copy goes to operations. If the supplier is ISO 9000 certified or doing business with a *Fortune* 500 company, we'll request a copy of its quality manual." ■

429

Proper Care and Feeding of Suppliers

Seal Power Corporation's OTC division in Owatonna, Minnesota, knows firsthand about the importance of developing good supplier relationships. The company produces specialized maintenance tools and equipment and high-pressure hydraulics. OTC's push for quality in manufacturing was part of a corporatewide effort that began in the 1980s. It recognized that if its own products were to get better, it had to help its suppliers get better. Its short-cycle production gave the company another compelling reason for pursuing effective suppliers. Because it frequently changes it manufacturing lines to accommodate changes in its products, it needed suppliers who could provide high-quality parts and respond quickly to the need for new kinds of components.

OTC decided to have just one supplier for each part it buys. With lead times of 12 to 26 weeks on many of its components, OTC was acutely aware of the risks associated with such a decision. However, by working closely with its suppliers, OTC has made this approach work. The company offers free training on statistical process controls and insists that its suppliers attend. Its purchasing manager does an audit at each supplier's company to find out what kinds of changes will be needed to maintain standards. (See Figure 16-1.) But the suggestions aren't all one-way. The purchasing manager stated, "There's lots of give and take. . . . We like to consider those suppliers an extension of this manufacturing house."

OTC's supply policy might be termed *single-source suppliers for multiple parts*. Overall, the system seems to work. Company officials report that acceptance rates for parts has risen from 75 percent to nearly 99 percent.

Source: Beverly Geber, "Keeping Your Suppliers in Step," Training: The Magazine of Human Resources Development (*July 1989*), pp. 28–34.

How Much Inventory Do You Need?

Managing inventory is like performing a balancing act. On one side of the scale, you have to keep an adequate supply of goods on hand. You don't want to shut down operations because you ran out of a needed part, and you don't want to lose a sale because customers find an empty shelf where they expected to find a product. On the other side of the scale, inventory represents money sitting idly on the shelf. And to complicate things, the more you try to decrease the risk of running out of more obscure items, the more you increase the risk that some items will become obsolete.

Retail Business. An important factor in considering the inventory needs of many small retail businesses is the time needed to get fresh inventory in and how much reordering will cost. If you can replace inventory quickly at a reasonable price, you can hold down your inventory costs by keeping fewer items yourself.

Retailers should be aware of the 80-20 principle, also called the Pareto rule. According to this rule, about 80 percent of the firm's revenue will come from about 20 percent of the inventory. What this principle does for the small retailer is that it reminds her to concentrate on the "vital few" rather than the "trivial many."

Small Business IN THE Service Industry

Even service businesses that aren't retail based must consider their inventory needs. For instance, a restaurant needs appropriate food and beverages, cleaning fluids, table service equipment, and miscellaneous supplies such as menus, toothpicks, cash register tape, and check slips. Financial service firms need adequate supplies of paper, pencils, accounting forms, and other types of office supplies. They might even need to have a supply of "cash" on hand to meet certain customer needs. Security firms need to keep things such as flashlights, mace or pepper spray, whistles or alarms, and, of course, office materials and supplies in their inventories. Auto repair shops must stock tires, batteries, wrenches, engine oil, grease, cleaning supplies, and other items. There are many other types of service businesses not mentioned here. The point is that small service business managers should pay just as much attention to inventory control as their counterparts in manufacturing and retail.

Manufacturing Business. Inventory needs for a small manufacturer are different than those of retailers. Manufacturers' needs are based on production rate, lead time required to get in new stock, and the order amount that delivers the optimum economic quantity. Common techniques of manufacturers include just-in-time (JIT) inventory control and materials requirement planning (MRP), considered later in this chapter.

Costs of Carrying Inventory

There are several obvious and not-so-obvious costs of carrying inventory of any type. **Financing** is the most apparent cost of inventory. Since inventory is an asset, it must be offset by a liability—the cost of borrowing money or diverting your own cash from other uses. If you can sell merchandise and collect payment before you have to pay the supplier who provided you with that merchandise, you can avoid direct finance costs. Since that usually isn't the case, most inventory has a cash cost to the business.

Inventory **shrinkage** is another cost to your business. Shrinkage can come from theft or spoilage. Employee theft and shoplifting by customers result in inventory that you had to pay for that is not available for sale. Spoilage is inventory you have purchased that is not fit for sale because of damage or deterioration.

shrinkage The loss of goods held in inventory due to theft or spoilage.

Obsolescence, in which products become outdated or out of fashion, produces the same effect as spoilage: unrecoverable inventory costs caused by merchandise you can't sell. Such merchandise is known as "dead stock." Obsolescence is a problem for a wide variety of businesses, especially ones in which styles, tastes, or technology change quickly, such as clothing, automobile parts, or computer parts and accessories. You may be able to salvage some money from inventory that is obsolete (or on its way) through price reductions or recycling, but dead stock is still a major cost.

Holding costs are what you incur for keeping extra goods on hand—warehouse building expenses (either purchase and upkeep or rent), added utilities,

holding costs Expenses related to keeping inventory on hand.

insurance, and taxes on the building. Then there is insurance on the value of the inventory and taxes on the inventory. Merchandise that spoils, becomes obsolete, depreciates, or is pilfered is part of holding costs. Finally, you have interest expenses if you borrow money to pay for the goods.

ordering costs Expenses related to procuring inventory.

Ordering costs are the expenses you incur in either ordering or producing inventory. Ordering costs tend to be fixed, meaning that they cost about the same no matter what quantity of goods you order. They include all the clerical expenses of preparing purchase orders, processing orders and invoices, analyzing vendors, and receiving and handling incoming products.

If holding costs were your only inventory expense, you would want to order as few items at a time as possible to minimize your cost of holding on to inventory. Ordering one part at a time would cut down on your storage expenses, but think of the cost in time, paper, and people needed to process that many order forms and receive goods one at a time; your total costs would go through the roof. Likewise, if ordering costs were your only inventory expense, you would want to send for as many goods as possible at a time to minimize your costs of ordering. While your clerical needs would be cut by just making out one order, think of the size of the storage facility you would need and the cash flow problems created by having all your money tied up in inventory.

In the real world, every business incurs both holding and ordering costs. Striving to maintain a balance between them is part of the difficult job of controlling inventory.

Controlling Inventory

Inventory, like cash flow, can make or break your business. Because you will invest up to 80 percent of your company's capital in inventory, you must manage it wisely.

Since inventory is such a significant expense, most businesses carefully look for ways to determine the right levels of and control for their inventory. Inventory control is the process of establishing and maintaining the supply of goods you need to keep on hand. Inventory control is important because inventory represents about 25 percent of a manufacturing firm's capital and up to 80 percent of a retailer's. There are many techniques used to control inventory, depending upon the type of business and the kind of inventory. Several techniques are described in this section.

Reorder Point and Quantity. Controlling your inventory begins with determining when you need to restock inventory and how much you need to reorder. These are called **reorder point** and **reorder quantity.** The time period that begins when an item is at its highest desired stocking level, continues as the item is used or sold, and ends when it is replenished is called an **inventory cycle.**

inventory cycle The period of time from the point when inventory is at its highest until it is replenished.

lead time The period of time from order placement until the goods are received.

For example, say that you are a retailer who sells a certain product—such as Elvis Presley statuettes—with an average weekly demand of ten units. (See Figure 16-2.) The **lead time** (time from order placement until delivery) is three weeks. You would need to reorder when inventory drops to 30 Elvises so you don't completely run out before the ordered items arrive. The reorder quantity would be 100 statuettes so you would have a ten-week supply of goods on hand at your highest desired stocking level.

Visual Control. Many small businesses operate without a formal or complex inventory control system. If you run a one- or two-person business that sells a relatively narrow selection of items, visual control may be the only inventory system you need. Visual inventory control means you look at the goods you have on hand and reorder when you appear to be running low on items. It depends on

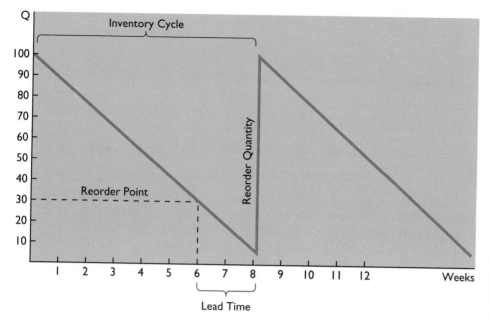

FIGURE 16-2
Inventory Cycles
An inventory cycle lasts from the time the goods are used or sold until replenished. The re-order point indicates when you need to order goods. The reorder quantity is how many items you wish to put back in stock.

your being in the business during most business hours and your knowledge of usage rate and reorder time needed.

Economic Order Quantity (EOQ). Economic order quantity is a traditional method of controlling inventory that minimizes total inventory costs by balancing annual ordering costs with annual holding costs for an item.

EOQ balances these two types of costs to minimize your total costs. (See Figure 16-3.) Several models exist for the EOQ approach that go beyond the scope of this book, so in practice you simply need to find a model that fits the cost structure of your business and use it. The basic model of EOQ assumes that: (a) you can't take advantage of volume discounts, (b) you can accurately predict annual demand, and (c) your average inventory level is equal to your maximum level minus your minimum level divided by 2.

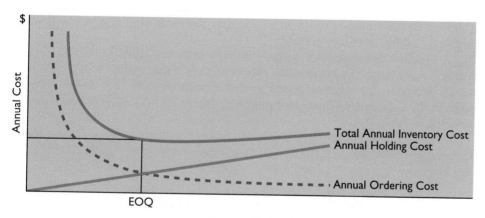

FIGURE 16-3
Economic Order Quantity
Economic order quantity (EOQ) is a way to minimize total inventory expenses by balancing holding costs and ordering costs.

If your business meets these assumptions, you can use the following formula:

$$EOQ = \sqrt{\frac{2DO}{C}}$$

where

D = annual demand for the product (in units)

O = average ordering cost for the product (in dollars per year)

C = average holding cost for one of the products (in dollars per year)

To illustrate, imagine a sporting goods store that meets the assumptions stated previously. This sporting goods store usually sells 12,000 pairs of hiking boots per year. The ordering costs are $10 per order. The holding costs run $0.96 per pair per year. The EOQ for hiking boots for this store would be 500.

$$EOQ = \sqrt{\frac{2 \times 12,000 \times 10}{0.96}}$$

$$= 500$$

This tells us that to minimize total inventory costs and balance ordering and holding costs, the sporting goods store would need to order 500 pairs of hiking boots at a time. That means in selling 12,000 pairs of boots and ordering 500 pairs each time, the store would need to make 24 orders of hiking boots per year.

$$\text{Orders per year} = \frac{D}{EOQ}$$

$$24 = \frac{12,000}{500}$$

ABC Classification. In the process of handling many types of goods, some can get misallocated. A reason for misallocation can be that the person in charge of inventory is spending as much attention on an item that costs $5 and is sold twice per year as on items that cost $500 and are sold many times per month.

An inventory system that helps to allocate more appropriate time and attention to items is ABC classification. This system classifies items based on the total dollar volume of sales each generates. To calculate the total dollar volume, multiply the cost of an item by the number of units sold annually. The greater the weighted dollar volume generated by an item, the more attention you will want to give it in your inventory control.

Items that generate high dollar volume will be classified in the A category and will receive the highest priority. Proportionally less attention will be given to the moderate dollar volume goods in the B category, and low dollar volume items in the C category. A rule of thumb for percentage allocation for each group is shown in Table 16-1.

The use of a computer database in your inventory control makes monitoring your ABC classification system relatively quick and easy to adjust if necessary.

Electronic Data Interchange (EDI). Electronic data interchange (EDI) is an electronic means of inventory control. It is made possible through the use of **bar coding,** the black and white parallel bars on packaged goods. (See p. 16 [Zebra Tech-

TABLE 16 ▪ 1   ABC Inventory Investment Classification

CLASSIFICATION		PERCENTAGE OF TOTAL INVENTORY INVESTMENT
A	(high dollar volume)	60–80%
B	(moderate dollar volume)	10–40%
C	(low dollar volume)	5–15%

nologies Global Small Business feature in Ch. 1].) When goods are scanned into your inventory system by employees receiving them in a shipment or ringing them up as a sale at the cash register, the transactions are updated in the company's computer inventory program. By using this technology, you can track sales, determine what needs to be ordered, and transmit the inventory data to your suppliers through the same EDI system. EDI is one type of **perpetual inven-**

perpetual inventory system
An inventory system which indicates how many units of an item are on hand at any given time.

Computer Applications

There are a number of software programs you can use to help you better control your inventory. Peachtree Complete Accounting and Peachtree Accounting for Windows (Peachtree Software) are particularly good programs for tracking inventories and accounts receivable. Also you can customize these packages to your unique inventory needs. Intuit Corporation's QuickBooks for Windows is another popular software package that you can use to track inventory. These three software packages are relatively inexpensive, ranging from $99 to $199.

However, you might decide to invest a little more in a more extensive software/hardware package called SellWise from CAP Automation. This program (list price of $1,495) handles sales, tracks customers, produces reports, controls inventory, and reads bar codes. This package is particularly good for small retail businesses. Finally, one of the newest software programs to come out is called Big Business from Automatic Software

Inc. (list price of $379 for single user or $749 for multiple users on a network version). This program is ideal for many different small business applications since it integrates four critical business functions: sales, marketing, inventory, and finance. Its creators say it's perfect for individuals who have limited accounting knowledge. This program may be just the ticket for helping you control your inventory.

Regardless of the specific software that you choose to help you manage your inventory, be sure to select one that you'll *use*. After all, this is one area of your business that you *can* control. So why not be effective and efficient at it?

Sources: Leon Erlanger, "Small-Office Software: The Essentials," PC Magazine, June 13, 1995, pp. 120–121; Bronwyn Fryer, "How to Succeed with Software," Working Woman (November 1995), pp. 55–60; Arden Hoffman, "Perfect Picks," Working Woman (November 1995), pp. 63–68; and Dennis James, "Level the Field with the Accounting Equalizer," Success (January/February 1996), p. 58.

Global Small Business

EDI can be beneficial to both supplier and customer. But what if the supplier is domestic and the customer is in a different country? And what if the cost of implementing an EDI system is just too expensive for a small business? Well, some industry trade associations are taking the lead by helping their members garner the benefits of EDI and being able to compete globally. They're doing this by creating networking collaborations among small businesses in a certain location. For instance, the National Tooling and Machining Association helped Kansas Manufacturer's Inc. in Wichita, a consortium of approximately 20 job shops, none with annual sales revenues over $4.5 million, by providing seed money for EDI links. This newly developed networking capability helped the Kansas job shops capture a $1.7 million order for auto parts from a Swedish corporation. *Source: Otis Port, "A Cutting-Edge Strategy Called Sharing,"* Business Week Special Report on Enterprise, *November 20, 1995, pp. ENT4–ENT6.*

Entering the Internet

The benefits to be gained from conducting business on-line can be numerous. However, you should also be alert to some of the security concerns that arise from electronic commerce. That's because the Internet's accessibility is one of the biggest advantages—and one of its biggest liabilities. The free-flow exchange of information among millions of users creates the possibility of a scenario in which your transactions or even your personal computer files on your PC are susceptible to outsider tampering. But there are ways to protect yourself.

If you've got a Web page, it's probably worth the time and expense to install what computer experts call a "firewall." The firewall guards your PCs and your Web site and includes both hardware and software to detect break-ins. If unauthorized activity is taking place, your firewall will automatically shut your system down before any damage can be done. Unless you have a solid knowledge of computers and software, you'll probably want to pay a consultant to help you erect this safety feature. If you're going to be doing a lot of business via the Internet, it's a wise investment.

Another protection to help secure confidential transactions (such as those taking place in EDI) is to use encryption software. Encryption software scrambles a message so that only the intended receiver can decode it. Both Netscape and Open Market (Internet firms with popular Web browsers) have built-in encryption software. Or you can use software programs such as IStore, Merchant Solution, or WebTrader to help you secure your transactions. However, if the security of financial transactions on the Internet still concerns you, you can always print a toll-free number on your home page and let customers contact you by phone or fax. *Sources: Kathy Reilly, "EDI Requires Prudent Management,"* Folio: The Magazine for Magazine Management, *August 1, 1995, p. 45; Anne Knowles, "Electronic Commerce: Securing Transactions Over the Net,"* PC Week, *October 30, 1995, pp. 102+; and Jenny C. McCune, "Stop, Thief!"* Success *(March 1996), p. 54.*

tory system that allows you to know how many items you have in stock at any given time.

Just-in-Time (JIT).   A Japanese approach to inventory management that has received a lot of attention in the last few years is called *just-in-time* (JIT). The basic idea of JIT is to reduce order sizes and to time orders to that goods arrive as close to the time they are needed as possible. The intent is to minimize a business's dependence on inventory and cut the costs of moving and storing goods. JIT is used more by producers than by retailers.

There are notable differences between a JIT approach and a more traditional approach (which you could think of as just-in-case). Table 16-2 highlights some of these differences.[4]

JIT is based on a **kanban** (pronounced KAHN-bahn) system, which translates roughly as *card*. Kanban was developed by Toyota, which used cards to initiate and authorize many activities within the business such as production, purchasing, and moving goods.

JIT is most effective when it is part of an overall philosophy. For example, American Standard, Inc., producer of bathroom fixtures, calls its JIT system "demand-flow manufacturing" and considers it to be part of its overall TQM philosophy. By concentrating on keeping the product moving continuously and eliminating dead time, everyone is looking for adjustments that need to be made to free up bottlenecks. With this mindset, continuous improvement, which is the overall goal of TQM, becomes automatic. At American Standard, efficiency has improved 20 percent, its cycle time to produce a toilet has decreased from 180 hours to about four hours, and inventory has been cut drastically.[5]

JIT works best in situations that allow accurate forecasting of both demand and production. Since JIT is based on actual rather than projected demand, a small business may have to be in operation for a while before it can take advantage of it, as a company called Lifeline Systems learned. When Lifeline first began making its voice-activated personal-response devices that allow people to call for help in an emergency, production lead time was 30 days from order to shipment.

TABLE 16 ▪ 2   JIT and Traditional Inventory Comparison

JIT INVENTORY	TRADITIONAL INVENTORY
Small orders/frequent deliveries.	Large orders/infrequent deliveries.
Single-source supplier for a given part with long-term contract.	Multiple sources of suppliers for same part with partial or short-term contracts.
Suppliers expected to deliver quality product, delivery performance, and price. No rejects acceptable.	Suppliers expected to deliver acceptable level of product quality, delivery performance, and price.
Objective of bidding is to secure the highest-quality product through long-term contract.	Objective of bidding is to find lowest possible price.
Less emphasis on paperwork.	Requires more time and formal paperwork. Changes in delivery time and quantity require new purchase orders.
Delivery time and quantity can be changed with direct communication.	

After adopting JIT, TQM, and manufacturing resource planning, that figure has dropped to four days. John Giannetto, corporate manager of materials and purchasing, stated, "What comes in the back door [in parts and materials] is gone four days after it gets here."[6] Keeping in line with JIT philosophies, Lifeline has cut the number of suppliers from 300 to 75, 85 percent of whom offer service and quality at a level that makes inspection unnecessary.

A caveat of JIT is that everyone involved *must* be able to do what they say they can, when they say they can do it. If you are operating with enough inventory to support one day's production, which is common with JIT, one unexpected trucking strike, breakdown, or shortage can shut down your entire operation. Just-about-in-time or almost-in-time won't cut it.

Materials Requirements Planning (MRP). Another new inventory control method for producers is materials requirements planning. MRP depends on computers to coordinate product orders, raw material in stock, and the sequence of production. A master schedule ensures that goods are available at the time they are needed in the production cycle.

While JIT is a *pull* system, based on actual customer demand, MRP relies on the *push* of estimated demand. MRP is an inventory management technique for use when demand for some materials depends on the demand for others. For example, if your business makes customized mountain bikes and you anticipate sales of 1,000 bikes next month, you know how many components you will need. You need 1,000 frames, 2,000 pedals, 4,000 wheel nuts, and so on. The demand for each of these items depends on the demand for bikes. Rather than keep all

R eality Check

Getting It There Just-in-Time

As businesses adopt just-in-time inventory systems to keep costs down, they must depend on trucking and distribution companies to get goods where they have to be. To meet this need, trucking companies like Star Delivery of Morton, Illinois, are beginning to specialize in time-sensitive deliveries.

Since starting in 1986, Star Delivery has grown from a company with 60 tractor-trailers to one with 500. Each truck is equipped with two-way satellite communications equipment called OmniTRACS. With this system, fleet manager Bernie Quin can pinpoint a truck location to within 1,000 feet at any given moment.

Drivers have a keyboard in their trucks, which they use to contact dispatchers from anywhere, anytime they want. The satellite tracks each truck's location every hour or upon demand. The exact location is then reported to the home office. With this information, Star can tell its customers the exact location of their shipments anywhere in North America. Just-in-time inventory depends on plenty of real-time communication.

Source: Adapted from Julie Candler, "Just-In-Time Deliveries," Nation's Business (April 1993), pp. 64–65.

those supplies in stock, as with EOQ, MRP is a process to determine the number of components and subassemblies needed and to coordinate their ordering and delivery.

A more advanced control system that has evolved from MRP is **manufacturing resource planning II (MRPII).** MRPII coordinates inventory management with all other functions of a business like marketing, accounting, financial planning, cash flow, and engineering. Since it is more complex and expensive, it is used mainly in large businesses but is worth noting here because techniques and processes often find their ways into small businesses after a period of time.

Summary

■ The importance of purchasing and its procedures.

Purchasing is an important part of a small business because the goods or raw materials that you bring into your business become the products you will, in turn, have available to sell to your customers. A savings gained from the cost of purchased items has a larger impact on your profit level than an increase in sales revenue.

■ Considerations for selecting suppliers.

Small manufacturers must first decide whether to make parts needed in their production or to purchase components from another business. Retailers must decide whether to hire personnel or to outsource needed services. Both of these are examples of the make or buy decision. Factors like product quality, location of supplier, services that suppliers offer, and credit terms available need to be considered when selecting suppliers.

■ How to determine inventory needs.

If the small business that you run requires inventory, you must maintain a balance between having enough goods on hand to prevent lost sales due to items being out of stock and having inventory dollars laying idle on a shelf. Retailers and manufacturers need to heed the Pareto rule by paying attention to the "vital few" rather than the "trivial many" items in your inventory. Shrinkage, obsolescence, holding costs, and ordering costs are factors to be considered in determining the inventory needs of your business.

■ Procedures for different types of inventory control.

To control your inventory, you must begin by determining your reorder point (when you need to reorder) and your reorder quantity (how much you need to reorder). Many small businesses depend on visual control to maintain inventory. Economic order quantity, ABC classification, electronic data interchange, just-in-time, and materials requirements planning are common tools for controlling inventory.

Questions for Review and Discussion

1. What factors should be considered when purchasing for a small business?
2. Explain how the Pareto rule is important to a small business owner.
3. What impact can shrinkage have on an inventory system?

4. Assume that you are the owner of the sporting goods store used in the example of economic order quantity inventory control on page 434. You typically sell 14,500 sweatshirts per year. Your ordering costs are still $10 per order. Holding costs are $0.60 per sweatshirt per year. What is your EOQ for sweatshirts? How many sweatshirt orders would you place per year?

5. When would an ABC inventory system be appropriate?

6. Besides reducing inventory levels, what does the just-in-time philosophy promote?

7. What is the difference between a pull system and a push system of inventory control?

8. Consider the make or buy decision. Give three examples of situations when a business should make, rather than buy. Give three examples of situations when a business should buy, rather than make.

Critical Incident

Costume Specialists Inc. Storybook characters like Madeline, Babar the Elephant, and even Stinky Cheese Man come alive under the watchful eye of Wendy Goldstein of Columbus, Ohio. Her company, Costume Specialists Inc., fashions the complicated costumes from scratch and sells the creations to book publishers and bookstore chains. Each costume takes about 60 to 80 hours of artistic effort and costs up to $3,000 in materials and labor to produce. Goldstein's business brings in $600,000 annually.

Catch the Wave. Catch the Wave is a marketing information and graphics design firm located in Minneapolis. The firm designs Web pages for clients wanting to get on the Internet. The firm's 20 employees have varied experience in design, advertising, writing, photography, and computer graphics. Prices charged clients depend on the desired sophistication and interactivity of their Web site. The popularity of the Internet and World Wide Web has sent the company's annual revenues soaring to $7 million. And this figure is expected to continue to go up as more and more clients want to "catch the wave."

Margaritaville Store. Of course, it has to be in Key West! Where else to find Jimmy Buffett's 400-square foot shop—Margaritaville Store. And what else would you expect to find there but T-shirts and other beach paraphernalia. The first store did so well that Buffett expanded the retail store and even added a cafe in New Orleans. Total annual sales revenues for Jimmy Buffett's empire exceed $50 million. That's a lot of CDs, tapes, books, T-shirts, trinkets, and food—even in Margaritaville!

Questions

1. Select one of the companies described and write a short paper (no more than two pages) about the type of inventory control techniques that the business should use. Explain what you think would be an appropriate number of suppliers for this company and why.

2. Effective inventory management also means being ready to cope with problems. Divide into groups according to the companies you selected and then discuss how you could design an inventory system that would adapt to such "shocks." (Read on for additional information.)

Costume Specialists Inc. You just found out that your long-time supplier of flexible costume mouthpieces has just been purchased by a Japanese conglomerate that has strict purchasing guidelines and wants you to go EDI.

Catch the Wave. You were hoping it would never happen, but now it has. A computer virus has wiped out all but two of your firm's computers.

Margaritaville Store. Trouble in paradise comes in the form of hurricanes. Even though you've been lucky so far, the 1996 hurricane season came a little too close for comfort.

Take it to the Net

We invite you to visit the Hatten page on the Prentice Hall Web site at: http://www.prenhall.com/~hattensb for this chapter's World Wide Web exercise.

VIDEO CASE
The Art of Barter

RATHER THAN PAYING WITH CASH, many businesses both large and small, are using barter to trade for many goods or services. For example, Paul Kola trades pizza for advertising in a local student newspaper, and Pepsi has traded soft drinks for Russian vodka.

Businesses that cannot find another business with which to trade directly can still barter by using a commercial barter agent such as Lance Lundberg. Lundberg trades for such products as barbeque sauce, laptop computers, or credit for hotel rooms and then makes matches with other companies.

Barter can be an attractive tool for increasing sales as long as the business has enough cash to pay its fixed expenses. Another danger of bartering is finding a place to sell the goods for which you have traded—you could get stuck with a white elephant, or worse. *Source: The Wall Street Journal Report, Show #659, May 13, 1995.*

Discussion Questions:

- What advantages could the use of barter provide for a small business?
- What problems could extensive use of barter create for most small businesses?

Chapter Focus

After reading this chapter, you should be able to:

- Discuss the importance and uses of financial records to a small business.
- Itemize the accounting records needed for a small business.
- Explain the 11 ratios used to analyze financial statements.
- Illustrate the importance of and procedures for managing cash flow.

Accounting Records and Financial Statements

O MOST OF US, NUMBERS ON accounting statements are simply a welter of information it takes an expert to interpret. But, at Mid-States Technical Staffing Services in Davenport, Iowa, those numbers take on a concrete meaning for employees. How? Through company president Steve Wilson's "bucket plan"—which offers an innovative spin on a new style of accounting practice known as *open-book management.*

Wilson was looking for a way to keep his 37 employees motivated and excited about doing their jobs—placing technical people in positions in client firms. That's when he devised this plan as a way to share profits and to educate staffers. As a certain level of revenue is reached, various "buckets" (boxes, actually), each representing different areas of expense (taxes, rent, and so on), as well as profit, are filled with paper money. This distribution of paper money enables employees to literally see where the company's revenues are going. Eventually, the money in the profit bucket (in real dollars) is distributed to employees. Each employee receives 7.5 percent of the first bucket and 2.5 percent of each succeeding bucket. In addition, if sales have increased by 25 percent at the time a bucket is filled, the bonus percentage is doubled.

While Wilson's bucket game has taught employees about cash flow and profit analysis, it has actually benefited both the company and the employees. Employees have received regular and frequent bonus profit distributions. In 1995, employees filled nine $75,000 profit buckets, eight of which were double-bonus. The company has also benefited from tremendous sales growth, exceeding $8 million in 1995. Rather than seeing cash flow and profits as just a bunch of foreign numbers on accounting statements, Mid-States's bucket game provides employees with a real understanding of the importance of the bottom line. *Source: Howard Scott, "Bonus Programs with a Motive,"* Nation's Business (December 1995), pp. 46R–47R.

The accounting process helps you to translate numbers—the language of business—into plain English.

Are you intimidated by the thought of accounting systems, with row after row and column after column of numbers? If you are, you are not alone. But you should not be frightened by or dread the numbers of your business because accounting is not about making rows and columns of numbers. It is about organizing and communicating what is going on in your business. Think of numbers as the language of business.

Computers help us take piles of raw data and turn them into usable information with which to make a managerial decision. For example, consider a marketing research project you have conducted. You have received thousands of

FIGURE 17-1
The Accounting Process
An accounting system works on a cycle to convert raw data into usable information for making decisions about how to run your small business.

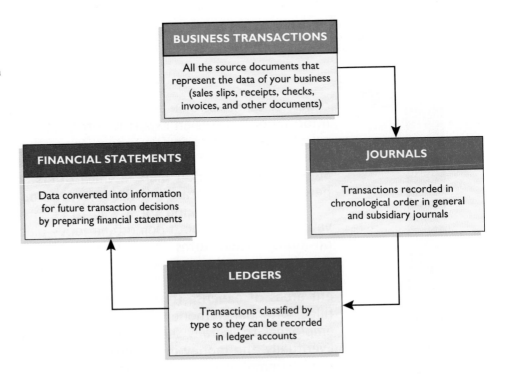

BUSINESS TRANSACTIONS

All the source documents that represent the data of your business (sales slips, receipts, checks, invoices, and other documents)

JOURNALS

Transactions recorded in chronological order in general and subsidiary journals

LEDGERS

Transactions classified by type so they can be recorded in ledger accounts

FINANCIAL STATEMENTS

Data converted into information for future transaction decisions by preparing financial statements completed questionnaires, each with 20 responses. You would have a very hard time interpreting these thousands of pages because they contain raw, unprocessed **data.** If you were to enter all your data into a statistical program on a computer, you could organize these data into means, trends, and a few meaningful numbers, or **information,** which would allow you to make marketing decisions.

    Accounting systems accomplish a similar purpose. Think of all the piles of checks, receipts, invoices, and other papers your business generates in a month as data. Everything you need to know about the financial health of your business is in those piles, but it is not in a usable form. Accounting systems funnel piles of data into usable information by recording every transaction that occurs in your business in journals, then transferring (or posting) them into ledgers. The process is basically the same whether you use pencil and paper or an accounting program on a PC. From the ledger you make financial statements like a balance sheet, income statement, and statement of cash flow. These statements communicate what is going on in your business much better than the piles of papers you started with.

    The last step in the accounting process is to take certain numbers from your financial statements to compute key ratios which can be compared to industry averages or historical figures from your own business to help you make financial decisions. The intent of this chapter is not to turn you into an accountant, but rather to understand the communication process—or language—better. (See Figure 17-1.)

> **accounting** The system within a business for converting raw data from source documents (like invoices, sales receipts, bills, and checks) into information which will help a manager make business decisions.

How Important are Financial Records?

Financial records are important to businesses for several reasons. Remember when we discussed the reasons for failure of small businesses in Chapter 1? Most of the mismanagement decisions that spell the doom of many small businesses are related to finance.

Accurate Information for Management

You need to have accurate financial information to know the financial health of your business. To make effective management decisions, you must know things like the value of your accounts receivable, the age of each account, how quickly your inventory is turning over, which items are not moving, how much your firm owes, when debts are due, and how much your business owes in taxes and FICA (Social Security taxes). Good records are needed to answer these and many other similar questions. Without good records, these questions would be impossible to answer. Accurate financial records also allow you to identify problems before they become threats to your business.

Banking and Tax Requirements

The information on your financial statements is needed to prepare your tax returns. If your business is audited by the Internal Revenue Service, you will be expected to produce the relevant accounting records and statements.

Bankers and investors use your financial statements to evaluate the condition of your business. If you need the services of either, you must not only produce statements, you must also be ready to explain and defend their contents.

Small Business Accounting Basics

The accounting system provides you with information for making decisions about your small business. To access this information, you need to understand the entry systems you can use and how accounting equations work. Your accounting system should be easy to use, accurate, timely, consistent, understandable, dependable, and complete.

Double- and Single-entry Systems

double-entry accounting An accounting system in which every business transaction is recorded in an asset account **and** a liability or owner's equity account in order for the system to balance.

asset Any resource that a business owns and expects to use to its benefit.

liability A debt owed by a business to another organization or individual.

owner's equity The amount of money the owner of a business would receive if all of the assets were sold and of the liabilities were paid.

Double-entry accounting systems revolve around three elements: assets, liabilities, and owner's equity. **Assets** are what your business owns. **Liabilities** are what your business owes. **Owner's equity** is what you (the owner) have invested in the business (it can also be called *capital* or *net worth*).

As the name implies, with a double-entry system, all transactions are recorded in two ways—once as a *debit* to one account and again as a *credit* to another account. Every "plus" must be balanced by a "minus" so that each transaction shows how assets are affected on one side and how liabilities and owner's equity are affected on the other.

A double-entry accounting system increases the accuracy of your system and provides a self-checking audit. If you make a mistake in recording a transaction, your accounts will not balance, indicating to you that you need to go back over the books to find the error. Debits must always equal credits. To increase an asset, you debit the account. To increase a liability or equity, you credit the account.

A **single-entry accounting system** does exist and may be used by small sole proprietorships. With a single-entry system, you record the flow of income and expenses in a running log, basically like a checkbook. It allows you to produce a monthly statement but not to make a balance sheet, an income statement, or other financial records. The single-entry system is simple but is not self-balancing as a double-entry system is.

Popular computer programs like Quicken employ a single-entry accounting system. These programs provide attractive features like the ability to track expense categories, to post amounts to those accounts, and to print reports, but they are still pretty much electronic checkbook registers. Many small one-person businesses begin with them because of their simplicity and graduate to more powerful, full-feature systems like Peachtree or Great Plains accounting programs. There is no one-size-fits-all computer accounting program for your small business.[1] You may have to adjust as you grow.

On the subject of beginning simply: *Always* use separate checkbooks for your business and your personal life. Avoid the temptation to combine the two by thinking that "the business money and personal money is all mine—I'll just keep them together." At some point you will need to separate them, which can be very difficult to do later.

Manager's Notebook

Computerized Accounting Packages

A computerized accounting information system can help a small business manager get accounting information efficiently and quickly. Some of the benefits of computerized accounting are the time saved by the structural methods of entering accounting data and generating accounting statements, the better and more detailed information obtained than with manual systems, the improved traceability of income and expenses (which could prove important for audits), and the increased timeliness and frequency of accounting statements. However, selecting appropriate hardware and accounting software can be a major challenge. To make your decision easier, let's examine some of the better-known accounting packages.

Businessworks 10.0. This full-featured accounting program has a modular design that can grow with a small business. You might start out with the basic modules and add more as your business grows and the financial records become more complex. Businessworks is a comprehensive program that covers the basic accounting functions such as general ledger, accounts payable, inventory, and payroll. The program will also integrate information such as point-of-sale transactions and time clock/payroll. In addition, you can add specialized industry package modules to the basic program.

DacEasy 6.0 This is also a modular program offering many basic accounting functions. Available add-on programs include payroll, order entry, point-of-sale, estimating, job costing, and executive information system. Although the name implies that it's "easy," DacEasy actually requires a solid understanding of basic accounting.

Peachtree 9.0. This comprehensive accounting package comes with payroll, inventory, job cost, and order entry functions included in the basic price. Although Peachtree allows great versatility

in creating accounting documents, the user needs a good understanding of debits, credits, and basic accounting principles. It's probably best suited for a well-established business wanting considerable sophistication in its accounting system and extensive flexibility in creating accounting reports. However, the program is probably too complex for a very small business that just wants to automate basic functions.

Quickbooks 2.0. Ads for this simple accounting package proclaim, "No need to know a debit from a credit—ever!" And it's true. Quickbooks 2.0 is a straightforward package and an excellent choice for a small business that doesn't require perpetual inventory. It will automate basic accounting functions such as check writing, invoicing, billing, and receipts.

One Write Plus 4.5. This no-frills program features many of the basic accounting functions. However, its usefulness is limited. For instance, the inventory function is restricted to tracking quantities, using tracking cards, and using a single cost and selling price for each item. Also, while the program creates many standard reports, it allows no customization. On the plus side, the program is easy to install and use. Only a basic understanding of debits and credits is needed.

Keep in mind that your choice of an accounting software package depends on the size of your business and its accounting needs. Generally speaking, the more features and customization options provided in the package, the more expensive it will be and the more complex to install and use. However, as you can see, there's a wide variety of packages to choose from. Be sure to get one that meets your particular needs!

Sources: *Bhaun Raghunathan and Suzanne L. Wobser, "Accounting Software Selection by Small Business Organizations," The National Public Accountant (September 1995), pp. 20+; and Amy Diller Haas, "DOS-based Accounting Software for Small Businesses," The CPA Journal (November 1995), pp. 30–35.*

Accounting Equations

As stated earlier, numbers are the language of business. Three equations set the foundation for that language.

$$Assets = Liabilities + Equity$$

$$Profit = Revenue - Expense$$

$$Cash\ Flow = Receipts - Disbursements$$

The first equation, Assets = Liabilities + Equity, is the basis of the *balance sheet*. Any entry that you make on one side of the equation must also be entered on the other to maintain a balance. For example, say you have a good month and decide to pay off a $2,000 note you took out at the bank six months ago. You would credit your cash account (an asset) by $2,000 and debit your notes payable account (a liability) by $2,000. Your balance sheet remains in equilibrium. Of course, any equation can be rearranged if you understand it. For example:

$$Equity = Assets - Liabilities$$

You can also think of it this way.

$$What\ you\ have = What\ you\ own - What\ you\ owe$$

The second equation, Profit = Revenue − Expense, represents the activity of the *income statement*. In other words, the money you get to keep equals the money your business brings in minus what you have to spend.

The third equation, Cash Flow = Receipts − Disbursements, is the basis of the *cash flow statement*. The money you have on hand at any given time equals the money you bring in minus what you have to pay out.

We will discuss the balance sheet, the income statement, and the cash flow statement in more detail later in this chapter.

Cash and Accrual Methods of Accounting

One decision you need to make in your accounting system is whether to use cash or accrual accounting. The difference between the two is how each shows the timing of your receipts and your disbursements.

accrual basis A method of accounting in which income and expenses are recorded at the time they are incurred, rather than when they are paid.

Most businesses use the **accrual basis method** of accounting. In using this method, you report your income and expenses at the time they are earned or incurred rather than when they are collected or paid. Sales you make on credit are recorded as accounts receivable that have not yet been collected. The accrual method also allows you to record payment of expenses over a period of time even if the actual payment is made in a single installment. For example, you may pay for insurance once or twice a year, but you can record payment on a monthly basis.

cash basis A method of accounting in which income and expenses are recorded at the time they are paid, rather than when they are incurred.

With a **cash basis method** of accounting, you record transactions when cash is actually received and expenses are actually paid. The cash method is simpler to keep than the accrual method. While it may be appropriate for very small businesses, for businesses with no inventory, or for businesses that deal strictly in cash, the cash method can distort financial results over time. You should not use the cash basis if your business extends credit because credit sales would not be recorded as sales until you receive payment. Also your accounts payable would not be recorded as an expense until the bill is paid.

What Accounting Records Do You Need?

To turn data into management information, you need to follow certain guidelines or standards called **generally accepted accounting principles (GAAP).** The group that monitors the appropriateness of these principles is the Financial Accounting Standards Board (FASB). These GAAP guidelines are intended to create financial statement formats that are uniform across industries. Since business is complex, flexibility in GAAP methods is acceptable as long as consistency is maintained within the business.

GAAP Generally accepted accounting principles, which are standards established so all businesses produce comparable financial statements.

Journals and Ledgers. Your accounting actually begins when you record your raw data from sources such as sales slips, purchase invoices, and check stubs in **journals.** A journal is simply a place to write down the date of your transactions, the amounts, and the accounts to be debited and credited. You will have several journals, such as sales, purchases, cash receipts, and cash disbursements journals.

journal A chronological record of all financial transactions of a business.

At some regular time interval (daily, weekly, or monthly), you will post the transactions recorded in all your journals in a **general ledger.** A general ledger is a summary book for recording all transactions and account balances. One of the advantages of using a computerized accounting system is that it can perform the monotonous task of posting electronically. To speed the posting process and to facilitate access to accounts, each account is assigned a two-digit number. The first digit indicates the class of the account (1 for assets, 2 for liabilities, 3 for capital, 4 for income, and 5 for expenses). The second digit is assigned to each account within the class. For example, your cash account could be assigned account number 11. The first 1 shows that the account is an asset, while the second means that it is your first asset listed. Your inventory could be assigned the account number 13, meaning that it is the third asset listed.

general ledger A record of all financial transactions divided into accounts and usually compiled at the end of each month.

At the end of your accounting period or fiscal year, you will close and total each individual account in your general ledger. At this point, or at any time you wish if you are using a computerized accounting package, you can prepare your financial statements to see where your business stands financially. The three most important statements for providing financial information about your business are the income statement, the balance sheet, and the statement of cash flow.

Income Statement. The **income statement** is also called the profit and loss (P&L) statement. It summarizes the income and expenses that your company has totaled over a period of time. (See Figure 17-2.) The income statement illustrates the accounting equation Profit = Revenue − Expense. Your income statement can generally be broken down into the following sections:

income statement A financial statement which shows the revenue and expenses of a firm in order to calculate the profit or loss produced in a specific period of time.

- Net sales
- Cost of goods sold
- Gross margin
- Expenses
- Net income (or loss)

Not only does the income statement show an itemization of your sales, cost of goods sold, and expenses, but it also allows you to calculate the percentage relationship of each item of expense to sales. Including these percentages on your financial statements produces what is known as a **common-size income statement.** Common-size financial statements are valuable tools for checking the

common-size financial statement A financial statement which includes a percentage breakdown of each item.

INCOME:		% OF SALES
Net Sales	$450,000	100.00%
Cost of Goods Sold	270,000	60.00%
GROSS PROFIT ON SALES	$180,000	40.00%
EXPENSES:		
Selling Expense		
Advertising	$ 12,000	2.67%
Delivery and Freight	10,000	2.22%
Sales Salaries	25,000	5.56%
Miscellaneous Selling Expenses	1,000	0.22%
Administrative Expense		
Licenses	$ 150	0.03%
Insurance	2,400	0.53%
Nonsales Salaries	38,000	8.44%
Payroll Taxes	6,300	1.40%
Rent/Mortgage	12,400	2.76%
Utilities	6,000	1.33%
Legal Fees	1,500	0.33%
Depreciation	42,000	9.33%
Miscellaneous Administrative Expenses	500	0.11%
TOTAL EXPENSES	$157,250	34.94%
INCOME FROM OPERATIONS	$ 22,750	5.06%
OTHER INCOME		
Interest Income	$ 300	0.07%
OTHER EXPENSES		
Interest Expense	$ 15,000	3.33%
NET PROFIT (LOSS) BEFORE TAXES	$ 8,050	1.79%
INCOME TAXES	$ 3,220	0.72%
NET PROFIT (LOSS) AFTER TAXES	$ 4,830	1.07%
NOTE:		
Cash Flow From Operations Equals Net Profit or Loss After Taxes Plus Depreciation	$ 46,830	

FIGURE 17-2
Stereo City Income Statement

efficiency trends of your business by measuring and controlling individual expense items.

Consider the example of Stereo City, a retail company which sells home electronic equipment. Stereo City's net sales for the accounting period were $450,000. The business held a 40 percent gross profit (or margin), which means that out of net sales, Stereo City had acquired $180,000 with which to cover its operating expenses. Total expenses were $157,250 (34.94 percent of sales). After adding interest income and deducting interest expenses and taxes, the company's net profit—the bottom line—was $4,830.

Balance Sheet. While the income statement shows the financial condition of your business over time, the **balance sheet** provides an instant "snapshot" of your business at any given moment (usually at the end of the month, quarter, or fiscal year). (See Figure 17-3.) A balance sheet has two main sections—one showing the assets of the business, and one showing the liabilities and capital of the business. As explained previously under "Accounting Equations," these two sides must balance.

On Stereo City's sample balance sheet, you will see a column of percentages of total assets, liabilities, and capital. As with the common-size income statement, these percentages on the common size balance sheet can indicate accounts and areas that are out of line compared to industry averages, such as those pub-

balance sheet A financial statement which shows a firm's assets, liabilities, and owner's equity.

ASSETS

Current Assets:

		Percent of Total Assets
Cash	$ 3,500	1.08%
Accounts Receivable	12,000	3.71%
Inventory	125,000	38.64%
Prepaid Expenses	5,000	1.55%
Short-term Investments	10,000	3.09%
Total Current Assets	$155,500	48.07%

Fixed Assets:

Building	$150,000	46.37%
Equipment	25,000	7.73%
Leasehold Improvements	20,000	6.18%
Other Fixed Assets	15,000	4.64%
Gross Fixed Assets	$210,000	64.91%
Less: Accumulated Depreciation	42,000	12.98%
Net Fixed Assets	$168,000	51.93%
Total Assets	$323,500	100.00%

LIABILITIES AND OWNERS' EQUITY

Current Liabilities:

		Percent of Liability and Equity
Accounts Payable	$ 75,000	23.18%
Accruals	7,500	2.32%
Current Portion of Long-term Debt	17,500	5.41%
Other Current Liabilities	5,000	1.55%
Total Current Liabilities	$105,000	32.46%

Long-term Liabilities:

Mortgage Loan	$ 93,000	28.75%
Term Loan	39,500	12.21%
Total Long-term Liabilities	$132,500	40.96%
Total Liabilities	$237,500	73.42%

Owners' Equity

Paid-in Capital	$ 75,000	23.18%
Retained Earnings	11,000	3.40%
Total Owners' Equity	$ 86,000	26.58%
Total Liabilities and Owners' Equity	$323,500	100.00%

FIGURE 17-3
Stereo City Balance Sheet

lished by Financial Research Associates, Robert Morris Associates, or by trade associations.

Statement of Cash Flow. The **statement of cash flow** highlights the cash coming into and going out of your business. It is summarized by the accounting equation, Cash Flow = Receipts − Disbursements. The importance of tracking and forecasting your cash flow is difficult to overstate because it is often more critical to survival of the business than profits. Many businesses show considerable profit but have problems paying their bills—meaning that they have a cash flow problem.

It is common for new businesses to experience a situation in which more cash goes out than comes in, which is called a negative cash flow. This condition is not too alarming if it happens when the business is very young or if it happens only occasionally. However, if you experience negative cash flow regularly, you may be undercapitalized, which is a serious problem.[2] More on managing your cash flow will be covered later in this chapter.

statement of cash flow A financial statement which shows the cash inflows and outflows of a business.

What if You are Starting a New Business? If you are starting a new business, you don't have historical data to compile in financial statements. Still, you must estimate how much money you will need, what your expenses will be at different sales levels, and how much money you can expect to make. Financial planning and budgeting are important parts of the business planning process. Making financial projections can even show you whether or not you should start the business. Are the financial risks you are about to take worth the *realistic* return you can expect?

pro forma financial statements Financial statements which project what a firm's financial condition will be in the future.

In this case, you will need to produce **pro forma** statements for your business plan. Pro forma statements are either full or partial estimates, since you are making projections rather than recording actual transactions. (*Pro forma* is Latin for "provided in advance to prescribe form.") Since these statements help you determine your future cash needs and financial condition, a new business should prepare them at least every quarter, if not every month.

In preparing pro forma statements, you need to state the assumptions you are making for your projections. How did you come up with the numbers? Did you grab them out of the air? Did the owner of a similar (but noncompeting) business share his actual numbers for you to use as a base? Are they based on industry averages, such as *Robert Morris Associates Annual Statement Summaries?*

Manager's Notebook

Financial Status Checklist

What should you know about the financial status of your business at any given time? According to SBA sources, you should know the following on a daily, weekly, and monthly basis.

Daily

1. Your cash balance on hand.
2. Your bank balance.
3. Daily summaries of sales and cash receipts.
4. Any problems in your credit collections.
5. A record of any money paid out.

Weekly

1. Accounts receivable—especially slow-paying accounts.
2. Accounts payable—noting discounts offered.

3. Payroll—the accumulation of hours worked and the total payroll owed.
4. Taxes—when tax items are due and which reports are required.

Monthly

1. If you use an outside accounting service, provide records of your receipts, disbursements, bank accounts, and journals to them.
2. Review income statement.
3. Review balance sheet.
4. Reconcile your business checking account.
5. Balance your petty cash account.
6. Review federal tax requirements and make deposits.
7. Review and age your accounts receivable.

Source: Recordkeeping in Small Business, *U.S. Small Business Administration Management Development series.*

Analyzing Financial Statements

Your ability to make sound financial decisions will depend upon how well you can understand, interpret, and use the information contained in your company's financial statements. The purpose of this section is to give an overview of the most common form of financial analysis: **ratio analysis.**

Ratio Analysis

Suppose that two entrepreneurs are comparing how well their respective businesses performed last year. The first entrepreneur, Ms. Alpha, determines that her store made 50 percent more profits last year than the second entrepreneur, Mr. Beta's store. Should Ms. Alpha feel proud? To answer this question, we need more information.

The profit figures tell us only part of the story. While generating 50 percent more profits *seems* good, we need to see how profit relates to other aspects of each business. For example, what if Ms. Alpha's store is four times the size of Mr. Beta's store? Or what if Ms. Alpha's store made three times as many sales as Mr. Beta's store? Now does 50 percent more profits seem as good?

The reality is that fair comparisons can only be made when we demonstrate the relationships between profit and other financial features of the businesses. The relationships that show the relative size of some financial quantity to another financial quantity of a firm are called **financial ratios.** Four important types of financial ratios are the **liquidity, activity, leverage,** and **profitability** ratios.[3]

financial ratios Calculations which compare important financial aspects of a business.

Liquidity Ratios

Liquidity ratios are used to measure a firm's ability to meet its short-term obligations to creditors as they come due. The financial data used to determine liquidity are the firm's current assets and current liabilities found on the balance sheet. There are two important liquidity ratios: the **current ratio** and the **quick (or acid-test) ratio.**

Current Ratio. The current ratio measures the number of times the firm can cover its current liabilities with its current assets. The current ratio assumes that both accounts receivable and inventory can be easily converted to cash. Current ratios of 1.0 or less are considered low and indicative of financial difficulties. Current ratios more than 2.0 often suggest excessive liquidity that may be adverse to the firm's profitability.

$$\text{Current Ratio} = \frac{\text{Current Assets}}{\text{Current Liabilities}}$$

Using the data from Stereo City's balance sheet, the company's current ratio is computed as:

$$\frac{\$155,000}{\$105,000} = \underline{\underline{1.48}}$$

This means that Stereo City can cover its current liabilities 1.48 times with its current assets. Another way of looking at this is that the company has $1.48 of current assets for each dollar of current liabilities.

Quick Ratio. The quick ratio measures the firm's ability to meet current obligations with the most liquid of its current assets. The quick ratio is computed as:

$$\text{Quick Ratio} = \frac{\text{Current Assets} - \text{Inventory}}{\text{Current Liabilities}}$$

With the data from Stereo City's balance sheet the quick ratio is:

$$\frac{\$155,000 - \$125,000}{\$105,000} = \underline{\underline{0.29}}$$

This means that Stereo City has only $0.29 in liquid assets for each dollar of current liabilities. The company obviously counts on making sales to pay its current obligations.

Activity Ratios

Activity ratios measure the speed with which various accounts are converted into sales or cash. These ratios are often used to measure how efficiently a firm uses its assets. There are four important activity ratios.

Inventory Turnover. Inventory turnover measures the liquidity of the firm's inventory—how quickly goods are sold and replenished. The higher the inventory turnover, the more times the firm is selling or "turning over" its inventory. A high inventory ratio generally implies efficient inventory management. Inventory turnover is computed as:

$$\text{Inventory Turnover} = \frac{\text{Cost of Goods Sold}}{\text{Inventory}}$$

Using data from Stereo City's income statement and balance sheet, the firm's inventory turnover is:

$$\frac{\$270,000}{\$125,000} = \underline{\underline{2.16}}$$

This means that Stereo City restocked its inventory 2.16 times last year.

Average Collection Period. The average collection period is a measure of how long it takes a firm to convert a credit sale into a usable form (cash). All firms that extend credit must compute this ratio to determine the effectiveness of their credit-granting and collection policies. High average collection periods usually indicate many uncollectible receivables, while low average collection periods may indicate overly restrictive credit-granting policies. The average collection period is computed as:

$$\text{Average Collection Period} = \frac{\text{Accounts Receivable}}{\text{Average Sales Per Day}}$$

Using the data from Stereo City's balance sheet and income statement, average collection period is:

$$\frac{\$12,000}{\dfrac{\$450,000}{365}} = \underline{\underline{9.93}}$$

This means that Stereo City collects its receivables in less than ten days.

Fixed Asset Turnover. The fixed asset turnover ratio measures how efficiently the firm is using its assets to generate sales. The higher the ratio, the more effective the firm's asset utilization. A low ratio often indicates that marketing efforts are ineffective or that the firm's core business areas are not currently feasible. The fixed asset turnover ratio is calculated as:

$$\text{Fixed Asset Turnover} = \frac{\text{Sales}}{\text{Net Fixed Assets}}$$

Using the data from Stereo City's income statement and balance sheet, the fixed asset turnover is:

$$\frac{\$450,000}{\$168,000} = \underline{\underline{2.68}}$$

This means that Stereo City turns over its net fixed assets 2.68 times per year.

Total Asset Turnover. The total asset turnover ratio measures how efficiently the firm uses all of its assets to generate sales, so a high ratio generally reflects good overall management. A low ratio may indicate flaws in the firm's overall strategy, poor marketing efforts, or improper capital expenditures. The total asset turnover is calculated as:

$$\text{Total Asset Turnover} = \frac{\text{Sales}}{\text{Total Assets}}$$

Using data from Stereo City's income statement and balance sheet, total asset turnover is:

$$\frac{\$450,000}{\$323,500} = \underline{\underline{1.39}}$$

This means that Stereo City turns its assets over 1.39 times per year.

Leverage Ratios

Leverage ratios measure the extent to which a firm uses debt as a source of financing and its ability to service that debt. The term *leverage* refers to the magnification of risk and potential return that comes with using other people's money to generate profits. The more debt a firm uses, the more financial leverage it has. Two important leverage ratios are the **debt ratio** and the **times interest earned ratio.**

Debt Ratio. The debt ratio measures the proportion of a firm's total assets that is acquired with borrowed funds. Total debt includes short-term debt, long-term debt, and long-term obligations such as leases. A high ratio indicates a more aggressive approach to financing and is evidence of a high risk, high (expected) return strategy. A low ratio indicates a more conservative approach to financing. The debt ratio is calculated as:

$$\text{Debt Ratio} = \frac{\text{Total Debt}}{\text{Total Assets}}$$

Using the data from Stereo City's balance sheet, the debt ratio is:

$$\frac{\$237,500}{\$323,500} = \underline{0.73}$$

This means that the company has financed 73 percent of its assets with borrowed funds. Or, $0.73 out of every dollar of funding for Stereo City has come from debt.

Times Interest Earned. The times interest earned ratio calculates the firm's ability to meet its interest requirements. It shows how far operating income can decline before the firm will likely have difficulties servicing its debt obligations. A high ratio indicates a low-risk situation, but may also indicate an inefficient use of leverage. A low ratio indicates that immediate action should be taken to ensure no debt payments will go into default status. Times interest earned is computed as:

$$\text{Times Interest Earned} = \frac{\text{Operating Income}}{\text{Interest Expense}}$$

Using the data from Stereo City's income statement, times interest earned is:

$$\frac{\$22,750}{\$15,000} = \underline{1.52}$$

This means that the company has operating income 1.52 times as much as its interest obligations.

Profitability Ratios

Profitability ratios are used to measure the ability of a company to turn sales into profits and to earn profits on assets committed. Additionally, profitability ratios allow some insight into the overall effectiveness of the management team. There are three important profitability ratios.

Net Profit Margin. The net profit margin measures the percentage of each sales dollar that remains as profit after all expenses, including taxes, have been paid. This ratio is widely used as a gauge of management efficiency. While net profit margins vary greatly by industry, a low ratio indicates that expenses are too high relative to sales. Net profit margin can be seen on a common-size income statement or with the formula:

$$\text{Net Profit Margin} = \frac{\text{Net Income}}{\text{Sales}}$$

Using the data from Stereo City's income statement, net profit margin is:

$$\frac{\$4,830}{\$450,000} = \underline{0.0107}$$

This means that the company actually generates 1.07 cents of after-tax profit per each dollar of sales.

Return on Assets. Also known as **return on investment,** this ratio indicates the firm's effectiveness in generating profits from its available assets. The higher this ratio is, the better. A high ratio shows effective management and good chances for prospective future growth. The return on assets is found with the formula:

$$\text{Return on Assets} = \frac{\text{Net Profit After Taxes}}{\text{Total Assets}}$$

Using the data from Stereo City's income statement and balance sheet, return on assets is:

$$\frac{\$4,830}{\$323,500} = \underline{0.0149}$$

This means the company generates approximately 1.5 cents of after-tax profit for each dollar of assets the company has at its disposal.

Return on Equity. The return on equity measures the return the firm earned on its owners' investment in the firm. In general, the higher this ratio is, the better off the owners are. However, this ratio is highly affected by the amount of financial leverage (borrowed money) used by the firm and may not be an accurate measure of management effectiveness. The return on equity is calculated as:

$$\text{Return on Equity} = \frac{\text{Net Profit After Taxes}}{\text{Owners' Equity}}$$

Using the data from Stereo City's income statement and balance sheet, return on equity is:

$$\frac{\$4,830}{\$86,000} = \underline{0.0562}$$

This means that the company generates a little more than 5.5 cents of after-tax profit for each dollar of owners' equity.

The Use of Financial Ratios

Financial ratios by themselves tell us very little. For analysis purposes, ratios are only useful when compared with other ratios. Two types of ratio comparisons can be made: **cross-sectional** analysis, which compares different firms' financial ratios at the same point in time, and **time series,** which compares a single firm's present performance with its own past performance.

Cross-sectional analysis is often done by comparing an individual firm's ratios against the standard ratios for the firm's industry. Such industry ratios may be found in most college or large public libraries. Look for Robert Morris Associate's *RMA Annual Statement Studies* or Dun & Bradstreet's *Industry Norms and Key Business Ratios.* Another good source is *Financial Studies of the Small Business* from Financial Research Associates.[4]

Table 17-1 shows how some of Stereo City's ratios compare with the median ratios for stereo equipment retail stores with an asset size between $10,000 and $1,000,000. From the data we can conclude that Stereo City potentially has three major problems.

First, Stereo City's quick ratio is only about half the average of the industry. This could mean that it has excessive amounts of inventory and faces the possibility of illiquidity if the inventory does not sell in a timely manner.

Second, Stereo City appears to have an excessive amount of debt in relation to its sales. The firm's times interest earned ratio is less than one-fourth of the industry average, indicating a strong probability that the company will not be able to service its debt in the future.

TABLE 17 ▪ 1 Comparing Company and Industry Ratios

	STEREO CITY	INDUSTRY
Liquidity		
Current Ratio	1.48	1.60
Quick Ratio	0.29	0.50
Activity		
Average Collection	9.7	8.0
Total Asset Turnover	1.4	4.2
Leverage		
Debt Ratio	73.0	61.5
Times Interest Earned	1.5	6.1
Profitability		
Return on Assets*	2.5	6.2
* Uses pretax profits.		

Source: Financial Studies of the Small Business, 17th ed. *(Winter Haven, FL: Financial Research Associates, 1994).*

Third, Stereo City's total asset turnover and return on asset ratios are both considerably below industry average. The likely cause of this is having insufficient sales to support the size of the business. The company must either downsize by selling off some assets or work harder to increase sales.

Time series analysis is used to uncover trends in the firm's financial performance. If there is potential trouble in any of the four main areas of analysis (liquidity, activity, leverage, and profitability), managers will have time to correct these problems before the problems become overbearing. The key to potential solutions is found in the ratios themselves.

For example, if the time series analysis shows that the firm's liquidity is diminishing, the managers will want to take action to enhance the firm's liquidity position. By looking at the liquidity ratios, a number of possible solutions will become apparent.

Since ratio analysis has shown that Stereo City needs to increase its current assets (especially cash and short-term investments) without a commensurate in-

Global Small Business

Small businesses worldwide recognize that they must examine their financial ratios in order to determine how well they're doing. For instance, JCG Holdings Ltd., a Taiwanese-Japanese financial services company, makes loans to working-class people in Hong Kong. Its average loans range from $2,000 to $3,200 and typically mature in 12 months. The borrower pays an interest rate that runs about 30 percent on an annual basis. However, on its deposits, JCG pays an average interest rate of 6.5 percent. This spread has allowed the company to earn an incredible 12 percent return on assets. Compare this to the average U.S. financial services firm's ROA ratio of 1.5 percent. It doesn't take an accounting genius to recognize that JCG is doing well! However, JCG's managers wouldn't know this *if* they hadn't calculated and analyzed the financial ratios. *Source: Andrew Tanzer, "Your Passport, Please,"* Forbes *(November 6, 1995), pp. 252–253.*

Small Business
IN THE Service Industry

If you find that you enjoy working with accounting information or creating accounting systems, you might even consider starting a small business to provide those services. Finding a unique accounting services niche can be profitable. Take, for instance, what Combined Resource Technology (CRT) of Baton Rouge, Louisiana, did. CRT started out as a real estate development company. However, when the oil and gas price crash battered Louisiana's economy, CRT found itself owing some $14 million to banks on loans it had taken out to buy a shopping center and apartment buildings. To avoid failure, CRT partners Darwyn Williams and Chris Moran had to do something quickly. Although their properties' values had plunged, they found that the tax assessor's property valuations hadn't changed. Thus, out of desperation was born their new accounting services business, in which they peruse tax rolls to identify overassessed properties and contact the owners about getting the taxes reduced—for a fee, of course. They've since expanded their cost-reduction services beyond taxes to include utilities, waste disposal, freight, leases, and any other areas where they can help business owners reduce costs. CRT provides a unique accounting service that others have been willing to pay for. *Source: Jay Finegan, "Corporate Cost Cutters," Inc. (August 1995), p. 28.*

crease in current liabilities, possible solutions are to borrow cash through a long-term loan, get a cash infusion from the firm's owners, or sell off some fixed assets for cash. An alternative approach would be to reduce current liabilities by restructuring short-term debt into long-term debt or using the proceeds of the sale of a fixed asset to retire some accounts payable. Any action that results in boosting the firm's liquidity helps to avoid the risk of Stereo City's becoming insolvent because of diminishing liquidity.

Reviewing financial ratios annually can help prevent difficult situations before they have the opportunity to occur. Thus, ratio analysis allows small business owners and managers to become proactive directors of the financial aspects of their ventures.

Managing Cash Flow

Each business day, approximately one dozen U.S. small businesses declare bankruptcy. The majority of these business failures are caused by poor cash flow management.[5] Companies from the smallest startups to the largest conglomerates all share the same need for positive cash flow. A company that does not effectively manage its cash is poised for collapse.

Cash Flow Defined

The accounting definition of cash flow is the sum of net income plus any noncash expenses such as depreciation and amortization. This treatment of cash flow is largely misunderstood by many small business owners. A more "bottom line" approach is to define cash flow as the difference between the actual amount of cash a company brings in and the actual amount of cash a company disburses in a given time period.

The most important aspects of this refined definition are the inclusion of the terms *actual cash* and *time period*. The goal of good cash flow management is to have enough cash on hand when you need it. It does not matter if your company will have a positive cash balance three months from now when your payroll, taxes, insurance, and suppliers all need to be paid today.

Cash flow management requires as much attention as developing new customers, perfecting products and services, and all other day-to-day operating activities. The basic strategy underlying cash flow management is to maximize your use of cash. This means not only ensuring consistent cash inflows, but also developing a disciplined approach to cash outflows.

Computer Applications

Could your cash flow management system be computerized? As noted earlier in the chapter, there are single-entry general ledger accounting software packages that are easy to use. However, these packages can provide an unrealistic view of your business's *cash flow*. In a single-entry system, all cash coming into the business is put on the left-hand side of the ledger and cash flowing out of the business is put on the right-hand side. However, if your business has accounts receivable or accounts payable, a single-entry system can "fool" you into thinking you have enough cash on hand to meet expenses or to be used for business expansion.

To manage cash flow more effectively, here are some packages that monitor cash flow. For instance, Great Plains Profit (Great Plains Software) is a fully integrated small business accounting program that has an exceptional cash flow monitoring capability. Or you might want to look at a more sophisticated analysis program if you must make decisions in your small business that involve varying probability of profit payoffs. In that case, you might find Decision Analysis 2.5 from

TreeAge Software Inc. useful. It helps you perform specific decision analyses in order to determine potential profits of different decision alternatives. Although this program isn't designed for day-in, day-out cash flow management, it can produce objective data for making decisions that concern the profitability of certain activities.

Another tool you might find helpful isn't a cash flow package but rather a multimedia course that trains employees in the basics of financial management: Financial Competence by Competence Software. Its seven chapters include: Financial Statement Overview; Income Statement; Balance Sheet; Cash Flow; Linking the Statements; Analyzing the Statements; and Review, Exam, and Certificate of Completion. This software would be a good investment if you or your employees need to brush up on accounting and financial information.

Sources: Jeffrey Rothfeder, "Top Tips for the Bottom Line," Newsweek Special Supplement on Small Office/Home Office (Summer 1995), pp. N2–N4; Dennis James, "Find Funding," Success (October 1995), p. 57; and Dennis James, "Smart Strategies," Success (November 1995), pp. 68–69.

Cash Flow Specialist

One reason that so many small businesses run into cash flow problems is that too often no one is put in charge of it. John Conroy, a cash flow expert from West Haven, Connecticut, offers an effective solution: "Appoint a cash flow specialist with the authority to cross department lines as he or she follows the trail of cash coming into—or failing to come into—the company."[6]

The idea of having one individual in a firm responsible for cash management is also endorsed by Leslie N. Masonson, president of Cash Management Resources and a leader of the American Management Association's Corporate Cash Management course. He said that cash managers "should get help from financially savvy individuals, knowledgeable professionals, bankers, or colleagues in the financial profession. [They] should attend regional cash management seminars, read industry magazines, and read books on cash management."[7]

For most small businesses the responsibility of cash flow specialist will necessarily fall upon the owner. While this task may seem overwhelming, there are a few cash flow fundamentals that are not difficult to grasp and will help even the novice cash flow manager gain more control over this essential activity.

A company that does not effectively manage its cash flow—by balancing its income and expenses on a day-to-day basis—is poised for collapse.

Cash Flow Fundamentals

The first step in cash flow management is to understand the purpose and nature of cash flow. Why do you need cash flow? How is cash flow generated? How do firms become insolvent even though they are profitable? To answer these questions we need to look at the motives for having cash, the cash-to-cash cycle, and the timing of cash inflows and outflows.

Motives for Having Cash. Three reasons for which a firm needs cash are: (1) to make transactions, (2) to protect against unanticipated problems, and (3) to invest in opportunities as they arise. Of these, the primary motive is to make transactions—the ability to pay the bills incurred by the business. If a business cannot meet its obligations, it is insolvent. Continued insolvency leads directly to bankruptcy.

Businesses, like individuals, occasionally run into unanticipated problems. Thefts, fires, floods, and other natural and man-made disasters affect businesses in the same way they affect individuals. Those businesses that have "saved for a rainy day" are able to withstand such setbacks. Those that have not planned ahead often suffer—and may even fail—as a result.

Finally, there are times when a business is presented with an opportunity to invest in a profitable venture. If the business has cash on hand to do so, it may reap significant rewards. If not, it has lost a chance to add to its cash flow in a way other than through normal operations.

Each of the three motives is important to understand as they combine to create the proper mentality for the cash flow manager. Without proactively managing a firm's cash flow, the firm is exposed to many risks, each of which can spell disaster.

Cash-to-Cash Cycle. The **cash-to-cash cycle** of the firm, sometimes known as the *operating cycle*, tracks the way cash flows through the business. It identifies how long it takes from the time a firm makes a cash outlay for raw materials or

cash-to-cash cycle The period of time from when money is spent on raw materials until it is collected on the sale of a finished good.

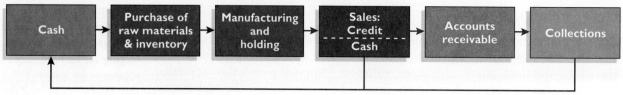

FIGURE 17-4
Cash-to-Cash Cycle
A chart of the cash-to-cash cycle of your small business shows the amount of time that passes between spending money for raw materials or inventory and collecting money on the sale of finished goods.

inventory until the cash is collected from the sale of the finished good. Figure 17-4 shows a typical cash-to-cash cycle.

The firm begins with cash which is used to purchase raw materials or inventory. The firm will normally take some time to manufacture or otherwise hold finished goods until they sell. As sales are made, cash is replenished immediately by cash sales, but accounts receivable are created by credit sales. Then the firm must collect the receivables in order to secure cash.

The cash flow process is continuous, with all activities occurring simultaneously. When the process is operating smoothly, cash flow is easy to monitor and control. However, for most firms, it is often erratic and subject to many complications, which makes cash flow management a challenge.

The Timing of Cash Flows. The major complication to cash flow management is timing. While some cash inflows and outflows will transpire on a regular schedule (such as monthly interest income or payroll costs), other cash flows occur on no schedule whatsoever. For example, when a firm needs to make periodic purchases of capital equipment, which are not part of the daily cash-to-cash process, it will cause a major disruption in the firm's cash flow.

Even though a firm might send out all of its billings to credit customers at one time, you can be sure that these customers will not all pay at the same time. Uncollected receivables may count as revenue on an accrual-based income statement, but they are worthless from a cash flow standpoint until they turn into real money.

The cash flow specialist needs to become well-versed in the patterns of cash inflows and outflows of the firm. The nuances of timing become critical. There are a few tools that can assist in this process.

Cash Flow Management Tools

Once you have a good idea about the purpose and nature of cash flow, you are ready to take steps to manage it. Using cash budgets, aging schedules, and float to control the inflow and outflow of cash is paramount for effective management.

Cash Budgets. Cash budgets (also known as *cash forecasts*) allow the firm to plan its short-term cash needs, with particular attention to periods of surplus and shortage. Whenever the firm is likely to experience a cash surplus, it can plan to make a short-term investment. When the firm is expected to experience a cash shortage, it can plan to arrange for a short-term loan.

A cash budget typically covers a one-year period which is divided into smaller intervals. The number of intervals is dictated by the nature of the business. The more uncertain the firm's cash flows, the more intervals there need to be. Using monthly intervals is common, but some firms require daily cash budgets.

The cash budget requires the cash flow specialist to determine all the known cash inflows and outflows that will occur during the year. Both the amount of cash involved and the cycle's length of time must be disclosed. This information is then put into a format as shown in Table 17-2.

Table 17-2 lists some of the most common types of cash inflows and outflows experienced by a typical small business. Categories should be modified to fit the particulars of each individual business. The most important point is to include all relevant sources of and demands for cash.

Many businesses find that adding a reconciliation component to the bottom of the cash budget is helpful. An example of the reconciliation follows:

Cash Receipts

minus: Cash Disbursements = Net Cash Flow

plus: Beginning Cash = Ending Cash

minus: Minimum Cash Balance = Excess Cash or (Required Financing)

This reconciliation summarizes the total cash inflows and outflows for the period. When added to the beginning cash balance, you have the current cash status of the firm. Since there will be some minimum cash balance required to

TABLE 17 ▪ 2 Cash Budget Format

BEGINNING CASH
Plus Receipts:
Cash Sales
Receivable Collections
Interest
Owner Contributions
Other Receipts
Total Receipts
Minus Disbursements:
Cash Purchases
Payment of Accounts Payable
Wages and Salaries
Payroll Taxes
Advertising
Office Supplies
Rent/Mortgage
Utilities
Telephone
Insurance
Legal/Accounting
Taxes and Licenses
Interest Payments
Loan Principal Payments
Dues and Subscriptions
Travel
Miscellaneous Disbursements
Total Disbursements
Ending Cash (Beginning Cash + Receipts − Disbursements)

begin the next period, the ending cash figure is compared to this minimum figure. If there is a positive difference (ending cash minus minimum cash balance), the firm has cash to invest. If there is a negative difference, the firm must arrange for financing before beginning the new cycle.

By forecasting the inflows and outflows of cash, the cash flow specialist will have a picture of when the firm will have cash surpluses and cash shortages. This knowledge allows the cash flow to be managed proactively rather than reactively.

Reality Check

Open-Book Management

At bulletin boards in the lobbies, conference rooms, and cafeterias of businesses across the country, employees are studying a type of information that had been off limits for years—the company's financial statements. The practice is called *open-book management* and it simply involves showing everyone in the business the numbers that are critical to the business's performance. When employees know and understand the numbers, they can measure their contribution to the company's bottom line and how their performance can make a difference in those numbers.

Open-book management gives logic and a rationale to many of today's management ideas such as employee empowerment, total quality management, and self-directed work teams. Employees are more motivated to work harder when they can see that they have a direct stake in the company's ultimate success.

Open-book management is being used successfully by many small businesses. However, you cannot simply hand out income statements and expect employees to care about the information or understand how their efforts affect it. You must teach them what the numbers mean to them.

One of the first proponents of open-book management was Jack Stack, president and CEO of Springfield Remanufacturing Company. In the book Stack wrote on the topic, *The Great Game of Business*, he stated that for open-book management to work you need to teach employees the rules of the game, give them the information (the financials) they need to play the game, and make sure they share in the risks and rewards.

Stack draws an analogy between open-book management and a game of baseball. He asked, "Can you imagine taking a spectator to a baseball game and not explaining the rules, not showing them how they keep score, and not giving them a stake in the outcome? Can you imagine sitting in those stands trying to figure out why those crazy people are running around on that field and hitting this little ball with a stick? The same thing occurs every single day when someone goes to work. They aren't taught the rules, they don't know what business is all about. They're only taught a little circle, a little piece of the process. We tried to convert it into a game—move everybody from a spectator to a player."

Sources: John Case, "The Open-Book Revolution," Inc. (June 1995), pp. 26–43; David Whitford, "Before & After," Inc. (June 1995), pp. 44–50; Michael Cronin, "Like Cookie, Like Company," Inc. (May 1994), p. 149; Chris Lee, "Open-Book Management," Training (July 1994), pp. 21–27; "Managing by the (Open) Book," Supervisory Management (July 1995), pp. 1–6; Nancy Austin, "When Honesty Is the Best Management Policy," Working Woman (May 1994), pp. 25–26; Catherine Romano, "When Money Talks," Management Review (November 1994), pp. 44–47.

TABLE 17·3 Macro-Aging Schedule

AGE OF RECEIVABLES	PERCENTAGE
0–30 days	25%
31–60 days	50%
61–90 days	20%
Over 90 days	5%

Cash budgeting is, however, not always easy to do. As noted earlier, there are always disruptions to the process. Unforeseen cash outflows and inconsistent cash inflows plague many small businesses. Another tool that helps reduce the uncertainty of the cash flow cycle is the aging schedule.

Aging Schedules. Aging schedules are listings of a firm's accounts receivable according to the length of time they are outstanding. A **macro-aging schedule** simply lists categories of outstanding accounts with the percentage of accounts that falls within each category. For example, see Table 17-3.

macro-aging schedule A list of accounts receivables by age category.

This schedule allows the cash flow specialist to forecast the collection of receivables. Say, for instance, that the firm made credit sales of $10,000 three months ago, $12,000 two months ago, $5,000 last month, and that it predicts it will make credit sales of $7,500 this month. Expected receivables collections for this month will be: $(0.25 \times \$7{,}500) + (0.5 \times \$5{,}000) + (0.2 \times \$12{,}000) + (0.05 \times \$10{,}000) = \$7{,}275$. This is the amount the cash flow manager will place in the Receivables Collection slot of the cash budget for that month.

The **micro-aging schedule** offers another approach to showing receivables. This technique lists the status of each credit customer's account (usually in alphabetical order). This allows the cash flow specialist to concentrate collection efforts on the specific companies that are delinquent in their payments. (See Table 17-4.)

micro-aging schedule A list of accounts receivables which shows each customer, the amount they owe, and the amount that is past due.

This aging schedule is invaluable for controlling receivables. Not only do you have the same information as shown in the macro schedule, but you also have specific information on each credit customer that will enable you to make future credit decisions.

Float. The last cash flow management tool of note is called **float.** Float has two definitions. First, it is the difference between the company's checking account balance and the account balance shown in the bank. Second, it is the period of time between sending a check and when that check clears your bank.

As anyone with a checking account knows, float can be "played" to your advantage. By investing cash in interest-bearing accounts until the checks that

float The difference between the balance in a checking account and the amount shown in the account or the period of time between writing a check and the check clearing the account.

TABLE 17·4 Micro-Aging Schedule

CUSTOMER	AMOUNT	CURRENT	PAST DUE DAYS 1–30	31–60	61–90	+90
Aardvark Supply	$1,500	$1,000	$200	$ 500		
Beaver Trucking	$2,250	$ 0	$ 0	$ 0	$2,250	
Canary Labs	$1,000	$ 500	$500			
. . .						
Total	$11,000	$5,000	$750	$3,000	$2,250	
Percentage	100%	45%	7%	27%	21%	

have been written are expected to clear, the business exploits the cash flow leverage of float. Many banks will do that for businesses using a service called the *zero-balance account*.

With a zero-balance checking account, you sustain a zero balance and deposit money to cover checks on the account only when the check reaches the bank. Typically, the firm keeps deposits in an interest-bearing account at the bank, such as a money market deposit account, and simply transfers the exact amount of funds from this account into the checking account.

Float exists because of the delays caused by the mail system, the processing (recording and depositing) of checks by the recipient, and the bank clearing system. Float has been decreasing due to faster mail service and electronic transfers of funds, but opportunities still remain for those who play the float.

Strategies for Cash Flow Management

Once the cash flow specialist understands some of the basic tools of cash flow management, he should develop a strategy for his firm. Upon which accounts should you concentrate? At what intervals are cash budgets needed? What information is available or needs to be made available to track cash flow? Is the firm's bank providing services to assist in cash flow management? The answers to these questions, among others, help shape cash flow strategy.

Manager's Notebook

Accounts Receivable Tips

Managing your accounts receivable is an important step in controlling your cash flow. The following advice can help you keep a handle on them:

1. **Obtain customer orders by faster means than mail.** For example, invite customers to use fax machines or on-line computer hookups to place orders.

2. **Process orders quickly.** Ensure that each order is handled on or before the date specified by the customer.

3. **Prepare the invoice the same day as the order is received.** Especially on large dollar amounts, do not wait until some "billing date," just because that is when you normally do it.

4. **Mail the invoice the same day it is prepared.** The sooner the bill is in the mail, the sooner it is likely to be paid.

5. **Smartly design your invoice.** Make sure that the amount due, due date, discount for early payment, and penalty for late payment are clearly laid out.

Some additional strategies for managing receivables include calling or personally visiting overdue accounts, creating strict guidelines for extending credit, creating a rigid collection policy, and using micro-aging schedules to ferret out poor credit customers.

Source: Leslie Manonson, "Cash Is King," Management Review *(October 1990), p. 37.*

Accounts Receivable. The first place to look for ways to improve cash flow is in accounts receivable. John Conroy, the West Haven, Connecticut cash flow expert, maintains that the key to an effective cash flow management system is the "ability to collect receivables quickly."[8]

Receivables have inherent procedural problems in most small businesses. Information often gets lost or delayed between salespeople, shipping departments, and the accounting clerks who create the billing statements. Most firms bill only once a month, and may delay that if busy with other activities.

Inventory. Inventory is another area that can drain cash flow. According to James Howard, chairman of the board of Asset Growth Partners, Inc., a New York City financial consulting firm for small businesses, inventory costs are often overlooked or understated by many small businesses. "A typical manufacturing company pays 25 to 30 percent of the value of the inventory for the cost of borrowed money, warehouse space, materials handling, staff, lift-truck expenses, and fixed costs."[9]

Cash flow determines how much inventory can be safely carried by a firm while still allowing sufficient cash for other operations. The inventory turnover ratio lends insight to this situation. If, for example, a firm has an inventory ratio of 12, it only has to keep a month's worth of projected sales in stock before enough cash returns to pay for the next month's worth of inventory.

However, if the firm has a ratio of 4, it must keep three months' worth of projected sales on the shelves. This ties up cash for as much as 90 days. In this case the firm should try to find suppliers that have terms extending to 90 days.

Reality Check

Cash before *Delivery*

Often a small business's inventory decisions can be based on very simple factors of survival—such as managing cash flow. For instance, look at Logo Athletics of Indianapolis. A company which wholesales a complete line of jackets, sweatshirts, hats, shorts, and other merchandise, Logo is the second-largest licensee of the National Football League. Under this arrangement, Logo has purchased the right to sign contracts with manufacturers to produce the goods, which it then distributes to retailers. If it has an NFL logo on it, there's a good chance it's a Logo product. Athletes such as Troy Aikman of the Dallas Cowboys and Steve Young of the San Francisco 49ers are under contract to wear Logo products on the sidelines. Although it's now a well-recognized business, the company had its fair share of early startup crises to weather. In its early days, Tom Shine, the company founder, used leverage to help Logo get off the ground. Everything he did—advertising, endorsements, publicity, pricing, and so forth—was designed to get the cash in from customers first. Then, and only then, would Shine order the products from the manufacturer. This simple policy worked for his business.

Source: Jay Finegan, "Leveraging: A Contact Sport," Inc. (August 1995), p. 32.

Otherwise, it may have to borrow to meet current cash needs. The cash flow management goal is to commit just enough cash to inventory to meet demand.[10]

Banks. Ideally, your bank should be your partner in cash flow management. The cash flow specialist should request the firm's bank to provide an *account analysis*. This analysis shows the banking services the business used during the month, the bank's charge for each service, the balances maintained in all accounts during the month, and the minimum balances required by the bank to pay for the services.

A review of the account analysis will indicate whether any excess account balances are on deposit. These should immediately be removed and invested. Also your firm may be better off removing all account balances that are earning little or no interest and reinvesting them at higher rates even if it means having to pay fees for bank services.

Finally, determine how quickly checks that your firm deposits in the bank become available as cash. Banks normally require delays up to two business days. Banks should have an availability schedule and the cash flow specialist needs to request one from each bank in the area to determine if his bank is competitive. Remember that the faster a deposited check becomes available as cash, the sooner your business has use of the money for other purposes.

Other Areas of Cash Flow Concern. Although receivables, inventory, and bank services are the most likely places on which to concentrate cash flow management strategies, several other areas also deserve attention. They include:

Entering the Internet

What types of accounting information and help can you find on the Internet? Plenty! At the Small Business Administration site, you can find files on Cash Flow Analysis, Recordkeeping in Small Business, and any other number of good topics: gopher://www.sbaonline.sba.gov

With the St. Louis University Entrepreneurship Gopher, you'll find easily accessible files on various business functions including accounting: gopher://egopher.slu.edu:71/

If you want additional information on cash flow analysis, check out the Canada/British Columbia Business Service Centre. Here, under the "On-Line Small Business Workshop," you'll find information on preparing a cash flow forecast and other financial topics: http://www.sb.gov.bc.ca/smallbus/sbhome.html

The CorpFiNet Directory provides access to accounting directories: http://www.corpfinet.com/

At AccountingNet, you'll find links to international, federal, and state sites. These accounting links include governmental tax resources and state tax and general state information: http://www.accountingnet.com/

Finally, you might want to access additional on-line accounting services information and consultants using any of the Web search tools (Yahoo, AltaVista, WebCrawler, and so forth).

1. **Compensation.** Look for duplication of effort and lack of productivity within the firm's work force. Cut personnel hours in those areas to save on wage and payroll tax costs.

2. **Supplies.** Review all petty cash accounts. Show employees the cost of supplies by marking the cost of each item, such as tablets, on the boxes.

3. **Deliveries.** Keep track of local delivery costs to the business. It may be cheaper to hire a part-time worker to pick up supplies than to pay other companies to deliver items.

4. **Insurance.** Ask insurance carriers about ways to reduce premiums. One independent grocery store reduced premiums for its stock personnel by 15 percent simply by requiring them to wear back supports while working.

5. **Borrowing.** Take the cost of borrowing into account when determining operational expenses. Even short-term loans can have a large impact on profit and cash flow.[11]

The process of cash flow management may be confusing to you in the beginning, but you may find it relatively easy to monitor once everything is in place. Armed with a cash budget, aging schedules, and a set of feasible strategies, you can evade cash flow problems and maximize your use of this precious resource.

Summary

◼ The importance of financial records to a small business.

You need financial records so you can make managerial decisions on topics concerning how much money is owed to your business, how much money you owe, and how to identify financial problems before they become serious. Financial records are also needed to prepare your tax returns and to inform your banker and investors of your financial status. Without accurate financial records, you cannot exercise the kind of clear-sighted management control needed to survive in a competitive marketplace.

◼ The accounting records needed for a small business.

The accounting records of your small business need to follow generally accepted accounting principles (GAAP) standards. From your source documents like sales slips, purchase invoices, and check stubs, you record all the transactions into journals. Information from your journals will then be posted (transferred) into a general ledger. Financial statements like your balance sheet, income statement, and statement of cash flow are produced from the transactions in your general ledger.

◼ Ratios used to analyze financial statements.

Ratio analysis is a way for you to compare the financial condition of your business to its performance in previous time periods or to similarly sized businesses within your industry. Four important types of financial ratios discussed in this chapter are liquidity, activity, leverage, and profitability.

◼ The importance of managing cash flow.

Cash flow is the difference between the amount of cash actually brought into your business and the actual amount paid out in a given period of time. Cash flow represents the lifeblood of your business because if you do not have enough money to pay for your operating expenses, you are out of business.

Questions for Review and Discussion

1. How can financial records allow you to identify problems in your business?
2. Assets = Liabilities + Owner's Equity. How would you restate this equation if you wanted to know what your liabilities are? Your owner's equity?
3. What purpose do GAAP and FASB serve for a small business owner?
4. Explain the difference between cash and accrual accounting.
5. Define the term "leverage" as it applies to accounting.
6. How can profitability ratios allow insight into the effectiveness of management? liquidity ratios? activity ratios? leverage ratios?
7. Why would a cash flow specialist be valuable to a small business?
8. Explain the difference between macro-aging and micro-aging accounts receivable schedules.
9. Choose a type of small business that is of interest to you and find industry standard ratios in *Robert Morris Associates Annual Statement Studies* or *Dun & Bradstreet's Industry Norms & Key Business Ratios*. What do these standards tell you about the financial needs for this type of business?
10. Cash flow is described as the life-blood of a business. How would you explain this description to someone who does not understand business finance?

Critical Incident

The popularity of soccer as a participation sport attracted Leo Hernandez and Gil Ferguson to open an indoor soccer arena with retail shops selling soccer-related merchandise. Last year's financial statements for their business OnGoal are shown here. Leo and Gil are hoping to expand their business by opening another facility. However, before they approach banks or potential investors, they need to look closely at what the accounting statements show them.

OnGoal
Balance Sheet
December 31, 19__

Assets:		
Current Assets:		
Cash	$ 7,120	
Accounts receivable	12,400	
Merchandise inventory	18,200	
Prepaid expenses	3,040	
Total current assets		$ 40,760
Fixed assets:		
Fixtures	$16,800	
Less accumulated depreciation	3,600	
Building	78,000	
Less accumulated depreciation	7,800	

Equipment	12,000	
Less accumulated depreciation	4,000	
Total fixed assets		$ 91,400
Total Assets		$132,160
Liabilities/Equity:		
Current Liabilities:		
Accounts payable	$ 6,000	
Notes payable	4,000	
Contracts payable	8,000	
Total Current Liabilities		$ 18,000
Fixed Liabilities:		
Long-term note payable	$75,000	
Owners' Equity:		
Shares held by Hernandez and Ferguson	$39,160	
Total Liabilities/Equity		$132,160

OnGoal
Income Statement
Year Ended December 31, 19__

Sales			$178,000
Cost of Goods Sold			
Beginning Inventory, January 1	$18,000		
Purchases during year	$22,000		
Less Ending Inventory, December 31	$18,200		
Cost of Goods Sold		$ 21,800	
Gross Margin			$156,200
Operating Expenses:			
Payment on building note	$34,000		
Salaries	68,000		
Supplies	7,460		
Advertising/promotion	3,000		
Insurance expense	18,000		
Utilities expense	10,000		
Miscellaneous expenses	4,000		
Total operating expenses		$144,460	
Net profit from operations			$ 11,740

Questions

1. Calculate liquidity, activity, leverage, and profitability ratios for OnGoal.
2. Pair off and compare your ratios. Discuss which of the ratios look weak and which look positive. Develop a one-page explanation of the company's ratios that you can show to potential lenders.

Take it to the Net

We invite you to visit the Hatten page on the Prentice Hall Web site at: http://www.prenhall.com/~hattensb for this chapter's World Wide Web exercise.

Chapter Focus

After reading this chapter, you should be able to:

- Determine the financing needs of your business.
- Define basic financing terminology.
- Explain where to look for sources of funding.

18

Small Business Finance

F INDING MONEY TO FINANCE your small business can be a real challenge. You might look to the traditional avenues such as using personal funds, tapping the resources of family and friends, or even relying on partners for financial backing. In the mid-1990s, however, a new approach to finding financing has emerged—one that utilizes the networking capability of the Internet. And that's what Pam Marrone of AgraQuest Inc. tapped into when she needed additional financing.

Marrone's Davis, California, company develops and manufactures all-natural pesticides. She needed $2.5 million to pay the research, development, and production costs of two pest-control products. Marrone knew how to find money the "old-fashioned" way. After all, she had raised $300,000 in startup financing to launch her company. But when she began looking to expand her business's product line, she decided to experiment with a more direct link to potential investors via the Internet.

Marrone chose to list her business idea (at a minimal charge) with Venture Connect, a World Wide Web site designed to match investors and entrepreneurs. Also she developed her own company home page, which included an extensive business summary and job postings, and promoted it through Yahoo's business directory. "This is a potential way to get directly to investors," Marrone said. "The responses have been fast." Marrone was confident that her unique search for financing would pay off, yet she was being just as cautious in her search for financing in this high-tech approach as if she had taken a more traditional approach. After all, we're still talking about money. *Source: Gianna Jacobson, "Raise Money Now," Success, November 1995, pp. 39–50.*

Although the story in the Reality Check feature (p. 479) illustrates that some entrepreneurs are well-versed in determining their need for capital and knowing where to find it, the failure of many businesses can be traced to undercapitalization. A common approach is to "not worry about it" until the situation gets out of hand. However, every small business owner should understand how to define the amount of funding required to efficiently operate her business. Furthermore, the ability to be a proactive manager of the financing aspects of the business is paramount in a dynamic economy. As we have seen in earlier chapters, as circumstances change quickly, you must be prepared to adapt. This chapter covers issues of financing that every entrepreneur should understand before starting a business.

Initial Capital Requirements

The fundamental financial building blocks for an entrepreneur are knowing what assets are required to open the business and how those assets will be financed. This knowledge is termed *initial capital requirements*. Recall from Chapter 17 the importance of the balance sheet. The balance sheet lists the investment decisions of the business owner in the asset column and the financing decisions in the liabilities and owners' equity column. The financing necessary to acquire each asset required for the business must come from either owner-provided funds (equity) or borrowed funds (liabilities).

The process of determining initial capital requirements begins with identifying the **short-term and long-term assets** necessary to get the business started. Once you have this list of required assets, you must then determine how to pay for them.

short-term assets Assets which will be converted into cash within one year.

long-term assets Assets which will not be converted into cash within one year.

Defining Required Assets

Every business needs a set of short-term and long-term assets in place before the business ever opens its doors. Typical short-term assets include cash and inventory but may also include prepaid expenses (such as rent or insurance paid in advance) and a working capital (cash) reserve. Since many businesses are not profitable in the first year or so of operation, having a cash reserve with which to pay bills can help you avoid becoming insolvent.

The most common long-term assets are buildings and equipment and may also include land, leasehold improvements, patents, and a host of other items. Each of these assets must be in the business *before* the enterprise earns its first dollar of sales. For this to happen, you must carefully evaluate your situation to determine exactly what *needs* to be in place in order for the business to effectively operate.

Small Business IN THE Service Industry

Because service businesses often require the purchase of fewer fixed assets at startup than do retailers or manufacturers, they can offer a good route to self-employment. And a survey by the national accounting and professional services firm Coopers & Lybrand found that many fast-growing companies now outsource certain service functions to outside providers. For small financial service firms, for instance, this means opportunity. How? This same survey found that the most commonly outsourced services were payroll services, tax compliance, employee benefits, and claims administration. It's a win-win situation for all parties involved. For the outsourcing firm, it's a way to reduce operating costs because providers of a single type of service have a lower cost structure resulting from economies of scale. For the small service business, it's a prime market to exploit. *Source: Dale D. Buss, "Growing More by Doing Less," Nation's Business (December 1995), pp. 18–24.*

A useful exercise to help accomplish this task is to prepare a list of the assets the business would have if money were no object. Then review the list and determine the essential assets that are needed to operate the business on a "bare bones" basis. Finally, try to determine the cost of these assets under each scenario.

For example, say you are an entrepreneur starting a restaurant and desire seating for 100 people. If money were no object, you could choose brand new oak dining sets at a cost of $1,200 per six-place setting. On the other hand, at an auction of restaurant supplies and equipment, you could purchase used pine dining sets at a cost of $200 per six-place setting. Either choice will allow the seating requirement to be met.

By carefully completing this exercise for all assets, you end up with a list of assets with a minimum dollar investment and another list of assets needed for the "dream" business. Often your actual business will wind up somewhere in the middle of those two lists as you make final decisions.

With the final list of required assets and corresponding dollar costs in hand, you can then determine your financing requirements. Remember that each dollar of assets must be supported by a dollar of equity or liability funds. How much equity can you contribute personally to the enterprise? This contribution does not necessarily have to be all in cash.

For example, if your business requires a delivery vehicle and you already own a van with a market value of $12,000 that would be suitable for deliveries, the asset will be listed as "Delivery Vehicle—$12,000" and the balancing entry would be $12,000 of owners' equity. The total market value of the owners' assets

Each business must have its assets in place—cash, inventory, patents, equipment, buildings, whatever it needs to operate—before it ever opens its doors.

Computer Applications

One capital investment you might be considering is a computer system for your small business. How can you be sure to make wise decisions as you purchase computer hardware and software? It's important not to get caught up in the "bells and whistles" of computer software and hardware, or to have a "gee whiz, look at what this thing can do" attitude. Approach these decisions as you would any major capital investment—with the utmost seriousness. Although technology advancements continue to force prices down, it's still money that you're spending and you want to make sure it's spent wisely. So what else should you do?

It's important first to *list what activities you do in your business*. For instance, do you sell merchandise, process information, serve people, crunch numbers, or manufacture products? By identifying those specific activities preformed in your business, you'll be able to better define which of these activities can be computerized efficiently and effectively. As this Computer Applications feature has illustrated throughout the text, there are many business areas—inventory control, desktop publishing, communication, and accounting are just a few—where computer software can prove helpful.

Once you've developed a list of these activities, you're ready to *decide which areas of your business are prime candidates for computerization and how much computerization you want to implement*. Look at activities where computerization would leverage what you're already doing well. You *don't* want to attempt to computerize areas where you have operational weaknesses, since computerizing a problem will only make it a computerized problem. It won't make the problem go away! This is also a good time to determine the level of investment you can, and are willing to, make in your computer system.

Next you're ready to *develop a flowchart outlining the information needed in these computerized activities*. Keep in mind that a computer only gives you the information that you ask it for. So define what information you absolutely need in that activity so you can make sure that the computer system you buy can do what you want it to.

Once you've done this, you're ready to *shop around for software packages that will do what you require*. Although software programs individually may seem expensive, keep in mind that you're investing in the "fuel" that will make your computer function efficiently and effectively. Suppliers of software—and hardware—include: computer superstores, warehouse clubs, consumer electronics stores, office supply stores, mass merchants, and mail order distributors. Research potential software by asking questions of sales representatives, reading about it in computer magazines, or talking to other users of the software.

Now you're ready to *choose your hardware or actual computer system*. You'll need to purchase hardware that has the processing power, speed, expandability, and compatibility needed to run your desired software packages. You'll also need to decide whether or not you're going to invest in a network of computers that will be linked to each other. Again, it's wise to thoroughly check out computer systems you're considering.

Finally, you're ready to *install your system*. Keep in mind that the cost of computerizing your business isn't just tied up in the software and hardware, it also includes the cost of training yourself or your employees to be proficient at using the system and perhaps hiring a consultant if needed. Be sure to plan for thorough training on the hardware and software to get the maximum benefit from your investment.

Sources: Ripley Hatch and Jon Pepper, "How to Buy Business Software," Nation's Business *(June 1994), pp. 20–28; Steve Bass and Dan Miller, "The Savvy Shopper,"* Newsweek Special Advertising Section, *August 24, 1994, pp. N2+; and* Inc. Special Technology Bonus Issue, *September 12, 1995.*

used in the business plus all cash contributions from the owner(s) to purchase assets or set up cash reserves is *owners' equity.*

The final step in the process is to subtract the total dollar value of owners' equity from the total dollar value of the required assets. Generally, this results in the dollar amount that must come from other sources. Sometimes there will be more owners' equity than needed to finance the required assets. In this situation the entrepreneur can afford to invest in more assets or in more expensive assets—such as the new oak dining sets rather than the used pine dining sets for the restaurant mentioned earlier. More commonly, however, businesses will need additional capital to finance the required assets. This additional capital will come from one or more sources, which are most likely external to the business.[1]

The Five Cs of Credit

When an entrepreneur decides to seek external financing, she must be able to prove her creditworthiness to potential providers of funds. A traditional guideline used by many lenders is the five Cs of credit, each *C* representing a critical qualifying element. These elements include:

Reality Check

The Evils of Undercapitalization

Let's say you had a marketable idea for a new venture, wrote a detailed business plan, secured some financing, and found a promising location. After two years the business was averaging $1,100 per day in revenues—a 40 percent jump from the first year's operations. Sounds pretty good, right?

Wrong!! The scenario just outlined is the true story of Rochelle Zabarkes, founder of Adriana's Bazaar, a specialty food shop in Manhattan. Despite being well organized, Zabarkes had a slight problem: she was broke—a victim of undercapitalization.

Undercapitalization simply means not having enough capital to effectively and efficiently run a business. The underlying causes are twofold: (1) the combined miscalculation of overestimated revenues and underestimated costs, and (2) the

owner's inability to secure adequate capital to cover cash shortages. The problem haunts many entrepreneurs and often leads to the failure of their ventures.

In Zabarkes's case, she wound up with stacks of unpaid bills from her creditors, a default notice on her SBA loan, and an eviction threat from her landlord. She had to seek to arrange a new loan that would enable her to get out of the red with her suppliers and other lenders while financing planned expansion.

Zabarkes's plight points out an important lesson for all entrepreneurs. According to *The Wall Street Journal,* "No matter how smart, industrious and experienced you are, if you miscalculate your costs, you might soon be headed for a going-out-of-business sale."

Source: Adapted from Brent Bowers, "This Store Is a Hit but Somehow Cash Flow Is Missing," The Wall Street Journal, *June 19, 1994, page B2. Reprinted by permission of the* Wall Street Journal, © *1994, Dow Jones & Co. Inc. All rights reserved worldwide.*

R eality Check

Vintage Financing

What help is available to assist small business owners and managers in thoroughly estimating assets? Patrick and Peggy Duffeler, owners of Williamsburg Winery, a $2 million-a-year wine producer in Williamsburg, Virginia, utilized different means. First of all, they scoured industry data for information. They learned the rule of thumb among wine producers: For every $1 worth of revenues that one hopes to produce, an initial investment of $2 to $3 in land, grapes, barrels, and laboratory equipment needs to be made. However, the would-be vintners also need to take into consideration whether they intend to produce upscale wines (which producers anticipate will appreciate in value over time), plus the prospect of unpredictable weather conditions and the uncertainties of competition and consumer tastes.

The Duffelers spent their initial investment of $180,000 on 2,500 grape plants, production equipment rental fees, and a trial production run. The test "crush" was a good way for the couple to test their processes—and to determine if their asset estimation was on target. The test run was so positive—from both angles—that they were able to raise the money to move the winery into full production.

Expanding also meant investing in 60 wine barrels that cost upwards of $500 each. Then the Duffelers had to plant new fields, buy fermenting equipment, and hire a wine specialist (viticulturist) and a wine maker to supervise the growing and producing processes. By carefully assessing their asset needs, the Duffelers have been able to build a successful small winery.

Source: Jill Andresky Fraser, "How to Finance Anything," Inc. (February 1994), pp. 38–46.

Capacity. Capacity refers to the applicant's ability to repay the loan. Capacity is usually estimated by examining the amount of cash and marketable securities available and both the historical and projected cash flows of the business.

Capital. Capital is a function of the applicant's personal financial strength. The net worth of a business—the value of its assets minus the value of its liabilities—determines its capital.

Collateral. Assets owned by the applicant that can be pledged as security for the repayment of the loan are collateral. If the loan is not repaid, the lender can confiscate the pledged asset(s).

Character. The applicant's character is considered important in that it indicates his apparent willingness to repay the loan. Character is judged primarily on the basis of the applicant's past repayment patterns, but lenders may consider other factors such as marital status, home ownership, and military service when attributing character to an applicant. The lender's prior experience with applicant repayment patterns his choice of factors in evaluating the character of a new applicant.

Conditions. The general economic climate at the time of the loan application may affect the applicant's ability to repay the loan. Lenders will usually not extend credit in times of economic recession or business downturns.[2]

Additional Considerations

In addition to the five Cs, potential investors will want to know more about you and your business. For startups, simply having a good idea will not be enough evidence to convince many investors to risk their capital in your business. You will need to show that you are a competent manager with a track record of prior business success. If possible, you should show an informal board of directors made up of the people whom you may contact for assistance. Potential members on such a board include bankers, attorneys, CPAs, and successful business owners.

If yours is a growing or emerging business, you will need to be ready to provide well-audited financial statements and show a solid record of earnings. It is difficult to attract investors without proven performance and a high likelihood of continued growth and success.

The old adage that "you have to have money to make money" is largely true in the area of financing. However, it might be amended to say "you have to show an ability to make money in order to attract money."

Basic Financial Vocabulary

Before an entrepreneur can begin looking for other sources of funds, two basic types of funds, as well as the terminology associated with them, must be understood.

Forms of Capital

Two kinds of funds are potentially available to the entrepreneur: debt and equity. Debt funds (also known as liabilities) are borrowed from a creditor and, of course, must be repaid. Using debt to finance a business creates **leverage,** which is money you can borrow against the money you already have. (See Chapter 17.) Leverage can enable you to magnify the potential returns expected due to investing your equity in the business.

leverage The ability to finance an investment through borrowed funds.

However, debt funding can also constrain the future cash flows generated by the business and can magnify losses as well. Debt creates the risk of becoming technically insolvent if the entrepreneur is unable to make each debt payment on time. Continued nonrepayment of debt will ultimately lead to the bankruptcy of the business. Debt as a funding source will be examined more closely in the next section.

Equity funds, by contrast, are supplied by investors in exchange for an ownership position in the business. They need not be repaid. Providers of equity funds forgo the opportunity to receive periodic repayments in order to share in the profits of the business. As a result, equity financing does not create a constraint upon the cash flows of the business.

However, equity providers usually demand a voice in the management of the business, thus reducing your autonomy to run the business as you would like. It is easy to see that the decision to seek outside funds is both critical and complex. Therefore, a more detailed view of each kind of financing is presented.

Figure 18-1 contains the results of a survey of the CEOs of some of the best-managed small businesses in the United States. In particular, the bar graph shows the anticipated sources of capital the CEOs expected to use in the subse-

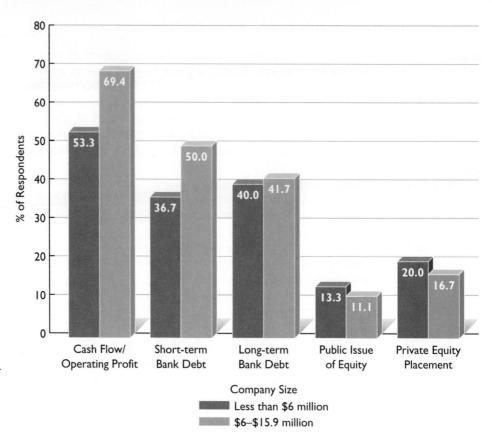

FIGURE 18-1
Where Capital Comes From
CEO responses to a survey question regarding where they intended to get their capital in the coming 18 months.

quent 18 months. While a majority predicted having operating profits available for their use, a significant number expected to use short-term and long-term debt. A smaller number anticipated using some form of equity financing.

debt financing The use of borrowed funds to finance a business.

Debt Financing. Three important parameters associated with **debt financing** are the amount of principal to be borrowed, the loan's interest rate, and the loan's length of maturity. Together they determine the size and extent of your obligation to the creditor. Until the debt is repaid, the creditor has a legal claim on a portion of the business's cash flows. Creditors can demand payment and, in the most severe case, force a business into bankruptcy because of overdue payments.

principal An amount of money borrowed from a lender.

The **principal** of the loan is the original amount of money to be borrowed. You should try to minimize the size of the loan to reduce your financial risk. The pro forma balance sheet estimates the amount of funds needed. (See Chapter 17.) The amount you need to borrow is the difference between the total of pro forma assets and total owner's equity.

interest The amount of money paid for the use of borrowed funds.

The **interest rate** of the loan determines the "price" of the borrowed funds. In most cases it will be based upon the current **prime rate of interest.** In the past the prime rate was defined as the rate of interest banks charge their "best" customers—those with the lowest risk. More recently it has also become a benchmark for determining many other rates of interest. Interest rates for small business loans are normally prime plus some additional percentage. For example, if the prime rate is 8.5 percent, a bank might offer small business loans at "prime plus four," or 12.5 percent. Additional factors such as default risk and maturity will also affect the cost of a loan.

The actual rate of interest the borrower will pay on a loan is called the **effective rate of interest.** It is often higher than the stated rate of interest for several reasons. A lender may require a **compensating balance,** meaning that the borrower is required to keep a minimum dollar balance (often as much as 10 percent of the principal) on deposit with the lender. This requirement reduces the amount of funds accessible to the borrower and increases the actual rate of interest since, over the life of the loan, the borrower pays the same amount of interest dollars for fewer available funds.

The frequency with which interest is compounded can also increase the cost of a loan. Compounding refers to the intervals at which you pay interest. Lenders may compound interest annually, semiannually, quarterly, monthly, weekly, daily, or even continuously. For example, quarterly compounding involves four compounding periods within a year—one-fourth of the stated interest rate is paid each quarter. The more compounding periods, the higher the effective rate. Financial institutions are required to inform borrowers of the effective rates of interest on all loans.

Whether a loan has a fixed rate or a variable rate of interest also affects its cost. A **fixed-rate loan** retains the same interest rate for the entire length of time for which the funds are borrowed. A **variable-rate loan** is one whose interest may fluctuate over time. Typically, the variable rate is tied to a benchmark such as the prime rate or federal funds rate. Every year (normally on the anniversary of the original loan date) a variable interest rate is adjusted according to changes in the benchmark.

fixed rate loan A loan with an interest rate which remains constant.

variable rate loan A loan with an interest rate which changes over the life of the loan.

A fixed-rate loan typically has a higher interest rate than the initial rate on a variable-rate loan. Therefore, the cost of a fixed-rate loan is higher in the first year (or longer). But because the variable interest rate could increase each year, it eventually might exceed the rate on the fixed loan by far. A variable-rate loan is much more of a gamble than a fixed-rate loan when borrowing for a long period of time.

Your goal is to find the lowest possible effective rate, given your current circumstances, by investigating different funding sources. For example, a particular bank may have excess funds available to lend and be willing to offer lower rates than its competitors. A startup business may want to consider a variable-rate loan to help offset its lower cash flows in the first year of operation.

The **maturity** of a loan refers to the length of time for which a borrower obtains the use of the funds. A **short-term loan** must be repaid within one year, an **intermediate-term loan** must be repaid within one to ten years, and a **long-term loan** must be repaid within ten or more years. Typically, the purpose of the loan will determine the length of maturity chosen.

maturity The length of time in which a loan must be repaid.

For example, you would use a short-term loan to purchase inventory that you expected to sell within one year, giving the funds to repay the loan. For the purchase of a building, which presumably will serve the business for decades, a long-term loan is preferable. The maturity of the loan essentially should match the borrower's use of the loan proceeds.

The maturity of the loan also affects its interest rate. Ordinarily, the longer the maturity, the higher the rate of interest. The reason for this rule is that a lender must be compensated for the opportunity cost of not being able to use those loaned funds in other ways. Lenders will add a "premium" to the price that the borrower pays for a longer-maturity loan.

Your goal regarding loan maturity is to obtain as much flexibility as possible. On one hand, a shorter maturity will usually have a lower rate of interest but must be quickly repaid, thus affecting cash flow. On the other hand, a longer maturity, despite its higher rate, gives you more time to repay the loan, resulting in smaller payments and reduced constraints on your current cash flow. Flexibility is created by maximizing the maturity of a loan while retaining the option of repaying the loan sooner than the maturity date if cash flows allow. Make sure that there is no penalty for early repayment.

Consider principal, effective rate of interest, and maturity very carefully when attempting to obtain debt financing. By ascertaining the proper amount of principal needed, comparing the effective rates of interest at your disposal, and matching the maturity of the loan with the projected availability of cash flows with which to make repayments, you will be able to make the greatest possible use of debt financing.

equity financing The sale of common stock or the use of retained earnings to provide long-term finance.

Equity Financing.   As stated earlier, **equity financing** does not have to be repaid. There are no payments to constrain the cash flow of the business. There is no interest to be paid on the funds. Providers of equity capital wind up owing a portion of the business and are generally interested in: (1) **dividends,** (2) **increased value of the business** (and thus their investment in it), and (3) **a voice in the management of the business.**

Dividends are payments that are based upon the net profits of the business and made to the providers of equity capital. These payments are often made on either a quarterly, semiannual, or annual basis. Many small businesses keep net profits in the form of retained earnings to help finance future growth, and dividends are only paid when the business has profits above the amount necessary to fund projected new development.

Increased value of the business is a natural result of a successful business enterprise. As a successful business grows and prospers, the owners prosper as well. Because the providers of equity capital own a "piece of the action," the value of their investment increases in direct proportion with the increase in value of the business. They are frequently not as concerned about dividends as they are about the business's long-term success. If the business is successful, the equity providers will have the opportunity to sell all or part of their investment for a considerable profit.

A **voice in management** is an additional consideration for providers of equity capital. The rationale underlying this concept is that because the owners of a business have the most to lose if the business fails, they are entitled to have a say about how their money is being used. Not all equity providers are interested in running a business, but many can contribute important expertise along with their capital contributions. They can enhance your business's chances of success.

Other Loan Terminology

Two additional sets of terms that you will often encounter while searching for financing have to do with *loan security* and with *loan restrictions*. These terms can be of great importance and should be well understood.

loan security Assurance to a lender that a loan will be repaid.

Loan Security.   **Loan security** refers to the borrower's assurance to lenders that loans will be repaid. If the entrepreneur's signature on a loan is not considered sufficient security by a lender, the lender will require another signature to guarantee the loan. Other individuals whose signatures appear on the loan are known as **endorsers.** Endorsers are contingently liable for the notes they sign. Two types of endorsers are **comakers** and **guarantors.**

Comakers create a joint liability with the borrower. The lender can collect from either the maker (original borrower) or the comaker. Guarantors insure the repayment of a note by signing a guarantee commitment. Both private and government lenders often require guarantees from officers of corporations in order to ensure continuity of effective management.

Loan Restrictions. Sometimes called **covenants,** loan restrictions spell out what the borrower cannot do *(negative covenants)* or what she must do *(positive covenants)*. These restrictions are built into each loan agreement and are generally negotiable—as long as you are aware of them!

Typical negative covenants will preclude the borrower from acquiring any additional debt without prior approval from the original lender, or will prevent the borrower from issuing dividends in excess of the terms of the loan agreement.

Common positive covenants will require that the borrower maintain some minimum level of working capital until the loan is repaid, carry some type of insurance while the loan is in effect, or provide periodic financial statements to the lender.

By understanding that lenders will sometimes require the additional assurance of an endorser and will likely create covenants on loan agreements, you can be better prepared to negotiate during the search for financing. Doing your homework on loan terminology and processes improves your chances for successfully obtaining funds.[3]

How Can You Find Capital?

Once you determine how much capital is needed for the startup or expansion, you are ready to begin looking for capital sources. To prepare for this search, you need to be aware of what these sources will want to know about you and your business before they are willing to entrust their funds. You also need to understand the characteristics of each capital source and the process for obtaining funds from them.

The Loan Application Process

Typically, to determine creditworthiness, a lending institution will collect relevant information from financial statements supplied by the applicant and by external sources such as local or regional credit associations, credit interchange bureaus, and the applicant's bank. This procedure is known as **credit scoring.**

If the applicant meets or exceeds some minimal score (set by the lender) on key financial and credit characteristics, the institution will be willing to arrange a loan. Most lenders are hesitant to make loans to startup businesses, however, unless either a wealthy friend or relative will cosign the loan or unless loan proceeds will be used to purchase assets that could be repossessed and easily resold in case of default.

Sources of Debt Financing

The wide array of credit options available confuses many entrepreneurs. A thorough understanding of the nature and characteristics of these debt sources will help ensure that you are successful in obtaining financing from the most favorable source possible.

Entering the Internet

With the wide availability of information on the Internet, you shouldn't be surprised to discover that you can find financial assistance and investigate financing sources there as well. In fact, recall the opening vignette from this chapter, which discussed how one small business owner used the Internet to investigate possible financing. Let's look closer at some Internet sites that you might find useful as you search for financial information.

At Entrepreneurs on the Web, under the section on Business Information, you'll find links to other financial sites including ones that list businesses looking for startup or expansion capital: http://www.einet.net

At another site, Venture Information Network for Entrepreneurs Inc., you'll find a virtual meeting place designed to bring together people in need of funding and people with available cash: VINE - found at http://www.thevine.com/

You might also want to check out FinanceHub, which is a site dedicated to helping entrepreneurs find financing: http://www.financehub.com/

Some other possible sites include:

The Small Business Resource Center: http://www.webcom.com/seaquest/sbrc/reports.html

The Corporate Finance Network: http://www.corpfinet.com/

The U.S. Small Business Administration:
gopher://www.sbaonline.sba.gov

Commercial Banks. Most people's first response to the question, "where would you borrow money?" is "a bank." Commercial banks are the backbone of the credit market, offering the widest assortment of loans to creditworthy small businesses.

Bank loans generally fall into two major categories: short-term loans (for purchasing inventory, overcoming cash flow problems, and meeting monthly expenditures) and long-term loans (for purchasing land, machinery, and buildings or renovating facilities).

unsecured loan A short-term loan for which collateral is not required.

Most short-term loans are **unsecured**—the bank does not require any collateral as long as the entrepreneur has a good credit standing. These loans are often **self-liquidating,** which means that the loan will be repaid directly with the revenues generated from the original purpose of the loan. For example, if an entrepreneur uses a short-term loan to purchase inventory, the loan is repaid as the inventory is sold. Types of short-term loans include lines of credit, demand notes, and floor planning.

line of credit An agreement which makes a specific amount of short-term funding available to a business as it is needed.

A **line of credit** is an agreement between a bank and a business which specifies the amount of unsecured short-term funds the bank will make available to the business over a specific period of time—normally one year. The agreement allows the business to borrow and repay funds up to the maximum amount specified in the agreement throughout the year. The business pays interest only on the amount of funds actually borrowed, but may be required to pay a setup or handling fee.

demand note A short-term loan which must be repaid (both principal and interest) in a lump sum at maturity.

A **demand note** is a loan made to a small business for a specific period of time to be repaid in a lump sum at maturity. With this type of loan, the bank reserves the right to demand repayment of the loan at any time. For example, a bank might loan a business $50,000 for one year at 12 percent interest. The business would repay the loan by making one payment of $56,000 ($50,000 principal plus 0.12 × $50,000 interest) at the end of one year. The only reason a bank is likely to demand repayment sooner is if the business appears to be struggling and potentially unable to repay the loan in full at the end of the specified time period.

Floor planning is a special type of loan used particularly for financing high-priced inventory items like new automobiles, trucks, recreational vehicles, and boats. A business borrowing money for this purpose is allowed to display the inventory on its premises, but the inventory actually is owned by the bank. When the business sells one of the items, it will use the proceeds of the sale to repay the principal of the loan. The business is generally required to pay interest monthly on each item of inventory purchased with the loan proceeds. Therefore, the longer it takes the business to sell each item, the more the business pays in interest expenses. This is one instance where the short-term loan is **secured.** The assets purchased with the loan proceeds serve as collateral.

Types of long-term bank loans include installment loans, balloon notes, and unsecured term loans. **Installment loans** are loans made to businesses for the purchase of fixed assets such as equipment and real estate. These loans are to be repaid in periodic payments that include accrued interest and part of the outstanding principal balance. In the case of many fixed assets, the maturity of the

floor planning A type of business loan generally made for "big-ticket" items. The business holds the item in inventory and pays interest, but it is actually owned by the lender until the item is sold.

secured loan A loan which requires collateral as security for the lender.

Manager's Notebook

Maintaining Good Banker Relationships

One way of ensuring that your business is getting the best rates and service from your bank is to nurture a strong relationship with your banker. Ron Siegle, vice president of commercial lending at a major Denver-based bank, offers these hints:

- Have routine meetings with your banker to keep him up to date on how your business is progressing.
- Tell your banker in person when your business is having trouble and explain how you intend to overcome the problem.
- Take time to educate your banker about your business and industry. The better your banker

understands your business, the better he can help you.

- Be timely with your payments and any financial information the bank may request from you.
- Give your banker all your business—both your personal and your firm's deposits. Use the bank's other services when appropriate.
- Refer potential customers to your banker.

By sustaining a good relationship with your banker, you can enhance your chances of getting the best possible assistance from him. This is especially helpful in troubled times.

Source: Frank Seffinger, "Maintain Good Relations with Your Banker," Rocky Mountain News, *Denver, Colorado, January 25, 1995, p. B1. Reprinted with permission of* Rocky Mountain News.

loan will equal the usable life of the asset, and the principal amount loaned will range from 65 to 80 percent of the asset's market value. For the purchase of real estate, banks will often allow a repayment schedule of 15 to 30 years and typically lend between 75 and 85 percent of the property's value. In every case the bank will maintain a security interest or **lien** in the asset until the loan is fully repaid.

balloon note A loan which requires the borrower to make small monthly payments (usually enough to cover the interest) with the balance of the loan due at maturity.

Balloon notes are loans made to businesses in which only small periodic payments are required over the life of the loan with a large lump-sum payment at maturity. A typical balloon note requires monthly payments to cover accrued interest with the entire principal due at the end of the term of the loan. This allows you more flexibility with your cash flow over the life of the loan. If you are unable to make the final balloon payment, it is common for the bank to refinance the loan for a longer period of time, allowing you to continue making monthly payments.

Unsecured term loans are loans made to established businesses which have demonstrated a strong overall credit profile. Eligible businesses must show excellent creditworthiness and have an extremely high probability of repayment. These loans are usually made for very specific terms and may come with restrictions on the use of the loan proceeds. For example, a bank might agree to lend a business a sum of money for a three-year period at a given rate of interest. You must then ensure that the funds are used to finance some asset or activity that will generate enough revenue to repay the loan within the three-year time horizon.

Commercial banks remain a primary source of debt financing for small businesses. The type, maturity, and other terms of each loan, however, are uniquely a function of the financial strength or creditworthiness of the borrower.

Commercial Finance Companies. Commercial finance companies extend short- and intermediate-term credit to firms that cannot easily obtain credit elsewhere. Since these companies are willing to take a bigger risk than the commercial banks, their interest rates are often considerably higher. Commercial finance companies perform a valuable service to small businesses that have yet to establish their creditworthiness.

Among the most common types of loans provided by commercial finance companies are: floor planning, leasing, and factoring accounts receivable.

Floor Planning. Finance company floor planning is similar to that offered by banks, with one important exception. The finance company can actually help generate retail sales by extending credit to the retail customers purchasing the floor-planned items. This in turn generates the need for more floor planning. Many small businesses seek finance companies that will finance both the wholesale (floor planning) and retail (customer purchases) aspects of their businesses.

Leasing. Leasing is a contract arrangement whereby a finance company purchases the durable goods needed by a small business and rents them to the small business for a specific period of time. The rent payment includes some amount of interest. This activity is very lucrative for finance companies due to current tax laws and often allows entrepreneurs to have the use of state-of-the-art equipment at a fraction of the cost.

factoring The practice of raising funds for a business through the sale of accounts receivable.

Factoring Accounts Receivable. Another important type of loan available from commercial finance companies is accounts receivable **factoring.** Under this arrangement a small business either sells its accounts receivable to a finance company outright or uses the receivables as collateral for a loan. The purchase price of the receivables (or the amount of the loan) is discounted from the face value of what the business is owed in order to allow for potential losses (in the form of unpaid accounts) and for the fact that the finance company will not receive full repayment of the loan until sometime in the future.

Typically, the finance company will either purchase the receivables for, or will lend the small business, somewhere between 55 and 80 percent of the face value of the business's accounts receivable, based upon their likelihood of being paid in a timely manner. If the finance company purchases the receivables outright, it will collect payments on them as they come due. If the small business uses its receivables as collateral for a loan in a process known as **pledging,** as the business collects these accounts due the proceeds are forwarded to the finance company to repay the loan.

Insurance Companies. For some entrepreneurs, life insurance companies have become a principal source of debt financing. The most common type of loan is called a **policy loan.** Policy loans are made to entrepreneurs based upon the amount of money paid in premiums on an insurance policy that has a cash surrender value. While each insurance company varies its methods for making these loans, a typical arrangement is for the insurance company to lend up to 95 percent of a policy's cash surrender value.

> **policy loan** A loan made to a business by an insurance company, using the business's insurance policy as collateral.

The collateral for the loan is the cash that the entrepreneur has already paid into the policy. In essence, the insurance company is lending the entrepreneur his own money. Since the default risk is virtually zero (defaulting on the loan merely reduces the cash surrender value of the policy), the rate of interest is often very favorable.

If an entrepreneur has been paying premiums into a whole life, variable life, or universal life policy, it is likely that the option to borrow funds against it will be available. Term insurance policies, however, have no borrowing capacity. One caution about this type of borrowing is that the amount of insurance coverage is usually reduced by the amount of the loan.

Federal Loan Programs. Government lending programs exist to stimulate economic activity. The underlying rationale for making these loans is that the borrowers will become profitable and create jobs, which in turn means more tax dollars in the coffers of government agencies providing the funds for the loans. The most active government lender is the Small Business Administration, a federal agency. **SBA loan** programs include guaranteed loans, direct loans, and the 504 loan program. The majority of the loan funds go to service, retail, and manufacturing businesses. (See Figure 18-2.)

> **SBA loan** A loan made to a small business through a commercial bank of which a portion of the loan is guaranteed by the Small Business Administration.

Guaranteed loans are generally known as the **7(a) program.** Under this program private lenders—usually commercial banks—make loans to entrepreneurs that are guaranteed up to 90 percent by the SBA. This means that the lender's risk exposure is reduced by the amount of the SBA guarantee. Since January 1, 1995, the SBA can guarantee as much as $500,000 per loan.

To be eligible for the 7(a) program, a business must be operated for profit and must fall within size standards set by the SBA. (See Chapter 1.) Loans cannot be made to businesses engaged in speculation or real estate rental. Existing businesses must provide, among other things, financial statements for the past three years and financial projections for the next three years. Startup businesses must provide three years of projected financial statements, a feasible business plan,

> *Government loan programs for small businesses are intended to help create jobs, prosperity, and tax revenues that make more loans available to other small businesses.*

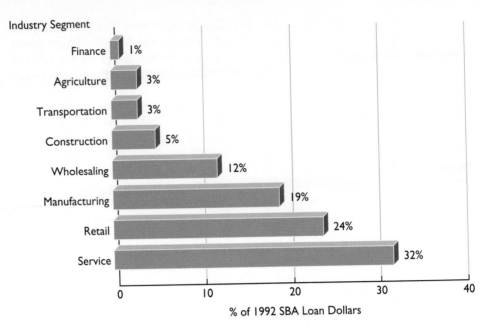

FIGURE 18-2
Who Gets SBA Loans?
In 1992 the SBA guaranteed
$7.5 billion in business loans.
The average loan was
$250,656 with a maturity of
11.5 years. Twenty-one percent of the loans went to businesses less than two years old.
Source: Small Business Administra-
tion, Washington DC, March 1993.

and proof of adequate investment by the owners (generally about 20 to 30 percent equity).

Successful applicants pay interest rates of up to 2.25 percent above the
prime rate for loans with maturities of less than seven years, and up to 2.75 percent above the prime rate for loans with maturities of seven years or longer. The
borrower will repay the loan in monthly installments, which include both principal and interest. The first payment may be delayed up to six months and the
loans carry no balloon payments, prepayment penalties, or application fees.[4]

Direct loans are those made directly by the SBA to a small business without
the participation of a bank or other lender. Most of these loans are made to special groups of individuals such as the **Vietnam Veteran and Disabled Veterans
Loan Program** and the **Handicapped Assistance Loan Program.** Generally, these
loans are limited to $150,000 and are made only when no other source of financ-
ing is available to the entrepreneur. These direct loan programs have come under
some criticism since they have the highest default rate among all of the SBA's
programs.

The **504 Loan Program** provides small businesses with funding for fixed assets when conventional loans are not possible. These funds are distributed
through a **certified development company,** which is a nonprofit organization
sponsored by either private interests or by state or local governments. In a typical
arrangement, a private lender will provide 50 percent of the total value of the
loan, the borrower 10 percent, and the certified development company the remaining 40 percent of the necessary funds. Since the 504 portion of the funds—
those contributed by the certified development company—are 100 percent guaranteed by the SBA, the private lender's risk exposure is significantly reduced.
The maturity for 504 financing is 10 years for equipment purchases and 20 years
for real estate.[5]

In addition to the preceding loan programs, the SBA offers loan programs
to support small businesses engaged in international trade, rural development,
those with women owners, and those with working capital needs. There is no
doubt that the SBA plays a very significant role in providing debt financing for

small businesses. However, the agency, like all other federal agencies, is subject to policy changes and budget cuts each year. The viability of the SBA in the future is dependent upon its ability to effectively service the small business community.

One of the main criticisms of the SBA loan programs has been the amount of paperwork required, especially for relatively small loans. In response to this concern, the SBA recently created the **LowDoc program.**[6] Under this program, qualified small businesses can borrow up to $100,000 with a one-page application, although the lender may require additional information from the applicant. Additionally, there is a **Small Loan Program** for businesses needing loans of less than $50,000. Each of these programs has been very successful.[7]

State and Local Government Lenders. Many state and local governments lend money to entrepreneurs through various programs. As noted earlier, they can sponsor a certified development company to assist small businesses with the acquisition of fixed assets. Other loan programs are usually tied in with economic development—for instance, some loans are made contingent upon the number of jobs that will be created by the small business. Most state and local government programs have lower interest rates than conventional loans, often with longer maturities. It is clearly to your advantage to find out if these programs would be available to you.

Trade Credit. The last major source of debt financing we will cover is the use of **trade credit** or accounts payable. Recall from Chapter 17 that accounts payable are the amounts owed by a business to the creditors who have supplied goods or services to the business. Although startups may find it difficult to obtain everything on credit right away, many manufacturers and wholesalers will ship goods at least 30 days before payment is required.

This 30-day grace period is essentially a loan to the small business. Since there is no interest charge for the first 30 days, the loan is "free." For this reason, you should take advantage of as much trade credit as possible. A 1994 survey of 300 small business owners by Dun & Bradstreet showed that 65 percent of the owners had used trade credit or lines of credit from vendors as their primary source of financing in the preceding twelve-month period.[8]

Sources of Equity Financing

From our discussion of debt financing, we know that lenders will expect entrepreneurs to provide equity funds in the amount of at least 20 percent—and possibly as much as 50 percent—of the business before approving a loan. The most common sources of equity financing are personal funds, family and friends, partners, venture capital firms, Small Business Investment Companies, angels, and stock offerings.

Personal Funds. Most new businesses are originally financed with their creators' funds. The Department of Commerce estimates that nearly two-thirds of all startups are begun without borrowed funds. The first place most entrepreneurs find equity capital is in their personal assets. Cash, savings accounts, and checking accounts are the most obvious sources of equity funds. Additional sources are the sale of stocks, bonds, mutual funds, real estate, or other personal investments.

Family and Friends. The National Federation of Independent Business reported that more than one-fourth of new businesses are at least partially funded by the

LowDoc program A relatively new loan program available through the SBA that simplifies the paperwork which has historically been required.

trade credit The purchase of goods from suppliers who do not demand payment immediately.

Credit from an Unlikely Source: Your Customers

For the owners of some fortunate service, retail, and manufacturing businesses, working capital is literally at their fingertips, provided by the people who know their firms' products and services best: their customers. Tapping this unique market requires the ability to show your customers how they will benefit from providing you with capital.

Take the case of OLI Systems, Inc., a New Jersey company that develops computer software for the environmentally sensitive chemical industry. OLI's founder, Marshall Rafal, was able to raise $600,000 from a consortium of four of his largest customers in order to develop specialized software that would help his customers treat waste from certain chemical processes.

In exchange for a $150,000 investment, OLI offered each consortium member a perpetual nonexclusive license for the new product and a place on its development committee. That meant not only unlimited use of the software for each in-vestor, but also the opportunity to ensure its unique pollutant problems were addressed. In addition, OLI repaid each investor 125 percent of its original investment from a royalty pool created with licensing revenues.

OLI's arrangement produced a win-win situation. OLI received the capital it needed for product development, while the investors were able to have a hand in product design and testing, as well as a sizeable return on their investments.

Similar agreements have been formed between equipment manufacturers and their customers. In these arrangements, the customers agree to make large initial payments to cover the manufacturers' costs for labor, materials, and other overhead. Without this up-front financing, the manufacturers would not be able to accept the customers' orders or to turn them out in a timely fashion.

Source: Ellyn E. Spragins, "Consumer Finance," Inc. (July 1990), pp. 110, 128. Adapted with permission, Inc. magazine. © 1990, Goldhirsh Group, Inc.

---

family and friends of the entrepreneurs. Family and friends are more willing to risk capital in a venture owned by someone they know than in ventures about which they know little or nothing. This financing is viewed as equity as long as there is no set repayment schedule.

Financing a business with capital from family and friends, however, creates a type of risk not found with other funding sources. If the business is not successful and the funds cannot be repaid, relationships with family and friends can become strained. You should explain the potential risk of failure inherent in the venture before accepting any funds from family and friends.

Partners. Acquiring one or more partners is another way to secure equity capital. (See Chapter 2.) Approximately 10 percent of U.S. businesses are partnerships. Many partnerships are formed to take advantage of diverse skills or attributes that can be contributed to the new business. For example, one person may have the technical skills required to run the business while another person has the capital to finance it. Together they form a partnership to accomplish a common goal.

Partners may play an active role in the venture's operation or may choose to be "silent," only providing funds in exchange for an equity position. The addition of one or more partners expands not only the amount of equity capital avail-

R eality Check

Succeeding in Spite of It All

Tae Wan Cho and Young Suk, husband and wife business partners, provide an excellent example of how to succeed when bank financing isn't available. In 1982, Tae Wan Cho left his native South Korea for the United States seeking, as many immigrants do, more freedom and opportunity. Young Suk and the couple's two daughters remained in Korea until he could get a business started—although he had no idea what type of business or where it would be!

Upon arriving in the United States, Tae stayed with an American friend in Harrisonville, Missouri. After reading a trade magazine article about the strong growth in sales of hair care products for African-Americans, he decided to open a store in St. Louis, an affordable metropolitan area. To get his business off the ground, Tae applied for a $10,000 loan from a local bank. Turned down by the bank, he borrowed $3,000 from his Harrisonville friend and another $2,000 from his landlord in St. Louis. His business, King's Beauty Supply, opened in a 500-square-foot space in a vacant downtown building. He sold $40 worth of merchandise his first day and $3,000 within the first month. However, because he couldn't afford to heat his shop that first winter, many of his prod-

ucts froze. Cash flow became such a severe problem that Tae could stock only two of many of his products.

Tae decided that everything he made would be reinvested in the business. He reminisced, "I spent no money on myself. I paid my bills before I ate. I had no radio, no television, no chair, no sofa, no bed. . . . All I had was a blanket and a 10-year-old Ford Pinto." For three years, Tae worked ten hours a day, seven days a week. When he finally was confident that the business would survive, Young Suk and their daughters made the move to St. Louis. Shortly afterward, they opened a second store which Young Suk managed. Was all this hard work and sacrifice worth it?

Well, today, Tae Wan Cho and Young Suk operate nine retail stores in St. Louis and wholesale their products all over the United States, generating around $8 million in sales by 1994. King's Beauty Supply Distributor, Inc. now occupies a 30,000-square-foot warehouse. And the bank that first turned Tae down has extended the firm a $1 million line of credit. The lesson, learned by millions of native-born and naturalized Americans, is that with initiative, focus, and sheer hard work, you *can* make it on your own.

Source: Cheryl Jarvis, "When Sacrifice Equals Success," Nation's Business *(July 1994), pp. 14–16.*

able for the business, but also the ability of the business to borrow funds. This is due to the cumulative creditworthiness of the partners versus that of only the entrepreneur alone.

Venture Capital Firms.   Venture capital firms are groups of individuals or companies that invest in new or expanding firms. Of the more than 600 venture capital firms operating in the United States, about 500 are private independent firms, about 65 are major corporations, and the rest are affiliated with banks.[9] Obtaining capital from them is not easy.

Most venture capital firms have investment policies that outline their preferences relative to industry, geographic location, investment size, and investment maturity. These firms look for businesses with the potential for rapid growth and high profitability. They provide funds in exchange for an equity position, which they hope to sell out within five to ten years or less.

A Lucky Draw

Gerald Martens, owner of three retail uniform stores in Fresno, California, had placed many orders for Bettie Dawn uniforms. But in 1994, he was stunned to hear that the company had closed. Its owner, he learned, had become too ill to carry on the business, leaving 25 women out of work. However, Martens's luck—and Bettie Dawn's—was about to change in a most unpredictable manner.

A regular player of the California lottery, Martens hit the jackpot—worth $3 million—in March 1995. What does one do with an extra $150,000 per year, before taxes, for 20 years? Martens decided to use part of his winnings in reviving the Bettie Dawn sewing plant. He liked the idea of making uniforms in the United States, he said, because 80 percent of nursing uniforms and hospital scrub outfits are now produced overseas. He also wanted to share his good fortune with the women who had provided him with top-quality uniforms over the years.

Martens has since revived the factory and jazzed up its line of products. One of its newest products that's selling well is a maternity scrub uniform. Bettie Dawn has given its other uniforms and scrubs a new look, adding extra pockets, new styling, and bolder colors and prints. Although winning the lottery isn't a reliable approach to finding financing for your small business, it *did* happen to one individual!

Source: Jerry Nachtigal, "Man's Windfall Revives Factory," Springfield News Leader, February 13, 1996, p. 6A.

A recent study showed that the average sum invested by venture capital firms is between $1.5 and $2 million per business, with an overall range between $23,000 to more than $50 million.[10] An excellent business plan is essential when approaching a venture capital firm, and a referral from a credible source—such as a banker or attorney familiar to the venture capital firm—may also be necessary. It takes an average of six to eight months to receive a potential investment decision. It has been estimated that less than 10 percent of the plans submitted to venture capital firms are ultimately funded.

Global Small Business

Financing for your small business can come from some unusual sources. Dilip Barot, a native of India's Gujarat region, manages 2,000 public housing apartments in four states from Florida to Nevada. His Miami Beach-based company, Naimisha Group, utilized creative financing to get going. Barot tapped into the informal network of other successful Gujarati businesspeople—mostly doctors and engineers—and raised the financing he needed. He's used this "tried and true immigrant network" several times, and has even gone back to India for help with financing if he found himself in a real bind.

Using whatever financing sources are open and available is smart business as Barot has discovered. In 1994, the Naimisha Group earned a nifty $10 million on revenues of $50 million. *Source: Joel Millman, "Imported Entrepreneurs," Forbes, November 6, 1995, pp. 232–237.*

Reality Check

Hazards in the Search for Cash

The entrepreneur's search for capital is not without its hazards. Consider the plight of Dale Jacobs, chairman and cofounder of **Musicsource, U.S.A., Inc.,** a California firm that markets computerized sheet music printing systems. The company recently filed suit claiming that investment promoter M & M Investments Inc. defrauded the company out of 1.6 million shares of stock.

Jacobs claims that his company was promised assistance both in raising capital and in marketing its products by M & M. Instead, Jacobs asserts, M & M not only did not come through with its promised assistance, it also sold the shares of stock to the public, causing Musicsource's stock price to fall.

This case illustrates how entrepreneurs struggling in their search for capital can run into various predicaments. As Jacobs's case began to unfold, it was discovered that a principal partner in M & M Investments had served more than two years in jail for the possession and transfer of counterfeit money.

Each side claims no wrongdoing. But perhaps Jacobs said it best when, urging caution in dealing with strangers promising to help raise capital, he said, "You don't get cheated unless you trust somebody."

Source: John R. Emshwiller, "Entrepreneur's Claim of Fraud Suggests Perils of Quest for Cash," The Wall Street Journal, September 2, 1994, pp. B1–B2.

Venture capital firms rarely invest in retail operations. They tend to focus on high-technology industries, growth industries, and essential services. Ventures within these fields with strong, experienced management teams have the best chance of being funded. *Pratt's Guide to Venture Capital Success* is a good source for information.

Small Business Investment Companies. Small Business Investment Companies (SBICs) are venture capital firms licensed by the SBA to invest in small businesses. SBICs were authorized by Congress in 1958 to provide equity financing to qualified enterprises. In 1969 the SBA, in cooperation with the Department of Commerce, created Minority Enterprise Small Business Investment Companies (MESBICs) to provide equity financing to minority entrepreneurs. Any business that is more than 50 percent owned by blacks, Hispanics, Native Americans, Eskimos, or socially and economically disadvantaged Americans is eligible for funding.

SBICs and MESBICs are formed by financial institutions, corporations, or individuals, although a few are publicly owned. These investment companies must be capitalized with at least $500,000 of private funds. Once capitalized, they can receive as much as four dollars from the SBA for each private dollar invested.

SBICs and MESBICs are excellent sources of both startup and expansion capital. Like venture capital firms, however, they tend to have investment policies regarding geographic area and industry. There are about 300 SBICs and MESBICs currently in operation in the United States. They are listed in the *Directory of Operating Small Business Investment Companies* available from any SBA office.

angel A lender, usually a successful entrepreneur, who loans money to help new businesses.

Angels. An **angel** is a wealthy, experienced individual who has a desire to assist startup or emerging businesses. Most angels are self-made entrepreneurs who want to help sustain the system that allowed them to become successful. Usually they are knowledgeable about the market and technology areas in which they invest.

According to a study on business angels, there are more than 250,000 such investors in the United States. A typical investment ranges from $20,000 to $50,000, although nearly one-fourth are for more than $50,000. An angel can add much more than money to a business. His business know-how and contacts can be far more valuable to the success of the business than the capital he invests.

Finding an angel is not easy. The best ways for an entrepreneur to locate an angel are to maintain business contacts with tax attorneys, bankers, and accountants in their closest metropolitan area, and to find out if a regional venture capital network exists.

Stock Offerings. Selling company stock is another method of obtaining equity financing. This decision, however, must be considered very carefully by the entrepreneur. The sale of stock results in the entrepreneur losing a portion of the ownership of the business. Furthermore, certain state and federal laws govern the way stock offerings are made. Private placements and public offerings are the two types of stock sales.

Private Placements. A private placement involves the sale of stock to a selected group of individuals. This stock cannot be purchased by the general public. Sales may be in any amount, but placements less than $500,000 confront fewer government-imposed restrictions and disclosure requirements than those over $500,000. If the company selling the stock is located and doing business in only one state, and stock is sold only to individuals within that same state, the sale is considered an *intrastate stock sale* subject only to that state's regulations.

If the sale involves more than one state, then the sale is an *interstate stock sale* and the federal Securities and Exchange Commission's regulations will apply.

Public Offerings. A public offering involves the sale of stock to the general public. These sales always are governed by the Securities and Exchange Commission regulations. Complying with these regulations is both costly and time-consuming. For public offerings of $400,000 to $1 million the legal fees, underwriting fees, audits, printing, and other costs can easily exceed 15 percent.

initial public offering (IPO) The first sale of stock of a business made available to public investors.

The first time a company offers its stock to the general public it is called an **initial public offering (IPO).** In order to be a viable candidate for an IPO a company must be in good financial health and be able to attract an underwriter (typically a stock brokerage firm or investment banker) to help sell the stock offering. In addition, the market conditions must be favorable for selling equity securities.

There are three main reasons why companies choose public offerings:

1. When market conditions are favorable, more funds can be raised through public offerings than through other venture capital methods without the repayment burdens of debt.
2. Having an established public price for the company's stock enhances its image.
3. The owner's wealth can be magnified greatly when owner-held shares are subsequently sold in the market.

One critical caution about public stock offerings is that they require companies to make financial disclosures to the public. If a company fails to live up to its self-reported expectations, shareholders can sue the company, charging that the company withheld or misrepresented important information. There were 165 such cases in 1993.[11]

Choosing a Lender or Investor

This chapter has described many sources of financing. The key decision facing entrepreneurs is determining which sources to pursue. Your choice will often be limited by the degree to which you meet the requirements of each lending or investing source. If you decide to pursue debt financing, you must have the minimum down payment or other capital requirements necessary to secure the loan. Assuming that these requirements can be met, you will have to determine which lending source to approach. Usually the foremost criterion will be finding the lowest cost or interest rate available. However, other factors must also be considered.

According to small business expert G. B. Baty, other important lender selection criteria are:

1. *Size.* The lender should be small enough to consider the entrepreneur an important customer, but large enough to service the entrepreneur's future needs.
2. *Desire.* The lender should exhibit a desire to work with startup and emerging businesses rather than considering them too risky.
3. *Approach to problems.* The lender should be supportive of small businesses facing problems, offering constructive advice and financing alternatives.
4. *Industry experience.* The lender should have experience in the entrepreneur's industry, especially with startup or emerging ventures.[12]

These factors can help you make reasoned judgments about which lender to approach. The best guideline may be to seek the lenders with whom you feel the most comfortable. A loan relationship can last for a decade or more. Finding a lending source that is pleasant to work with is often as important as finding the lowest cost of debt.

If you decide to pursue equity financing, a number of different considerations emerge. While the use of funds obtained from family members, friends, or partners is perhaps conceivable, none of these sources may be acceptable or feasible for personal reasons. For example, close personal relationships can become strained when money is involved.

Autonomy is another important consideration. Equity financing always requires that you give up a portion of ownership in the venture. If independence is critical to you, then think carefully about the source of equity you pursue.

The most important criterion in choosing investors should be matching the needs of the business with what the investor(s) can offer. If the business requires only money, then you should attempt to find a "silent" partner—one who is willing to provide capital without playing an active role in the management of the business.

But if your business needs, in addition to money, a particular type of expertise, then you should seek an investor who can provide management advice or other assistance along with needed capital. For example, a new business in a high-tech industry might pursue angel financing from a successful individual who has prospered in that industry.

Entrepreneurial guru Jeffry A. Timmons offers a few more cautions when choosing an investor. Each of the following "sand traps," he says imposes a responsibility on the entrepreneur.

1. *Strategic Circumference.* A fund-raising decision can affect future financing choices. Raising equity capital may reduce your freedom to choose additional financing sources in the future due to the partial loss of ownership control that accompanies equity financing.
2. *Legal Circumference.* Financing deals can place unwanted limitations and constraints on the unwary entrepreneur. It is imperative to read and understand the details of each financing document. Competent legal representation is recommended.
3. *Opportunity Cost.* Entrepreneurs often overlook the time, effort, and creative energy required to locating and securing financing. A long search can exhaust the entrepreneur's personal funds before the business ever gets a chance to get off the ground.
4. *Attraction to Status and Size.* Many entrepreneurs seek financing from the most prestigious and high-profile firms. Often a better fit is found with lesser-known firms that have firsthand experience with the type of business the entrepreneur is starting.
5. *Being Too Anxious.* If the entrepreneur has a sound business plan, there will often be multiple venture capital firms interested in investing in it. By accepting the first offer, the entrepreneur may overlook a better deal from another source.[13]

Clearly, choosing a lender or investor takes time and patience. The process is similar to finding a spouse. The relationship that is forged between the entrepreneur and the source of financing can be long-lasting and should be mutually beneficial.

Summary

■ The financing needs of your business.

A straightforward process for determining financing need is to: (1) list the assets required for your business to operate effectively, (2) determine the market value or cost of each asset, (3) identify how much capital you are able to provide, and (4) subtract the total of the owner-provided funds from the total of the assets required. This figure represents the minimum amount of financing required.

■ Basic financing terminology.

To procure financing you must be able to understand basic financial vocabulary. Each major form of capital (debt and equity) has unique terminology that defines the details underlying financing agreements. Each form of capital has pros and cons that make it more or less desirable to the entrepreneur under given circumstances.

■ Where to look for sources of funding.

The search for capital can be unsettling as you sort through the various sources of funds. The loan application process is explained and major sources of debt financing, such as commercial banks, finance companies, government lenders, and insurance companies, are presented. Equity sources such as partners, venture capital firms, angels, and stock offerings are introduced.

Finding capital is one of the most important tasks you face in starting and managing a business. An understanding of this material will enhance your chances of finding the best source for your business.

Questions for Review and Discussion

1. Define "initial capital requirements." How can you determine these?
2. What are the 5 Cs of credit and how do lenders use them?
3. What are the differences between debt funds and equity funds?
4. What kinds of businesses would depend on floor plan financing?
5. What is pledging accounts receivable?
6. What are the advantages of borrowing through the SBA?
7. Why do suppliers extend trade credit to other businesses? What are the advantages and disadvantages of using trade credit?
8. How are private placements and public offerings different?
9. Discuss the types of interest which may apply to a loan.
10. What is the difference between a secured loan and an unsecured loan?

Critical Incident

We're going to take a different approach in this Critical Incident. For once, *you* get to choose the type of small business you want to look at. So think long and hard and select a hypothetical small business you'd like to start. Then answer the following questions.

Questions

1. Develop a listing of the assets that you'll need for this business. Be sure you're considering all the aspects of your business in determining these assets. Then write a short report describing the type of financing you're going to seek for your business.
2. Divide into teams. It's time to role play! Each person will take a turn presenting his or her idea to the other members of the group who are acting as potential investors. As the "entrepreneur," be sure to provide information that you think the investors will want to know. As the "investor group," be prepared to ask questions of the person requesting financing.

Take it to the Net

We invite you to visit the Hatten page on the Prentice Hall Web site at: http://www.prenhall.com/~hattensb for this chapter's World Wide Web exercise.

Chapter Focus

After reading this chapter, you should be able to:

- Discuss laws and regulations that affect small business.
- List the types of bankruptcy.
- Describe the elements of a contract.
- Understand how to protect intellectual property.

19 The Legal Environment

BA 8(a). Is it the governmental boondoggle that critics claim or is it the needed economic boost for minority-owned firms that proponents claim? Well, for one Miami-based firm it's proven to be an important stepping-stone in the company's growth.

Just what is SBA 8(a)? It's a Small Business Administration program named for the section where it's found in the law books, and that's designed to provide a way for thousands of minority-owned businesses to get started and grow. Under the program, the SBA acts as the prime contractor on selected federal contracts. As contractor, the SBA has the authority to award these contracts to "qualified" socially disadvantaged firms. Qualification of 8(a) firms is done through a certification process administered by the SBA. Critics claim that the 8(a) program deprives mainstream firms of public contracts without proving that these firms have discriminated. In fact, the decision by the U.S. Supreme Court in June 1995 that cast doubt on the constitutionality of federally-mandated affirmative action efforts, has led to legal challenges of the 8(a) program. These lawsuits are still winding their way through the legal system. Other critics claim that certified firms rely too heavily on receiving 8(a) contracts and don't develop any competitive capability for surviving in the marketplace. However, despite these criticisms and challenges, the program has had its share of success stories.

For Maria Elena Toraño, the 8(a) program has proven to be beneficial. Toraño started her company, META (Maria Elena Toraño Associates) Inc., as a public relations firm in the early 1980s. In fact, Toraño learned of the 8(a) program in 1986 while working on a project for the Small Business Administration. After achieving certification as an 8(a) company, META was awarded a management information systems contract with the Defense Contract Audit Agency. Moving away from public relations and into management and consulting, the firm subsequently completed contracts for the Department of Energy, preparing environmental impact statements on nuclear weapons facilities, and for the Resolution Trust Corporation, managing and helping to liquidate assets held by failed financial institutions. Although META didn't exclusively do 8(a) contract work, the federal program opened business opportunities that it might not otherwise have had. META has since grown from one office with four employees to six offices with 250 employees—creating a substantial number of new jobs. Annual revenues are in the neighborhood of $22 million.

Toraño, in turn, has parlayed her knowledge and experience back into the community by exercising civic leadership. She's a founding member of the National Hispana Leadership Institute, an organization dedicated to furthering the careers of Hispanic women. In 1993 she hosted a Hispanic Women's Conference that brought together leaders from business, entrepreneurship, academia, national organizations, and the media to discuss the barriers faced by Hispanic women and to propose possible solutions. In 1992 Toraño was awarded the National Latina Excellence Award in the Business Category, sponsored by *Hispanic Magazine* and Avon Products. And she has received the Top Woman-Owned Business Award from the National Association of Women Business Owners and the *Washington Business Journal.*

Whether or not Toraño's business would have achieved its level of success without the SBA 8(a) program cannot be known. But what we do know is that some governmental laws and regulations *can* benefit the small business owner. *Sources: Carole Boston Weatherford, "Women Who Make a Difference,"* Minorities and Women in Business *(January/February/March/April 1994), pp. 37+; Maria Elena Toraño, "New Opportunities, New Directions," reprinted by permission,* Nation's Business *(November 1994), p. 6, © 1994, U.S. Chamber of Commerce; Stephanie N. Mehta, "On Their Own,"* The Wall Street Journal Special Issue on Small Business, *May 22, 1995, p. R23; and Paul M. Barrett, "Main Program for Minority Firms Faces Challenges in Federal Courts,"* The Wall Street Journal, *November 22, 1995, p. B2.*

Small Business and the Law

Would you like to live in a place with no laws? You could drive as fast as you wanted. You could drink alcohol at any age. You could do whatever you wanted and, just think—no taxes to pay because there would be no government making up rules and regulations! While such absolute freedom may sound exciting at first glance, you don't have to think of this scenario long to realize that it also includes no protection for anyone or any groups—it would be chaos. Orderly, civilized societies are built upon laws.

We need laws to ensure fair competition between businesses, to protect the rights of consumers and employees, to protect property, to enforce contracts and agreements, and to permit bankruptcy when things go bad. And we need tax laws to collect the money needed for government to provide these protections. The balance of how much or how little protection we need or we want changes over time. Through elections and open debate, our laws evolve to reflect the needs and changes of society. But, as an old saying goes—It's a good thing that we don't get half the government we pay for.

One of the many problems facing small business owners is keeping up with the changes and understanding the laws and regulations that they must abide by. The wording of many laws and regulations is often baffling and easy to misunderstand. Another problem of regulations for small businesses is the enormous amount of paperwork required to generate reports and records. This paperwork imposes time and resource burdens on often-strapped business owners. A third problem is the cost (for administrative and actual expenses) and difficulty in complying with regulations.

We need laws to ensure competition, to enforce contracts, and to protect our rights as consumers, workers, and property owners.

Running a small business does not require a law degree, but you do need two things to avoid trouble. You need a working knowledge of legal basics and you need a good lawyer on retainer. The best time to get a lawyer for your small business is when you are writing your business plan—not when you are already in trouble.

The weight of government regulations has become a serious burden to small businesses. A study by the National Federation of Independent Business showed that a majority of people who start businesses underestimate the degree of government regulations and red tape more than any other factor. Almost 60 percent were unprepared for the volume of regulations they faced.[1] *The Wall Street Journal* polled 250 top executives of small to mid-sized manufacturing companies on what would benefit their businesses. Figure 19-1 shows that "less regulation" was their top priority.

Regulations and the legal environment of small business covers a lot of ground. This chapter will discuss several major areas of business affected by the law: regulations, licenses, bankruptcy, contracts, and protection of intellectual property.

Laws to Promote Fair Business Competition

Competition between businesses lies at the heart of a free enterprise system. (See Chapter 9.) Healthy competition provides the balance needed to ensure that buyers and sellers are both satisfied. It decreases the need for government intervention in the market.

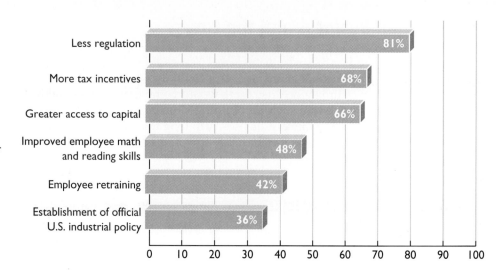

FIGURE 19-1
Get Off Our Backs
Most manufacturers wish for less government regulation. *Grant Thornton, "Wishing for a Lighter Load," The Wall Street Journal, Report on Small Business, Oct. 15, 1994, p. R6. Reprinted by permission of the Wall Street Journal, © 1994 Dow Jones & Co., Inc. All rights reserved worldwide.*

eality Check

Sometimes You Can't Win

Laws, regulations, "special interests." Is it really necessary for the U.S. government to be so involved in business affairs? As owner of a business, for instance, would you expect to have the right to fire an employee without providing a specific reason? Until the late 1980s you had that right in almost every state. But now courts have severely limited at-will powers in over 30 states, and even where it is allowed, the at-will doctrine is shaky and undermined by several other laws.

The pendulum of rights within the legal system has swung to dangerous territory for small business owners who lack resources to fight claims against them in court. Commercial litigator Joseph Ortego stated that legal fees for defending an employer can cost $100,000 by the time a verdict is reached. All a disgruntled employee has to do to start the legal process is fill out a form—at little or no cost. Unfortunately, laws created to protect hardworking employees also open doors for unscrupulous individuals, who may file a

costly suit—even if they don't have a legal case against the company. Whether or not more laws have increased the number of fraudulent claims, people are more comfortable contacting attorneys on the chance that they *may* have a case. Employees who may have little to lose can sue the business or they can sue the owner *personally*. Small business owners have trouble defending themselves. While many lawsuits against small businesses are legitimate, many more are not. Some examples of potential abuses include:

- When a sweet little elderly lady asked the founder of a small woman's clothing manufacturer for a job "at any wage, just to finish my time" he hired her to clean desks. After exactly 10 days of work she asked for a leave of absence. Still sentimental, the business owner said "give a call when you are ready to come back." The sweet lady didn't call back, but her lawyer did. She was filing a claim against the company claiming she had developed double carpel tunnel syndrome which prevented her from doing work of any kind—at the tune of $20,000 per wrist! Many months and many legal fees later the owner ended up settling on the courthouse steps, even though he found that she had lined up her lawyer even *before* she applied at the business.

- According to witnesses, a worker laying shingles for a siding chain was not following prescribed safety procedures and due to his own carelessness, fell from a scaffold. Workman's compensation laws call for wages and medical payments to be paid to injured employees for up to 160 months (13.3 YEARS)—no matter who is at fault. In this case, the siding company was faced with paying out $28,000/yr. and protested the claim on the grounds the worker was malingering. Since back injuries (the most common type of complaint) are difficult to prove, a doctor's statement convinced the judge to rule for the employee. Later, when the siding company had an opening for a management position, the injured worker applied. The company hired a person with management experience. The former employee sued for discrimination against the handicapped.

- A small Philadelphia equipment-repair company had a problem with an employee who was habitually absent without prior notification. The company was tolerant past the number of absences allowed by their policy. The employee claimed that bursitis would flare up randomly, leaving his arm incapacitated. One day a manager was driving by the employee's home and saw him vigorously polishing his car with the allegedly "bad" arm. When he came back to work, the employee was called into the managers office for a little talk. When the door was shut the employee did an immediate U-turn and left. The next day the sheriff served both managers with criminal charges including: interference with the exercise of civil rights, assault and battery, stalking and kidnapping. The employee claimed he was held in a locked room against his will, threatened, and injured permanently when the defendant pulled on his arm. Since it was a criminal, rather than civil trial the company's liability insurance did not cover legal expenses. The defendant spent nothing.

What can you do if you are a small business owner facing such circumstances? Sometimes, not much, but after reading this chapter you will find some ways to protect yourself and your business.

Source: Adapted from Robert Mamis, "Employees from Hell," Inc. (January 1995), pp. 50–57. Adapted with permission, Inc. magazine. © 1995 by Goldhirsh Group, Inc.

Antitrust laws like the Sherman Antitrust Act of 1890 and the Clayton Act of 1914 were written to prevent large businesses from forming *trusts*—large combinations of firms that can dominate an industry and stifle competition, preventing new or small businesses from participating. Under antitrust laws, any agreements or contracts that restrain trade are illegal and unenforceable. The Sherman Antitrust Act and Clayton Act are two of the best-known antitrust laws and are still widely used in preventing business mergers and acquisitions judged to decrease competition.

The Federal Trade Commission Act of 1914 created the Federal Trade Commission (FTC), the agency that regulates competition in our economy. The FTC has the power to issue cease-and-desist orders, which prohibit offending companies from unfair or deceptive practices such as collusion (acting together to keep prices artificially high). The five-member commission has the power to conduct hearings, direct investigations, and issue cease-and-desist orders to violators which are enforceable in federal court.

antitrust laws Legislation which prohibits firms from combining in a way that would stifle competition within that industry.

Laws to Protect Consumers

Up until the past few decades, U.S. Consumer laws were based on the rule of *caveat emptor*—let the buyer beware. Now laws have largely abandoned this precept to offer ever-increasing protection for consumers, administered by a wide variety of state and federal agencies. The most common practices that government protects consumers against involve extension of credit, deceptive trade practices, unsafe products, and unfair pricing.

The Federal Trade Commission, for instance, is involved in product labeling standards, banning hazardous products, ensuring consumer product safety, regulating the content and message of advertising, ensuring truth-in-lending practices, equal credit access to consumers, fair credit practices, and many other areas. Many laws which are intended to protect consumers fall under the jurisdiction of the FTC, including the Nutrition Labeling and Education Act of 1990, the Fair Debt Collection Practices Act of 1977, the Truth-in-Lending Act, the Consumer Product Safety Act, to name but a few. The FTC is an agency of the federal government with broad and deep power when it comes to protecting consumers.

Laws to Protect People in the Workplace

A major thrust of federal employment legislation today is equal opportunity employment. This goal is based on the belief that an individual should be considered for employment on the basis of individual merit rather than with regard to race, color, religion, sex, age, national origin, or disability. The origin of this goal dates back to the U.S. Constitution, and it was fortified by the Fourteenth and Fifteenth Amendments in the 1860s. However, beginning in the early 1960s, in response to great social change and unrest, Congress acted to strengthen the enforcement of this belief, passing several comprehensive pieces of legislation as outlined here.

Equal Pay Act of 1963. As an amendment to the 1938 Fair Labor Standards Act, this act requires businesses with two or more employees engaged in commerce or activities affecting commerce to pay men and women in the same organization performing equal work an equal wage. Equal work is defined in terms of skills, effort, job conditions, and responsibilities. The law does, however, permit wage differentials for reasons other than sex. These might include a bonafide seniority system, merit pay decisions, quantity and quality of production scales, or other practices such as shift differentials.

Compliance is regulated by the Equal Employment Opportunity Commission (EEOC). Employers covered by the law must provide upon request detailed records of compensation, including rates of pay, hours worked, overtime payments, deductions, and other related pay data. In addition, supporting documents, such as wage surveys, job descriptions, job evaluation studies, collective bargaining agreements, and the like, may also be requested.

Civil Rights Act of 1964. The Civil Rights Act (CRA) of 1964 prevents discrimination on the basis of sex, race, color, religion, or national origin in any terms, conditions, or privileges of employment. Discrimination on the basis of pregnancy, childbirth, and related medical conditions is also prohibited as a result of a 1978 amendment. Title VII of this landmark legislation applies to all organizations with 15 or more employees working 20 or more weeks a year in commerce or in any industry or activity affecting commerce. As amended, state and local governments, labor unions, employment agencies, and educational institutions are also covered. Religious organizations, private clubs, or places of employment connected with a Native American reservation are, however, not covered by the act.

Provisions of the act are enforced by the Equal Employment Opportunity Commission. Private employers with 100 or more employees are required to file annually Form EEO-1, detailing the makeup of the company's work force. In addition, all employers are required to keep employment-related documents for at least six months from the time of their creation, or in the case of a personnel action such as a discharge, from the date of the action.

Immigration Reform and Control Act of 1986. The Immigration Reform and Control Act (IRCA) was passed in 1986 with two intended goals. First, it seeks to discourage illegal immigration into the United States by denying employment to aliens who do not comply with the Immigration and Naturalization Service regulations. It achieves this goal by requiring employers to document worker eligibility. All U.S. employers must complete Form I-9 for new hires, for which the employee must provide documentation proving his or her identity *and* work authorization. Permissible documents include a birth certificate, a U.S. passport, certificate of U.S. citizenship, certificate of naturalization, unexpired foreign passport, resident alien card, or a combination of documents attesting to identity and employment authorization as outlined on Form I-9.[2]

A second goal of the act was to strengthen the national origin provisions of Title VII of the 1964 Civil Rights Act by extending coverage to "foreign-sounding" and "foreign-looking" individuals and to all employers with four or more employees (rather than the 15 or more established by the CRA). If found guilty of discrimination under the IRCA, you may be assessed back pay for up to two years and civil fines of up to $2,000 per violation and $10,000 for multiple violations.[3] Enforcement responsibilities were assigned to the Office of the Special Counsel for Immigration-Related Unfair Employment Practices, a division of the Department of Justice.

Americans with Disabilities Act of 1990. The 1990 Americans with Disabilities Act (ADA) was passed to guarantee individuals with disabilities the rights to obtain and hold a job, travel on public transportation, enter and use public facilities, and use telecommunication services. Almost all businesses, regardless of size, are affected by one or more of the act's provisions.

If you are a private employer with 15 or more employees (including part-time employees) working 20 or more calendar weeks a year, you are covered by Title 1, the employment discrimination provision. As such, you may not discriminate against *qualified disabled* individuals with regard to any employment practice or terms, conditions, and privileges of employment. Under the act, a disabled person is one who has (1) a physical or mental impairment that substantially limits one or more major life activities, (2) has a physical or mental impairment, or (3) is regarded as having such an impairment. Specially included within this definition are recovering drug addicts, alcoholics, and individuals infected with HIV and AIDS. In turn, a qualified applicant is one who (1) meets the necessary prerequisites for the job, such as education, work experience, or training, and (2) can perform the essential functions of the job, with or without reasonable accommodation.

Once a set of effective accommodations has been identified—which might include restructuring a job, modifying work schedules, providing readers and interpreters, or obtaining and modifying equipment—you are free to select the one that is the least expensive or easiest to provide. Even then, you need make the accommodation only if it does not present an undue hardship on the operation of your business. An undue hardship is an action that is "excessively costly, extensive, substantial, or disruptive, or that would fundamentally alter the nature or operation of the business."[4] In determining undue hardship, you should consider the nature and cost of the accommodation in relation to your business's size, financial resources (including available tax credits, as discussed later), the nature and structure of its operation, and the impact of the accommodation on its operation.

In addition to the issue of reasonable accommodation, you should also keep the following points in mind.

- Prior to a conditional offer of employment, inquiries of others about the applicant's disability, illness, and workers' compensation history are prohibited.

- Required medical or physical examinations are prohibited prior to a conditional offer of employment. Drug tests may be given, however, at any point in the employment process, since such tests are not considered medical examinations under the law.

- Any selection or performance standards should be job related, be based upon a thorough job analysis, and be prepared prior to advertising the position.

- Asking the applicant about the nature, origin, or severity of a known disability is prohibited. You may, however, question the applicant about his ability to perform the essential functions of the job and to describe or demonstrate how he might perform such functions.

- An employer may not refuse to hire an individual simply because he might or will require accommodation under the act.

- All application materials and processes from the application form to the interview and beyond must be free of references to or inquiries about disabilities.

Under Title III of the ADA, virtually all businesses serving the public must make their facilities and services accessible to the disabled. This may require you to modify your operational policies, practices, and procedures, remove structural barriers, and provide auxiliary aids and services to the disabled. Technical standards for building and site elements, such as parking, ramps, doors, and elevators, have been set forth in the *ADA Accessibility Guidelines for New Construction and Alterations* handbook. The handbook is available from the Office of the Americans with Disabilities Act, U.S. Department of Justice.

Tax incentives are available to aid businesses with ADA compliance. The Disabled Access Credit for small businesses allows one-half the cost of eligible access expenditures that are more than $250 but less than $10,500 to be taken.[5] You may also qualify for tax deductions under the Architectural and Transportation Barrier Removal, and Targeted Job Tax Credit provisions. You should contact your local IRS or vocational rehabilitation office for additional information.

Civil Rights Act of 1991. Congress passed the 1991 Civil Rights Act in reaction to several 1989 U.S. Supreme Court decisions which, it believed, unnecessarily

R eality Check

When Abilities Matter More Than Disabilities

Hiring disabled employees proved to be a winning formula for Exabyte, a manufacturer of computer storage tape drives located in Boulder, Colorado. When the company hired its first hearing impaired employee to work in the assembly plant, supervisors' intial concerns soon dissolved. In fact, the excellent organizational skills and work habits of the new hire led the company to promote him to the position of coordinating production in the assembly plant and to add more hearing impaired employees to its payroll. The company's rapid growth created a demand for good, reliable workers, and Exabyte found its hearing impaired employees to be a valuable addition to its human resources. Exabyte provides accommodations as needed—a translator for departmental meetings and sign language classes for other employees. In fact, one of the hearing impaired employees who supervises five "hearing" employees has taught them sign language for phrases such as "Good!" and more exotically, "Put on your antistatic jacket." As Exabyte has shown, what workers cannot do is less important than what they *can* do.

Source: Jennifer Reese, "If You Can Read This, You Can Get a Job," Fortune, *July 12, 1993, p. 11.*

---

shifted the focus of employment law in favor of U.S. business. The act amends Title VII and the ADA with the following provisions:

- It prohibits **race norming,** the practice of using different cut-off test scores for different groups.

- It provides that in cases where an otherwise neutral employment practice results in an underrepresentation of minorities (called *disparate impact cases*), employers must show that (1) the practice is job related, (2) the practice is consistent with a business necessity (that it exists in the best interest of the firm's employees and the general public), and (3) a less discriminatory practice does not exist.

- In cases of intentional discrimination, it provides for both compensatory and punitive damages and allows for jury trials.

- It places a cap on the amount of punitive and compensatory damages which may be awarded, depending on company size.

race norming An illegal activity of setting different test standards for divergent groups for purposes of hiring or promotion.

COMPANY SIZE	MAXIMUM AWARD
14 to 100 employees	$ 50,000
101 to 200 employees	100,000
201 to 500 employees	200,000
More than 500 employees	300,000

- It provides that *any* reliance on a discriminatory factor in an employment decision is grounds for litigation.

The impact of the 1991 Civil Rights Act on small business owners is clear: The legitimacy of any employment practice or decision is yours to prove. If you are challenged and cannot prove that you did not intend to discriminate, you face the possibility of both compensatory and punitive damage awards. Therefore, you must be sure that any employment decision is based on a business need rather than on the basis of race, sex, color, religion, disability, or national origin.

The Civil Rights Act of 1991 also added teeth to EEOC guidelines on **sexual harassment.** (See Chapter 3.) The Civil Rights Act of 1991 provides victims of discrimination, including sexual harassment, access to trial by jury, compensatory damages for pain and suffering, and punitive damages if employers are proven to have acted with "malice or reckless indifference."

Small businesses are certainly not immune from sexual harassment. Unfortunately, such unwelcome behavior can occur in any company. Yet the penalties faced by small businesses are proportionately higher than large businesses. Limits vary from state to state, but consider the disparity in awards. A business with 15 employees could be assessed a maximum fine of $50,000 for a harassment conviction, or $3,333 per employee. A business with 500 employees could be fined $200,000, or $400 per employee. Which award do you think would have a greater impact on the business—$50,000 from a business of 15, or $200,000 from a business of 500?[6]

Because they can be held legally responsible not only for their own actions, but also for the actions of their managers and employees, small businesses must be prepared by setting policies and procedures. Employees and managers need to be trained, as do subcontractors, since the business can be held liable for both. For example, the owners of a Florida hotel were required to pay $420,670 to a former employee who was harassed by the president of the hotel management company.[7] A business owner should be ready to investigate any complaint in a timely manner. Finally, if suspect behavior is found to have occurred by the investigation, the company should be ready to take appropriate action.[8]

Family and Medical Leave Act of 1993. The Family and Medical Leave Act (FMLA) of 1993 requires private employers with 50 or more employees who work for 20 or more calendar weeks per year to make at least 12 weeks of unpaid leave available to eligible employees. To be eligible, an employee must have worked for a covered employer for at least 12 months, putting in at least 1,250 hours over the prior 12 months at a location where at least 50 employees are employed by the employer within a 75-mile radius.[9] Due in part to the 75-mile restriction, it is estimated that as many as 60 percent of U.S. workers and about 95 percent of all employers are not affected by the act.[10]

Eligible employees may take leave for one or more of the following reasons: for the birth or placement of a child for adoption or foster care, to care for an immediate family member with a serious health condition, or to take medical leave when the employee is unable to work because of a serious health condition. This leave may be taken during any 12-month period in a block of time or intermittently through reduced work schedules. Within limitations, paid leave may be substituted for unpaid leave.

Covered employers are required to maintain group health insurance coverage for employees on FMLA leave and to provide equivalent job restoration upon completion of the leave. Employers are allowed to exempt "key" employees—an employee who is among the highest paid 10 percent of employees within 75 miles of the worksite—from the restoration requirement. In addition, employers

When Harassment Comes from Outside

Sexual harassment is difficult to deal with when it occurs within a business, but what about when it comes from a customer, a supplier, or an advisor? What is the victim to do? What is the business to do?

Caryn Wilde owned a secretarial services business in Minnesota. For over a year, her largest client became increasingly aggressive in his advances toward her. When she refused, Wilton Croonquist, head of a regional economic development agency, implied that if she took any action against him, he would take his business elsewhere. Because Croonquist's business represented 15 percent of Wilde's revenue, this was a serious threat.

As Croonquist continued to harass her, the normally gregarious Wilde became withdrawn, confiding only in her husband and a few close friends. Afraid of losing her business, she was also afraid of losing her health and her well-being. After 15 months, she filed a restraining order against Croonquist. Within minutes of receiving the order not to contact Wilde, Croonquist phoned her. She in turn called the police, who arrested Croonquist. Shortly afterward, Wilde's fears came true: Croonquist's agency canceled its agreement with Wilde's company.

Then things got even worse. Although Wilde had filed sexual harassment charges for workplace discrimination under Title VII of the Civil Rights Act of 1964, a loophole existed. The law was interpreted as applying only to employees and Wilde was not Croonquist's employee. Therefore, "by law," she said, "I could not be sexually harassed."

When Wilde finally had her day in court, with a jury, Croonquist denied any wrongdoing. The jury awarded Wilde $113,100 directly from him, and $36,900 from the agency. Unfortunately, the story does not end happily. Croonquist subsequently declared bankruptcy, leaving Wilde without her settlement. Shaken and denied her settlement, Wilde sold her house and put her business on the market, hoping to move as far away from the incident as possible. Third-party harassment will surely be the next battlefield in the fight against sexual harassment.

Source: Adapted from Frank Clancy, "When Customer Service Crosses the Line," Working Woman *(December 1994), pp. 36–39, 77–78.*

---

may require employees requesting FLMA leave to comply with certain notification and certification requirements, such as providing 30 days' advance notice when the leave is foreseeable, providing medical certification of serious health conditions, or requiring a fitness-for-duty certificate upon returning to work.

In addition to complying with FMLA leave requirements, employers must inform employees about their rights and responsibilities under the act. In response to specific notices of need, employers also must notify employees of the conditions under which the leave is being granted or denied. The Wage and Hour Division of the U.S. Department of Labor is responsible for enforcing the provisions of the act.

Occupational Safety and Health Administration (OSHA). Congress passed the Occupational Safety and Health Act of 1970 to "assure, so far as possible, every working man and woman in the nation safe and healthful working conditions and to preserve our human resources."[11] The act created three federal agencies: the Occupational Safety and Health Administration (OSHA), the enforcement arm; the National Institute of Occupational Safety and Health (NIOSH), the research center; and the Occupational Safety and Health Review Commission (OSHRC), the enforcement review board.

As the enforcement agency, OSHA establishes and enforces occupational safety and health standards in all places of employment affecting commerce. OSHA compliance officers have a right to enter your workplace (you may require them to obtain a search warrant first), inspect part or all of your workplace (you should negotiate the scope and conditions before voluntarily permitting entry), issue citations for alleged violations, and propose penalties and abatement periods. Inspections are conducted to investigate a reported accident, injury, or fatality at a worksite, an employee complaint alleging a violation, or as part of a regular or programmed schedule of inspections. As an employer, if you are cited for a violation, you may either correct the alleged violation, seek a variance, or appeal the penalty.

OSHA requires most employers with 11 or more employees to keep records of occupational injuries and illnesses. Employers must also post an approved state or federal OSHA poster and any citations, which must be displayed at or near the site of the alleged violation for three days, or until corrected, whichever is later.

As a small business owner, you may request information from one of ten regional OSHA offices or request a free on-site OSHA-supported consultation through your state's labor or health departments. No citations are issued or penalties proposed, nor is the name of your firm and any information regarding your firm given to OSHA. However, you will be expected to correct any serious job safety and health hazards identified.

Licenses, Restrictions, and Permits

Since there are different requirements for licenses and permits at the federal, state, regional, county, and city government levels, a comprehensive list is not possible. But there are some general guidelines in finding information on regulations at each level.

Double check license and permit rules. Check the appropriate government agency directly—don't rely on real estate agents, sellers, or anyone else's opinion.

At the federal level. Get an employer identification number for federal tax and Social Security withholdings. File Form 2553 if you are forming a corporation. Check with the appropriate agency for your specific type of business. For example, if you are starting a common carrier trucking company, you should contact the Interstate Commerce Commission.

At the state level. Professionals like lawyers, dentists, and architects need professional licenses. You need to register for a state tax number with the Department of Revenue. You need an employer identification number for state tax withholdings. Special licenses are usually needed for selling liquor, food, gasoline, or firearms.

At the regional level. Several counties may form regional agencies that oversee environmental regulations and water usage.

At the local level. Permits and licenses to comply with local and county requirements will vary from place to place.[12] You need answers from the local level—the local chamber of commerce and lawyers are good sources of information. Offices to check with would be:

City or county clerk

City or county treasurer

Zoning department

Building department

Health department

Fire department

Police department

Public works department

If your business involves the sale or preparation of food, you will not only need a permit from a local health department, you also will need regular inspections. Local health departments may also be involved with environmental concerns such as asbestos, radon testing, and water purity testing.

Zoning Laws. You need to be absolutely sure of how a property is zoned before you sign a lease. If it is not zoned properly, you can sign the lease with a contingency clause that the property will be rezoned. You can also apply to the local zoning commission to get a variance, which allows you to operate without complying with the regulation or the regulation being changed.

Entering the Internet

The Internet includes a variety of sites that you can access for information on laws and regulations. A federal government site (http://www.business.gov) has lots of good information for small businesses. One of the topic areas that you can access at this site is "Laws/Regulations," which links you to a variety of governmental agencies and information databases.

You might want to access some of these agencies directly. For instance, you can link to OSHA at http://www.osha.gov. You can connect to the U.S. Patent and Trade Office at http://www.uspto.gov. Or you might want to access the Small Business Administration's Gopher files at gopher://www.sbaonline. sba.gov and link to the one called "Legislation and Regulation."

Another good governmental source is Fedworld, which can be reached at http://www.fedworld.gov.

Nongovernmental sources which you might try include Cornell University's Institute of Labor Relations, which can be reached at http://www.ilr. cornell.edu/library/e_archive/Dunlop/dunlop.contents. html. This will link you to a site that provides the final report from the Commission on the Future of Worker-Management Relations, which has several sections relating to laws and regulations that apply to employees.

Finally, there's a site with the unusual name of THE SEAMLESS WEBsite™ that provides law-related information. The home page lists links such as State Law Resources, Federal Resources, International Legal Sites, and Legal Service Providers and Associations. You can access this site at http://www.seamless.com/road.html.

Computer Applications

A small business person might find the paperwork of staying in compliance with laws and regulations overwhelming. In fact, a Small Business Administration study showed that the average cost of federal regulation, including paperwork and taxpayer filing requirements in 1992, was $5,400 per employee for companies with fewer than 500 workers. For companies with more than 500 employees, the amount was $3,000. With this significant level of resources devoted to complying, you want to use every means you can to help make these activities efficient.

You might find that certain computer software can help you with selected legal and regulatory requirements. For instance, in the area of employee relations—such as performance appraisal, hiring, discipline, health and safety, and so forth—you can use software programs such as Personnel Readyworks, Employee Appraiser, and Performance Now! to effectively and efficiently handle these issues to ensure that you're within the bounds of the various employment laws and regulations.

If your business tax situation is such that you need to keep careful track of your business expenses, you might want to use a program called ExpensAble. This program was created by Intuit, the company that makes the popular Quicken accounting programs. If you already use Quicken, you can easily exchange data between it and ExpensAble, making tax form preparation much easier.

Finally, there are computer software programs available that have boilerplate (or standardized) legal forms. However, as mentioned in earlier chapters, you need to be cautious in your use of such software. Sometimes, in uncertain and complicated legal situations, it's better to pay a legal expert to help you with the required paperwork. After all, taking what appears to be the "inexpensive" approach may turn out to cost you more in the long run, particularly when it comes to points of the law.

Sources: Steve Bass, "Hot Picks for the Home Office," Newsweek *Special Advertising Section (Summer 1995), p. N19; Ripley Hatch and Jon Pepper, "They Could Just as Well Be Giants,"* Nation's Business *(July 1995), pp. 50–52; and Michael Selz, "Costs of Complying with Federal Rules Weigh More Heavily on Small Firms,"* The Wall Street Journal, *November 1, 1995, p. B2.*

---

zoning laws Local laws which control where and how businesses may operate.

Zoning laws control what a business can sell and where it can operate. They are typically used to control parking, waste disposal, and sign size and placement. You may not even be able to paint the building a certain color due to zoning restrictions. For example, a White Castle hamburger franchise in Overland Park, Kansas, was not allowed to paint the building white because a zoning ordinance prohibited white buildings.

How do zoning laws affect home-based businesses, since they are the fastest growing segment in business? (See Chapter 8.) Technology is making it possible for you to be productive at work from the comfort of your own living room. Are zoning boards as comfortable with the idea? While some zoning ordinances prohibit home businesses, most don't. Restrictions on what you can and can't do on the property are more common. Most are primarily looking to maintain the residential nature of the neighborhood.

You should check zoning laws before you start your business, whether or not it is home-based. At the Zoning Department at City Hall, find out not only about the written laws but also about the community attitudes of administrators, citizens, and the business community. Are other home-based businesses allowed? If you disagree with a zoning ruling, you may be able to appeal to a variance board, the city council, or local commissioners.

Bankruptcy Laws

Bankruptcy is a remedy for becoming insolvent. When an individual or a business gets in a financial condition in which there's no other way out, the courts administer the estate for the benefit of the creditors. The Bankruptcy Reform Act of 1978 established eight chapters for businesspeople seeking the protection of bankruptcy. Three of these chapters apply to most small business situations: Chapters 7, 11, and 13.

Bankruptcy can accomplish two different objectives: **liquidation,** after which the business ceases to exist; and **reorganization,** which allows the business owner to file a plan with the court that offers protection from creditors until the debt is satisfied.

bankruptcy A ruling granted by courts to release businesses or individuals from some or all of their debt.

Chapter 7 Bankruptcy

Chapter 7 bankruptcy means that the business is liquidated. All of the assets of the business are sold by a trustee appointed by the court. After the sale, the trustee distributes the proceeds to the creditors, who usually receive a percentage of the original debt. If any money is left over, it is divided among shareholders. About three of every four bankruptcy filings are under Chapter 7.

Declaring bankruptcy does not necessarily leave you penniless and homeless. Most states have provisions which allow individuals to keep the equity in their homes, autos, and some personal property.

Other businesses that declare bankruptcy may provide an opportunity for you. For instance, imagine you are in business and one of your key suppliers goes bankrupt. What are your options? You could try to continue doing business with that firm for as long as possible. You could try to find a new supplier. Or you could use your knowledge of the bankrupt company and industry to your advantage and buy the supplier at a bargain price, assuming you could operate the failed business more efficiently than the previous management.[13] Other strategic purchases could include buying a financially strapped competitor to increase your market share or buying a business that is a customer to provide an outlet for your products.

Chapter 11 Bankruptcy

Chapter 11 provides a second chance for a business that is in financial trouble but still has potential for success. Chapter 11 can be either voluntary or involuntary. Once you file for Chapter 11 protection, you file a reorganization plan with the bankruptcy court. The plan includes a repayment schedule for current creditors (which may be less than 100 percent of amount owed), and how the business will operate more profitably in the future. Only about 3 percent of bankruptcy filings are under Chapter 11.

This reorganization protection keeps creditors from foreclosing on debts during the reorganization period. The business continues to operate under court direction. The plan must be approved by the court and the creditors. The reorganization plan also spells out a specific time period for the reorganization. If the business cannot turn operations (and profits) around, the likelihood of its switching to a Chapter 7 liquidation is great.

Chapter 13 Bankruptcy

Chapter 13 bankruptcy allows individuals, including small business owners, who owe less than $250,000 in unsecured debts and secured debts of less than $750,000 to pay back creditors over a three- to five-year period. As with Chapter 11, a repayment plan is submitted to a bankruptcy judge who must approve the conditions of the plan. The plan must show how most types of your debt will be paid in full. Other types can be reduced or even eliminated by the court. About one-fourth of bankruptcies filed are under Chapter 13.

While much of the negative stigma attached to declaring bankruptcy of any type has decreased, it is still absolutely not an "easy way out." Bankruptcy stays on your credit report for at least seven years. It is expensive and time-consuming. Chapters 11 and 13 may be better than liquidation, but they are not a solution to all of your problems.

Contract Law for Small Business

contract An agreement between two or more parties that is enforceable by law.

A **contract** is basically a promise that is enforceable by law. **Contract law** comprises the body of laws that are intended to make sure that parties entering into contracts comply, and provides remedies to those parties harmed if a contract is broken.

A contract does not have to be in writing to be enforceable. While it is a good idea to get any important agreement in writing to help settle future disputes, the only contracts that *must* be in writing are those which:

- Involve the sale of real estate
- Involve paying someone else's debt
- Take longer than one year to perform
- Involve the sale of goods valued at $500 or more.

Even contracts that are written do not have to be complicated, formal documents written by a lawyer. While you may not want to rely on contracts that are too sketchy, a letter or memo that identifies the parties, the subject, and the terms and conditions of the sale can be recognized as a valid contract.

The Elements of a Contract

The four basic conditions or elements that a contract must meet to be binding are legality, agreement, capacity, and consideration.

Legality. A contract has to be intended to accomplish a legal purpose. For instance, you can't make a contract that charges an interest rate higher than legal restrictions allow. At the same time, just because a deal is unfair, it is not necessarily illegal. You can't get out of a deal later if you offer to pay $1,500 for a used computer that is worth only $150.

Agreement. A valid contract has to include a legitimate offer and a legitimate acceptance—called a *meeting of the minds.* If a customer tells you his traveling circus will pay your print shop $600 to print 200 circus posters and you say "it's a deal," you have a legally binding contract. In this case, it is an oral one, which is as legally binding as a written contract.

Consideration. Something of value must be exchanged between the parties involved in the contract. Without consideration, the agreement is about a gift, not a contract. In the preceding example, the $600 and the 200 posters are the consideration. If the circus owner picks up the posters, pays you the $600 and says "Wow, for doing such a great job, come to the circus and I'll give you a free elephant ride." Can you legally demand to ride the elephant later? No, you got what you agreed to—the $600, but there was no consideration for the bonus.

Capacity. Not everyone has the capacity to legally enter into a contract. Minors and persons who are intoxicated or who have diminished mental ability cannot be bound by contracts. This is an important point to remember when running a small business. For example, if you sell a used car to a person under the age of 18, you could end up with a problem. The minor could take the car, run it without oil, smash it into a tree, and come to you to get his money back. You would be legally obligated to return his money because a contract with a minor is not binding.

Small Business IN THE Service Industry

Michael Blair, the owner of a small Hollywood advertising and design studio called Blair Communications, learned about the dark side of federal laws and regulations the hard way. According to the Federal Bankruptcy Code, every person or company that has declared bankruptcy may, in certain circumstances, sue for the return of money paid out to others within three months of the bankruptcy filing. This section in the code applies when preferential payments were made to some creditors over others during that time period in order to give all creditors an equitable distribution of assets. However, what's happened to Blair shows the downside of this supposed protection.

Blair was sued by a company that he developed advertising for—a company by the name of PC Brand Computers, a subsidiary of Tandon Corporation. Tandon had filed for Chapter 11 bankruptcy protection in March 1993, two months after its last payment to Blair. What happened next was, for Blair, like a nightmare gone out of control. Blair received a parcel by registered mail containing a mass of legal documents—the gist of which was that Tandon was suing him for the return of the previous payment. He was asked to send a check reimbursing the company for the full amount. Is that what the law's creators had in mind when they wrote this particular "preference payments" section? Probably not. But this example illustrates how important it is for small businesses—especially for service businesses that deal in intangibles—to understand the legal environment. *Source: Michael Blair, "Business' Plight; Lawyers' Delight," The New York Times, June 18, 1995, p. F13.*

Contractual Obligations

breach of contract A violation of one or more terms of a contract by a party involved in the contract.

What can you do if a party with whom you signed a contract doesn't hold up her end of the agreement? This is called **breach of contract** and you have several remedies available. Usually either money or some specific performance is used to compensate the damaged party. With either remedy, the intent of litigation is to try to put you back to where you were before the agreement was made.

compensatory damages Money awarded by the courts to a party of the contract who has suffered a loss due to the actions of another party.

If the judge or arbitrator awards money, it is called **compensatory damages.** Go back to the circus poster example. If you were not able to complete the job as agreed and the circus owner had to pay someone else $800 to get the posters printed, you could be sued for $200 for breach of contract (probably in small claims court). Why $200? That amount represents the compensatory damages the circus owner suffered since you couldn't do the job for $600.

specific performance A nonmonetary award granted by the courts to a party of the contract who has suffered a loss due to the actions of another party.

In some contract dispute cases, money alone is insufficient to put a person back to her original state. In these cases a judge may order a **specific performance** by the damaging party to make sure justice is done. Specific performance requires one party to do exactly what he has agreed to do.

Consider buying an existing business and the sales contract includes a noncompete covenant. This means the previous business owner will not start or own a similar business within a specific geographic area for a certain amount of time. If the previous owner breaks the noncompete covenant and starts the same type of business, a single monetary award won't be enough. The judge can issue an

injunction A court order which prohibits certain activities.

injunction, which prohibits the previous owner from operating the new business for the duration of the agreement.

Specific performance is awarded only if the item involved is very unique and not substitutable. In this case, a judge will require the losing party to surrender the item in question.

Laws to Protect Intellectual Property

intellectual property Property which is created through the mental skills of a person.

Intellectual property is a broad term that refers to the product of some type of unique human thought. It begins as an idea that could be as simple as a new name or as complex as the invention of a new product. Intellectual property also includes symbols and slogans that describe your business or product and original expression whether it takes the form of a collection of words (like a published book), an artistic interpretation (like a videotape of a concert performance), or a computer program. These products of human thought have some value in the marketplace. A body of laws determines how, and for how long, a person can capitalize on his idea.

Safeguarded by the U.S. Constitution, copyright protection encourages entrepreneurs to invent new ideas and products.

The forms of legal protection for intellectual property that will be discussed in this section are patents, copyrights, and trademarks. Although commonly used, the term *protection* may be misleading when we are discussing intellectual property because it implies defense. Actually, patents, copyrights, and trademarks give the owner more offensive rights than defensive protection. They provide a tool for you to use in protecting your property against infringers. In the United States, this right has been considered so essential a part of the country's economic functioning that it was written into the Constitution.[14]

Patents

patent A form of protection for intellectual property provided to an inventor for a period of seventeen years.

A **patent** gives you the right to exclude someone else (or some other company) from making, using, or selling the property you have created and patented for a

Reality Check

If Only I'd Thought of That. . . .

Are you a potential inventor? Do you come up with ideas for new products the world can't live without when you are in the shower, or driving to work? Here are some products or services that have recently been patented. Keep thinking and you may come up with a patentable product!

- Ted Schott, who invents games, has patented a "stress-reducing" board game that involves up to six players in pillow fights. He says it is a good way for children to use up excess energy.

- John Dahman, a mechanical engineer by trade, came up with a solution to one form of household drudgery—ironing. Dahman patented a process for drying cotton pants so no ironing is needed by using an ordinary hair dryer.

- Leroy Forney designs medical devices. His latest patented invention looks like a pacifier, but it keeps people from snoring. Unfortunately, at this writing, the FDA has not yet approved the product.

- Raymond and Hilde Smith wanted more room in their recreational vehicle, so they invented and patented a two-story RV. The second story slides down into the first while traveling and goes up to double your floor space when parked.

- Ellis Gordon invented and patented a computerized kitchen appliance which can be programmed to mix ingredients together, then prepare a meal by cooking or cooling.

- Is kitty litter a problem? Traditionally used sodium bentonite does not decompose. Theodore Kiebke patented a more environmentally friendly version made from wheat.

- Optometrist Sidney Slavin had dreamed of being able to show driver's education students the deadly effects of driving drunk, so he invented and patented eyeglasses that distort, rather than clarify, vision. The glasses simulate the effects of drugs or alcohol (without the side-effects).

- William Holmes patented an insulated drinking bag that fits on bicycles. The rider does not have to remove his hands from the handlebars to search for a bottle, remove it, take a drink and return the bottle to its holder. Holmes's invention's unique attribute is a tube that extends from the handlebar. Riders just lean over to take a drink.

- Not all inventors think on a small scale. Retired aerospace engineer George Neumayr patented a design for a flying machine that can take off and land straight up and down, even over water. The design looks like a flying saucer and can carry up to 800 people. Sorry, Trekkies, beaming up is not yet an option.

- With some products, you have to wonder "Do we really need this product?" Who would invent something like synthetic human feces? Actually, Kimberly-Clark patented this invention, which it used as an odorless alternative in testing its diapers.

Sources: All adapted from The New York Times *patent column. "A Board Game to Inspire Fighting," January 2, 1995, p. A40; "Device to Aid Drying of Trousers," January 9, 1995, p. D2; "Anti-snoring Unit Resembles Pacifier," January 9, 1995, p. D2; "Recreation Vehicle With a 2d Story," January 2, 1995, p. A40; "Patents," December 26, 1994, p. A56; "A New Cat Litter, Made From Wheat," December 12, 1994, p. D2; "Patents," December 5, 1994, p. D2; "A Pressurized Bag for Thirsty Cyclists," November 21, 1994, p. D2; "Patents," November 7, 1994, p. B14; "An Odorless Way of Testing Diapers," October 24, 1994, p. D2.*

Patent Trademark Office The office of the U.S. government which grants protection for intellectual property.

period of 17 years. To receive this protection, you have to file for a patent through the **Patent Trademark Office** (PTO). This requires paying filing fees and maintenance fees. Three maintenance fees must be paid four, eight, and 12 years after the patent grant or the patent will expire before 17 years.

Although it is commonly believed that you have to hire a patent attorney to file a patent application, this is not the case. Actually regulations require the PTO to help individuals who do not use an attorney. Hundreds of patents are granted each year to inventors who go through the process alone. But just because you can complete the patent process without legal counsel, does that mean you *should* attempt it? It depends. Patent attorneys charge $3,000 to $5,000 to prepare a patent application. How many of the earth-changing widgets will you have to sell to cover that kind of overhead? If you are unsure of what the market for your widgets will be, books like *Patent It Yourself* by David Pressman contain all the instructions and forms you need to do it yourself.[15] Doing as much as you can yourself, while checking periodically with an attorney throughout the process, may be a reasonable compromise to offer you both expertise and cost savings.

Three types of patents exist. The most common type is the **utility patent.** This patent covers inventions that provide a unique or new *use* or *function*. If you could come up with a new way to keep shoes on people's feet without using laces, buckles, Velcro fasteners, zippers, or other ways currently used, you would need to file for a utility patent.

While utility patents cover use, **design patents** protect unique or new *forms* or *shapes*. If the new shape also changes the function of the object, then you need to apply for a utility patent. If looks alone are different, you need a design patent. For example, if you were to design a ball-point pen that looked like a fish, but which served no other function than that of a ball-point pen, you would file a design patent for your invention.

The third patent type is a **plant patent.** This patent covers living plants, such as flowers, trees, or vegetables which can be grown or otherwise reproduced.

What Can Be Patented? The PTO reviews each application and decides whether or not to grant a patent by four tests which come from the following questions:

- Does the invention fit a statutory class?
- Is the invention useful?
- Is it novel?
- Is it unobvious?

The invention must fit into one of the five statutory classes—which means you must be able to call it a machine, process, manufacture, chemical composition, or combination of those terms.

The invention must provide some legal utility. It must be useful in some way. If the invention has some commercial value, this test shouldn't be difficult to pass. If it doesn't, you will have a hard time building your small business on it. The invention must be possible to build and be workable to be granted a patent. You have to be able to show the examiner that the invention will operate as you say it will.

The invention must be novel. It must be different than all other things that have been previously made or described anywhere else in the world (called *prior art*). Meeting this test can be a difficult and confusing one to everyone involved.

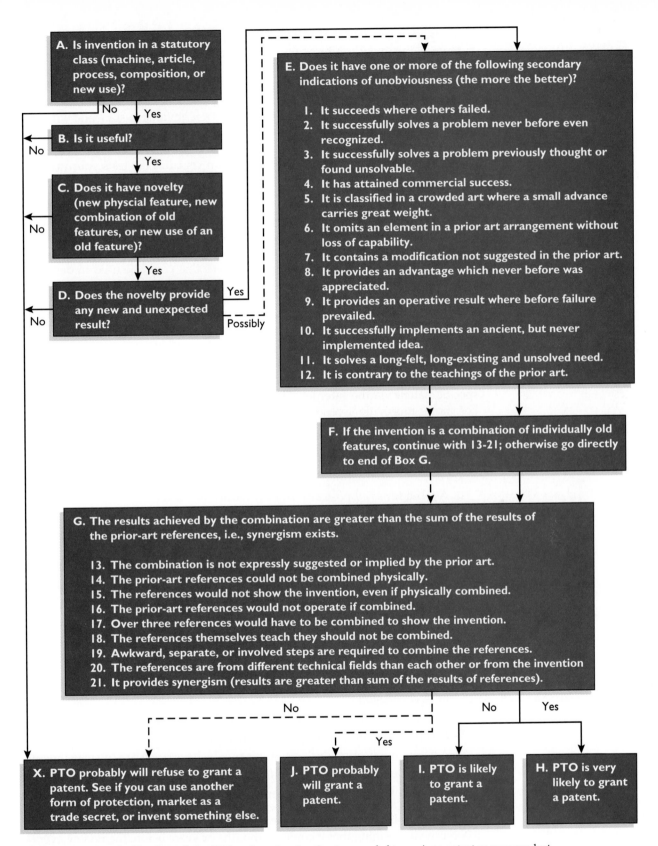

FIGURE 19-2 **How Do You Get a Patent?** Flowchart showing the steps needed to receive a patent on your product.

Reprinted with permission from Patent It Yourself *by David Pressman. © 1995. Published by Nolo Press, Berkeley, CA. Available in bookstores or by calling 1-800-992-6656.*

Three types of novelty that meet this requirement are those created by physical difference, by a new combination of existing parts, or by the invention of a new use.

The invention must be unobvious. While this rule is also difficult to understand, it is an important one. It means that the difference between your invention and other developments (or prior art) must be not obvious to someone with common knowledge in that field. The novelty of your invention needs to produce new or unexpected results.

The flowchart in Figure 19-2 can help you visualize the tests your invention must pass to get a patent.

Patent Searches. Before you file a patent application, you should conduct a patent search to save time and money later. You can conduct a search yourself, or hire a patent agent or patent attorney. What you are searching for is existing patents for inventions that are or may be similar to yours.

Start by coming up with several *key words* that could be used in describing your invention. These key words will be run through the primary patent reference publication at the Patent and Trademark Office in Arlington, Virginia, *The Index to the U.S. Patent Classification*. The CD-ROM version of the index greatly speeds this process. If you can't go to the PTO, you can search a Patent Depository Library. In these libraries, you can use the *Official Gazette of the U.S. Patent & Trademark Office*.

Recent developments allow you to conduct a patent search by subject or by specific patent via the Internet. This is done through the Shadow Patent Office. For more information, send an e-mail message to spo_patent@spo.eds.com or visit the PTO homepage at http://pioneer.uspto.gov through the Internet.

Patent Application. When submitting your patent application, you should include:

1. A self-addressed postcard to show receipt of packet.
2. Payment of filing fee.
3. A letter of transmittal.
4. Drawings of your invention.
5. Specification including:
    a. Title or name of your invention
    b. Cross-reference of similar inventions
    c. Description of the field of your invention
    d. Prior art
    e. Features and advantages of your invention
    f. Drawing descriptions
    g. Description of how your invention works
    h. A conclusion
6. The claim—patent details which define the scope of your invention.
7. An abstract—summarizing the whole project.
8. A patent application declaration form, which says you are the true inventor.
9. A statement that you have not transferred patent ownership to anyone else.
10. An information disclosure statement and a list of prior art.[16]

Your application will be reviewed by a PTO examiner in the order in which it is received, meaning that it could be months or years before the review ever be-

R eality Check

Keeping a Trademark in Shape

When you've got a good thing, you want to keep it. That's why it's particularly important for small business owners to register ideas and products as soon as possible and to monitor for any misuse of your trademark. Designer Nancy Ganz introduced the Hipslip™ in 1988. It's a product she created from nylon and Du Pont's Lycra to provide extra "support" for the body-hugging garments that she designed. Today her Manhattan-based company Bodyslimmers™ By Nancy Ganz ships more than 90,000 Hipslips a month and has annual sales of nearly $10 million.

Ganz recognized that new ideas and products are quickly imitated, so she registered Hipslip with the U.S. Patent and Trademark Office as soon as she coined the name. In addition, she feels that by keeping her company's name unique, she's been better able to protect her rights. For instance, instead of calling her company Bodyslimmers, which she felt was too generic, Ganz added her name and thus achieved both legal protection and added identity.

Ganz is also vigilant in her monitoring of any misuse of her registered trademark. How does she keep up? Ganz chose to hire a press-clipping service to track references to her company or products, including those in advertisements. This nationwide search costs her about $200 a month plus about $1.50 per clipping. And, as Ganz agrees, protecting your rights also means sometimes confronting the "bad guys."

When a problem does arise, Ganz has her lawyer send the offending party a letter notifying them of her trademark and position in the industry. In extreme instances, Ganz has had to take legal action to recover some of the proceeds that offenders have received using her trademarked name. Finally, Ganz feels it's important to get your name out and let people see it frequently. For instance, she often takes out full-page ads in trade publications. All of these actions help Nancy Ganz "protect" her good name.

Source: Nancy Ganz, "Protecting Your Good Name," Nation's Business (September 1995), p. 6.

gins. The examination process can take from one to three or more years with revisions and amendments.

If your patent is approved, you will be notified and a copy of the application will be sent to the U.S. Government Printing Office.

Copyrights

A **copyright** is the protection of literary, musical, or artistic works. Copyright laws protect the *expression* of ideas, not the ideas themselves. This is because lawmakers want to encourage the dissemination of ideas while protecting the rights of the original owner.

The length of copyright protection is the life of the author plus 50 years. If your corporation is the owner of a book's copyright, it will continue as owner for 75 years after the first publication, or 100 years after creation.

You don't have to register your work to receive copyright protection, but it does strengthen your rights to do so. If registered, you don't have to prove actual damages to collect up to $500,000. The act of creating the work begins the

copyright A form of protection for intellectual property provided to the creator of a literary, musical, or artistic work for a period of the creator's life plus fifty years.

copyright protection, whether or not it is published. If you do choose to register your work, all you need to do is complete the proper forms and send in the fees to the Copyright Office along with a copy of your work.

Many small businesses are involved in creating computer software. Should they seek a patent or a copyright for their creation? Actually, software could qualify for either or both, so which would be better? A patented computer program is difficult for competitors to simulate or design around and lasts for 17 years, but consider the disadvantages. Patents can be expensive, take a lot of work applying for and searching, and can take several years to obtain. Windows of opportunity open and shut quickly in the software market. Your software may be obsolete before a patent can even be granted.

Copyrighting software is quick and inexpensive but doesn't provide the offensive punch of a patent. You can't copyright what a program does, only the specific way it is written. So competing small business programmers only need to write the program for their software in a different manner to avoid copyright infringement.

So, what's the answer for "protecting" your software? Frankly, neither patents nor copyrights do a thorough job. Protecting intellectual property for quickly changing industries and global markets is a serious problem small businesses and regulators will have to face in the near future.

Trademarks

A **brand** is a name, term, symbol, design, or combination of these elements that clearly identifies and differentiates your products from those of your competitors. A **trademark** is a registered and protected brand. Therefore, all trademarks are brands, but not all brands are trademarks. A trademark can include a graphic as well as a brand name. For example, not only is the *Coke* name protected, but also the style of script writing make it a trademark.

Trademark rights continue as long as you continue to use the trademark. This is an advantage over patents or copyrights. Trademarks are useful because they provide brand recognition for your product and are a good way to create an image in your customer's mind.

Since there are over a million trademarks in use in the United States, how do you find one that isn't already taken? As with the patent search, you can either do the search yourself or hire someone to do it for you. The problem gets even more complicated since a 1989 regulation change makes it possible to reserve a trademark before it is even put into use.

Several businesses specialize in trademark searches of registered and unregistered marks. They include Trademark Service Corporation, 747 Third Avenue, New York, NY 10017 (212) 421-5730; Thompson & Thompson, 500 Victory Road, North Quincy, MA 02171-2126 (800) 692-8833; and Compu-Mark U.S., 1333 F Street NW, Washington, DC 20004 (800) 421-7881. You can conduct a search yourself with *The Trademark Register of the U.S.*, available in many libraries, or a similar directory. CD-ROM versions of these directories speed the process considerably.

You can file for a trademark with the Patent and Trademark Office, Washington, DC 20231 with an application and a fee that was $245 in 1996. You can also register your trademark in your state with the secretary of state at your state capitol.

Your trademark is worthless (and actually invalid) if you don't use it. Before your product is registered, use the symbol ™, and after it is registered use ®.

trademark A form of protection for intellectual property provided to the owner of a brand name or symbol.

Global Small Business

Complications associated with protecting intellectual property in global markets are bound to arise since there is no single body of international copyright law. But what protection *does* a small business person have over intellectual property when expanding into global markets? Through a series of international treaties, almost all nations—the former Soviet Union countries and China are the major exceptions—have agreed to give each other's citizens the same copyright protection given to their own citizens. So if you take the apropriate procedural steps, your copyright will be protected in virtually every global market.

The two most important and overlapping copyright treaties are the Berne Convention and the Universal Copyright Convention (U.C.C.). International copyright protection for works by U.S. citizens and permanent residents largely depends on the rights granted by these two international treaties.

The Berne Convention is the most important international copyright treaty, affording the highest standards of protection. Every country that has signed the Berne Convention (which the United States did in 1989) must give citizens or permanent residents of other Berne countries at least the same copyright protection it gives its own nationals. Under the Berne Convention, no formalities such as notice and registration may be required for basic copyright protection. However, some countries will provide greater copyright protection if a copyright is registered or carries a particular type of notice. Other countries have certain procedural requirements that must be followed. It's important for the small business person to determine what these requirements are for each country in which he hopes to do business—and to follow them in order to protect his intellectual property rights.

The United States joined the Universal Copyright Convention (U.C.C.) on September 16, 1995. The U.C.C. is very similar to the Berne Convention except that it allows member countries to establish and require some formalities. (When a country has signed both the Berne Convention and the U.C.C., the Berne Convention has priority over the U.C.C.) Again, it's important that a small business person determine the copyright protection formalities that are required in each country.

What happens if you find that your intellectual property is being used improperly and illegally? It's important to consult with an experienced U.S. copyright attorney to help you through the maze of how, when, and if to file a lawsuit. Although the United States has urged other foreign governments to take copyright infringement seriously, some countries still do not.

One of the newest challenges in the protection of intellectual property concerns the uncharted legal territories of cyberspace. The uncertainties and rapidly changing nature of linked global computer networks and the content that floats throughout these networks are creating their own sets of legal issues that are still being discussed and developed. If electronic publishing and digital information is what your small business does, be sure to get good legal help to protect your hard-earned intellectual property. *Sources: Stephen Fishman,* The Copyright Handbook, *2nd ed. Berkeley, CA: Nolo Press, 1994), pp. 13/2–13/7; Yogesh Malhotra, "Controlling Copyright Infringements of Intellectual Property: The Case of Computer Software—Part One,"* Journal of Systems Management *(June 1994), pp. 32–35; Samuel Rabino and Elizabeth Enayati, "Intellectual Property: The Double-Edged Sword,"* Long Range Planning *(October 1995), pp. 22–31; "Forcing the Issue on Intellectual Piracy: An Editorial of the Times,"* Los Angeles Times, *October 11, 1995, p. B10; Debra Gersh Hernandez, "Congress Considers Updating Copyright Law to Cover Online Information,"* Editor & Publisher, *November 25, 1995, p. 31; and James G. Kimball, "What's Yours Could Be Mine,"* Advertising Age, *November 27, 1995, p. 32.*

Global Protection

Protecting intellectual property in other countries is difficult. Your patent, copyright, or trademark protection in the United States does not apply in most foreign markets. You need separate protection in each country so you must check regulations and filing procedures for each market you intend to enter. Timing is critical. You should file before entering a foreign market or you may lose the right to do so later.

Summary

◼ Laws and regulations that affect small business.

Laws and regulations exist to protect competition, consumers, people in the workplace, intellectual property, to allow bankruptcy, and to establish contracts. Specific laws that owners of small businesses should know include the Equal Pay Act, the Civil Rights Acts of 1964 and 1991, the Immigration Reform and Control Act, the American with Disabilities Act, the Family and Medical Leave Act, and the Occupational Safety and Health Act.

◼ Types of bankruptcy.

The U.S. Bankruptcy Code is made up of nine chapters, only three of which apply to many small businesses (Chapters 7, 11, and 13). Chapter 7 uses *liquidation*, meaning that the business ceases to exist in order to provide the debtor with a fresh start. Liquidation involves selling all of the business assets and nonexempt personal assets to distribute the proceeds among creditors. Chapters 11 and 13 allow the business owner to file a plan with the court that offers protection from creditors until the debt is satisfied.

◼ The elements of a contract.

For a contract to be legally binding, it must be intended to accomplish a legal purpose. Both parties must come to an agreement including a legitimate offer and a legitimate acceptance. Consideration, or something of value, must be exchanged. Finally, all parties must have the capacity to enter a binding contract, meaning that they must not be underage, intoxicated, or of diminished mental ability.

◼ Ways to protect intellectual property.

Patents, copyrights, and trademarks are legal ways to protect intellectual property. A patent grants an inventor the exclusive right to make, use, and sell an invention for a period of 17 years. A copyright provides legal protection against infringement of an author's literary, musical, or artistic works. Copyrights usually last for the author's life plus 50 years. A trademark is a legally protected name, term, symbol, design, or combination of these elements used to identify products or companies. Trademarks last for as long as they are in use.

Questions for Review and Discussion

1. Will the antitrust laws established in the late 1800s and early 1900s still be pertinent in the 21st century? Why or why not?
2. What does the Federal Trade Commission do to protect consumers?
3. What rights does owning a patent protect? How do you get this protection?

4. What test must an invention pass in order to receive a patent?

5. What is the difference between a copyright and a trademark? between a trademark and a brand?

6. Name and explain the four elements that a contract must have to be valid.

7. List and briefly explain the laws that protect people in the workplace.

8. How are liquidation and reorganization used as different approaches to bankruptcy? What chapters of bankruptcy law accomplish these objectives?

9. What licenses does the owner of a small business need in order to comply with regulations?

10. What risk does an inventor assume when filing for a patent for an invention?

Critical Incident

The creativity of the human mind is often quite amazing. Read through the descriptions of the following entrepreneurial ideas, pick one that sounds interesting, and then answer the questions.

Harasser Flasher. This battery-operated pin enables wearers to "avoid harrassment with the touch of a button." The red light and siren can be used against offensive come-ons. The yellow light can signal "you're pushing the limits." And the green light can reinforce acceptable actions and speech.

Alan's X-Tenda Fork. This fork telescopes from standard size to 23 inches so that users can sample food of tablemates.

File-A-Way Desk Bed. This 36-inch by 72-inch desk quickly converts to a standard-sized double bed. How's that for your home office?

Automatic Umpire. This high-tech homeplate calls its own balls and strikes with the aid of embedded sensors and voice chips. Programmed phrases include: "Ball," "Strike," "Take Your Base," and, of course, "You're Out." *Source for ideas:* Springfield News Leader, *December 31, 1995, p. 4E.*

Questions

1. Draft a mock specification sheet (item #5 of Patent Application, p. 522) for the patent application. Try to make your drawing as coherent and realistic as possible.

2. Those who have selected the same "gadget" are to divide into teams of six. Two students are to compose Items #6 and #7 of Patent Application, p. 522, each working on one item individually. The remaining four students are to review the specifications done by each member and select the best submission. Be prepared to make a presentation of your best submission in front of the class.

Take it to the Net

We invite you to visit the Hatten page on the Prentice Hall Web site at: http://www.prenhall.com/~hattensb for this chapter's World Wide Web exercise.

Appendix A

Complete Sample Business Plans

The following business plans were written by undergraduate business students at Mesa State College in Grand Junction, Colorado, as part of a class in small business management. These plans (one for a service business, one for a retail business) are about fictitious (at least for now) businesses and are included to serve as examples of structure, content, and format for your business plan.

Business Plan 1: Western Slope Detailing

Executive Summary

A really great talent finds its happiness in execution.
—Johann Wolfgang von Goethe

Western Slope Detailing (WSD) is a business partnership that combines the talents of Michael Hyatt and Shawn Serviss. In hopes of soon utilizing these talents, the partners have created a comprehensive business plan to invite a prospective investor to assist Western Slope Detailing in raising the needed capital of $6,500 to begin the operations of an automotive detailing facility.

The Company

Western Slope Detailing is a company that provides a variety of detailing services for cars, trucks, and show vehicles. Detailing is a service that cleans, beautifies, and protects one's automotive investment. In addition to the usual detailing services, WSD will provide special services such as hand waxing and chassis detailing. By focusing on quality and striving for perfection, Western Slope Detailing will establish itself as the most prestigious and unique detailer in Grand Junction, Colorado. To make services easily accessible, the company will provide customer vehicle pick-up and delivery services.

A market analysis has identified three target market segments which combine to make a total base of over 13,000 customers. The analysis shows that Grand Junction can support the type of services that WSD will offer. We are confident that this type of upscale service is needed in the Grand Junction area and is one that people are willing to pay a premium price to receive.

The Plan

The partners of Western Slope Detailing have made a commitment to invest a total of $9,000 into this business venture. As the financial projections indicate, an additional investment of $6,500 is required to initiate operations. These funds will be committed to the startup costs, which include a work facility, equipment, and supplies.

The Partners

Western Slope Detailing is the product of unique and complementary skills and talents forged into a partnership. Mr. Hyatt brings with him extensive automotive detailing knowledge coupled with a degree in business management. In addition, he has a broad work history in management positions as well as in the automotive industry. On the other hand, Mr. Serviss has developed talents in the area of marketing and recently received his B.B.A. in Marketing. He also has experience in the detailing industry. As a team, Mr. Hyatt and Mr. Serviss have the knowledge and skills necessary to satisfy a demanding clientele and operate a successful detailing shop.

Conclusion

Considerable thought, planning, and time have gone into the concept, image, and organization of Western Slope Detailing. We believe that all the necessary elements are present to establish a successful business. There is a market for our services, the partners are experienced and motivated, and the business venture is definitely viable. Finally, Western Slope Detailing is projected to generate a positive cash flow every month. Projections also show a profit from the first year of operations forward.

Table of Contents

Concept History and Background

Idea History

The conception for Western Slope Detailing started as a brainstorm endeavor on how to earn a few extra dollars to supplement my income. After some deliberation, I decided that auto detailing was a service that I was capable of providing, and one that I would enjoy doing. I spent the next several weeks talking to friends and family about starting my own company. To my surprise there was much support, encouragement, and enthusiasm for my idea. I began talking to other companies that might be able to use my services. Within days, I was working, and my new company was in business.

Description of Services

The purpose of Western Slope Detailing is to provide an auto detailing service that is the best available in the Grand Valley. Typically, the customer's car is picked up and returned within four to eight hours. The following services are available:

- Hand wash exterior
- Hand wax or low-speed buff exterior
- Treat vinyl top
- Clean and detail wheels/tires
- Clean and detail undercarriage/chassis
- Clean and detail engine
- Vacuum interior and trunk
- Clean interior and windows
- Treat vinyl, rubber, leather, and plastic
- Re-dye carpet, dash, and interior panels
- Touch-up rock chips

Summary of Partners' Experiences

Michael Hyatt

Education: Bachelor of Business Administration with an emphasis in management
Associate of Applied Science in Machining Technology
Both degrees from Mesa State College

Work Experience: 1 year managing detail business
3 years of retail management
5 years in auto parts sales
2 years as auto mechanic
Previous Employment: Billing's Auto
Checker Auto
Champion Auto
Auto Zone
AAA Auto
B.U. Daughters
Gart Sports
Michael Garman Gallery
Other Experience: 10 years of maintaining and restoring personal car collection

Shawn Serviss

Education: Bachelor of Business Administration with an emphasis in marketing
Degree from Mesa State College
Work Experience: 3 years in auto detailing
2 years as owner/manager of auto dealership
3 years in auto parts sales
5 years buying/selling cars at auction
Previous Employment: Frank Dunn Co.
Western Slope Auto
West Star Aviation
Other Experience: 13 years of interest and exposure to the automotive industry

Goals and Objectives

Year 1

The company will have completed the construction of a two-bay facility. The facility will have all the necessary equipment and supplies that are needed to operate efficiently. Company policies and efficient operating systems will be determined and implemented. Estimated net income is $18,000.

Year 3

The company will be running at full capacity of the two-bay facility. The company will have two employees. A healthy customer base will be established. Estimated net income is $32,000.

Year 5

The company will be ready for relocation to a larger facility. An operations manager will be hired and trained, as well as two more employees. This will allow the partners to focus more on promotions and customer relations. Estimated net income is $60,000.

Year 10

The company will be viewed by the industry as a stable, strong, and profitable company. The partners will then decide whether to diversify, expand, open a new location, or sell the company for a substantial profit.

Marketing Plan

Western Slope Detailing's market strategy is to promote the fact that our services will be considered the best within the automotive detailing industry. The overall marketing plan for our services is based on the following fundamentals:

- Promote our services as prestigious and as the "ultimate in detailing." This concept will show in our company attitude as well as in our advertisements.

- Focus on providing the highest-quality service possible. Our commitment to quality is what will set us apart from the competition.

- Make it as convenient as possible for our customers to receive our services. We will offer free pick-up and delivery.

- Provide services that are not available elsewhere. We will be the only detail shop equipped to provide specialized services for show cars.

- Prove that customer satisfaction is our goal. It is our belief that the customer comes first.

- Educate our customers about the fact that we use only the finest products available. We use only top-quality cleaners, wax, and conditioners.

- Convey the concept to customers that our detailing is not just another "expense" of maintaining their vehicles. It is a service offered to help "protect" their investment.

- Establish Western Slope Detailing as the "best" automotive detailer in the Grand Valley of Mesa County. We are determined to outperform the competition and will set a new standard for automotive detailing.

- Plan on capturing at least 15 percent of the general detailing market and 40 percent of the show car detailing market within five years.

Consumers

There are three types of customers that Western Slope Detailing will focus on as primary market segments. The first type of customer is a newer vehicle owner with an annual income above $40,000. The average vehicle value will be above $25,000. The second market segment is the show car owner. The typical situation will be that the owners do not have time to detail their vehicles before a car show. Income and vehicle value will vary greatly for these customers. The third type of customer is the sport utility vehicle owner who is usually in the upper middle class. These customers usually have children and use the vehicle for family transportation.

Demographics

Group 1:

Customer's age: 30–75 years old

Customer's income: $45,000 and up

Customer's vehicle: Newer luxury and sports cars
Customer's family: Single, married, children or not

Group 2:

Customer's age: 20–60 years old

Customer's income: $25,000 and up

Customer's vehicle: Show car

Customer's family: Single, married, children or not

Group 3:

Customer's age: 25–45

Customer's income: $30,000 and up

Customer's vehicle: Sport utility and minivans

Customer's family: Married with children

Demand

As our society becomes busier, there is less time for people to spend on nonessential items. People are now focusing more on work, family, and leisure. Naturally, this creates a demand for automotive detailing. The following statistics reflect the growing demand for automotive detailing.

MESA COUNTY STATISTICS

Total population	105,000				
Percent within WSD's age range	49.90%				
Population within WSD's age range	52,395				
Age group	25–34	35–44	45–54	55–64	Totals
Percent of county population	14.90%	15.70%	10.20%	9.10%	49.90%
Number of population	15,645	16,485	10,710	9,555	52,395
Percent within WSD's income range	36.60%				
Population within income range	38,430				
Income group ($1,000)	25–34	35–49	50–74	75+	Totals
Percent of county population	14.90%	11.70%	6.40%	3.60%	
Numbers in population	15,645	12,285	6,720	3,780	38,430
Projected vehicle registrations	130,000				

Customer base	Group 1	Group 2	Group 3	Total
	6,000	600	7,000	13,600

We believe that a total customer base of 130,000 will be more than sufficient to generate the necessary revenue. We anticipate that our customer base will grow in proportion with the 1.2 percent population growth. In addition, the figures that were calculated are considered conservative.

Competitive Analysis

The following chart shows our local competitors and makes a comparison in different key areas:

NAME	PRICE (H,M,L)	LOCATION (B,S,W)	FACILITY (B,S,W)	TYPE (D,I)	RANK (1–9)
Auto Prep	H	B	S	D	1
Auto Works	M	B	S	D	2
Crest Auto	M	B	S	D	3
Pro Clean	M	B	S	D	4
Cindy's Detailing	M	B	S	D	5
Fine Line	M	B	S	D	6
Dave's Car Wash	L	B	W	I	7
Cindy's Car Wash	L	B	W	I	8
Buggy Bath	L	B	W	I	9

H, M, L = high, medium, low   B, S, W = better, same, worse   D, I = direct, indirect

Note: All competitors listed are located in Grand Junction.

Competitors that have Failed

T & L Auto has failed in the last year. Although the cause of this failure is not known for certain, it is rumored that it was due to poor management. There have been several individuals that have attempted to cater strictly to used car dealerships. In general these businesses fail within six months. The reasons for these failures were due to poor management and a highly fluctuating flow of business. Gary's Wash and Wax is an example of this type of failure.

Competition Strengths

Many of our competitors are well-established detailers and many have been active in the Grand Valley area for many years. Auto Prep, which has been in business for over 15 years, is an example of this.

Some competitors have excellent locations. This is essential in attracting the walk-in customer. Cindy's Car Wash is one of these competitors that bases its business on the walk-in customers. Cindy's is strategically located on North Avenue.

A few of our competitors are equipped to handle volume. This creates convenience for the customer through shorter waiting times. One example is Dave's, which has the facilities to handle volume and has been able to provide this type of quick service.

Competition Weaknesses

Because most of our competitors focus on volume, it is impossible for them to focus on small details while providing their service. Precision detailing is time-consuming and the competition is unwilling to take the extra steps necessary to ensure perfection. In addition, it appears that none of our competitors are currently offering any special services to show car customers. This market segment has been almost ignored by our competition.

Observations and Conclusions

Our number-one competitor is Auto Prep. Its advertisements claim that it is the only professional detail shop in the area. Western Slope Detailing will soon make it impossible for Auto Prep to make that claim. Our competitor's greatest strength is that it is established with a large clientele. Soon we will share this strength with our competition. Mediocre service is our competition's greatest weakness. We plan on taking advantage of this weakness by providing superior service.

Western Slope Detailing Strengths and Weaknesses

Strengths

Western Slope Detailing has several distinct advantages over the competition. First, because our commitment is to detail and not to volume, we are able to provide a better-quality service than our competition. We are convinced that our focus on high-quality service will give us our greatest edge on the competition.

Second, our facility will be equipped to provide services that the competition is not able to offer. Our facility will have a pit which will allow access to the underside of vehicles. This asset will enable us to detail the chassis on show cars.

Third, we will be the only detailing business located in Grand Junction. We consider this location both a strength and a weakness. As a strength, this location will make our service convenient for customers living on the east side of the Grand Valley. The key to this strength is increasing the public's awareness of our location.

Weaknesses

The management of Western Slope Detailing has also recognized some weaknesses. As stated, our location also represents a weakness. We are not located in a business district. This means that our walk-in business will be minimal. We plan to overcome this weakness by emphasizing our pick-up and delivery service. In addition, we are not building our business around the walk-in customer. We anticipate less than 5 percent of our customers will be considered walk-in business.

Finally, because our facility will not be designed for volume, a waiting list may result, which will discourage some customers. However, we believe that our service will be so outstanding that our customers will discover that it is worth waiting for.

Geographic Market

The customer base for Western Slope Detailing will be drawn from across the Grand Valley of Mesa County. As we become established and our reputation increases, our aim is to draw customers from other areas of the Western Slope. We believe that word of mouth will continue to bring us customers from an ever increasing geographical area.

Pricing Policy

Our pricing will be reflective of our superior service. Because we plan to provide service that our competition cannot, our prices will be on the high end of the scale in this industry.

Customers can expect to pay between $100 to $150 to have their newer vehicles completely detailed. A sport utility/minivan detail usually will cost between $125 to $175. Show car details will range from $150 to $250. Other specialized services will also be available ranging from $50 to $100.

We plan to review our pricing every six months. The volume of business will help to determine whether we will raise or lower our prices. We will also utilize customer surveys to help us obtain a price-to-service comparison.

Advertising and Promotions

Western Slope Detailing recognizes that the key to success is a reputation for superior service. It is essential that the public is aware of the services that we provide. In this industry, the best way to establish a reputation and a strong customer base is through word of mouth. However, there are other approaches that may prove helpful in establishing a clientele.

Objectives

- Establish Western Slope Detailing as the best detail shop in the area.
- Increase the public's awareness of the unique services offered by Western Slope Detailing.
- Maximize our promotion budget dollars by reaching as much of the target market as possible. Because our advertising budget is very limited, we will reach as many potential customers as possible per dollar spent.

Promotions

We will set up a booth at local car shows to promote our services to show car owners. In addition, we will send fliers to car club representatives.

Phone Directory

An ad in the local Yellow Pages will be placed to target newer car customers.

Newspaper Service Directory

We will place ads in *Thrifty Nickel* and *Shopping News* for the purpose of targeting both newer car customers and show car customers.

Legal Requirements

The principals of Western Slope Detailing will select a law firm to be retained to serve as legal counsel for all contracts, agreements, and other legal concerns. This law firm will also represent Western Slope Detailing in the event of a suit brought by or against Western Slope Detailing.

Contracts

It may become necessary to sign certain agreements and contracts during the course of business. These contracts may include, but are not limited to, a partnership agreement, supplier contracts, and agreements for professional services. These will be reviewed and accepted on an individual basis. As expressed in the partnership agreement, the signatures of both partners will be required for a contract to be agreed to by Western Slope Detailing.

Insurance

Due to the nature of today's litigious climate, it is very important that Western Slope Detailing carry ample insurance coverage. Liability coverage will be carried to cover damage that might occur to the personal property of customers. The insurance policy will also cover our workmanship.

Form of Ownership

The principals of Western Slope Detailing have chosen a partnership as the form of ownership. The reason that this form of ownership was chosen is because it is the best way to pool the talents and capital of the principals. Second, the partnership can be quickly set up without many of the legal procedures involved in creating a corporation. The following agreement is subject to change, pending legal advise from an attorney.

Partnership Agreement

THIS AGREEMENT is made by and between Michael Hyatt ("Hyatt") and Shawn Serviss ("Serviss") and Western Slope Detailing ("WSD") to be effective as of the effective date, as herein defined. All parties hereto are sometimes referred to herein collectively as "partners" and individually as "partner." WSD is sometimes referred to herein as the "Corporate Partner."

WITNESSETH:

WHEREAS, the Partners desire to form a Colorado general partnership for the purpose of pursuing the establishment of an Automotive Detailing Business in Grand Junction, CO, all pursuant to the terms and conditions hereinafter set forth,

NOW THEREFORE, in consideration of the mutual promises made and for other good and valuable consideration the receipt of which is hereby acknowledged, the parties agree as follows:

1. *Name, Principal Office, Purchase and Terms of the Partnership.*
   A. *Partnership Name.* The partnership shall operate under the name of Western Slope Detailing Partnership (the "partnership"), which shall be a Colorado general partnership, and except as otherwise provided for herein, shall operate and be governed in accordance with the Uniform Partnership Act of Colorado, as amended from time to time.
   B. *Principal Office.* The principal office of the Partnership shall be 226 3rd St., Grand Junction, CO, with such other places of business as may be agreed upon by the Partners from time to time.
   C. *Purpose.* The purpose of the Partnership shall be to pursue the establishment of an automotive detailing business (the "Shop") to be located in Grand Junction, CO, and to be operated by one or more entities to be subsequently formed, which may include an S corporation and/or a Colorado Limited Partnership (such affiliated operating entity(s) to be hereinafter referred to collectively as the "Venture"). Specifically, the Partnership shall exist for the purpose of carrying out the following initial steps in organizing the Venture and establishing the Shop, some of which may have already been completed by the Managing Partners (through WSD, which is a Colorado company, wholly owned by them) at the time of the Effective Date of this Agreement:
      (1) WSD shall obtain a binding commitment from Michael Hyatt who owns a desirable parcel of Real Property (the "Site") upon which to locate the Shop.
      (2) Upon securing a commitment concerning the Site, the partnership shall organize the Venture. Unless otherwise determined by a unanimous vote of the partners, the Venture shall be organized as a Colorado Partnership.
      (3) In the event that the above steps are not successfully completed, as determined by a Unanimous Vote of the partners, the Partnership shall be dissolved and liquidated in the manner hereinafter prescribed. The Partnership shall also be permitted to conduct such other business of lawful nature as the Partners may from time to time agree.
   D. *Term of the Partnership.* The partnership shall continue its existence unless terminated as hereinafter provided; and from the date hereof shall operate pursuant to the terms and conditions hereof.
2. *Initial Partnership Capital.* The Partners shall initially have no interest in the Capital of the Partnership but shall agree, in exchange for their interest in the Partnership, to contribute to the Partnership, immediately prior to the organization of the Venture, all of their interest in and to WSD, which owns proprietary interest in the service mark "Ultimate in Detailing"; the Building Design for the Shop; and contracts and/or preliminary agreements in principle which have already been or which are in the process of being entered into with such as vendors of equipment and supplies who have given binding price quotes on supplies and equipment which will be needed to outfit the Shop and conduct initial operations at the Shop.
3. *Capital Accounts.* The initial capital accounts of each Partner shall be equal to the amount of his initial contribution to the Capital of the Partnership. The capital accounts of each Partner shall be adjusted at the end of each month to account for contributions to and distribution from the Capital of the Partnership occurring during each month and also for the allocation of Partnership profits and losses experienced during such month.

4. *Division of Profits or Losses.* The net profits and net losses of the Partnership shall be credited and/or charged to the capital accounts of the Partners at the end of each month in the same ratio which the capital account of each Partner at the beginning of such month bears to the total Capital of the Partnership at such time.

5. *Salaries to Partners.* No salary shall be paid to any Partner for his services to the Partnership.

6. *Distributions.* When agreed upon by both Partners, distributions shall be made to the Partners from the available funds of the Partnership in proportion to each Partner's interest in Profits and Losses of the Partnership, to the extent that such distributions are made from accumulated and undistributed capitalized profits of the Partnership, and in proportion to each Partner's interest in the Capital of the Partnership, to the extent that such distributions are made following the distribution of all accumulated profits of the Partnership.

7. *Accounting Method.* The Partnership shall keep its accounting records and shall report its income for income tax purposes on the cash basis of accounting. The accounting for Partnership purposes shall be in accordance with generally accepted accounting principles. The Partnership shall keep its records and file its tax returns on a calendar-year basis.

8. *Books of the Partnership.* The Partnership's books shall be maintained at the principal place of business of the Partnership, and each Partner shall at all reasonable times have access thereto.

9. *Administrative Provisions.*
   A. *Managing Partners.* The management and conduct of the business of the Partnership shall be vested in the Partners, who shall have an equal voice in the management of all affairs of the Partnership except as otherwise stated herein. Such fact notwithstanding, the signature of both Partners shall be necessary in order to draw checks upon the bank accounts of the Partnership. Both of the Partners shall be in charge of handling the Partnership books; tax returns; and in general, communicating any information concerning the Partnership business to the employees. Provided, however, that in the event of any deadlock between the Partners, either Partner shall submit the matter to a vote of all the Partners and Employees. Furthermore, the Partners shall be entitled to vote upon any decision to initiate or modify step 3 in the organization of the Venture as set forth in Section 1C above. If a Partner becomes unwilling or unable, by reason of permanent mental or physical disability to carry out his duties in the management of the Partnership, a successor Partner will not be elected and the Partnership shall then become a Sole Proprietorship.

   B. *Voting of the Partners and Employees.* On all matters to be decided by a vote of the Partners and Employees, each Partner and Employee shall be entitled to cast the following number of votes:

Partner	No. of Votes
WSD	0
Hyatt	45
Serviss	35
Employees	A total of 20 votes. Each employee shall receive a proportionate share of the 20 votes, corresponding to his or her salary, as a percent of the Total Employee Salary Expense.

   Any reference in this Agreement to a "majority vote" shall mean the majority of those votes entitled to be cast as prescribed above. All matters to be decided by a vote shall be decided by a majority vote as thus defined, unless otherwise specifically provided in this Agreement.

   C. *Authority.* All deeds, notes, mortgages, security agreements, leases, assignments, options, contracts to sell or purchase real property, or any encumbrances shall be signed by both Partners. No Partner shall, on the behalf of the Partnership, borrow or lend money; or make, deliver, accept, or endorse any commercial paper; or execute any mortgage, security agreement, bond, or lease; or purchase or contract to purchase any property for the Partnership; or sell or contract to sell any property for the Partnership; or bind the Partnership for the payment of any amount without the consent of the Partners.

D. *Conflicts of Interest.* It is expressly understood that the Partners may engage in any other business, investment, or profession, including the ownership of, or investment in, real estate and the operation and management of real estate, and neither the Partnership nor the remaining Partner shall have any rights in or to said business, professions, or investments, or the income or profits derived therefrom.

The Partners may employ, on behalf of the Partnership, such persons, firms, or corporations as they, in their sole judgment, shall deem advisable for the operation and management of the business of the Partners, including such management agents, attorneys, architects, engineers, accountants, appraisers, and experts on such terms and for such terms and for such compensation as they, in their sole judgment, shall determine. The fact that a Partner or a member of his family is directly or indirectly interested in or connected with any person, firm, or corporation employed by the Partnership to render or perform a service or from whom the Partnership may buy merchandise or other property shall not prohibit the Partners from employing such person, firm, or corporation, or from dealing with him, her, or it, and neither the Partnership nor the Partner thereof shall have any rights in or to any income of profits derived therefrom.

E. *Agency Relationship.* Any action taken by either Partner shall be as an agent for the other Partner. Nothing contained herein shall create any fiduciary responsibility of any Partner beyond that of a Partnership under the laws of the State of Colorado. Furthermore, and notwithstanding any law or any other provision contained herein, no Partner including a Partner, shall be responsible to another Partner for mere errors of judgment as to any action taken by him in the management of the Partnership, except in the case of fraud, dishonesty, or the gross abuse of his discretion as a Partner.

F. *Meetings.* Partnership meetings shall be held at least annually and more frequently as determined by the Partners. Meetings may be held by means of telephone, or other electronic or mechanical means of communication agreed to by the Partners.

10. *Retirement, Death of a Partner, and Transferability of a Partnership Interest.*

A. *Transferability of a Partnership Interest.* During his lifetime, no partner shall give, sell, transfer, encumber, or otherwise dispose of any portion or all of his interest in the Partnership, nor shall any interest of a Partner be transferred by operation of the law unless and until such interest shall first be offered to the remaining partner at a price determined under Paragraph C below. If the interest is not purchased by the remaining Partner within 30 days of the receipt of the offer to them, the Partner desiring to give, sell, transfer, or encumber his interest may do so, but the transfer or encumbrance of such interest shall not entitle the recipient of such transfer or encumbrance to be a Partner but shall only effect a transfer of the economic rights of the transferring Partner to the recipient, unless the remaining Partner consents to the admission of such recipient as a Partner.

B. *Death of a Partner.* The surviving Partners shall have an option to purchase all of a Deceased Partner's interest in the Partnership by giving notice of the exercise of such option to the Personal Representative of the estate of the Deceased Partner within 60 days after the qualification and appointment of such Personal Representative. The purchase price for such interest shall be computed in accordance with the provisions of Paragraph C below. Upon the exercise of the option to purchase the stock of a Deceased Partner, if this agreement is funded by insurance and if the purchase price exceeds the proceeds of the insurance, then the proceeds shall be applied against the purchase price and the balance of the purchase price, of all of the purchase price if this agreement is not funded by insurance, shall be paid in ten (10) equal consecutive annual payments beginning twelve (12) months after the date of the Partner's death. Such unpaid balance of the purchase price shall be evidenced by a series of negotiable promissory notes executed by the purchasing Partner to the order of the estate of the Deceased Partner with annual interest at the greater of the Applicable Federal Rate of the prime lending rate of Nations Bank, or its successor in interest, determined as of the date of the Deceased Partner's death. Such notes shall provide for the acceleration of the due date of all unpaid notes in the series on default in the payment of any note of interest thereon and shall provide that upon the default in the payment of interest of principal, all notes shall become due and payable immediately and shall give the purchasing Partner the option of prepayment in whole or in part at any time. Neither the Partnership nor any Partner shall be under any duty to purchase policies of insurance on the lives of any Partner in order to fund the purchase of a Deceased Partner's Interest in the Partnership.

C. *Value of Partnership Interest.* Unless and until changed as hereinafter provided, the value of the interest in the Partnership held by each Partner shall be equal to the Capital Account of such Partner, plus a pro rata share and any unrealized appreciation in the assets of the Partnership plus a pro rata share of any Partnership income which has not been credited to the Capital Account of such Partner less any pro rata share of any Partnership expense which has not been debited to the Capital Account of such Partners, all as of the time that such determination of value is to be made. This method of computing the purchase price has been agreed upon by the Partners as a method which will result in a purchase price representing the fair value of the interest of each partner, including his interest in the goodwill of the Partnership. The date upon which such purchase price is to be determined shall be the last day of the most recent fiscal year of the Partnership, in the case of a Partner desiring to sell his interest, or the date of death, in the case of a Deceased Partner. If because of disagreement concerning the application of the preceding formula, the value of such Partner's interest cannot be agreed upon by the Purchasing Partner and the Selling Partner or the Personal Representative of the Deceased Partner, if applicable, then the price for the Deceased or Selling Partner's interest shall be determined by arbitration as follows: The remaining or surviving Partner and the Selling Partners or the Personal Representative of the Deceased Partner, as applicable, shall each name one arbitrator: if the two arbitrators cannot agree upon a value within 30 days, they shall appoint a third arbitrator and the decision of the majority shall be binding upon all parties. When determining the value of the Company after the death of a Partner, if this agreement is funded by insurance, the value of the insurance proceeds shall not be taken into account.

D. *Life Insurance.* In order to fund the optional purchase under this Agreement upon the death of a Partner, the Partners and the Partnership shall have the right to become applicants, owners, and beneficiaries of life insurance policies on the life of any Partner which, if purchased, shall be identified on Exhibit B attached hereto.

E. *Binding Effect.* The remaining Partners and the Selling Partner or Personal Representative of the Deceased Partner, as applicable, shall make, execute, and deliver any documents necessary to carry out the purchase and sale of a Selling or Deceased Partnership Interest in the Partnership.

11. *Waiver of Right to Court Decree of Dissolution.* The Partners agree that irreparable damage would be done to the goodwill and reputation of the Partnership if any Partner should bring an action in court to dissolve this Partnership. Each party hereby waives and renounces his right to seek a court decree of dissolution or to seek the appointment by a court of a liquidator for the Partnership. Each Partner hereby irrevocably waives any and all rights with respect to the undivided interest of said Partner in any asset of the Partnership.

12. *Arbitration.* If any controversy or claim arising out of this Partnership Agreement cannot be settled by the Partners, or in the event of any deadlock between the Partners regarding any decision involving the business of the Partnership, which controversy, claim, or deadlock cannot be settled in the manner herein provided, such controversy, claim, or deadlock shall be settled by submitting the matter to the majority vote of an arbitration panel consisting of one arbiter selected by the parties on one side of the claim, controversy, or deadlock; one arbiter selected by the parties on the other side of the controversy, claim, or deadlock; and one arbitrator selected by the two arbiters, respectively, selected by the parties.

13. *Tax Elections.* All tax elections for the Partnership shall be made by the Partners.

14. *Dissolution and Liquidation.* In the event the Partnership is dissolved for any reason, the Partnership assets shall be liquidated and the proceeds thereof shall be applied first to satisfy the debts of the Partnership to persons other than the Partners, then

the debts of the Partnership to any Partner. Any remaining balance shall then be allocated and distributed to the partners as follows:

A. The balance of the Partnership assets, if any, shall be distributed to the Partners pro rata based on the respective balances in their capital accounts, provided, however, that if any Partner to another Partner, then such indebtedness shall first be satisfied out of the share that would otherwise be distributed to such indebted Partner before any remaining amounts shall be distributed to such indebted Partner. Anything herein to the contrary notwithstanding, if the Partner(s) decide, by a majority vote of the Partners, to dissolve and liquidate the Partnership, the Partner acting against such dissolution and liquidation shall have a first option to purchase the interest of the Partner voting in favor of such liquidation and dissolution at the price as determined pursuant to the terms of Section 11-C above before such dissolution and liquidation occur. Such option must be exercised within thirty (30) days after the majority vote of the Partner(s) to liquidate the Partnership.

15. *Miscellaneous.*

A. In the event any portion of this Agreement is declared invalid or unenforceable, the remaining portions of this agreement shall remain in full force and effect.

B. This Agreement shall at all times be construed and interpreted in accordance with the laws of the State of Colorado and unless otherwise provided for herein, more particularly, in accordance with the Uniform Partnership Act of Colorado.

C. The necessary grammatical changes required to make provisions of this Partnership Agreement applicable in the plural sense and the necessary changes in the gender of pronouns shall in all instances be assumed.

D. This Agreement may be executed in several counterparts and all so executed shall constitute one Agreement binding on all parties hereto, notwithstanding that all parties have not signed the original or some counterpart.

E. The covenants and agreements contained herein shall extend to and be binding and obligatory upon the Partners hereto, and their respective executors, administrators, heirs, and assigns.

F. This Agreement may be amended only with the written consent of all Partners.

IN WITNESS WHEREOF, The undersigned Partners and those Partners whose signatures are incorporated herein by this reference have executed this Partnership Agreement to be effective the _____ day of _____, _____.

WITNESSES:

_____

_____   _____
                                     Michael Hyatt

_____   _____

_____   Shawn Serviss

Financial Plan/Requirements

Initial Capitalization Plan

The startup costs required by Western Slope Detailing are outlined on the following pages. As indicated by the plan, the required financing to launch Western Slope Detailing into operation is $15,370 (p. 542, top). With the capitalization from the partners of $9,000, the company requires additional financing in the amount of $6,370. The additional financing will come in the form of a bank loan.

Cash Flow Projection

The projected cash flow for Western Slope Detailing is $19,469 in the first year of operation. The business is expected to generate a positive cash flow every month, after initial capitalization. A consolidated summary shows the Statement of Cash Flows (p. 542, bottom). More information can be found in the Monthly Cash Flow Projection (p. 543).

Pro Forma Statement
Western Slope Detailing
Initial Capitalization

Detailing Supplies	$105	Other Costs		
Cleaners, Conditioners, and Wax	$140	Advertising		$1,000
Total Beginning Inventory	$245	Legal Fees		$1,000
		Utilities		$150
Buffer	$150	Telephone		$200
Pressure Washer	$1,500	Computer Equipment		$1,500
Shop Vacuum	$125	Insurance		$300
Air Compressor	$1,400	Miscellaneous Items		$200
Total Equipment	$3,175	Total Other Costs		$4,350
Shop Construction	$7,000	Total Initial Capitalization Cost		$15,370
Office		Less: Principals' Portion		
Equipment	$500	M. Hyatt		$5,000
Supplies	$100	S. Serviss		$4,000
Total Office	$600	Required Financing		$6,370

Western Slope Detailing
Statement of Cash Flows
Year Ended December 1996

Cash flows from operating activities			
Net Income per Income Statement		$18,264	
Add:			
Depreciation	$1,200		
Increase Accounts/Payable	$0	$1,200	
		$19,464	
Less:			
Purchases	$4,445		
Increase in Inventory	$245	$4,690	
Net cash flow from operating activities:			$14,774
Cash flows from financing activities:			
Cash received—Note Payable (Bank)		$6,370	
Net cash from financing			$6,370
Cash flows from investing activities:			
Less:			
Purchase P, P, & E	$10,675	$10,675	
Net cash flows from investing activities:			($10,675)
Increase in cash flow			$10,469
Cash at beginning of the year			$9,000
Cash at the end of the year			$19,469

Western Slope Detailing
Monthly Cash Flow Projection
for 1996

	PRE-STARTUP	JANUARY	FEBRUARY	MARCH	APRIL	MAY	JUNE	JULY	AUGUST	SEPTEMBER	OCTOBER	NOVEMBER	DECEMBER	TOTAL
Cash on Hand		$0.00	$22.00	$1,119.00	$2,406.00	$4,033.00	$5,890.00	$7,782.00	$9,954.00	$12,126.00	$14,163.00	$16,165.00	$18,012.00	
Total Cash receipts	$15,370.00	$1,700.00	$2,000.00	$2,300.00	$2,600.00	$2,900.00	$3,100.00	$3,400.00	$3,400.00	$3,200.00	$3,000.00	$2,800.00	$2,600.00	$33,000.00
Total Cash Available	$15,370.00	$1,700.00	$2,022.00	$3,419.00	$5,006.00	$6,933.00	$8,990.00	$11,182.00	$13,354.00	$15,326.00	$17,163.00	$18,965.00	$20,612.00	$33,000.00
Cash Paid Out														
(a) Detailing Inventory	$245.00	$100.00	$120.00	$140.00	$155.00	$175.00	$185.00	$200.00	$200.00	$190.00	$180.00	$170.00	$155.00	$1,970.00
(b) Equipment	$3,175.00													$0.00
(c) Shop Construction	$7,000.00													$0.00
(d) Office Equipment	$500.00													$0.00
(e) Office Supplies	$100.00	$50.00	$50.00	$50.00	$50.00	$50.00	$50.00	$50.00	$50.00	$50.00	$50.00	$50.00	$50.00	$600.00
(f) Advertising	$1,000.00	$900.00	$100.00	$100.00	$150.00	$200.00	$250.00	$350.00	$350.00	$200.00	$150.00	$100.00	$100.00	$2,950.00
(g) Legal Fees	$1,000.00													$0.00
(h) Utilities	$150.00	$90.00	$95.00	$85.00	$80.00	$80.00	$85.00	$90.00	$90.00	$85.00	$80.00	$95.00	$100.00	$1,055.00
(i) Telephone	$200.00	$50.00	$50.00	$50.00	$50.00	$50.00	$50.00	$50.00	$50.00	$50.00	$50.00	$50.00	$50.00	$600.00
(j) Computer Equipment	$1,500.00													$0.00
(k) Insurance	$300.00	$100.00	$100.00	$100.00	$100.00	$100.00	$100.00	$100.00	$100.00	$100.00	$100.00	$100.00	$100.00	$1,200.00
(l) Accounting Fees				$100.00			$100.00			$100.00			$200.00	$500.00
(m) Loan Payments		$213.00	$213.00	$213.00	$213.00	$213.00	$213.00	$213.00	$213.00	$213.00	$213.00	$213.00	$213.00	$2,556.00
(n) Repair and Maintenance		$100.00	$100.00	$100.00	$100.00	$100.00	$100.00	$100.00	$100.00	$100.00	$100.00	$100.00	$100.00	$1,200.00
(o) Miscellaneous	$200.00	$75.00	$75.00	$75.00	$75.00	$75.00	$75.00	$75.00	$75.00	$75.00	$75.00	$75.00	$75.00	$900.00
Total Cash Paid Out	$15,370.00	$1,678.00	$903.00	$1,013.00	$973.00	$1,043.00	$1,208.00	$1,228.00	$1,228.00	$1,163.00	$998.00	$953.00	$1,143.00	$13,531.00
Cash Position	$0.00	$22.00	$1,119.00	$2,406.00	$4,033.00	$5,890.00	$7,782.00	$9,954.00	$12,126.00	$14,163.00	$16,165.00	$18,012.00	$19,469.00	$19,469.00
Essential Operating Data (noncash flow information)														
A. Sales Volume	$1,700.00	$1,700.00	$2,000.00	$2,300.00	$2,600.00	$2,900.00	$3,100.00	$3,400.00	$3,400.00	$3,200.00	$3,000.00	$2,800.00	$2,600.00	$33,000.00
B. Inventory on Hand	$245.00	$245.00	$245.00	$245.00	$245.00	$245.00	$245.00	$245.00	$245.00	$245.00	$245.00	$245.00	$245.00	$245.00
C. Depreciation	$100.00	$100.00	$100.00	$100.00	$100.00	$100.00	$100.00	$100.00	$100.00	$100.00	$100.00	$100.00	$100.00	$1,200.00

Western Slope Detailing
Forecasted Monthly Income Statement
before taxes (1996)

	1996	JANUARY	FEBRUARY	MARCH	APRIL	MAY	JUNE	JULY	AUGUST	SEPTEMBER	OCTOBER	NOVEMBER	DECEMBER
Sales	$33,000.00	$1,700.00	$2,000.00	$2,300.00	$2,600.00	$2,900.00	$3,100.00	$3,400.00	$3,400.00	$3,200.00	$3,000.00	$2,800.00	$2,600.00
COGS	$1,970.00	$100.00	$120.00	$140.00	$155.00	$175.00	$185.00	$200.00	$200.00	$190.00	$180.00	$170.00	$155.00
Gross Margin	$31,030.00	$1,600.00	$1,880.00	$2,160.00	$2,445.00	$2,725.00	$2,915.00	$3,200.00	$3,200.00	$3,010.00	$2,820.00	$2,630.00	$2,445.00
Expenses:													
Advertising	$2,950.00	$900.00	$100.00	$100.00	$150.00	$200.00	$250.00	$350.00	$350.00	$200.00	$150.00	$100.00	$100.00
Depreciation	$1,200.00	$100.00	$100.00	$100.00	$100.00	$100.00	$100.00	$100.00	$100.00	$100.00	$100.00	$100.00	$100.00
Insurance	$1,200.00	$100.00	$100.00	$100.00	$100.00	$100.00	$100.00	$100.00	$100.00	$100.00	$100.00	$100.00	$100.00
Office supplies	$600.00	$50.00	$50.00	$50.00	$50.00	$50.00	$50.00	$50.00	$50.00	$50.00	$50.00	$50.00	$50.00
Accounting	$500.00			$100.00			$100.00			$100.00			$200.00
Telephone	$600.00	$50.00	$50.00	$50.00	$50.00	$50.00	$50.00	$50.00	$50.00	$50.00	$50.00	$50.00	$50.00
Utilities	$1,060.00	$90.00	$95.00	$85.00	$80.00	$80.00	$85.00	$90.00	$90.00	$85.00	$80.00	$95.00	$105.00
Loan Payments	$2,556.00	$213.00	$213.00	$213.00	$213.00	$213.00	$213.00	$213.00	$213.00	$213.00	$213.00	$213.00	$213.00
Repair and Maintenance	$1,200.00	$100.00	$100.00	$100.00	$100.00	$100.00	$100.00	$100.00	$100.00	$100.00	$100.00	$100.00	$100.00
Miscellaneous Expense	$900.00	$75.00	$75.00	$75.00	$75.00	$75.00	$75.00	$75.00	$75.00	$75.00	$75.00	$75.00	$75.00
Total Expenses:	$12,766.00	$1,678.00	$883.00	$973.00	$918.00	$968.00	$1,123.00	$1,128.00	$1,128.00	$1,073.00	$918.00	$883.00	$1,093.00
Net Income:	$18,264.00	($78.00)	$997.00	$1,187.00	$1,527.00	$1,757.00	$1,792.00	$2,072.00	$2,072.00	$1,937.00	$1,902.00	$1,747.00	$1,352.00

Projected Income

The forecasted net income for Western Slope Detailing is expected to be $18,264 for the first year. Other pertinent information regarding income and expenses can be found in detail in the Forecasted Monthly Income Statement (p. 544). Following the Forecasted Monthly Income Statement is a graphical representation of the net income projection (see below). In addition, a pie chart showing the expenses and the percentages that they represent has been included on this page.

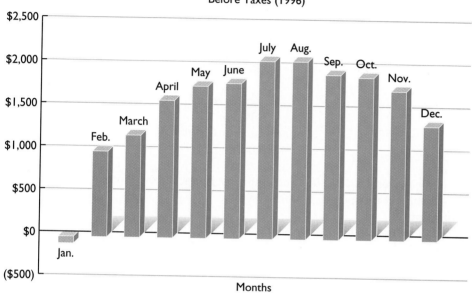

Net Income Projection
Before Taxes (1996)

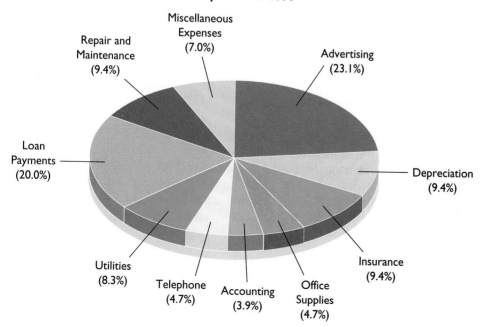

Expenses for 1996

Organization, Management, and Staffing Plan

The Management and Organization

The owners of Western Slope Detailing have created a partnership that incorporates detailing experience, business management skills, and an overwhelming level of enthusiasm for this type of business. Michael Hyatt and Shawn Serviss will equally share the responsibilities of managing the operation. The education, experience, skills, and knowledge of the partners are complementary. This fact will give the management of Western Slope Detailing a pool of resources, which will enable them to manage effectively. The résumés of the partners are shown here and on page 547 along with business references.

Résumé
of
Shawn Serviss
555 Wilson Ct.
Grand Junction, Colorado
(970) 555-5555

Goals

My current goal is to contribute my financial and human resources to a small but prosperous detailing facility.

Education

I obtained a B.B.A. in Marketing from Mesa State College in 1996.

Work Experience

Frank Dunn Co.   1984–1991

I worked as manager/owner during the last two years of employment. My duties included selling new/used auto parts, and supervising employees.

Western Slope Auto Co.   1991–1993

I was employed to transport inventory to both Denver and Salt Lake City auto auctions.

Board and Buckle Co.   1993

Employment with this company was primarily during the summer as a bicycle mechanic.

West Star Aviation   1993–1994

West Star Aviation employed me part-time as a building and equipment maintenance assistant.

Hobbies and Special Interests

In 1992 I volunteered for the reelection campaign of Tim Foster, a state representative for Colorado. As a hobby, I enjoy playing soccer and am currently a member of the Grand Mesa Youth Soccer Association (GMYSA). Also I am a men's and co-ed soccer team representative and head coach of a women's soccer team called The Mummies. In addition, I am a certified referee. Finally, I enjoy downhill and cross-country skiing as well as mountain biking.

Résumé

of

Michael A. Hyatt

P.O. Box 555

Clifton, Colorado

(970) 555-5555

Goals

My current goal is to become the owner of a growing yet stable detailing facility. I plan to use my background, education, and skills to make this business profitable while setting new standards for the industry.

Education

I have received two degrees from Mesa State College, which is located in Grand Junction, Colorado. The first is an A.A.S. degree in Machining and Manufacturing Trades. The second degree is a B.B.A. with an emphasis in Management. I graduated in spring 1996 with an accumulative grade point average of 3.1.

Work Experience

B.U. Daughters Construction   1994

Initially, this company hired me to design and construct heavy road construction equipment. Following the completion of those duties, I became a heavy equipment operator. Soon thereafter, I was promoted to job foreman.

Billing's Auto Parts Inc.   1993–1994

My duties at Billing's were primarily as a parts person and secondarily as a automotive machinist. I was known for my automotive knowledge and expertise.

Gart Sports   1993–1994

My main position at this sporting goods retailer was the department manager of hunting and firearm sales. I was promoted after being with the company for only one month.

Western Slope Industries   1993

This company hired me as a manual operator machinist. Within two months I was promoted to a CNC programmer/operator. Shortly thereafter, I was again promoted to Quality Control as an inspector.

Mesa State Housing   1990

Mesa State Housing hired me as a resident assistant. I was responsible for the welfare of 39 residents on the third floor of Mary Rait Hall. In general, the residents considered me a friend and looked up to me as a leader.

Michael Garman Gallery   1986–1989

I was the assisstant manager at the Michael Garman Gallery. My duties included bookkeeping, inventory control, and sales.

Hobbies and Special Interests

Most of my hobbies are automotive related. I enjoy drag racing and circle track racing. I am also an avid car collector with an unusual collection of rare vehicles. Finally, I enjoy outdoor activities such as hunting, camping, and off-road four-wheeling.

Special Considerations

Facility Needs

The principals of Western Slope Detailing have decided to build the facility on the property currently owned by Michael Hyatt. This property is located at 555 1st St. in Grand Junction, Colorado. The facility will be 575 square feet and will accommodate two vehicles at a time. The facility will be constructed with certain considerations in mind. First, a below ground level pit will be constructed. This pit will be the appropriate size to facilitate chassis detailing. Second, a proper grease trap and floor drains will be installed. Third, one 9-foot overhead door will be included to allow for the servicing of tall vehicles. Finally, proper power, water, heating, and cooling will be included.

Since the partners possess the necessary skills and knowledge to design and construct a facility, they have chosen to do so. It is estimated that $8,000 will be saved by not having the construction contracted out. As reflected in the Initial Capitalization Plan, the total cost of the facility construction will be reduced to $7,000.

Business Plan 2: Excalibur Traditional Men's Clothier, LTD. (Excalibur)

Executive Summary

This is what quality is all about: the customer's perception of excellence.
*And quality is our response to that perception.**

Tom Peters

Excalibur Traditional Men's Clothier, LTD. (Excalibur) by and through its owners, has created this comprehensive business plan in order to invite First of America Bancorp to assist Excalibur in raising the needed capital of $80,000 to begin the operations of a men's clothing store in Monroe, Michigan.

The Program

The development of Excalibur can be attributed to the two principal investors, B. Mark Springsteel and Karl E. Hall. A men's clothing store, yes, but that is where the similarity ends. By reintroducing an old concept "customer service and satisfaction," Excalibur intends to aggressively promote its *value-added* pricing policy to attract the professional businessman. It is the intention of Excalibur to assist the executive in image building through successful marketing of the proper apparel for his position in the company. Inasmuch as the only available service is off-the-rack type of purchasing, Excalibur intends to tailor-make to the needs of the customer. Excalibur will also provide the service of going, if need be, to the office of the executive for proper measurements and selection of fabric, color, and styling. Excalibur is confident that the professional male is more than willing to pay for this type of value-added service. A survey of the Monroe area indicated there was no store that catered to the executive.

The principals of Excalibur are confident that there is a strong demand for

---

* Tom Peters, *Thriving on Chaos* (New York: Harper & Row, 1987), p. 101.

this type of merchandise which is not available in the Monroe area. Monroe is a bedroom community for both the Detroit Metro and Toledo areas; however, the principals discovered that executives preferred to shop in their home community as opposed to either metropolitan area, provided the merchandise they sought was available to them.

The Plan

Financial projections for Excalibur indicate an investment of approximately $80,000, in addition to the principals' investment of $100,000, is required for a startup cost in order to initiate operations. These funds will be committed to beginning inventory and store equipment and supplies, and will provide working capital for the first year of operations.

The Players

Excalibur has three distinct and complementary players. B. Mark Springsteel, president, brings to Excalibur his expertise in the area of finance and marketing along with retail sales and management experience. Karl Hall, treasurer, with his varied background in accounting and finance, has the hands-on experience and know-how of the internal workings of a small business. Craig Hall, who will manage the store, had in the past developed his own clientele base while employed with a men's retail store in the Monroe area. His ease with people and ability to merchandise adds to the diversity of this group.

The Game Summary

Collectively, the players have spent the past five months developing the concept and image of Excalibur. With confidence in their abilities, knowledge, and professionalism, the players anticipate a net profit in the first year of operations.

Table of Contents

Concept History and Background

Description of Product

The merchandise being offered by Excalibur Traditional Men's Clothier, Ltd. will consist of men's professional wear; business suits of the finest quality along with dress slacks and sports jackets. In addition, Excalibur will offer accessories to complement the professional's image; dress shirts, ties, sweaters, vests, socks, belts, and undergarments. There will also be available seasonal wear such as overcoats, gloves, and scarves.

Idea History

The concept of Excalibur was first discussed in late 1993 by K. Evan Hall and his brother, Craig. However, the plan never proceeded beyond the preliminary discussions and ultimately the idea never materialized. At the beginning of this year K. Evan Hall approached Mark Springsteel with the business idea. Subsequent talks evolved into a decision to form the corporation.

Summary of Principals' Experience

K. Evan Hall completed his bachelor's degree in Business Administration with a Finance major from Mesa State College, Grand Junction, Colorado. Mr. Hall's experience includes five years in retail sales, ten years in accounting, and seven years in management of personnel.

B. Mark Springsteel also completed his bachelor's degree in Business Administration with a Finance major from Mesa State College. Mr. Springsteel's experience includes six years in retail sales and three years in retail management. He also has broad experience in the valuation of the stocks of retail clothing companies.

Craig Hall is in the process of working toward a degree in business management. Mr. Hall's 19 years of retail sales experience will allow him to act in the capacity of sales manager for Excalibur. In addition he has represented several retail stores, such as Neiman-Marcus, Bally, and Steve Petix, in the capacities of buyer, merchandiser, advertising and sales manager.

Goals and Objectives

The main, long-term goal of Excalibur Traditional Men's Clothier, Ltd. is to open a chain of men's clothing stores in the midwestern area of the United States. The initial capital requested will go toward the purchase of inventory, fixtures, and the securing of an initial place of business. After the first store is established in the Monroe County, Michigan area, expansion into other areas of the Midwest will be implemented.

The final goal is to position Excalibur as being the archetype of the finest in men's clothing retailers. This will be accomplished through sincere and unyielding service to our clientele and uncompromising dedication to selling quality products at prices that reflect the value-added features of our stores.

Management feels that the main target customer, namely the professional male, is currently seeking such a store and has become frustrated with the lack of style and value that is currently available through current retail outlets. This clientele will be willing to pay a premium for such value-added features as personalized attention, custom fitting, and "office-call" measurings (measurings done at the client's office or home).

The following one-year objectives have been determined by management:

1. Rent, remodel, and occupy the store in the Monroe, Michigan area upon receiving debt financing.
2. Purchase fixtures and inventory.
3. Hire competent, professional sales staff.
4. Advertise innovatively and heavily toward our target market.
5. Establish immediate cash inflows sufficient to meet 18-month breakeven point.

Intermediate goals are to establish a strong base and system of operations at the Monroe, Michigan location from which to launch other branches. This means establishing an early breakeven point and developing rapid profit growth at the Monroe, Michigan store in order to support the expansions.

In addition, management has established the following five-year goals:

1. Average 20 percent annual growth rate as measured by revenues.
2. Total sales over $5 million for the first five years combined.
3. Net income before taxes is expected to be $250,000 for that same period.
4. The opening of a second Excalibur store.

In order to establish our reputation as the finest in men's clothing, the following criteria for success will be kept in mind:

1. Focus on the value-added service features to our clientele and build within them an emotional attachment to Excalibur.
2. Incorporate a high-spirited yet professional atmosphere among employees by respecting their skills and humanity, both monetarily and by treating them with autonomy.
3. Develop a culture and value system that pivots and grows from a passion for excellence in product and superiority in service.
4. Grow without becoming big. Be profitable without being greedy. Maintain sharp pencils and sharp minds without losing the gracefulness of flexibility.

Marketing Plan

Market Profile—Consumers and Demand

The typical customer of Excalibur products will be a professional male between the ages of 21 and 64 earning a median income of $37,500 annually. Management believes that any ancillary demand will be derived from this customer and therefore any forecasted demand is inclusive of this group. In addition, the principle decision makers will be of this customer profile and consequently any promotions will be directed toward this group. Within our customer group there reside five subcategories segmented according to age. The following are descriptions of each subcategory.

Generation X-ers

Age 21–24
Income . . . . $20,000–$30,000
Family. . . . . Married, no children
Occupation . . . . Salesman, intern, entrepreneur
Personality. . . . . Progressive, trend setter
Percent Demand . . . . 5 percent

In-Betweens

Age 25–34
Income . . . . $25,000–$35,000
Family. . . . . Married with young children
Occupation . . . . Salesman, entrepreneur, middle management
Personality. . . . . Risk sensitive, trend follower
Percent Demand . . . . 15 percent

Young Baby Boomers

Age 35–44
Income . . . . $30,000–$45,000
Family . . . . Full nest or divorced single parent
Occupation . . . . Management, professional service provider
(i.e., attorney)
Personality. . . . . Risk averse, conservative
Percent Demand . . . . 25 percent

Older Baby Boomers

Age 45–54
Income . . . . $40,000–$60,000
Family. . . . . Married or divorced with older children
Occupation . . . . Management, professional service provider
Personality. . . . . Risk averse, conservative
Percent Demand . . . . 35 percent

The Old Guard

Age 55–64
Income . . . . $50,000 and up
Family. . . . . Empty nest
Occupation . . . . Senior management, early retiree
Personality. . . . . Risk averse, conservative
Percent Demand . . . . 20 percent

Management anticipates a strong demand for Excalibur products due to two important demographic features of the Detroit PMSA in which Excalibur is located. First, Monroe County itself has a relatively high median family income of $40,532, which management believes will help support a demand for the premium-quality goods which Excalibur will market. Second, the city of Monroe is a bedroom community for both Detroit to the north and Toledo, Ohio to the south. Management presupposes that much of the demand will come from the professionals who work in these cities but reside in Monroe. The following table shows the statistics and estimates used to calculate demand:

Monroe County statistics						
Total population	135,962					
Males per 100 females	97.2					
Total males	66,077					
Percent within Excalibur's age range	56.40%					
Males within Excalibur's age range	37,267					
Age group	21–24	25–34	35–44	45–54	55–64	Totals
Percent total males	5.30%	16.30%	15.50%	10.80%	8.50%	56.40%
Number of males	3,502	10,771	10,242	7,136	5,617	37,267
Estimated derived demand	8.00%	12.00%	15.00%	18.00%	12.00%	
Customer base by age group	280	1,292	1,536	1,285	674	5,067

As with the startup of any new business, the estimation of a product's demand is replete with assumptions; however, management believes this to be a conservative estimation of demand for Excalibur products. Additionally, the 5,067 customer base seems sufficient with regard to revenue needs. This customer base is anticipated to stay fairly constant due to a slow growth rate of approximately 1 percent per annum in Monroe County.

Market Profile—Competitors

The management of Excalibur used the following information to evaluate past and present competition:

REASONS FOR FAILURE

NAMES	POOR MANAGEMENT	UNDER-CAPITALIZATION	LACK OF KNOWLEDGE	COMPETITION	OTHER
Top Hat Men's Wear	yes	no	yes	yes	yes
Uptown Clothing	yes	no	no	yes	no
J.C. Penneys					
Southern Monroe City	yes	no	no	yes	yes
Creeks Brothers	no	no	no	yes	yes

Direct and Indirect Competition

Competitors	Price (H,M,L)	Location (B/W/S)	Facility (B/W/S)	Direct/ Indirect	Rank 1-Most, 10-Least
T.J.'s Mens' Clothing	M	Same	Same	Direct	1
*Sears	L	Better	Better	Indirect	6
*J.C. Penneys	L	Better	Better	Indirect	5
Sachs	H	Better	Better	Indirect	3
Macy's	H	Better	Better	Indirect	7
*Elder Berman	M-H	Better	Better	Indirect	2
*Hudson's	M-H	Better	Better	Indirect	4

* Indicates mall locations

Four businesses offering approximately the same product as Excalibur are no longer in the competitive market. Three of the former competitors were located in or near downtown Monroe. Top Hat Men's Wear and Creeks Brothers were situated on the main street through downtown Monroe. Uptown Clothing was within walking distance of the downtown locale. Excalibur will be located in the same proximity as the former competitors.

Both Top Hat Men's Wear and Uptown Clothing were forced to close their doors because of poor management decisions. Both businesses attempted to leave their respective market niches and expand the existing product lines in order to compete with Sears and J.C. Penney. Sears and J.C. Penney both established new locations in a mall just north of the city of Monroe. Top Hat Men's Wear and Uptown Clothing were no longer able to meet the demands of their customers after adding to their product lines. Customers then sought other locations to fulfill their demands. Shopping in Toledo and the malls became the norm for local residents.

Top Hat and Uptown both faced the same problems: outdated products, too large a product line to compete, and overpricing due to lack of business. Additionally, poor credit and accounts receivable management haunted both businesses.

Creeks Brothers Men's Wear recently closed its doors. The proprietor passed away and the family lost interest in the retail business. Upon talking with the eldest son, he indicated a loss of market share because of outdated goods. Trying to deplete current inventory and reestablish an updated inventory was just not feasible at this time.

Creeks Brothers, Top Hat, and Uptown were all direct competitors. The only local indirect competitor to discontinue operations was J.C. Penney located in southern Monroe County. This store was also in close proximity to downtown Monroe. J.C. Penney continued to operate both stores because of the distances between locations. Although prices were about the same, the mall store continued to attract the business and J.C. Penney finally made the decision to close the old store. Another factor prime to the decision was a fire that swept through half of the shopping center where the old J.C. Penney was located.

The chart also shows how the management of Excalibur ranked both the direct and indirect competition. Management believes that reestablishing a downtown Monroe location will produce enough business traffic to be successful. In the past, clothing stores in Monroe have all met with success. Keeping abreast of market demand, service, and quality goods has been the common denominator for these types of business.

New Business Strengths and Weaknesses

Strengths:
1. Excalibur will supply the current demand for a quality product that is nonexistent in Monroe County.
2. Commitment to professional personal service along with custom fitting and quick turnaround tailoring for our customers.

Weaknesses:
1. Excalibur will be selling at premium prices that will be recession sensitive. To combat this weakness, cash flows and retained earnings will be kept at higher levels than industry average.
2. Reintroducing the concept of professional service and adding to it a premium price.

Excalibur will attack this problem head on using aggressive ad campaigns, personal selling, and through the satisfied customer's word-of-mouth advertising.

Geographic Market

The geographic market for Excalibur will include a 20-mile radius from our location in downtown Monroe. Although this radius extends into other counties, we remain committed to establishing Monroe County as our geographic market and any business that develops from outside Monroe County will be incidental and appreciated.

Although most of the competition, both direct and indirect, have mall locations and similar products, the management of Excalibur believes that the professional service and quality products offered will enable us to establish a customer base. Our intention is to draw the bedroom community workers away from the competition, both in Toledo and the Detroit PSMA, back to Monroe to purchase their professional wear.

Pricing Policy

Excalibur will employ several pricing theories in the operation of its business.

1. The pricing strategy for our main product line, professional men's wear, will requisition a unique value-added price. The value-added price embodies personal service, custom tailoring, and delivery of a quality product.
2. The product lines of sports jackets and dress pants will entail a status quo pricing strategy along with the value-added strategy for quality and service.
3. Accessories and complements to professional men's wear will be priced using a status quo pricing policy.

The value added component of the pricing strategy for Excalibur will not remove us from the competitive market. On the contrary, we anticipate that the prestige pricing policy established at Excalibur will distinguish us from the rest of the competition. Most of the competition does not offer, on the same scale, the type of personal service or quality of merchandise of Excalibur. We firmly believe that our customer base is willing to purchase a quality product and professional service at a premium price.

Promotion

Excalibur's promotional strategy will focus on delivering a clear, concise message distinctly directed to the extent possible toward the previously described target customer. All advertising, personal selling, and merchandising will have a common core and fulcrum in the philosophy that to sell quality one must manifest quality in all that one does. The real-world application of this philosophy demands that all promotions communicate, both explicitly and implicitly, to the target market, the quality and value-added properties.

More specifically, Excalibur's advertising will focus on newspaper and radio. Management plans to utilize the daily newspapers, *The Toledo Blade* and *The Monroe Evening News* along with the weekly *Frenchtown News*. Newspapers will be Excalibur's primary advertising medium based on two assumptions. First, management concludes that the target customers are very apt to read the newspaper regularly. Second, because the demand for the products that Excalibur will market is based on visual appeal, newspaper advertisement will have more impact due to its visual nature. For this reason newspaper ads will be used somewhat uniformly and continually throughout the year. A heavier emphasis will be placed on this type of advertising prior to and during high seasonally driven demand. During the seasonal demand times, radio advertisement will be utilized to augment the base of newspaper advertisement. The concentration of radio advertisement will be on radio stations that appeal to the target markets. However, because radio audiences are primarily segmented by age, Excalibur will only be able to target a section of the whole target market with each advertisement. To utilize the medium of radio as a comprehensive demand inducer, a variety of radio stations will need to be employed. Primarily radio stations with an older listenership will be used because the majority of the customer base is in an older category.

In addition to the above Excalibur will sponsor an annual charitable fund raiser in the form of an auction of men dressed in suits from Excalibur. The bidders will bid for dates with these men and the proceeds will benefit charities that the management of Excalibur deems appropriate at the time.

The service that Excalibur delivers with its personal selling will be the distinctive character of the business. The management wishes to position itself in the midst of consumers as the epitome of superior customer service. To do this Excalibur will offer such services as "office call" measuring, custom fitting, and quick turnaround tailoring. Initial training and continual education of the sales staff will be of the utmost importance to support a high level of service. The management of Excalibur is committed to such training and education. These types of value-added services for our customers will initiate a word-of-mouth advertising campaign.

Legal Requirements

The law firm of Dewey, Cheatum and Howe has been retained to serve as legal counsel for all of Excalibur's contracts, agreements, and other legal concerns. This law firm will also represent Excalibur in the event of a suit brought by or against Excalibur.

Contracts

The contracts that are relevant to the operation of Excalibur include a site lease agreement and licenses to sell certain products. The management expects to sign standard agreements and most suppliers with regard to shipping arrangements and agreements to sell. These will be reviewed and accepted on an individual basis. As of the writing of this plan, the signatures of both the president and treasurer are required for a contract to be agreed to by Excalibur but, as laid down in the bylaws, this requirement can be changed by vote of the shareholders.

Insurance

It is impossible to cover every risk contingency but the management believes that ample insurance coverage is a necessity in today's litigious climate. Management also understands that the best way to deal with risk is to plan for it and work to reduce it. Under these considerations Excalibur will carry a strong insurance package. Liability insurance will be carried to cover injuries to the person or property of customers. Worker's compensation will be carried in accordance to state statutes. In addition, key-employee insurance will be included to cover the contingency of the death or disability of key personnel. All employees with access to funds will be bonded.

Form of Ownership

The form of ownership that the management has elected to use is the Subchapter S Corporation form. There are numerous positive aspects to this form of ownership, including:

- The fact that S corporations are taxed as partnerships.
- The limited liability faced by the shareholders.
- The transferability of ownership.
- The continuity of life of the corporation.
- The ability to increase equity capital by selling shares.

Each one of these advantages can be found in other forms of ownership, but the management feels that the mix of advantages found with this form is the best suited for this enterprise. A partnership would have left any general partners open to unlimited liability. The form of a C corporation would have entailed double taxation and reduced the ability of Excalibur to retain the earnings needed for growth. A limited liability company would have been the next best option but because its only advantage would be its ability to have unlimited shareholders and because we believe we will not need more than the 35 shareholders legally allowed to an S corporation, the limited liability company seemed like an incorrect match for our purposes.

A copy of the articles of incorporation and the bylaws for Excalibur can be found on pages 568-571.

Financial Plan and Requirements

Initial Capitalization Plan

The startup costs required by Excalibur are outlined on the following pages. As indicated by the plan, the required financing to launch Excalibur into operation is $126,975. With capitalization from the principals of $50,000, along with the principal's loan to Excalibur for $50,000, the company requires additional financing in the amount of $80,000. We fully anticipate receiving the necessary funding from First of America Bancorp in Monroe, MI. The terms of the debt will be 1 percent over prime, or an 11 percent rate of interest on the principal. Required debt payments during our first year in operation will apply $12,700 to the principal balance and $8,172 to interest.

The principal players for Excalibur have agreed to accept responsibility for a portion of the required funding for startup costs. A schedule listing their respective liabilities for payment can be found in the Initial Capitalization Plan. The principals consider the "Total Other Costs" as sunk costs and accept the risk associated with these costs in the formation of a new business venture.

Projected Income

Forecasted net income for Excalibur's first year is expected to be $5,281. This includes taking into account the debt payment to First of America Bancorp. Other pertinent information regarding income and expense for 19X6 can be found in detail in the Forecasted Income Statement. The projected Income Statement, Balance Sheets, and Cash Flow for Excalibur can be viewed in the following pages.

	Pro Forma Statements Excalibur Initial Capitalization	
Suits	Sizes 36R to 48L	$58,000
Dress shirts	Sizes 14 to 18, Long & Short Slv	$4,000
Ties	Assorted	$3,600
Casual Shirts	Sizes 14 to 18, Long and Short Slv	$2,500
Dress Slacks	Sizes 28 to 42, Assorted	$5,000
Sport Coats	Sizes 36R to 48L	$7,000
Sweaters	Assorted Colors, Sm to XL	$2,500
Overcoats	All Weather, Sizes 36R to 48L	$7,500
Casual Jackets	Assorted 36R to 48L	$6,500
Belts	Assorted Sizes and Lengths	$1,150
Socks	Assorted, Sizes 8 to 13	$1,500
Undergarments:		
Briefs	Sizes 28 to 42	$300
Boxer	Sizes 28 to 42	$325
T-Shirts	Sizes 28 to 42	$300
Scarves	Assorted colors and lengths	$900
Gloves	Assorted Sizes, Black and Brown	$1,100
Miscellaneous Attire	Tie-Tacks, Buttons, Cuff Links, etc.	$1,200
Total Beginning Inventory		$103,375
Retail Store		
Equipment	Desks, Racks, File Cabinets, Mannequins, Phone, Shelves, etc.	$20,000
Supplies	Letterheads, Envelopes, Stamps, etc.	$3,600
Total Retail Store		$23,600
Other Associated Costs		
Advertising	Initial Campaign	$4,500
Legal Fees	Associated with License and Registration	$3,500
Heat, Light, Power, and Telephone Hook-up	Initial Startup Costs/Deposits	$2,000
Computer Equipment Deposit	Secure Equipment	$1,000
Insurance Deposit	Fees Associated with Startup Policy	$300
Miscellaneous Items	Keys, Alarm Fees, Safe Setup	$450
Total Other Costs		$11,750
Total Initial Capitalization Costs		$138,725
Less: Principals Portion	K. Hall, 50% of 75% of Total Other Costs	$4,406
	B. Springsteel, 50% of 75% of Total Other Costs	$4,406
	C. Hall 25% of Total Other Costs	$2,938
Required Financing	Inventory $103,375; Retail Store $23,600	$126,975

Excalibur
Forecasted Income Statement
19X6

	19X6	JANUARY	FEBRUARY	MARCH	APRIL	MAY	JUNE	JULY	AUGUST	SEPTEMBER	OCTOBER	NOVEMBER	DECEMBER
Sales	$810,000	$39,919	$32,756	$30,496	$35,107	$42,363	$52,894	$60,875	$76,707	$91,583	$102,141	$117,450	$127,709
COGS	$283,500	$13,972	$11,465	$10,674	$12,287	$14,827	$18,513	$21,306	$26,847	$32,054	$35,749	$41,108	$44,698
Gross Margin	$526,500	$25,947	$21,291	$19,822	$22,820	$27,536	$34,381	$39,569	$49,860	$59,529	$66,392	$76,343	$83,011
Expenses:													
Advertising:													
Mediums	$30,000	$2,500	$2,500	$2,500	$2,500	$2,500	$2,500	$2,500	$2,500	$2,500	$2,500	$2,500	$2,500
Postage	$5,000	$417	$417	$417	$417	$417	$417	$417	$417	$417	$417	$417	$417
Depreciation	$2,800	$233	$233	$233	$233	$233	$233	$233	$233	$233	$233	$233	$233
Wages:													
Employee	$80,760	$6,730	$6,730	$6,730	$6,730	$6,730	$6,730	$6,730	$6,730	$6,730	$6,730	$6,730	$6,730
Commissions	$20,250	$998	$819	$762	$878	$1,059	$1,322	$1,522	$1,918	$2,290	$2,554	$2,936	$3,193
Officers' Salary	$100,000	$8,333	$8,333	$8,333	$8,333	$8,333	$8,333	$8,333	$8,333	$8,333	$8,333	$8,333	$8,333
Tailor Expense	$81,000	$3,992	$3,276	$3,050	$3,511	$4,236	$5,289	$6,088	$7,671	$9,158	$10,214	$11,745	$12,771
Benefits	$8,289	$691	$691	$691	$691	$691	$691	$691	$691	$691	$691	$691	$691
Payroll Taxes	$30,152	$2,409	$2,382	$2,374	$2,391	$2,418	$2,458	$2,488	$2,547	$2,603	$2,643	$2,700	$2,738
Credit Card Expense	$8,505	$419	$344	$320	$369	$445	$555	$639	$805	$962	$1,072	$1,233	$1,341
H, L, & P	$11,800	$983	$983	$983	$983	$983	$983	$983	$983	$983	$983	$983	$983
Telephone	$4,200	$350	$350	$350	$350	$350	$350	$350	$350	$350	$350	$350	$350
Store Supplies	$3,200	$1,500	$155	$155	$155	$155	$155	$155	$155	$155	$155	$155	$155
Lease Expense/Computer	$22,800	$1,900	$1,900	$1,900	$1,900	$1,900	$1,900	$1,900	$1,900	$1,900	$1,900	$1,900	$1,900
Repair/Maintenance	$3,700	$308	$308	$308	$308	$308	$308	$308	$308	$308	$308	$308	$308
Miscellaneous Expense	$4,300	$1,500	$255	$255	$255	$255	$255	$255	$255	$255	$255	$255	$255
Dues/Subscription	$1,200	$100	$100	$100	$100	$100	$100	$100	$100	$100	$100	$100	$100
Travel/Entertainment	$9,500	$792	$792	$792	$792	$792	$792	$792	$792	$792	$792	$792	$792
Donations	$2,500			$625			$625			$625			$625
Rent	$22,592	$2,884	$1,792	$1,792	$1,792	$1,792	$1,792	$1,792	$1,792	$1,792	$1,792	$1,792	$1,792
Legal/Accting	$8,400	$3,500	$445	$445	$445	$445	$445	$445	$445	$445	$445	$445	$445
Insurance	$3,500	$292	$292	$292	$292	$292	$292	$292	$292	$292	$292	$292	$292
State Sales Tax	$48,600	$2,395	$1,965	$1,830	$2,106	$2,542	$3,174	$3,653	$4,602	$5,495	$6,128	$7,047	$7,663
Interest Expense	$8,172	$733	$724	$715	$706	$696	$686	$678	$667	$656	$648	$637	$627
Total Expenses:	$521,220	$43,959	$35,785	$35,951	$36,236	$37,672	$40,385	$41,342	$44,486	$48,064	$49,534	$52,574	$55,233
Net Income:	$5,281	($18,012)	($14,494)	($16,129)	($13,416)	($10,136)	($6,004)	($1,773)	$5,374	$11,465	$16,857	$23,769	$27,778

Excalibur Pro Forma Balance Sheet January 19X6			Excalibur Pro Forma Balance Sheet December 19X6		
Assets:			Assets:		
Cash		$52,325	Cash		$47,335
Inventory		$103,375	Inventory		$137,750
P.P, & E		$20,000	P.P, & E		$20,000
Less: Depreciation		$0	Less: Depreciation		$2,800
Net P.P, & E		$20,000	Net P.P, & E		$17,200
Pre Paid Rent		$4,300	Pre Paid Rent		$2,508
Total Assets		$180,000	Total Assets		$204,793
Liabilities:			Liabilities:		
Notes Payable:			Notes Payable:		
Shareholders		$50,000	Shareholders		$50,000
Bank-Current Portion		$12,700	Bank-Current Portion		$14,170
			A/P		$32,213
LTD		$67,300	LTD		$53,129
Total Liabilities		$130,000	Total Liabilities		$149,512
Owners Equity		$50,000	Owners Equity		$55,281
Total Liabilities and Equity		$180,000	Total Liabilities and Equity		$204,793

Excalibur Projected Income Statement Year Ended 19X6	
Sales:	$810,000
COGS:	$283,500
Gross Margin	$526,500
Expenses:	
Advertising:	$35,000
Depreciation:	$2,800
Wages/Salaries:	$201,010
G,S,&A	$194,645
Professional Fees:	$8,400
Rent	$22,592
State Sales Tax:	$48,600
Net Income before interest:	$13,453
Interest Expense:	$8,172
Net Income:	$5,281

Excalibur
Statement of Cash Flows
Year Ended December 31, 19X6

Cash flows from operating activities:			
Net Income, per Income Statement:		$5,281	
Add:			
Depreciation	$2,800		
Increase Accounts Payable	$32,213		
Decrease prepaid expenses	$1,792	$36,805	
		$42,086	
Less:			
Purchases	$103,375		
Increase in Inventory	$34,375	$137,375	
Net cash flow from operating activities:			($95,289)
Cash flows from financing activities:			
Cash received-Note Payable (Bank)	$80,000		
Cash received-Note Payable (Owners)	$50,000	$130,000	
Net cash from financing:			$130,000
Cash flows from investing activities:			
Less:			
Purchase PP&E	$20,000		
Payment of Note Payable Bank Principal & Interest	$19,701	$39,701	
Net cash flow from investing activities:			($39,701)
Increase/(Decrease) in cash flow:			($4,990)
Cash at beginning of the year:			$52,325
Cash at the end of the year:			$47,335

Organization, Management, and Staffing Plan

The Management and Organization

The management team of Excalibur is an exciting mix of retail industry knowledge, business management skills, and experience in clothing sales. B. Mark Springsteel and Karl E. Hall will serve as president and treasurer, respectively, for Excalibur and upon the inception of the corporation both gentlemen will be the sole shareholders of the corporation. Craig Hall will serve as sales manager. The following organizational chart represents the structure that will be used at the initial startup of the company.

The résumés of all three gentlemen can be seen on the following pages along with personal financial statements of the two equity shareholders.

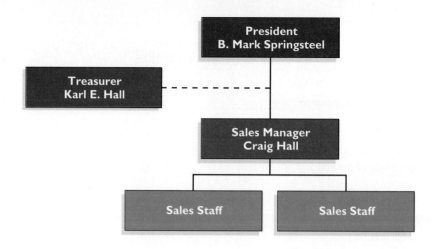

Résumé
of
B. Mark Springsteel
Grand Junction, Colorado 81501

Goals

My current goal is to become the co-owner and operator of a stable, growing men's clothier. I hope to see the company through the infancy and maturity stages and then to divest myself of my share of the company, the proceeds of which I will use in other profitable ventures.

Education

I graduated from Mesa State College located in Grand Junction, Colorado with a bachelor's degree in finance in 1990. My cumulative GPA was 3.96 and I received honors upon graduating.

Work Experience

Options Trader, Salomon Brothers Inc.   1993–1995

My main duty at Salomon Brothers was the trading of stock options on the Pacific Exchange. My main focus was stock options that derived their values from retail clothing stocks.

Stockbroker, Merrill Lynch & Co.   1991–1993

My duties at Merrill Lynch included the buying and selling of stock for over 40 accounts. I specialized in specialty retail clothing stocks such as The Gap Inc. and other broader retail stocks such as Nordstrom Inc.

Stockbroker Trainee, Merrill Lynch & Co.   1990–1991

During this time I was trained specifically in the field of retail stocks for my subsequent duties as a stockbroker for Merrill Lynch.

Salesperson, Fridays Men's Clothing   1987–1990

This was a part-time position that I held during college. My responsibilities encompassed all duties in the retail selling of men's clothing including measuring of customers and the selling, ordering, and stocking of merchandise.

Honors and Awards

Rookie Broker of the year, Merrill Lynch Co., 1991
Graduated Summa Cum Laude from Mesa State College
Who's Who Among Students in American Universities and Colleges, 1989
Third Place in Poetry; Mesa State College *The Literary Review,* 1989

Personal Financial Statements
of
B. Mark Springsteel

B. Mark Springsteel
Balance Sheet
April 30, 1995

ASSETS			LIABILITIES	
Current assets			Current Liabilities	
Cash		$756.00	Credit card debt	$532.00
Savings		2,193.00	Current portion of long-term debt	1,076.59
Investments (value as of 04/28/95)			Miscellaneous short-term debt	152.36
LSI Logic, 200 shares	$13,300.00			
Gap Inc., 150 shares	4,781.25		Long-Term Liabilities	
TeleEspana, 200 shares	5,493.75		Mortgage	58,263.54
Oppenheimer Fd: GrowthA 500 shares	14,220.00		Education debt	7,638.00
Total investment		37,795.00		
			Total Liabilities	67,662.49
Long-Term Assets				
Condominium (appraised value)		85,000.00	Net Worth	
			Net worth, B. Mark Springsteel	58,081.51
Total Assets		$125,744.00	Total Liabilities and Net Worth	$125,744.00

B. Mark Springsteel
Income Statement
For the Month Ended April 30, 1995

Monthly After-tax Income		$3,256.25
Monthly Expenses		
Mortgage	$820.27	
Education debt	256.32	
Insurance	235.16	
Automobile lease	356.54	
Telephone and Utilities	220.00	
Food and Entertainment	321.54	
Clothing	185.00	
Miscellaneous expenses	150.00	
Total monthly expenses		2,544.83
Monthly Net Income		$711.42

Résumé
of
Karl E. Hall
Parachute, CO 81635

Goals

My current goal is to own a fine men's clothing store, catering to the executive. With my background and experience, I will provide the financial expertise to see the inauguration of the business and to guide the finances during its growing phase.

Education

I received my B.B.A. from Mesa State College in Grand Junction, CO, and am in the process of working toward an M.B.A. Other course work included financial planning seminars and banking seminars.

Work Experience

Financial Program Manager, USAF, Italy   1992–1994

In this capacity, I developed and conducted comprehensive seminars on the effective uses of credit in today's society, and I wrote a financial guide for transitional and relocating military personnel on the evaluation of personal finances, budgeting, and savings plans. In addition, I processed and disbursed funds for the Air Force Aid Society (AFAS) loans to assist military personnel during emergencies and financial hardships.

Controller, Cutter Ceramics, Inc., MA   1990–1992

At this company I was responsible for payroll, incoming and outgoing orders, and all financials. At this time I developed a spreadsheet program for tracking outstanding money orders, bank checks, and accounts payable checks.

Assistant to the Treasurer, Lexington Savings Bank, Lexington, MA   1989–1991

Among my duties were the completion of quarterly FDIC Call Reports, which included loan loss reserve calculation; and the calculation of investment income for FNMA, FHLMC, Treasury bonds and notes, and other securities using computer software programs.

Customer Service Representative, Great Lakes Bancorp, MI   1987–1988

In this capacity, I assisted new and existing customers in choosing financial products to meet their financial needs.

Military Experience   1982–1987

During my five years in the military I received Air Force supervisor training as well as leadership training.

Personal Financial Statements
of
Karl E. Hall

Karl E. Hall
Balance Sheet
April 30, 1995

ASSETS			LIABILITIES	
Current Assets				
Cash		$1,050	Current Liabilities	
Savings		$13,596	Credit Card Debt	$1,076
Investments			Current portion-LTD	$2,087
20th Ultra, 325 shares	$3,546			
Berger 101 Fund, 475 shares	$5,582		Long Term Liabilities	
Tenneco Inc, 200 shares	$9,224		Mortgages on Rentals	$187,550
2-6 month CD's	$2,096		Education Debt	$11,596
Total Investments:		$20,448		
			Total Liabilities	$202,309
Long Term Assets:				
Real estate rental Property:			Net Worth	
Illinois (appraised value)		$136,850	Net worth, K. E. Hall	$74,535
Michigan (appraised value)		$104,900		
Total Assets:		$276,844	Total liabilities and Net Worth	$276,844

Karl E. Hall
Income Statement
For the Month Ended April 30, 1995

Monthly After-tax Income		$4,135
Monthly Expenses		
Mortgage Payments	$1,958	
Education Debts	$325	
Insurance	$196	
Auto Payment	$225	
Telephone and Utilities	$215	
Food and Entertainment	$276	
Clothing	$100	
Miscellaneous	$75	
Total Monthly Expenses		$3,370
Monthly Net Income		$765

Résumé
of
Craig R. Hall
Rochester Hills, MI 48309

Goals

My current goal is to manage a men's retail outlet, catering to the executive, in which I can best utilize my communication, organization, and merchandising skills. Future goals include assisting the executive in developing his image through the choice of proper apparel. I would also like to offer made-to-order clothing where it would not be necessary for the executive to leave his office to receive this service.

Business Experience

Store Manager, Bally, Inc.   1994–Present

In this position I oversee all store operations including staff management, inventory control, merchandising, promotional events, and daily business analysis.

Department Manager, Neiman-Marcus   1992–1994

Soon after I was hired, I became acting interim manager of men's clothing, during which time sales exceeded plan. I also initiated and implemented a program for special gift items and was responsible for contacting and arranging for personal appearances by designers. Within ten months after hire, I was promoted to manager of fashion accessories, a $1.2 million grossing department.

Duplication Specialist, Account Executive   1992

Chief duties here consisted of the management of major educational and municipal accounts.

Systems Specialist, Albin Business Copiers   1988–1991

During the time with Albin Business Copiers, I was Salesman of the Month five times.

Additional Experience   1982–1988

During this period, I was engaged in various retail and outside sales positions.

Education   1980–1982

I attended Monroe County Community College where I majored in marketing and management. In addition I received training in Dallas with the Neiman-Marcus Sales Management Program as well as other intensive corporate programs which stressed sales and management techniques.

Summary of Qualifications

Previous experience has proven my expertise in merchandising, buying, and display in a retail setting; success in managing and motivating sales associates through training, example, and leadership; strong organizational skills; the ability to compile and present reports concerning department status and fiscal goals; and excellent verbal and written communication skills.

Employee Requirements

Along with the above management who will be active members of the sales team, two additional part-time employees will be required in order to serve the customer to the degree desired by management. The following chart is a tentative scheduling and shows that at no time will there be fewer than three people on duty on any day. This is, of course, contingent upon demand and the principals have decided to err on the side of customer service and not on cost cutting.

Tentative Weekly Schedule							
DAY	MONDAY	TUESDAY	WEDNESDAY	THURSDAY	FRIDAY	SATURDAY	SUNDAY
President	O	O	O	O	O	O	X
Treasurer	O	O	O	O	O	O	X
Sales Manager	O	O	O	O	O	X	X
Salesperson 1	X	O	X	O	O	O	X
Salesperson 2	X	X	O	O	O	O	X

Note: O-on duty, X-off duty; Excalibur will be closed on Sunday.

The management believes that the human resource is the most valuable resource a business has. The people who work on the Excalibur team will be hired not simply on the merits of their experience and knowledge but because of their potential to grow with the business.

The management of Excalibur has decided to outsource the tailoring services for a time in order to see if demand for such services warrants hiring an in-house tailor. Again, the management will allow customer service to drive this decision.

Special Considerations

Facility Needs

The principals of Excalibur have signed an option to lease the facility located at 124 E. Front Street, Monroe, Michigan. Due to the fact that this location was previously used as a retail clothing store, it will need very little reworking in order to fit Excalibur's needs. The location is 2,000 square feet and the option states a lease price of $10.25 per square foot, the price of which includes building management fees.

Employee Training

Due to the high degree of customer service desired by the management, it is imperative that Excalibur have a highly trained staff. The goal is to ensure no less than 20 contact hours of training per employee per year. This training will focus on customer service, selling techniques, industry trends, teamwork, and management training. A battery of trainings will be given to each new hire before any customer contact takes place. This training will include an introduction to the goals and direction of Excalibur and will attempt to instill an enthusiasm for the Excalibur team.

Most people wish for riches, but few provide the definite plan and the burning desire which pave the road to wealth. ▪

Napolean Hill*

Articles of Incorporation
of
Excalibur Traditional Men's Clothier, Ltd.

ARTICLE ONE
Name of Corporation

The name of the corporation is Excalibur Traditional Men's Clothier, Ltd.

ARTICLE TWO
Period of Duration

The period of the duration of the corporation shall be perpetual.

ARTICLE THREE
Purposes and Powers

Purposes. The purpose for which the corporation is organized is the transaction of all lawful business for which corporations may be incorporated pursuant to the Michigan Corporation Code.

Powers. The corporation shall have all of the rights, privileges, and powers now or hereafter conferred upon corporations by Michigan Corporation Code. The corporation shall have and may exercise all powers necessary or convenient to effect any of the purposes for which the corporation has organized.

ARTICLE FOUR
Capital Structure

Aggregate Shares, Classes, and Series. The aggregate number of shares that the corporation shall have authority to issue is 1,000,000 shares of capital stock without par value. The authorized shares are not to be divided into classes or series. There shall be only one class of stock which shall be common stock.

Consideration for Shares. Each share of stock, when issued, shall be fully paid and nonassessable. The shares of the corporation may be issued for consideration as may be fixed from time to time by the president and chief executive officer of the corporation. Consideration may consist of money, property, services, or any consideration that the president and chief executive officer of the corporation shall, in the absence of fraud or bad faith, deem of appropriate value.

ARTICLE FIVE
Conditions to Commencement

The corporation will not commence business until it has received for the issuance of its shares consideration of the value of $50,000.

ARTICLE SIX
Regulation of Internal Affairs

Bylaws. The initial bylaws shall be adopted by the shareholders. The power to alter, amend, or repeal the bylaws or to adopt new bylaws shall be vested in the shareholders. The bylaws may contain any provision for the regulation and management of the affairs of the corporation not inconsistent with law or these articles of incorporation.

ARTICLE SEVEN
Initial Registered Office and Agent

The address of the corporation's registered office is 124 Front Street, Monroe, and the name of its agents at such address are Karl Evan Hall and Brian Mark Springsteel.

* Napolean Hill, *Think and Grow Rich* (New York: Hawthorn, 1966), p. 245.

ARTICLE SEVEN
Cumulative Voting

Voting shall be done on a cumulative per share basis. There will be no directors of the corporation and the shareholders have sole power to repel or amend the bylaws of the incorporation.

ARTICLE EIGHT
Incorporators

The names and addresses of the incorporators are Karl Evan Hall, 1011 Main Street, Parachute, Colorado 81304 and Brian Mark Springsteel, 606 Chipeta Avenue, Grand Junction, Colorado 81501.

Incorporator   Karl Evan Hall

Incorporator   Brian Mark Springsteel

Sworn to on _____ by the above named incorporators.
       (date)

Notary Public, Monroe County, Monroe

Bylaws
of
Excalibur Traditional Men's Clothier, Ltd.

ARTICLE ONE
Meetings of Shareholders

Annual Meetings. Meetings of the shareholders shall be held at the principal place of business of the corporation located at 124 E. Front Street, Monroe, Michigan, unless another place shall have been determined and notice has been given to all shareholders. Annual meetings shall be held on the twentieth day of the month of March, at 9:30 a.m., unless a holiday, and then on the next business day.

Special meetings. Special meetings may be called by any shareholder with a 10 percent or greater share of the total outstanding shares on five days' notice given personally or by telephone, telex, telegraph, or electronic mail, or on fourteen days notice by mail. Special meetings shall be pursuant on the aforementioned location and holiday requirements and restrictions.

Telephone or Video Meetings. The shareholders may participate in any meeting of the shareholders by means of conference telephone or similar communication equipment that enables all participants in the meeting to hear and speak to each other at the same time. Such participation shall constitute presence in person at the meeting.

ARTICLE TWO
Voting

Voting of Shares. Each outstanding share shall be entitled to one vote upon each matter submitted to a meeting of shareholders.

Proxies. At the meeting of shareholders, a shareholder may vote in person or by proxy appointed in writing by the shareholder or by his duly authorized attorney-in-fact. Such writing must be shown at the meeting of the shareholders.

ARTICLE THREE
Informal Action by Shareholders

Any action required or permitted to be taken at a meeting of the shareholders may be taken without a meeting if consent in writing, setting forth the action to be taken, shall be signed by all of the shareholders entitled to vote with respect to the subject matter thereof.

ARTICLE FOUR
Officers

Number and Qualifications. The principle officers of the corporation shall be a president, a secretary, and a treasurer, each of whom shall be elected by the shareholders. Any two or more offices may be held by the same person, except the offices of president and secretary. The officers of the corporation shall be natural persons, eighteen years of age or older.

Election and Term of Office. The principal officers shall be elected annually by vote of the shareholders at the annual meeting of the shareholders.

Removal of Officer. Any officer or agent may be removed by the shareholders whenever in their collective judgment the interests of the corporation shall be best served thereby. Such removal shall be without prejudice to the contract rights, if any, of the person so removed.

President. The president shall be the principal executive officer of the corporation and shall in general, supervise and control all of the business and affairs of the corporation. The president shall, when present, preside at all the meetings of the shareholders. The president shall, at each annual meeting, present a report of the business of the corporation for the preceding fiscal year. The president may sign, with the secretary, certificates for shares of the corporation, any deeds, mortgages, bonds, contracts, or other instruments which the shareholders have authorized to be executed; and in general perform all duties incident to the office of president.

Secretary. The secretary shall: (a) attend and keep the minutes of the proceedings of the shareholders; (b) see that notice of shareholder meetings are given; (c) be custodian of the corporate records and of the seal of the corporation and see that the seal is affixed to any documents requiring the seal; (d) sign with the president, certificates for shares of the corporation, or any deeds, mortgages, bonds, contracts or other instruments which the shareholders have authorized to be executed; (e) keep a complete record of the shareholders on file and have general charge of the stockholder transfer books of the corporation; and (f) in general, perform all duties incident to the office of secretary.

Treasurer. The treasurer shall: (a) keep correct and complete books and records of account on file in the principal place of business of the corporation; (b) have custody of and be responsible for all funds and securities of the corporation; (c) receive monies due and payable to the corporation; (d) immediately deposit all corporate funds in a bank or other depository as may be designated by the shareholders; (e) disburse the funds of the corporation as may be ordered by the president or shareholders as a group; (f) render to the president and to the shareholders an account of all the transactions of the treasurer and the financial condition of the corporation; and (g) in general, perform all duties incident to the office of treasurer.

Vice President. In the absence of the president or in the event of the president's death, inability, or refusal to act, the most senior vice president, but not if the vice president acts also as secretary, shall perform the duties of the president, and when so acting, shall have all the powers and be subject to all the restrictions of the office.

Salaries. The salaries of the officers shall be fixed from time to time by the shareholders and no officer shall be prevented from receiving such salary by reason of the fact that he is also a shareholder of the corporation.

ARTICLE FIVE
Contracts, Loans, and Checks

Contracts. The shareholders may authorize any officer or officers, agent or agents, to enter into any contract or execute and deliver any instrument in the name of and on behalf of the corporation, and such authority may be general or confined to specific instances or restricted as to time.

Loans. No loans shall be contracted on behalf of the corporation and no evidence of indebtedness shall be issued in its name unless authorized by a voting of the shareholders. Such authority may be general or confined to specific instances.

Checks and Drafts. All checks, drafts, or other orders for the payment of money, notes, or other evidences of indebtedness issued in the name of the corporation, shall be signed by both the president and the secretary of the corporation.

ARTICLE SIX
Certificates for Shares and Their Transfer

Certificates for Shares. Each purchaser of shares of the corporation shall be entitled to a certificate, signed by the president and secretary and sealed with the corporate seal or a facsimile thereof certifying the number of shares owned in the corporation. Each certificate shall be consecutively numbered. The certificate representing shares shall state on the face that the corporation is organized under the laws of this state; the name of the person to whom issued; the number of shares; and a statement that the shares are without par value. Restrictions imposed on the transferability of the shares shall be noted conspicuously on the certificate.

Transfer of Shares. The name and address of the person to whom the shares represented thereby are issued, with the number of shares and date of issue, shall be entered on the stock transfer books of the corporation. All certificates surrendered to the corporation for transfer shall be canceled and no new certificate shall be issued until the former certificate for a like number of shares shall have been surrendered and canceled. Transfer of the shares of the corporation shall be made only on the stock transfer books of the corporation by the holder of record thereof or by his or her legal representative, who shall furnish proper evidence of authority to transfer, or by an attorney thereunto authorized by power of attorney duly executed and filed with the secretary of the corporation, and on surrender for cancellation of the certificate for such shares. The person in whose name shares stand on the books of the corporation shall be deemed by the corporation to be the owner thereof for all purposes, except as otherwise authorized or provided in the bylaws.

ARTICLE SEVEN
Corporate Seal

The shareholders shall adopt a corporate seal which shall be circular in form and shall have inscribed on the periphery the name of the corporation and the state of incorporation. In the center of the seal there shall be the word "Seal".

ARTICLE EIGHT
Miscellaneous

Fiscal Year. The fiscal year for the corporation shall run from March 1 to February 28, or 29 in the event of a leap year.

Shareholder's Inspection of Corporate Records. Any shareholder, at any reasonable time may request to inspect, and must be granted access within reasonable standards to, the books, minutes, or other records of the corporation.

ARTICLE NINE
Amendments

The power to alter, amend, or repeal the bylaws or adopt new bylaws shall be vested in the shareholders. The bylaws may contain any provision for the regulation and management of the affairs of the corporation not inconsistent with law or the articles of incorporation.

Appendix B

Tax Forms and Information

This appendix includes publications available from the Internal Revenue Service, types of taxes to which your small business may be subject, and tax forms that you will need.

IRS Publications

The following is a list of tax publications available from the Internal Revenue Service (IRS) to help you prepare your income tax returns. Even if you have your tax returns prepared by someone else, you should still be familiar with tax regulations. You can do this by creating a file of publications that pertain to you and your business. Update these files annually.

These IRS publications are available at no charge by visiting your local IRS office, by calling (800) TAX-FORM, or on the World Wide Web at http://www.ustreas.gov. A CD-ROM containing over 600 current-year and previous-year IRS tax forms, instructions, and tips is available for $46.

Form Number	Title

General Guides

1	Your Rights as a Taxpayer
17	Your Federal Income Tax (For Individuals)
225	Farmer's Tax Guide
334	Tax Guide for Small Business **(Note: This is a very good comprehensive tax and accounting guide that every small business should get every year.)**
509	Tax Calendars for 1996
553	Highlights of 1994 Tax Changes
595	Tax Guide for Commercial Fishermen
910	Guide to Free Tax Services

Employer's Guides

15	Employer's Tax Guide (Circular E)
51	Agricultural Employer's Tax Guide (Circular A)
80	Federal Tax Guide for Employers in the Virgin Islands, Guam, American Samoa, and the Commonwealth of the Northern Mariana Islands (Circular SS)
926	Household Employer's Tax Guide

Specialized Publications

349	Federal Highway Use Tax on Heavy Vehicles
378	Fuel Tax Credits and Refunds
463	Travel, Entertainment, and Gift Expenses
505	Tax Withholding and Estimated Tax
510	Excise Taxes for 1996
515	Withholding of Tax Nonresident Aliens and Foreign Corporations
517	Social Security and Other Information for Members of the Clergy and Religious Workers
527	Residential Rental Property
533	Self-Employment Tax
535	Business Expenses
536	Net Operating Losses
537	Installment Sales
538	Accounting Periods and Methods
541	Tax Information on Partnerships
542	Tax Information on Corporations
544	Sales and Other Dispositions of Assets
551	Bases of Assets
556	Examination of Returns, Appeal Rights, and Claims for Refund
560	Retirement Plans for the Self-Employed
561	Determining the Value of Donated Property
583	Taxpayers Starting a Business

Federal Taxes

Some of the federal taxes for which a sole proprietor, a corporation, or a partnership may be liable are listed on page 575. If a due date falls on a Saturday, Sunday, or legal holiday, it is postponed until the next day that is not a Saturday, Sunday, or legal holiday. A statewide legal holiday delays a due date only if the IRS office where you are required to file is located in that state. Certain exceptions to these due dates may apply. For more information, see Publication 509, *Tax Calendars*.

YOU MAY BE LIABLE FOR:	IF YOU ARE:	USE IRS FORM:	DUE ON OR BEFORE:
Income tax	Sole proprietor	Schedule C or C-EZ (Form 1040)	File with Form 1040
	Individual who is a partner or S corporation shareholder	1040	15th day of 4th month after end of tax year
	Corporation	1120 or 1120-A	15th day of 3rd month after end of tax year
	S Corporation	1120S	15th day of 3rd month after end of tax year
Self-employment tax	Sole proprietor, or an individual who is a partner	Schedule SE (Form 1040)	File with Form 1040
Estimated tax	Sole proprietor or an individual who is a partner or S corporation shareholder	1040-ES	15th day of 4th, 6th, and 9th months of tax year, and 15th day of 1st month after the end of tax year
	Corporation	1120-W (WORKSHEET) 8109 (to make deposits)	15th day of 4th, 6th, 9th, and 12th months of tax year
Annual return of income	Partnership	1065	15th day of 4th month after end of tax year
Social Security and Medicare taxes (FICA taxes and the withholding of income tax)	Sole proprietor, partnership, or corporation	941	April 30, July 31, October 31, and January 31
		8109 (to make deposits)	See Chapter 33 of publication 334
Providing information on Social Security and Medicare taxes (FICA taxes) and the withholding of income tax	Sole proprietor, corporation, S corporation, or partnership	W-2 (to employee)	January 31
		W-2 and W-3 (to the Social Security Administration)	Last day of February
Federal unemployment (FUTA) tax	Sole proprietor, corporation, S corporation, or partnership	940-EZ or 940	January 31
		8109 (to make deposits)	April 30, July 31, October 31, and January 31, but only if the liability for unpaid tax is more than $100
Information returns for payments to nonemployees and transactions with other persons	Sole proprietor, corporation, S corporation, or partnership	See Chapter 36 of publication 334	Form 1099 to the recipient by January 31 and to the IRS by February 28
Excise taxes	Sole proprietor corporation, S corporation, or partnership	See Chapter 35 of publication 334	See instructions to the forms

Source: Department of Treasury, Tax Guide for Small Business (Washington, DC: IRS Publication number 334, 1995), p. 223.

Tax Forms

Form SS-4 Application for Employer Identification Number

All businesses are required to obtain an employer identification number (EIN). If your business is a sole proprietorship without employees, your EIN can be your social security number. Your EIN stays the same for the life of your business unless you change forms of ownership, such as changing from sole proprietorship to corporation. If you have more than one business, you must get a different EIN for each business. (See form on page 578).

Form 1040 U.S. Individual Income Tax Return

As a sole proprietor, partner, shareholder in an S corporation, or member of a Limited Liability Company, you must file your individual taxes and business earnings and losses on Form 1040 (pages 579–580). It is the form on which many of your calculations from other schedules, such as profit or loss (Schedule C) or self-employment tax (Schedule SE), are recorded.

Schedule C (Form 1040) Profit or Loss from Business

Income and expenses from your business are reported on Schedule C (pages 581–582) and filed on line 12 of your 1040 form. If your total business receipts are $25,000 or less or your expenses are $2,000 or less, you may use Schedule C-EZ.

Schedule SE (Form 1040) Self-Employment Tax

You must file Schedule SE (page 583) to report your self-employment tax if your net earnings for the year are over $400. Schedule SE helps you calculate your net earnings for the year to be multiplied by the self-employment tax rate (15.3 percent for 1995). A flow chart is included on the schedule to determine whether you need to use the short or long schedule.

Form 1065 U.S. Partnership Return of Income

Partnership businesses are not taxed directly as the profits of the business pass through the firm and are taxed on the partners' 1040 forms. Still, the partnership must report its income, deductions, and other required information to the IRS by filing Form 1065. If a Limited Liability Company is treated as a partnership, it must file Form 1065 (page 584). Schedule K reports partner's shares of income, credits, and deductions. Form 1065 and its schedules are informational returns.

Form 1120 U.S. Corporation Income Tax Return

Every corporation must file a tax return regardless of gross income, even if it had no taxable income for the year. Form 1120 (page 585) is the income tax return for ordinary corporations. Small corporations which have gross receipts, total income, and total assets all under $500,000, and which meet some other requirements may save time by using Form 1120-A. Form 1120 or 1120-A are due on or before the fifteenth day of the third month after the end of the tax year.

Form 1120S U.S. Income Tax Return for an S Corporation

An eligible domestic corporation can avoid double taxation by forming an S corporation under the rules of the IRS code. Like proprietorships and partnerships, S corporations pass on income, loss, deduction, and credits to their shareholders to be included on their separate returns. Form 1120S is the tax return to be filed by S corporations. Form 1120S (page 586) is due on or before the fifteenth day of the third month after the end of the tax year.

Form 941 Employer's Quarterly Federal Tax Return

Employers who withhold income tax on wages, Social Security tax, or Medicare tax must file Form 941 (page 587) quarterly, unless the business employs seasonal farm workers or household employees (see IRS instructions for exceptions). Social Security, Medicare, and withheld income taxes are reported on Form 941. This form is due on or before April 30, July 31, October 31, and January 31.

Form 940-EZ Employer's Annual Federal Unemployment (FUTA) Tax Return

Federal unemployment tax (FUTA) must be paid by employers into the unemployment insurance system. Form 940 or 940-EZ (page 588) is due on or before January 31 each year. If you pay your state unemployment tax on time, a credit will be allowed against your federal FUTA. Most small businesses qualify to use the simpler 940-EZ form (see IRS instructions).

Form **SS-4**	**Application for Employer Identification Number**	EIN
(Rev. December 1993) Department of the Treasury Internal Revenue Service	(For use by employers, corporations, partnerships, trusts, estates, churches, government agencies, certain individuals, and others. See instructions.)	OMB No. 1545-0003 Expires 12-31-96

Please type or print clearly.

1 Name of applicant (Legal name) (See instructions.)

2 Trade name of business, if different from name in line 1	**3** Executor, trustee, "care of" name
4a Mailing address (street address) (room, apt., or suite no.)	**5a** Business address, if different from address in lines 4a and 4b
4b City, state, and ZIP code	**5b** City, state, and ZIP code

6 County and state where principal business is located

7 Name of principal officer, general partner, grantor, owner, or trustor—SSN required (See instructions.) ▶

8a Type of entity (Check only one box.) (See instructions.)

☐ Sole Proprietor (SSN) _____ ☐ Estate (SSN of decedent) _____ ☐ Trust
☐ REMIC ☐ Personal service corp. ☐ Plan administrator-SSN _____ ☐ Partnership
☐ State/local government ☐ National guard ☐ Other corporation (specify) _____ ☐ Farmers' cooperative
☐ Other nonprofit organization (specify) _____ ☐ Federal government/military ☐ Church or church controlled organization
☐ Other (specify) ▶ _____ (enter GEN if applicable) _____

8b If a corporation, name the state or foreign country (if applicable) where incorporated ▶

State	Foreign country

9 Reason for applying (Check only one box.)

☐ Started new business (specify) ▶ _____ ☐ Changed type of organization (specify) ▶ _____
☐ Hired employees ☐ Purchased going business
☐ Created a pension plan (specify type) ▶ _____ ☐ Created a trust (specify) ▶ _____
☐ Banking purpose (specify) ▶ ☐ Other (specify) ▶

10 Date business started or acquired (Mo., day, year) (See instructions.)

11 Enter closing month of accounting year. (See instructions.)

12 First date wages or annuities were paid or will be paid (Mo., day, year). **Note:** *If applicant is a withholding agent, enter date income will first be paid to nonresident alien. (Mo., day, year)* . . . . ▶

13 Enter highest number of employees expected in the next 12 months. **Note:** *If the applicant does not expect to have any employees during the period, enter "0."* . . . . ▶	Nonagricultural	Agricultural	Household

14 Principal activity (See instructions.) ▶

15 Is the principal business activity manufacturing? . . . . ☐ Yes ☐ No
If "Yes," principal product and raw material used ▶

16 To whom are most of the products or services sold? Please check the appropriate box. ☐ Business (wholesale)
☐ Public (retail) ☐ Other (specify) ▶   ☐ N/A

17a Has the applicant ever applied for an identification number for this or any other business? . . . . ☐ Yes ☐ No
Note: *If "Yes," please complete lines 17b and 17c.*

17b If you checked the "Yes" box in line 17a, give applicant's legal name and trade name, if different than name shown on prior application.

Legal name ▶ Trade name ▶

17c Enter approximate date, city, and state where the application was filed and the previous employer identification number if known.

Approximate date when filed (Mo., day, year)	City and state where filed	Previous EIN

Under penalties of perjury, I declare that I have examined this application, and to the best of my knowledge and belief, it is true, correct, and complete. | Business telephone number (include area code)

Name and title (Please type or print clearly.) ▶

Signature ▶   Date ▶

Note: *Do not write below this line. For official use only.*

Please leave blank ▶	Geo.	Ind.	Class	Size	Reason for applying

For Paperwork Reduction Act Notice, see attached instructions.   Cat. No. 16055N   Form **SS-4** (Rev. 12-93)

Form 1040

Department of the Treasury—Internal Revenue Service

U.S. Individual Income Tax Return (U) **1995**

IRS Use Only—Do not write or staple in this space.

For the year Jan. 1–Dec. 31, 1995, or other tax year beginning _____ , 1995, ending _____ , 19 ___ | OMB No. 1545-0074

Label

(See instructions on page 11.)

Use the IRS label. Otherwise, please print or type.

L A B E L H E R E

| Your first name and initial | Last name | Your social security number |
| If a joint return, spouse's first name and initial | Last name | Spouse's social security number |

Home address (number and street). If you have a P.O. box, see page 11. | Apt. no.

City, town or post office, state, and ZIP code. If you have a foreign address, see page 11.

For Privacy Act and Paperwork Reduction Act Notice, see page 7.

Presidential Election Campaign (See page 11.)

| | Yes | No |
Do you want $3 to go to this fund? . . . . | | |
If a joint return, does your spouse want $3 to go to this fund? . . . . . | | |

Note: Checking "Yes" will not change your tax or reduce your refund.

Filing Status

(See page 11.)

Check only one box.

1 ☐ Single
2 ☐ Married filing joint return (even if only one had income)
3 ☐ Married filing separate return. Enter spouse's social security no. above and full name here. ▶
4 ☐ Head of household (with qualifying person). (See page 12.) If the qualifying person is a child but not your dependent, enter this child's name here. ▶
5 ☐ Qualifying widow(er) with dependent child (year spouse died ▶ 19 ___). (See page 12.)

Exemptions

(See page 12.)

6a ☐ **Yourself.** If your parent (or someone else) can claim you as a dependent on his or her tax return, **do not** check box 6a. But be sure to check the box on line 33b on page 2

b ☐ **Spouse** . . . .

c **Dependents:**

(1) First name Last name	(2) Dependent's social security number. If born in 1995, see page 13.	(3) Dependent's relationship to you	(4) No. of months lived in your home in 1995

If more than six dependents, see page 13.

No. of boxes checked on 6a and 6b _____

No. of your children on 6c who:
• lived with you _____
• didn't live with you due to divorce or separation (see page 14) _____

Dependents on 6c not entered above _____

d If your child didn't live with you but is claimed as your dependent under a pre-1985 agreement, check here ▶ ☐
e Total number of exemptions claimed . . . .

Add numbers entered on lines above ▶ _____

Income

Attach Copy B of your Forms W-2, W-2G, and 1099-R here.

If you did not get a W-2, see page 14.

Enclose, but do not attach, your payment and payment voucher. See page 33

7	Wages, salaries, tips, etc. Attach Form(s) W-2	7	
8a	**Taxable** interest income (see page 15). Attach Schedule B if over $400	8a	
b	**Tax-exempt** interest (see page 15). DON'T include on line 8a 8b		
9	Dividend income. Attach Schedule B if over $400	9	
10	Taxable refunds, credits, or offsets of state and local income taxes (see page 15) . .	10	
11	Alimony received	11	
12	Business income or (loss). Attach Schedule C or C-EZ	12	
13	Capital gain or (loss). If required, attach Schedule D (see page 16) . . .	13	
14	Other gains or (losses). Attach Form 4797	14	
15a	Total IRA distributions . 15a	b Taxable amount (see page 16)	15b	
16a	Total pensions and annuities 16a	b Taxable amount (see page 16)	16b	
17	Rental real estate, royalties, partnerships, S corporations, trusts, etc. Attach Schedule E	17	
18	Farm income or (loss). Attach Schedule F	18	
19	Unemployment compensation (see page 17)	19	
20a	Social security benefits 20a	b Taxable amount (see page 18)	20b	
21	Other income. List type and amount—see page 18 _____	21	
22	Add the amounts in the far right column for lines 7 through 21. This is your **total income** ▶	22	

Adjustments to Income

23a	Your IRA deduction (see page 19)	23a	
b	Spouse's IRA deduction (see page 19)	23b	
24	Moving expenses. Attach Form 3903 or 3903-F . .	24	
25	One-half of self-employment tax	25	
26	Self-employed health insurance deduction (see page 21)	26	
27	Keogh & self-employed SEP plans. If SEP, check ▶ ☐	27	
28	Penalty on early withdrawal of savings	28	
29	Alimony paid. Recipient's SSN ▶	29	
30	Add lines 23a through 29. These are your **total adjustments** . . . . . . ▶	30	

Adjusted Gross Income

| 31 | Subtract line 30 from line 22. This is your **adjusted gross income.** If less than $26,673 and a child lived with you (less than $9,230 if a child didn't live with you), see "Earned Income Credit" on page 27 ▶ | 31 | |

Cat. No. 14087D

Form **1040** (1995)

579

Tax Compu-tation (See page 23.)	**32**	Amount from line 31 (adjusted gross income)	**32**	
	33a	Check if: ☐ **You** were 65 or older, ☐ Blind; ☐ **Spouse** was 65 or older, ☐ Blind. Add the number of boxes checked above and enter the total here . . . . ▶ **33a** ☐		
	b	If your parent (or someone else) can claim you as a dependent, check here . ▶ **33b** ☐		
	c	If you are married filing separately and your spouse itemizes deductions or you are a dual-status alien, see page 23 and check here . . . . ▶ **33c** ☐		
	34	Enter the larger of your: { **Itemized deductions** from Schedule A, line 28, **OR** **Standard deduction** shown below for your filing status. **But if you checked any box on line 33a or b,** go to page 23 to find your standard deduction. If you checked **box 33c,** your standard deduction is zero. • Single—$3,900 • Married filing jointly or Qualifying widow(er)—$6,550 • Head of household—$5,750 • Married filing separately—$3,275 }	**34**	
	35	Subtract line 34 from line 32	**35**	
	36	If line 32 is $86,025 or less, multiply $2,500 by the total number of exemptions claimed on line 6e. If line 32 is over $86,025, see the worksheet on page 23 for the amount to enter	**36**	
If you want the IRS to figure your tax, see page 35.	**37**	**Taxable income.** Subtract line 36 from line 35. If line 36 is more than line 35, enter -0- .	**37**	
	38	Tax. Check if from **a** ☐ Tax Table, **b** ☐ Tax Rate Schedules, **c** ☐ Capital Gain Tax Work-sheet, or **d** ☐ Form 8615 (see page 24). Amount from Form(s) 8814 ▶ **e** _____	**38**	
	39	Additional taxes. Check if from **a** ☐ Form 4970 **b** ☐ Form 4972	**39**	
	40	Add lines 38 and 39 . . . . ▶	**40**	
Credits (See page 24.)	**41**	Credit for child and dependent care expenses. Attach Form 2441	**41**	
	42	Credit for the elderly or the disabled. Attach Schedule R . .	**42**	
	43	Foreign tax credit. Attach Form 1116	**43**	
	44	Other credits (see page 25). Check if from **a** ☐ Form 3800 **b** ☐ Form 8396 **c** ☐ Form 8801 **d** ☐ Form (specify) _____	**44**	
	45	Add lines 41 through 44	**45**	
	46	Subtract line 45 from line 40. If line 45 is more than line 40, enter -0- . . . . ▶	**46**	
Other Taxes (See page 25.)	**47**	Self-employment tax. Attach Schedule SE	**47**	
	48	Alternative minimum tax. Attach Form 6251	**48**	
	49	Recapture taxes. Check if from **a** ☐ Form 4255 **b** ☐ Form 8611 **c** ☐ Form 8828	**49**	
	50	Social security and Medicare tax on tip income not reported to employer. Attach Form 4137 .	**50**	
	51	Tax on qualified retirement plans, including IRAs. If required, attach Form 5329 . .	**51**	
	52	Advance earned income credit payments from Form W-2	**52**	
	53	Household employment taxes. Attach Schedule H	**53**	
	54	Add lines 46 through 53. This is your **total tax** . . . . ▶	**54**	
Payments Attach Forms W-2, W-2G, and 1099-R on the front.	**55**	Federal income tax withheld. If any is from Form(s) 1099, check ▶ ☐	**55**	
	56	1995 estimated tax payments and amount applied from 1994 return .	**56**	
	57	**Earned income credit.** Attach Schedule EIC if you have a qualifying child. Nontaxable earned income: amount ▶ _____ and type ▶ _____	**57**	
	58	Amount paid with Form 4868 (extension request)	**58**	
	59	Excess social security and RRTA tax withheld (see page 32) .	**59**	
	60	Other payments. Check if from **a** ☐ Form 2439 **b** ☐ Form 4136	**60**	
	61	Add lines 55 through 60. These are your **total payments** . . . . . . ▶	**61**	
Refund or Amount You Owe	**62**	If line 61 is more than line 54, subtract line 54 from line 61. This is the amount you **OVERPAID** . .	**62**	
	63	Amount of line 62 you want **REFUNDED TO YOU** . . . . ▶	**63**	
	64	Amount of line 62 you want **APPLIED TO YOUR 1996 ESTIMATED TAX** ▶	**64**	
	65	If line 54 is more than line 61, subtract line 61 from line 54. This is the **AMOUNT YOU OWE.** For details on how to pay and use **Form 1040-V,** Payment Voucher, see page 33 . . ▶	**65**	
	66	Estimated tax penalty (see page 33). Also include on line 65	**66**	

Sign Here Keep a copy of this return for your records.	Under penalties of perjury, I declare that I have examined this return and accompanying schedules and statements, and to the best of my knowledge and belief, they are true, correct, and complete. Declaration of preparer (other than taxpayer) is based on all information of which preparer has any knowledge.		
	▶ Your signature	Date	Your occupation
	▶ Spouse's signature. If a joint return, BOTH must sign.	Date	Spouse's occupation

Paid Preparer's Use Only	Preparer's signature ▶	Date	Check if self-employed ☐	Preparer's social security no.
	Firm's name (or yours if self-employed) and address ▶		EIN	
			ZIP code	

580

⊛ *Printed on recycled paper*   *U.S.GPO:1995-389-067

Profit or Loss From Business

(Sole Proprietorship)

▶ **Partnerships, joint ventures, etc., must file Form 1065.**

▶ **Attach to Form 1040 or Form 1041.** ▶ **See Instructions for Schedule C (Form 1040).**

OMB No. 1545-0074

1995

Attachment Sequence No. **09**

Name of proprietor

Social security number (SSN)

A Principal business or profession, including product or service (see page C-1)

B Enter principal business code
(see page C-6) ▶

C Business name. If no separate business name, leave blank.

D Employer ID number (EIN), if any

E Business address (including suite or room no.) ▶ ....
City, town or post office, state, and ZIP code

F Accounting method: **(1)** ☐ Cash **(2)** ☐ Accrual **(3)** ☐ Other (specify) ▶ ....

G Method(s) used to value closing inventory: **(1)** ☐ Cost **(2)** ☐ Lower of cost or market **(3)** ☐ Other (attach explanation) **(4)** ☐ Does not apply (if checked, skip line H) | Yes | No

H Was there any change in determining quantities, costs, or valuations between opening and closing inventory? If "Yes," attach explanation

I Did you "materially participate" in the operation of this business during 1995? If "No," see page C-2 for limit on losses.

J If you started or acquired this business during 1995, check here . . . . ▶ ☐

Part I   Income

1	Gross receipts or sales. **Caution:** If this income was reported to you on Form W-2 and the "Statutory employee" box on that form was checked, see page C-2 and check here . . . . ▶ ☐	1
2	Returns and allowances	2
3	Subtract line 2 from line 1	3
4	Cost of goods sold (from line 40 on page 2)	4
5	**Gross profit.** Subtract line 4 from line 3	5
6	Other income, including Federal and state gasoline or fuel tax credit or refund (see page C-2) . .	6
7	**Gross income.** Add lines 5 and 6 . . . . ▶	7

Part II   Expenses. Enter expenses for business use of your home **only** on line 30.

8	Advertising	8		19 Pension and profit-sharing plans	19
9	Bad debts from sales or services (see page C-3) . .	9		20 Rent or lease (see page C-4):	
10	Car and truck expenses (see page C-3)	10		a Vehicles, machinery, and equipment .	20a
11	Commissions and fees. . .	11		b Other business property . .	20b
12	Depletion.	12		21 Repairs and maintenance . .	21
13	Depreciation and section 179 expense deduction (not included in Part III) (see page C-3) . .	13		22 Supplies (not included in Part III)	22
				23 Taxes and licenses	23
14	Employee benefit programs (other than on line 19) . . .	14		24 Travel, meals, and entertainment:	
15	Insurance (other than health) .	15		a Travel	24a
16	Interest:			b Meals and entertainment .	
a	Mortgage (paid to banks, etc.) .	16a		c Enter 50% of line 24b subject to limitations (see page C-4) .	
b	Other	16b		d Subtract line 24c from line 24b	24d
17	Legal and professional services	17		25 Utilities	25
				26 Wages (less employment credits) .	26
18	Office expense	18		27 Other expenses (from line 46 on page 2)	27

28	**Total expenses** before expenses for business use of home. Add lines 8 through 27 in columns. ▶	28
29	Tentative profit (loss). Subtract line 28 from line 7	29
30	Expenses for business use of your home. Attach **Form 8829**	30
31	**Net profit or (loss).** Subtract line 30 from line 29.	

 • If a profit, enter on **Form 1040, line 12,** and ALSO on **Schedule SE, line 2** (statutory employees, see page C-5). Estates and trusts, enter on Form 1041, line 3.

 • If a loss, you MUST go on to line 32.

| 31 |

32 If you have a loss, check the box that describes your investment in this activity (see page C-5).

 • If you checked 32a, enter the loss on **Form 1040, line 12,** and ALSO on **Schedule SE, line 2** (statutory employees, see page C-5). Estates and trusts, enter on Form 1041, line 3.

 • If you checked 32b, you MUST attach **Form 6198.**

32a ☐ All investment is at risk.

32b ☐ Some investment is not at risk.

For Paperwork Reduction Act Notice, see Form 1040 instructions.   Cat. No. 15786J   **Schedule C (Form 1040) 1995**

| **Part III** | **Cost of Goods Sold** (see page C-5) | | |

33	Inventory at beginning of year. If different from last year's closing inventory, attach explanation . .	**33**	
34	Purchases less cost of items withdrawn for personal use	**34**	
35	Cost of labor. Do not include salary paid to yourself	**35**	
36	Materials and supplies	**36**	
37	Other costs	**37**	
38	Add lines 33 through 37	**38**	
39	Inventory at end of year	**39**	
40	**Cost of goods sold.** Subtract line 39 from line 38. Enter the result here and on page 1, line 4 . .	**40**	

| **Part IV** | **Information on Your Vehicle.** Complete this part **ONLY** if you are claiming car or truck expenses on line 10 and are not required to file Form 4562 for this business. See the instructions for line 13 on page C-3 to find out if you must file. |

41   When did you place your vehicle in service for business purposes? (month, day, year) ▶ ..../.........../........ .

42   Of the total number of miles you drove your vehicle during 1995, enter the number of miles you used your vehicle for:

a   Business .... b Commuting .... c Other ....

43   Do you (or your spouse) have another vehicle available for personal use? . . . . ☐ Yes   ☐ No

44   Was your vehicle available for use during off-duty hours? . . . . ☐ Yes   ☐ No

45a Do you have evidence to support your deduction? . . . . ☐ Yes   ☐ No
 b   If "Yes," is the evidence written? . . . . ☐ Yes   ☐ No

| **Part V** | **Other Expenses.** List below business expenses not included on lines 8–26 or line 30. |

....		
....		
....		
....		
....		
....		
....		
....		
....		
46 Total other expenses. Enter here and on page 1, line 27	**46**	

Printed on recycled paper   ☆ **U.S. GOVERNMENT PRINTING OFFICE:** 1995-389-520

Self-Employment Tax

▶ See Instructions for Schedule SE (Form 1040).

▶ Attach to Form 1040.

OMB No. 1545-0074

1995

Attachment
Sequence No. **17**

Name of person with **self-employment** income (as shown on Form 1040)

Social security number of person
with **self-employment** income ▶

Who Must File Schedule SE

You must file Schedule SE if:

- You had net earnings from self-employment from **other than** church employee income (line 4 of Short Schedule SE or line 4c of Long Schedule SE) of $400 or more, **OR**
- You had church employee income of $108.28 or more. Income from services you performed as a minister or a member of a religious order **is not** church employee income. See page SE-1.

Note: *Even if you have a loss or a small amount of income from self-employment, it may be to your benefit to file Schedule SE and use either "optional method" in Part II of Long Schedule SE. See page SE-3.*

Exception. If your only self-employment income was from earnings as a minister, member of a religious order, or Christian Science practitioner **and** you filed Form 4361 and received IRS approval not to be taxed on those earnings, **do not** file Schedule SE. Instead, write "Exempt–Form 4361" on Form 1040, line 47.

May I Use Short Schedule SE or MUST I Use Long Schedule SE?

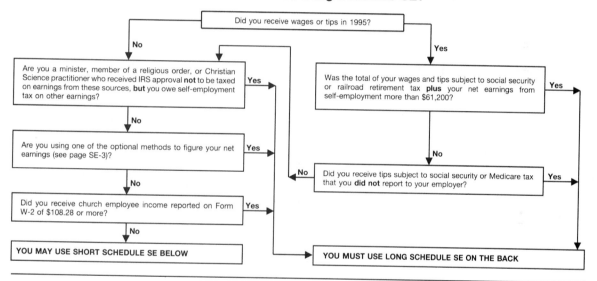

Did you receive wages or tips in 1995?

No

Are you a minister, member of a religious order, or Christian Science practitioner who received IRS approval **not** to be taxed on earnings from these sources, **but** you owe self-employment tax on other earnings?　**Yes** ▶

No

Are you using one of the optional methods to figure your net earnings (see page SE-3)?　**Yes** ▶

No

Did you receive church employee income reported on Form W-2 of $108.28 or more?　**Yes** ▶

No

YOU MAY USE SHORT SCHEDULE SE BELOW

Yes

Was the total of your wages and tips subject to social security or railroad retirement tax **plus** your net earnings from self-employment more than $61,200?　**Yes** ▶

No

No ◀ Did you receive tips subject to social security or Medicare tax that you **did not** report to your employer?　**Yes** ▶

YOU MUST USE LONG SCHEDULE SE ON THE BACK

Section A—Short Schedule SE. Caution: *Read above to see if you can use Short Schedule SE.*

1 Net farm profit or (loss) from Schedule F, line 36, and farm partnerships, Schedule K-1 (Form 1065), line 15a	**1**	
2 Net profit or (loss) from Schedule C, line 31; Schedule C-EZ, line 3; and Schedule K-1 (Form 1065), line 15a (other than farming). Ministers and members of religious orders see page SE-1 for amounts to report on this line. See page SE-2 for other income to report	**2**	
3 Combine lines 1 and 2	**3**	
4 **Net earnings from self-employment.** Multiply line 3 by 92.35% (.9235). If less than $400, **do not** file this schedule; you do not owe self-employment tax . . . . ▶	**4**	
5 **Self-employment tax.** If the amount on line 4 is: • $61,200 or less, multiply line 4 by 15.3% (.153). Enter the result here and on **Form 1040, line 47.** • More than $61,200, multiply line 4 by 2.9% (.029). Then, add $7,588.80 to the result. Enter the total here and on **Form 1040, line 47.**	**5**	

6 **Deduction for one-half of self-employment tax.** Multiply line 5 by 50% (.5). Enter the result here and on **Form 1040, line 25** . . . . | **6** |

For Paperwork Reduction Act Notice, see Form 1040 instructions.　　　Cat. No. 11358Z　　　**Schedule SE (Form 1040) 1995**

U.S. Partnership Return of Income

For calendar year 1995, or tax year beginning .... , 1995, and ending .... , 19 .... .
▶ **See separate instructions.**

OMB No. 1545-0099

1995

A Principal business activity	Use the IRS label. Otherwise, please print or type.	Name of partnership	D Employer identification number
B Principal product or service		Number, street, and room or suite no. (If a P.O. box, see page 10 of the instructions.)	E Date business started
C Business code number		City or town, state, and ZIP code	F Total assets (see page 10 of the instructions) $

G Check applicable boxes: (1) ☐ Initial return (2) ☐ Final return (3) ☐ Change in address (4) ☐ Amended return

H Check accounting method: (1) ☐ Cash (2) ☐ Accrual (3) ☐ Other (specify) ▶ ....

I Number of Schedules K-1. Attach one for each person who was a partner at any time during the tax year ▶ ....

Caution: *Include **only** trade or business income and expenses on lines 1a through 22 below. See the instructions for more information.*

Income

1a Gross receipts or sales	1a		
b Less returns and allowances	1b		1c
2 Cost of goods sold (Schedule A, line 8)			2
3 Gross profit. Subtract line 2 from line 1c			3
4 Ordinary income (loss) from other partnerships, estates, and trusts *(attach schedule)*			4
5 Net farm profit (loss) *(attach Schedule F (Form 1040))*			5
6 Net gain (loss) from Form 4797, Part II, line 20			6
7 Other income (loss) *(attach schedule)*			7
8 **Total income (loss).** Combine lines 3 through 7			8

Deductions (see page 11 of the instructions for limitations)

9 Salaries and wages (other than to partners) (less employment credits)			9
10 Guaranteed payments to partners			10
11 Repairs and maintenance			11
12 Bad debts			12
13 Rent			13
14 Taxes and licenses			14
15 Interest			15
16a Depreciation (if required, attach Form 4562)	16a		
b Less depreciation reported on Schedule A and elsewhere on return	16b		16c
17 Depletion **(Do not deduct oil and gas depletion.)**			17
18 Retirement plans, etc.			18
19 Employee benefit programs			19
20 Other deductions *(attach schedule)*			20
21 **Total deductions.** Add the amounts shown in the far right column for lines 9 through 20			21
22 **Ordinary income (loss)** from trade or business activities. Subtract line 21 from line 8			22

Please Sign Here

Under penalties of perjury, I declare that I have examined this return, including accompanying schedules and statements, and to the best of my knowledge and belief, it is true, correct, and complete. Declaration of preparer (other than general partner or limited liability company member) is based on all information of which preparer has any knowledge.

▶ _____
Signature of general partner or limited liability company member

▶ _____
Date

Paid Preparer's Use Only

Preparer's signature ▶	Date	Check if self-employed ▶ ☐	Preparer's social security no.
Firm's name (or yours if self-employed) and address ▶		EIN ▶	
		ZIP code ▶	

For Paperwork Reduction Act Notice, see page 1 of separate instructions.

Cat. No. 11390Z

Form **1065** (1995)

Form 1120

Department of the Treasury
Internal Revenue Service

U.S. Corporation Income Tax Return

For calendar year 1995 or tax year beginning .... , 1995, ending .... , 19 ...
▶ **Instructions are separate. See page 1 for Paperwork Reduction Act Notice.**

OMB No. 1545-0123

1995

A Check if a:
1 Consolidated return (attach Form 851) ☐
2 Personal holding co. (attach Sch. PH) ☐
3 Personal service corp. (as defined in Temporary Regs. sec. 1.441-4T— see instructions) ☐

Use IRS label. Otherwise, print or type.

Name

Number, street, and room or suite no. (If a P.O. box, see page 6 of instructions.)

City or town, state, and ZIP code

B Employer identification number

C Date incorporated

D Total assets (see page 6 of instructions)
$

E Check applicable boxes: (1) ☐ Initial return (2) ☐ Final return (3) ☐ Change of address

Income	**1a** Gross receipts or sales [____] **b** Less returns and allowances [____] **c** Bal ▶		**1c**	
	2 Cost of goods sold (Schedule A, line 8)		**2**	
	3 Gross profit. Subtract line 2 from line 1c		**3**	
	4 Dividends (Schedule C, line 19)		**4**	
	5 Interest		**5**	
	6 Gross rents		**6**	
	7 Gross royalties		**7**	
	8 Capital gain net income (attach Schedule D (Form 1120)) . . .		**8**	
	9 Net gain or (loss) from Form 4797, Part II, line 20 (attach Form 4797) .		**9**	
	10 Other income (see page 7 of instructions—attach schedule) . . .		**10**	
	11 **Total income.** Add lines 3 through 10 . . . . ▶		**11**	

Deductions (See instructions for limitations on deductions.)	**12** Compensation of officers (Schedule E, line 4)		**12**	
	13 Salaries and wages (less employment credits)		**13**	
	14 Repairs and maintenance		**14**	
	15 Bad debts		**15**	
	16 Rents		**16**	
	17 Taxes and licenses		**17**	
	18 Interest		**18**	
	19 Charitable contributions (see page 9 of instructions for 10% limitation)		**19**	
	20 Depreciation (attach Form 4562) **20**			
	21 Less depreciation claimed on Schedule A and elsewhere on return . . **21a**		**21b**	
	22 Depletion		**22**	
	23 Advertising		**23**	
	24 Pension, profit-sharing, etc., plans		**24**	
	25 Employee benefit programs		**25**	
	26 Other deductions (attach schedule)		**26**	
	27 **Total deductions.** Add lines 12 through 26 . . . . . ▶		**27**	
	28 Taxable income before net operating loss deduction and special deductions. Subtract line 27 from line 11		**28**	
	29 **Less:** **a** Net operating loss deduction (see page 11 of instructions) . . **29a**			
	b Special deductions (Schedule C, line 20) **29b**		**29c**	

Tax and Payments	**30** **Taxable income.** Subtract line 29c from line 28		**30**	
	31 **Total tax** (Schedule J, line 10)		**31**	
	32 **Payments: a** 1994 overpayment credited to 1995 **32a**			
	b 1995 estimated tax payments . . **32b**			
	c Less 1995 refund applied for on Form 4466 **32c** ( ) **d** Bal ▶ **32d**			
	e Tax deposited with Form 7004 . . . . **32e**			
	f Credit from regulated investment companies (attach Form 2439) . . **32f**			
	g Credit for Federal tax on fuels (attach Form 4136). See instructions **32g**		**32h**	
	33 Estimated tax penalty (see page 12 of instructions). Check if Form 2220 is attached . . . ▶ ☐		**33**	
	34 **Tax due.** If line 32h is smaller than the total of lines 31 and 33, enter amount owed . . .		**34**	
	35 **Overpayment.** If line 32h is larger than the total of lines 31 and 33, enter amount overpaid .		**35**	
	36 Enter amount of line 35 you want: **Credited to 1996 estimated tax** ▶ **Refunded** ▶		**36**	

Sign Here

Under penalties of perjury, I declare that I have examined this return, including accompanying schedules and statements, and to the best of my knowledge and belief, it is true, correct, and complete. Declaration of preparer (other than taxpayer) is based on all information of which preparer has any knowledge.

▶ _____   _____   ▶ _____
Signature of officer   Date   Title

Paid Preparer's Use Only

Preparer's signature ▶	Date	Check if self-employed ☐	Preparer's social security number
Firm's name (or yours if self-employed) and address ▶		EIN ▶	
		ZIP code ▶	

Cat. No. 11450Q

<table>
<tr>
<td>Form 1120S</td>
<td colspan="2">U.S. Income Tax Return for an S Corporation</td>
<td>OMB No. 1545-0130</td>
</tr>
</table>

Form **1120S**

Department of the Treasury
Internal Revenue Service

U.S. Income Tax Return for an S Corporation

▶ Do not file this form unless the corporation has timely filed
Form 2553 to elect to be an S corporation.
▶ See separate instructions.

OMB No. 1545-0130

19**95**

For calendar year 1995, or tax year beginning _____ , 1995, and ending _____ , 19____

	Use IRS label. Other-wise, please print or type.		
A Date of election as an S corporation		Name	**C** Employer identification number
B Business code no. (see Specific Instructions)		Number, street, and room or suite no. (If a P.O. box, see page 9 of the instructions.)	**D** Date incorporated
		City or town, state, and ZIP code	**E** Total assets (see Specific Instructions) $

F Check applicable boxes: (1) ☐ Initial return (2) ☐ Final return (3) ☐ Change in address (4) ☐ Amended return

G Check this box if this S corporation is subject to the consolidated audit procedures of sections 6241 through 6245 (see instructions before checking this box) ▶ ☐

H Enter number of shareholders in the corporation at end of the tax year ▶

Caution: *Include **only** trade or business income and expenses on lines 1a through 21. See the instructions for more information.*

Income

1a Gross receipts or sales _____	**b** Less returns and allowances _____	**c** Bal ▶ **1c**
2 Cost of goods sold (Schedule A, line 8)		**2**
3 Gross profit. Subtract line 2 from line 1c		**3**
4 Net gain (loss) from Form 4797, Part II, line 20 *(attach Form 4797)*		**4**
5 Other income (loss) *(attach schedule)*		**5**
6 **Total income (loss).** Combine lines 3 through 5 ▶		**6**

Deductions (see page 10 of the instructions for limitations)

7 Compensation of officers		**7**
8 Salaries and wages (less employment credits)		**8**
9 Repairs and maintenance		**9**
10 Bad debts		**10**
11 Rents		**11**
12 Taxes and licenses		**12**
13 Interest		**13**
14a Depreciation *(if required, attach Form 4562)*	**14a**	
b Depreciation claimed on Schedule A and elsewhere on return	**14b**	
c Subtract line 14b from line 14a		**14c**
15 Depletion **(Do not deduct oil and gas depletion.)**		**15**
16 Advertising		**16**
17 Pension, profit-sharing, etc., plans		**17**
18 Employee benefit programs		**18**
19 Other deductions *(attach schedule)*		**19**
20 **Total deductions.** Add the amounts shown in the far right column for lines 7 through 19 ▶		**20**
21 Ordinary income (loss) from trade or business activities. Subtract line 20 from line 6		**21**

Tax and Payments

22 **Tax: a** Excess net passive income tax *(attach schedule)*	**22a**	
b Tax from Schedule D (Form 1120S)	**22b**	
c Add lines 22a and 22b (see page 13 of the instructions for additional taxes)		**22c**
23 **Payments: a** 1995 estimated tax payments and amount applied from 1994 return	**23a**	
b Tax deposited with Form 7004	**23b**	
c Credit for Federal tax paid on fuels *(attach Form 4136)*	**23c**	
d Add lines 23a through 23c		**23d**
24 Estimated tax penalty. Check if Form 2220 is attached ▶ ☐		**24**
25 **Tax due.** If the total of lines 22c and 24 is larger than line 23d, enter amount owed. See page 3 of the instructions for depositary method of payment ▶		**25**
26 **Overpayment.** If line 23d is larger than the total of lines 22c and 24, enter amount overpaid ▶		**26**
27 Enter amount of line 26 you want: **Credited to 1996 estimated tax** ▶	**Refunded** ▶	**27**

Please Sign Here

Under penalties of perjury, I declare that I have examined this return, including accompanying schedules and statements, and to the best of my knowledge and belief, it is true, correct, and complete. Declaration of preparer (other than taxpayer) is based on all information of which preparer has any knowledge.

▶ _____   _____   ▶ _____
Signature of officer   Date   Title

Paid Preparer's Use Only

Preparer's signature ▶	Date	Check if self-employed ▶ ☐	Preparer's social security number
Firm's name (or yours if self-employed) and address ▶		EIN ▶	
		ZIP code ▶	

For Paperwork Reduction Act Notice, see page 1 of separate instructions. Cat. No. 11510H Form **1120S** (1995)

Form **941**
(Rev. January 1995)
Department of the Treasury
Internal Revenue Service (O)

4141

Employer's Quarterly Federal Tax Return

▶ **See separate instructions for information on completing this return.**
Please type or print.

Enter state code for state in which deposits made . ▶ ☐
(see page 3 of instructions).

Name (as distinguished from trade name)	Date quarter ended	OMB No. 1545-0029
		T
Trade name, if any	Employer identification number	FF
		FD
Address (number and street)	City, state, and ZIP code	FP
		I
		T

If address is different from prior return, check here ▶ ☐

IRS Use

1 1 1 1 1 1 1 1 1 1   2   3 3 3 3 3 3   4 4 4

5 5 5   6   7   8 8 8 8 8   9 9   10 10 10 10 10 10 10 10 10 10

If you do not have to file returns in the future, check here ▶ ☐   and enter date final wages paid ▶

If you are a seasonal employer, see **Seasonal employers** on page 1 of the instructions and check here ▶ ☐

1	Number of employees (except household) employed in the pay period that includes March 12th ▶		
2	Total wages and tips, plus other compensation	**2**	
3	Total income tax withheld from wages, tips, and sick pay	**3**	
4	Adjustment of withheld income tax for preceding quarters of calendar year	**4**	
5	Adjusted total of income tax withheld (line 3 as adjusted by line 4—see instructions)	**5**	
6a	Taxable social security wages . . . . $_____ × 12.4% (.124) =	**6a**	
b	Taxable social security tips . . . . $_____ × 12.4% (.124) =	**6b**	
7	Taxable Medicare wages and tips . . . . . $_____ × 2.9% (.029) =	**7**	
8	Total social security and Medicare taxes (add lines 6a, 6b, and 7). Check here if wages are not subject to social security and/or Medicare tax . . . . ▶ ☐	**8**	
9	Adjustment of social security and Medicare taxes (see instructions for required explanation) Sick Pay $_____ ± Fractions of Cents $_____ ± Other $_____ =	**9**	
10	Adjusted total of social security and Medicare taxes (line 8 as adjusted by line 9—see instructions)	**10**	
11	**Total taxes** (add lines 5 and 10)	**11**	
12	Advance earned income credit (EIC) payments made to employees, if any	**12**	
13	Net taxes (subtract line 12 from line 11). **This should equal line 17, column (d) below** (or line D of Schedule B (Form 941))	**13**	
14	Total deposits for quarter, including overpayment applied from a prior quarter	**14**	
15	**Balance due** (subtract line 14 from line 13). Pay to Internal Revenue Service	**15**	

16 **Overpayment,** if line 14 is more than line 13, enter excess here ▶ $_____
and check if to be: ☐ Applied to next return   **OR**   ☐ Refunded.

- **All filers:** If line 13 is less than $500, you need not complete line 17 or Schedule B.
- **Semiweekly depositors:** Complete Schedule B and check here . . . . ▶ ☐
- **Monthly depositors:** Complete line 17, columns (a) through (d), and check here . . . . ▶ ☐

17	**Monthly Summary of Federal Tax Liability.**		
(a) First month liability	**(b)** Second month liability	**(c)** Third month liability	**(d)** Total liability for quarter

Sign Here   Under penalties of perjury, I declare that I have examined this return, including accompanying schedules and statements, and to the best of my knowledge and belief, it is true, correct, and complete.

Signature ▶ _____   Print Your Name and Title ▶ _____   Date ▶ _____

For Paperwork Reduction Act Notice, see page 1 of separate instructions.   Cat. No. 17001Z   Form **941** (Rev. 1-95)

Form 940-EZ

Department of the Treasury
Internal Revenue Service (O)

Employer's Annual Federal Unemployment (FUTA) Tax Return

OMB No. 1545-1110

1994

	T
	FF
	FD
	FP
	I
	T

Name (as distinguished from trade name)

Calendar year

Trade name, if any

Address and ZIP code

Employer identification number

Follow the chart under **Who May Use Form 940-EZ** on page 2. If you cannot use Form 940-EZ, you must use Form 940 instead.

A Enter the amount of contributions paid to your state unemployment fund. (See instructions for line A on page 4.) ▶ $ ....

B (1) Enter the name of the state where you have to pay contributions . . . . ▶ ....
(2) Enter your state reporting number as shown on state unemployment tax return. ▶

If you will not have to file returns in the future, check here (see **Who Must File,** on page 2) **complete, and sign the return** . . . . . ▶ ☐

If this is an Amended Return check here . . . . ▶ ☐

Part I   Taxable Wages and FUTA Tax

1	Total payments (including payments shown on lines 2 and 3) during the calendar year for services of employees	**1**	

Amount paid

2 Exempt payments. (Explain all exempt payments, attaching additional sheets if necessary.) ▶ ....
....

		2	

3 Payments for services of more than $7,000. Enter only amounts over the first $7,000 paid to each employee. Do not include any exempt payments from line 2. Do not use your state wage limitation. The $7,000 amount is the Federal wage base. Your state wage base may be different . . . .

3	

4 Total exempt payments (add lines 2 and 3) . . . . ▶   **4**

5 **Total taxable wages** (subtract line 4 from line 1) **5**

6 **FUTA tax.** Multiply the wages on line 5 by .008 and enter here. (If the result is over $100, also complete Part II.) .   **6**

7 Total FUTA tax deposited for the year, including any overpayment applied from a prior year (from your records) ▶   **7**

8 **Amount you owe** (subtract line 7 from line 6). This should be $100 or less. Pay to "Internal Revenue Service."   **8**

9 **Overpayment** (subtract line 6 from line 7). Check if it is to be: ☐ **Applied to next return, or** ☐ **Refunded** ▶   **9**

Part II   Record of Quarterly Federal Unemployment Tax Liability (Do not include state liability.) Complete only if line 6 is over $100.

Quarter	First (Jan. 1 – Mar. 31)	Second (Apr. 1 – June 30)	Third (July 1 – Sept. 30)	Fourth (Oct. 1 – Dec. 31)	Total for year
Liability for quarter					

Under penalties of perjury, I declare that I have examined this return, including accompanying schedules and statements, and, to the best of my knowledge and belief, it is true, correct, and complete, and that no part of any payment made to a state unemployment fund claimed as a credit was, or is to be, deducted from the payments to employees.

Signature ▶   Title (Owner, etc.) ▶   Date ▶

Cat. No. 10983G

Form **940-EZ** (1994)

DO NOT DETACH

Form 940-V-EZ

Department of the Treasury
Internal Revenue Service

Form 940-EZ Payment Voucher

1994

Complete boxes 1, 2, 6, and 7. **Do not send cash and do not staple your payment to this voucher.** Make your check or money order, with your employer identification number clearly written on it, payable to the **Internal Revenue Service.**

1 Your employer identification number	2 Enter the first four letters of your business name	3 MFT	4 Tax year	5 Transaction code
		1 0	9 4 1 2	6 1 0
	6 Your name and address		7 Amount of payment	
			$.	
Do not staple your payment to this voucher.			Do not send cash.	

Case I

Testing the Limits

Testing the limits is an apt description of Yvon Chouinard in both his personal and professional life, which tend to overlap to the point of being indistinguishable. Chouinard, a lifelong avid outdoors adventurer, is the founder and owner of Patagonia, Inc., the Ventura, California-based maker and retailer of outdoor clothing and equipment. His unique approach to managing his business is an interesting story of how a business owner can succeed—and succeed, not just in the usual sense of being profitable, but in a variety of ways that some business-people might consider atypical—by following his dream.

This story begins in 1957 when the 19-year-old Chouinard began selling handmade mountain-climbing equipment out of his car. Frustrated with the standard climbing pitons (pegs pounded into rock or ice as a climbing support) that were used and then left behind, Chouinard had designed a removable hard-steel piton that could be used repeatedly and with less waste. His other innovative designs revolutionized mountain climbing equipment.

By 1964 Chouinard had moved to the coastal city of Ventura, California, in search of good surf, where he eventually set up shop in a tin shed behind a meat-packing plant. His legendary reputation among extreme adventurers attracted other self-described "dirt bags" and "fun hogs" seeking work. Chouinard hired workers not on the basis of any particular business skills but because they had climbed, surfed, or fished with him and wanted to work with him because it seemed like a fun thing to do. Chouinard's management style included making decisions from the "gut." For instance, when he realized that his climbing pitons were severely pitting and scarring rock faces, Chouinard denounced them in an essay in the company catalog about "clean climbing." At that time, such products constituted 70 percent of his company's sales. He then introduced an environmentally responsible aluminum alternative.

By the early 1970s Chouinard had added a line of outdoor clothing that became so immensely popular that he created a new name for it: Patagonia. (The name comes from the southern region of Argentina.) The 1980s were a bonanza for the company as it continued to post increasing sales revenues. Customers bought not only Patagonia's products—rain gear, foul-weather sailing wear, ski clothes, and casual pants, shirts, and shorts—but the lifestyle they represented. By the late 1980s Patagonia offered 375 different styles and the company's annual growth rate was nearly 30 percent.

Patagonia was regularly heralded in the business press for its atypical business atmosphere. With an on-site sand volleyball court for aggressive lunchtime matches, surfboards propped in office corners for employees to catch the best afternoon waves, and a company cafeteria serving gourmet pizzas and fresh-cut organic vegetables, the company's image was "one of cool Patagonia people selling cool products to cool people."

However, that image was tarnished in 1991 when Patagonia, whose sales had become flat, found itself with a warehouse full of stuff that wasn't selling. Expenses had spiraled out of control and the company faced a cash crunch, so it took on millions of dollars in additional debt just to stay afloat. An uncertain economic environment and a mild winter contributed to the problems.

Chouinard also found himself at a crossroads in deciding what he wanted for his business. Chouinard and his wife Malinda (who is co-owner) sought counsel from Michael Kami, president of the Center for Strategic Management in Miami. In Kami's blunt assessment, entrepreneurial businesses like Patagonia which were at the outer limits of their capacity generally had two options: sell the company or adopt a more "normal" or businesslike management style. The Chouinards and key company colleagues went on a retreat to Argentina to discuss the "next 100 years." They concluded that the only way to reconcile the company's values with its environmental impact was to "use the company as a tool for social change." But what exactly did this assertion mean? Sidestepping Kami's advice, it established a policy of "slow growth" to return the company to its original mission of producing the highest-quality products and donating a portion of its profits.

To achieve this new goal, Chouinard downsized the company by 20 percent, cut the clothing line by 30 percent, reduced catalog production from four to two times a year, and replaced the direct-mail tactic of prospecting with rented mailing lists. Chouinard described the change to customers in an essay called "Reality Check" in the fall 1991 catalog. "Everything pollutes," he wrote. "Well, last fall you had a choice of five ski pants; now you may choose between two. This is, of course, un-American, but two styles of ski pants are all that anyone needs."

The company's accountant said that Patagonia became a much better company from a traditional financial management perspective because of the slow, controlled growth. At the same time, the company's commitment to social accountability has made a difference. To some entrepreneurs, Chouinard's decision to live within self-prescribed limits may seem to contradict the American ethic of pursuing growth at any cost. Yet Chouinard has learned from his life-long pursuit of risk sports that one should never exceed one's resources. "The ultimate is to be right on the edge, but you never go over it because then you'd be dead," he said. "Living on that edge and breaking a lot of the rules in business to do things our own way is what unifies the company."

Chouinard's visionary management style arises from his strong philosophical principles about the relationship between business and the environment. It's best reflected in the simple description of the company's mission: "Building really good products for your friends and being able to do some good." His idea of "doing good" means donating 1 percent of the company's annual sales to environmental groups. And Patagonia's commitment to priorities beyond the bottom line is a critical success factor: In 1994, Chouinard was named one of the retailing industry's "Entrepreneurs of the Year." Today the company manufactures and retails outdoor clothing and equipment worldwide. By the end of its fiscal year in April 1995, Patagonia's sales had reached $150 million and checks written to environmental groups totaled $1.5 million. Chouinard, and Patagonia's current managers, know that they need to keep focused on the company's values. They've recently reaffirmed those core principles: commitment to the environment, dedication to employees and community, and pursuit of highest quality. A glowing testament to the company's ability to do this comes from one of its competitors, Jack Gilbert, president of Mountain Hardware of Berkeley, California. "It would appear to be difficult to stay on the cutting edge over such an extended period, and to be true to such lofty environmental goals, but Patagonia manages to do both well," Gilbert said. "Plus, they're honorable businesspeople, a company which is true to its word." Chouinard's approach to business and sports has marked him as an innovator. And he has proven that you can "test the limits" and succeed.

Sources:

"Retailing's Entrepreneurs of the Year," *Chain Store Age Executive* (December 1994), pp. 46–50; Polly LaBarre, "Patagonia Comes of Age," *Industry Week*, April 3, 1995, pp. 42–48; and Mary Scott, "Interview with Yvon Chouinard," *Business Ethics* (May/June 1995), pp. 31–34.

Questions:

1. How and why did Chouinard start his business? Is this typical for small business owners? Explain.

2. Can company growth become a problem? What are some ways that small business owners or managers can solve these problems?

3. Do you think that many small business owners or managers make decisions from the "gut"? What are the advantages of doing so? What might the drawbacks be?

4. What role have Chouinard's personal values played in the company's growth and operations?

5. Why does a nontraditional approach to doing business appear to work for Patagonia? Could it work for other companies? Why or why not?

Case II

Preston's Cleaners*

Family businesses are often described as constituting the "bedrock" of America—especially by politicians on the campaign trail. However, those same politicians are creating a tangle of laws and regulations that are threatening to strangle the family business as families attempt to pass the business from one generation to the next. Preston's Cleaners is a classic example.

Preston's Cleaners was incorporated in 1969 by Mark and Sylvia Preston of Lincoln, Illinois, and eventually taken over by the Prestons' son Glen. Having received a degree in business, Glen worked in Tennessee for ten years as a manager for a large publicly owned company. Then his parents began looking for someone besides themselves to manage the family dry cleaning business. After a year of wavering back and forth, Glen decided in 1991 to return home and buy into the family firm. But, Glen admits, the actual transfer of the business from parents to son has been like walking a financial tightrope.

The company run by Mark and Sylvia had a single location—a "package plant" as it's called in the industry, where both the customer service facility and

* The story of Preston's Cleaners describes a real situation, although the names and locations have been disguised at the owner's request.

the dry cleaning equipment were housed. However, Glen realized that in order to support both his family—a wife, two young daughters—and his parents, he would need a larger volume of business. So he decided to double the size of the first store and to add a second location. Although the site he chose for Preston's #2 was not in a "demographically desirable" area, Glen said, he received a good deal from the landlord, who was also the landlord for Preston's #1. At Preston's #2, Glen installed a shirt laundry making it the first cleaners to wash shirts "in-house" rather than sending them to a commercial laundry operation. The dry cleaning equipment was still located at Preston's #1. Although it was an expensive proposition, Glen felt that he gained control over the quality of the cleaning process. However, his competitors soon added their own shirt laundries.

One of Preston's competitive advantages is that it provides pick-up and delivery service to homes and businesses. However, this service has had its drawbacks too. For instance, Glen recalled, one of his delivery employees was caught stealing goods from customers' homes, which he had hidden in the attic of another customer's home. Because this individual had access to customers' homes, it was easy for him to do. And, it was pretty safe, really. After all, how often do people actually get into their attics? He was finally caught when the customer whose attic was the storage site had to unexpectedly stay home with a sprained ankle, heard someone enter her house and go up into the attic. After calling the police, she retrieved a pistol and was able to get off a shot, hitting the employee in the ankle as he was coming down the stairs. That's when she discovered that her attic had become the storage site for goods stolen from other customers' houses. Needless to say, Glen fired the employee immediately and revised the way that pick-ups and deliveries were made.

In Glen's first three years, sales volume continued to increase, so he considered opening a third location. Because the northeast side of the city was growing rapidly, he decided that Preston's #3 should be located there and found a new strip shopping center in the area that offered a very attractive demographic location. However, Glen's biggest competitors also decided to build stores in the area. Still Glen went ahead with his plans and opened Preston's #3 in 1994. The store provided drop-off and pick-up service, but did not have any cleaning equipment, thus reducing his capital expenses.

Unfortunately, 1995 was a bad year for the entire dry cleaning industry. Although Glen did not detect any significant decrease in sales revenues, five new competitors opened their doors, which could affect future sales. And Glen, who had always been pretty confident in his ability to project sales, found that none of his past guidelines fit.

One factor affecting the overall climate, he felt, was the economy, because of the concerns it caused his customers about their job security. The stagnant retail sales of clothing that resulted also had an impact on the dry cleaning business. Fewer clothes purchased meant fewer clothes to be dry cleaned or laundered. Not only were customers taking fewer clothes in to be cleaned, they were leaving them for longer periods of time. For instance, Preston's inventory used to be 8 days; it has become closer to 24 days.

Changes in people's lifestyles and expectations further threaten the demand for dry cleaning services. For instance, Glen sensed that the trend toward more casual dressing could ultimately affect his sales revenues. His target market had always been professionals—doctors, attorneys, managers, accountants, and so forth. As firms institute practices such as "casual Fridays," the number of suits, ties, and other professional clothing that need to be cleaned is likely to decline.

Glen cited globalization and other market pressures as having an impact on his business. It used to be that the big-name clothing manufacturers would stand behind their products. Now, as manufacturers chase price and negotiate contracts all over the world, often at the expense of quality, the local dry cleaner has to deal with the shoddily made clothes that customers bring in for cleaning. When these clothes fall apart easily, the angry customer sometimes blames the closest suspect—the dry cleaner—for the problem.

Finally, Glen noted the labor shortage that he faced in 1995. Finding good employees and keeping them has always been a problem for small service businesses. But Glen found it particularly trying in 1995. He tells this story: "I hired a young man (I'll call him Joe) who appeared to be a hard worker. One of the requirements for this particular job is that you have to be at work at 4 a.m. During his first couple of weeks on the job, Joe was catching a ride with a friend, but that individual didn't have to be at work until 5 a.m. and got tired of getting up earlier than he really needed to. I decided that Joe had potential and I wanted to keep him. So I went out to a local used-car auction and bought a 1982 blue Cadillac for $760 and loaned it to Joe. He appreciated the gesture and for the next couple of weeks was at work right on time. Then, one Friday afternoon, Joe turned the keys over, saying he'd found a better-paying job. He quit and I haven't seen him since. Now my wife is hollering at me to get that darned car out of the driveway. I don't know what else I can do to get or keep good employees."

All of these factors led Glen to shut down Preston's #2. "You're in business to make a profit," he said. "It didn't make a profit." Then he added, "You can have the best product, the best-quality product, but if people don't have money to pay for it, you won't be in business." He said he continues to struggle with the plans for transferring the business from his parents to himself without incurring a significant, and potentially costly, tax bite. He recommends getting as much advice on the process as you can.

Despite all the pressures and risks, Glen doesn't regret making the decision to come back in the family business. For one thing, he said, his parents are there for him and they back him completely. Also he enjoys the freedom to make his own decisions. He still strongly believes in the power of family businesses, although he is worried about the climate that they face.

Source:
Personal interview with the owner, March 1996.

Questions:

1. Research family businesses at the library. How prevalent are they? What types of issues and challenges do family businesses face? In what ways is Preston's Cleaners a "typical" family business?

2. Preston's Cleaners is obviously a service-type business. Would Glen Preston have faced similar problems if the family business were in manufacturing? Why or why not?

3. Look at the location decision behind Preston's #2. Do you think this is a typical way for small business owners to make this decision? What are the problems with doing so? How would you have made this decision?

4. What are Preston's Cleaners' competitive advantages? Are they sustainable? Might the company develop other competitive advantages? Describe.

5. Glen Preston described some of the challenges that his industry faces. Do you think a small business owner needs this information? Why or why not?

6. Although there are no financials included, Glen states that he shut down Preston's #2 because it didn't make a profit. Do you think you would have made the same decision? Are there some instances when a small business might keep a location open even though it's not making a profit? Explain.

7. Discuss the implications of Glen's statement, "You can have the best product, the best-quality product, but if people don't have money to pay for it, you won't be in business."

8. What do you think the advantages of starting or running a family business are? What are the drawbacks?

Case III

Home, Sweet Home

Bob Gray of Baltimore, Maryland, operates a small business out of his home. He shared his experiences and thoughts in a telephone interview about the rewards and drawbacks of starting and operating his home-based business.

Describe your company. How long have you been in this business? I started my own business—Robert Gray Writing and Editing—in June 1987. It's a marketing communications and consulting business, which means that I help organizations to write marketing literature. That may take the form of anything from a product capabilities brochure to an annual report. On the corporate side, I do product brochures, product literature, or service descriptions for a service company. I also do a lot of nonprofit organization work and my clients have ranged from hospitals to museums to colleges and universities. I'm not really a marketing specialist. I'm a copywriter with skills in the area of marketing communications.

My work is done mostly as part of a creative team that's hired by a client to develop these communications pieces. Typically what happens is that an end client, an organization that has a particular marketing communications need, will retain a graphic design studio to help put together the materials it needs. And then, that design studio will serve as a kind of general contractor and will hire other members of this creative team. All of us—graphic designer, illustrator, photographer, or other specialists, as needed—then work together as a team to pull together the desired materials. But I've also dealt on my own with organizations as end clients. Essentially I deal with two types of clients: graphic design studios who hire me as part of a creative team to work on a specific project, and organizations who hire me directly.

I'm the sole employee of my company and I usually work about 40 hours a week, although those 40 hours aren't all billable. As a one-person operation, there are lots of things I have to do besides making the acutal product for clients. My billing is based upon my estimate of what a single project will cost. This takes into account the actual hours I think I'll spend doing it, the prevailing market value of what I'm actually writing, and a certain margin to cover the expenses of maintaining my business and earning a profit. I very rarely actually work on an hour-by-hour basis. I usually work toward a single dollar amount that we (myself and the client) have agreed upon.

In my office, I have a Macintosh computer, a laser printer, fax machine, modem, an external disk drive, and a removable cartridge Syquest disk drive. I also have a photocopier, file cabinets, and the usual basic office equipment. Plus I have a portable computer that I take with me when I'm out of the office. Both of my computer systems have e-mail access through the Internet and through my account with America Online, an online service provider. (And like any other business I have an account with a security agency to protect my equipment.)

How did you get into this particular type of business? Before I opened my business, I worked for about three years in a small advertising agency. Before that, I worked for a year in a corporate communications office in a software publishing company. And, before that, I was a high school English teacher.

The advertising agency that I was working for was preparing to close its Baltimore office. In fact, they'd laid off every other employee except me. I was the creative staff for this ad agency, which was good in a way because it allowed me to hire other freelancers. That gave me the opportunity for about a year to explore the freelance community in Baltimore and see what it was like. During that time, I knew that I was either going to have to move with this company to New York or stay here and do something on my own. At this point in my life I was also diligently pursuing one of my other hobbies, playing tenor saxophone, and I wasn't really interested in the corporate lifestyle or in moving up the corporate ladder, which is what moving to New York would have meant. Plus, the ad agency really wasn't offering me what I felt was enough money to move to New York compared to what I thought I could make in Baltimore as a freelancer. All these factors conspired together so that when the ad agency finally did ask me to move, I said no. I feel very fortunate that I was in the forefront of the home-office boom in the United States. I felt at the time that it was the right decision for me and I still feel that way.

What problems and challenges did you face in going into business for yourself? How did you deal with these? I started my business with next to nothing. I think I had less than $1,000 in my savings account. I had a computer at home, but I didn't really know much about it. Early challenges were, as you might expect, making it from month to month. I was never afraid that I would fail—and that was very important. Fortunately, I lived in a very inexpensive place and I was young enough that I didn't have a lot of financial commitments beyond the simplest ones. I did have a line of credit that I used a couple of times to get me through some difficult days.

Also, when I started, I didn't know what the business was necessarily going to turn into. A writing business constantly evolves. For the first three years I was not making a lot of money but doing okay—actually I was making a little bit more than at the ad agency. As I became a known entity, work began to flow in more regularly. Now I'm constantly busy and can select the projects that I want to work on rather than taking everything that comes in. I still have qualms about doing that. It's difficult for me to turn down work, although I will do it, whereas before I never would. And a lot of times I don't have to turn down work because I can tap into other resources and have other people help me.

What problems and challenges do you face currently in running your own business? How do you deal with these? One of the challenges is directing the business. It's like steering a ship, turning it in the direction you want it to go. A problem that many businesses face as they become known for or experienced in certain areas is that people tend to call on them for certain things. If you've been the one steering the ship and you attempt to turn it to another direction, it can be a difficult thing to do. For instance, when I get requests for work in a certain area that I may not particularly want to work in, I examine the project and try to determine whether or not the benefits of working on it outweigh the drawbacks of doing so. If I decide that it's not something I want to work on, I describe to the client what I feel are my areas of strength, saying that I'd love to work with the client in the future if he or she has any needs in those areas. Then I try to give the client the name of somebody else who I think would do a really good job. It's a tough balancing act because you don't want to burn any bridges.

Another challenge that I always face is keeping current on billing and keeping the whole financial end of my business moving along smoothly. On paper, I do fine, but then I still have extreme ups and downs when maybe ten projects will be finished and I receive checks for them. But then I might face a month where I don't get much money, so I have to balance all this out. One of the bittersweet ironies of becoming more successful is that you take on fewer but larger projects. When you're billing the way I do (which is in chunks at the beginning, middle, and end), you may get a check, then not get another for three months, and then another in three months. So bigger projects—while they're typically more prestigious, more fun, and pay more money—have much longer billing cycles. I have to figure out how to deal with that.

Another challenge I face now is managing other people. As I said before, I've been subcontracting some work and I do face the challenge of being a manager. I've got to assemble their work and put it together. I've got to be concerned about the relationships with these writers and the client and how these relationships reflect on me.

Finally, I've got to face the question of expansion. All of the advantages I have of working out of my home, working for myself, and having the freedom to work as I want to could disappear if I expanded the business to the point where I had to rent out space and have a staff of two or three writers working with me. When I'm really, really busy, I think about this and whether I should simply be more selective about the work I take on or be more aggressive about getting clients.

What's the favorite and least favorite parts of running your own business? My favorite part is coming up with the solution to a creative problem that's dictated by the project. The most fun is solving a problem in a creative and purposeful way. My least favorite part has to be collecting on deadbeats—trying to get money out of people who don't want to pay. On balance, though, I'd say it's a good life. In fact, sometimes I think it's the most incredible life you can have. At other times, of course, it's terrible when you're under tremendous deadline pressures and projects aren't working out right—people hate what you're doing, they think your writing stinks, and they let you know that. But most of the time, I think it's fantastic.

What "words of wisdom" can you give to students studying about small business ownership and management? There are no rules, there's no formula, there's no single method, there's no academic program in business—especially in small business—that can *fully* prepare you for being in business for yourself. You need to have a lot of faith in your own ability to prevail. You have to be very optimistic and very positive. There's an old saying that talent is 90 percent perspiration and 10 percent inspiration, or something like that. If you have faith and optimism in your ability to have a business, and you have 90 percent of that and 10 percent of talent and skills, you'll go much further than if you have 90 percent talent and 10 percent faith, optimism, and perseverance.

Source:

Personal telephone interview with Bob Gray, Baltimore, Maryland, March 1996.

Questions:

1. Research home-based businesses at the library. Is the number of home-based businesses growing? Why?

2. What are some of the advantages of running a home-based business? What are the challenges?

3. Describe how Bob Gray got into his own business. Do you think this is a typical approach? Explain.

4. Develop a list of the supplies and equipment that you think a home office might need. Draw what you think would be an ideal layout for a home office. Explain your rationale for placing equipment and supplies where you did.

5. Do you think that the problems and challenges that Gray first faced in starting his business are normal? What others might a small business owner face?

6. Gray cited four current challenges in running his business: directing the business; keeping current on billing and other financial matters; managing other people as he subcontracts work; and expansion. Do you think these are typical for small businesses? Why or why not? What other types of challenges might a small business that's beyond the startup phase face? How might these challenges be dealt with?

7. Discuss Gray's "words of wisdom" on small business ownership and management.

Case IV

Another Look at Open-book Management

It's been described as nothing less than a "revolution" in management thinking. But opening up the financial statements (the "books") is just the beginning of what it means to practice open-book management. Let's look at the concept more closely and at some of the companies that have put it into practice.

What is open-book management? It's an approach to managing an organization that encourages everyone in the organization to focus on improving the financials—in other words, on making more money—or, How is this strategy different from what owners and employees have always done? Haven't owners always wanted to make money and haven't employees always wanted to be employed and so they'd do whatever was necessary to keep their jobs? Well, what makes it different is that with open-book management, employees are given the information needed to understand *why* they're asked to solve problems, cut costs, decrease defects, and provide excellent customer service. Armed with this information they can see the link between their actions and the bottom line.

John Case, author of *Open-Book Management: The Coming Business Revolution*, cities the three essential features of a business that's open book. First, "Every employee sees—and learns to understand—the company's financials, along with all the other numbers that are critical to tracking the business's performance." Every employee has access to the numbers and knows whether or not the business is making money and why. Second, "Employees learn that, whatever else they do, part of their job is to move those numbers in the right direction." Warehouse employees and checkout clerks, no less than sales managers, understand their role in the company's financial performance. Finally, "Employees have a direct stake in the company's success." That is, if the business makes a profit, employees get a cut of it.

In implementing open-book management in your small business, you should recognize that there's no "recipe" to follow. A plant manager at Pace Industries' Cast-Tech Division explained, "It's more a philosophy than a how-to-do-it, step-by-step program." However, according to Case, you'll need to take four steps before open-book management can work.

Step 1 is *to get the information out*. Determine what your business's key operational numbers are: customer returns, on-time deliveries, lines of code written, floral arrangements designed, or whatever. Show employees the financial statements: income statement, cash flow statement, and balance sheet. How do you distribute this information? You might use bulletin boards, paper handouts at meetings, or messages posted on your internal e-mail system. (You may also wish to request confidentiality.) For instance, at Manco, a distributor of tape and other consumer products that is located near Cleveland, big charts on the lunchroom walls post the previous day's sales, year-to-date revenues and expenses, year-to-date profits, return on operating assets, and other key financial numbers. Herman Miller, the furniture maker based in Zeeland, Michigan, distributes videos that detail and explain the company's numbers. And at an engineering firm in Blacksburg, Virginia, the financials are loaded on the company's computer network. It doesn't matter which approach you choose to get the information out as long as you do get the information to employees.

The next step is *to teach the basics of business*. Although most people work in organizations, it's surprising how little they know about business. For instance, some people think that revenues are the same as profits. Others consider profits to be whatever cash the business has in the bank. How can you teach people about the way businesses operate? You'll probably have to start off in a classroom-type setting in which you go through the financials step by step. For instance, at Foldcraft, a manufacturer of institutional seating based in Kenyon, Minnesota, employees begin by learning about personal finances, compiling personal income statements and balance sheets. Then they're introduced to a fictional chocolate chip cookie company with simplified financials. They look at the expenses and how changes in the price of flour, for example, will change the results. Next employees are shown Foldcraft's actual financials and how they compare to this simplified fictional chocolate chip cookie company. Once you've taught employees the basics, it's time to reinforce these lessons every day on the job. And that's exactly what practicing open-book management means. As Case has said, "What reinforces the learning best, of course, is the open-book system itself. When people see important information regularly, they find ways to learn what it says. If part of their income depends on that bottom line, you can be sure they will soon understand which numbers have the biggest impact on it."

The third step in preparing your company for open-book management is *to empower people to make decisions based on what they know*. Many companies claim to practice empowerment or employee involvement. But if employees don't know how their work affects the bottom line, how empowered are they really? In

Case's analogy, it's like giving someone the authority to drive a truck and then not giving him or her a map or a destination. One approach followed by Eric Gershman, founder of Published Image, a financial newsletter publisher in Boston, was to establish teams that act like self-contained businesses. These teams line up their own clients, negotiate prices, take responsibility for producing the client's newsletter from start to finish, and collect their own accounts receivable. They're even learning to keep their own books. Another approach, pioneered by Springfield Remanufacturing Company, is called the "huddle" system. Here representatives from the company's various departments and divisions meet (or "huddle") once every two weeks to report numbers and share opinions about the upcoming months. These groups also generate an income statement, cash flow statement, and a forecast which representatives take back to their own unit.

The final step in implementing open-book management is *to make sure everyone—EVERYONE!—shares directly in the company's success and in the risk of failure.* As Case put it, "If you want people to think like owners, they must be rewarded like owners." At many conventionally managed companies, profit sharing is used as a means of involving employees. However, these plans often don't have the intended motivational effects because employees don't understand the numbers or don't believe what managers tell them. In an open-book company, employees know what they're working toward at the beginning of each year. They track their progress by watching the numbers and at the end of the time period, they know whether or not they've been successful and why. For example, at Kacey Fine Furniture in Denver, employees were paid a bonus based on net profits and return on assets during the first year of open-book management. The next year, a factor designed to minimize customer returns was included. At Engines Plus, a Springfield, Missouri, company that buys diesel engines and converts them to stationary power plants, employees were paid bonuses linked both to profit before taxes and to inventory accuracy. In their situation, inventory accuracy was a key operational number and the CEO wanted to keep it in sharp focus.

Whether or not you choose to give open-book management a try in your small business, it's important to consider what you want your business to be like, how you intend to keep employees motivated, and how you can achieve the performance levels you want. After all, since you've chosen to take the plunge into small business ownership, doesn't it make sense to do the very best that you can?

Source:

John Case, "The Open-Book Revolution," *Inc.* (June 1995), pp. 26–50.

Questions:

1. Describe in your own words what open-book management is.
2. The case emphasized open-book management in business organizations. Could the practice be implemented in not-for-profit organizations? If so, how? If not, why not?
3. Do you think that there are risks to sharing financial information with employees? Explain. Why don't these risks seem to bother companies who have implemented open-book management?
4. Working in teams, design a short course for teaching the basics of business. Assume that employees have no previous knowledge about business. Ex-

plain *what* you want to teach; *how* you're going to teach it; and *how long* each unit should last.

5. Do research on any one of the following topics, looking for the most current information. Describe what it is, how it's being used, and any advantages or disadvantages.

- empowerment
- employee stock ownership plans (ESOPs)
- employee participation
- self-managed work teams
- profit-sharing planes

6. Why do you think open-book management is being called a "revolution" in management thinking?

7. Do you think that you'd ever try open-book management in your own business? Why or why not?

Endnotes

Chapter 1

1. *Small Business Primer.* NFIB Foundation/Visa Business Card, (August 1993), p. 2.
2. Ibid.
3. *Code of Federal Regulations 13:121,* Standard Industrial Classification Codes and Size Standards (Washington, DC: U.S. Government Printing Office, January 1, 1994), pp. 354–367.
4. *Standard & Poor's Register of Corporations, Directors and Executives,* Volume 1 (New York: McGraw-Hill, 1995), pp. 161, 1733.
5. John A. Byrne, "How Entrepreneurs Are Reshaping the Economy and What Big Companies Can Learn," *Business Week,* Enterprise edition (October 1993), pp. 12–18.
6. Therese Eiben and Joyce Davis, "A New 500 for the New Economy," *Fortune,* May 15, 1995, p. 166.
7. B. Baumohl, "When Downsizing Becomes Dumbsizing," *Time,* March 15, 1993, p. 55.
8. Byrne, "How Entrepreneurs Are Reshaping the Economy," p. 14.
9. *Statistical Abstract of the United States, 1993.*
10. Ibid.
11. *Small Business Primer.* NFIB Foundation/Visa Business Card, (August 1993), p. 16.
12. Byrne, "How Entrepreneurs Are Reshaping the Economy," p. 12.
13. "Small Business Job Creation in 1993," *The Small Business Advocate* (May 1994), p. 6.
14. "They Create Winners: The Boom in Entrepreneurial Education," *Success* (September 1994), p. 43.
15. Faye Rice, "How to Make Diversity Pay," *Fortune,* August 8, 1994, pp. 79–86.

16. *Competing in a Seller's Market: Is Corporate America Prepared?* Workforce 2000, (Washington, DC: Towers Perrin, 1990).

17. "Workforce Diversity Stirs Little Concern," *The Wall Street Journal*, May 22, 1992, p. B1.

18. Russell Mitchell and Michael Oneal, "Managing by Values," *Business Week*, August 1, 1994, pp. 46–52.

19. Ibid., p. 46.

20. Faye Rice, "How to Make Diversity Pay," p. 79.

21. Andrew Serwer, "Lessons From America's Fastest-Growing Companies," *Fortune* (August 1994), p. 59.

22. Dorothy Gaiter, "Short-Term Despair, Long-Term Promise," *The Wall Street Journal*, April 3, 1992, p. R1.

23. Therese Eiben and Joyce Davis, "A New 500 for the New Economy," p. 170.

24. Ibid.

25. Myron Magnet, "The New Golden Rule of Business," *Fortune*, February 21, 1994, pp. 60–63.

26. Brenda Paik Sunoo and Jennifer Laabs, "Winning Strategies for Outsourcing Contracts," *Personnel Journal* (March 1994), pp. 69–78.

27. "Farming Out Your Financials," *Inc.* (April 1994), p. 116.

28. Byrne, "How Entrepreneurs Are Reshaping the Economy and What Big Companies Can Learn," p. 12.

29. John Case, "The Wonderland Economy," *Inc. The State of Small Business*, March 16, 1995, p. 29.

30. Ibid.

31. Howard Gleckman, "Meet the Giant-Killers," *Business Week*, Enterprise edition (October 1993), pp. 68–73.

32. "Report Examines Small Business Innovative Activity," *The Small Business Advocate* (December 1993), p. 10.

33. George Gendron, Michael Hopkins, and David Birch, "Managing in the New Economy," *Inc.* (April 1990), pp. 33–41.

34. "The Whiz Kids—Never Stop Learning," *Success* (September 1994), pp. 38–42.

35. Michael Barier, "Learning the Meaning of Measurement," *Nation's Business* (June 1994), pp. 72–74.

36. David Greising, "Quality—How To Make It Pay," *Business Week*, August 8, 1994, pp. 54–74.

37. Dun & Bradstreet, Business Economics Division, *The Business Failure Record, 1990* (New York, 1990).

38. "Avoiding the Pitfalls," *The Wall Street Journal Report on Small Business*, May 22, 1995, p. R1.

39. Case, "The Wonderland Economy," p. 24.

40. James Aley, "Debunking the Failure Fallacy," *Fortune,* September 6, 1993, p. 21.

41. *1994 Information Please Almanac* (Boston: Houghton Mifflin, 1994), p. 839.

42. "Sharp Increase Seen in New Firm Formation," *The Small Business Advocate* (July 1994), p. 5.

43. Michael Selz, "Small Business Survival Rate Expected to Rise in 1994," *The Wall Street Journal*, February 18, 1994, p. B2.

Chapter 2

1. Robert Hisrich, "Entrepreneurship/Intrapreneurship," *American Psychologist* (February 1990), p. 209.

2. P. VanderWerf and C. Brush, "Toward Agreement on the Focus of Entrepreneurship Research: Progress Without Definition," *Proceedings of the National Academy of Management Conference*, Washington, DC, 1989.

3. Carol Moore, "Understanding Entrepreneurial Behavior: A Definition and Model," in J. A. Pearce, II and R. B. Robinson, Jr. (eds.), *Academy of Management Best Paper Proceedings*. Forty-sixth Annual Meeting of the Academy of Management, Chicago, pp. 66–70. Also see William Bygrave, "The Entrepreneurial Paradigm (I): A Philosophical Look at Its Research Methodologies, *Entrepreneurship: Theory and Practice* (Fall 1989), pp. 7–25, and William Bygrave and Charles Hofer, "Theorizing About Entrepreneurship," *Entrepreneurship: Theory and Practice* (Winter 1991), pp. 13–22.

4. A. Shapiro and L. Sokol, "The Social Dimensions of Entrepreneurship," in J. A. Kent, D. L. Sexton, and K. H. Vesper (eds.), *Encyclopedia of Entrepreneurship* (Englewood Cliffs, NJ: Prentice Hall, 1982).

5. J. A. Schumpeter, *History of Economic Analysis* (New York: Oxford University, 1934).

6. William Gartner, " 'Who Is an Entrepreneur?' Is the Wrong Question," *Entrepreneurship: Theory and Practice* (Summer 1989), p. 47. Also see J. W. Carland, F. Hoy, W. R. Boulton, and J. A. C. Carland, "Differentiating Entrepreneurs From Small Business Owners: A Conceptualization," *Academy of Management Review,* Vol. 9, no. 2 (1984), pp. 354–359, and William Gartner, "What Are We Talking About When We Talk About Entrepreneurship?" *Journal of Business Venturing,* 5, (1990), pp. 15–28.

7. Steven Covey, *The Seven Habits of Highly Effective People* (New York: Simon and Schuster, 1989), p. 95.

8. Peter Drucker, *Innovation and Entrepreneurship: Practice and Principles*, (New York: Harper & Row, 1985).

9. Christopher Caggiano and Susan Greco, "Boot Me Up," *Inc.* (November 1993), pp. 44–45, "Start-ups From Scratch," *Inc.* (September 1994), pp. 76–77. *Inc.* magazine publishes an article annually on very successful businesses that were started with very little money.

10. Jon Goodman, "What Makes an Entrepreneur?" *Inc.* (October 1994), p. 29.

11. David C. McClelland, *The Achieving Society* (New York: Van Nostrand Reinhold, 1961). Also see David McClelland, "Achievement Motivation Can Be Developed," *Harvard Business Review* (November/December 1965), pp. 6+, and David Miron and David McClelland, "The Impact of Achievement Motivation Training on Small Business," *California Management Review* (Summer 1979), pp. 13–28.

12. Robert Brochhaus and Pamela S. Horwitz, "The Psychology of the Entrepreneur," in Donald Sexton and Raymond W. Smilor (eds.), *The Art and Science of Entrepreneurship* (Cambridge, MA: Ballinger Publishing Co., 1986), pp. 25–48.

13. Timothy S. Hatten, "Student Entrepreneurial Characteristics and Attitude Change Toward Entrepreneurship as Affected by Participation in an SBI Program," *Journal of Education for Business,* March/April 1995.

14. Michael Oneal, "Just What Is an Entrepreneur?" *Business Week,* Enterprise 1993, pp. 104–112.

15. Ingrid Abramovitch, "Myth of the Gunslinger," *Success* (March 1994), p. 37.

16. *A Small Business Primer.* NFIB Foundation/American Express Travel.

17. Jerome Katz, "The Institution and Infrastructure of Entrepreneurship," *Entrepreneurship: Theory and Practice* (Spring 1991), pp. 85–102.

18. "They Create Winners," *Success* (September 1994), p. 43.

19. Ibid., p. 43.

20. William Bygrave, *The Portable MBA in Entrepreneurship* (New York: John Wiley & Sons, 1994), p. 2.

21. "Never Stop Learning," *Success* (September 1994), p. 41.

22. "Two Who Made Good," *Inc.* (June 1994), p. 40.

23. Fred Steingold, *Legal Guide for Starting and Running a Small Business* (Berkeley, CA: Nolo Press, 1993), p. 1/9.

24. James Hopson and Patricia Hopson, "Helping Clients Choose the Legal Form for a Small Business," *The Practical Accountant* (October 1990), pp. 67–84.

25. Steingold, *Legal Guide for Starting and Running a Small Business.*

26. William Cohen, *The Entrepreneur and Small Business Problem Solver,* 2nd ed. (New York: John Wiley and Sons, 1990), p. 10.

27. Ibid., p. 1/20.

28. Ibid., p. 1/19.

Chapter 3

1. For a more complete discussion of corporate social responsibility, see Stephen P. Robbins and Mary Coulter, *Management* 5th ed. (Upper Saddle River, NJ: Prentice Hall, 1996). Also see Archie Carroll, "The Pyramid of Corporate Social Responsibility: Toward the Moral Management of Organizational Stakeholders," *Business Horizons* (July/August 1991), pp. 39–48; and Richard Rodewald, "The Corporate Social Responsibility Debate: Unanswered Questions About the Consequences of Moral Reform," *American Business Law Journal* (Fall 1987), pp. 443–466.

2. O. C. Ferrell and John Fraedrich, *Business Ethics: Ethical Decision Making and Cases,* 2nd ed. (Boston: Houghton Mifflin, 1994), p. 67.

3. Milton Friedman and Rose Friedman, *Free to Choose* (New York: Harcourt Brace Jovanovich, 1980); and Milton Friedman, *Capitalism and Freedom* (Chicago: University of Chicago Press, 1963) p. 133.

4. Jack Gordon, "Rethinking Diversity," *Training* (January 1992), p. 23.

5. Anne Fisher, "Sexual Harassment: What To Do," *Fortune,* August 23, 1993, pp. 84–88.

6. 29 CFR 1604.11 (a)

7. Gordon, "Rethinking Diversity," p. 85.

8. Jan Bohren, "Six Myths of Sexual Harassment," *Management Review* (May 1993), pp. 61–63.

9. Letter from T. Gordon Roddick dated September 22, 1994.

10. Marjorie Kelly, "To Tell the Truth," *Business Ethics* (September–October 1994), pp. 6–7; Jon Entine, "Shattered Image," *Business Ethics* (September–October 1994), pp. 23–28; and letter from Marjorie Kelly, publisher of *Business Ethics.*

11. Anne Murphy, "The Seven (Almost) Deadly Sins of High-Minded Entrepreneurs," *Inc.* (July 1994), pp. 47–51.

12. Ferrell and Fraedrich, *Business Ethics,* p. 10.

13. George Manning and Kent Curtis, *Ethics at Work: Fire in a Dark World* (Cincinnati: South-Western Publishing, 1988), p. 74.

14. Ibid., p. 77.

15. Karen Berney, "Finding the Ethical Edge," *Nation's Business* (August 1987), pp. 18–26.

16. Ibid.

17. Gary Stern, "Guns for Toys," *Hispanic* (April 1994).

18. For a more detailed discussion of the strategic planning process, see Henry Mintzberg, James Brian Quinn, and John Voyer, *The Strategy Process* (Englewood Cliffs, NJ: Prentice Hall, 1995).

19. Tom Peters, *Thriving on Chaos* (New York: Knopf, 1988).

20. Tom Ehrenfeld, "The (Handbook) Handbook," *Inc.* (November 1993), p. 58.

21. Robert Linneman and John Stanton, "Mining For Niches," *Business Horizons* (May–June 1992), pp. 43–51.

22. Fran Tarkenton and Joseph Boyett, "Taking Care of Business," *Entrepreneur* (February 1990), pp. 18–23.

23. Sheila Eby, "Pssssssst! (Do You Want to Know a Secret?)" *Inc. Magazine Guide to Small Business Success,* 1993 Supplement Issue.

24. M. A. Lyles, I. S. Baird, J. B. Orris, and D. F. Kuratko, "Formalized Planning in Small Business: Increasing Strategic Choices," *Journal of Small Business Management* (April 1993), pp. 38–50.

25. Kenneth Hatten and Mary Louise Hatten, *Strategic Management: Analysis and Action* (Englewood Cliffs, NJ: Prentice Hall, 1987), p. 13.

26. Jill Andresky Fraser, "Plans to Grow By," *Inc.* (January 1990), pp. 111–113.

27. Ferrell and Fraedrich, *Business Ethics*, p. 114.
28. Ibid.

Chapter 4

1. George Gendron and Bo Burlingham, "Thriving on Order," *Inc.* (December 1989), pp. 47–62.
2. Karl Albrecht, "The Power of Bifocal Vision," *Management Review* (April 1994), pp. 42–46.
3. Roger Thompson, "Business Plans: Myth and Reality," *Nation's Business* (August 1988), pp. 16–23.
4. Bo Burlingham, "How to Succeed in Business in 4 Easy Steps," *Inc.* (July 1995), pp. 30–42.
5. Stanley Rich and David Gumpert, "How to Write a Winning Business Plan," *Harvard Business Review* (May–June 1985), pp. 156–163.
6. *Guideline for Entrepreneurs* of the Colorado Small Business Development Center.
7. J. Tol Broome, Jr., "How to Write a Business Plan," *Nation's Business* (February 1993), pp. 29–30.
8. David H. Bangs, *Financial Troubleshooting: An Action Plan For Money Management in the Small Business* (Dover, NH: Upstart Publishing Company, 1992) p. 46.
9. Ibid., p. 50.

Chapter 5

1. Thomas Dicke, *Franchising in America: The Development of a Business Method, 1840–1980* (Chapel Hill, NC: University of North Carolina Press, 1992), p. 13.
2. U.S. Department of Commerce, *Franchise Opportunities Handbook* (Washington, DC: U.S. Government Printing Office, October 1994), p. vii.
3. *Franchising in the Economy.* (International Franchise Association: Washington, DC, 1993).
4. Robert Justis and Richard Judd: *Franchising* (Cincinnati: South-Western, 1989).
5. Robin Pogrebin, "What Went Wrong With Mrs. Fields?" *Working Woman* (July 1993), pp. 9–11.
6. U.S. Department of Commerce, *Franchise Opportunities Handbook.*
7. Joan Delaney, "10 Danger Signs to Look for When Buying a Franchise," *Black Enterprise* (September 1994), pp. 118–122.
8. "Franchise Industry Resources," *Black Enterprise* (September 1994), p. 122.
9. Heather Page, "No Sub-stitute," *Entrepreneur*, (January, 1996), pp. 192–194.
10. U.S. Department of Commerce, *Franchise Opportunity Handbook.*
11. Andrew Sherman, "Structuring the Financial Agreement," *The Franchising Handbook* (New York: AMACOM American Management Association, 1993), p. 297.
12. Ibid., p. 300.
13. David Baucus, Melissa Baucus, and Sherrie Human, "Choosing a Franchise: How Base Fees and Royalties Relate to the Value of the Franchise," *The Journal of Small Business Management* (April 1993), pp. 91–104.
14. Andrew Sherman, "Hard Data on Franchisees," *Nation's Business* (February 1994), p. 54.
15. Andrew Serwer, "Trouble in Franchise Nation," *Fortune* (March 6, 1995), p. 118.
16. Ibid., pp. 115–129.
17. Jeffrey Tannenbaum, "U.S. Franchisors Expect NAFTA to Boost Mexican Business," *The Wall Street Journal*, November 17, 1993, p. B2.
18. Meg Whittemore, "An International Touch in Expansion Plans," *Nation's Business* (January 1992), p. 62.

Chapter 6

1. William Cohen, *The Entrepreneur and Small Business Problem Solver,* 2nd ed. (New York: John Wiley & Sons, 1990), pp. 90–91.

2. Fleming Meeks and Nancy Rotenier, "Am I Going to Mind Sweeping the Floors?" *Forbes,* November 8, 1993, pp. 142–148.

3. Gustav Berle, *SBA Hotline Answer Book* (New York: John Wiley & Sons, 1992), pp. 78–80. Also contact your local Service Corp of Retired Executives (SCORE) for a complete management consultant's checklist.

4. Joshua Hyatt, "Should You Start a Business?" *Inc.* (February 1992), pp. 48–58.

5. *RMA Annual Statement Studies 1994* (Philadelphia: Robert Morris Associates, 1994).

6. Joseph Anthony, "Maybe You Should *Buy* a Business," *Kiplinger's Personal Finance Magazine* (May 1993), pp. 83–87.

7. John Johansen, "How to Buy or Sell a Business," *Small Business Administration Management Aid, Number 2.029* (Washington, DC: U.S. Small Business Administration Office of Business Development).

8. Gary Schine, "How to Buy a Business Without Overpaying," *Home Office Computing* (August 1993), pp. 26–27.

9. William Bygrave, *The Portable MBA in Entrepreneurship* (New York: John Wiley & Sons, 1994), pp. 63–66.

10. Wendy Handler, "Key Interpersonal Relationships of Next-Generation Family Members in Family Firms," *Journal of Small Business Management* (July 1991), p. 21.

11. John Ward and Craig Aronoff, "Two 'Laws' for Family Businesses," *Nation's Business* (February 1993), pp. 52–53.

12. Jeffrey Barsch, Joseph Gantisky, James Carson, and Benjamin Doochin, "Entry of the Next Generation: Strategic Challenges for Family Members in Family Firms," *Journal of Small Business Management* (April 1988), pp. 49–56.

13. David Bork, "If Family Members Ask for a Job," *Nation's Business* (April 1992), pp. 50–52.

Chapter 7

1. Louise Washer, "Home Alone," *Working Woman* (March 1993), p. 46.

2. Ibid.

3. Laurel Toube, "Starting a Business on the Side," *Working Woman* (September 1992), p. 44.

4. Leslie Brokaw, "The Truth About Start-ups," *Inc.* (March 1993), pp. 56–64.

5. Jeffry A. Timmons, Daniel Muzyka, Howard Stevenson, and William Bygrave, "Opportunity Recognition: The Core of Entrepreneurship," *Frontiers of Entrepreneurship Research: 1987* p. 409.

6. Stephanie Mehta, "Small Talk," *The Wall Street Journal—Small Business,* May 22, 1995, p. R16.

7. Diane Goldner, "Ahead of the Curve," *The Wall Street Journal—Small Business,* May 22, 1995, p. R19.

8. C. D. Peterson, *How to Leave Your Job & Buy a Business of Your Own* (New York: McGraw-Hill Book Company, 1988), p. 76.

9. David Kopcso, Robert Ronstadt, and William Rybolt, "The Corridor Principle: Independent Entrepreneurs Versus Corporate Entrepreneurs," *Frontiers of Entrepreneurship Research, 1987,* pp. 259–271.

10. Karl Vesper, "When's the Big Idea?" *Frontiers of Entrepreneurship Research, 1989,* pp. 334–343.

11. Barbara Marsh, "Want to be a Success? Try Opening Only Twice a Week," *The Wall Street Journal,* June 6, 1994, p. B2.

12. Anne Murphy, "Where Great Business Ideas Come From," *Inc.* (September 1993), pp. 59–60.

13. Phaedra Hise, "Where Great Business Ideas Come From," *Inc.* (September 1993), pp. 59–60.
14. Michael Treacy and Fred Wiesema, "How Market Leaders Keep Their Edge," *Fortune*, February 6, 1995, pp. 88–98.
15. Lori Stones and Kelly Lynn, "Entrepreneurism + Customer Service = Success," *Management Review* (November 1993), pp. 38–44.
16. Ibid., p. 41.

Chapter 8

1. John Case, "Where the Growth Is," *Inc.* (June 1991), p. 66.
2. "The Power of the Buying Survey," *Sales and Marketing Management*, August 30, 1994, pp. a6–a14.
3. James Aley, "Startup 'Hoods," *Fortune*, October 18, 1993, p. 24.
4. Richard Stern and Toddi Gutner, "A Helluva Place to Have a Business," *Forbes*, December 21, 1992, pp. 114–136.
5. William Barrett, "A Great Place to Visit, But . . . ," *Forbes* (May 1993), pp. 92–94.
6. Michael Cronin, "Where the Growth Is," *Inc.* (October 1993), pp. 72–80.
7. Ellyn Spragins, "Working Far Afield," *Inc.* (July 1991), pp. 79–80.
8. Gary Brockway and W. Blynn Mangold, "The Sales Conversion Index: A Method for Analyzing Small Business Market Opportunities," *The Journal of Small Business Management* (April 1988), pp. 38–48.
9. Michael Weiss, *The Clustering of America* (New York: Harper & Row Publishers, 1988).
10. Benjamin Weiner, "Sources of Information (and Misinformation)," *Management Review* (January 1992), pp. 24–25.
11. Troy Segal, "Feathered Nests for Your Fledgling Business," *Business Week*, February 19, 1990, pp. 139–140.
12. Bradford McKee, "Achieving Access for the Disabled," *Nation's Business* (June 1991), pp. 31–34.
13. Ripley Hotch, "All the Comforts of a Home Office," *Nation's Business* (July 1993), pp. 26–28.

Chapter 9

1. Paul Argenti, *The Portable MBA Desk Reference* (New York: John Wiley & Sons, 1994), p. 101.
2. Anil Gupta, "Business-Unit Strategy: Managing the Single Business" in *The Portable MBA in Strategy*, Liam Fahey and Robert Randall, eds. (New York: John Wiley & Sons Publishing, 1994), pp. 84–107.
3. Michael Porter, "Know Your Place," *Inc.* (September 1991), pp. 90–95.
4. David Cravens and Shannon Shipp, "Market-Driven Strategies for Competitive Advantage," *Business Horizons* (January/February 1991), pp. 53–61.
5. Michael Porter, "Know Your Place," *Inc.* (September 1991), pp. 90–95.
6. Robert Hartley, *Marketing Mistakes*, 5th ed. (New York: John Wiley & Sons, 1992), p. v.
7. Leslie Cauley, "Perils of Progress," *The Wall Street Journal Report—Technology*, June 27, 1994, p. R12.
8. Ibid.
9. Ibid.
10. Christopher Power, Kathleen Kerwin, Ronald Grover, Keith Alexander, and Robert Hof, "Flops," *Business Week*, August 16, 1993, pp. 76–82.
11. John Czepiel, *Competitive Marketing Strategy*, (Englewood Cliffs, NJ: Prentice Hall, 1992), p. 41.

12. Michael Porter, *Competitive Advantage: Creating and Sustaining Superior Performance* (New York: Free Press, 1985).

13. Jenny McCune, "In the Shadow of Wal-Mart," *Management Review* (December 1994), pp. 10–16.

14. Lee Iacocca, *Iacocca: An Autobiography* (New York: Bantam Books, Inc., 1984).

15. Oren Harari, "The Secret Competitive Advantage," *Management Review* (January 1994), pp. 45–47.

16. Susan Greco, "On-the-Road Research," *Inc.* (July 1992), p. 115.

17. "New Marketing Research Definition Approved," *Marketing News*, January 2, 1987, p. 1.

18. J. Ford Laumer, Jr., James Harris, and Hugh Guffey, Jr., "Learning About Your Market," *Management Aid No. 4.019*, Small Business Administration Management Assistance Office.

19. George Kress and John Snyder, *Forecasting and Market Analysis Techniques: A Practical Approach* (Westport, CT: Quorum Books, 1994), pp. 29–54.

20. Vera Gibbons, "The Scoop on 'Info Brokers," *Inc.* (December 1992), p. 27.

21. Susan Greco, "Fact Finders for Hire," *Inc.* (December 1992), p. 27.

22. Fahri Karakaya, "Market Research: A Pocket Guide for Managers," *SAM Advanced Management Journal* (Summer 1991), pp. 34–40.

23. "Do-it-yourself Techniques to Solve Marketing Problems," *Profit-Building Strategies for Business Owners* (December 1992), pp. 14–16.

24. Allan Magrath, *The 6 Imperatives of Marketing: Lessons From the World's Best Companies* (New York: AMACOM, 1992), pp. 40–41.

25. Oren Harari, "The Tarpit of Marketing Research," *Management Review* (March 1994), pp. 42–44.

26. Ibid., p. 43.

27. Gary Hamel and C. K. Prahalad, "Seeing the Future First," *Fortune*, September 5 1994, p. 70.

Chapter 10

1. Peter Drucker, *People and Performance: The Best of Peter Drucker on Management* (New York: Harper's College Press, 1977), p. 90.

2. Ibid., p. 91.

3. Regis McKenna, *Relationship Marketing* (Reading, MA: Addison Wesley Publishing Co., 1991).

4. Ibid.

5. Earl Naumann and Patrick Shannon, "What Is Customer-Driven Marketing?" *Business Horizons* (November/December 1992), pp. 44–52.

6. David Cravens and Shannon Shipp, "Market-Driven Strategies for Competitive Advantage," *Business Horizons* (January/February 1991), pp. 53–61.

7. Meg Whittemore, "Survival Tactics for Retailers," *Nation's Business* (June 1993), pp. 20–27.

8. Avraham Shama, "Marketing Strategies During Recession: A Comparison of Small and Large Firms," *Journal of Small Business Management* (July 1993), pp. 62–72.

9. William Bygrave, *The Portable MBA in Entrepreneurship* (New York: John Wiley & Sons, 1994), p. 85.

10. Pierre Loewe and Dominique Hanssens, "Taking the Mystery Out of Marketing," *Management Review* (August 1994), pp. 32–34.

11. *The 1994 Information Please Almanac* (Boston: Houghton Mifflin Company, 1994) p. 748.

12. For a more complete description of the "Black Box" model, see Warren Keegan, Sandra Moriarty, and Tom Duncan, *Marketing,* 2nd ed. (Englewood Cliffs, NJ: Prentice Hall, 1995).

13. Bob Isenhour and Kathryn Payne, "Getting Serious About Product Development," *Management Review* (April 1991), pp. 19–22.

14. William Barbach, "Developments to Watch," *Business Week*, June 28, 1993, p. 85.

15. Roberta Maynard, "What's In a Name?" *Nation's Business*, (September 1994), p. 54.

16. Alexander Hiam and Charles Schewe, *The Portable MBA in Marketing* (New York: John Wiley & Sons, 1992), p. 243.

17. Ibid., p. 242.

18. Hiam and Schewe, *The Portable MBA in Marketing*, p. 242.

19. Ibid., pp. 367–368.

20. Paul Hawkin, *Growing a Business* (New York: Simon and Schuster, 1987), p. 33.

21. Melanie Wells, "Making For Strange Bedfellows," *Advertising Age*, March 29, 1993, p. 30.

22. Minda Zetlin, "It's All the Same to Me," *Sales and Marketing Management* (February 1994), pp. 71–75.

23. "The Cost of a Sales Call," *Inc.* (May 1991), p. 86.

24. Susan Greco, "The Art of Selling," *Inc.* (June 1993), pp. 72–80.

25. David Whitford, "This Year's Model," *Inc.* (February 1995), pp. 45–52.

26. Jane Applegate, "Building Your Business With Good PR," *Working Woman* (December 1993), p. 69.

27. Larry Light, "Promotion Has Bigger Role Than Ads, But 'Short-term Bribes' Are Suicidal," *Advertising Age*, March 29, 1993.

Chapter 11

1. Edward Welles, "When Wal-Mart Comes to Town," *Inc.* (July 1993), pp. 76–88.

2. Ibid., p. 79.

3. Ibid.

4. For a complete discussion of demand and price elasticity, see Warren Keegan, Sandra Moriarty, and Tom Duncan, *Marketing*, 2nd ed. (Englewood Cliffs, NJ: Prentice Hall, 1995).

5. Paul Argenti, *The Portable MBA Desk Reference* (New York: John Wiley & Sons, 1994), p. 313.

6. For a concise article on break-even analysis, see Kevin Thompson, "Planning for Profit," *Black Enterprise* (April 1993), pp. 93–98.

7. Michael Mondello, "Naming Your Price," *Inc.* (July 1992), pp. 80–83.

8. Kelly Holland and Greg Burns, "Plastic Talks," *Business Week*, February 14, 1994, pp. 105–107.

9. Ibid., p. 107.

10. Timothy O'Brien, "Merchant's Ire Flares Over Fees on Credit Cards," *The Wall Street Journal*, October 11, 1993, p. B1.

11. Carolyn Brown, "How to Secure a Line of Credit," *Black Enterprise* (January 1994), pp. 64–67.

12. Jill Andresky Fraser, "Getting Paid," *Inc.* (June 1990), pp. 58–69.

13. Jill Andresky Fraser, "The Outstanding Bill Collection System," *Inc.* (May 1993), pp. 93–95.

Chapter 12

1. Johnathan Calof, "The Impact of Size on Internationalization," *The Journal of Small Business Management* (October 1993), pp. 60–69.

2. Amy Barrett, "It's a Small (Business) World", *Business Week*, April 17, 1995, pp. 96–101.

3. Michael Barrier, "A Global Reach for Small Firms," *Nation's Business* (April 1994), p. 66.

4. Ibid.

5. *Breaking Into the Trade Game: A Small Business Guide to Exporting* (U.S. Small Business Administration/AT&T Printing, 1993), pp. 4–5.

6. Thomas Gaspar of the New Jersey Governor's Commission on International Trade, "International Business Planning: A 'How-to' Workshop Sponsored by the New Jersey DEC," *Business America*, June 28, 1993, p. 16.

7. Inga Baird, Marjorie Lyles, and J. B. Orris, "The Choice of International Strategies by Small Businesses," *The Journal of Small Business Management* (January 1994), pp. 48–59.

8. *Breaking Into the Trade Game*, p. 3.

9. Ibid., p. 4.

10. Robert Mamis, "Not So Innocent Abroad," *Inc.* (September 1993), pp. 110–111.

11. Clark Cassell, *The World Is Your Market: The Export Guide for Small Business* (Washington, DC: Braddock Communications, 1990), p. 20.

12. Ibid., p. 25.

13. Joseph Pattison, "Global Joint Ventures," *Overseas Business* (Winter 1990), pp. 24–29.

14. Ibid.

15. Ibid.

16. Ted Rakstis, "Going Global," *Kiwanis* (October 1991), pp. 39–43.

17. Roberta Maynard, "A Good Time to Export," *Nation's Business* (May 1994), p. 24.

18. Jill Andresky Fraser, "How Bad Can Collections Get?" *Inc.* (March 1993), p. 94.

19. *Breaking Into The Trade Game*, p. 86.

20. Margitta Wulker-Mirback, "New Trends in Countertrade," *The OECD Observer* (April/May 1990), p. 63.

21. Matt Schaffer, "Countertrade as an Export Strategy," *Journal of Business Strategy* (May/June 1990).

22. Susan Greco, "Export Experts Close to Home," *Inc.* (July 1992), p. 117.

23. "Understand and Heed Cultural Differences," *Business America* (September 1992), pp. 30–31.

24. Joann Lublin, "Companies Use Cross-Cultural Training to Help Their Employees Adjust Abroad," *The Wall Street Journal*, August 24, 1992, pp. B1, B9.

25. Sylvia Odenwald, "A Guide for Global Training," *Training and Development* (July 1993), pp. 22–31.

26. Ibid.

27. Cassell, *The World Is Your Market*, p. 90.

28. Kevin Walsh, "How to Negotiate European-Style," *Journal of European Business* (July/August 1993), pp. 45–47.

29. *Trilateral Customs Guide to NAFTA* (Ottowa, Ontario, Canada: Department of Customs, Excise and Taxation, 1994) p. 2.

30. *NAFTA Rules of Origin* (Ottowa, Ontario, Canada: Department of Customs, Excise, and Taxation, 1994), p. 1.

31. Geoffrey Brewer, "New World Orders," *Sales and Marketing Management* (January 1994), pp. 59–63.

32. Patricia Raiken, "Business Guide to Planning for the NAFTA," *Business America*, October 18, 1993, pp. 33–35.

33. Kim Howard, "GATT Bridges the Gap," *Business Credit* (March 1994), pp. 22.

34. Leslie Brokaw, "ISO 9000: Making the Grade," *Inc.* (June 1993), pp. 98–99.

35. Ibid., p. 99.

Chapter 13

1. Linda Hill, "Hardest Lessons for First-time Managers," *Working Woman* (February 1994), pp. 18–21.

2. Henry Mintzberg, "The Manager's Job: Folklore and Fact," *Harvard Business Review* (March/April 1990), pp. 163–176.

3. Ibid., p. 175.

4. Jacquelyn Denalli, "Keeping Growth Under Control," *Nation's Business* (July 1993), pp. 31–32.

5. John Case and Elizabeth Conlin, "Second Thoughts on Growth," *Inc.* (March 1991), pp. 46–57.

6. Donna Fenn, "When To Go Pro," *Inc. 500 1995*, p. 72.

7. Ibid., p. 4.

8. David Terpstra and Philip Olson, "Entrepreneurial Start-up and Growth: A Classification of Problems," *Entrepreneurship Theory and Practice* (Spring 1993), pp. 5–20.

9. Howard Stevenson and David Gumpert, "The Heart of Entrepreneurship," *Harvard Business Review* (March/April 1985), p. 85.

10. Theodore Kinni, "Leadership Up Close," *Industry Week*, June 20, 1994, pp. 21–25.

11. Theodore Kinni, "The Credible Leader," *Industry Week*, June 20, 1994, pp. 25–26.

12. Warren Bennis, "Why Leaders Can't Lead," *Training and Development Journal* (April 1989), pp. 35–39.

13. Genevieve Capowski, "Anatomy of a Leader: Where Are the Leaders of Tomorrow?" *Management Review* (March 1994), pp. 10–17.

14. Ibid.

15. For examples of applying Maslow's hierarchy in small businesses, see Mark Henricks, "Motivating Force," *Entrepreneur* (December 1995), pp. 68–72.

16. Michael Cronin, "Motivation the Old Fashioned Way," *Inc.* (November 1994), p. 134.

17. W. Edwards Deming, *Out of Crisis* (Cambridge, MA: MIT Press, 1986), p. 24.

18. David Bowen and Edward Lawler, "Total Quality-Oriented Human Resource Management," *Organizational Dynamics* (Spring 1992), pp. 29–41.

19. David Greising, "Quality: How To Make It Pay," *Business Week*, August 8, 1994, pp. 54–59.

20. Oren Harari, "Ten Reasons Why TQM Doesn't Work," *Management Review* (January 1993), pp. 33–37. Also see related articles: Selwyn Becker, "TQM Does Work: Ten Reasons Why Misguided Attempts Fail," *Management Review* (May 1993), pp. 30–33, and Oren Harari, "The Eleventh Reason Why TQM Doesn't Work," *Management Review* (May 1993), pp. 31–35.

21. Catherine Romano, "Report Card on TQM," *Management Review* (January 1994), p. 22.

22. Ibid., p. 23.

23. Howard Rothman, "Quality's Link to Productivity," *Nation's Business* (February 1994), pp. 33–34.

24. Greising, "Quality: How to Make It Pay," p. 55.

25. Martha Davis, Matthew McKay, and Elizabeth Robbins Eshelman, *The Relaxation & Stress Reduction Workbook*, 2nd ed. (Oakland, CA: New Harbinger Publications, 1982).

26. Kenneth Hart, "Introducing Stress and Stress Management to Managers," *Journal of Managerial Psychology*, vol. 5, no. 2 (1990), pp. 9–16.

Chapter 14

1. *The Wall Street Journal*, March 20, 1980, p. A1.

2. Asron Bernstein and Paul Magnusson, "How Much Good Will Training Do?" *Business Week*, February 22, 1993, p. 77.

3. Martin John Yate, *Hiring the Best: A Manager's Guide to Effective Interviewing* (Holbrook, MA: Bob Adams, Inc. 1988), p. 18.

4. Peter F. Drucker, "How to Save the Family Business," *The Wall Street Journal*, August 19, 1994, p. A10.

5. *Griggs* v. *Duke Power Company*, 401 U.S. 424 (1971).

6. "Technical Assistance Manual of the Employment Provisions (Title 1) of the Americans with Disabilities Act," *HR News*, Society for Human Resource Management, p. C30.

7. Ibid.

8. "SHRM-BNA Survey No. 59: Human Resource Activities, Budgets, and Staffs: 1993–94," *HR Bulletin to Management*, June 30, 1994, p. 31.

9. Michael Barrier, "Now You Hire Them, Now You Don't," *Nation's Business* (January 1994), p. 31.

10. Marvin Selter, "On the Plus Side of Employee Leasing," *Personnel Journal* (April 1986), pp. 87–91.

11. John Naisbitt, "Employee Leasing Takes Off," *Success* (April 1986), p. 12.

12. Rosalind Resnick, "Leasing Workers," *Nation's Business* (August 1993), pp. 34–35.

13. "Business Realities Clash with Training Needs and Turnover," *HR Focus* (January 1994).

14. Ibid.

15. Jill Andresky Fraser, "Financial Strategies," *Inc.* (November 1993), p. 137.

16. "Employee Benefit Costs," *BNA Bulletin to Management*, January 16, 1992, pp. 12–13.

17. *Public Attitudes on Flexible Benefits, 1994: Summary Report* (Washington, DC: Employee Benefit Research Institute, 1994), p. 10.

18. Ibid.

19. Joseph S. Placentini and Jill D. Foley, *EBRI Databook on Employee Benefits*, 2nd ed. (Washington, DC: Employee Benefit Research Institute, 1992), p. 52.

20. Richard I. Henderson, *Compensation Management: Rewarding Performance* (Englewood Cliffs, NJ: Prentice Hall, 1994) p. 491.

21. "Employer Contributions Spur 401(k) Participation Modestly," *HR News* (April 1994), p. 13.

22. Mary Rowland, "Pension Options for Small Firms," *Nation's Business* (March 1994), p. 27.

23. *Public Attitudes on Flexible Benefits, 1994: Summary Report* (Washington, DC: Employee Benefit Research Institute, 1994), p. 20.

24. "Employees Pitch in for Working Parents," *Parents* (July 1994), p. 132.

25. Joseph S. Placentini and Jill D. Foley, *EBRI Databook on Employee Benefits*, 2nd ed. (Washington, DC: Employee Benefit Research Institute, 1992), p. 18.

Chapter 15

1. Shawn Tully, "You'll Never Guess Who Really Makes . . . ," *Fortune*, October 3, 1994, pp. 124–128.

2. Otis Port, "Custom-Made, Direct From the Plant," *Business Week*, 21st Century Capitalism edition, pp. 158–159.

3. Ronald Henkoff, "Make Your Office More Productive," *Fortune*, February 25, 1991.

4. Dan Gutman, "Always in Touch," *Success* (March 1995), p. 54.

5. "Office Ergonomics: Not the Same as in a Plant," *Industry Week*, December 5, 1994, p. 37.

6. Gwen Fontenot, Alicia Gresham, and Ravi Behara, "Using Six Sigma to Measure and Improve Customer Service," *Proceedings of 1994 National Small Business Consulting Conference*, Small Business Institute Director's Association, San Antonio, pp. 298–304.

7. Ibid., p. 303.

8. *Breaking Into the Trade Game: A Small Business Guide to Exporting* (U.S. Small Business Administration Publication, 1994), p. 74.

9. Ronald Henkoff, "The Hot New Seal of Quality," *Fortune*, June 28, 1993, pp. 116–117.

10. Michael Barrier and Amy Zuckerman, "Quality Standards the World Agrees On," *Nation's Business* (May 1994), pp. 71–72.

11. Henkoff, "The Hot New Seal of Quality," p. 116.

12. Barrier and Zuckerman, "Quality Standards the World Agrees On," p. 72.

13. Steven Ashley, "Nondestructive Evaluation with Laser Ultrasound," *Mechanical Engineering* (October 1994), pp. 63–66.

Chapter 16

1. Verona Beguin, ed., *Small Business Institute Student Consultant's Manual* (Washington, DC: Small Business Administration, 1992), Appendix F7.

2. Stephanie Gruner, "The Smart Vendor-audit Checklist," *Inc.* (April 1995), pp. 93–95.

3. Eliyahu Goldratt, "Late-Night Discussions," *Industry Week,* August 5, 1991, pp. 28–29.

4. Sang Lee and Marc Schniederjans, *Operations Management* (Boston: Houghton Mifflin Co., 1994), p. 256.

5. Michael Barrier, "When 'Just In Time' Just Isn't Enough," *Nation's Business* (November 1992), pp. 30–31.

6. Julie Candler, "Just-in-Time Deliveries," *Nation's Business* (April 1993), pp. 64–65.

Chapter 17

1. "Making Sense of Your Dollars," *Home Office Computing* (November 1993), pp. 79–88.

2. For a concise source on reading financial statements, see Frank Evans, "A Roadmap to Your Financial Report," *Management Review* (October 1993), pp. 39–47.

3. Kathryn Stewart, "On the Fast Track to Profits," *Management Accounting* (February 1995), pp. 44–50.

4. For more depth in the use of numbers in running your business, see Tom Richman, "The Language of Business," *Inc.* (February 1990), pp. 41–50 and an interview with "Accounting Critic: Robert Kaplan," *Inc.* (April 1988), pp. 55–67.

5. Andrew J. Potts, "Cash Flow—The Oil that Keeps the Small and Family Business Organization Running Smoothly," *Journal of Small Business Strategy,* Vol. 4, no. 2 (Fall 1993), pp. 63–71.

6. "Cash Flow: Who's in Charge," *Inc.* (November 1993), p. 140.

7. Leslie Manonson, "Cash Is King," *Management Review* (October 1990), pp. 36–38.

8. "Cash Flow," *Inc.* (November 1993), p. 140.

9. Roberta Maynard, "Smart Ways to Manage Cash," *Nation's Business* (August 1992), pp. 43–44.

10. For a more detailed treatment of inventory management, see Robert A. Mamis, "Money In, Money Out," *Inc.* (March 1993), pp. 96–103.

11. Adapted from Maynard, "Smart Ways to Manage Cash," p. 44.

Chapter 18

1. For a more thorough explanation and example of the process of defining required assets, see *The Business Planning Guide, 6th ed.* by David H. Bangs, Jr., Upstart Publishing Company, Dover, NH.

2. More detailed treatments of the Five Cs of Credit can be found in any Financial Management textbook, such as *Foundations of Managerial Finance, 4th ed.,* by Lawrence J. Gitman, HarperCollins Publishers, New York, NY.

3. "The ABC's of Borrowing," U.S. Small Business Administration Office of Business Development, Management Aids Number 1.001.

4. "Business Loans & the SBA," U.S. Small Business Administration, Washington, DC, FI-0006, July 1994.

5. Joseph J. Vassallo, "Tapping Capital for Small Companies," *Journal of Accountancy* (August 1993), pp. 44–46.

6. "LowDoc Quick & Easy Lending Program," U.S. Small Business Administration, Washington, DC, ED-0001, June 1994.

7. "The Facts About . . . Small Loan Program," U.S. Small Business Administration, Washington, DC, FS-0001, September 1992.

8. "Small Business Credit Survey," Dun & Bradstreet, New York, NY, August 1994.

9. Jeffry A. Timmons, *Planning and Financing the New Venture* (Acton, MA: Brick House Publishing Company, 1991), p. 49.

10. Ibid., p. 50.

11. "Small Fast-Growth Firms Feel Chill of Shareholder Suits," Enterprise Section, *The Wall Street Journal*, April 5, 1994, p. B2.

12. G. Baty, *Entrepreneurship: Playing to Win* (Reston, VA: Reston Publishing, 1990), pp. 157–159.

13. Jeffry A. Timmons, *New Venture Creation, Entrepreneurship in the 1990s, 3rd ed.* (Homewood, IL: Irwin Publishers, 1990), pp. 463–467.

Chapter 19

1. William Dennis, *Small Business Primer*, National Federation of Independent Business (August 1993), pp. 32–33.

2. 8 U.S.C. § 1324a.

3. 8 U.S.C. § 1324(B) (g) (2) (B) (iv) (I)–(III).

4. Ibid., p. C4.

5. Ibid., p. 19–20.

6. William Jackson, Geralyn McClure-Franklin, and Diana Hensley, "Sexual Harassment: No Immunity for Small Business," *Proceedings of 1995 Small Business Consulting Conference*, Nashville, TN, pp. 161–165.

7. Jennifer Laabs, "HR Puts Its Questions on the Line: Sexual Harassment," *Personnel Journal* (February 1995), pp. 36–45.

8. Jackson, McClure-Franklin, and Hensley, "Sexual Harassment," p. 164.

9. *Compliance Guide to the Family and Medical Leave Act*, U.S. Department of Labor, Employment Standards Administration, Wage and Hour Division (June 1993), p. 16.

10. Ibid., p. 16.

11. 29 U.S.C. § 651(b).

12. Fred Steingold, *The Legal Guide for Starting and Running a Small Business* (Berkeley, CA: Nolo Press, 1992).

13. Alan Zeiger, "Bankruptcy Can Also Mean Smart Investment," *Management Review* (May 1992), pp. 36–39.

14. The Constitution of the United States of America, Article I, Section 8. In Daniel J. Boorstin, *An American Primer* (Chicago and London: The University of Chicago Press, 1966), p. 94.

15. David Pressman, *Patent It Yourself* (Berkeley, CA: Nolo Press, 1991).

16. Ibid., p. 6/41.

Further Readings

Chapter 2

You can find additional information on legal forms of business ownership in the following publications.

1. Denis Clifford and Ralph Warner, *The Partnership Book: How to Write a Partnership Agreement,* 4th ed. (Berkeley, CA: Nolo Press, 1991).

2. William Cohen, *The Entrepreneur and Small Business Problem Solver,* 2nd ed. (New York: John Wiley and Sons, 1990).

3. Frederick Daily, *The Small Business Tax Survival Handbook,* (Berkeley, CA: Nolo Press, 1994).

4. Robert Friedman, *The Complete Small Business Legal Guide* (Dover, NH: Upstart Publishing, 1993).

5. Anthony Mancuso, *How to Form Your Own Nonprofit Corporation* (Berkeley, CA: Nolo Press, 1994).

6. Ted Nicholas, *The Complete Guide to Business Agreements* (Dover, NH: Upstart Publishing, 1993).

7. Ted Nicholas, *The Complete Guide to Corporate Forms* (Dover, NH: Upstart Publishing, 1994).

8. Ted Nicholas, *The Complete Guide to "S" Corporations* (Dover, NH: Upstart Publishing, 1994).

9. Fred Steingold, *The Legal Guide for Starting and Running a Small Business* (Berkeley, CA: Nolo Press, 1992).

Chapter 12

Do's and Taboos Around the World (1990) by Roger Axtell; *Do's and Taboos of Hosting International Visitors (1990)* by Roger Axtell; *The Global Edge: How Your Company Can Win in the International Marketplace* (1986) by Sondra Snowdon; *When in Rome . . . A Business Guide to Cultures and Customs in 12 European Countries* (1990) by John Mole; and *Management in Two Cultures: Bridging the Gap between U.S. and Mexican Managers* (1989) by Eva Kras.

Index